漢字リスト • Kanji List 『とびらⅡ』

L11	140	141	142	143	14[illegible]	[illegible]	[illegible]	[illegible]	[illegible]	149
	勉	強	着	自	[illegible]	[illegible]	[illegible]	[illegible]	[illegible]	肉
	150	151	152	153	1[illegible]	[illegible]	[illegible]	[illegible]	[illegible]	
	鳥	魚	絵	例	力	[illegible]	[illegible]	[illegible]	[illegible]	
L12	159	160	161	162	163	164	165	166	167	168
	集	配	動	働	走	当	荷	由	計	画
	169	170	171	172	173	174	175	176	177	
	映	仕	事	初	東	京	同	半	士(E8)	
L13	178	179	180	181	182	183	184	185	186	187
	拾	返	守	変	止	電	車	神	様	注
	188	189	190	191	192	193	194	195	196	
	意	味	色	々	世	界	記	昨	若	
L14	197	198	199	200	201	202	203	204	205	206
	開	閉	消	汚	乗	遅	困	運	転	痛
	207	208	209	210	211	212	213	214	215	
	医	者	薬	服	店	部	屋	教	室	
L15	216	217	218	219	220	221	222	223	224	225
	続	助	調	忘	図	館	質	問	宿	題
	226	227	228	229	230	231	232	233	234	
	試	験	受	練	習	飯	族	夕	馬(E9)	
L16	235	236	237	238	239	240	241	242	243	244
	取	泣	笑	起	始	終	決	歌	洗	台
	245	246	247	248	249	250	251	252	253	
	旅	駅	朝	昼	晩	夜	漢	字	竹(E10)	
L17	254	255	256	257	258	259	260	261	262	263
	北	南	西	合	送	活	近	歩	急	授
	264	265	266	267	268	269	270	271	272	
	卒	業	写	真	研	究	顔	幸	正	
L18	273	274	275	276	277	278	279	280	281	282
	院	通	考	答	残	留	重	便	利	不
	283	284	285	286	287	288	289	290	291	
	弱	用	地	球	野	空	港	両	他	
L19	292	293	294	295	296	297	298	299	300	301
	覚	貸	借	待	落	違	死	多	少	工
	302	303	304	305	306	307	308	309	310	
	主	員	去	風	経	春	夏	秋	冬	
L20	311	312	313	314	315	316	317	318	319	320
	結	婚	果	予	約	定	全	伝	感	暑
	321	322	323	324	325	326	327	328	329	
	寒	犬	赤	青	白	黒	銀	紙	葉	

TOBIRA
BEGINNING JAPANESE

初級日本語
とびら

岡まゆみ Mayumi Oka
近藤純子 Junko Kondo
[文法解説] 筒井通雄 Michio Tsutsui
森祐太 Yuta Mori
奥野智子 Tomoko Okuno
榊原芳美 Yoshimi Sakakibara
曽我部絢香 Ayaka Sogabe
安田昌江 Masae Yasuda

Kurosio Publishers

CONTENTS

CONTENTS

Welcome to the world of Japanese!

『とびらⅡ』をはじめる前に
Before we begin

『とびら Ⅱ』の使い方
How to use *TOBIRA II*

To the *TOBIRA* Learners

- This section explains how to use *TOBIRA II*. Some aspects of this textbook are different from *TOBIRA I*, so please go over this section before you proceed.

教師の皆様へ

- 『とびらⅡ』の使い方についての説明です。『とびらⅠ』と異なる部分があるので、使い始める前に目を通してください。

◎ The Structure of *TOBIRA II*

◎ 『とびらⅡ』の構成

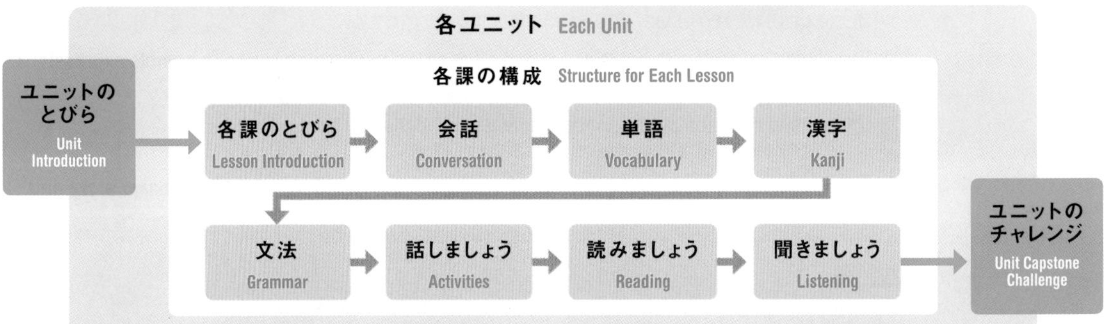

◎ The Lesson *Tobira* ("Portal") Page and *Dekiru* List

- The *Tobira* (or "portal") page in each lesson summarizes the content to be learned in the lesson and features a *Dekiru* (or "can do") List that specifies what you will be able to do by the end of the lesson. Before beginning each lesson, you will perform an "Entry Check" to ascertain the lesson's learning objectives. Then, when you finish the lesson, you will perform an "Exit Check" to see what you have learned to do and to make sure you have met those objectives.

◎ 各課の扉のページと「できるリスト」

- 各課の「扉」にはその課で勉強する内容のまとめと「できるリスト」があります。「できるリスト」にはその課を終えたら何ができるようになるか示してあります。課に入る前に「Entry Check」、課が終わったら「Exit Check」をして、学習成果を確認してください。

◎ Conversations

- In each lesson there are 3 to 4 conversations and some "Conversation Tips" for more natural speech.
- The conversations align with the lesson's *Dekiru* List, covering each topic on it in order.

◎ 会話

- 一課に3つから4つの会話と、自然な話し方をするためのワンポイントアドバイスが入っています。
- 会話の内容は「できるリスト」に順番に対応しています。

◎ Vocabulary

- Vocabulary to memorize for each lesson is presented on both a "Vocabulary with Pictures" page, where words are grouped by theme, and a "Vocabulary List" page, where words are sorted by part of speech, as seen below.
- We have chosen 40 to 70 commonly used words as vocabulary to memorize for each lesson.

◎ 単語

- 単語セクションには「絵入り単語」と「品詞別単語リスト」があります。
- 覚える単語として日常生活でよく使う言葉を各課で40〜70選んであります。

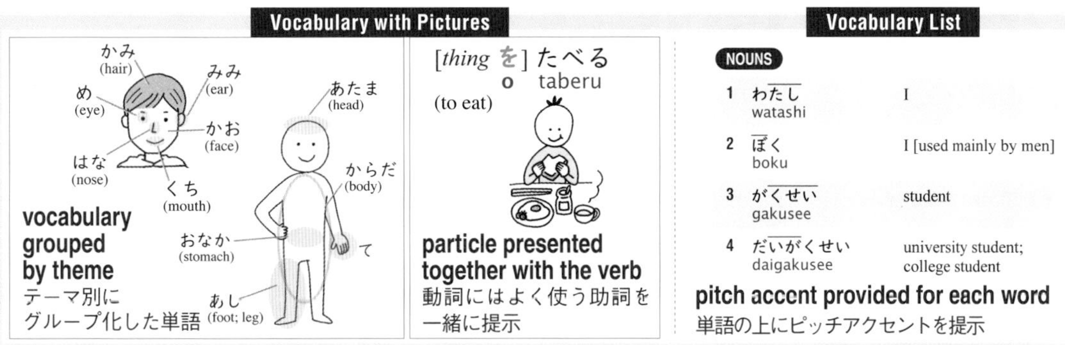

◎ Kanji

- In each lesson, 19 new kanji are introduced, for a total of 190 characters. In each lesson, we link the new kanji and new vocabulary to each other whenever possible.
- Furigana (hiragana pronunciation guides) are presented along with unlearned kanji and new kanji for the lesson, with two exceptions:
  - No furigana are given for new kanji in the kanji practice and reading practice sections.
  - Furigana are provided for all kanji in the grammar explanation example sentences.

◎ 漢字

- 11課から20課までの各課に、初級レベルの漢字が19字、全部で190字紹介してあります。漢字は各課の新出単語とできるだけリンクしています。
- 未習の漢字にはルビがつきます。新出漢字はその課の漢字練習と読解練習にはルビがついていません。文法例文に出てくる漢字には全てルビがつけてあります。

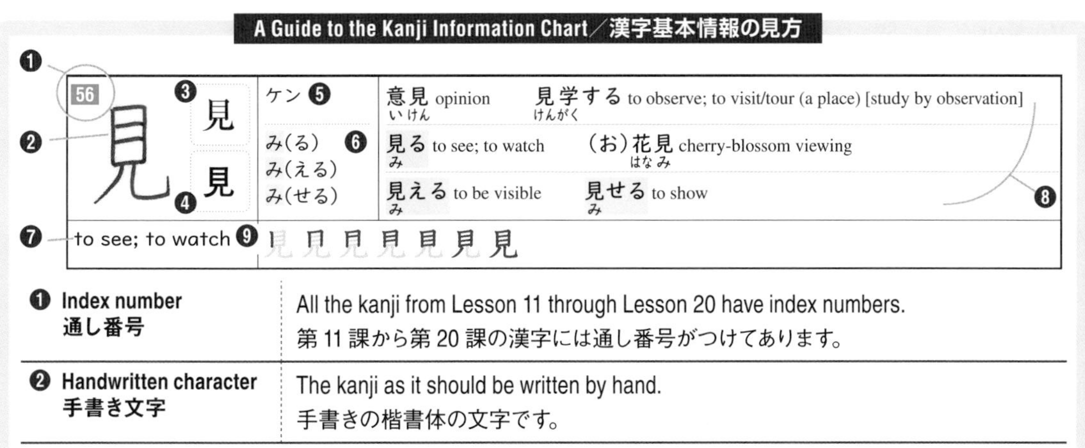

❶ **Index number 通し番号**	All the kanji from Lesson 11 through Lesson 20 have index numbers. 第11課から第20課の漢字には通し番号がつけてあります。
❷ **Handwritten character 手書き文字**	The kanji as it should be written by hand. 手書きの楷書体の文字です。

How to use *TOBIRA II*

❸ **Mincho font** **明朝フォント**	One of the most common font styles in Japanese, Mincho is a family of fonts equivalent to Roman alphabet serif fonts such as Times New Roman. 英語の Times New Roman のように、日本語でよく使われるフォントの一つです。
❹ **Gothic font** **ゴシックフォント**	Another common Japanese font style, Gothic is a font family that corresponds to Roman alphabet sans-serif fonts such as Arial. 英語の Arial のように、日本語でよく使われるフォントの一つです。
❺ ***On*-reading** **音読み**	A reading borrowed from Chinese; as such, it is written here in katakana. All readings to be memorized for the current lesson are highlighted. カタカナで書いてあります。各課で覚える読み方にはハイライトがしてあります。
❻ ***Kun*-reading** **訓読み**	A reading native to Japanese; as such, it is written here in hiragana. All readings to be memorized for the current lesson are highlighted. ひらがなで書いてあります。各課で覚える読み方にはハイライトがしてあります。
❼ **English meaning** **英訳**	The kanji's basic meaning in English. 漢字の基本的な意味が英語で書いてあります。
❽ **Vocabulary list** **単語リスト**	A list of frequently used words in which the kanji appears. All words to be memorized for the current lesson are highlighted. 漢字を含むよく使われる単語のリストです。各課で覚える単語にはハイライトがしてあります。
❾ **Stroke order** **書き順**	The order in which the strokes that make up the kanji are to be written. Following this order will help you write the character neatly and with good proportions. 漢字を構成している線や点を書く順番が提示してあります。この書き順で書くと漢字がきれいに書けます。

◎ Grammar

- The explanation for each grammar point includes the grammar point's function, an English equivalent or equivalents, the sentence structure it is used in, and example sentences. Each grammar point is also clearly linked to an item on the lesson's *Dekiru* List.
- The "GID" that sometimes appears in grammatical explanations refers to the "Grammar In Depth" supplement provided on the *TOBIRA* website.

◎ 文法

- 文法解説は、項目見出し・機能・対応英語・文型・説明・例文からなっています。各文法項目は「できるリスト」とのつながりがすぐに分かるようになっています。
- 解説中にある「GID」は Grammar in Depth のことで、文法をより深く理解するための情報が「とびら初級 WEB サイト」で提供されています。本冊から QR コードで直接各項目に飛ぶことができます。

Abbreviation／略語 Symbol／記号	Meaning／意味	Examples／例
Adj	Adjective／形容詞	大きい(*I*-adjective); べんり(*Na*-adjective)
Adj(*i*)	*I*-adjective／イ形容詞	大きい；おもしろい
A(*i*)-stem	Stem of *i*-adjective／イ形容詞の語幹	大き；おもしろ
Adj(*na*)	*Na*-adjective／ナ形容詞	べんり(な); しずか(な)
Adv	Adverb／副詞	すぐ；ゆっくり
Conj	Conjunction／接続詞	が；から；でも
N	Noun／名詞	学生；日本；バス
Prt	Particle／助詞	は；が；を；に；よ；ね
Q-word	Question word／疑問詞	何；だれ；どこ
S	Sentence／文	私は学生です。
V	Verb／動詞	話す；食べる；する
V-*masu*	Stem of the *masu*-form of a verb／ 動詞の「ます形」の語幹	話し~~ます~~；食べ~~ます~~
V-*nai*	*Nai*-form of a verb minus ない／ 動詞の「ない形」から「ない」を取ったもの	話さ~~ない~~；食べ~~ない~~；し~~ない~~

V-plain	Plain form of a verb／動詞の普通形	食べる；食べた；食べない；食べなかった
V-*te*	*Te*-form of a verb／動詞の「て形」	話して；食べて；して
ø	No particle or *da*／助詞や「だ」が不要な場合	先生 ø みたいです。
×	Ungrammatical or unacceptable／非文・不適格文	×リサさんはスキーをできません。
??	Extremely unnatural／非常に不自然	?? 雨がふっていません。
GID	Grammar in Depth／より深い文法説明	
⚠	Important note on a frequently misunderstood point／間違いやすいポイントの説明	
FYI	Grammar item that you only need to learn to understand; no exercises are provided／理解するだけでいい文法	

◎ Activities

- In this section, you will practice speaking in incremental steps, using grammatical items and expressions to fulfill the goals presented in the lesson's *Dekiru* List.
- The examples for some exercises have parts of them underlined. When practicing, substitute in the given words and phrases for the underlined segments.
- Blue text in an example indicates particles or expressions you should pay particular attention to.
- The exercises that use casual speech are marked with a t-shirt icon.

◎ 話しましょう

- 「できるリスト」を達成するために、必要な文法項目や表現を使いながら、段階的に話す練習をします。
- 練習の例に下線がある場合は置き換え練習をするという意味です。
- 青字は注意する助詞や表現を示しています。
- カジュアルスピーチの練習にはのマークがついています。

◎ Reading

- In L11 to L17, this section is divided into three subsections: "Information Gathering," "Reading Comprehension," and "Writing Practice." In the "Reading Comprehension" subsection, you will learn how to read accurately using various reading strategies.
- In L18 to L20, you will engage in comprehensive reading practice, so we provide a reading goal on the lesson's *Dekiru* List. In order to advance to the intermediate level, you will practice thoroughly analyzing written works and passages through pre-reading, reading comprehension, and post-reading activities.
- In L18 to L20, information gathering practice and reading strategies are not included.

◎ 読みましょう

- 1課から17課には「情報取り」「読み物」「書く練習」があります。「読み物」では「読みのストラテジー」を用いて、正確に読む練習をします。
- 18課から20課では、読みの総合的な練習をするため、読解の「できるリスト」を設けました。中級への橋渡しとなるように前作業、読み物、後作業の活動を通して、文章や作品をより深く理解する訓練をします。
- 18課から20課には、「情報取り」の練習と「読みのストラテジー」は入れてありません。

◎ Listening

- This section contains listening practice where you will make use of a variety of different listening strategies to understand spoken Japanese. These strategies build on each other from lesson to lesson, allowing you to develop your overall listening comprehension abilities as you go.

◎ 聞きましょう

- 日本語の聴解に役立つストラテジーを用いて聴く練習をします。ストラテジーを積み上げていくことにより、総合的な聴解力を身につけることが目標です。

◎ Instructional Videos

- There are instructional videos available to view on the *TOBIRA* website. You can use these to familiarize yourself with material before class or to review and deepen your understanding afterwards.

◎ 反転授業 (flipped classroom) 用動画について

- 反転授業用動画は「とびら初級WEBサイト」にあります。これを見ることを予習課題とすれば、授業ではより実践的、応用的な練習に時間を使うことができます。その他にも、授業内で使用する、学習者が復習や自律学習に使うなど多様な使い方が可能です。特に、オンライン授業やハイブリッド授業に役に立ちます。

◎ The *TOBIRA* Website

- You can access a variety of different supplementary materials on the *TOBIRA* website.

□ Audio materials: These include audio recordings for the vocabulary, conversation, activities, and listening sections in each lesson. Content for which there is audio available is marked by LX-X in the textbook.

□ Audio recordings for the Reading Comprehesion section in each lesson.

□ Instructional videos: Content for which there are instructional videos available is noted in the textbook.

□ Grammar in Depth (GID)

□ Links to web content related to each lesson's activities.

■とびら初級 WEB サイト
https://tobirabeginning.9640.jp/

◎ 「とびら初級WEBサイト」について

- 「とびら初級 WEB サイト」からは、教科書を補助したり、学習を助けたりする各種教材にアクセスできます。

□ 音声教材 LX-X ：各課の「会話」「単語」「話しましょう」の基本練習、「聞きましょう」の音声

□ 各課の「読み物」の音声

□ 反転授業用動画

□ GID (Grammar in Depth)

□ 各課活動の関連サイトリンク集

□ スケジュール、小テスト、試験、宿題のサンプル

□ 「聞きましょう」「読み物」の練習問題の模範解答

□ 「会話」「読み物」の英訳

□ 「聞きましょう」の音声教材のスクリプト

日本の地図（ちず）

先生方へ：授業で必要な時に使ってください。「とびら初級 WEB サイト」の「リンク集」のページにも同じ地図があります。

Students: Refer to this map to see where the various regions and prefectures of Japan are located. A link to the same map can be found on the *TOBIRA* website under "Links."

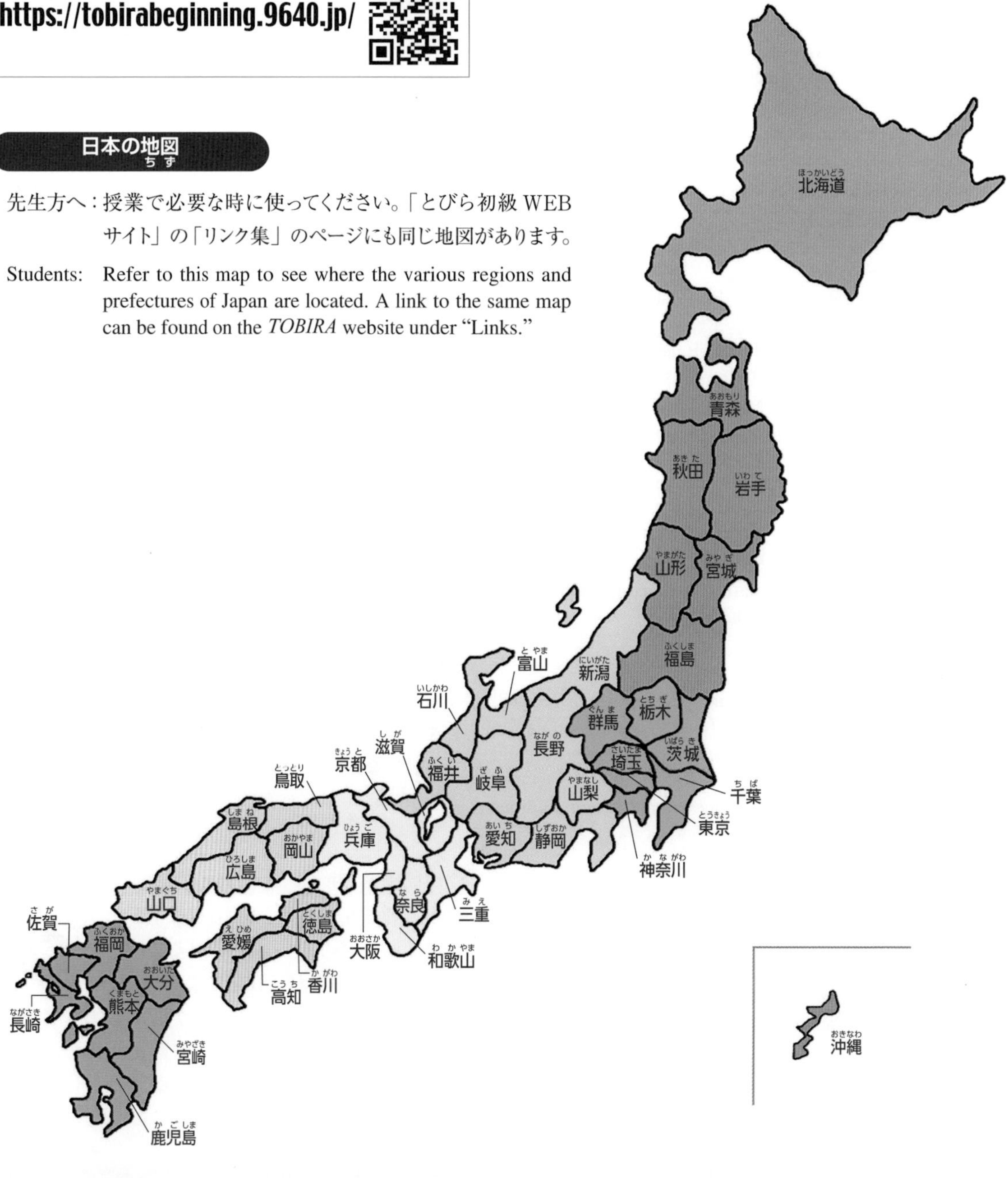

北海道
青森
秋田
岩手
山形
宮城
富山
新潟
福島
石川
群馬
栃木
滋賀
長野
茨城
京都
福井
岐阜
埼玉
鳥取
山梨
千葉
島根
兵庫
東京
岡山
愛知
静岡
広島
神奈川
山口
奈良
三重
佐賀
徳島
福岡
愛媛
大阪
和歌山
大分
香川
高知
熊本
長崎
宮崎
沖縄
鹿児島

Unit 4

世界に飛び出す
せかい　と　だ

Going forth into the world

04

Pre-activity

Unit4の前に

The theme of this unit is "Going forth into the world." In the past, many Japanese people have ventured outside their country and made an impact on the world. The Japanese continue to play an active role in various fields worldwide today.

1 誰(だれ)か有名な日本人を知っていますか。クラスメートとその人の名前と仕事(しごと)について話してみましょう。

2 下の写真(しゃしん)は世界(せかい)で有名な６人の日本人です。名前を聞いたことがありますか。

Useful expressions	～を知っています／知りません　～という名前を聞いたことがあります

① 山中伸弥(やまなかしんや)

京都大学 iPS 細胞研究所

[　　　]（　　　）

② 坂茂(ばんしげる)

[　　　]（　　　）

③ 紫舟(ししゅう)

Photo by Noriaki Ito

[　　　]（　　　）

④ 近藤麻理恵(こんどうまりえ)

©KonMari Media Inc.

[　　　]（　　　）

⑤ 羽生結弦(はにゅうゆづる)

写真：YUTAKA/ アフロスポーツ

[　　　]（　　　）

⑥ 村上春樹(むらかみはるき)

写真：The New York Times/ Redux/アフロ

[　　　]（　　　）

Q1. ①～⑥の人は何をしていますか。写真(しゃしん)の下の［　　］に a.～f. を入(い)れてください。

a. 作家　　b. 医学者(いがくしゃ) (medical scientist)　　c. かたづけコンサルタント

d. 書道家(しょどうか) (calligrapher)　　e. 建築家(けんちくか) (architect)　　f. フィギュアスケーター

Q2. ①～⑥の人の作品(さくひん) ((a piece of) work) やしたことは下のどれだと思いますか。写真(しゃしん)の下の（　　）に (1)～(6) を入(い)れてください。

(1) ベストセラー小説(しょうせつ) (novel)

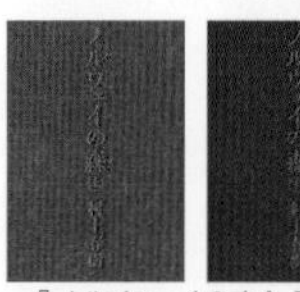

『ノルウェイの森』講談社

(2) 紙(かみ)の教会(きょうかい)

© 平井広行

(3) こんまり®メソッドが大人気(だいにんき) (wildly popular)

(4) うかぶ文字(もじ) (floating letters)

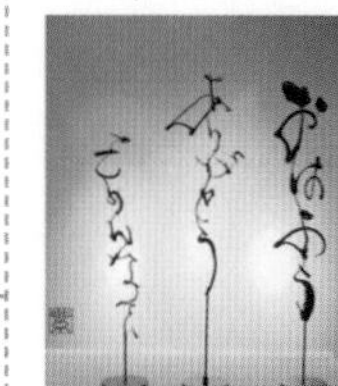

(5) 二つの冬(ふゆ)のオリンピックの金メダル

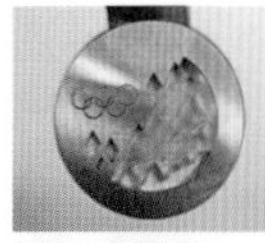

写真：AP/アフロ　写真：ロイター/アフロ

(6) iPS細胞(さいぼう)の発見(はっけん)とノーベル賞(しょう) (Discovery of iPS cells and Nobel Prize)

京都大学教授 山中伸弥

Q3. あなたの国で有名な人は誰(だれ)ですか。その人は何を{していますか／しましたか}。

Lesson 11

私に漢字の覚え方を教えてくれない？

Can you teach me how to memorize kanji?

Instructional Video Lesson 11

DEKIRU List

できるCheck ☑

できるI **Describe and explain things and people around you in detail.**
自分の回りの物や人について、具体的に描写したり説明したりできる。
Entry ☐ Exit ☐

できるII **Draw comparisons to give easy-to-understand explanations of familiar things.**
自分がよく知っている物事について、何かに例えたり分かりやすく説明したりできる。
Entry ☐ Exit ☐

できるIII **Ask and answer questions about how to use, make, and do things in your everyday life.**
身近な物の使い方や作り方などについて、尋ねたり答えたりできる。
Entry ☐ Exit ☐

STRATEGIES

Conversation Tips .... • Contracted forms ～てる, ～てた, and そっか／そう

Reading .... • Getting information from visual clues: Solving Japanese riddles
• Grasping the structure of noun phrases containing noun modification clauses
• Identifying noun modification clauses
• Understanding demonstratives: そ-words

Listening .... • Understanding sequence words

GRAMMAR

1. の [Indefinite pronoun] できるI
2. Noun modification clauses できるI
3. ～時 "when" できるII
4. ～みたい／よう [Resemblance] できるII
5. XはYことです "X is to Y; X is V-ing; X is that Y" できるII
6. V-*te*から "after V-ing; after X has V-ed" できるIII
7. V-*masu* 方 [Method, manner] できるIII

Conversation

会話(かいわ)

1 できる I **Ai is talking with Keita about her study abroad plans.** L11-1

アイ　：圭太(けいた)さん、今ちょっといいですか。

圭太(けいた)　：うん、何？

アイ　：夏(なつ)に京都(きょうと)の宇治(うじ)という町でホームステイをするんですが、

宇治(うじ)を知っていますか。

圭太(けいた)　：宇治(うじ)？　うん、知ってるよ。

アイ　：どんな町ですか。

圭太(けいた)　：お茶(ちゃ)が有名で、自然(しぜん)がたくさんあるいい所(ところ)だよ。

アイ　：そうですか。実(じつ)は、ホストファミリーは宇治(うじ)でお茶(ちゃ)の店(みせ)をやっているんです。

圭太(けいた)　：そっか、じゃ、毎日おいしいお茶(ちゃ)を飲むことができるね。

日本のお茶(ちゃ)は色々(いろいろ)あるけど、僕(ぼく)は宇治(うじ)のが一番おいしいと思うよ。

アイ　：へえ、そうなんですか。

これはホストファミリーの写真(しゃしん)です。

このめがねをかけている人はお父さんです。

圭太(けいた)　：そう、やさしそうな人だね。

アイ　：ええ。お父さんの右にいる人はお姉さんで、

それから、弟さんとお母さんです。

2 できる II **Mark and Tao are talking at the Japan House.** L11-2

ライバル：rival

マーク　：タオちゃん、アイちゃんと圭太(けいた)は最近(さいきん)仲(なか)がいいね。

タオ　：ええ。よく二人で美術館(びじゅつかん)に行っていますよ。

マーク　：一緒(いっしょ)にいる時、とても楽しそうだね。

タオ　：はい、でも、アイちゃんは最近(さいきん)ジャンさんともよく話しています。

マーク　：アイちゃんは留学(りゅうがく)する場所(ばしょ)を決(き)める時、ジャンに相談(そうだん)したと言ってたね。

にゃんた：ニャーニャー！

タオ　：あ、ここにも圭太(けいた)さんのライバルがいる！

Ai and Riemann are talking at the Japan House.

L11-3

学習(がくしゅう)スタイル：learning style

アイ　：リーマンさん、私に漢字(かんじ)の覚(おぼ)え方(かた)を教(おし)えてくれない？

リーマン：ええ、いいですよ。僕(ぼく)の趣味(しゅみ)は漢字(かんじ)を覚(おぼ)えることですから…

アイさんは自分(じぶん)の学習(がくしゅう)スタイルを知っていますか。

アイ　：え、私の学習(がくしゅう)スタイル？

リーマン：はい、それを知ってから一番(いちばん)いいのを考(かんが)えましょう。

<Ai takes a learning style quiz online.>

アイ　：えっと、私の学習(がくしゅう)スタイルはビジュアルタイプだと思う。

リーマン：そうですか。じゃ、レッスン11の漢字(かんじ)を絵(え)で覚(おぼ)えましょう。

アイ　：え？　絵(え)で覚(おぼ)える？

リーマン：はい。まず、この「肉(にく)」の漢字(かんじ)を使って絵(え)を描(か)いてみてください。

<Ai is drawing.>

アイ　：これはどう？

リーマン：あ、とてもいいですね。バーベキューの肉(にく)みたいです！

じゃ、次に、「鳥(とり)」の漢字(かんじ)の絵(え)を描(か)いてみてください。

<Ai draws another picture.>

リーマン：アイさんは本当(ほんとう)に絵(え)を描(か)くのが上手ですね！

この富士山(ふじさん)みたいな山もいいですね。

アイ　：リーマンさん、この漢字(かんじ)の覚(おぼ)え方(かた)は楽しいね。

リーマン：そうですか。よかったです。

最後(さいご)に、漢字(かんじ)の書き方(かた)も練習(れんしゅう)してくださいね。

アイ　：うん、分かった。どうもありがとう！

CONVERSATION TIPS

Contracted forms ～てる, ～てた, and そっか／そう: When speaking casually, it is common to use contracted forms. For example, ～ている becomes ～てる, ～ていた becomes ～てた, and そうか becomes そっか or そう.

＜電話(でんわ)で＞

Ａ：もしもし、今、何してる？

Ｂ：今？　宿題(しゅくだい)してる。

Ａ：そっか／そう。じゃ、また、あとで電話(でんわ)するね。

Vocabulary with Pictures

単語（たんご）

▶ **The words written in gray** are supplemental vocabulary.

描写する（びょうしゃ） Describing people, things, and feelings

[*thing* に] かんどうする
(to be moved;
to be (emotionally) touched)

おこる
(to get angry)

おどろく
(to be surprised)

ふとい
(thick [line];
big [body shape])

↔ ほそい
(thin [line];
small [body shape])

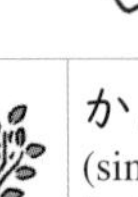

かんたん(な)
(simple; easy)
[not used
for people]

↔ むずかしい

まるい
(circular; round)

まる
(circle; oval)

しかくい
(square; box-shaped)

しかく
(square; box (on a form))

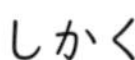

場所（ばしょ） Places

[*thing* を] チェックする
(to check (out/on))

ざっし
(magazine)

[*thing/place* を] よやくする
(to reserve)

[*place* に] つく
(to arrive)

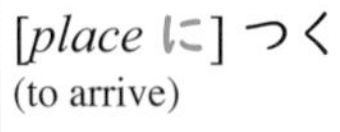

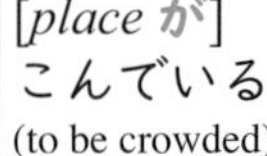

[*place* が] こむ
(to get crowded)

[*place* が] こんでいる
(to be crowded)

[*thing* を] ちゅうもんする
(to order)

わしょく
(Japanese cuisine)

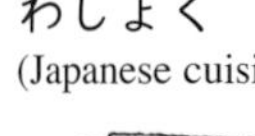

[*place* に *thing/person* を] はこぶ
(to carry;
to transport)

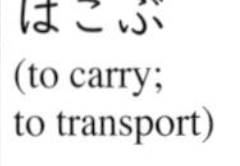

[*place* に] よる
(to stop by)

[*thing* が] おわる
(to (come to an) end)

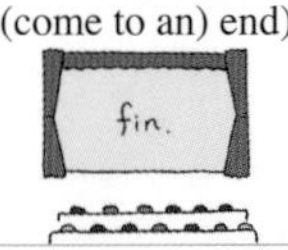

ばしょ
(place; area;
location)

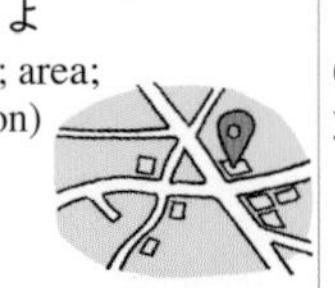

にわ
(garden;
yard)

けしき
(scenery;
view)

しぜん
(nature)

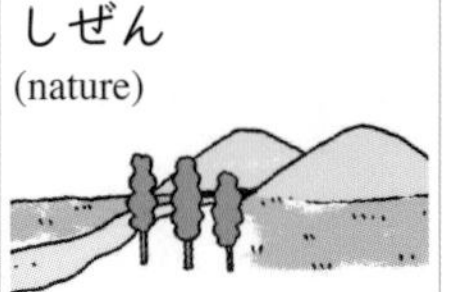

身（み）のまわりの物／こと Things around you

[*clothes/shoes* を] ぬぐ
(to take off;
to remove)

くつした
(sock)

[*thing* を] やる
(to do) [more casual than する]

もんだい
(problem; question;
issue)

みせをやる／する
(to run a shop)

SHOP

ゆっくりする
(to relax; to stay for long)

けしゴム
(eraser)

かいわ
(conversation)

ことば
(word; phrase; language)

すうじ
(number [numeral]; digit)

0 1 2 3 4 5

もじ
(character; letter)

あいうえお
かきくけこ

Lesson 11

料理（りょうり） Cooking

- [*thing* を] きる (to cut) 
  - りんご (apple)
- [*thing* を] まぜる (to mix) 
- [*thing X* に *thing Y* を] いれる (to put (Y) in (X); to insert (Y in X)) 
  - おゆ (hot water)
  - Ex. おゆにラーメンをいれる (to put ramen in hot water)
- [*thing* を] いためる (to stir-fry) 
  - フライパン (frying pan)
- [*thing* を] ゆでる (to boil (in water to cook)) 
  - なべ ((cooking) pot)
- [*thing* を] やく (to bake; to broil; to grill; to toast; to sear) 
- [*thing* を] あたためる (to warm; to heat up) 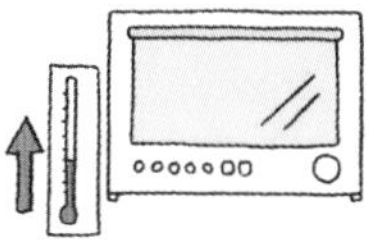
  - でんしレンジ (microwave)
- [*thing* を] ひやす (to chill; to cool down) 
  - れいぞうこ (refrigerator)
- [*thing X* に *thing Y* を] はさむ (to put/insert/sandwich (Y) between (X)) 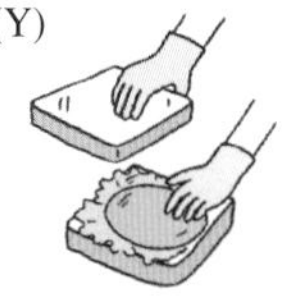
  - Ex. パンにハムをはさむ (to put ham between slices of bread)
- [*thing X* に *thing Y* を] のせる (to put (Y) on (X); to top (X) with (Y)) 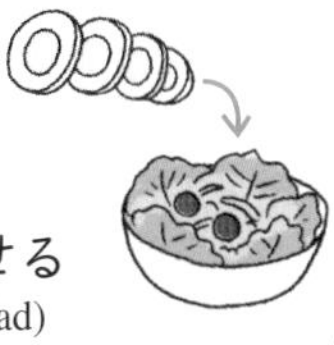
  - Ex. サラダにたまごをのせる (to put egg on salad)
- [*thing X* に *thing Y* を] かける (to pour/drizzle/sprinkle (Y onto X)) 
  - Ex. サラダにドレッシングをかける (to pour dressing onto salad)
- [*thing X* に *thing Y* を] つける (to spread (Y on X); to dip (X in Y)) 
  - Ex. (お)すしにしょうゆをつける (to dip sushi in soy sauce)
- ざいりょう (ingredient; material) 
  - たまご (egg) 
  - とりにく (chicken (meat)) 
  - ぎゅうにく (beef) 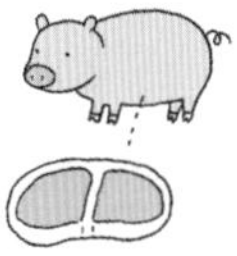
  - ぶたにく (pork)
- ちょうみりょう (seasoning) 
  - しお (salt)
  - さとう (suger)
  - しょうゆ (soy sauce) 
- できあがりです (It is done; It is ready (to eat).)

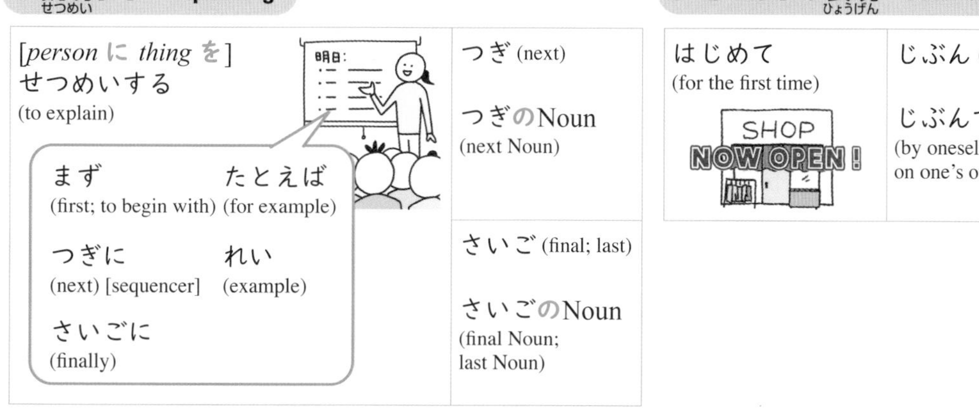

説明（せつめい）する Explaining

- [*person* に *thing* を] せつめいする (to explain)
  - まず (first; to begin with)
  - たとえば (for example)
  - つぎに (next) [sequencer]
  - れい (example)
  - さいごに (finally)
- つぎ (next)
- つぎのNoun (next Noun)
- さいご (final; last)
- さいごのNoun (final Noun; last Noun)

そのほかの表現（ひょうげん） Other expressions

- はじめて (for the first time)

- じぶん (oneself)
- じぶんで (by oneself; on one's own)

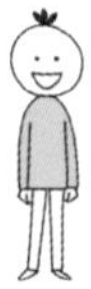

Vocabulary List

単語リスト

L11-5

Highlighted kanji words contain kanji you have learned previously.

RU-VERBS

1	あたためる	温める	to warm; to heat up [*thing* を]
2	いためる		to stir-fry [*thing* を]
3	いれる	入れる	to put (Y) in (X); to insert (Y in X) [*thing X* に *thing Y* を]
4	かける		to pour/drizzle/sprinkle (Y onto X) [*thing X* に *thing Y* を]
5	つける		to spread (Y on X); to dip (X in Y) [*thing X* に *thing Y* を]
6	のせる		to put (Y) on (X); to top (X) with (Y) [*thing X* に *thing Y* を]
7	まぜる	混ぜる	to mix [*thing* を]
8	ゆでる		to boil (in water to cook) [*thing* を]

U-VERBS / U-VERB PHRASES

9	おこる	怒る	to get angry
10	おどろく		to be surprised
11	おわる	終わる	to (come to an) end [*thing* が]
12	きる	切る	to cut [*thing* を]
13	こむ	混む	to get crowded [*place* が]
	こんでいる	混んでいる	to be crowded [*place* が]
14	つく	着く	to arrive [*place* に]
15	ぬぐ		to take off; to remove [*clothes/shoes* を]
16	はこぶ	運ぶ	to carry; to transport [*place* に *thing/person* を]
17	はさむ		to put/insert/sandwich (Y) between (X) [*thing X* に *thing Y* を]
18	ひやす	冷やす	to chill; to cool down [*thing* を]
19	やく	焼く	to bake; to broil; to grill; to toast; to sear [*thing* を]
20	やる		to do [*thing* を] [more casual than する]
21	みせをやる／する	店をやる／する	to run a shop
22	よる	寄る	to stop by [*place* に]

SURU-VERBS

23	かんどうする	感動する	to be moved; to be (emotionally) touched [*thing* に]
24	せつめいする	説明する	to explain [*person* に *thing* を]
25	チェックする		to check (out/on) [*thing* を]
26	ちゅうもんする	注文する	to order [*thing* を]
27	ゆっくりする		to relax; to stay for long
28	よやくする	予約する	to reserve [*thing/place* を]

I-ADJECTIVES

29	しかくい	四角い	square; box-shaped
30	ふとい	太い	thick [line]; big [body shape]
31	ほそい	細い	thin [line]; small [body shape]
32	まるい	丸い	circular; round

NA-ADJECTIVE

33	かんたん	簡単	simple; easy [not used for people]

NOUNS

34	おゆ	お湯	hot water
35	かいわ	会話	conversation
36	ぎゅうにく	牛肉	beef
37	とりにく	鳥肉／鶏肉	chicken (meat)
38	ぶたにく	豚肉	pork

39	くつした	くつ下	sock
40	けしき	景色	scenery; view
41	けしゴム	消しゴム	eraser
42	ことば	言葉	word; phrase; language
43	さいご	最後	final; last
	さいごの Noun	最後の～	final Noun; last Noun
44	ざいりょう	材料	ingredient; material
45	ざっし	雑誌	magazine
46	さとう	砂糖	sugar
47	しお	塩	salt
48	しょうゆ		soy sauce
49	しかく	四角	square; box (on a form)
50	しぜん	自然	nature
51	じぶん	自分	oneself
52	すうじ	数字	number [numeral]; digit
53	たまご	卵／玉子	egg
54	つぎ	次	next
	つぎの Noun	次の～	next Noun
55	でんしレンジ	電子レンジ	microwave (oven)
56	なべ		(cooking) pot
57	にわ	庭	garden; yard
58	ばしょ	場所	place; area; location
59	フライパン		frying pan
60	まる	丸	circle; oval
61	もじ	文字	character; letter [symbol used to write words]
62	もんだい	問題	problem; question; issue
63	りんご		apple
64	れい	例	example
65	れいぞうこ	冷蔵庫	refrigerator
66	わしょく	和食	Japanese cuisine

ADVERBS

67	はじめて	初めて	for the first time
68	まず		first; to begin with

OTHER WORDS AND PHRASES

69	さいごに	最後に	finally
70	じぶんで	自分で	by oneself; on one's own
71	たとえば	例えば	for example
72	つぎに	次に	next [sequencer]
73	できあがりです		It is done; It is ready (to eat).

Kanji

漢字（かんじ）

140	勉 勉 勉	ベン	勉強する（べんきょう） to study　勤勉（な）（きんべん） hardworking 勉強になる（べんきょう） to be informative; to teach one something
	to make effort		勉 (stroke order)
141	強 強 強	キョウ	勉強する（べんきょう） to study　勉強になる（べんきょう） to be informative; to teach one something 強力（な）（きょうりょく） powerful
		つよ(い)	強い（つよ） strong　強く（つよ） strongly [adverbial form of 強い（つよ）]
	strong		強 (stroke order)
142	着 着 着	チャク	着払い（ちゃくばら） payment on delivery　到着する（とうちゃく） to arrive [formal]
		き(る) つ(く) ぎ	着る（き） to put on (clothes above the waist)　着物（きもの） kimono　着がえる（き） to change clothes 着く（つ） to arrive　水着（みずぎ） swimsuit
	to wear; to arrive		着 (stroke order)
143	自 自 自	ジ シ	自分（じぶん） oneself　自分で（じぶん） by oneself　自己紹介する（じこしょうかい） to introduce oneself 自信を持つ（じしん・も） to have confidence　自転車（じてんしゃ） bicycle; bike　自動車（じどうしゃ） automobile; car 自動で（じどう） automatically　自慢する（じまん） to brag; to boast 自由（じゆう） freedom　自由（な）（じゆう） free　自由に（じゆう） freely　自然（しぜん） nature
	self		自 (stroke order)
144	場 場 場	ジョウ	会場（かいじょう） venue; meeting place　工場（こうじょう） factory　駐車場（ちゅうしゃじょう） parking lot/garage
		ば	場所（ばしょ） place; area; location　場合（ばあい） case; occasion　場面（ばめん） scene; situation
	location		場 (stroke order)
145	所 所 所	ショ ジョ	場所（ばしょ） place; area; location　市役所（しやくしょ） city hall　住所（じゅうしょ） address 名所（めいしょ） famous place　近所（きんじょ） neighborhood
		ところ	所（ところ） place
	place		所 (stroke order)
146	茶 茶 茶	チャ サ	お茶（ちゃ） (green) tea　お茶をいれる（ちゃ） to make tea　紅茶（こうちゃ） black tea 茶色（ちゃいろ） brown [noun]　茶色い（ちゃいろ） brown [adjective]　抹茶（まっちゃ） powdered green tea 喫茶店（きっさてん） coffee shop; café　茶道（さどう） (Japanese) tea ceremony
	tea		茶 (stroke order)

147	料	ingredient; fare	リョウ	～料理(りょうり) ... cuisine (Ex. 日本料理(にほんりょうり) Japanese cuisine)　料理(りょうり)する to cook 給料(きゅうりょう) salary; wage　材料(ざいりょう) ingredient; material　授業料(じゅぎょうりょう) tuition 無料(むりょう) free of charge　料金(りょうきん) fee
148	理	logic	リ	～料理(りょうり) ... cuisine (Ex. 日本料理(にほんりょうり) Japanese cuisine)　料理(りょうり)する to cook 心理学(しんりがく) psychology　地理(ちり) geography　無理(むり)(な) impossible 無理(むり)(を)する to push oneself too hard　理解(りかい)する to understand　理由(りゆう) reason
149	肉	meat	ニク	肉(にく) meat　牛肉(ぎゅうにく) beef　鳥肉(とりにく)／鶏肉(とりにく) chicken (meat) 豚肉(ぶたにく) pork　肉屋(にくや) butcher shop　筋肉(きんにく) muscle
150	鳥	bird	チョウ	白鳥(はくちょう) swan
			とり	鳥(とり) bird　鳥肉(とりにく)／鶏肉(とりにく) chicken (meat)　小鳥(ことり) small bird 鳥居(とりい) *torii*; gate (at a Shinto shrine)
151	魚	fish	ギョ	魚介類(ぎょかいるい) seafood　金魚(きんぎょ) goldfish
			さかな ざかな	魚(さかな) fish　魚屋(さかなや) fishmonger; fish shop 小魚(こざかな) small fish; baitfish
152	絵	drawing	カイ	絵画(かいが) painting
			え	絵(え) picture; painting; drawing　絵本(えほん) picture book
153	例	example	レイ	例(れい) example
			たと(えば)	例えば(たとえば) for example
154	方	direction	ホウ	XよりYの方(ほう)が Y is more ... than X　地方(ちほう) region; area　方言(ほうげん) dialect 方向(ほうこう) direction　方法(ほうほう) method　両方(りょうほう) both (sides/parties)
			かた がた	～方(かた) how to ... (Ex. 使い方(つかいかた) how to use)　夕方(ゆうがた) early evening

155 次 次 次	ジ	次回（じかい） next time　目次（もくじ） table of contents
	つぎ	次（つぎ） next [noun]　次に（つぎに） next [sequencer]
		次の（つぎの） Noun next Noun　次の日（つぎのひ） the next day
next	次次次次次次	

156 最 最 最	サイ	最後（さいご） final; last　最後に（さいごに） finally　最後の（さいごの） Noun final Noun; last Noun
		最悪（さいあく） worst　最近（さいきん） recently　最高（さいこう） highest; awesome　最初（さいしょ） the first　最低（さいてい） lowest
	もっと(も)	最も（もっとも） most
utmost	最最最最最最最最最最最最	

Kanji as elements

These kanji are used in many other kanji as elements, so you will encounter them frequently as you continue to study Japanese.

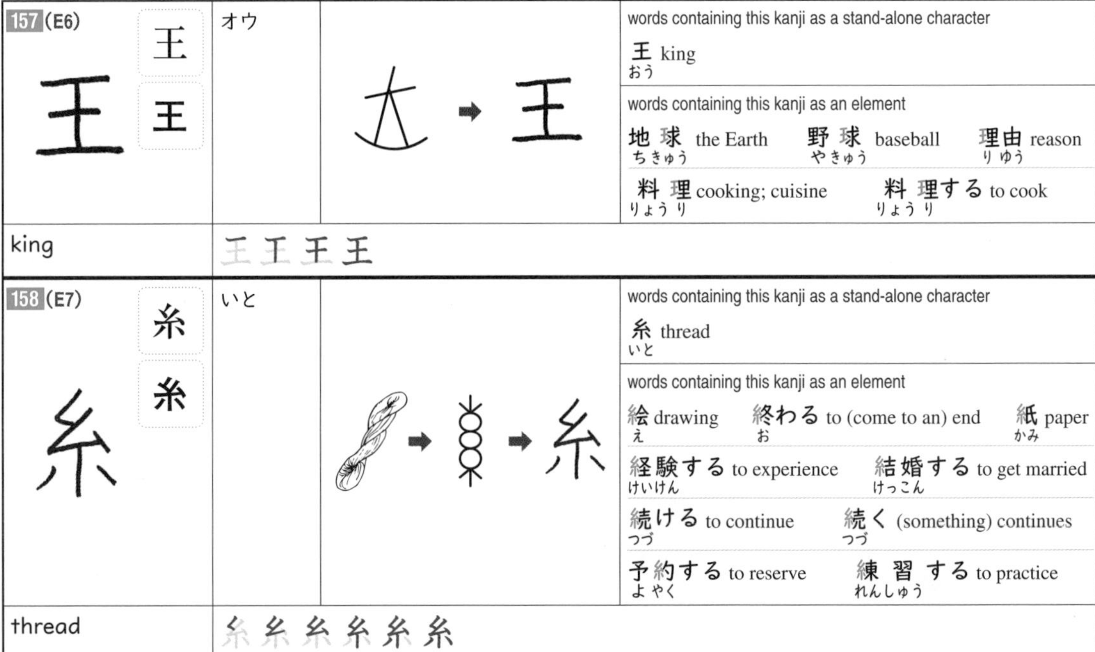

157 (E6) 王 王 王	オウ		words containing this kanji as a stand-alone character: 王（おう） king
			words containing this kanji as an element: 地球（ちきゅう） the Earth　野球（やきゅう） baseball　理由（りゆう） reason
			料理（りょうり） cooking; cuisine　料理する（りょうりする） to cook
king	王王王王		

158 (E7) 糸 糸 糸	いと		words containing this kanji as a stand-alone character: 糸（いと） thread
			words containing this kanji as an element: 絵（え） drawing　終わる（おわる） to (come to an) end　紙（かみ） paper
			経験する（けいけんする） to experience　結婚する（けっこんする） to get married
			続ける（つづける） to continue　続く（つづく） (something) continues
			予約する（よやくする） to reserve　練習する（れんしゅうする） to practice
thread	糸糸糸糸糸糸		

新しい読み方（かた）

The following are new readings for kanji that you have already learned. Read each word aloud.

1) 入（い）れる　2) 会話（かいわ）　3) 牛肉（ぎゅうにく）　4) 切（き）る　5) 自分（じぶん）／自分（じぶん）で

習（なら）った漢字（かんじ）で書ける新しい単語（たんご）

The following are other new vocabulary in this lesson that contain kanji you have already leaned. Read each word aloud.

1) くつ下（した）

練習(れんしゅう)

1 Find and circle 10 words that contain kanji you have learned so far, then write the words and their readings in the spaces provided. The words may appear either vertically or horizontally.

勉	強	お	茶
場	い	着	く
Ex. (所)	魚	る	自
会	話	絵	分

Ex. 所 （ ところ ）

1） ______（　　　）　2） ______（　　　）

3） ______（　　　）　4） ______（　　　）

5） ______（　　　）　6） ______（　　　）

7） ______（　　　）　8） ______（　　　）

9） ______（　　　）　10） ______（　　　）

2 Below is a post Lin-san made on social media about how to make Japanese-style curry. Read the post aloud, then write the readings for the underlined words.

週末はよく友達のりかさんと一緒(いっしょ)に遊(あそ)びます。例えば、日本の料理を作ったり、人気があるカフェにお茶を飲みに行ったりします。今週はカレーライスを作りました。すごくおいしかったから、作り方を紹介(しょうかい)します。まず、肉と野菜(やさい)を小さく切ります。肉は牛肉か鳥肉を使いますが、私は牛肉の方が好きです。次に、なべに油(あぶら) (oil) を入れて、肉と野菜(やさい)をいためます。それから、そのなべに水を入れて、20 分ぐらいにます (to simmer)。そして、カレールーを入れて、よく混(ま)ぜます。最後に、10 分ぐらいにて、できあがりです。とても簡単(かんたん)だから、みなさんもぜひ作ってみてください！

The Story of Kanji

■ Special readings

You learned in Lesson 4 that most kanji have both *kun-yomi* (native Japanese readings) and *on-yomi* (imported Chinese-style readings), as shown below.

Ex.1 音が聞こえます。　　**Ex.2** 音楽を聞きます。

In Ex.1, 音 is read as おと, which is the *kun-yomi*. On the other hand, in Ex.2, 音 is read as おん, which is the *on-yomi*. The *kun-yomi* is commonly used when you see one kanji alone, while the *on-yomi* is commonly used for kanji compound words. For many kanji compound words (e.g., 音楽(おんがく)), the reading is a combination of the *on-yomi* of each of the kanji (e.g., 音(おん) and 楽(がく)).

Some kanji compound words, however, have a single special reading that is assigned to the word as a whole. One such example is 今日(きょう), the reading of which is neither a combination of the *on-yomi* nor of the *kun-yomi* of 今 and 日. In cases like these, it is impossible to assign each kanji in the compound a particular part of the reading.

練習(れんしゅう)

You have already learned the following kanji compound words with special readings. Write the reading for each compound word 1)-3), as well as the reading and meaning of each kanji in it. Can you figure out how the meanings of compound words are created?

読み方	読み方と意味(いみ)			意味(いみ)
Ex. 今年 [ことし]	今 [いま now]	+	年 [ねん year]	this year
1) 明日 [ ]	明るい [ ]	+	日 [ ]	
2) 上手 [ ]	上 [ ]	+	手 [ ]	
3) 一人 [ ]	一 [ ]	+	人 [ ]	

文法（ぶんぽう）

1 の [Indefinite pronoun] "one"

[1]

Topic	Adj			
パソコンは	軽い（かる）	の	が	いいです。
As for computers, light ones are good.				

You can use の in place of a specific noun when what の refers to is clear to the listener from the situation or context. In [1], の is used instead of repeating パソコン.

⚠ Note that の cannot be used by itself. It is typically modified by adjectives or noun modification clauses. (See #2 below.)

Exs. (1) 音楽（おんがく）はにぎやかで楽（たの）しい音楽（おんがく）が好（す）きです。*As for music, I like lively and fun music.*

→ 音楽（おんがく）はにぎやかで楽（たの）しいのが好（す）きです。*As for music, I like the lively and fun kind.*

(2) <インド料理（りょうり）のレストランで>

A: どんなカレーがいいですか。*What kind of curry do you prefer?*

B: あまりからくないカレーがいいです。*I prefer a curry that is not very spicy.*

→ あまりからくないのがいいです。*I prefer one that is not very spicy.*

The indefinite pronoun の is typically used to refer to a specific subgroup of a category, as in (1) and (2). In (1), for example, にぎやかで楽（たの）しい specifies "interesting and fun" music out of the various types of music.

の cannot be used in the following sentence because 甘（あま）くておいしい simply describes the apples the speaker received and does not refer to a specific subgroup of a larger category (i.e., it is not specifying all of the sweet and delicious apples out of the larger group of all apples).

× りんごをもらいました。甘（あま）くてとてもおいしいのです。

→ りんごをもらいました。甘（あま）くてとてもおいしいりんごです。

Someone gave me (lit. I received) some apples. They are sweet and very delicious apples.

Similarly, の cannot be used in B's line in the following conversation because here, とてもいいの does not specify a certain type of person among many; it simply describes what kind of person Yamada-san is.

A: 山田（やまだ）さんはどんな人（ひと）ですか。*What kind of person is Yamada-san?*

B: × とてもいいのです。 → とてもいい人（ひと）です。*She is a very nice person.*

The indefinite pronoun の is also used to refer to a specific item in a group when the referent is clear from the situation, as in (3) below.

Ex. (3) <服（ふく）の店（みせ）で> その赤（あか）いセーターを見（み）せてください。*Show me that red sweater, please.*

→ その赤（あか）いのを見（み）せてください。*Show me that red sweater (lit. that red one), please.*

When this pronoun の comes after the particle の, the indefinite pronoun の drops, as in (4) below.

Ex. (4) 田中（たなか）さんのくつはイタリアの~~の~~ですが、私（わたし）の~~の~~は日本（にほん）の~~の~~です。

Tanaka-san's shoes are Italian (lit. Italian ones), but mine are Japanese (lit. Japanese ones).

2 Noun modification clauses

We have already learned how to modify a noun with another noun or with an adjective, as in (a)-(c) below.

(a) にゃんたはジャパンハウスのネコです。*Nyanta is the Japan House's cat.*

(b) にゃんたはかわいいネコです。*Nyanta is a cute cat.*

(c) にゃんたは元気(げんき)なネコです。*Nyanta is an energetic cat.*

Similarly, you can modify a noun with a clause (i.e., a sentence within a sentence), as in [2-a].

[2-a]

Topic	NP (= noun phrase)		
	Noun modification clause	N	
にゃんたは	ジャパンハウスに住(す)んでいる	ネコ	です。
Nyanta is a cat that lives in the Japan House.			

By using noun modification clauses, you can explain objects, people, places, etc. in a more compact, efficient fashion. For example, you can express the ideas described in two sentences in (d) below in a single sentence, as in (e), using a noun modification clause.

(d) にゃんたはネコです。にゃんたはジャパンハウスに住(す)んでいます。

Nyanta is a cat. Nyanta lives in the Japan House.

(e) にゃんたは<u>ジャパンハウスに住(す)んでいる</u>[ネコ]です。(= [2-a])

Nyanta is a cat that lives in the Japan House.

(The <u>underline</u> and [ ] indicate the noun modification clause and the modified noun, respectively. The same notations are used in other examples below.)

The following are the steps for making a sentence with a noun modification clause:

Step 1 Put the noun modifying clause directly before the noun to be modified. (No relative pronoun, such as *who* and *which* in English, is used between the noun modification clause and the modified noun.)

にゃんたは <u>ジャパンハウスに住(す)んでいます</u>[ネコ]です。

Step 2 Change the predicate in the noun modification clause into the plain form.

にゃんたは <u>ジャパンハウスに住(す)んでいる</u>[ネコ]です。

[2-b] is an example of a noun modification clause with a subject.

[2-b]

Topic	NP				
	Noun modification clause			N	
	Subject		V-plain		
これは	私(わたし)	が	焼(や)いた	ケーキ	です。
This is a cake (that) I baked.					

Here, the two sentences in (f) are combined into one sentence, presented again in (g).

(f) これはケーキです。<u>私(わたし)は</u>(このケーキを)焼(や)きました。*This is a cake. I baked it (= this cake).*

(g) これは <u>私(わたし)が焼(や)いた</u>[ケーキ]です。*This is a cake (that) I baked.* (= [2-b])

As seen in (g), when a subject is necessary in the noun modification clause, it is marked with が. Note that は is used to present the topic of the entire sentence (e.g., これは in (g)).

Exs. (1) これはみかさんにあげる[おみやげ]です。*This is a present I will give Mika.*

(2) 昨日(きのう)見(み)た[映画(えいが)]はおもしろかったです。*The movie I saw yesterday was interesting.*

(3) 渋谷(しぶや)はアイさんが初(はじ)めてジャンさんに会(あ)った[所(ところ)]です。
Shibuya is the place where Ai met Jean for the first time.

(4) <寮(りょう)の食堂(しょくどう)で> あそこでピザを食(た)べている[人(ひと)]を知(し)っていますか。
Do you know the person eating pizza over there?

The following sentence patterns present noun modification clauses with an *i*-adjective, a *na*-adjective, and a noun in the predicate position.

[2-c]

	NP				
	Noun modification clause			N	
	Subject		Adj(*i*)-plain		
クラスで一番(いちばん)	背(せ)	が	高(たか)い	人(ひと)	はトムさんです。
The tallest person in the class is Tom. (lit. The person who is the tallest in the class is Tom.)					

[2-d]

NP					
Noun modification clause				N	
Subject		Adj(*na*)			
研(けん)さん	が	得意(とくい)	な	スポーツ	は何(なん)ですか。
What is {the/a} sport you are good at, Ken? / What is {the/a} sport Ken is good at?					

[2-e]

NP					
Noun modification clause				N	
Subject		N			
専攻(せんこう)	が	歴史(れきし)	の	人(ひと)	は誰(だれ)ですか。
Who is a history major? (lit. Who is {the/a} person whose major is history?)					

The ending forms of noun modification clauses are as follows:

	Affirmative	Negative
Verbs (always plain forms)	勉強(べんきょう)する[漢字(かんじ)] 勉強(べんきょう)した[漢字(かんじ)]	勉強(べんきょう)しない[漢字(かんじ)] 勉強(べんきょう)しなかった[漢字(かんじ)]
I-adjectives (always plain forms)	おいしい[店(みせ)] おいしかった[店(みせ)]	おいしくない[店(みせ)] おいしくなかった[店(みせ)]
Na-adjectives + だ (plain forms except for な)	きれいな[ホテル] きれいだった[ホテル]	きれいじゃない[ホテル] きれいじゃなかった[ホテル]
Nouns + だ (plain forms except for の)	お金持(かねも)ちの[人(ひと)] お金持(かねも)ちだった[人(ひと)]	お金持(かねも)ちじゃない[人(ひと)] お金持(かねも)ちじゃなかった[人(ひと)]

Exs. (5) 庭(にわ)が大(おお)きい［家(いえ)］に住(す)みたいです。

I want to live in a house with a big yard (lit. where the yard is big).

(6) 日本(にほん)の子(こ)どもが好(す)きな［スポーツ］を教(おし)えてください。

What's the sport Japanese children like? (lit. Please tell me the sport Japanese children like.)

(7) ルームメートを探(さが)しているんですが、趣味(しゅみ)が料理(りょうり)の［人(ひと)］を知(し)りませんか。

I'm looking for a roommate—do you know of anyone whose hobby is cooking?

Note that noun phrases consisting of a noun modification clause and a noun are considered noun equivalents. Therefore, the particles that occur with nouns (e.g., に, を, etc.) can be attached to noun phrases, as in (5)-(7).

☞ GID (vol.2): E. Special topics 3. Noun modification clauses

3 ～時(とき) "when"

[3-a]

	Time clause (Action 1)			Main clause (Action 2)
		V-plain.non-past		
私(わたし)は	日本(にほん)に	行(い)く	時(とき)、	大(おお)きいスーツケースを買(か)いました。
I bought a large suitcase when I was going to Japan.				

[3-b]

	Time clause (Action 1)			Main clause (Action 2)
		V-plain.past		
私(わたし)は	日本(にほん)に	行(い)った	時(とき)、	漢字(かんじ)のＴシャツを買(か)いました。
I bought a kanji T-shirt when I was in (lit. had gone to) Japan.				

You can express ideas like "when I go to Japan" and "when I went to Japan" using 時(とき) with verbs. Because 時(とき) is a noun, the clause immediately preceding it (i.e., the time clause in [3-a] and [3-b]) is a noun modification clause. Thus, the verb before 時(とき) is always in the plain form.

In Japanese the tense of a verb before 時(とき) is determined as follows:

Rule 1 If Action 1 in the time clause (日本(にほん)に行(い)く) is not completed before Action 2 in the main clause (大(おお)きいスーツケースを買(か)う) occurs, the non-past form is used.

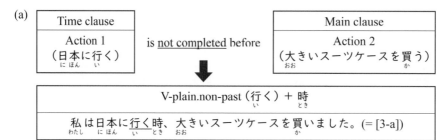

(a)

Time clause
Action 1 (日本(にほん)に行(い)く)

is not completed before

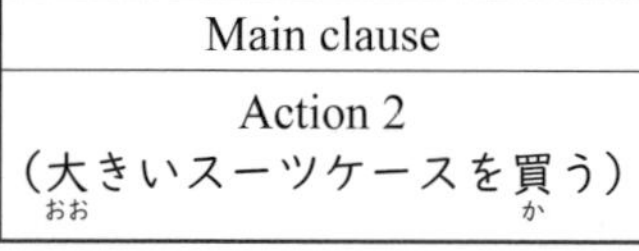

Main clause
Action 2 (大(おお)きいスーツケースを買(か)う)

⬇

V-plain.non-past (行(い)く) ＋ 時(とき)
私(わたし)は日本(にほん)に行(い)く時(とき)、大(おお)きいスーツケースを買(か)いました。(= [3-a])

Rule 2 If Action 1 in the time clause (日本に行く) is completed before Action 2 in the main clause (漢字のTシャツを買う) occurs, the past form is used.

(b)

Time clause		Main clause
Action 1 (日本に行く)	is completed before	Action 2 (漢字のTシャツを買う)

⬇

V-plain.past (行った) ＋ 時
私は日本に行った時、漢字のTシャツを買いました。(= [3-b])

As seen above, regardless of the tense of the main clause, when Action 1 (= the time clause action) is not completed before Action 2 (= the main clause action), the non-past tense is used before 時, whereas when Action 1 is completed before Action 2, the past tense is used.

Exs. (1) 料理する時、まず手を洗います。*When I'm going to cook, I first wash my hands.*

(2) 大学に入った時、ホームシックになりました。*When I started college, I became homesick.*

(3) トムさんはケーキが好きだから、トムさんの家に行く時、ケーキを買いました。
Since Tom likes cakes, I bought some (cakes) when I was going to his house. (= I bought cakes before going to his house.)

(4) 先生：クラスを休む時はメールしてください。
Please email me when you are going to miss class.

(5) 明日会った時、お金を返します。*When we meet tomorrow, I will pay you back.*

When the subject of a time clause and that of the main clause are different, the subject in the time clause is marked by が. (See #2 Noun modification clauses above.)

Ex. (6) ワンさんが来た時、私は晩ご飯を作っていました。／私は、ワンさんが来た時、晩ご飯を作っていました。*When Wang-san came, I was making dinner.*

You can also use adjectives and nouns before 時. The forms before 時 are the same as those used in noun modification clauses. (See #2 above.)

	Affirmative	Negative
I-adjectives	(クラスが)おもしろい時	(クラスが)おもしろくない時
Na-adjectives	(仕事が)大変な時	(仕事が)大変じゃない時
Nouns	(学校が)休みの時	(学校が)休みじゃない時

Exs. (7) ひまな時、よくカフェにコーヒーを飲みに行きます。
When I'm free, I often go to a café to drink coffee.

(8) 父は若い時、すごくかっこよかったです。*My father was quite cool when he was young.*

(9) リーマンさんは高校の時、漢字の勉強を始めました。
Riemann started studying kanji when he was in high school.

(10) 料理したくない時、よくインスタントラーメンを食べます。
When I don't want to cook, I often eat instant ramen.

⚠ As in (7)-(10), when the predicate of a 時 clause (i.e., a clause before 時) expresses a state with an adjective or a noun as its predicate, you usually use a non-past form regardless of the tense of the main clause. The same rule applies to a 時 clause with a state verb such as ある, いる, and V-*te*いる, as in (11)-(13).

Exs. (11) 私は日本にいる時、よく京都に行きました。*I often went to Kyoto when I was in Japan.*

(12) テストの勉強をしている時、頭が痛くなりました。
I got a headache when I was studying for a test.

(13) 去年、忙しい時はよくコンビニで晩ご飯を買いましたが、時間がある時は自分で作りました。*Last year, I often bought dinner at the convenience store when I was busy, but I made it myself when I had the time.*

☞ **GID** (vol.2): A. Time expressions 1. 時 vs. 時に
E. Special topics 4. Tense in time clauses

4 ～みたい／よう [Resemblance] "be like; look like; be similar to"

[4-a]

Topic	N		
この絵は	写真	ø	みたいです。
		の	ようです。
This painting looks like a photograph.			

Using みたい or よう, you can express the idea that X resembles or is otherwise similar to Y. みたい and よう essentially mean the same thing. The only difference is that みたい is more colloquial than よう. Note that みたい can be directly attached to the preceding noun, while よう requires の after the noun, as in [4-a]. (In this lesson, we mainly practice with みたい.)

Exs. (1) <春に> 今日はすごく暑いですね。夏{みたい／のよう}ですね。
It's really hot today, isn't it? It's like summer.

(2) スミスさんは料理が上手で、プロのシェフ{みたい／のよう}だね。
Smith-san is good at cooking; it's like he's a professional chef, don't you think?

As resemblance expressions, みたい and よう are generally used in the affirmative form. Thus, the idea "X is not like Y" is not expressed using Y{みたい／のよう}じゃないです. Instead, 違います "be different" (L12) is used to express this concept.

?? 奈良は京都{みたい／のよう}じゃないです。 → 奈良は京都とちょっと違います。
Intended meaning: *Nara is not like Kyoto.* *Nara is somewhat different from Kyoto.*

[4-b]

Topic	N				N	
私(わたし)は	写真(しゃしん)	ø	みたい	な	絵(え)	はあまり好(す)きじゃないです。
		の	よう			
I don't like paintings that look like photographs very much.						

[4-c]

Topic	N				Adj
みかさんは	歌手(かしゅ)	ø	みたい	に	歌(うた)が上手(じょうず)です。
		の	よう		
Mika is as good at singing as a professional singer.					

みたい and よう behave like *na*-adjectives. That is, when they modify nouns, な follows, and when they modify adjectives and verbs, に follows, as in [4-b] and [4-c].

Exs. (3) 田中(たなか)さん{<u>みたい</u>／<u>のよう</u>}<u>な</u>人(ひと)と結婚(けっこん)したいです。
I want to marry someone like Tanaka-san.

(4) このロボットは魚(さかな){<u>みたい</u>／<u>のよう</u>}<u>に</u>泳(およ)ぐことができます。*This robot can swim like a fish.*

(5) リーマンさんはアインシュタイン{<u>みたい</u>／<u>のよう</u>}<u>に</u>頭(あたま)がいいと思(おも)います。
I think Riemann is smart like Einstein.

5 XはYことです "X is to V; X is V-ing; X is that Y"

[5]

	NP			
		V-plain	Nominalizer	
私(わたし)の趣味(しゅみ)は	歌(うた)を	作(つく)る	こと	です。
My hobby is making songs.				

You can talk about your hobbies, dreams, problems, etc. by using こと. こと is used to change a phrase that ends with a verb, adjective, or other part of speech into a noun phrase, which can be used anywhere a noun would be.

こと in this use is a grammatical element called a nominalizer. The こと in the experience expression "V-plain.pastことがある" (L9 #7) and the one in the ability expression "V-plain.non-pastことができる" (L10 #7) are also, in fact, instances of this nominalizer.

Although the nominalizer こと carries no meaning, it is grammatically a noun. Thus, Yこと in "XはYことです" is a type of noun modification structure.

Exs. (1) 私(わたし)の夢(ゆめ)はシェフになる<u>こと</u>です。*My dream is to become a chef.*

(2) 今(いま)の問題(もんだい)はお金(かね)がない<u>こと</u>です。*The current problem is that we don't have money.*

(3) 私(わたし)が好(す)きな<u>こと</u>は友達(ともだち)と話(はな)す<u>こと</u>です。*What I like (doing) is talking with my friends.*

The following sentences are ungrammatical. To make them grammatical, こと is necessary.

× 私(わたし)の趣味(しゅみ)は鳥(とり)を{見(み)ます／見(み)るです}。 → 私(わたし)の趣味(しゅみ)は鳥(とり)を見(み)る<u>こと</u>です。
Intended meaning: *My hobby is birdwatching.*

You have previously learned that の can also be used as a nominalizer. While both の and こと have the same function, which nominalizer is more natural depends on the structure of the sentence. See the GID for more detailed information.

☞ **GID** (vol.2): E. Special topics 5. Nominalizers の vs. こと and 3. Noun modification clauses

6 V-*te* から "after V-ing; after X has V-ed"

[6]

V_1-*te*		V_2
宿題(しゅくだい)をして	から	ゲームをします。
I'm going to play a game after doing my homework.		

You can express the idea of "after V-ing" using V-*te* から.

Exs. (1) 今(いま)ねむいから、コーヒーを飲(の)んでから勉強(べんきょう)します。
I'm sleepy now, so I'm going to study after I drink coffee.

(2) 私(わたし)のルームメートは毎朝(まいあさ)シャワーを浴(あ)びてから朝(あさ)ご飯(はん)を食(た)べます。
Every morning my roommate eats breakfast after taking a shower.

(3) 留学(りゅうがく)する大学(だいがく)は先生(せんせい)に相談(そうだん)してから決(き)めました。
I decided which university to study abroad at after consulting with my professor.

☞ **GID** (vol.2): D. Sentence patterns 1. V_1-*te* V_2 vs. V_1-*te* から V_2

7 V-*masu* 方(かた) [Method; manner] "how to V; a way of V-ing"

[7-a]

<table>
<tr><td colspan="4">NP</td></tr>
<tr><td rowspan="2">N (direct object)</td><td rowspan="2"></td><td colspan="2">NP</td></tr>
<tr><td>V-masu</td><td></td></tr>
<tr><td>メール</td><td>の</td><td>書(か)き</td><td>方(かた)</td></tr>
<tr><td colspan="4">how to write emails / {a/the} way to write emails</td></tr>
</table>

[7-b]

<table>
<tr><td colspan="4">NP</td></tr>
<tr><td rowspan="2">N (subject)</td><td rowspan="2"></td><td colspan="2">NP</td></tr>
<tr><td>V-masu</td><td></td></tr>
<tr><td>タオさん</td><td>の</td><td>話(はな)し</td><td>方(かた)</td></tr>
<tr><td colspan="4">the way Tao talks / Tao's way of talking</td></tr>
</table>

You can express the ideas of (1) how to do something and (2) the way someone does something, using V-*masu* 方(かた). Here is how to make the V-*masu* 方(かた) form:

Step 1 Attach 方(かた) to the stem of the *masu*-form.

Exs. 書(か)き~~ます~~＋方(かた) → 書(か)き方(かた)　　話(はな)し~~ます~~＋方(かた) → 話(はな)し方(かた)

Step 2 If a direct object or a subject is involved, change the direct object marker を or the subject marker が to の.

Exs. メールを書(か)き方(かた) → メールの書(か)き方(かた) (= [7-a])
タオさんが話(はな)し方(かた) → タオさんの話(はな)し方(かた) (= [7-b])

Therefore, the following forms are ungrammatical:

× メールを書き方　　× タオさんが話し方

Exs. (1) このケーキの作り方はとても簡単だよ。
It's very easy to make this cake. (lit. How to make this cake is very easy.)

(2) 私はこの歌手の歌い方が大好きです。
I love this singer's singing. (lit. I love the way this singer sings.)

(3) ツアーガイド：今から美術館(へ)の行き方について説明します。
Tour guide:　I am going to explain how to get to the art museum now.

(4) 初めて日本に行った時、バスの乗り方が分かりませんでした。
When I went to Japan for the first time, I didn't know how to use the buses (lit. get on buses).

Note that the particle に cannot be used before the particle の. Thus, in some situations に is optionally replaced by the destination particle へ (see GID (vol.1): B. Particles 1-4. へ), as in (3). In others, に drops before の, as in (4). The following forms are ungrammatical:

× 美術館にの行き方　　× バスにの乗り方

The particles と and で do not drop before "の+V-*masu*方," as in (5) and (6) below.

Exs. (5) 先生との話し方 *the way to talk to your teachers (lit. how to talk to your teachers)*

(6) 日本での温泉の入り方
the ways of using the facilities at hot springs (lit. how to enter hot springs) in Japan

[7-c]

N (direct object)		VN *		V-*masu* of する	
漢字	の	勉強	の	し	方
how to study kanji					

* VN is the noun portion of a *suru*-verb.

You need to use a slightly different structure for *suru*-verbs. Here's how to make the V-*masu*方 phrase from *suru*-verbs:

Step 1 Change する to し方. (し is the stem of the *masu*-form of する.)

Exs. 勉強する → 勉強し方　　説明する → 説明し方

Step 2 Insert の between the noun portion (= VN) and し.

Exs. 勉強し方 → 勉強のし方　　説明し方 → 説明のし方

Step 3 If a direct object or a subject is involved, change the direct object marker を or the subject marker が to の.

Exs. 漢字を勉強のし方 → 漢字の勉強のし方 (= [7-c])
黒田先生が説明のし方 → 黒田先生の説明のし方 *the way Prof. Kuroda explains*

Because "VNし方" is an ungrammatical form, the following phrases are also ungrammatical:

× 漢字の勉強し方　　× 黒田先生の説明し方

Exs. (7) この魚の料理のし方を知っていますか。*Do you know how to cook this fish?*

(8) すみません。予約のキャンセルのし方を教えてくださいませんか。

Excuse me. Could you show me how to cancel the reservation?

言語ノート Language Note　Extended use of "XはYです"

We have learned the sentence structure XはYです, which means "X is Y," as in (1) and (2).

(1) 私はゴーブル大学の学生です。*I am a student of Goble University.*

(2) あの建物は図書館です。*That building is a library.*

However, this structure can be used to express more than just identity or equivalence. For example, in (3), です is used in place of にあります to give a location.

(3) A: トイレはどこです (= にあります) か。*Where is the restroom?*

B: (トイレは) あそこです (= にあります)。*It's over there.*

In fact, にあります・います is often replaced by です.

(4) and (5) provide other examples. Here, です is used to avoid repeating the same predicates.

(4) A: 私は経済を専攻しています。*I'm majoring in economics.*

B: そうですか。私はコンピュータ科学です (= を専攻しています)。

Is that so? I'm majoring in computer science. (lit. As for me, [it's] computer science.)

(5) <A and B are talking about music.>

A: Bさんは何が好きですか。*B-san, what do you like?*

B: (私は) ジャズです (= が好きです)。*I like jazz. (lit. As for me, [it's] jazz.)*

As seen in the above examples, です can be used in place of the particle and predicate when they are clear from the situation or other context. Can you think of what situations the following sentence could be used in and what it would mean in those situations?

(6) 私はすしです。

話しましょう

▶ **Words written in purple** are new words introduced in this lesson.

できる I Describe and explain things and people around you in detail.

できるI-A Indefinite pronoun の

1 You are helping your partner create an avatar for social media. Ask your partner's preferences about the facial features listed below and draw an image according to the responses you receive. L11-6

Ex. face shape (形(かたち)): round / square

A: どんな顔(かお)の形(かたち)がいいですか。

B: 丸(まる)いのがいいです。 or 四角(しかく)いのがいいです。

1) face shape: round / square
2) eye: big / small
3) eyebrows (まゆげ): thick / thin
4) nose: big / small
5) mouth: big / small
6) hair: long / short / strange

2 Suppose you are seeing your guests off after a party and handing out their belongings. Take turns asking and answering to whom each item belongs. L11-7

Ex. You: これは誰(だれ)のジャケットですか。

Guest: ヒルさんのです。

Ex. ヒル
1) 山川
2) 私
3) トラン
4) パク
5) ルイス
6) ケリー

3 You are planning to have a movie night with your classmates.

Step 1 First, check what kind movies are available to watch.

Ex. A: 色々(いろいろ)な映画(えいが)がありますね。

B: そうですね。有名なのがありますね。

A: それから… <Continue>

Step 2 Talk about what kind of movie you would like to watch.

Ex. A: ○○さんはどんな映画(えいが)が見たいですか。

B: 私はこわいのが見たいです。△△さんは？

A: 私はこわいのはちょっと… こわくないのがいいです。

B: じゃ、有名なのはどうですか。

Group Work

4 You are checking out some costumes online with your classmates for an upcoming Halloween party.

Step 1 Describe the following costumes based on their colors and motifs.

Ex. {黄色(きいろ)い／バナナの} コスチューム

Ex. 
1) 
2) 
3) 
4) 
5) 

Step 2 Decide which costume you'd like to wear and state a reason for your decision.

Ex. A: 〇〇さんはどのコスチュームが着(き)たいですか。

B: そうですね、一番おもしろいと思うから、バナナのが着(き)たいです。

C: 私はむらさき (purple) が好きだから、むらさきのが着(き)たいです。

Step 3 The costumes you ordered online have been delivered! Take turns asking and answering which costume is whose.

Ex. A: バナナのコスチュームは誰(だれ)のですか。

B: {〇〇さんの／私の} です。

5 Now, you are at the Halloween party and being offered some fancy cookies. Take turns and say which cookie you'd like by specifying its shape.

Ex. A: クッキーを焼(や)いたんですが、食べませんか。

B: わあ、すごいですね。

じゃ、このお化(ば)け (ghost) のとネコのをください。

できるI-B Noun modification clauses

1 Let's practice using noun modification clauses to describe people at a gathering.

Step 1 First, describe what the people in the picture on the previous page are doing, then make a noun modification clause based on each description. L11-8

Ex. 写真(しゃしん)をとっています → 写真(しゃしん)をとっている[人]

Step 2 Now, suppose you are at the party. Take turns checking the names of the people at the party.

Ex. A: 写真(しゃしん)をとっている人はウッドさんですね。

B: はい。それから、すしを食べているのは… <Continue>

2 Noun modification is often used in hashtags on social media. Let's try making some hashtags in Japanese!

Step 1 First, describe each illustrated topic below by modifying it with the information provided.

Ex. ＃誕生日(たんじょうび)に行く[レストラン]

Ex. 誕生日(たんじょうび)に行きます
1) 和食(わしょく)があります
2) 学生がよく行きます
3) 毎日混(こ)んでいます

4) 若(わか)い人があまり読みません
5) 人気がありません
6) 本屋(ほんや)で売っていません

7) 昨日(きのう)着ました
8) 母にもらいました
9) 少(すこ)し古くなりました

友達(ともだち)

10) 絵(え)が上手です
11) 髪(かみ)が長いです
12) 出身(しゅっしん)がパリです

Step 2 Now, try making hashtags for things/people/animals around you using noun modification clauses as in the examples.

Ex.1 ＃毎日使う[教科書(きょうかしょ)]

Ex.2 ＃コンビニで買った[コーラ]

Ex.3 ＃クラスで一番背(せ)が高い[人]

Ex.1

Ex.2

Ex.3

Step 3 Finally, share the hashtags you made in Step 2 with your classmates as shown in the example.

Ex. A: これは毎日使う[教科書(きょうかしょ)]です。

B: ○○さんはクラスで一番背(せ)が高い[人]です。

<Continue>

3 You are showing your partner a photo album of your trip to Japan.

Step 1 Create a title in Japanese for each photo below based on the English cues provided. L11-10

Ex. 山 → 私が京都(きょうと)で登(のぼ)った 山

Step 2 Answer your partner's questions using the phrases you made in Step 1.

Ex. A: これはどこですか。

B: （これは）私が京都(きょうと)で登(のぼ)った 山 です。

A: へえ。きれいですね。（← Comment）

Ex. **[mountain]** I climbed in Kyoto

1) **[garden]** I saw in the temple

Taizoin Zen Buddhist Temple

2) **[Japanese sweets]** I ate with my friend

3) **[sushi erasers]** my friend bought

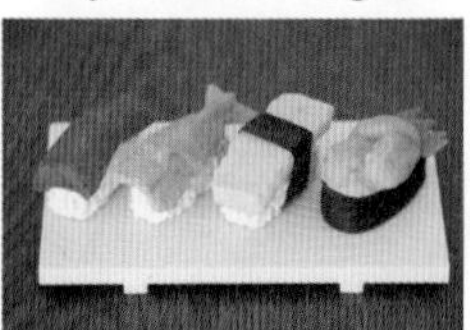

4) **[toy]** my Japanese friend gave me

5) **[Japanese-style inn]** I stayed at in Kyoto

6) **[friends]** I went on the trip together with

7) **[café]** I ate tasty cake at

4 Do you like simulation games? Talk about what kind of world you would like to make in a simulation game. L11-11

Ex.1 A: どんな家を作りたいですか。

B: 広いおふろがある 家 を作りたいです。

Ex.1 has a spacious bath	1) friends can stay
2) the garden is big	3) your own

Ex.2 A: どんな人と友達になりたいですか。

B: 趣味(しゅみ)が料理(りょうり)の 人 と友達になりたいです。

Ex.2 hobby is cooking	4) likes animals
5) plays tennis	6) your own

Ex.3 A: どんな町にしたいですか。

B: 親切な人がたくさん住んでいる 町 にしたいです。

Ex.3 a lot of kind people live	7) the scenery is beautiful
8) has a lot of nature	9) your own

5 Describe your favorite character, including all information about the character in one sentence.

Ex. A: 私は『とびら』のにゃんたが好きです。

B: にゃんたはどんなキャラクターですか。

A: 体が茶色(ちゃいろ)くて、食べるのが好きで、ちょっと太(ふと)っているキャラクターです。

B: そうですか。にゃんたはかわいいですね。(← Comment / Follow-up question)

Ex. にゃんた	1) とびら先生	2) アイ	3) your favorite manga/anime/movie character

・brown body ・likes eating ・a bit chubby	・smart ・very kind ・knows a lot about Japan	・good at speaking Japanese ・has a lot of friends ・lives in the Japan House	

できるII Draw comparisons to give easy-to-understand explanations of familiar things.

できるII-A ～時

1 Explain on what occasions you relax at home. L11-12

Ex. 時間があります → 時間がある時、家でゆっくりします。

1) ストレスがあります　2) 天気が悪いです　3) 何もしたくないです

4) 気分がよくないです　5) ひまです　6) 学校が休みです

2 Ai is describing her experience in Japan. Fill in each ____ with the most appropriate verb from the box below, paying attention to the tense in the 時 clause. L11-13

Ex. 行く	着(つ)く	いる	見る	食べる	会う	帰る

Ex. 日本に＿行く＿時、新しいスーツケースを買いました。

1) 日本の空港(くうこう)に＿＿＿＿＿時、人がたくさんいたから、おどろきました。

2) ジャンさんに初(はじ)めて＿＿＿＿＿時、かっこいいと思いました。

3) 日本に＿＿＿＿＿時、よく秋葉原(あきはばら)に行きました。

4) レストランで＿＿＿＿＿時、日本語で注文(ちゅうもん)しました。

5) アメリカに＿＿＿＿＿時、日本の空港(くうこう)でおみやげをたくさん買いました。

3 Explain when to use the following Japanese expressions based on the cues provided. 

Ex.1 いただきます（ご飯を食べます）

ご飯を**食べる**時、「いただきます」と言います。

Ex.2 ごちそうさまでした（ご飯を食べます）

ご飯を**食べた**時、「ごちそうさまでした」と言います。

1）はじめまして（初めて人に会います）
2）おはよう（朝、友達に会います）
3）いってきます（出かけます）
4）すみません（悪いことをします）
5）失礼します（先生のオフィスに入ります）
6）your own

4 Suppose you are teaching English (or your preferred language) in Japan. Explain how to use some colloquial expressions, including ones used on the internet.

Step 1 First, brainstorm what kind of colloquial expressions you use (Exs. sweet, epic, totally).

Step 2 Next, explain when you use those expressions, making sure to provide specific situations as examples.

Ex. アメリカの英語のスラングの "lit" は「とてもいい」という意味です。

例えば、すごくおもしろいパーティーに行った時、"The party was lit." と言います。

5 Have you felt emotional lately? Take turns asking and answering when you had the following emotional experiences, then ask follow-up questions.

Ex. 泣きます

A: 〇〇さんは最近、どんな時に泣きましたか。

B: えっと、動物のビデオを｛見ている／見た｝時、泣きました。

A: そうですか。どんなビデオでしたか。（← Follow-up question）

1）泣きます　2）感動します　3）怒ります　4）笑います

できるⅡ-B Resemblance ～みたい／よう

1 Clouds can form all different kinds of shapes. Describe the clouds in the pictures below using ～みたい／よう. L11-15

Ex.1 この雲はウマ (horse) **みたい**です。ウマ**のよう**です。

これはウマ (horse) **みたいな**雲です。ウマ**のような**雲です。

Ex.1

1)

2)

3)

4)

Ex.2 この雲(くも)は<u>ドーナツ</u>みたいに見えます。<u>ドーナツ</u>のように見えます。

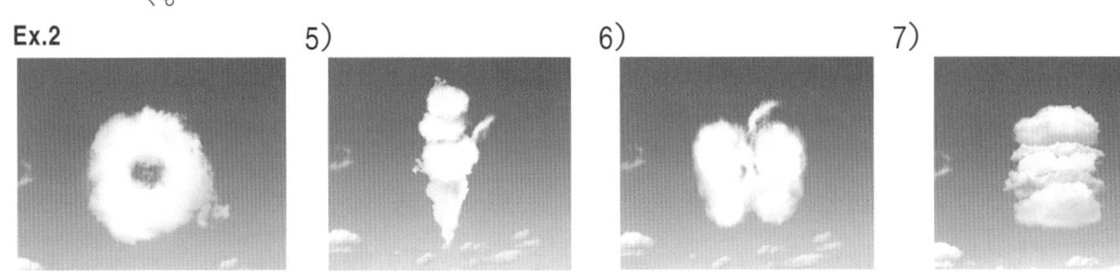

2 Describe what the following things resemble in appearance, characteristics, or actions using ～みたい／よう. L11-16

Ex.1 この美術館(びじゅつかん)は船(ふね){みたい／のよう}です。

or これは船(ふね){みたいな／のような}美術館(びじゅつかん)です。

Ex.1 美術館(びじゅつかん)　1) すし　2) バナナ　3) くつ下　4) スリッパ　5) your own

Ex.2 この鳥(とり)は人{みたいに／のように}話します。

Ex.2 話します
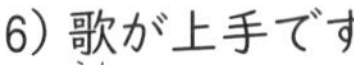
6) 歌(うた)が上手です
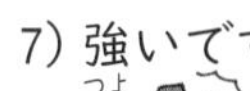
7) 強(つよ)いです
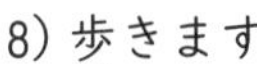
8) 歩(ある)きます

9) your own

3 A simile is a figure of speech that compares two different things to emphasize a description. In English, the comparison is generally preceded by "like" or "as."

Step 1 What kind of similes do you use in the language(s) you know? Draw a picture illustrating a simile, translate the phrase into Japanese, and write when you use it in the spaces provided below.

Ex.1

Ex.2

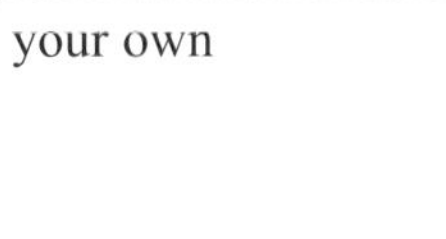

	何語(なにご)？	どんな時？	何と言う？
Ex.1	日本語	とても明るい人に会った時	太陽(たいよう)みたいだ
Ex.2	英語	たくさんお酒(さけ)を飲む人を見た時	魚(さかな)みたいにお酒(さけ)を飲む
your own			

Step 2 Explain the simile you chose in Step 1 and provide one example sentence as shown in the examples below.

Ex.1 日本語ではとても明るい人に会った時、「太陽(たいよう)みたいだ」と言います。

例(たと)えば、「私のルームメートはいつも笑(わら)っていて、太陽(たいよう)みたいな人です」と言います。

Ex.2 英語ではたくさんお酒(さけ)を飲む人を見た時、「魚(さかな)みたいにお酒(さけ)を飲む」と言います。

例(たと)えば、「父は昨日(きのう)のパーティーで魚(さかな)みたいにお酒(さけ)を飲みました」と言います。

できるII-C　XはYことです

1 Let's practice the sentence structure "XはYことです."

Step 1 Describe the dreams, hobbies, weak/strong points, and little moments of happiness the Japan House members have based on the cues provided. L11-17

Ex. アイ：dream / becoming a curator at an art museum

アイさんの夢(ゆめ)は美術館(びじゅつかん)のキュレーターになることです。

1) タオ　：hobby / baking cakes and cookies

2) マーク　：dream / buying a big house that has a spacious garden

3) 圭太(けいた)　：weak point（苦手(にがて)なこと）/ doing homework early

4) にゃんた：strong point（得意(とくい)なこと）/ getting up early in the morning

5) リーマン：little moments of happiness（小さい幸(しあわ)せ）/ relaxing at home, playing with numbers, etc.

Step 2 Now, talk about yourself using verb phrases as in Step 1.

Ex. 夢(ゆめ) → 私の夢(ゆめ)はプログラマーになることです。

1) 夢(ゆめ)　2) 趣味(しゅみ)　3) 苦手(にがて)なこと　4) 得意(とくい)なこと　5) 小さい幸(しあわ)せ

2 Talk about your dream and your role model following the prompts in the shaded box below.

Ask about your partner's dream
Ask for details (what kind, role model)
Follow-up question

Ex. A: ○○さんの夢(ゆめ)は何ですか。

B: 私の夢(ゆめ)はプログラマーになることです。

A: そうですか。どんなプログラマーになりたいですか。

B: ゲームのプログラマーになりたいです。

A: そうですか。例(たと)えば、誰(だれ)みたいになりたいですか。

B: 宮本茂(みやもとしげる)みたいになりたいです。「スーパーマリオ」を作った人です。

できるIII Ask and answer questions about how to use, make, and do things in your everyday life.

できるIII-A Actions in sequence V-*te*から

1 Let's practice talking about actions in sequence.

Step 1 The following are two sequential actions performed by Riemann. Connect them into one sentence using V-*te*から. L11-18

Ex. 毎朝(まいあさ)シャワーを浴(あ)びる → 朝(あさ)ご飯(はん)を食べる
リーマンさんは毎朝(まいあさ)シャワーを浴(あ)びてから、朝(あさ)ご飯(はん)を食べます。

1) いつも漢字(かんじ)を 10 覚(おぼ)える → 寝(ね)る
2) よくカフェに寄(よ)る → 学校に来る
3) 今朝(けさ)起(お)きた → すぐにシャワーを浴(あ)びた
4) 昨日(きのう)クラスが終(お)わった → 買い物に行った

Step 2 Using Step 1 as a reference, talk about your own sequential actions.

Ex. A: 私は毎朝(まいあさ)シャワーを浴(あ)びてから、朝(あさ)ご飯(はん)を食べます。○○さんはどうですか。
B: そうですね、私は… <Continue>

2 You and your roommate are preparing a meal for a party.

Step 1 First, review the vocabulary for cooking activities on p.17.

Step 2 You are making salad and grilled chicken. Take turns asking permission to do something and giving directions about how to do something based on the cues provided. L11-19

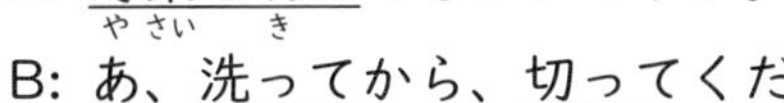

Ex. A: 野菜(やさい)を切(き)ってもいいですか。
B: あ、洗(あら)ってから、切(き)ってください。
A: 分かりました。洗(あら)ってから、切(き)ります。

Ex. cut vegetables?

1) put broccoli into the salad? (ブロッコリー)

2) put eggs on the salad?

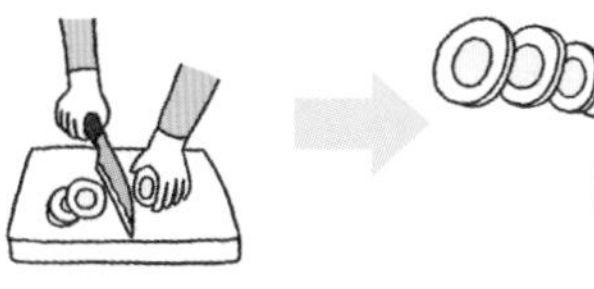

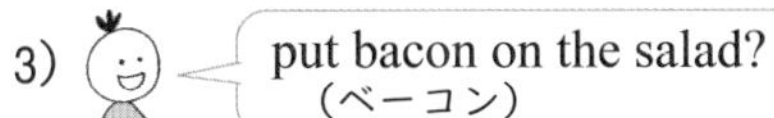

3) put bacon on the salad? (ベーコン)

4) pour dressing over the salad? (ドレッシング)

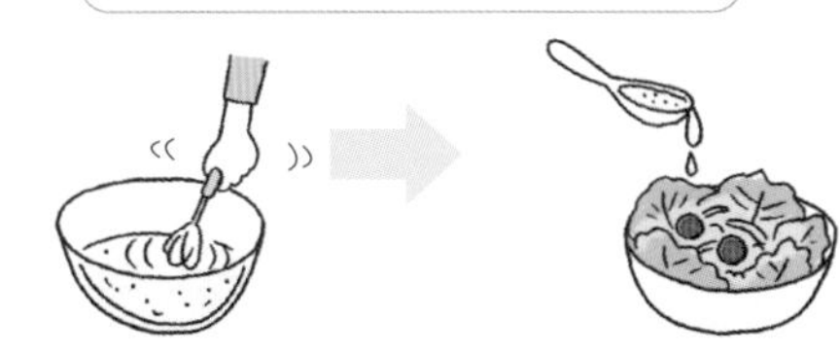

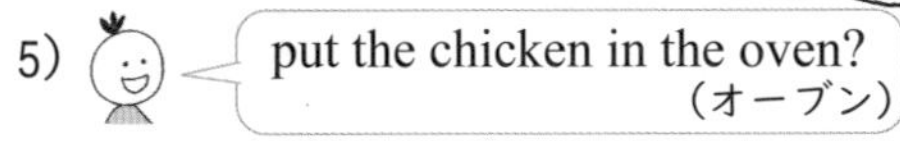

5) put the chicken in the oven? (オーブン)

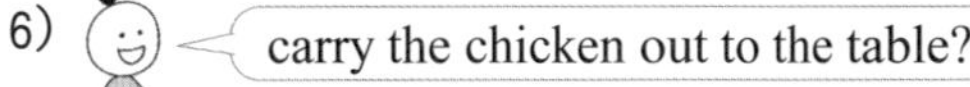

6) carry the chicken out to the table?

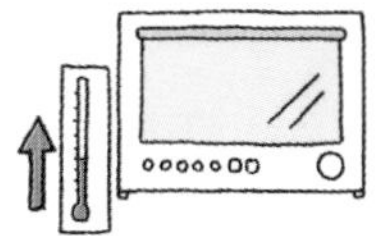

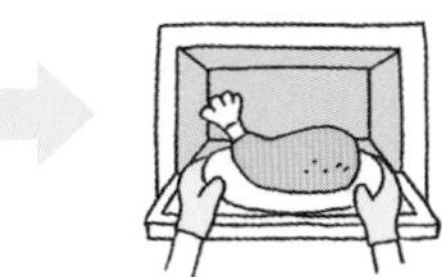

3 Let's practice explaining a sequence of actions related to cooking.

Step 1 Suppose you have prepared the following dishes for your classmates. Give your partner tips on how to eat them.

Useful vocabulary	冷(ひ)やす	温(あたた)める	混(ま)ぜる	かける	のせる	つける

Ex. A: これは私が作ったコーヒーゼリーです。冷蔵庫(れいぞうこ)でよく冷(ひ)やして、ミルクを混(ま)ぜてから、食べてくださいね。

B: わあ、ありがとうございます。おいしそうですね。（← Comment）

1) サラダ　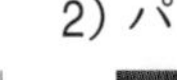　2) パンケーキ　3) ピザ　4) チキンナゲット

Step 2 Show a photo of a dish that you like and give some tips on how to eat it.

できるIII-B Method and manner V-*masu*方(かた)

1 Change each of the following words/phrases into a V-*masu*方(かた) expression. L11-20

Ex.1 読(よ)む → 読(よ)み方(かた)

1) 覚(おぼ)える　2) 調(しら)べる　3) 行(い)く　4) 作(つく)る　5) 使(つか)う

Ex.2 漢字(かんじ)を読(よ)む → 漢字(かんじ)の読(よ)み方(かた)

6) 単語(たんご)を覚(おぼ)える　7) 辞書(じしょ)を使(つか)う　8) 日本語(にほんご)のメールを書(か)く　9) 先生(せんせい)が話(はな)す

10) 先生(せんせい)のオフィスに行(い)く

Ex.3 勉強(べんきょう)する → 勉強(べんきょう)のし方(かた)

11) 練習(れんしゅう)する　12) 準備(じゅんび)する　13) 予約(よやく)する　14) チェックする　15) 説明(せつめい)する

Ex.4 漢字(かんじ)を勉強(べんきょう)する → 漢字(かんじ)の勉強(べんきょう)のし方(かた)

16) 文法(ぶんぽう)を勉強(べんきょう)する　17) 会話(かいわ)を練習(れんしゅう)する　18) 料理(りょうり)を注文(ちゅうもん)する

2 Practice asking your partner to teach you how to do the following activities in Japan.

Ex. buy a train ticket

A: すみません。電車(でんしゃ)のきっぷの買い方(かた)を教(おし)えてくれませんか。

B: はい、いいですよ。

1) use a luggage locker（コインロッカー）　2) search for good restaurants　3) go to Tokyo Station

4) make a reservation at a restaurant　5) order ramen　6) your own

3 Let's practice giving some simple step-by-step instructions for cooking.

Step 1 Below is a recipe for a ham sandwich（ハムサンドイッチ）. Explain the ingredients and the steps for making it.

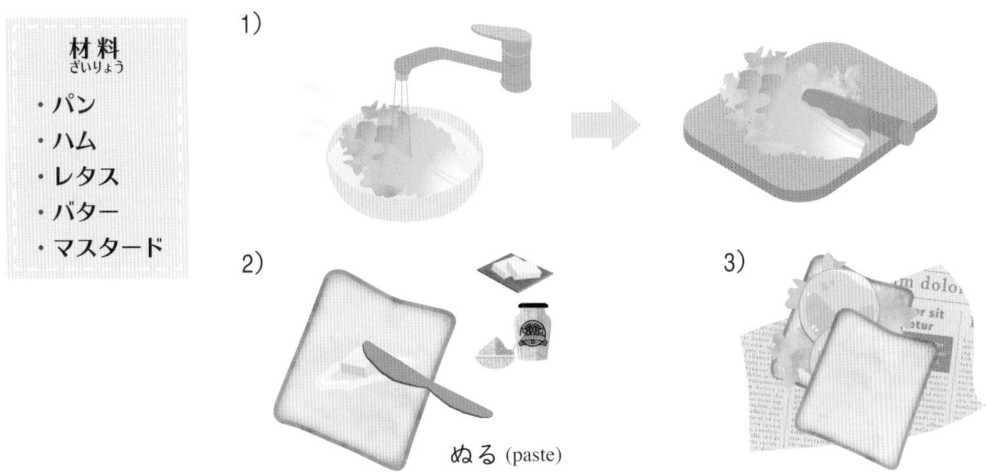

Step 2 Do you know any recipes for simple yet tasty dishes (Exs. ramen, a sandwich)? Using the following step-by-step instructions for how to make a ham sandwich as a model, share your recipe with your classmates.

Ex. 今日は簡単(かんたん)で、おいしい「ハムサンドイッチ」の作り方(かた)を説明(せつめい)します。
材料(ざいりょう)は、パンとハムとレタスとバターとマスタードです。
まず、レタスを洗(あら)ってから、切(き)ります。
次(つぎ)に、パンにバターとマスタードをぬります。
最後(さいご)に、そのパンに切(き)ったレタスとハムをはさんでください。
おいしいハムサンドイッチのできあがりです！

Review

Now you can give detailed explanations on how to do things you like/are good at.

Possible topics 漢字(かんじ)／単語(たんご)の覚(おぼ)え方(かた)　〇〇の上手なやり方(かた)／作り方(かた)／使い方(かた)

Step 1 Brainstorm what you would like to explain and what steps you need for your activity.

Q1. 何を説明(せつめい)しますか。 ________________方(かた)

Q2. どんなステップがありますか。 Step 1: ________________

Step 2: ________________

Step 3: ________________

Step 2 Explain the steps you've come up with to your partner.

Ask if your partner knows how to do X **Explain the steps & share any tips you have**

Ex. A: ○○さん、SNSの上手なやり方(かた)を知っていますか。

B: いいえ、知りません。教(おし)えてください。

A: はい。まず、ハッシュタグをチェックします。ハッシュタグは人気があるのを調(しら)べてください。

B: 分かりました。

A: 次(つぎ)に、おもしろい写真(しゃしん)をとります。写真(しゃしん)をとる時は、スマホのカメラを使ってください。

B: スマホのカメラですね。分かりました。

A: 最後(さいご)に、アプリで写真(しゃしん)をきれいにしてから、SNSにアップします。アップする時間は、夜(よる)８時から１０時がおすすめです。

Reading

読みましょう

Getting information from visual clues: Solving Japanese riddles

1 Do you like solving brain-teasers? Riemann introduces two such brain-teasers, known as なぞとき in Japanese, below—see if you can solve them!

Check Point: Pay attention to the noun modification clauses you have learned in this lesson so that you understand the problems correctly; each underlined part is modifying the noun in the adjacent [ ].

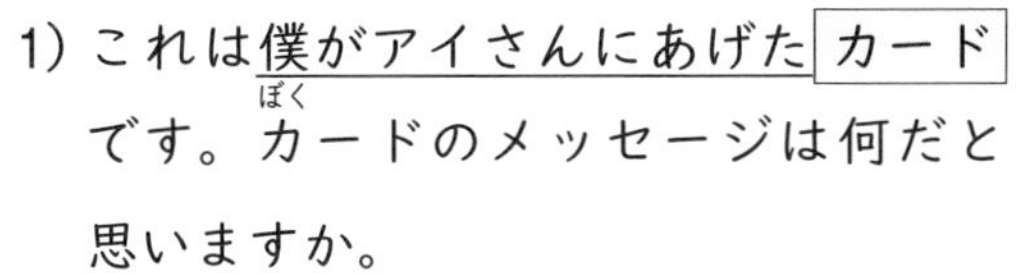

1) これは僕(ぼく)がアイさんにあげた[カード]です。カードのメッセージは何だと思いますか。

ヒント「あり」がいくつありますか。

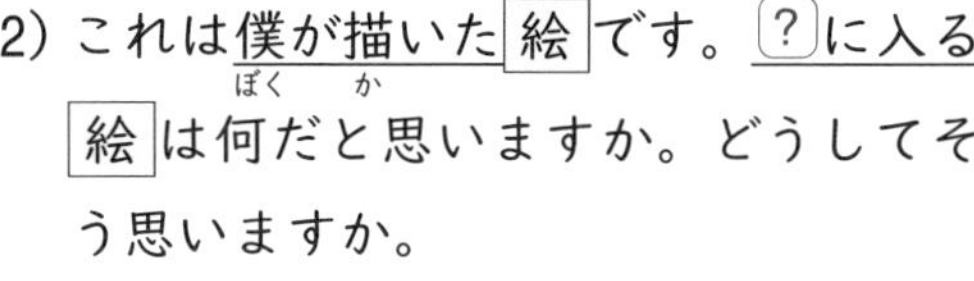

2) これは僕(ぼく)が描(か)いた[絵]です。[?]に入る[絵]は何だと思いますか。どうしてそう思いますか。

Grasping the structure of noun phrases containing noun modification clauses

Noun modification clauses are often used in written texts because they allow you to explain things and people in a compact, efficient fashion. On the other hand, if you do not recognize a noun modification clause correctly while reading, you are more likely to misinterpret the sentence. One effective strategy for understanding noun modification is to identify where a modifying clause begins and ends by looking at the structure of the sentence that contains it.

To identify a noun modification clause, ask yourself which part of the sentence is describing a particular noun and underline the part that answers the question. For instance, consider なぞとき 1) again, and think about what kind of カード the sentence is referring to (i.e., which part is modifying カード). The answer is 僕(ぼく)がアイさんにあげた (I gave Ai), and thus this is the modifying clause for the noun [カード]. In the same manner, you can identify that the underlined parts in なぞとき 2) are the noun modification clauses for the two [絵] respectively. In Japanese, a noun modification clause always precedes the noun to be modified.

If you are not sure whether the part you have underlined is the correct noun modification clause, try reading the same sentence without the underlined part. The sentence should still make sense grammatically without it if it is the correct noun modification clause.

Now, using the strategies explained so far, underline the noun modification clause for each of the boxed words a.-d. in the following passage that Riemann wrote about なぞとき.

なぞとき(をする)：(to do a) brain-teaser　解く：to solve

昨日インターネットで「なぞとき」というゲームについて読みました。なぞときは日本でとても人気がある a. [ゲーム] で、なぞときをする b. [人] は言葉や文字や数字を使った c. [問題] の答えを考えます。僕は漢字を覚えたり数学の問題を解いたりするのが好きだから、初めてなぞときを知った d. [時]、すごくおもしろいと思いました。

2 リーマンさんはジャパンハウスのメンバーになぞときを紹介したかったから、「にゃんたはどこ？」という問題を作りました。みなさんもこのなぞときをしてみてください。

表：table　続けて：one after the other; in succession　では：Moving on [conjunction for changing topics]

今、僕は日本の「なぞとき」がおもしろいと思っています。今日は僕が作った a. [なぞときの問題] と①その解き方を説明します。三つの問題を解いて、にゃんたを見つけてください。

まず、問題１を見てください。この表をどこかで見たことがありませんか。みんなは日本語の勉強を始めた b. [時] にこの表を見たと思います。１から４を続けて読んでください。にゃんたはこの部屋にいます。答えが分からない c. [人] はヒントを見てください。

次に、問題２を見てください。これは部屋にある d. [物] です。この問題にはヒントはありません。

では、問題３です。この問題の答えが分かった e. [時]、にゃんたがいる f. [所] が分かります。問題３も自分で考えてみてください。

どうですか。分かりましたか。じゃ、答えをチェックしてみましょう。

最後に、問題４を見てください。問題４の答えの場所に、僕がにゃんたがいる所を描いた絵があります。②その絵がある所を考えてください。左の漢字を読んで右に③その読み方を書いてください。そして、赤い丸のひらがなを続けて読んでみてください。その言葉が問題４の答えです。

問題１

N	W	R	Y	M	H	N	T	S	K	
3										あ
		1			2゛					い
									4゛	う
										え
										お

問題２

四角や丸の木の体に足が４本あります。

問題３

wat__：水　riv__：川
fath__：父　und__：？

問題４

勉強：○○○○○
魚：○○○
場所：○○○

Identifying noun modification clauses

1） Underline the part that modifies each noun in boxes a.-f.

Understanding demonstratives: そ-words

2） What do the そ-word + noun combinations ①-③ in the passage refer to? Rewrite the phrases by identifying the referents.

① l.2 その解き方 ____________________解き方

② l.19 その絵 ____________________絵

③ l.20 その読み方 ____________________読み方

Comprehension check

3） 全部読んでから、次の質問に答えてください。

a. 問題１の答えは何ですか。

b. 問題２の答えは何ですか。

c. 問題３の答えは何ですか。

d. どれがリーマンさんが描いた絵だと思いますか。

(1) 

(2) 

(3) 

(4) 

e. 問題４の答えは何ですか。

問題１のヒント

これはひらがなの表です。数字の１のひらがなは「り」です。数字の２は「ひ」で、てんてんがあるから「び」です。３は「ん」です。４は「く」にてんてんがあるから「ぐ」です。

書く練習 Writing Practice

Do you know any なぞとき problems like the ones you tried in this section? Try your hand at creating one in Japanese. If you cannot think of any, go online and find one that you think might be fun for your classmates to try.

聞きましょう

リスニング・ストラテジー：Listening strategy

Understanding sequence words

Listening to and understanding sequential procedures and step-by-step instructions is an important skill for everyday life. It will facilitate your comprehension if you pay attention to the words and expressions that indicate sequence when listening to procedures or step-by-step instructions.

L11-22

1 **Pre-listening activity:** Your friends are explaining how to make their favorite foods. Listen to each description and identify what food they are talking about. Then, choose the correct food from a.-c. below. You may hear unknown words, but you do not need to understand everything to correctly answer the questions.

1) ____________

2) ____________

3) ____________

a. 
b. 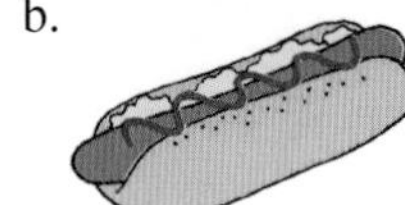
c. 

L11-23

2 **Listening:** Listen to monologues 1) and 2) and arrange pictures a.-e. in the correct order according to each explanation.

1) You are participating in an orientation for new students at a Japanese university, and the orientation leader is explaining the orientation schedule.

(　　　　) → (　　　　) → (　　　　) → (　　　　) → (　　　　)

a. 
b. 

c. 

d. 
e. 

2) You are visiting a スーパー銭湯(せんとう) (deluxe bathhouse & spa), and a staff member is explaining how to use the facilities.

(　　　　) → (　　　　) → (　　　　) → (　　　　) → (　　　　)

a. 
b. 
c. 
d. 
e. 

Exit Check

Now it's time to go back to the DEKIRU List for this chapter (p.13) and do the exit check to see what new things you can do now that you've completed the lesson.

Lesson 12

今度日本に来たら、何がしたい？

When you come to Japan next time, what do you want to do?

DEKIRU List

できるCheck

できる I **Ask and answer questions about your abilities and what you can do in a particular place.**
自分の能力やある場所でできることについて、尋ねたり答えたりできる。
Entry ☐ Exit ☐

できる II **Talk about preparations for trips, parties, events, etc.**
旅行、パーティー、イベントなどの準備について、話すことができる。
Entry ☐ Exit ☐

できる III **Talk briefly about hypothetical situations.**
仮定の状況について、簡単に話すことができる。
Entry ☐ Exit ☐

できる IV **Express what you infer about a situation based on what you see and hear.**
見たり聞いたりした情報をもとに、推測したことを言うことができる。
Entry ☐ Exit ☐

STRATEGIES

Conversation Tips .... ・かな(ぁ) in a self-addressed question

Reading .... ・Getting information from a website: Book recommendations
・Recognizing event sequence
・Understanding demonstratives: そ-words
・Summarizing

Listening .... ・Guessing unknown words from context (1)

GRAMMAR

1. Potential forms of verbs できるI
2. V前に "before V-ing" and V後で "after V-ing" できるII
3. ～ておく "V (ahead of time); V ~ and leave it as is" できるII
4. ～たら "if; when" できるIII
5. ～みたい／よう [Conjecture] できるIV

会話

1 できるI **Ai is talking with Prof. Kuroda in her office.** L12-1

アイ　：黒田先生、ホームステイする家が決まりました！京都でお茶の店をしている家族です。

先生　：あ、ホームステイにしたんですか。

アイ　：はい、寮よりホームステイの方が日本の文化がよく分かると思ったんです。

先生　：そうですか。お茶の店でホームステイをするのはめずらしいですよ。いい経験ができそうですね。

アイ　：はい、私もそう思います。でも、ちょっと心配していることがあるんです。

先生　：心配？　どんなことですか。

アイ　：ホームステイの生活です。例えば、家族のみんなと仲良くなれるかな、食事は全部食べられるかな、とよく考えます。

先生　：だいじょうぶですよ。食べられない時は、食べられないと言ってもいいんですよ。

アイ　：そうですか。分かりました。じゃ、そうします。

2 できるII **Ai is asking Keita for advice on studying abroad.** L12-2

アイ　：あのう、圭太さんはアメリカに留学に来る前に、どんな準備をしておきましたか。

圭太　：そうだね…　留学する大学の授業や単位について調べておいたよ。

アイ　：ああ、それは大切ですね。私もそうします。

圭太　：あ、アイちゃん、ホストファミリーにあげるおみやげ、もう買った？

アイ　：いいえ、まだ買っていません。何がいいと思いますか。

圭太　：うーん、難しいね。何がいいかなぁ。

アイ　：圭太さん、よかったら、日曜日に一緒に買い物に行ってくれませんか。

圭太　：うん、いいよ。じゃ、買いに行く前に、いいおみやげをチェックしておくよ。

アイ　：ありがとうございます。日曜日は昼ご飯を食べた後で、出かけましょう！

3 できるIII Ai and Tao are talking about Nyanta.

L12-3

タオ　：アイちゃん、もうすぐ日本に行くんだね。
アイちゃんがいなくなったら、にゃんたはさびしくなるね。

アイ　：うん…　そうだね…

タオ　：アイちゃんが日本に行ったら、私が毎日にゃんたと寝(ね)てもいいかなぁ。

アイ　：うん、もちろんだよ、ぜひ！　あ、それから、朝(あさ)にゃんたが起(お)きたら、ご飯(はん)あげてくれない？

タオ　：うん、分かった。

アイ　：タオちゃん、どうもありがとう！

にゃんた：ニャー！

4 できるIV Ai is on a video call with Jean in Japan.

L12-4

アーティスト：artist　作品(さくひん)：(a piece of) work

ジャン：アイちゃん、留学(りゅうがく)の準備(じゅんび)、終(お)わった？

アイ　：はい。今はちょっと緊張(きんちょう)していますが、すごく楽(たの)しみにしています。

ジャン：今度日本に来たら、何がしたい？

アイ　：去年(きょねん)日本に行った時はあまり美術館(びじゅつかん)に行けなかったから、
今度は色々(いろいろ)な美術館(びじゅつかん)に行ってみたいです。

ジャン：美術館(びじゅつかん)？　あ、じゃ、直島(なおしま)はどう？

アイ　：直島(なおしま)？　ああ、人気があるみたいですね。
島(しま)の色々(いろいろ)な所で美術(びじゅつ)が楽(たの)しめると聞きました。

ジャン：うん、アイちゃんが好きなアーティストの作品(さくひん)もあるみたいだよ。

アイ　：あ、草間彌生(くさまやよい)ですね。時間があったら、ぜひ行ってみます。

CONVERSATION TIPS

かな(ぁ) in a self-addressed question: かな(ぁ) is a sentence-final particle indicating that the sentence is a self-addressed question, similar in meaning and use to the English phrase "I wonder..." It is usually used in casual conversation, and the forms used before かな(ぁ) are the same as those before みたい.

1) 来週の日本語のテスト、難(むずか)しいかな(ぁ)。

2) 日本にいる友達、元気かな(ぁ)。

3) 来年、東京(とうきょう)に行けるかな(ぁ)。

Vocabulary with Pictures

単語（たんご）

▶ **The words written in gray** are supplemental vocabulary.

趣味（しゅみ）・特技（とくぎ） Hobbies and skills

- [*thing* を] けいさんする (to calculate)
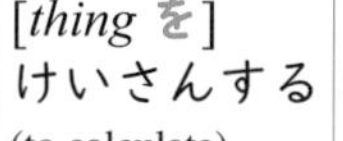
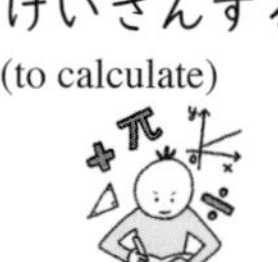
- はしる (to run)
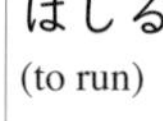

- とぶ (to fly; to jump)
  そらをとぶ (to fly in a sky)

- きんトレ(を)する (to do strength training; to lift weights)
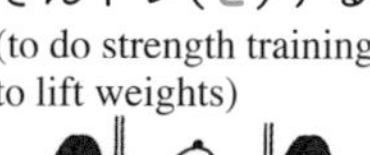

- がっき (musical instrument)

- どうが (video; animated image)

描写する（びょうしゃ） Describing people, things, and feelings

- おちこむ (to get depressed; to feel down)

- きんちょうする (to get nervous; to feel tense)

- こまる (to be in trouble; to have a hard time)

- [*thing* を／について] しんぱいする (to worry)

- [*thing* を] たのしむ (to enjoy)

- [*person* と] なかよくなる (to become good friends)

- すばらしい (wonderful; fantastic)

- めずらしい (rare; unusual; unique)

- ひどい (terrible [thing/person]; serious [injury])
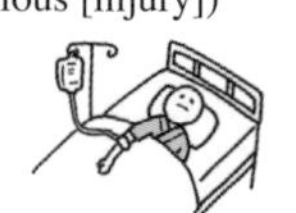
- じゆう (freedom)
  じゆう(な) (free)
  じゆうに (freely)
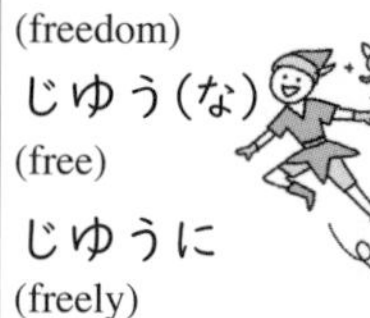
- びんぼう(な) (poor) [lacking money/food/possessions to live]

- [*thing X* は *thing Y* と] ちがう ((X is) different (from Y))
  [*thing X* と *thing Y* は] ちがう ((X and Y are) different)
- [*thing X* は *thing Y* と] おなじ
  [*thing X* と *thing Y* は] おなじ
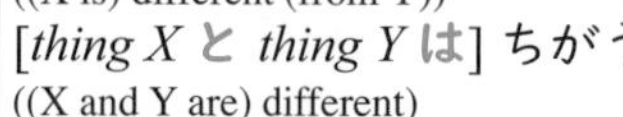

生活（せいかつ） Daily life

- しょくじ(を)する (to have a meal; to dine)

- (お)べんとう (boxed lunch)

- おにぎり (rice ball) [Japanese food]

- [*thing* を] みがく (to polish)
  くつをみがく (to polish shoes)
  はをみがく

- おかねをおろす (to withdraw money)

- [*money* を] はらう (to pay)

- ねだん (price) [monetary]

- ただ (free of charge)

- [*person/animal* が] いなくなる (to disappear)

- [*thing* が] なくなる (to disappear)

- ひるね(を)する (to take a nap)

- [*thing X* を *thing Y* に] かえる (to change (X into Y))
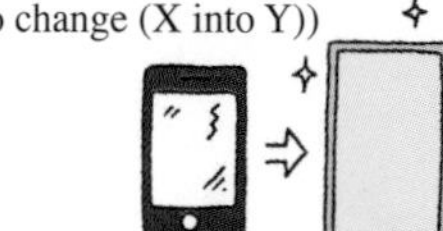
- たからくじ {に／が} あたる (to win a lottery)
  たからくじ (lottery (ticket))
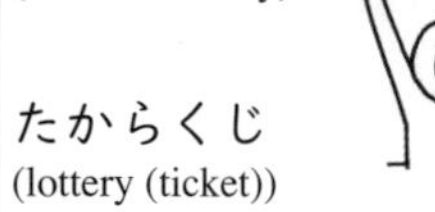
- こと ((intangible) thing)
  言ったこと
  聞いたこと
- にもつ (package; baggage)

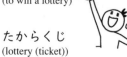

学校・仕事 (しごと) School and work

- [*thing* を] よしゅうする (to do preparatory study/research)
- [*thing* を] ふくしゅうする (to review)
- [*school* を] そつぎょうする (to graduate)
- たんい ((academic) credit)
- ろんぶん (thesis; dissertation; academic paper)
- [*thing* を／について] はっぴょうする (to present; to announce)
- はっぴょう (presentation)
- データ (data)
- [*thing* を] コピーする (to make a copy)
- [*thing* を] けいけんする (to experience)
- [*thing/person* を] あつめる (to collect; to gather)
- [*person/place* に *thing* を] かえす (to return; to give back)
- けいかくをたてる (to make a plan)
- けいかく (plan)
- [*thing* が] きまる (to be decided)
- [*issue* を] きめる
- りれきしょ (résumé)
- めんせつ ((job) interview)
- めんせつをうける (to have a (job) interview)
- [*workplace* に] しゅうしょくする (to get a (full-time) job)

人・場所 People and places

- おや (parent)
- かがくしゃ (scientist)
- かがく (science)
- ～たち [plural marker for people, animal, etc.]
  - **Ex.1** わたしたち (we)
  - **Ex.2** こどもたち (children)
- [*person* と] つきあう (to go out; to date)
- [*person* と] やくそく(を)する (to make a promise; to make an appointment)
- [*person/animal* が] うまれる (to be born)
- [*body part* を] しゅじゅつする (to undergo surgery; to perform surgery)
- ひだりて (left hand)
- みぎて (right hand)
- ゆび (finger)
- [*thing/person* が] うごく ((something/someone) moves; (something) functions)
- たいしかん (embassy)
- (お)しろ (castle)
- しま (island)
- ちず (map)
- じこ (accident) [traffic, etc.]

そのほかの表現 (ひょうげん) Other expressions

- たのしみ (pleasure; enjoyment)
- [*event/activity* を] たのしみにしています (to look forward to)
- もちろん (of course; certainly)
- **もちろんです** (Of course.)

- はじめ (beginning; first)
- ほかの Noun (other/another Noun)
- ほかに (besides)
- もし(～たら) (if) [emphasizes the conditional meaning]
- もうすぐ (soon)

Vocabulary List

単語(たんご)リスト

L12-6

▶Highlighted kanji words contain kanji you have learned previously.

RU-VERBS / RU-VERB PHRASE

1	あつめる	集める	to collect; to gather [thing/person を]
2	うまれる	生まれる	to be born [person/animal が]
3	かえる	変える	to change (X into Y) [thing X を thing Y に]
4	けいかくをたてる	計画を立てる	to make a plan

U-VERBS / U-VERB PHRASES

5	いなくなる		to disappear [person/animal が]
6	なくなる		to disappear [thing が]
7	うごく	動く	(something/someone) moves; (something) functions [thing/person が]
8	おかねをおろす	お金をおろす	to withdraw money
9	おちこむ	落ち込む	to get depressed; to feel down
10	かえす	返す	to return; to give back [person/place に thing を]
11	きまる	決まる	to be decided [thing が] Ex. めんせつの日がきまった the job interview date has been decided
12	こまる	困る	to be in trouble; to have a hard time
13	たからくじ{に/が}あたる	宝くじ{に/が}当たる	to win a lottery
14	たのしむ	楽しむ	to enjoy [thing を] Ex. カラオケを楽しむ enjoy karaoke
15	ちがう	違う	(X is) different (from Y) [thing X は thing Y と]; (X and Y are) different [thing X と thing Y は]
	↔ おなじ [L9]	同じ	(X is) the same (as Y) [thing X は thing Y と]; (X and Y are) the same [thing X と thing Y は]
16	つきあう	付き合う	to go out; to date [person と]
17	とぶ	飛ぶ	to fly [sky, etc を]; to jump
18	なかよくなる	仲良くなる	to become good friends [person と]
19	はしる	走る	to run
20	はらう	払う	to pay [money を]
21	みがく		to polish [thing を]; to brush (one's teeth) [teeth を]

SURU-VERBS

22	きんちょうする	緊張する	to get nervous; to feel tense
23	きんトレ(を)する	筋トレ(を)する	to do strength training; to lift weights
24	けいけんする	経験する	to experience [thing を]
25	けいさんする	計算する	to calculate [thing を]
26	コピーする		to make a copy [thing を]
27	しゅうしょくする	就職する	to get a (full-time) job [workplace に]
28	しゅじゅつする	手術する	to undergo surgery; to perform surgery [body part を]
29	しょくじ(を)する	食事(を)する	to have a meal; to dine
30	しんぱいする	心配する	to worry [thing を/について]
31	そつぎょうする	卒業する	to graduate [school を]
32	はっぴょうする	発表する	to present; to announce [thing を/について]
33	ひるね(を)する	昼寝(を)する	to take a nap
34	ふくしゅうする	復習する	to review [thing を]
35	やくそく(を)する	約束(を)する	to make a promise; to make an appointment [person と]

Lesson 12

36	よしゅうする	予習する	to do preparatory study/research [*thing* を] **Ex.** じゅぎょうのよしゅう preparation for a class

I-ADJECTIVES

37	すばらしい		wonderful; fantastic
38	ひどい		terrible [thing/person]; serious [injury]
39	めずらしい		rare; unusual; unique

NA-ADJECTIVES

40	じゆう	自由	free
41	びんぼう	貧乏	poor [lacking money/food/possessions to live]

NOUNS

42	おにぎり		rice ball [Japanese food]
43	おや	親	parent
44	かがくしゃ	科学者	scientist
45	がっき	楽器	musical instrument
46	けいかく	計画	plan
47	こと		(intangible) thing **Ex.1** 分からないことがある to have things that (one) does not know **Ex.2** いろいろなことをする to do various things
48	じこ	事故	accident [traffic, etc.]
49	しま	島	island
50	じゆう	自由	freedom
51	しろ／おしろ	(お)城	castle
52	たいしかん	大使館	embassy
53	たからくじ	宝くじ	lottery (ticket)
54	ただ		free of charge
55	たんい	単位	(academic) credit
56	ちず	地図	map
57	データ		data
58	どうが	動画	video; animated image
59	にもつ	荷物	package; baggage
60	ねだん	値段	price [monetary]
61	はじめ	初め	beginning; first
62	ひだりて	左手	left hand
	みぎて	右手	right hand
63	べんとう／おべんとう	(お)弁当	boxed lunch
64	めんせつ	面接	(job) interview
65	ゆび	指	finger
66	りれきしょ	履歴書	résumé
67	ろんぶん	論文	thesis; dissertation; academic paper

ADVERBS

68	じゆうに	自由に	freely
69	もうすぐ		soon
70	もし(～たら)		if [emphasizes the conditional meaning]

SUFFIX

71	～たち	～達	[plural marker for people, animal, etc.] **Ex.1** 私たち we **Ex.2** 子どもたち children

OTHER WORDS AND PHRASES

72	ほかのNoun	他の～	other/another Noun
73	ほかに	他に	besides
74	もちろん		of course; certainly **Ex.** もちろんです Of course.
75	たのしみにしています	楽しみにしています	to look forward to [*event/activity* を]
	たのしみ	楽しみ	pleasure; enjoyment

漢字（かんじ）

▶ ＊Special reading

159	集	シュウ	集合する（しゅうごう） to assemble
		あつ(める) あつ(まる)	集める（あつ） to collect; to gather 集まる（あつ） to be collected; to gather together
	to gather		
160	配	パイ ハイ	心配する（しんぱい） to worry 配信する（はいしん） to stream live online　配達する（はいたつ） to deliver
		くば(る)	配る（くば） to distribute; to hand out
	to distribute		
161	動	ドウ	動画（どうが） video; animated image　動物（どうぶつ） animal　運動する（うんどう） to (get) exercise 活動（かつどう） activity　感動する（かんどう） to be moved　行動する（こうどう） to act 自動で（じどう） automatically　自動車（じどうしゃ） automobile; car　動詞（どうし） verb　動物園（どうぶつえん） zoo
		うご(く) うご(かす)	動く（うご） (something/someone) moves; (something) functions　動かす（うご） to move (something)
	to move		
162	働	ドウ	労働（ろうどう） labor; work
		はたら(く)	働く（はたら） to work
	to work		
163	走	ソウ	走者（そうしゃ） runner　逃走する（とうそう） to flee
		はし(る)	走る（はし） to run
	to run		
164	当	トウ	本当に（ほんとう） really; actually　本当ですか（ほんとう） Really?; Is it true?　(お)弁当（べんとう） boxed lunch
		あ(たる) あ(てる)	宝くじ{に／が}当たる（たから・あ） to win a lottery　当たる（あ） (something) hits 当てる（あ） to hit (something)
	to hit		
165	荷	に	荷物（にもつ） package; baggage　手荷物（てにもつ） hand luggage; carry-on luggage
	baggage		

166 由

由 由

reason; cause

ユウ
- 自由(じゆう) freedom
- 自由(じゆう)(な) free
- 自由(じゆう)に freely
- 理由(りゆう) reason
- 不自由(ふじゆう)(な) inconvenient; with limited capacity [disability]

167 計

計 計

to measure

ケイ
- 計画(けいかく)を立(た)てる to make a plan
- 時計(とけい)* watch; clock
- 温度計(おんどけい) (air) thermometer
- 会計学(かいけいがく) accounting [field of study]
- 会計士(かいけいし) accountant
- 計算(けいさん)する to calculate
- 合計(ごうけい)する to sum; to total up
- 統計(とうけい) statistics
- 統計学(とうけいがく) statistics [field of study]

168 画

画 画

picture; stroke

カク
ガ
- 計画(けいかく)を立(た)てる to make a plan
- 画数(かくすう) number of strokes (of a kanji)
- 映画(えいが) movie
- 動画(どうが) video; animated image
- 映画館(えいがかん) movie theater
- 映画監督(えいがかんとく) film director
- 画家(がか) painter
- 画像(がぞう) image; picture
- 漫画(まんが) comic book; manga

169 映

映 映

to reflect

エイ
- 映画(えいが) movie
- 映画館(えいがかん) movie theater
- 映画監督(えいがかんとく) film director
- 反映(はんえい)する to reflect

うつ(す)
うつ(る)
- 映(うつ)す to reflect; to project
- 映(うつ)る to be reflected; to be projected

170 仕

仕 仕

to serve; to work

シ
- 仕事(しごと) job; work
- 仕方(しかた)がない cannot be helped
- ～の仕方(しかた) how to ... (Ex. 料理(りょうり)の仕方(しかた) how to cook)

171 事

事 事

thing; matter

ジ
- お大事(だいじ)に Get well soon; Take care of yourself.
- 火事(かじ) fire [destructive]
- 食事(しょくじ)(を)する to have a meal
- 家事(かじ)をする to do housework
- 記事(きじ) (media) article
- 行事(ぎょうじ) (seasonal/annual) event
- 事故(じこ) accident [traffic, etc.]
- 事故(じこ)にあう to have an accident
- 大事(だいじ)(な) precious
- 返事(へんじ)をする to answer; to respond
- 用事(ようじ) errand

ごと
こと
- 仕事(しごと) job; work
- 事柄(ことがら) matter

172 初

初 初

first; beginning

ショ
- 最初(さいしょ) the first
- 初級(しょきゅう) elementary level
- 初心者(しょしんしゃ) beginner

はじ(め)
はじ(めて)
- 初(はじ)め beginning; first
- 初(はじ)めて for the first time

No.	Kanji	Reading	Words
173	東	トウ	東京(とうきょう) Tokyo　東京駅(とうきょうえき) Tokyo Station　関東地方(かんとうちほう) the Kanto region
			東北地方(とうほくちほう) the Tohoku region　中東(ちゅうとう) the Middle East　東南(とうなん)アジア Southeast Asia
		ひがし	東(ひがし) east　東口(ひがしぐち) east entrance/exit (of a train station)
east			東
174	京	キョウ	東京(とうきょう) Tokyo　東京駅(とうきょうえき) Tokyo Station　京都(きょうと) Kyoto
			上京(じょうきょう)する to go to the capital (Tokyo)　北京(ペキン)* Beijing
capital			京
175	同	ドウ	同級生(どうきゅうせい) classmate　同時(どうじ)に at the same time
			同情(どうじょう)する to sympathize　同僚(どうりょう) colleague
		おな(じ)	同(おな)じ the same　同(おな)じ Noun same Noun
same			同
176	半	ハン	～半(はん) ... half (Exs. 九時半(くじはん) half past nine [time], 一時間半(いちじかんはん) one and a half hours,
			一歳半(いっさいはん) one and a half years old)　半額(はんがく) half price　半分(はんぶん) half
			半日(はんにち) half a day　半月(はんつき) half a month　半年(はんとし) half a year
half; middle			半

Kanji as elements

This kanji is used in many other kanji as elements, so you will encounter it frequently as you continue to study Japanese.

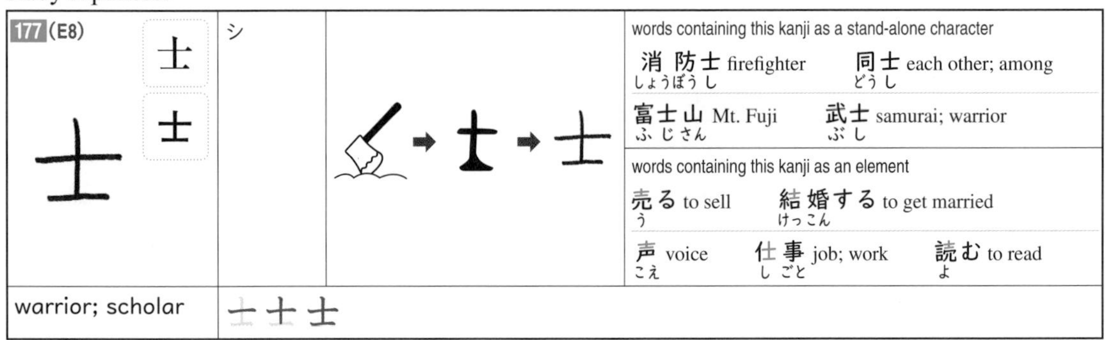

No.	Kanji	Reading	Words
177 (E8)	士	シ	words containing this kanji as a stand-alone character
			消防士(しょうぼうし) firefighter　同士(どうし) each other; among
			富士山(ふじさん) Mt. Fuji　武士(ぶし) samurai; warrior
			words containing this kanji as an element
			売(う)る to sell　結婚(けっこん)する to get married
			声(こえ) voice　仕事(しごと) job; work　読(よ)む to read
warrior; scholar			士

新しい読み方

The following are new readings for kanji that you have already learned. Read each word aloud.

1) 生(う)まれる　2) 親(おや)　3) 計画(けいかく)を立(た)てる　4) 食事(しょくじ)(を)する　5) 心配(しんぱい)する
6) 楽(たの)しみにしています　7) 楽(たの)しむ　8) 動物(どうぶつ)　9) 荷物(にもつ)　10) 私達(わたしたち)

習った(なら)漢字(かんじ)で書ける新しい単語(たんご)

The following are other new vocabulary in this lesson that contain kanji you have already leaned. Read each word aloud.

1) お金(かね)をおろす　2) 左手(ひだりて)　3) 右手(みぎて)

練習(れんしゅう)

1 Complete sentences 1)-8) by selecting the most appropriate kanji word/phrase from a.-i. in the box below. Where applicable, conjugate the verbs appropriately, then write the letter and reading of each kanji word in (　　).

a. 計画を立てる	b. 荷物	c. 自由	d. 集める	e. 動物
f. 宝(たから)くじに当たる	g. 動く	h. 時計	i. 仕事	

Ex. 母は旅行(りょこう)の（ a. けいかくをたてる ）のが好きだから、いつも旅行(りょこう)に行く前にガイドブックをたくさん買って読みます。

1) 大学を卒業(そつぎょう)したら、日本語を使う（　　　　　　　　）がしたいです。

2) （　　　　　　　　）てお金持ちになって、一年間世界(せかい)を旅行(りょこう)したいです。

3) となりの部屋(へや)に住んでいる山田さんが引(ひ)っこしするみたいです。昨日(きのう)大きい（　　　　　　　　）をたくさん運(はこ)んでいたんです。

4) 私の趣味(しゅみ)は色々(いろいろ)な町で売っているマグネットを（　　　　　　　　）ことです。

5) 私は親と住んでいるから、あまりしたいことができません。だから、今一番ほしいのは（　　　　　　　　）です。

6) スマホで時間が分かるから、最近(さいきん)は（　　　　　　　　）を買う人が少(すく)なくなりました。

7) ネコやイヌが好きだから、将来(しょうらい)は（　　　　　　　　）の医者(いしゃ)になりたいです。

8) 田中さんは電気(でんき) (electricity) で（　　　　　　　　）車(くるま)を買ったそうです。

2 Kim-san wrote about a memorable trip she took in Japan to present to her class. Read the presentation script, then write the readings for the underlined words.

私は去年(きょねん)日本に行った時、東京から滋賀(しが)まで自転車(じてんしゃ)で旅行(りょこう)しました。滋賀(しが)では「琵琶湖(びわこ)」という日本で一番大きい湖(みずうみ)を見ました。湖(みずうみ)を見た後で、湖(みずうみ)の近(ちか)くの道を自転車(じてんしゃ)で一時間半ぐらい走りました。

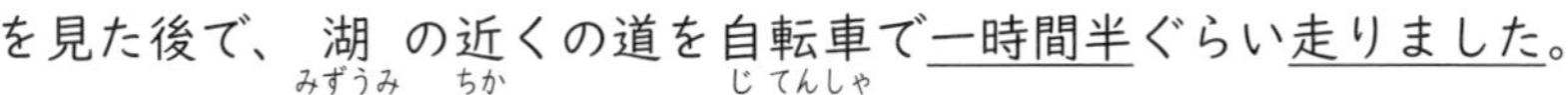

休んでいる時、私と同じ大学のＴシャツを着ている人に会ったから、一緒(いっしょ)に写真(しゃしん)をとりました。その後で、滋賀(しが)で働いている友達と会って、琵琶湖(びわこ)の映画フェスティバルに行ったり、湖(みずうみ)の魚を使った料理のレストランで食事したりしました。一人で旅行(りょこう)したことがなかったから、初めは少(すこ)し心配でしたが、本当に楽しくて、いい旅行(りょこう)でした。

漢字の話 The Story of Kanji

■ When to use kanji

When writing in Japanese using kanji, a reader-friendly paragraph is thought to be one that contains a good mixture of both hiragana and kanji. However, there are some occasions in which kanji are not (commonly) used.

Ex.1 子どもの時、よく家でアニメを見ました。

Ex.2 抹茶スイーツがおいしそうだったから、食べてみました。

As you can see in Ex.1, when the verb 見る is used to describe an action, it is written in kanji. However, in Ex.2, you can see that みる is written in hiragana, not kanji, because it is used as an auxiliary verb (as in Vてみる, which adds a sense of "try and see").

Other expressions with auxiliary verbs that are written in hiragana include ～ておきます and ～ています. The phrase ～てください is also commonly written in hiragana, but sometimes you see it written as ～て下さい as well.

In addition, as in Exs.3-6 below, the words あります／います and こと are also commonly written in hiragana. In Ex.5, the words こと in 田中さんの事 and できる in ギターが出来る can be written using either kanji or hiragana. However, for the phrase ことができる, as in ピアノをひくことができません, the kanji 事 and 出来る cannot be used. In the same way, the phrase ことがある, as in 日本に行ったことがありません in Ex.6, is also not written in kanji.

Ex.3 大学の図書館には、日本のまんががたくさんあります（×有ります）。

Ex.4 スミスさんは兄弟が三人います（×居ます）。

Ex.5 田中さんの｛こと／事｝を知っていますか。田中さんは歌が得意で、ギターが｛できます／出来ます｝。でも、ピアノをひくことができません（×事が出来ません）。

Ex.6 私は日本に行ったことがありません（×事が有りません）。

When you write sentences with kanji, keep these rules in mind, and make sure not to use kanji indiscriminately for every word.

練習

Read Ai's post on social media below. For each of the underlined segments 1)-7), mark ○ if it can be written in kanji and × if it cannot.

日本に行く飛行機を予約した！　日本には行った Ex. ことが 1) ある けど、その時はあまり観光する 2) ことが 3) できなかった。だから、今度日本に行って一番したい 4) ことは、雑誌で 5) みた有名なお寺や神社の観光だ。それから、日本には虫のような和菓子 (Japanese sweets) が 6) あると聞いた。おもしろそうだから、食べて 7) みたい。

(Ex. ×)

文(ぶん)法(ぽう)

1 Potential forms of verbs

In Lesson 10 #7, we studied the expression Vことができる "can V; be able to V." The potential forms of verbs express the same meaning in a single word. The rules for making the verb potential forms are as follows:

(a) *Ru*-verbs: Change the final る of the dictionary form to られる.

Exs. 食(た)べ~~る~~ → 食(た)べられる; 見(み)~~る~~ → 見(み)られる

(b) *U*-verbs: Change the final /u/ sound of the dictionary form to the /e/ sound and attach る.

Exs. 書(か)く (/kaku/) → 書(か)ける (/kake/ +る); 買(か)う (/kau/) → 買(か)える (/kae/ +る)

More examples of *u*-verb potential forms are shown in the following conjugation table, along with the other forms we have learned that use different vowels in their conjugations:

帰(かえ)らない	話(はな)さない	行(い)かない	言(い)わない	← /a/ row: Plain negative forms
帰(かえ)ります	話(はな)します	行(い)きます	言(い)います	← /i/ row: *Masu*-forms
帰(かえ)る	話(はな)す	行(い)く	言(い)う	← /u/ row: Dictionary forms (= plain affirmative forms)
帰(かえ)れる	話(はな)せる	行(い)ける	言(い)える	← /e/ row: **Potential forms**

(c) Irregular verbs: する → できる; 来(く)る → 来(こ)られる

Note that the potential forms are not used for the following types of verbs:

(i) Verbs that express a state:

Exs. 分(わ)かる (× 分(わ)かれる), ある (× あれる), (１時間(じかん)) かかる (× かかれる)

(ii) Verbs that are used with a non-animate subject:

Exs. (雨(あめ)が) 降(ふ)る (× 降(ふ)れる), 晴(は)れる (× 晴(は)れられる)

All potential forms are *ru*-verbs. For example, 話(はな)せる conjugates as follows:

	Polite		Plain		*Te*-form
Non-past	話(はな)せます	話(はな)せません	話(はな)せる	話(はな)せない	話(はな)せて
Past	話(はな)せました	話(はな)せませんでした	話(はな)せた	話(はな)せなかった	

[1-a]

	N (direct object)		V (potential)
私(わたし)は	フランス語(ご)	が／を	話(はな)せます。
I can speak French.			

Using potential forms, you can talk about a person's abilities, talents, and skills. The direct objects of potential verbs can be marked by either が or を.

Exs. (1) 田中さんは上手にギター{が／を}ひけます。*Tanaka-san can play the guitar well.*

(2) 子どもの時、野菜{が／を}全然食べられませんでした。
When I was a kid, I could not eat vegetables at all.

Note that the direct object of できる (the potential form of する) can be marked only by が. Thus, the following sentence is ungrammatical.

× リサさんはスキーをできません。 → リサさんはスキーができません。*Lisa cannot ski.*

[1-b]

	N (direct object)		VN	
この大学では	アラビア語	が／を	勉強	できます。
You can study Arabic at this university.				

You can make the potential form of a *suru*-verb by adding できる to its noun portion. As seen in [1-b], although the potential forms of *suru*-verbs involve できる, the direct object can be marked by を as well.

[1-b] can be rephrased as この大学ではアラビア語の勉強ができます. In this sentence, できる is used as the main verb, so the direct object アラビア語の勉強 can be marked only by が.

Another important point regarding [1-b] is that potential forms can also be used when one can do something as a result of certain facilities, resources, services, etc. being available.

Exs. (3) このアプリで漢字のテストが受けられます。*Using this app, you can take kanji tests.*

(4) A: この抹茶のお菓子はおいしいね。どこで買えるの？
This powdered green tea snack is delicious. Where can we buy it?

B: 実はコンビニで買えるんだよ。*Actually, you can buy it at a convenience store.*

To make the potential form of the ～たり～たりする structure, you change する to できる, as in (5). Note here that in the phrase ～たり～たりできる, the direct object "Wi-Fi" is marked by を rather than が.

Ex. (5) 日本のコンビニではWi-Fiを使ったり、コピーしたりできます。
You can do things like use the Wi-Fi and make photocopies at convenience stores in Japan.

☞ **GID** (vol.2): D. Sentence patterns 2. Potential forms of verbs vs. Vことができる

2 V前に "before V-ing; before ~ V" and V後で "after V-ing; after ~ have V-ed"

[2-a]

V-plain.non-past		
朝ご飯を食べる	前に、	シャワーを浴びました。
I took a shower before eating breakfast.		

[2-b]

V-plain.past		
シャワーを浴びた	後で、	朝ご飯を食べました。
I ate breakfast after taking a shower.		

You can express the ideas of "before doing something" and "after doing something" using V前に and V後で, respectively. Note that the tense of the verb before 前に is always non-past, and that of the verb before 後で is always past, regardless of the tense of the main clause. (See L11 #3.)

Exs. (1) 私はたいてい寝る前に、スマホでまんがを読みます。でも、昨日は（寝る前に）アニメを見ました。*I usually read manga on my smartphone before going to bed. Yesterday, though, I watched anime (before going to bed).*

(2) 妹はよく学校から帰った後で、スポーツをします。昨日は（帰った後で）サッカーをしました。*My younger sister often plays sports after returning home from school. She played soccer (after returning home) yesterday.*

(3) A: 今日学校が終わった後で、ラーメンを食べに行かない？
Do you wanna go to eat ramen after school is over today?

B: いいね。あ、でも、ラーメン屋に行く前に、コンビニに寄ってもいい？
Sounds good. Oh, but can I stop by a convenience store before going to the ramen place?

In the same manner as the 時 clause (L11 #3), when the subject of a 前に／後で clause is different from that of the main clause, it is marked by が, as in (4).

Ex. (4) ルームメートが起きる前に、私は学校に行きます。／私は、ルームメートが起きる前に学校に行きます。*I go to school before my roommate gets up.*

☞ **GID** (vol.2): A. Time expressions 2. V-*te*から vs. 後で;
E. Special topics 4. Tense in time clauses

3 ～ておく "V (ahead of time); V ~ and leave it as is"

[3]

	V-*te*	
飲み物を	冷やして	おきます。
I'm going to chill the drinks (ahead of time).		

Using V-*te*おく, you can express the idea that someone does something ahead of time in preparation for something. For example, you can use [3] when you are having a party and plan to serve chilled drinks. The おく in this structure is an auxiliary *u*-verb.

Exs. (1) 試験の前に、もう一度文法をよく勉強しておきます。
I'm going to study grammar thoroughly one more time before the exam.

(2) A: あ、12時。もうすぐ田中さんが来ますね。
Oh, it's 12:00. Tanaka-san should be arriving soon, huh?

B: そうですね。田中さんが来る前に、ピザを温めておきましょう。
That's right. Let's warm the pizza before Tanaka-san comes.

(3) 先生：次のクラスの前に、教科書を30ページから40ページまで読んでおいてください。*Please read pp.30-40 in the textbook before the next class.*

FYI

"Xを V-*te*おく" can also be used to mean either "V X and leave it that way" or "leave X in its (already) V-ed state." (4) can be interpreted in either of these ways, depending on the context.

Ex. (4) 暑(あつ)いから、窓(まど)を開(あ)けておきましょう。
It's hot, so let's {open the window (and leave it open) / leave the (already opened) window open}.

4 ～たら "if; when" 

[4-a]

	たら clause		Main clause
	S-plain.past		
この本(ほん)は	ネットで買(か)った	ら、	安(やす)いです。
As for this book, it'll be cheap(er) if you buy it online.			

You can express ideas such as "if X does Y" and "if X is Y" using たら (to be more accurate, using a sentence in the plain past form with ら at the end). Examples of たら forms are below:

	Affirmative	Negative
Verbs	買(か)ったら	買(か)わなかったら
I-adjectives	おいしかったら	おいしくなかったら
Na-adjectives	上手(じょうず)だったら	上手(じょうず)じゃなかったら
Nouns	学生(がくせい)だったら	学生(がくせい)じゃなかったら

Exs. (1) 週末(しゅうまつ)、雨(あめ)が降(ふ)ったら、出(で)かけません。でも、降(ふ)らなかったら、キャンプに行(い)きます。
If it rains this weekend, we won't go out. But if it doesn't, we'll go camping.

(2) 安(やす)かったら、買(か)いますが、安(やす)くなかったら、買(か)いません。
I'll buy it if it's cheap, but I won't if it's not cheap.

(3) 暇(ひま)だったら、手伝(てつだ)ってください。でも、暇(ひま)じゃなかったら、いいです。
If you're free, please help. If you're not, though, that's okay.

(4) もし明日(あした)晴(は)れだったら、公園(こうえん)を散歩(さんぽ)しましょう。いい天気(てんき)じゃなかったら、ボウリングに行(い)きましょう。
If it's sunny tomorrow, let's take a walk in the park. If it's not good weather, let's go bowling.

もし in (4) above is an adverb that makes it clear or emphasizes that the たら clause indicates the condition for what is stated in the main clause.

[4-b]

たら clause		Main clause
S-plain.past		
夏休(なつやす)みになった	ら、	旅行(りょこう)したいです。
I want to go on a trip when summer vacation begins.		

たら can also be used when the たら clause represents an event that will definitely take place, as in [4-b], in which case, the corresponding English is not "if" but "when." (5) is another example of this use.

Ex. (5) 宿題(しゅくだい)が終(お)わったら、一緒(いっしょ)にゲームをしませんか。
When we are done with our homework, would you like to play games with me?

Because たら can be used in "*if* situations" and "*when* situations," as in [4-a] and [4-b], the meaning of a たら sentence can be ambiguous without proper situational or contextual information. (6) below provides an example. Here, the たら clause can mean either (i) if Yamada-san comes (the speaker is not sure if that will happen), or (ii) when Yamada-san comes (the speaker is certain it will happen). In either case, this sentence indicates that the condition that will prompt the speaker to go home is Yamada-san's coming to where the speaker is.

Ex. (6) 山田(やまだ)さんが来(き)たら、私(わたし)は帰(かえ)ります。*I'll go home if/when Yamada-san comes.*

If もし is used in the たら clause, the sentence is not ambiguous; it can only mean "I'll go home if Yamada-san comes."

[4-c]

たら clause		Main clause (action/event in the past)
S-plain.past		
図書館(としょかん)に行(い)った	ら、	休(やす)みでした。
When I went to the library, I found it closed.		

たら can be used when the main clause represents a past action or event, as in [4-c]. In this case, however, the たら clause represents a time rather than a condition, and the main clause represents an unexpected action or event (e.g., the speaker discovered something at that time; something happened unexpectedly at that time; etc.). For this reason, when たら is used, volitional actions (i.e., actions performed on one's own will, such as 話(はな)す and 質問(しつもん)する) cannot appear in the main clause. The following sentence, for instance, is ungrammatical:

× 黒田先生(くろだせんせい)に会(あ)ったら、留学(りゅうがく)のことを話(はな)しました。
→ 黒田先生(くろだせんせい)に会(あ)った時(とき)、留学(りゅうがく)のことを話(はな)しました。
When I saw Prof. Kuroda, I talked to her about studying abroad.

The two sentences in (7) further illustrate the above point.

Exs. (7) a. カフェに行(い)って、彼女(かのじょ)に会(あ)いました。*I went to the café and met with my girlfriend.*
b. カフェに行(い)ったら、彼女(かのじょ)に会(あ)いました。*When I went to the café, I ran across my girlfriend.*

In (7a), the speaker had a plan to meet with his girlfriend at the café. On the other hand, in (7b), the speaker had no plan to meet with his girlfriend at the café; rather, he went to the café and unexpectedly encountered her there. (Note that 会(あ)う can mean both "meet" and "encounter.")

☞ GID (vol.2): B. Connecting sentences 4-1. たら

5 ～みたい／よう [Conjecture] "It looks like ~; seems ~; appears ~" 

We studied the resemblance expressions みたい and よう in Lesson 11 #4. In this lesson, we will study another use for these expressions. (We mainly practice with みたい.)

[5-a]

Topic		V-plain	
リサさんは	今晩(こんばん)トムさんと	出(で)かける	みたいです／ようです。
It looks like Lisa is going out with Tom tonight.			

[5-b]

Topic		Adj(*i*)-plain	
田中(たなか)さんは	今週(こんしゅう)	忙(いそが)しい	みたいです／ようです。
It seems that Tanaka-san is busy this week.			

[5-c]

Topic		Adj(*na*)		
山田(やまだ)さんは	料理(りょうり)が	上手(じょうず)	ø	みたいです。
			な	ようです。
It seems like Yamada-san is good at cooking.				

[5-d]

Topic		N		
あの人(ひと)は	この大学(だいがく)の	先生(せんせい)	ø	みたいです。
			の	ようです。
It looks like that person is a professor at this university.				

You can express your conjecture based on your direct observation using みたい or よう. Your conjecture can also be based on what you actually hear, taste, and smell. みたい is more conversational than よう.

The forms before みたい and よう are always plain forms, except for だ. Before みたい, だ drops, while before よう, だ changes to な after *na*-adjectives and to の after nouns, respectively, as in [5-c] and [5-d].

Exs. (1) リサさんは今日(きょう)ねむそうですね。昨日(きのう)あまり寝(ね)なかった{みたい／よう}です。
Lisa looks sleepy today. It appears that she didn't sleep much yesterday.

(2) <レストランの前(まえ)で>
誰(だれ)もいないから、今日(きょう)は休(やす)み{みたい／のよう}ですね。
No one's inside, so it seems like they're closed today.

(3) リーマンさんはカラオケに行(い)きません。歌(うた)が苦手(にがて){みたい／なよう}です。
Riemann does not go to karaoke. It looks like he is not confident in singing.

Note that sentences before みたい and よう can be either affirmative or negative, but みたいです and ようです themselves do not occur in the negative form. Therefore, the following sentence is ungrammatical:

× トムさんは昨日(きのう)のパーティーに行(い)った{みたい／よう}じゃないです。
→ トムさんは昨日(きのう)のパーティーに行(い)かなかった{みたい／よう}です。
It doesn't look like Tom went to yesterday's party. (lit. It looks like Tom didn't go to yesterday's party.)

☞ **GID** (vol.2): C. Auxiliaries 1. ～そう vs. ～みたい／よう;
E. Special topics 7. Adj(*na*)/Nだ: Why does だ drop in some situations?

話しましょう

▶ **Words written in purple** are new words introduced in this lesson.

Ask and answer questions about your abilities and what you can do in a particular place.

できるI-A Potential forms of verbs (ability)

1 Let's practice conjugating verbs into their potential forms.

Step 1 First, change the verbs below into their base potential forms.

Ex. 食(た)べる → 食(た)べられる → 食(た)べられます

1) 起(お)きる　2) 覚(おぼ)える　3) 借(か)りる　4) 話(はな)す　5) 書(か)く　6) 泳(およ)ぐ
7) 買(か)う　8) 持(も)つ　9) する　10) 来(く)る　11) 変(か)える　12) 飛(と)ぶ
13) お金(かね)をおろす　14) 計算(けいさん)する

Step 2 Next, practice conjugating all the base potential forms from Step 1 into all of their plain forms and the *te*-form, as shown below. L12-8

Ex. 食(た)べる

2 Let's talk about what some animals can and can't do.

Step 1 Change the verb phrases below into their potential forms. L12-9

Ex. 文字(もじ)を書く → 文字(もじ){が／を} 書けます。

1) 速(はや)く走(はし)る　2) 空(そら)を飛(と)ぶ　3) 自由(じゆう)に泳(およ)ぐ　4) 人の言葉(ことば)を話す
5) 高い木に登(のぼ)る　6) 熱(あつ)い物を食べる　7) 人の顔(かお)を覚(おぼ)える　8) 人と仲良(なかよ)くなる

Step 2 Choose some of the animals shown below and describe what they can and can't do using the verb phrases in Step 1.

Ex. 人は文字(もじ)が書けます。でも、空(そら)を飛(と)べません。

Group Work

3 Let's find out your classmates' strengths.

Step 1 Ask your classmates if they can do the things listed in the table below. Before starting, create question sentences to ask your classmates. Don't limit your answers to yes or no — give additional information as well.

Ex. A: ○○さんはからい物が食べられますか。

B: はい、食べられます。大好きです。よく料理にタバスコをかけて食べます。

C: 私はからい物が食べられません。おなかが痛(いた)くなります。△△さんは？

<Continue>

質問(しつもん)	さん	さん	私
Ex. からい物を食べる	はい・いいえ	はい・いいえ	はい・いいえ
1) 朝早(あさ)く起(お)きる	はい・いいえ	はい・いいえ	はい・いいえ
2) 人に何か教(おし)える	はい・いいえ	はい・いいえ	はい・いいえ
3) 上手に絵を描(か)く	はい・いいえ	はい・いいえ	はい・いいえ
4) 速(はや)く計算(けいさん)する	はい・いいえ	はい・いいえ	はい・いいえ
5) your own	はい・いいえ	はい・いいえ	はい・いいえ

Step 2 Report to the class what your group members can or can't do.

Ex. ○○さんはからい物が食べられます。でも、△△さんはからい物が食べられません。

4 Let's get to know more about each other! Use casual speech to ask your partner about things they can or can't do.

Possible topics 歌(うた)　楽器(がっき)　スポーツ　料理　外国語　絵

Ex. A: ○○さんは日本語の歌(うた)が歌(うた)える？

Yes

B: うん、歌(うた)えるよ。

A: 何が歌(うた)える？

B: てフォームの歌(うた)やアニメの歌(うた)が歌(うた)えるよ。

A: へえ、すごいね。

B: △△さんは？

<Continue>

No

B: ううん、歌(うた)えない。

A: そっか。

B: △△さんは日本語の歌(うた)が歌(うた)える？

<Continue>

できるI-B　Potential forms of verbs (availability)

1 Nowadays, you see convenience stores all over the world. Talk about what you can do at a convenience store.

Step 1 First, say what services Japanese convenience stores typically do (○) and do not (×) offer using the cues provided. L12-10

Ex. 日本のコンビニではおにぎりやお弁当(べんとう){が／を}買えます。

Ex. ○ buy rice balls, boxed lunches, etc.　1) ○ use free Wi-Fi

2) ○ withdraw money from the ATM　3) ○ send luggage to the airport

4) ○ make photocopies　5) ○ dine in the store

6) ○ buy various tickets　7) × send packages to foreign countries

8) × buy lottery (tickets)

Step 2 Now, compare convenience stores in Japan with those in other places in the world and talk about their similarities and differences.

Ex. A: 日本のコンビニではおにぎりやお弁当(べんとう)が買えます。でも、アメリカのコンビニではお弁当(べんとう)は買えませんね。

B: そうですね。でも、アメリカのコンビニ{でも／では}…　<Continue>

2 Talk about things that make your life easier and more interesting.

Step 1 Describe the various things you can do using the tools shown below.

Ex. スマートスピーカーで簡単(かんたん)に音楽を聞いたり、知りたいことを調(しら)べたりできます。それから…　<Continue>

Ex. スマートスピーカー　1) スマホ　2) タブレット　3) ○○というSNS　4) ○○というアプリ　5) your own

Step 2 Exchange opinions about the convenient tools in Step 1 with your partner. Make sure to give reason(s) for your opinions as well.

Ex. A: ○○さんは何が便利(べんり)だと思いますか。

B: そうですね、私はスマートスピーカーが便利(べんり)だと思います。スマートスピーカーで簡単(かんたん)に音楽を聞いたり、知りたいことを調(しら)べたりできるからです。△△さんは何が便利(べんり)だと思いますか。

<Continue>

Group Work

3 If you were to invent a new gadget, what would you like to create?

Step 1 The following are newly invented gadgets. Add a gadget you want to invent and brainstorm what you can do using the product as in the examples.

Exs.

カラオケが楽(たの)しめる

自由(じゆう)に飛(と)べる

your own

Step 2 Explain the best uses for the product that you want to invent in three sentences.

Ex. A: ①これは「カラオケペン」です。②このめずらしいペンでカラオケを楽(たの)しめて、人気がある歌(うた)が歌(うた)えます。③それから、自分の声(こえ)が変(か)えられます。

B: へえ、すばらしいペンですね。すごくほしいです。(⇄ Comment or follow-up question)

C:「カラオケペン」でアニメの歌(うた)も歌(うた)えますか。

できる II Talk about preparations for trips, parties, events, etc.

できるII-A V前に and V後で

1 Let's practice using the structures V前に and V後で to describe a specific sequence of events.

Step 1 The following are sequences of events in Lewis-san's life. Use V前に to describe them, paying attention to the tense of each clause. L12-11

Ex.1 コーヒーを飲む ➡ 授業(じゅぎょう)に行く

ルイスさんは授業(じゅぎょう)に行く前に、コーヒーを飲みます。

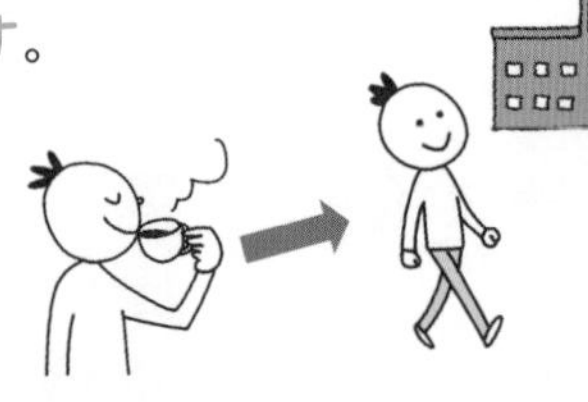

1) 宿題(しゅくだい)をする ➡ 晩(ばん)ご飯(はん)を食べる
2) ホテルを予約(よやく)する ➡ 旅行(りょこう)に行く
3) 筋(きん)トレする ➡ 走(はし)る
4) 安い店(みせ)を探(さが)す ➡ 古いパソコンを新しいのに変(か)える

Ex.2 アルバイトを始(はじ)めた ➡ 大学に入った

ルイスさんは大学に入る前に、アルバイトを始(はじ)めました。

5) 面接(めんせつ)を受(う)けた ➡ インターンシップをした
6) 日本語のクラスを取(と)った ➡ 日本に留学(りゅうがく)した
7) 上手な話し方の練習(れんしゅう)をした ➡ ユーチューバー (YouTuber) になった
8) 家賃(やちん)を調(しら)べた ➡ アパートを借(か)りた

Step 2 Describe the same sequences of events as in Step 1, but this time, use V後で. Again, pay attention to the tense of each clause. L12-12

Ex.1 コーヒーを飲む ➡ 授業(じゅぎょう)に行く

ルイスさんはコーヒーを飲んだ後で、授業(じゅぎょう)に行きます。

Ex.2 アルバイトを始(はじ)めた ➡ 大学に入った

ルイスさんはアルバイトを始(はじ)めた後で、大学に入りました。

2 Talk about your routines with your partner using the cues provided.

Ex. before eating dinner

A: ○○さんは晩(ばん)ご飯(はん)を食べる前に、たいてい何をしますか。

B: そうですね、私は晩(ばん)ご飯(はん)を食べる前に、授業(じゅぎょう)の復習(ふくしゅう)をしたり、イヌの散歩(さんぽ)をしたりします。△△さんは？ <Continue>

1) before going on a trip　2) before going to sleep　3) before renting a new apartment

4) after class is over　5) after returning home　6) after ○○ (your own)

3 It's important to familiarize yourself with local customs before visiting a country.

Step 1 Describe what people usually do/don't do in Japan using V前に and V後で. 

Ex.1 日本では食事(しょくじ)する前に、「いただきます」と言います。

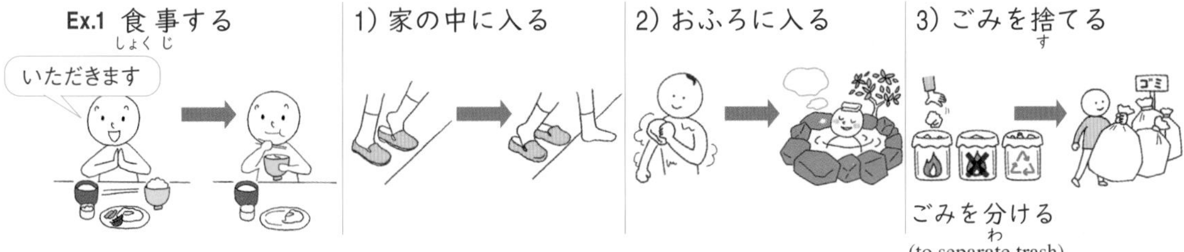

Ex.2 日本では食事(しょくじ)した後で、「ごちそうさま」と言います。

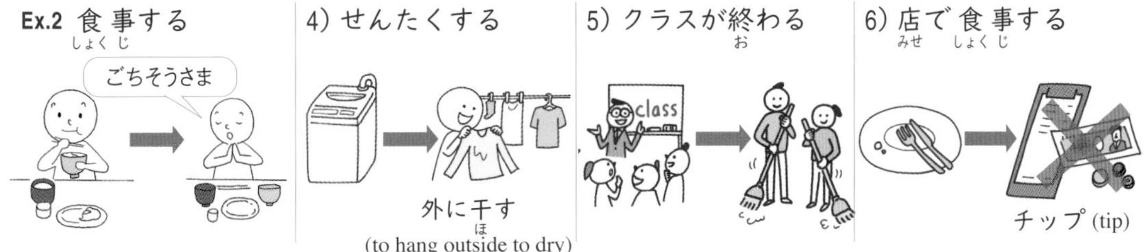

Step 2 Now, compare and contrast the customs in Japan with those in another country/culture you are familiar with.

Ex. A: 台湾(たいわん)も日本と同(おな)じです。家の中に入る前に、くつをぬぎます。

B: そうですか。オランダ (Netherlands) は日本と違(ちが)います。たいてい部屋(へや)に入る前に、くつをぬぎません。でも、私の家では家の中に入る前に、くつをぬぎます。

4 Let's play a bingo game. Before starting, create question sentences to ask your classmates using the cues provided in the table below. If someone answers yes, write down their name in the space under each cue.

Ex. A: ○○さんは昼(ひる)ご飯(はん)を食べた後で、昼寝(ひるね)しますか。

B: はい、私は時々(ときどき)昼寝(ひるね)します。

Ex. take a nap after eating lunch _____________さん	1) often forget after making a promise _____________さん	2) worry before taking an exam _____________さん
3) change a password (パスワード) after using (it) for a year _____________さん	4) your own question using 前に or 後で _____________さん	5) look at the price before buying something _____________さん
6) get depressed after receiving a bad grade _____________さん	7) get nervous before presenting in class _____________さん	8) started studying Japanese before entering university _____________さん

5 Talk casually about which of two things you tend to do first.

Ex. 漢字(かんじ)の書き方 vs. 読み方

A: ○○さんは漢字(かんじ)の書き方を覚(おぼ)える前に、読み方を覚(おぼ)える？

それとも (or)、書き方を覚(おぼ)えた後で、読み方を覚(おぼ)える？

B: 私は漢字(かんじ)の読み方を覚(おぼ)えた後で、書き方を覚(おぼ)えるよ。△△さんは？

<Continue>

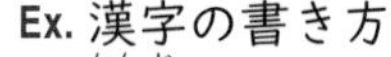

Ex. 漢字(かんじ)の書き方　読み方　1) 食事(しょくじ)　運動(うんどう)　2) レビュー　映画(えいが)

VS

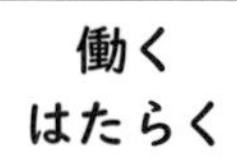

VS

MOVIE REVIEWS

VS

3) 店(みせ)に入る　食べる物を決(き)める　4) your own

VS

VS ?

できるII-B Preparation ～ておく

1 If you are going to travel abroad or have a job interview, what should you do beforehand? Describe what people often do to prepare for these occasions. L12-14

Ex. 外国に旅行(りょこう)に行く前に、ホテルを予約(よやく)しておきます。

外国に旅行(りょこう)に行く前に	インターンシップの面接(めんせつ)を受(う)ける前に
Ex. ホテルを予約(よやく)する	6) 履歴書(りれきしょ)を準備(じゅんび)する
1) パスポートやビザを取(と)る	7) 会社について調(しら)べる
2) 大使館(たいしかん)の場所を調(しら)べる	8) 面接(めんせつ)の練習(れんしゅう)をする
3) 計画(けいかく)を立(た)てる	9) 質問(しつもん)の答(こた)え方を考(かんが)える
4) 行く所の地図(ちず)を見る	10) くつをみがく
5) your own	11) your own

2 Suppose you are a Japan travel expert. Answer the following questions using the cues provided. L12-15

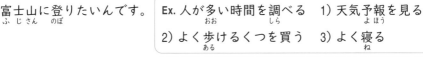

Ex. A: 富士山(ふじさん) (Mt. Fuji) に登(のぼ)りたいんですが、アドバイスがありますか。

B: 登(のぼ)る前に、人が多(おお)い時間を調(しら)べておいてください。それから… <Continue>

富士山(ふじさん)に登(のぼ)りたいんです。

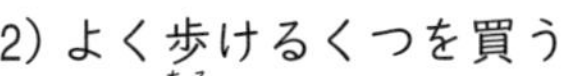

Ex. 人が多(おお)い時間を調(しら)べる　1) 天気予報(よほう)を見る

2) よく歩(ある)けるくつを買う　3) よく寝(ね)る

おいしい和食(わしょく)が食べたいんです。

4) 食べたい物を決(き)める

5) ネットで食べ方の動画(どうが)を見る

6) 箸(はし)の使い方を練習(れんしゅう)する

人気があるバンドのライブに行きたいんです。

7) 早くチケットを買う

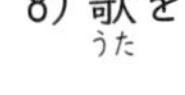

8) 歌(うた)を覚(おぼ)える

9) your own

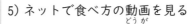

3 Do you have any good advice to give to your classmates? Choose a topic and give the three best pieces of advice you have on it. Take turns with your partner and ask follow-up questions.

Possible topics　いい成績(せいせき)を取(と)る　動物(どうぶつ)を飼(か)う　筋(きん)トレをする　楽しい旅行(りょこう)をする

Ex. 私はいい成績(せいせき)の取(と)り方が教(おし)えられます。

①まず、授業(じゅぎょう)に行く前に予習(よしゅう)しておきます。②その時、分からないことをチェックしておきます。③そして、授業(じゅぎょう)を受(う)けた後で、すぐに宿題(しゅくだい)をして、習(なら)ったことを復習(ふくしゅう)します。ぜひやってみてください。

Group Work

4 Do you have any genius party ideas for the class? As the class party organizers, make a plan.

Step 1 Discuss the following things with your groupmates.

① パーティーのテーマ (theme) は何ですか。 ______________________

② パーティーでどんなことができますか。 ______________________

③ パーティーの前に何をしておきますか。 ______________________

④ パーティーに来る人に何をお願(ねが)いしますか。 ______________________

Step 2 Share your party plan with the class.

Ex. ① 私達(わたしたち)のパーティーはJ-POPパーティーです。

② このパーティーではみんなでJ-POPのいい歌(うた)を聞いたり、みんなと好きな歌(うた)を歌(うた)ったりできます。

③ パーティーの前に、みんなで歌(うた)いたい歌(うた)を選(えら)んで、動画(どうが)を探(さが)しておきます。それから、飲み物やペンライト (glow stick) を準備(じゅんび)しておきます。

④ パーティーに来る時、みんなで食べられる物を一つ持ってきてください。

できるIII Talk briefly about hypothetical situations.

できるIII-A ～たら ("if")

1 Let's practice ～たら form conjugations.

Step 1 First, change the following verbs into their ～たら forms. L12-16

Ex. 食(た)べる → 食(た)べたら → 食(た)べなかったら

1) 見(み)る　2) いる　3) ある　4) 行(い)く　5) 言(い)う　6) する　7) 来(く)る　8) できる
9) 会(あ)える　10) 行(い)ける　11) 見(み)られる　12) 宝(たから)くじに当(あ)たる　13) 仲良(なかよ)くなる　14) 就職(しゅうしょく)する

Step 2 This time, change the following adjectives and nouns into their ～たら forms. 

Ex.1 高(たか)い → 高(たか)かったら → 高(たか)くなかったら

Ex.2 好(す)き → 好(す)きだったら → 好(す)きじゃなかったら

1) 安(やす)い　2) 多(おお)い　3) おもしろい　4) いい　5) 頭(あたま)がいい　6) 危(あぶ)ない
7) きれい　8) 静(しず)か　9) 休(やす)み　10) 雨(あめ)　11) 貧乏(びんぼう)　12) 自由(じゆう)

2 Make sentences about whether you would feel happy or sad in the following situations. L12-18

Ex. いい友達がいる → いい友達がいたら、うれしいです。

いい友達がいなかったら、悲(かな)しいです。

1) 宝(たから)くじに当(あ)たる	2) 自由(じゆう)がある	3) 日本語が上手になる
4) 難(むずか)しい試験(しけん)がなくなる	5) 新しい単語(たんご)が覚(おぼ)えられる	6) クラスメートと仲良(なかよ)くなれる
7) いい経験(けいけん)ができる	8) 冬(ふゆ)休みが長い	9) 教科書(きょうかしょ)の値段(ねだん)が安い
10) 成績(せいせき)がいい	11) 部屋(へや)がきれい	12) 水がただ　13) your own

3 Talk about what you would do to survive on a desert island in the following situations.

Ex. きれいな水がありません

A: ○○さんは、きれいな水がなかったら、どうしますか。

B: 私はきれいな水がなかったら、ココナッツを取(と)って飲みます。△△さんは？

A: んー、私は… <Continue>

1) 食べる物がありません
2) 雨が降(ふ)ります
3) 一人でさびしいです
4) 夜(よる)、寝(ね)られません
5) 助(たす)け (rescue) がほしいです
6) your own

Group Work

4 If something/someone you take for granted disappeared, what would happen to you? Choose a topic and brainstorm about it for a few minutes. Then, discuss the positives and negatives of the situation.

Possible topics	インターネット	スマホ	学校	友達

Ex. A: インターネットがなかったら、色々(いろいろ)なことが分からないと思います。

B: そうですね。でも、もしインターネットがなかったら、もっと友達と会って話すと思います。

C: それから、もしインターネットがなかったら、もっと長く寝(ね)られると思います。

<Continue>

できるⅢ-B ～たら ("when; after")

1 Tanaka-san is texting his friends. Read his messages aloud using the cues provided. 

Ex. 12時になったら、電話してください。

Ex. 12時になる → 電話する
1) 日本語の本を読む → 貸す
2) レポートを書く → 見せる
3) いい写真をとる → 送る

4) バイトが終わる → カフェに来る
5) 夏休みになる → 楽器を教える
6) 大学を卒業する → 僕と付き合う
7) your own

2 Ask and answer questions about when you typically do the things listed below, as in the example.

Ex. A: 私はたいてい7時になったら、晩ご飯を食べます。〇〇さんは？
B: 私はいつもおなかがすいたら、晩ご飯を食べます。

Ex. 晩ご飯を食べる　1) 昼寝する　2) 親に電話する　3) 就職する
4) 感動する　5) 落ち込む　6) {甘い物／からい物} を食べる　7) your own

3 What are you going to do after you graduate? Talk about your plan in four sentences.

Plan	**Ex.** 私は大学を卒業したら、日本や他の外国に行って、子ども達に英語を教えたいです。
Reason	色々な国の文化を知りたいからです。
Subsequent action	その経験をした後で、たぶん就職すると思います。
Alternative plan	でも、いい仕事がなかったら、自分の会社を作ります。

できるⅣ Express what you infer about a situation based on what you see and hear.

できるⅣ-A Conjecture ～みたい／よう

1 Let's practice using みたいです and ようです to express conjecture. L12-20

Step 1 First, practice ～みたいです conjugations as in Ex.1.

Ex.1 食べる

	affirmative	negative
non-past	食べるみたいです	食べないみたいです
past	食べたみたいです	食べなかったみたいです

Ex.2 食べる

	affirmative	negative
non-past	食べるようです	食べないようです
past	食べたようです	食べなかったようです

1) いる　2) できる　3) ある　4) 分かる　5) 来る　6) いい
7) 悪い　8) 好き　9) ひま　10) 学生　11) 動いている　12) 事故

Step 2 This time, practice ～ようです conjugations as in Ex.2 using the cues in Step 1. Pay attention to the conjugation patterns for *na*-adjctives and nouns. L12-21

2 Suppose you are traveling in Japan with your classmate. Make various conjectures based on the information provided. L12-22

Ex. 飛行機は早く着く？

A: 飛行機は早く着きますか。

B: ええ、少し早く着く{みたいです／ようです}よ。

1) 店でWi-Fiが使える？
2) お金がおろせる？
3) 中で食べられる？

4) この店はおいしい？
5) 有名？
6) ベジタリアンメニューがある？

7) 事故？
8) 地震？
9) 電車は動いている？

10) もうバスは来た？
11) 雨が降った？

3 You and your classmate are renting a private room you found on a home-sharing website. Make guesses about the owner based on what you see in the room. Make sure to include the reasoning behind your conjecture.

Ex. 歴史が好き？

A: さむらいやお城のポスターがあるから、この部屋の人は歴史が好きみたいですね。

B: そうですね。それから… <Continue>

1) 学生？
2) 英語が分かる？
3) 動物を飼っている？
4) 今朝、部屋をそうじした？
5) 私達にケーキを焼いた？
6) your own

4 You hear some sounds coming from the apartment next door. Listen to the audio on the *TOBIRA* website and make some conjectures about what is happening there. L12-23

Ex. A: となりの人はパーティーをしているみたいだね。

B: そうだね。楽しそうだね。(← Comment)

5 Look at the Japanese memes below and make guesses about the creator and the meaning of each meme. Share your thoughts with your classmates.

Ex. A: この人はカタカナの「シ」と「ツ」が分からないみたいです。

B: そうですね。この人は私と同(おな)じです。

1)

2)

3)

4)

Review

Now you can give tourist information and make recommendations for a place you are familiar with.

Step 1 Pick a place and brainstorm the things you want to tell your classmates.

Q1. おすすめの所はどこ？ ____________________

Q2. どうして？ ____________________

Q3. そこで何ができる？ ____________________

Q4. 行く前に準備(じゅんび)しておく物やことは？ ____________________

Q5. 他(ほか)に？ ____________________

Step 2 Give a presentation to the class using the information you brainstormed in Step 1. Your classmates will ask some questions after your presentation.

Place you recommend	**Ex.** 私のおすすめの所はケニアのワイルドサファリです。
Reason	自然(しぜん)の中で動物(どうぶつ)を見たら、すごく感動(かんどう)するからです。
Details: • what you can do there • what to do to prepare for your visit, etc.	サファリではめずらしい動物(どうぶつ)や鳥がたくさん見られます。気球(ききゅう) (balloon) に乗(の)って、空(そら)からサファリを見ることもできます。サファリに行く前に、ホテルで双眼鏡(そうがんきょう) (binoculars) を借(か)りておいてください。そして、旅行(りょこう)が終(お)わった後で、SNS にぜひ写真(しゃしん)をアップしてください。
Additional information	サファリは7月から 10 月に行くのがいいみたいです。
Closing	みなさんもチャンスがあったら、ぜひワイルドサファリを楽(たの)しんでください。

読みましょう

Getting information from a website: Book recommendations

1 みなさんはネットで日本語の本について調(しら)べたことがありますか。下の写真(しゃしん)はネットにある本屋(ほんや)の「おすすめの本」のページです。

1） Talk with your partner about what kind of information you can get from the covers of books a.-f. Try to guess unknown words from visual clues, then discuss the main topic of each book.

a.

『SCRAP ヒラメキナゾトキ BOOK』
SCRAP［著］ SCRAP 出版

b.

『日本のスゴイ科学者 29人が教える発見のコツ』
日本科学未来館・朝日小学生新聞［編著］
朝日学生新聞社

c.

『おとなが愉しむ 文房具の世界』
ぴあ

d.

『和菓子の絵本 和菓子っておいしい！』
平野恵理子［著］ あすなろ書房

e.

『お札のはなし その歴史、肖像と技術』
植村峻［著］ 印刷朝陽会

f.

『キャラとストーリーがつくれる！
まんがのかき方マスターBOOK』
清水めぐみ［監修］ 朝日新聞出版

2） Which of the following blurbs would be the most appropriate for each book? Insert the corresponding letter from a.-f. in each (　　).

(　　　) 日本人でノーベル賞(しょう) (Nobel Prize) をもらった人は何人？　知っておきたいすごい人達！

(　　　) この本を読んだら、日本のお菓子(かし)のことが分かる。日本の自然(しぜん)や歴史(れきし)や文化も分かる。

(　　　) 日本のお札(さつ) (bill) になった人は誰(だれ)？　どんなことをした人？　知っていますか。

(　　　) 楽しいデザインでカラーも色々(いろいろ)。おもしろい文房具(ぶんぼうぐ)がたくさん見られる。

(　　　) 難(むずか)しいクイズにチャレンジしたかったら、この本がおすすめ！

(　　　) キャラクターやストーリーが簡単(かんたん)に作れる！　自分のまんがを描(か)いてみよう。

3） a.～f. の本の中で、どの本を読んでみたいと思いましたか。どうしてですか。

2 次の話を読んで、質問に答えましょう。

みなさんの国のお札はどんなデザインですか。日本のお札にはたいてい有名でりっぱな人の顔がありますが、みなさんの国ではどうですか。

150年ぐらい前、日本に野口英世というすばらしい科学者がいました。世界でも有名な学者で、彼の顔は日本のお札になったことがあります。野口は色々な病気の研究をして、3回ノーベル賞の候補になりました。日本人はたいてい子どもの時に、彼の話を読んだことがあります。

野口は1876年にいなかの貧乏な農家で生まれました。1才半の時に左手にひどいやけどをしましたが、家が貧乏だったから病院に行けませんでした。だから、子どもの時は左手の指が全然動きませんでした。

その時代はお金がなくて学校に行けない a. 人 がたくさんいましたが、野口のお母さんは手が自由に使えない b. 野口 には教育が必要だと思って、野口の学校のために、たくさん働きました。だから、野口は学校で勉強することができました。野口は成績がとてもよかったですが、初めは学校に行くのが楽しくなかったようです。子ども達が野口の左手を見て、ひどいことを言ったからです。

15才の時、野口はクラスで自分の左手について書いた c. 作文 の発表をしました。①それを聞いて感動した d. 先生やクラスメート達 は、野口の手の手術のためにお金を集めました。そして、手術をしたら、全然動かなかった e. 左手の指 が少し動きました。②その時、野口は自分も医者になって人を助けたいと思いました。

野口は東京に行って医者になった後で、24才の時にアメリカの大学に留学しました。そして、色々な病気の研究をして、いい論文をたくさん発表しました。彼の研究は病気の人達を助けましたが、アフリカで黄熱病の研究をしている f. 時 に、自分も同じ病気になって、51才で死にました。

野口は本当にすごい科学者でしたが、お酒を飲んだり遊んだりするのも大好きで、よくお金を借りました。でも、③そのお金を返せなくていつも困っていました。実はお金にはとてもルーズな人だったようです。

これが野口の顔がお札になった g. 千円札 です。野口みたいな人がお札になったことについて、どう思いますか。

(お)札：bill; bank note
りっぱな：admirable
学者：scholar
ノーベル賞の候補：Nobel Prize candidate
農家：farmer
やけどをする：to get burned
時代：era; period
(〜に)教育が必要：education is necessary (for ~)
Noun のために：for Noun
黄熱病：yellow fever
お金にルーズな：irresponsible with money

Recognizing event sequence

1） Based on the story, complete the following biographical timeline for Hideyo Noguchi.

年	才	主な出来事 (major events)
1876	0	いなかの貧乏な農家で生まれました。
	1才半	
		自分の左手について書いた作文を発表しました。
1900		
〜		色々な病気の研究をして、病気の人達を助けました。
1928		

Understanding demonstratives: そ-words

2） What do the そ-words ①-③ in the passage refer to? Rewrite the phrases by identifying the referents.

① l.17　それ　＿＿＿＿＿＿＿＿＿＿＿＿＿＿＿＿を

② l.19　その時　＿＿＿＿＿＿＿＿＿＿＿＿＿＿＿＿時

③ l.27　そのお金　＿＿＿＿＿＿＿＿＿＿＿＿＿＿＿＿お金

Summarizing

3） 野口はどんな人でしたか。いいことと悪いことについて、書いてください。

＿＿＿＿＿＿＿＿＿＿＿＿＿＿が、＿＿＿＿＿＿＿＿＿＿＿＿＿＿。
☺　　☹

Comprehension check

4） Underline the part of the text that modifies each noun in boxes a.-g.

5） Mark ○ if the statement is true and × if it is false.

（　　）野口は日本だけで有名だ。世界の人はあまり知らない。

（　　）野口は左手を手術した後で、医者になりたいと思った。

（　　）野口は研究が大好きで、全然遊ばなかったようだ。

（　　）野口はお金を使う前に、計画を立てる人だった。

6）「野口みたいな人がお札になった」(ll.30-31) ことについてどう思いますか。

書く練習

Write about a person who inspires you and/or makes you strive for self-improvement. Support your selection with episodes that would make your readers want to know more about that person.

聞きましょう

リスニング・ストラテジー：Listening strategy

Guessing unknown words from context (1)

You will often encounter unknown words as you go about your daily life in a foreign language environment. You cannot always pause a conversation to check the meaning of those words, so it is important to learn to guess their meaning based on other information you hear.

L12-24

1 **Pre-listening activity:** Yamada-san and Tanaka-san are talking about their friends. The words 1)-3) below describe their friends' personalities and may not be familiar to you. Listen to their conversations carefully and choose the correct meaning for each word from a.-f. in the box on the right based on what you hear.

1) ようきな人：＿＿＿＿

2) しゃこうてきな人：＿＿＿＿

3) まえむきな人：＿＿＿＿

a. positive person	b. negative person
c. cheerful person	d. procrastinator
e. laid-back person	f. social person

L12-25

2 **Listening:** Tom, a senior in college, is talking with Aya, a Japanese exchange student, at a Japanese conversation table event about his experience traveling around Japan. Listen to their conversation carefully and try to define each of the phrases 1)-3) below based on what you hear. You may use whatever language you prefer, but do not use a dictionary.

	Phrase to define based on the dialogue	Your proposed definition of the phrase (in your preferred language)
1)	日本語がつうじる	
2)	地下鉄(ちかてつ)や新幹線(しんかんせん) (bullet train) が うんきゅうしました	
3)	へんこうしました	

Exit Check

Now it's time to go back to the DEKIRU List for this chapter (p.51) and do the exit check to see what new things you can do now that you've completed the lesson.

Lesson 13

明日行ってみようと思います。

I think I'll go tomorrow.

DEKIRU List

できるCheck ☑

できる I **Talk about things you are planning on doing.**
自分がしようと思っていることを言うことができる。
Entry ☐ Exit ☐

できる II **Report and share interesting and useful information you have heard or read.**
聞いたり読んだりした情報を共有して、それについて話すことができる。
Entry ☐ Exit ☐

できる III **Talk about things that are prohibited.**
禁止されていることについて話すことができる。
Entry ☐ Exit ☐

できる IV **Talk about things you have or do not have an obligation to do.**
守らなくてはいけないこと、守らなくてもいいことについて話すことができる。
Entry ☐ Exit ☐

STRATEGIES

Conversation Tips .... • Japanese interjections: わあ and えっ

Reading .... • Getting information from photos and captions
• Guessing the meaning of katakana words from context
• Identifying the 5Ws and 1H

Listening .... • Guessing unknown words from context (2)

GRAMMAR

1. Volitional forms (V-vol) and V-volと思う "I think I'll V" できるI
2. ～も [Emphasis] できるII
3. ～そうだ [Hearsay] できるII
4. ～ながら [Simultaneous/concurrent actions] できるIII
5. ～てはいけない [Prohibition] できるIII
6. ～なくてはいけない [Obligation/necessity] できるIV
7. ～なくてもいい [Lack of obligation/necessity] できるIV

会　話

1 できる I,II Ai has arrived at her host family's house in Japan and is having dinner with them for the first time. L13-1

抹茶(まっちゃ): powdered green tea　スーパー銭湯(せんとう): deluxe bathhouse & spa

母　：アイちゃん、晩(ばん)ご飯(はん)はどう？

アイ：全部(ぜんぶ)おいしいです！　このお茶もとても
　　　おいしいですね。何ばいも飲めます。

弟　：宇治(うじ)のお茶はおいしくて、有名だからね！

姉　：アメリカでも日本のお茶は人気があるそう
　　　だけど、本当？

アイ：はい、抹茶(まっちゃ)ラテや抹茶(まっちゃ)アイスクリームがとても人気がありますよ。

抹茶(まっちゃ)ラテ

母　：へえ、そうなんだ。ところで、アイちゃん、明日の予定(よてい)は？

アイ：まだ一度も大学に行っていないから、明日行ってみようと思います。
　　　キャンパスを見ておきたいんです。

<The conversation continues.>

アイ：あのう、友達によると、スーパー銭湯(せんとう)がおもしろいそうですが…

姉　：えっ、スーパー銭湯(せんとう)？　うん、私も時々(ときどき)行くよ。
　　　駅(えき)の近(ちか)くにあるから、一緒(いっしょ)に行ってみない？

アイ：本当ですか？　ありがとうございます！

姉　：じゃ、明日行こう！

湯の森 所沢

スーパー銭湯(せんとう)

The conversation over dinner continues. L13-2

父　：アイちゃん、ビール、飲む？

アイ：いえ、ちょっと…　私はまだ二十歳(はたち)になっていないから、
　　　お酒(さけ)を飲んではいけないんです。

父　：なるほど、そっか…　でも、これ、お酒(さけ)を飲みながら食べたら、おいしいんだけど…

母　：お父さん、また何か食べながら話してる。やめてくれない？

父　：はーい、お母さん。

姉　：お父さん、子どもみたい。

アイ：ふふふ。

弟　：ははは。

Ai and her host sister are at a spa.

L13-3

<At the entrance>

くつ箱(ばこ) (shoe cubby)

アイ　：あ、ここでくつをぬがなくてはいけませんか。

姉　：うん、ぬいでからそのくつ箱(ばこ)に入れるんだよ。

<At the reception desk (受付(うけつけ))>

受付(うけつけ)　：二人で 1,500 円です。

姉　：あ、今日は私が払(はら)うから、アイちゃんは払(はら)わなくてもいいよ。

アイ　：えっ、でも…

姉　：だいじょうぶ、だいじょうぶ。

アイ　：そうですか。どうもありがとうございます。

<In the bathing area>

アイ　：わあ、広くて、きれい！
えっと、おふろに入る前に、まず体を洗(あら)わなくてはいけませんね。

姉　：うん、あそこで洗(あら)おうか。

<After washing up>

姉　：あ、アイちゃん、タオルはちょっと…

アイ　：えっ、おふろの中に入れてはいけないんですか。すみません。

<In the bathtub>

コーヒー牛乳(ぎゅうにゅう)

アイ　：お姉さん、大きいおふろはすごく気持ちがいいですね！

姉　：うん、おふろを出たら、冷(つめ)たいコーヒー牛乳(ぎゅうにゅう)、飲もうか。

アイ　：わあ、コーヒー牛乳(ぎゅうにゅう)ですか。はい、ぜひ！

CONVERSATION TIPS

ワンポイント　L13-4

Japanese interjections わあ and えっ: Using interjections like わあ and えっ properly will make your speech sound more natural. First, try to guess the functions of わあ and えっ from the preceding 会話, then check with the dialogue below to see if you guessed them correctly.

＜クラスで＞

先生：みなさん、テストを始(はじ)めましょう。

学生：えっ、今日テストがあるんですか。（← Surprised exclamation）

先生：えっ、知らなかったんですか。（← Surprised exclamation）

学生：わあ（← Overwhelmed/impressed exclamation）、全然(ぜんぜん)勉強してない…

Vocabulary with Pictures 単語（たんご）

▶ The words written in gray are supplemental vocabulary.

生活（せいかつ） Daily life

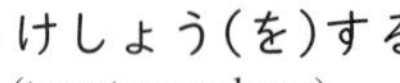

- けしょう(を)する (to put on makeup)

- かみをそめる (to color (one's) hair)

- びよういん (hair salon)

- コーヒー／おちゃをいれる (to make coffee/tea)
- [*thing* が] でる (to go/come out)

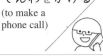

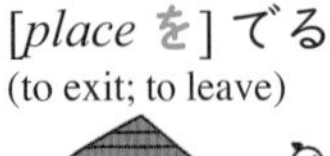

- [*place* を] でる (to exit; to leave)
- [*meeting/event/media* に] でる (to attend; to appear)
- しゅくだいがでる (homework is assigned)

- でんわにでる (to answer the phone)

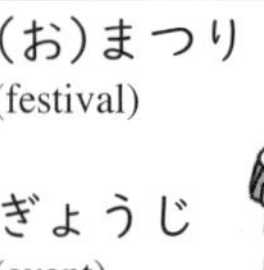

- [*person* に] でんわをかける (to make a phone call)

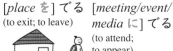

- [*thing* に] もうしこむ (to apply (to/for))
- [*event* に] さんかする (to participate)

- (お)まつり (festival)
- ぎょうじ (event)

- おどり ((traditional Asian) dance)
- つりをする (to fish)

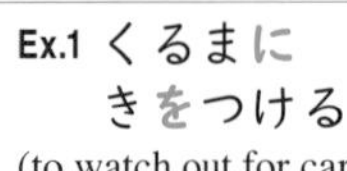

- きもち (feeling; mood)

- きもちがいい (nice-feeling; comfortable; pleasant) ⟷ きもちがわるい (to feel sick/creepy/gross/unpleasant)

- タオル (towel)

- ぎゅうにゅう (milk)

トラブル Troubles

- [*thing* に] きをつける (to be careful; to watch out; to take care)
  - **Ex.1** くるまにきをつける (to watch out for cars)
  - **Ex.2** からだにきをつける (to take care of oneself)
- [*thing/person* に] ちゅういする (to pay attention)
- [*person* に／を] ちゅういする (to warn)

- [*person* に] あやまる (to apologize)
- [*activity/event* に] ちこくする (to be late)
- ガムをかむ (to chew gum)

- [*person* と] しゃべる (to chat; to talk; to speak) [informal]
- [*work/class* を] サボる (to skip (work, class, etc.))
- カンニング(を)する (to cheat (on a test, etc.))

数える（かぞえる） Counting

〜ど (... time(s))

1	2	3	?
いちど	にど	さんど	なんど

〜こ [Counter for small objects]

1	2	3	4	5	6	7	8	9	10	?
いっこ	にこ	さんこ	よんこ	ごこ	ろっこ	ななこ	はっこ	きゅうこ	じ(ゅ)っこ	なんこ

〜さつ [Counter for bound/printed materials (books, brochures, etc.)]

いっさつ	にさつ	さんさつ	よんさつ	ごさつ	ろくさつ	ななさつ	はっさつ	きゅうさつ	じ(ゅ)っさつ	なんさつ

〜ほん [Counter for long, cylindrical objects]

いっぽん	にほん	さんぼん	よんほん	ごほん	ろっぽん	ななほん	はっぽん	きゅうほん	じ(ゅ)っぽん	なんぼん

〜はい [Counter for food/drink in cups, glasses, bowls, etc.]

いっぱい	にはい	さんばい	よんはい	ごはい	ろっぱい	ななはい	はっぱい	きゅうはい	じ(ゅ)っぱい	なんばい

ルール・マナー　Rules and manners

[*thing* を] とめる (to stop)	くるまをとめる (to park/stop a car)	[*thing* が] とまる ((something) stops)	[*road/corner* を *direction* に] まがる (to turn)
シートベルトをする (to fasten a seat belt; to buckle up)	[*thing* を] やめる (to stop (doing); to quit)	[*place* に *thing* を] もってくる (to bring (along) (to the speaker's location))	[*thing* を] ひろう (to pick up (off the ground))
かさをさす (to hold up an umbrella) かさ (umbrella)	さわぐ (to make noise)	たたみ (*tatami*) [traditional Japanese straw mat]	ふとん (*futon*) [Japanese-style bedding]

社会・学校　Society and schools

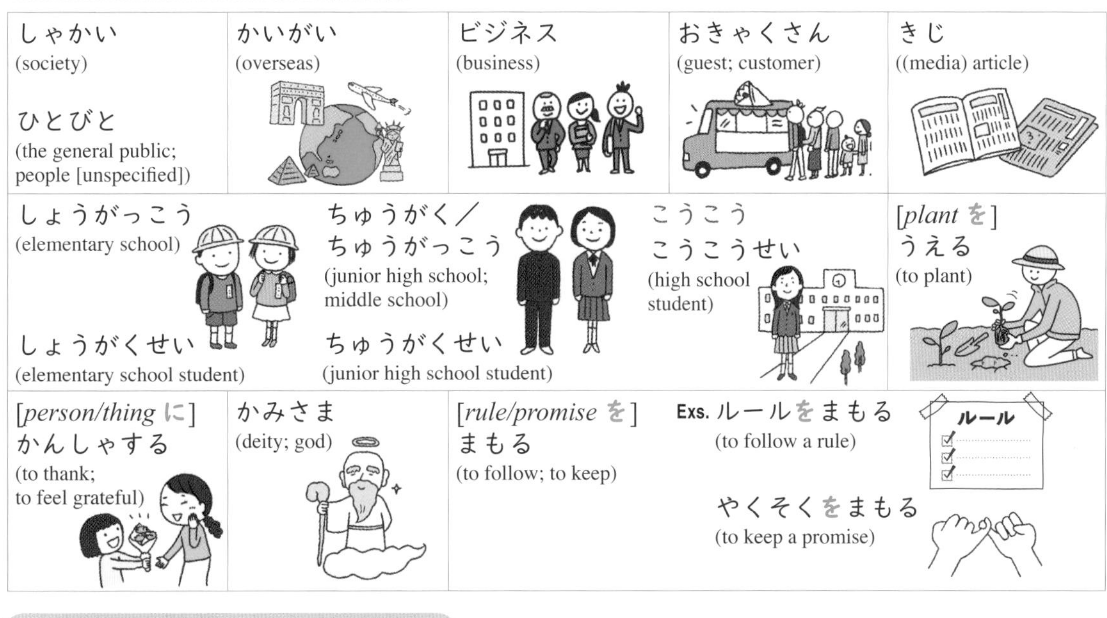

しゃかい (society) ひとびと (the general public; people [unspecified])	かいがい (overseas)	ビジネス (business)	おきゃくさん (guest; customer)	きじ ((media) article)
しょうがっこう (elementary school) しょうがくせい (elementary school student)	ちゅうがく／ちゅうがっこう (junior high school; middle school) ちゅうがくせい (junior high school student)		こうこう こうこうせい (high school student)	[*plant* を] うえる (to plant)
[*person/thing* に] かんしゃする (to thank; to feel grateful)	かみさま (deity; god)	[*rule/promise* を] まもる (to follow; to keep)	**Exs.** ルールをまもる (to follow a rule) やくそくをまもる (to keep a promise)	

そのほかの表現　Other expressions

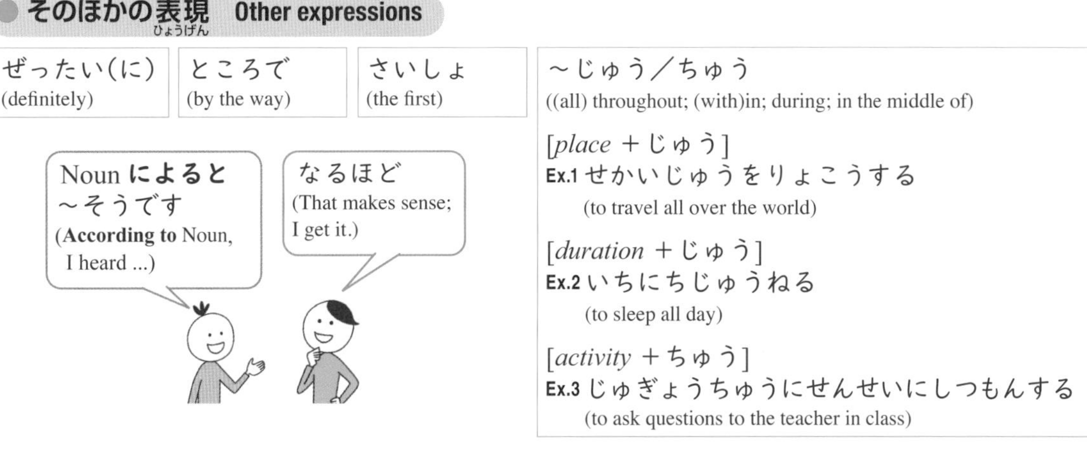

ぜったい(に) (definitely)	ところで (by the way)	さいしょ (the first)

Noun によると～そうです (**According to** Noun, I heard ...)

なるほど (That makes sense; I get it.)

～じゅう／ちゅう
((all) throughout; (with)in; during; in the middle of)

[*place* ＋じゅう]
Ex.1 せかいじゅうをりょこうする
(to travel all over the world)

[*duration* ＋じゅう]
Ex.2 いちにちじゅうねる
(to sleep all day)

[*activity* ＋ちゅう]
Ex.3 じゅぎょうちゅうにせんせいにしつもんする
(to ask questions to the teacher in class)

Vocabulary List

単語リスト

L13-5

▶**Highlighted kanji words** contain kanji you have learned previously.

RU-VERBS / *RU*-VERB PHRASES

1	うえる	植える	to plant [*plant* を]
2	かみをそめる	髪を染める	to color (one's) hair
3	きをつける	気をつける	to be careful; to watch out; to take care [*thing* に] **Ex.1** くるまに気をつける to watch out for cars **Ex.2** 体に気をつける to take care of oneself (lit. one's body)
4	コーヒー/おちゃをいれる	コーヒー/お茶をいれる	to make coffee/tea
5	とめる	止める	to stop [*thing* を]
	くるまをとめる	車を止める	to park/stop a car
6	でる	出る	to go/come out [*thing* が]; to exit; to leave [*place* を]; to attend; to appear [*meeting/event/media* に]
	しゅくだいがでる	宿題が出る	homework is assigned
	でんわにでる	電話に出る	to answer the phone
7	でんわをかける	電話をかける	to make a phone call [*person* に]
8	やめる		to stop (doing); to quit [*thing* を]

U-VERBS / *U*-VERB PHRASES

9	あやまる	謝る	to apologize [*person* に]
10	かさをさす		to hold up an umbrella
11	ガムをかむ		to chew gum
12	サボる		to skip (work, class, etc.) [without good reason] [*work/class* を]
13	さわぐ		to make noise
14	しゃべる		to chat; to talk; to speak [*person* と] [informal]
15	とまる	止まる	(something) stops [*thing* が]
16	ひろう	拾う	to pick up (off the ground) [*thing* を]
17	まがる	曲がる	to turn [*road/corner* を *direction* に]
18	まもる	守る	to follow; to keep [*rule/promise* を]
	ルールをまもる	ルールを守る	to follow a rule
	やくそくをまもる	約束を守る	to keep a promise
19	もうしこむ	申し込む	to apply (to/for) [*thing* に]

IRREGULAR VERB

20	もってくる	持ってくる	to bring (along) (to the speaker's location) [*place* に *thing* を]

SURU-VERBS / *SURU*-VERB PHRASES

21	かんしゃする	感謝する	to thank; to feel grateful [*person/thing* に]
22	カンニング(を)する		to cheat (on a test, etc.)
23	けしょう(を)する	化粧(を)する	to put on makeup
24	さんかする	参加する	to participate [*event* に]
25	シートベルトをする		to fasten a seat belt; to buckle up
26	ちこくする	遅刻する	to be late [*activity/event* に]
27	ちゅういする	注意する	to pay attention [*thing/person* に]; to warn [*person* に/を]
28	つりをする		to fish

I-ADJECTIVE PHRASES

29	きもちがいい	気持ちがいい	nice-feeling; comfortable; pleasant [thing, person, stimulus, etc.]

30	きもちがわるい	気持ちが悪い	to feel sick/creepy/gross/unpleasant [thing, person, stimulus, etc.]

NOUNS

31	おきゃくさん	お客さん	guest; customer
32	おどり		(traditional Asian) dance
33	かいがい	海外	overseas
34	かさ		umbrella
35	かみさま	神様	deity; god
36	きじ	記事	(media) article
37	きもち	気持ち	feeling; mood
38	ぎゅうにゅう	牛乳	milk
39	ぎょうじ	行事	(seasonal/annual) event
40	しゃかい	社会	society
41	しょうがくせい	小学生	elementary school student
42	ちゅうがくせい	中学生	junior high school student
43	こうこうせい	高校生	high school student
44	しょうがっこう	小学校	elementary school
45	ちゅうがく／ちゅうがっこう	中学／中学校	junior high school; middle school
46	タオル		towel
47	たたみ	畳	*tatami* [traditional Japanese straw mat]
48	ビジネス		business
49	ひとびと	人々	the general public; people [unspecified] **Ex.1** せかい中の人々 people in the world **Ex.2** アニメが好きな人達 people who like anime (not アニメが好きな人々)
50	びよういん	美容院	hair salon
51	ふとん	布団	*futon* [Japanese-style bedding]
52	まつり／おまつり	(お)祭り	festival

ADVERBIAL NOUN

53	さいしょ	最初	the first

ADVERB

54	ぜったい(に)	絶対(に)	definitely

COUNTERS

55	～こ	～個	[counter for small objects]
56	～さつ	～冊	[counter for bound/printed materials (books, brochures, etc.)]
57	～ど	～度	... time(s) [not commonly used with numbers 4 and above]
58	～はい	～杯	[counter for food/drink in cups, glasses, bowls, etc.]
59	～ほん	～本	[counter for long, cylindrical objects]

SUFFIX

60	～じゅう	～中	(all) throughout [*place* + 中] **Ex.1** せかい中をりょこうする to travel all over the world [*duration* + 中] **Ex.2** 一日中ねる to sleep all day
	～ちゅう	～中	(with)in; during; in the middle of [*activity* + 中] **Ex.3** じゅぎょう中に先生にしつもんする to ask questions to the teacher in class

CONJUNCTION

61	ところで		by the way

OTHER WORDS AND PHRASES

62	なるほど		That makes sense; I get it.
63	Noun によると		according to Noun

Kanji

漢字（かんじ）

▶ ＊Special reading

178 拾	ひろ(う)	拾う（ひろう） to pick up (off the ground)　拾い物（ひろいもの） found article; find; bargain
to pick up		
179 返	ヘン	返金する（へんきん） to refund　返事をする（へんじ） to answer; to respond 返信する（へんしん） to reply (to an email, a letter, etc.)
	かえ(す)	返す（かえ） to return; to give back　くり返す（かえ） to repeat; to do over again
to return		
180 守	ス	留守（るす） absence; being away (from home, etc.)　留守にする（るす） to be away (from home, etc.) 留守番（るすばん） housesitting　留守番電話（るすばんでんわ） voice mail; answering machine
	まも(る)	守る（まも） to follow; to keep; to protect　お守り（まも） (protective) amulet; talisman
to protect		
181 変	ヘン	大変(な)（たいへん） tough [situation]　変(な)（へん） strange; unusual 変化する（へんか） to change [formal]
	か(える) か(わる)	変える（か） to change (something)　変わる（か） (something) changes
to change; strange		
182 止	シ	禁止する（きんし） to prohibit　中止する（ちゅうし） to cancel; to discontinue　停止する（ていし） to halt
	と(める) と(まる)	止める（と） to stop (something) 止まる（と） (something) stops
to stop		
183 電	デン	電車（でんしゃ） train　電子レンジ（でんし） microwave (oven)　電気（でんき） light; electricity　電池（でんち） battery 電話を{かける／する}（でんわ） to make a phone call　電話を切る（でんわ　き） to hang up the phone 電話番号（でんわばんごう） phone number　携帯電話（けいたいでんわ） mobile phone 充電する（じゅうでん） to charge (battery, etc.)　停電する（ていでん） to lose power; to have a power outage
electricity		
184 車	シャ	電車（でんしゃ） train　救急車（きゅうきゅうしゃ） ambulance　自転車（じてんしゃ） bicycle　自動車（じどうしゃ） automobile; car 駐車場（ちゅうしゃじょう） parking lot/garage　駐車する（ちゅうしゃ） to park a car
	くるま	車（くるま） car
vehicle		

185	神 god	ジン シン コウ	神社（じんじゃ） (Shinto) shrine　神道（しんとう） Shinto 神戸市（こうべし） Kobe City
		かみ	神様（かみさま） deity; god
186	様 situation; Mr./Ms./Mx.	ヨウ	様子（ようす） appearance; condition
		さま	神様（かみさま） deity; god　お客様（きゃくさま） customer [formal]　様々（さまざま）(な) various ～様（さま） [honorific title added to a name to show respect] (Ex. 田中様（たなかさま） Tanaka-sama)
187	注 to pour	チュウ	注意（ちゅうい）する to pay attention; to warn　注文（ちゅうもん）する to order 注射（ちゅうしゃ） injection; shot　不注意（ふちゅうい）(な) careless
		そそ(ぐ)	注（そそ）ぐ to pour
188	意 mind	イ	意味（いみ） meaning　注意（ちゅうい）する to pay attention; to warn 意外（いがい）(な) unexpected　意見（いけん） opinion　意思（いし） intention; will 得意（とくい）(な) to be confident in; to be good at [subjective]　用意（ようい）する to prepare
189	味 taste	ミ	意味（いみ） meaning　興味（きょうみ） interest　興味（きょうみ）を持（も）つ to take an interest (in)　趣味（しゅみ） hobby
		あじ あじ(わう)	味（あじ） taste; flavor　味（あじ）わう to taste; to savor; to enjoy
190	色 color	シキ ショク	景色（けしき）* scenery; view　一色（いっしょく） one color
		いろ	色（いろ） color　色々（いろいろ）(な) various　茶色（ちゃいろ） brown [color]　茶色（ちゃいろ）い brown 何色（なにいろ） what color　黄色（きいろ） yellow [color]　黄色（きいろ）い yellow
191	々 symbol for repetition of a kanji		色々（いろいろ）(な) various　時々（ときどき） sometimes　人々（ひとびと） the general public; people [unspecified] 国々（くにぐに） various countries　様々（さまざま）(な) various　次々（つぎつぎ）(に) one after another 昔々（むかしむかし） once upon a time
192	世 generation	セ セイ	世界（せかい） world　世界中（せかいじゅう） all over the world　お世話（せわ）になる to be in (someone's) care 世話（せわ）をする to take care (of)　～世紀（せいき） ... century (Ex. 21世紀（せいき） twenty-first century)
		よ	世（よ）の中（なか） society

Lesson 13

193	界 界 界	カイ	世界(せかい) world　世界中(せかいじゅう) all over the world 世界一(せかいいち) number one in the world　世界遺産(せかいいさん) World Heritage
	boundary; limit		界 (stroke order)
194	記 記 記	キ	記事(きじ) (media) article　暗記する(あんき) to memorize　記者(きしゃ) reporter 記入する(きにゅう) to fill out　記録する(きろく) to record　日記(にっき) diary
	to write down		記 (stroke order)
195	昨 昨 昨	サク	昨日*(きのう)／昨日(さくじつ) yesterday　一昨日*(おととい)／一昨日(いっさくじつ) the day before yesterday 昨年(さくねん) last year　昨晩(さくばん) yesterday evening　昨夜(さくや) last night 一昨年*(おととし)／一昨年(いっさくねん) the year before last
	yesterday; previous		昨 (stroke order)
196	若 若 若	わか(い)	若い(わか) young　若者(わかもの) young people
	young		若 (stroke order)

新しい読み方

The following are new readings for kanji that you have already leaned. Read each word aloud.

1) 海外(かいがい)　2) 行事(ぎょうじ)　3) 最初(さいしょ)　4) 小学生(しょう)　5) 小学校(しょう)
6) 神社(じんじゃ)　7) 注文する(ちゅうもん)　8) 電子レンジ(でんし)　9) ～中(じゅう) (Ex. 世界中(せかいじゅう))

習った漢字で書ける新しい単語(ならったかんじでかけるあたらしいたんご)

The following are other new vocabulary in this lesson that contain kanji you have already learned. Read each word aloud.

1) お茶(ちゃ)をいれる　2) 気持(きも)ちがいい／悪(わる)い　3) 気(き)をつける　4) 高校生(こうこうせい)　5) 中学生(ちゅうがくせい)
6) 中学(ちゅうがく)／中学校(ちゅうがっこう)　7) 社会(しゃかい)　8) 出(で)る　9) 持(も)ってくる　10) ～中(ちゅう) (Ex. 授業中(じゅぎょうちゅう))
11) ～度(ど) (Ex. 一度(いちど))　12) ～本(ほん／ぽん／ぼん) (Exs. 一本(いっぽん)／二本(にほん)／三本(さんぼん))

練習(れんしゅう)

1 Find and circle 12 words that contain kanji you have learned so far, then write the words and their readings in the spaces provided. The words may appear either vertically or horizontally.

電	話	行	海
Ex. (車)	記	事	外
神	様	注	文
社	会	意	味

Ex. 車 (くるま)

1) ______ (　　　) 2) ______ (　　　)

3) ______ (　　　) 4) ______ (　　　)

5) ______ (　　　) 6) ______ (　　　)

7) ______ (　　　) 8) ______ (　　　)

9) ______ (　　　) 10) ______ (　　　)

11) ______ (　　　) 12) ______ (　　　)

2 Ivanov-san is studying Japanese in Tokyo and talking about his findings, experiences, etc. Read the speech bubbles aloud, then write the readings for the underlined words.

1) 日本で新しいスマホに変える時、注意してください。私は古いデータがなくなったから大変でした。

2) 東京では電車やバスが便利(べんり)です。車を止める所がないから、若い人はあまり車を持っていません。

3)「守る」という言葉(ことば)には色々な意味があります。例えば、「約束(やくそく)を守る」の "keep" や「ルールを守る」の "follow" です。

4) 日本の小学校や中学校にはそうじの時間があります。ごみを拾ったり、教室(きょうしつ)をきれいにしたりします。

5) 昨日、神社に行きました。神社は日本の神様がいる所で、茶色や赤(あか)の建物(たてもの)が多(おお)いです。

6) 新聞で「笑い(わらい)祭(まつり)」という行事についての記事を読みました。世界中から人が見に来るそうです。

Wakayama Tourism Federation

漢字の話 The Story of Kanji

■ Use of kanji for homophones

Japanese has fewer sounds (or phonemes) than many other languages including English, Korean, and Chinese. Because of this, the Japanese language has many homophones (i.e., words that are pronounced the same but have different meanings). One of the characteristics of kanji is that they represent the meaning of words. If you know the meanings of kanji, it will help facilitate your understanding of homophones and the sentences that include them.

For example, try reading the following sentences. Which sentences give you a clear meaning?

1. きてください。　2. 着てください。　3. 来てください。

As you probably noticed, sentence 1. may be easy to read, but its meaning is ambiguous. On the other hand, it is easier to understand the meanings of sentences 2. and 3. because of their use of kanji. This is especially true for sentences containing words that have homophones.

Here are some examples of kanji that have the same sounds but different meanings:

Pronunciation	かみ			あつい			きる	
Kanji	紙	神	髪	暑い	熱い	厚い	着る	切る
Meaning	paper	god	hair	hot [air temperature]	hot [to the touch]	thick	to wear	to cut

Note that homophones may have different pitch accents, as in 着る and 切る.

練習

Circle the appropriate kanji words in sentences 1)-4) based on the context.

1) スミスさんは【日本／二本】に行ったことがないと言っていました。

2) すみません。もう少し大きい声で【行って／言って】ください。

3) 私は野菜を小さく【着る／切る】のが苦手です。

4) すみません。【神／紙】を一枚ください。

> Here is a Japanese tongue twister. Can you say it? Can you guess its meaning?
>
> にわにはにわにわとりがいる。

文(ぶん)法(ぽう)

1 Volitional forms (V-vol) and V-volと思(おも)う

1-1 Volitional forms of verbs

In Lesson 3 #6-2, we studied the expression V-*masu*ましょう (e.g., 行(い)きましょう, 食(た)べましょう). In this expression, verbs are in their "polite volitional forms," which politely express a person's volitional action (i.e., an action performed of one's own will). In this lesson, we will study plain volitional forms. Using plain volitional forms, you can casually invite your listener to do something together or make a suggestion. (From now on, we use "volitional forms" to refer to plain volitional forms.)

The rules for making volitional forms are as follows:

(a) *Ru*-verbs: Change the final る of the dictionary form to よう.

Exs. 食(た)べ~~る~~ → 食(た)べよう; 見(み)~~る~~ → 見(み)よう

(b) *U*-verbs: Change the final /u/ sound of the dictionary form to the /oo/ sound. In writing, the second /o/ sound is spelled as う.

Exs. 書(か)く (/kaku/) → 書(か)こう (/kakoo/); 買(か)う (/kau/) → 買(か)おう (/kaoo/)

More examples of *u*-verb volitional forms are shown in the following conjugation table along with the other forms we have learned that use different vowels in their conjugations:

帰(かえ)らない	話(はな)さない	行(い)かない	言(い)わない	← /a/ row: Plain negative forms
帰(かえ)ります	話(はな)します	行(い)きます	言(い)います	← /i/ row: *Masu*-forms
帰(かえ)る	話(はな)す	行(い)く	言(い)う	← /u/ row: Dictionary forms (= plain affirmative forms)
帰(かえ)れる	話(はな)せる	行(い)ける	言(い)える	← /e/ row: Potential forms
帰(かえ)ろう	話(はな)そう	行(い)こう	言(い)おう	← /o/ row: **Volitional forms**

(c) Irregular verbs: する → しよう; 来(く)る → 来(こ)よう

Exs. (1) 土曜日(どようび)に僕(ぼく)の部屋(へや)で一緒(いっしょ)に映画(えいが)を見(み)よう。*Let's watch movies together in my room on Saturday.*

(2) A: 明日(あした)バーベキューをしようか。*Do you wanna (lit. shall we) have a BBQ tomorrow?*

B: うん、そうしよう。*Yeah, let's do that.*

(3) アイ：今晩(こんばん)、どこかに晩(ばん)ご飯(はん)を食(た)べに行(い)きましょうか。
Would you like to (lit. Shall we) go out somewhere for dinner tonight?

圭太(けいた)：うん、いいね。行(い)こう。*Yeah, that sounds good. Let's go.*

1-2 V-volと思(おも)う "I think I'll V"

[1-a]

Subject (first person)		V-vol (plain volitional form)	
(私(わたし)は)	明日(あした)から朝(あさ)6時(じ)に	起(お)きよう	と思(おも)います。
I think I'll get up at six in the morning starting tomorrow.			

You can express your decision to do something using "V-vol と思(おも)います." This expression is used when you have made a decision to do something and are telling the listener that you think you will act on it.

Exs. (1) 頭(あたま)が痛(いた)いから、今日(きょう)は早(はや)くうちに帰(かえ)ろう<u>と思(おも)います</u>。

I have a headache, so I think I'll go home early today.

(2) あのレストランはいつも混(こ)んでいるから、予約(よやく)しておこう<u>と思(おも)います</u>。

That restaurant is always crowded, so I think I'll make a reservation in advance.

[1-b]

Subject (first person)		V-vol	
(私(わたし)は)	来年日本(らいねんにほん)に	留学(りゅうがく)しよう	と思(おも)っています。
I'm thinking of going to Japan to study next year.			

You can express your plan or intention using "V-vol と思(おも)っています." The difference between "V-vol と思(おも)います" and "V-vol と思(おも)っています" is the following:

(a) "V-vol と思(おも)います" is used when the decision was made just before the moment of speech.

(b) "V-vol と思(おも)っています" is used when a decision was made some time ago and the decision remains in effect at the moment of speech.

Ex. (3) 来月(らいげつ)の母(はは)の日(ひ)に母(はは)に会(あ)いに行(い)こう<u>と思(おも)っています</u>。

I'm thinking of going to see my mother on Mother's Day next month.

[1-c]

Subject (third person)		V-vol	
ジョンさんは	日本(にほん)で	働(はたら)こう	と思(おも)っています。
John is thinking of working in Japan.			

When the subject is a third person, you always use 思(おも)っています instead of 思(おも)います. (See L9 #4 and L9 Language Note.) For example, the following sentence is not grammatical:

× リサさんは明日(あした)から朝(あさ)6時(じ)に起(お)きようと<u>思(おも)います</u>。

→ リサさんは明日(あした)から朝(あさ)6時(じ)に起(お)きようと<u>思(おも)っています</u>。(cf. [1-a])

Lisa is thinking of getting up at six in the morning staring tomorrow.

Ex. (4) みかさんは新(あたら)しい車(くるま)を買(か)おう<u>と思(おも)っています</u>。*Mika is thinking of buying a new car.*

2 ～も [Emphasis]

The particle も can be used to emphasize that a number of objects, people, etc. or an amount of something is very large or very small in the speaker's opinion.

2-1 Number + Counter + も (+ V (affirmative)) "as many/much as"

[2-a]

	Number + Counter		V (affirmative)
パーティーでケーキを	5個(こ)	も	食(た)べました。
I ate as many as five cakes at the party.			

You can stress that you find a number or amount to be very large by using "Number + Counter + も" with an affirmative form of a verb. Compare [2-a] with the following sentence that does not include the emphatic も:

パーティーでケーキを５個(こ) ø 食(た)べました。*I ate five cakes at the party.*

In English the type of emphasis expressed in [2-a] is often conveyed through intonation and syllabic stress, so this structure is difficult to translate directly into natural written English. "As many as [number]" or "as much as [amount]" would be a rough equivalent.

Exs. (1) 田中(たなか)さんは日本(にほん)のまんがを200冊(さつ)も持(も)っています。
Tanaka-san has 200 Japanese manga [and I think that's a lot].

(2) リサさんは10回(かい)も日本(にほん)に行(い)ったことがあります。
Lisa has been to Japan as many as 10 times.

(3) 研(けん)さんは昨日(きのう)３キロも泳(およ)いだと言(い)っていました。
Ken said he'd swum 3 kilometers yesterday [and I think that's a lot].

2-2 何(なん) + Counter + も (+ V (affirmative)) "a great number of; many"

[2-b]

	Q-word	Counter		V (affirmative)
新(あたら)しい漢字(かんじ)を	何(なん)	度(ど)	も	練習(れんしゅう)しました。
I practiced the new kanji many times.				

You can emphasize the largeness of an unspecified number or amount using "何(なん) + Counter + も" with an affirmative form of a verb.

Exs. (1) スミスさんは何年(なんねん)も日本(にほん)に住(す)んでいます。*Smith-san has been living in Japan for many years.*

(2) この歌(うた)が大好(だいす)きだから、毎日(まいにち)何回(なんかい)も聞(き)きます。
I love this song, so I listen to it many times every day.

(3) 先生(せんせい)に聞(き)きたい質問(しつもん)がいくつもあります。*I have many questions that I want to ask my teacher.*

2-3 一 + Counter + も (+ V (negative)) "not a single; not any"

[2-c]

		Counter		V (negative)
今年(ことし)はクラスを	一(いち)	度(ど)	も	休(やす)みませんでした。
I didn't miss any class this year.				

You can express the idea of "not a single; not any" using "一 + Counter + も" with a negative form of a verb.

Exs. (1) 今日(きょう)はまだコーヒーを一(いっ)ぱいも飲(の)んでいません。*I haven't had a single cup of coffee yet today.*

(2) 私(わたし)は一度(いちど)もアルバイトをしたことがありません。*I've never once had a part-time job.*

(3) 昨日(きのう)のパーティーには知(し)っている人(ひと)が一人(ひとり)も来(き)ませんでした。
Nobody I knew came to the party yesterday.

3 ～そうだ [Hearsay] "I hear that ~; I heard that ~" 

[3]

S-plain (what you heard)	
山下(やました)さんはもうすぐ結婚(けっこん)する	そうです。
I heard that Yamashita-san is going to marry soon.	

You can tell others what you have learned from someone else or from media (e.g., TV, internet, etc.) using そうです. The sentence before そうです must be in the plain form.

Exs. (1) 森(もり)さんは卒業(そつぎょう)したら一人(ひとり)で世界中(せかいじゅう)を旅行(りょこう)するそうです。
I heard Mori-san is going to travel around the world alone after graduation.

(2) A: 先週(せんしゅう)のテストは簡単(かんたん)だったそうですね。
I heard last week's test was easy. (Is that correct?)

B: ええ、みんな成績(せいせき)がよかったそうですよ。*Yes, I heard everyone received good grades.*

The information source can be indicated using によると, as seen in the following examples:

Exs. (3) 天気予報(てんきよほう)によると、明日(あした)は雨(あめ)だそうです。
According to the weather forecast, it's going to rain tomorrow.

(4) A：「さくら」という新(あたら)しいレストラン、おいしい？
Is the new restaurant called "Sakura" good (lit. tasty)?

B1: うん、研(けん)さんによると、おいしいそうだよ。
Yeah, Ken says (lit. according to Ken,) it's good.

B2: ううん、リサさんによると、あまりおいしくないそうだよ。
No, Lisa says (lit. according to Lisa,) it's not very good.

Note that the hearsay そう is used only with だ and です. That is, the past and negative forms of だ and です are not used with the hearsay そう. The sentences with × below are ungrammatical:

× トムさんは日本(にほん)の会社(かいしゃ)に就職(しゅうしょく)したそうでした。
→ トムさんは日本(にほん)の会社(かいしゃ)に就職(しゅうしょく)したそうです。
I heard that Tom got a job at a Japanese company.

× 天気予報(てんきよほう)によると、明日(あした)は雨(あめ)が降(ふ)るそうじゃないです。
→ 天気予報(てんきよほう)によると、明日(あした)は雨(あめ)が降(ふ)らないそうです。
According to the weather forecast, it's not going to rain tomorrow.

Hearsay can also be expressed using the verbs 聞(き)く and 言(い)う, as in (5) and (6) below:

Exs. (5) （私(わたし)は、）山下(やました)さんはもうすぐ結婚(けっこん)すると聞(き)きました。
I heard that Yamashita-san is going to marry soon.

(6) リサさんは、山下(やました)さんはもうすぐ結婚(けっこん)すると言(い)っていました。
Lisa said that Yamashita-san is going to marry soon.

In casual speech, Sって is commonly used instead of Sそうだ and Sと聞きました.

Exs. (7) 山下さんはもうすぐ結婚するって。(cf. [3] and (5))

(8) 森さんは卒業したら一人で世界中を旅行するって。(cf. (1))

The hearsay そうだ and the impression そうだ (L9 #3) must be clearly distinguished. Compare the following sentences:

(a) 友達によると、この店のケーキはおいしいそうですよ。
According to my friend, the cake at this place is delicious.

(b) あ、このケーキはすごくおいしそうですね。*Oh, this cake looks very delicious, doesn't it?*

The differences between the two expressions are summarized below:

	Forms before そうだ	Usable forms of そうだ
そうだ [Hearsay]	Any plain form can be used.	そうだ; そうです
そうだ [Impression]	Only V-*masu*, Adj(*i*)-stem, Adj(*na*), and the negative ending ～なさ can be used. (Nそうだ is ungrammatical.)	そうだ; そうです そうなN そうにV

4 ～ながら [Simultaneous/concurrent actions] "while"

[4]

	V1-*masu*			V2
私はたいていスマホを	見	ながら	昼ご飯を	食べます。
I usually eat lunch while looking at my smartphone.				

You can express the idea that someone performs one action while performing another at the same time using V-*masu*ながら.

Exs. (1) 私はたいてい音楽を聞きながら勉強します。*I usually listen to music while I study.*

(2) 運転しながらスマホを見るのは危ないです。
It is dangerous to look at your smartphone while driving.

(3) クリスさんは毎日働きながら大学に行っています。
Chris goes to college while working every day.

Note that in the "V_1-*masu*ながらV_2" structure, the subjects of the two verbs must be the same. Thus, the following sentence is ungrammatical:

× ルームメートが晩ご飯を作りながら、私はリビングをそうじしました。

Intended meaning: *While my roommate was fixing dinner, I cleaned the living room.*

Note also that when one action is primary and the other is secondary, V-*masu*ながら has to represent the secondary action. Thus, in [4], looking at the speaker's smartphone is usually interpreted as the secondary action. (In English the action represented by "while V-ing" is not necessarily secondary.)

When it is not clear which of the two simultaneous or concurrent actions is primary or secondary, you simply attach ながら to one of them.

Ex. (4) 私(わたし)はよく{歯(は)をみがきながらニュースを聞(き)きます／ニュースを聞(き)きながら歯(は)をみがきます}。

I often listen to the news while brushing my teeth. / I often brush my teeth while listening to the news.

Note that when V-*masu*ながら is used to express one's simultaneous or concurrent actions, it cannot be used with the action-in-progress expression V-*te*いる. For example, the following sentence is ungrammatical:

× 私(わたし)はたいてい音楽(おんがく)を聞(き)いていながら勉強(べんきょう)します。
→ 私(わたし)はたいてい音楽(おんがく)を聞(き)きながら勉強(べんきょう)します。(= (1))

5 ～てはいけない [Prohibition] "not allowed to ~; may not ~; should not ~"

[5]

	V-*te*		
ここで写真(しゃしん)を	とって	は	いけません。
You are not allowed to take pictures here.			

You can express the idea of prohibition using V-*te*はいけない. (Its literal meaning is "You cannot go if you V.") This expression and the permission expression V-*te*もいい (See L8 #10) convey opposite ideas, as shown below:

Permission	
+	− (= prohibition)
Doing X is permitted.	Doing X is NOT permitted (= is prohibited).
(食(た)べ)てもいい may (eat)	(食(た)べ)てはいけない may not (eat)

V-*te*はいけない is commonly used to tell the listener that a certain act is not allowed in a certain place or on a certain occasion. Note that this expression should not be used unless the speaker is in a position to prohibit the listener from doing something.

Exs. (1) 学生(がくせい)：先生(せんせい)、試験(しけん)の時(とき)、辞書(じしょ)を使(つか)ってもいいですか。
Professor, is it all right to use a dictionary during the test?

先生(せんせい)：いいえ、使(つか)ってはいけません。*No, it is not.*

(2) 図書館(としょかん)や映画館(えいがかん)で大(おお)きい声(こえ)で話(はな)してはいけません。
You may not talk loudly in the library or at the movie theater.

(3) 危(あぶ)ないから、歩(ある)きながらスマホを使(つか)ってはいけません。
You should not use your smartphone while walking because it is dangerous.

6 〜なくてはいけない [Obligation/necessity] "must ~; have to ~"

[6]

	V (negative *te*-form)		
今晩(こんばん)	勉強(べんきょう)しなくて	は	いけません。
{You/I} have to study tonight.			

You can express obligation or necessity using 〜なくてはいけない. なくて is the *te*-form of the negative ending ない. (The literal meaning of this expression is "You cannot go if you do not V.")

Exs. (1) 明日(あした)は８時(じ)にクラスがあるから、７時(じ)に家(いえ)を出(で)なくてはいけません。
I have a class at eight o'clock tomorrow, so I have to leave home at seven.

(2) 車(くるま)を運転(うんてん)する時(とき)はシートベルトをしなくてはいけません。
You must fasten your seatbelt when you drive a car.

(3) ペットが病気(びょうき)になったから、病院(びょういん)に連(つ)れていかなくてはいけませんでした。
My pet became sick, so I had to take it to the veterinarian (lit. the hospital).

Note that 〜なくてはいけない cannot be used for recommendation, as in the following sentence:

× この映画(えいが)はとてもおもしろいから、見(み)なくてはいけません。

Intended meaning: *This movie is very interesting, so you must watch it.*

→ この映画(えいが)はとてもおもしろいから、ぜひ見(み)てください。

7 〜なくてもいい [Lack of obligation/necessity] "do not have to ~; it's all right not to ~"

[7]

	V (negative *te*-form)		
日本(にほん)ではレストランでチップを	払(はら)わなくて	も	いいです。
You don't have to leave a tip at restaurants in Japan.			

You can express a lack of obligation or necessity using 〜なくてもいい. Its literal meaning is "It is all right even if you don't ~."

Exs. (1) 金曜日(きんようび)は授業(じゅぎょう)がないから、学校(がっこう)に行(い)かなくてもいいです。
I don't have class on Friday, so I don't have to go to school.

(2) 学生(がくせい)：このワークショップは予約(よやく)しなくてはいけませんか。
Do we have to make a reservation for this workshop?

先生(せんせい)：いいえ、しなくてもいいですよ。*No, you don't have to.*

〜なくてもいい expresses the opposite idea of 〜なくてはいけない (#6) as shown below:

Obligation / necessity	
＋	−
It is necessary to do X.	It is NOT necessary to do X.
(食(た)べ)なくてはいけない have to (eat)	(食(た)べ)なくてもいい don't have to (eat)

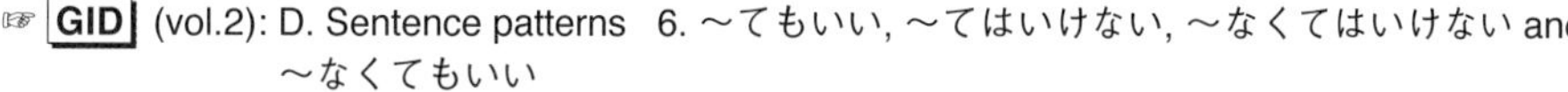
☞ GID (vol.2): D. Sentence patterns 6. 〜てもいい, 〜てはいけない, 〜なくてはいけない and 〜なくてもいい

話しましょう

▸ **Words written in purple** are new words introduced in this lesson.

できる I　Talk about things you are planning on doing.

できるI-A　Volitional forms of verbs

1 Let's practice conjugating verbs into their volitional forms. L13-6

Ex. 食べる → 食べよう

1) 見る　2) 寝る　3) 出かける　4) 行く　5) 帰る　6) 買う　7) 遊ぶ
8) なる　9) する　10) 準備する　11) 連れてくる　12) しておく
13) 電話をかける　14) 気をつける　15) 髪を染める　16) 謝る　17) つりをする

2 Suppose you are planning on doing the following things after class. Invite your friend and decide on the details.

Ex. ご飯を食べる　A: 授業の後で、一緒にご飯を食べない？
B: いいね、食べよう！　どこで食べようか。
<Continue>

1) どこかでしゃべる　2) 明日のクラスの予習をする　3) 筋トレをする　4) your own

3 Now, let's practice talking about your upcoming plans.

Step 1 Suppose you have just decided to do the following things right away. Make sentences about what you are about to do based on the cues provided. L13-7

Ex. 今から出かけようと思います。

Ex. 出かける　1) コーヒーをいれる　2) 部屋をかたづける　3) 友達に電話をかける
4) 美容院に行く　5) せんたくをする　6) クラスの復習をする　7) your own

Step 2 Suppose you decided some time ago to do the following things tonight. Make sentences about what you are going to do tonight based on the cues provided. L13-8

Ex. 今晩、旅行の計画を立てようと思っています。

Ex. 旅行の計画を立てる　1) 髪を切る　2) 食事してから帰る　3) クッキーを焼く
4) ワークショップに参加する　5) 来週の発表の準備をしておく　6) your own

Step 3 Now, talk about your actual plans for tonight.

Ex. A: ○○さん、今晩、何をしますか。
B: 夏のインターンシップに申し込もうと思っています。
A: へえ、どんなインターンシップに申し込むんですか。（← Follow-up question）
B: ロボットの研究をしている会社のインターンシップです。　<Continue>

4 Do you have any plans for your next vacation?

Step 1 Talk about your plans for your next vacation with your partner.

Ex. A: ○○さんは次の休みに何をしますか。

😆	😕?
B: 台湾(たいわん)に行こうと思っています。 A: そうですか。台湾(たいわん)で何をしようと思っていますか。 B: そうですね、牛肉麺(めん) (noodles) を食べたり、お祭(まつ)りに行ったりしようと思っています。それから… <Continue> A: いいですね。旅行(りょこう)を楽しんでください。	B: うーん、まだ決(き)めていません。 A: そうですか。あのう、とびら公園(こうえん)に行ったことがありますか。 B: いいえ、ありません。どんな所ですか。 <Continue> B: じゃ、次の休みにとびら公園(こうえん)に行ってみようと思います。

Step 2 Report to the class what you heard from your partner in Step 1.

Ex. ○○さんは次の休みに台湾(たいわん)に行って、牛肉麺(めん)を食べようと思っています。

できる II Report and share interesting and useful information you have heard or read.

できるII-A Emphasis ～も

1 Let's practice using ～も to emphasize numbers.

	Ex.	1)	2)	3)	4)	5)	6)
Step 1	1-10 & how many?						
Step 2	50 / a lot	1000 / a lot	20 / a lot	10 / a lot	8 / a lot	300 / a lot	70 / a lot
Step 3	none						

Step 1 First, say which counter you use for the objects listed in the table above, count them from 1-10, and end with the question word for "how many." L13-9

Ex. 枚(まい) → 一枚(いちまい) → 二枚(にまい) … 十枚(じゅうまい) → 何枚(なんまい)？

Step 2 Suppose there is a large number of the objects listed in the table above. Make sentences based on the cues provided in the second row. L13-10

Ex.1 チケットが50枚(まい)もあります。　**Ex.2** チケットが何枚(なんまい)もあります。

Step 3 Suppose there is none of these things. Make sentences accordingly. L13-11

Ex. チケットが一枚(まい)もありません。

2 Suppose a survey is being conducted targeting both students and businesspeople. Answer the questions from both perspectives based on the cues provided. L13-12

Ex. 毎日まんがを読みますか。　**A1.** 学生　：はい、何冊(なんさつ)も読みます。
A2. 会社員(かいしゃいん)：いいえ、一冊(いっさつ)も読みません。

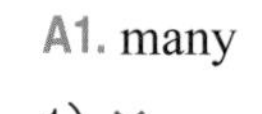

	A1. many	A2. ×
Ex. 毎日まんがを読みますか。		
1) 毎日コーヒーを飲みますか。	×	many
2) 毎日エナジードリンクを飲みますか。	many	×
3) 時計を持っていますか。	×	many
4) いい先輩(せんぱい)がいますか。	many	×
5) 白(しろ)いシャツを持っていますか。	×	many
6) 去年(きょねん)、海外(かいがい)に行きましたか。	×	many

3 Talk about what kind of people バリバリさん and ゴロゴロさん are. L13-13

Ex. バリバリさんは友達が600人もいますが、
ゴロゴロさんは友達が一人もいません。

	バリバリさん	ゴロゴロさん
Ex. 友達がいる？	600	×
1) ペットがいる？	8 pets	×
2) ファッション雑誌(ざっし)を持っている？	200	×
3) 誕生日(たんじょうび)にプレゼントをもらった？	50	×
4) テレビに出たことがある？	15 times	×
5) 走れる？	42 km（キロ）	×
6) your own		

4 Let's have a bragging contest!

Step 1 Brag about yourself to your partner. Feel free to exaggerate for the sake of the exercise!

Ex.1 A: 私はSNSに毎日写真(しゃしん)を10回もアップしますよ。
B: わあ、多(おお)いですね。でも、私はフォロワーが800人もいますよ。

Ex.2 A: 私は今まで、日本語の授業(じゅぎょう)を{一回／一度}も休んだことがありませんよ。
B: えっ、すごいですね。でも、私は日本語のテストで何度もいい成績(せいせき)を取(と)ったことがありますよ。

Step 2 Report which one of you is the better bragger. Remember to include the reason(s) for your judgement.

Ex. 私より〇〇さんの方がすごいと思います。SNS にフォロワーが 800 人もいるからです。

できるII-B Hearsay ～そうだ

1 Let's review plain forms and practice using them with ～そうです. L13-14

Ex. 食べます

	affirmative	negative
non-past	食べるそうです	食べないそうです
past	食べたそうです	食べなかったそうです

1) 出かけます　2) できます　3) 行きます　4) あります　5) 旅行します
6) 来ます　7) 住んでいます　8) おいしいです　9) いいです　10) 好きです
11) 学生です　12) 楽しみです　13) しゃべります　14) 謝ります　15) 勉強中です

2 Share some gossip about the *TOBIRA* characters. L13-15

Ex. A: ジャンさんは来月、アイさんに会いに行くそうですよ。
B: へえ、そうですか。知りませんでした。(← Comment)

Ex. 来月、アイさんに会いに行きます。

ジャン

1) 毎日朝早く起きます。
2) 外国語が四つもできます。
3) 絶対にクラスをサボりません。
4) 今学期は大変だから、ひまな時間がありません。

リーマン

5) 先月、新しいアルバイトを始めました。
6) 最近、アルバイトがとても忙しくなりました。
7) 昨日はあまり寝ませんでした。
8) 週末は一秒 (second) も勉強できませんでした。

タオ

9) アイさんが近くにいないから、さびしいです。
10) アイさんと電話で話すのが楽しみです。
11) 今の生活はあまり楽しくないです。
12) 昨日は予定が何もなかったから、ひまでした。

圭太

3 Let's practice introducing someone to others.

Step 1 Ask the following questions to learn more about your partner.

Ex. 専攻(せんこう)は何ですか。　　A: 専攻(せんこう)は何ですか。
B: ビジネスです。

1) 専攻(せんこう)は何ですか。
2) 好きな食べ物は何ですか。
3) 週末はよく何をしますか。
4) この近(ちか)くでどのレストランが一番好きですか。
5) 日本に行ったことがありますか。
6) your own

Step 2 Change your partner and share two pieces of information you heard about your previous partner.

Ex. A: 私は〇〇さんと話しました。〇〇さんの専攻(せんこう)はビジネスだそうです。
それから、好きな食べ物は…　<Continue>

C: へえ、そうですか。私の専攻(せんこう)もビジネスです。

Group Work

4 Try to get some interesting stories from your classmates.

Step 1 Ask the following questions to some of your classmates. Make sure to ask follow-up questions as well.

1) 最近(さいきん)、どんな時に笑(わら)いましたか。
2) 最近(さいきん)、どんな時に謝(あやま)りましたか。
3) 最近(さいきん)、どんな時に家族(かぞく)に電話(でんわ)をかけましたか。
4) your own

Step 2 Report to the class the stories you heard from your classmates.

Ex. 〇〇さんは先週日本語のクラスに遅刻(ちこく)した時に、先生に謝(あやま)ったそうです。
それから、△△さんは…　<Continue>

5 Do you follow what's going on in the world?

Step 1 Brainstorm some news you saw/read/heard recently and think of how to explain it in Japanese.

Step 2 Share the news you thought of in Step 1 with your partner.

Possible topics	商品(しょうひん) (products)	政治(せいじ)	IT	大学	天気

Ex. A: ネットの記事(きじ)によると、最近(さいきん)日本ではからいチョコレートが人気がある
そうですよ。知っていますか。

Yes	No
B: はい、知っています。日本人の友達に聞きました。〇〇さんは食べたことがありますか。　<Continue>	B: いいえ、知りません。ここでも買えますか。　<Continue>

できるIII Talk about things that are prohibited.

できるIII-A Simultaneous/concurrent actions ～ながら

1 Describe what Ai often does using ～ながら based on the cues provided. L13-16

Ex. アイさんはよくコーヒーをいれながら、朝(あさ)ご飯(はん)を作ります。

Ex.

1) Check

2) タオさん

3)

4)

5)

6)

7)

Group Work

2 Let's play charades! One student will act out two simultaneous actions while others guess what those actions are.

Ex. A: (performs charade)

B: ガムをかみながら、運転(うんてん)しています。

A: はい、そうです。or いいえ、違(ちが)います。

3 Are you good at multitasking?

Step 1 Talk about what kind of things you often do simultaneously.

Ex. A: 私はよく音楽を聞きながら、勉強します。

B: そうですか。どんな音楽をよく聞きますか。

A: クラシックをよく聞きます。○○さんは何かしながら、勉強しますか。

<Continue>

Step 2 Report to the class what your partner does simultaneously. Add your own information as well.

Ex. ○○さんはよく音楽を聞きながら、勉強するそうです。私 {は／も}… <Continue>

できるIII-B Prohibition ～てはいけない

1 Let's practice forming the expression ～てはいけない in the plain and polite forms.

Ex. 食(た)べる → 食(た)べてはいけない → 食(た)べてはいけません

1) 見(み)る　2) 寝(ね)る　3) 出(で)かける　4) 使(つか)う　5) 話(はな)す　6) 取(と)る　7) する
8) 持(も)ってくる　9) 電話(でんわ)をかける　10) 髪(かみ)を染(そ)める　11) さわぐ　12) サボる
13) ガムをかむ　14) カンニングする

2 Let's practice describing what actions are prohibited in certain places.

Step 1 Describe what you are not allowed to do in your Japanese class. L13-18

Ex. 授業(じゅぎょう)中に食べ物を食べてはいけません。

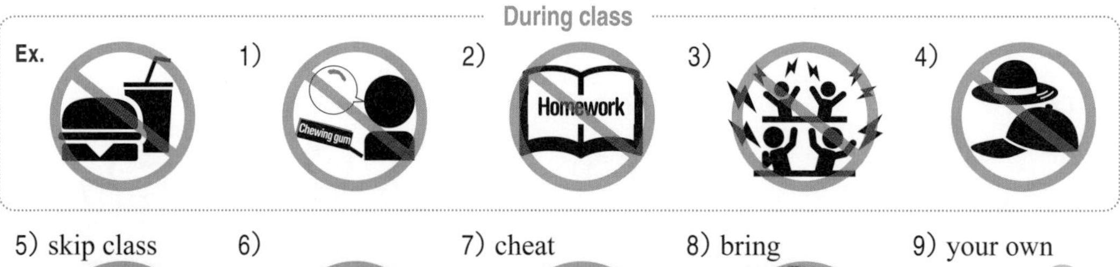

5) skip class　6)　7) cheat　8) bring　9) your own

Step 2 Answer your partner's questions about what is allowed in the following places.

Ex. A: この川でバーベキューをしてもいいですか。

B: いいえ、バーベキューをしてはいけません。

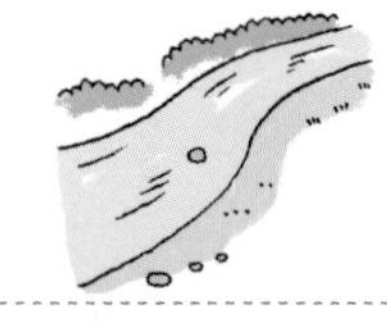

Ex.

1)

2)

3)

4) Tシャツで行く

5)

3 Many high schools in Japan have various rules for their students.

Step 1 Say what is commonly prohibited among Japanese high school students.

Ex. 日本の高校生はたいていピアスをしてはいけません。

Ex. ピアス　1) アルバイト　2) 化粧(けしょう)　3) 髪(かみ)　4) バイク　5) ゲーム

Step 2 Discuss if these actions are also prohibited in countries/cities/schools you are familiar with.

Ex. A: {ベトナムの／ハノイの／○○(school name)の} 高校生は（たいてい）

バイクで学校に行ってもいいです。

B: 中国の高校でも同じです。バイクで学校に行ってもいいです。

or 中国の高校では違(ちが)います。 <Continue>

4 Are you aware of safety rules?

Step 1 You saw your partner do the following things. Give them a warning.

Ex. A: ○○さん、スマホを見ながら、バイクに乗(の)ってはいけませんよ。
ルールを守(まも)ってください。(← Comment)
B: あ、すみません。すぐやめます。

Step 2 What two actions are people prohibited from doing simultaneously in the countries you are familiar with or in more specific places (e.g., library, class, lab)?

Ex. A: 日本語のクラスでは、ガムをかみながら、授業(じゅぎょう)を受(う)けてはいけません。
B: そうですか。私の経済(けいざい)のクラスでは、ガムをかみながら、授業(じゅぎょう)を受(う)けてもいいです。
A: そうですか。 <Continue>

できるⅣ Talk about things you have or do not have an obligation to do.

できるⅣ-A Obligation/necessity ～なくてはいけない

1 Let's practice forming the expression ～なくてはいけない in the plain and polite forms. 

Ex. 食(た)べる → 食(た)べない → 食(た)べなくてはいけない → 食(た)べなくてはいけません

1) 決(き)める　2) 覚(おぼ)える　3) 行(い)く　4) 言(い)う　5) やる　6) 働(はたら)く
7) する　8) 持(も)ってくる　9) しておく　10) 話(はな)せる　11) 止(と)まる　12) 曲(ま)がる
13) 拾(ひろ)う　14) 注意(ちゅうい)する

2 What kind of things do you have to do when preparing for guests? 

Step 1 Suppose you are in Japan and your parents are coming to visit you. List up what you have to do to prepare for their visit.

Ex. 旅行(りょこう)の計画を立てる → 旅行(りょこう)の計画を立てなくてはいけません

1) 両親(りょうしん)に電話(でんわ)をかける　2) 食事する所を探(さが)す
3) ホテルを予約(よやく)しておく　4) ホテルの場所をチェックする
5) 両親(りょうしん)を空港(くうこう)まで迎(むか)えに行く　6) 両親(りょうしん)を空港(くうこう)で待(ま)つ

Step 2 Your parents are coming to visit your apartment to have drinks after dinner. What do you have to do beforehand?

Useful vocabulary 拾(ひろ)う　かたづける　洗(あら)う　ゴミを出す　せんたくする

Ex. 両親(りょうしん)が来る前に、ゴミを拾(ひろ)わなくてはいけません。
それから… <Continue>

3 Can you explain what the following signs indicate in Japanese? L13-23

Ex.1 これを見たら、ゆっくり運転(うんてん)しなくてはいけません。

Ex.2 これを見たら、自転車(じてんしゃ)で入ってはいけません。

できるIV-B Lack of obligation/necessity ～なくてもいい

1 Let's practice forming the expression ～なくてもいい in the polite form. Use the cues from できるIV-A-1 on the previous page. L13-24

Ex. 食(た)べる → 食(た)べない → 食(た)べなくてもいいです

2 Suppose you have a day off from work tomorrow. Say what you don't have to do. 

Ex. 仕事をする → 明日は休みだから、仕事をしなくてもいいです。

1) 朝早(あさはや)く起(お)きる　2) 寝(ね)る時間に気をつける　3) 化粧(けしょう)する　4) 電車(でんしゃ)に乗(の)る
5) 会社に行く　6) 仕事の電話(でんわ)に出る　7) お客(きゃく)さんと会う　8) your own

3 Talk about your schedule for this weekend.

Step 1 You have to do the following activities this weekend, but your roommate does not. Describe both of your circumstances based on the cues provided. L13-26

Ex. 私は週末、日本語の宿題(しゅくだい)をしなくてはいけません。

でも、ルームメートは日本語の宿題(しゅくだい)をしなくてもいいです。

Ex. Japanese

1) article on economics

2)

3) return

4) participate

5) apply

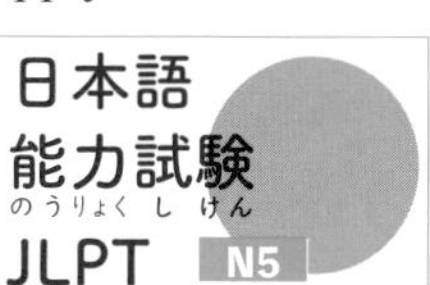

6) early

7) your own

Step 2 Take turns with your partner asking if you are busy this weekend. When you answer, say what you have to/don't have to do along with a reason.

Ex. A: ○○さんは、週末忙(いそが)しいですか。

B: はい、宿題(しゅくだい)がたくさん出たから、宿題(しゅくだい)をしなくてはいけません。
△△さんは？

A: 私は宿題(しゅくだい)をしなくてもいいから、あまり忙(いそが)しくないです。

<Continue>

ROLE PLAY

4 A prospective student is visiting your university.

Role A You are a prospective student from Japan. Ask your partner, who works in the administration office, whether you have to do the things listed below if you attend the university and live in the city.

Role B You are working at the university admissions office, where your partner is visiting as a prospective student. Answer your partner's questions.

Ex. A: 寮(りょう)に住まなくてはいけませんか。

B: はい、○○さんは一年生だから、寮(りょう)に住まなくてはいけません。

or いいえ、住まなくてもいいです。

Ex. live in the dormitory　1) take a foreign language class　2) purchase a car

3) participate in an orientation（オリエンテーション）　4) decide on a major before entering university

5) be able to speak English well　6) your own

5 Do you have any family rules?

Step 1 Recall what family rules you had when you were a child.

Step 2 Take turns with your partner asking about the family rules you had when you were a child. When answering, list at least three rules.

Ex. A: ○○さんは、子どもの時、どんなルールがありましたか。

B: 一週間に一回、部屋(へや)をそうじしなくてはいけませんでした。(← Obligation)

それから、食事をしながら、テレビを見てはいけませんでした。(← Prohibition)

でも、食事をした後で、お皿(さら)を洗(あら)わなくてもよかったです。(← Lack of obligation)

そして、何時間もゲームをしてもよかったです。(← Permission)

A: そうですか。私の家では、食事をした後で、自分でお皿(さら)を洗(あら)わなくてはいけませんでした。 <Continue>

Group Work

6 Hold a small debate session with your groupmates!

Step 1 Brainstorm what pros and cons there are on the following topics related to foreign language education.

学校で外国語を勉強する	外国語の授業(じゅぎょう)は毎日ある
日本語の授業(じゅぎょう)中にいつも日本語で話す	your own (any topic)

Step 2 Choose one topic from Step 1 and discuss it with your groupmates.

Ex. A:「学校で外国語を勉強する」について話しましょう。○○さんはどう思いますか。

B: 私は学校で外国語を勉強しなくてはいけないと思います。

A: どうしてですか。

B: 今はとてもグローバルな社会だからです。外国語を勉強したら、世界中(せかいじゅう)の人とビジネスができます。

C: 私は勉強しなくてもいいと思います。 <Continue>

Review

Now that you can talk about rules and social customs, try creating a booklet with helpful tips for your classmates.

Step 1 Decide on a topic with your partner and then individually brainstorm what you must do, don't have to do, and must not do when engaging in activities related to the topic you have chosen.

Possible topics ○○の楽しみ方　　○○の上手な作り方／やり方

トピック：＿＿＿＿＿＿＿＿＿＿

・しなくてはいけないこと：＿＿＿＿＿＿＿＿＿＿

・しなくてもいいこと：＿＿＿＿＿＿＿＿＿＿

・してはいけないこと：＿＿＿＿＿＿＿＿＿＿

Step 2 Exchange your ideas from Step 1 with your partner and decide what tips you want to include in your booklet. Make sure to include at least three tips.

Topic
What you have to/ don't have to do
What you must not do
Additional tips if any

Ex. A: じゃ、「アメリカンフットボールの楽しみ方」を考(かんが)えましょう。

B: まず、アメフトのルールを覚(おぼ)えなくてはいけませんね。

A: そうですね。私は試合(しあい)を見ながら覚(おぼ)えましたよ。

B: それから、選手(せんしゅ)の名前を知らなくてはいけませんね。

A: うーん、私は知らなくてもいいと思います。私はあまり選手(せんしゅ)の名前を知りませんが、試合(しあい)が楽しめます。

B: なるほど、そうですか。じゃ、試合(しあい)を見る時、何をしてはいけませんか。

A: そうですね、スタジアムで見る時は、相手(あいて) (opponent) のチームの色(いろ)のTシャツを着てはいけませんね。 <Continue>

Step 3 Present your ideas to your classmates. Include all the tips you talked about in order.

Ex. 私達のガイドのタイトルは「みんなでアメフトを楽しもう！」です。

まず、ルールを覚(おぼ)えなくてはいけません。

それから… <Continue>

Reading

読みましょう

Getting information from photos and captions

1 There are many traditional events and festivals celebrated in all corners of Japan in every season. Look at the photos below and read the captions that describe them. Try to guess any unknown words in the captions using the photos as clues.

a.

六月　お田植え祭り（岡山）

提供：岡山後楽園

お米に感謝する歌を歌いながら、お米の苗を植える。

b.

七月　秩父川瀬祭（埼玉）

提供：秩父市役所産業観光部観光課

350年の歴史がある秩父神社の夏祭り。みんなで400キロもある神輿を持って川の中を歩く。

c.

八月　よさこい祭り（高知）

提供：高知商工会議所・よさこい祭振興会

人々がチームでおどりながら町の中を進む。世界中からたくさんの人々が見に来る。

d.

九月　大覚寺観月の夕べ（京都）

提供：旧嵯峨御所　大本山大覚寺

千年も前から京都にある行事。舟に乗って、夜空に見える月と水の上に見える月、二つの月を楽しむ。

Now, discuss the following questions with your classmates.

1）a.～d. の祭りや行事はいつどこでありますか。その場所は p.10 の日本地図のどこにありますか。

2）a. の「お米」は何だと思いますか。

3）b. の「神輿」の中には何があると思いますか。

4）a.～d. は下の①～④のどのタイプの行事だと思いますか。

① みんなでおどりを楽しむ祭り　　② 食べ物に感謝する祭り

③ 自然を楽しむ行事　　④ 神様を大切にする (to revere god) 祭り

5）あなたの出身や住んでいる所にも①～④のような行事がありますか。

6）a.～d. の中で、どの行事を見てみたいですか。どうしてそう思いますか。

2 「よさこい祭り」の記事を読んで、質問に答えましょう。

四国高知のよさこい祭り

鳴子

毎年八月の初めに、四国の高知で「よさこい祭り」という祭りがある。たくさんの人がチームでおどりながらパレードをしたり、大きいステージでおどりを見せたりする楽しいa.祭りだ。

この祭りは一九五四年に高知の人達が戦後の町を元気にしようと思って始めたb.祭りで、初めは「よさこいおどり」という伝統的な盆おどりだった。「よさこい」は「夜さ来い」＝「夜に遊びに来てください」というc.意味だそうだ。

最初に参加した人は七五〇人だったが、今は四日間で約二百チームが参加して、全部で二万人もおどるd.祭りになった。そして、毎年観光客が百万人も見に来る。

おどる人達はカラフルなコスチュームを着たり、ユニークな化粧をしたりして、ゲームやアニメのキャラクターみたいに見える。みんなとてもかっこいい。

おどり方はチームの自由で、音楽は何を使ってもいいが、守らなくてはいけないルールが二つあるそうだ。まず、鳴子というカスタネットのようなものを鳴らしながらおどらなくてはいけない。それから、音楽の中に「よさこいおどり」のメロディを少し入れなくてはいけない。

その二つのルールを守ったら、おどりはロック、ヒップホップ、サンバ、フラメンコ、フラダンス…何でもいいそうだ。日本の古い音楽と外国の音楽をミックスした音楽でおどるのはとても楽しそうだ。

祭りには幼稚園の子ども達や小学生のチームから大学生や会社のチームまで色々なe.人々が参加する。海外から参加するチームもあって、一日中とてもにぎやかだ。

祭りの最後の日には、全部のチームの中で一番よかったf.チームが大きいステージでおどって、祭りが終わる。

日本には昔から色々な祭りがあるが、古い祭りにはたいてい絶対に守らなくてはいけないことと、絶対にやってはいけないことがある。でも、「よさこい祭り」はルールを二つだけ守ったら、あとは自由だ。

この自由なスタイルの祭りは一九九〇年代から日本中に広がった。そして、今は日本の色々な所でその町の「よさこい祭り」をやっている。毎年夏に、他の所にいる若い人達が祭りのために帰ってくるから、静かな町がとても元気になるそうだ。

最近は世界中の色々な所の日本紹介イベントでも、若い人達が「よさこいダンス」をおどっているそうだ。四国の町から始まった祭りが世界に広がっている。

四国の高知：City of Kochi in Shikoku
戦後：postwar [after WWII]
伝統的な盆おどり：traditional Bon dance
約：approximately
観光客：tourist
鳴らす：to play (a rattle)
幼稚園：preschool
あとは：after that
1990年代：1990s
広がる：to spread
Nounのために：for Noun

Guessing the meaning of katakana words from context

1） There are many katakana words in this article. Find the following words in the article and guess their meanings.

パレード	ステージ	カラフルなコスチューム		カスタネット
メロディ	フラメンコ	フラダンス	ミックスする	スタイル

Identifying the 5Ws and 1H

2） The 5Ws (who, what, when, where, and why) and 1H (how) can be used to get at the important information about an event. Complete the table below by answering the questions (1)-(6) based on the information in the article.

(1) いつ	(2) どこで	(3) 何がありますか。
(4) 誰が、どんなことをしますか。		
(5) いつ、誰が、どうして始めましたか。		
(6) 最近どう変わりましたか。		

Comprehension check

3） Draw a line on the right side of the part of the text that modifies each noun in boxes a.-f.

4） Mark ○ if the statement is true and × if it is false.

（　　）「よさこい祭り」に参加する人は、日本人じゃなくてはいけない。

（　　）記事によると、音楽の中に日本のメロディが全然入っていなくてもいいそうだ。

（　　）記事によると、日本の古い祭りにはルールがたくさんあるようだ。

（　　）記事によると、「よさこい祭り」のおどりが見られるのは日本だけだそうだ。

5）「よさこいおどり」はどうして「よさこいダンス」(l.51) になったと思いますか。

書く練習

Write about a famous or interesting festival/event held in your community or place of origin. Make sure to share some interesting episodes that would make your readers want to visit the event.

聞きましょう

リスニング・ストラテジー：Listening strategy

Guessing unknown words from context (2)

As we discussed in Lesson 12, you cannot always pause a conversation to check the meaning of unknown words as they come up. Let's do some more practice guessing the meaning of unknown words from context to facilitate your listening comprehension.

1 **Pre-listening activity:** Your Japanese instructor is describing some terms in Japanese. Listen to monologues 1)-3) and try to infer the meaning of the words in question. Then, check to see if your guesses were correct.

Words	Meaning (in your preferred language)
Ex. わしつ	Japanese-style room
1) しゅと	
2) るすでん	
3) こうそく	

L13-28

2 **Listening:** Han-san is studying abroad in Japan and staying with a host family. Listen to conversations 1)-3) and choose the most appropriate picture from a.-c. that shows what Han-san will do next.

1) a.  b.  c. 

2) a.  b.  c. 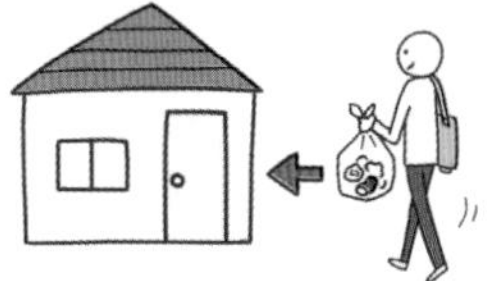

3) a.  b.  c. 

Now it's time to go back to the DEKIRU List for this chapter (p.85) and do the exit check to see what new things you can do now that you've completed the lesson.

Unit4 チャレンジ

1 How to master kanji

As Riemann said in the conversation in Lesson 11 (p.15), there are many learning strategies that could make your kanji learning more efficient, effective, and enjoyable.

Search online to see what kind of learning strategies are available, find one that you think would suit your learning style, and share it with the class! You can find some useful links on the *TOBIRA* website.

2 Unique rules around the world

Various places around the world have unique rules and manners for their visitors to follow. Think of an example of such a place and share its rules and manners with your classmates.

Ex. 日本の鹿島神社(かしまじんじゃ)の中にある「鹿園(しかえん)」という公園(こうえん)のルールを紹介(しょうかい)します。例えば、鹿園(しかえん)のシカ (deer) に食べ物をあげてもいいですが、イヌを連(つ)れてきてはいけません。それから、食べ物はにんじん (carrot) をあげなくてはいけません。

3 Meme contest

Humor is one of the most difficult linguistic elements in any language to communicate and yet one of the most valuable ways to enhance intercultural understanding. Try making your own meme in Japanese. Post it online and see whose meme is the funniest! You can find some useful links on the *TOBIRA* website.

Ex.1

Ex.2

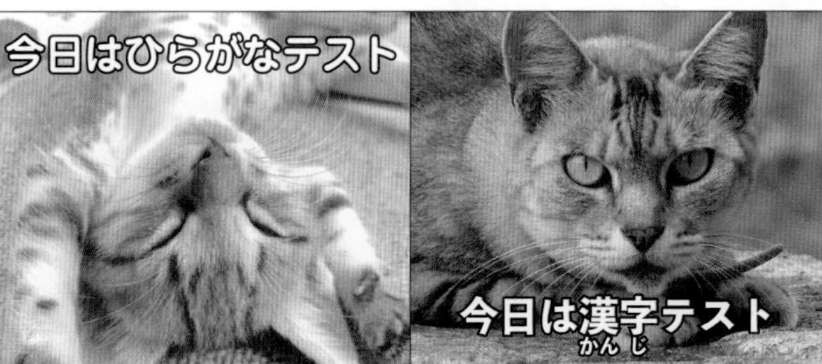

Unit 5

異文化を体験する

いぶんか　たいけん

Experiencing different cultures

05

Pre-activity

Unit5の前に

The theme of this unit is “Experiencing different cultures.” In Japan, you can enjoy many fun and interesting cultural activities such as calligraphy, tea ceremony, and flower arrangement, as well as visiting temples, shrines, castles, and hot springs. You will also have various opportunities to enjoy more immersive cultural experiences during your stay in Japan.

1 下の写真(しゃしん)は「日本でできる文化体験(たいけん) (hands-on experience)」です。何をしていると思いますか。クラスメートと話してください。その後で［　　］の中から説明(せつめい)を選(えら)んで (to choose) ください。

a

提供：NINJA DOJO and STORE

b

提供：築地玉寿司

c

写真：三木光 / アフロ

d

提供：「acosta!」by HACOSTA inc.

e

提供：夢アカデミー　和太鼓夢蔵 MUSASHI

f

提供：両足院

① 太鼓(たいこ)という日本の楽器(がっき)を楽しむ	② 夏(なつ)の祭(まつ)りでみんなでおどる	③ 忍者(にんじゃ)になる
④ 日本料理の作り方を習(なら)う	⑤ お寺で座禅(ざぜん) (Zen meditation) をする	
⑥ コスプレをして、まんがやアニメのイベントに行く		

Q1. a～f の中で何か体験(たいけん)したことがありますか。いつどこでしましたか。どうでしたか。

Q2. a～f の中でどれをしてみたいですか。どうしてですか。

Q3. 他(ほか)に、日本でどんなことがしてみたいですか。

Q4. あなたの国や他(ほか)の国ではどんなおもしろい体験(たいけん)ができますか。何がおすすめですか。

Lesson 14

大阪(おおさか)を案内(あんない)してほしいんですけど…

I'd like you to show me around Osaka...

DEKIRU List

できるCheck ☑

できる I **Describe the state of things and places in detail.**
場所や物などがどのような状態か、詳しく描写することができる。
Entry ☐ Exit ☐

できる II **Ask and answer questions about troubles someone is having.**
困ったことについて、尋ねたり答えたりできる。
Entry ☐ Exit ☐

できる III **Ask for and give suggestions about familiar topics.**
身近な問題について相談したり、相談を受けて提案したりできる。
Entry ☐ Exit ☐

STRATEGIES

Conversation Tips .... • Demonstratives for referring to items in discourse

Reading .... • Getting information from a website: Event information
• Visualizing
• Understanding Japanese sentence structure: Transitive and intransitive verbs

Listening .... • Getting the gist

GRAMMAR

1. Transitive verbs and intransitive verbs できるI
2. Intransitive verb＋ている [State resulting from change] できるI
3. Transitive verb＋てある [State resulting from purposeful action] できるI
4. ～てしまう "V (to one's regret); finish V-ing" できるII
5. ～かもしれない [Uncertainty; possibility] できるII
6. ～すぎる "too Adj; V too much/many (N)" できるII
7. S_1し、S_2し [Multiple reasons] できるIII
8. ～てほしい "want (someone) to V" できるIII
9. ～たらどうですか [Suggestion] できるIII

Conversation

会話

1 できるI Ai is not feeling well.

L14-1

保険に入る：to sign up for (health) insurance

アイ　：あのう、お母さん…

母　：あれ？　アイちゃん、どうしたの？

アイ　：ちょっと気持ちが悪いんです。それから、おなかも痛いんです。

母　：えっ、だいじょうぶ？　病院、行く？

アイ　：でも、あの、お母さん、お店が開いていますけど…

母　：今、閉めるから、だいじょうぶ。すぐに行きましょう！

アイ　：じゃ、お願いします。すみません…

母　：あ、アイちゃん、保険はある？

アイ　：はい、日本に来る前に入りました。
スマホに保険の ID がダウンロードしてあります。

母　：そう、よかった。

<Ai's host mother checks around the house.>

母　：えっと、お店の窓を閉めて、電気を消して、かぎもかけたから、オッケー！
じゃ、行きましょう。

2 できるII Ai is meeting with a doctor at the clinic.

L14-2

医者　：どうしましたか。

アイ　：えっと、気持ちが悪くて、おなかが痛いです。

医者　：今日は何を食べましたか。

アイ　：えっと、朝はヨーグルトとパンを食べて、
昼はおにぎりを食べました。

医者　：飲み物は？

アイ　：飲み物は水と…　あ、大学から帰ってから、冷蔵庫に入っているお茶を
飲みました。

母　：アイちゃん、あれはそば茶よ。

医者　：ああ、じゃ、そばアレルギーかもしれませんね。調べてみましょう。

<After allergy tests have been performed>

医者　：ブルーノさん、そばアレルギーですよ。

アイ　：えっ、そばアレルギー？　おいしかったから、たくさん飲んでしまいました…

医者　：そうですか。これからは絶対にそばを食べたり、そば茶を飲んだりしないでくださいね。それから、今日は晩ご飯を食べすぎないでください。

アイ　：はい。

医者　：この紙にそばアレルギーについて書いてありますから、よく読んでおいてください。

アイ　：はい、分かりました。どうもありがとうございました。

3 できるIII Ai is on a video call with Keita and Nyanta.

L14-3

圭太　：あ、アイちゃん、久しぶり。元気？

アイ　：はい。でも、おとといは病院に行ったんですよ。

圭太　：え？　病院？

にゃんた：ニャ、ニャーイン？

アイ　：ええ、そば茶を飲んでしまって…　実は私、そばアレルギーだったんです。

圭太　：本当？　だいじょうぶ？

アイ　：ええ、よく休んだし、薬も飲んだし、今はだいじょうぶです。

圭太　：そっか、よかった。ところで、アイちゃん、今度、大阪に遊びに行ってみたらどう？　食べ物がおいしいし、にぎやかだし、とても楽しい所だよ。

アイ　：あ、圭太さんの出身は大阪ですね。絶対に行こうと思っています。

圭太　：うん、ぜひ。本当は僕がアイちゃんを案内したいんだけど…

アイ　：ええ、私も圭太さんに大阪を案内してほしいんですけど…

CONVERSATION TIPS

Demonstratives for referring to items in discourse: You can refer to something out of sight using a そ-word or an あ-word, but they do not function quite the same as "it" and "that" in English. Use a そ-word if the topic is something only the listener or the speaker is familiar with; use an あ-word, on the other hand, if the topic is familiar to both the speaker and the listener. Read the conversation below and see if you can determine which speakers are already familiar with the café mentioned.

A：昨日、「ソレイユ」というカフェに行ったんですよ。

B：ああ、あの店のコーヒーはおいしいですね。私もよく行きます。

C：えっ、そのカフェはどこにありますか。私も行ってみたいです。

単語（たんご）

▶ **The words written in gray** are supplemental vocabulary.

動作・変化を描写する（どうさ・へんか・びょうしゃ） Describing actions and changes

[*thing* が] あく ((something) opens) 	[*thing* を] あける (to open) 	[*thing* が] しまる ((something) closes) 	[*thing* を] しめる (to close) 	[*thing* が] おちる ((something) drops/falls) 	[*thing* を] おとす (to drop) 
[*thing* が] よごれる ((something) becomes dirty) 	[*thing* を] よごす (to make (something) dirty) 	[*thing* が] つく ((something) turns on) 	[*thing* を] つける (to turn on (the lights, etc.))  でんき (light; electricity)	[*thing* が] きえる ((something) turns off/goes out) 	[*thing* を] けす (to turn off (the lights, etc.); to erase; to delete (messages, etc.)) 
[*thing* が] こわれる ((something) breaks) 	[*thing* を] こわす (to break; to damage) 	[*thing* が] われる ((something) shatters/cracks/breaks) 	[*thing* を] わる (to shatter; to crack; to break) 	[*thing* に] かぎがかかる ((something) locks (itself)) 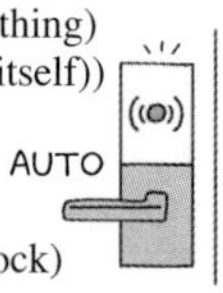 かぎ (key; lock)	[*thing* に] かぎをかける (to lock) 
[*thing* が／に] つながる ((something) connects) 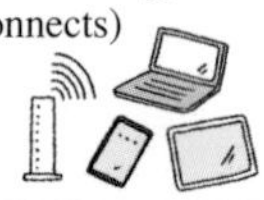	[*thing* を／に] つなげる (to connect) 	おゆがわく (water boils) 	おゆをわかす (to boil water) 	ゆか (floor) 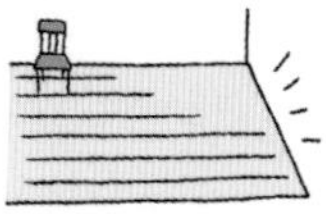	じどうで (automatically) 
みずがでる (water comes out) 	みずをだす (to turn on the water) 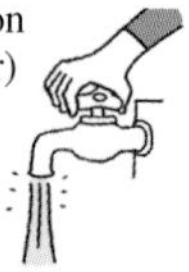	[*thing* が] はいる ((something) enters; to get/be inside)) 	[*thing* を] いれる (to put/place (in)) 	[*thing* が] とまる ((something) stops) 	[*thing* を] とめる (to stop/park) 

状態を描写する（じょうたい・びょうしゃ） Describing states

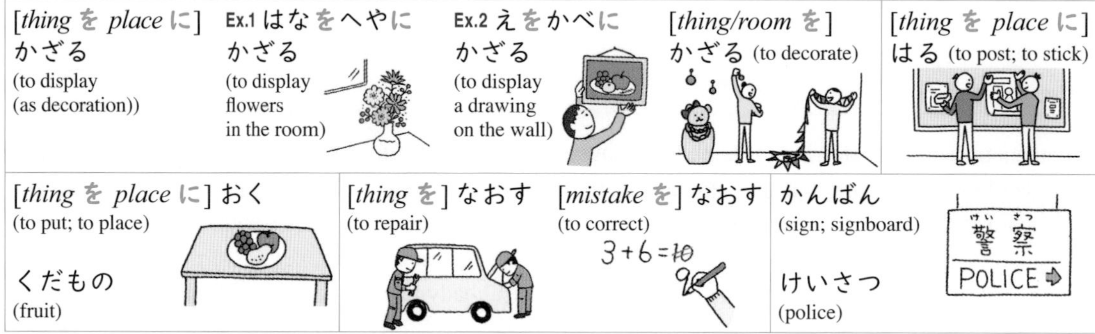

[*thing* を *place* に] かざる (to display (as decoration))	Ex.1 はなをへやにかざる (to display flowers in the room)	Ex.2 えをかべにかざる (to display a drawing on the wall)	[*thing/room* を] かざる (to decorate)	[*thing* を *place* に] はる (to post; to stick)
[*thing* を *place* に] おく (to put; to place) くだもの (fruit)	[*thing* を] なおす (to repair)	[*mistake* を] なおす (to correct)	かんばん (sign; signboard) けいさつ (police)	

そのほかの表現（ひょうげん） Other expressions

Noun のこと (about Noun)	おととい (the day before yesterday)

体調 Health conditions

たいちょう

せきがでる (to cough) せき (cough)	けがをする (to get injured) ち (blood)	ふつかよい (hangover)	アレルギー (allergy) アレルギーがある (to have an allergy) そば (buckwheat (noodles))	くすり (medicine; drug) くすりをのむ (to take medicine)

[*body part* が] いたい: のど (throat), くび (neck), おなか, かた (shoulder), こし (back hip), おしり ((one's) backside; buttocks)

Lesson 14

失敗 Mistakes

しっぱい

[*transportation* に] のりおくれる (to miss (a train, bus, etc.))	あさねぼう(を)する (to oversleep (in the morning))	[*thing/person* に] ぶつかる (to bump into; to crash into)	ころぶ (to fall over; to trip)	にげる (to escape; to run away)

[*thing* を] まちがえる (to make a mistake)

まちがい (mistake; error)

[*thing/person* に／と] にる (to resemble; to be similar/alike)

Ex.1 えいごはスペインご{に／と}にている (English is similar to Spanish)

[*thing/person X* と *thing/person Y* は／が] にる ((X and Y are) similar)

Ex.2 えいごとスペインご{は／が}にている (English and Spanish are similar)

[*thing* が] なくなる	[*thing* を] なくす (to lose)	くさい (foul-smelling; stinky)	さいあく (worst) Ex. さいあくのひ (the worst day)

仕事・イベント Jobs and events

ボランティア(を)する (to volunteer)

ボランティア (volunteer)

[*person/place* に] れんらくする (to contact; to get in touch)

[*person/place* から] れんらくがある (to be contacted; to hear (from))

MAIL

[*person* を *place* に] あんないする (to guide)

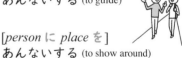

[*person* に *place* を] あんないする (to show around)

[*place* に *thing* を] もっていく (to take (along) (to a different location)) ↔ [*place* に *thing* を] もってくる

[*thing* を] あきらめる (to give up)

リラックスする (to relax)

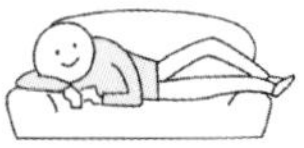

[*person/thing* が] できる (to come into existence; to gain)

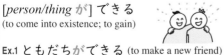

Ex.1 ともだちができる (to make a new friend)

Ex.2 おもいでができる (to create memories)

[*thing* が] できる (to do well; to be good at)

Ex.3 べんきょうができる (smart; to be good at studies)

きょうしつ (classroom)

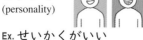

いりぐち (entrance)

でぐち (exit)

おもいで (memory)

ALB

せいかく (personality)

Ex. せいかくがいい (to have a nice personality)

にんぎょう (doll)

おばけ (ghost; spooky imaginary creature)

ろうそく (candle)

ひ (fire)

Vocabulary List

単語リスト

(たんご)

L14-5

▶ **Highlighted kanji words** contain kanji you have learned previously.

RU-VERBS / *RU*-VERB PHRASES

1	あきらめる		to give up [*thing* を]
2	あける	開ける	to open [*thing* を]
3	おちる	落ちる	(something) drops/ falls [*thing* が]
4	かぎをかける		to lock [*thing*に]
5	きえる	消える	(something) turns off/ goes out [*thing* が]
6	こわれる		(something) breaks [*thing* が]
7	しめる	閉める	to close [*thing* を]
8	せきがでる	せきが出る	to cough
9	つける		to turn on (the lights, etc.) [*thing* を]
10	つなげる		to connect [*thing* を／に]
11	できる		to come into existence; to gain [*person/thing* が] **Ex.1** 友達ができる to make a new friend **Ex.2** 思い出ができる to create memories to do well; to be good at [*thing* が] **Ex.3** 勉強ができる smart; to be good at studies
12	にげる		to escape; to run away
13	にる	似る	to resemble; to be similar/alike [*thing/person* に／と] **Ex.1** 英語はスペイン語{に／と}にている English is similar to Spanish [*thing/person X* と *thing/person Y* は／が] **Ex.2** 英語とスペイン語{は／が}にている English and Spanish are similar
14	のりおくれる	乗り遅れる	to miss (a train, bus, etc.) [*transportation* に]
15	まちがえる	間違える	to make a mistake [*thing* を]
16	よごれる	汚れる	(something) becomes dirty [*thing* が]
17	われる	割れる	(something) shatters/ cracks/breaks [*thing* が]

U-VERBS / *U*-VERB PHRASES

18	あく	開く	(something) opens [*thing* が]
19	おく	置く	to put; to place [*thing* を *place* に]
20	おとす	落とす	to drop [*thing* を]
21	おゆがわく	お湯がわく	water boils
22	おゆをわかす	お湯をわかす	to boil water
23	かぎがかかる		(something) locks (itself) [*thing* に]
24	かざる		to display (as decoration) [*thing* を *place* に] **Ex.1** 花をへやにかざる to display flowers in the room **Ex.2** 絵をかべにかざる to display a drawing on the wall to decorate [*thing/room* を]
25	けす	消す	to turn off (the lights, etc.); to erase; to delete (messages, etc.) [*thing* を]
26	ころぶ	転ぶ	to fall over; to trip
27	こわす		to break; to damage [*thing* を]
28	しまる	閉まる	(something) closes [*thing* が]
29	つく		(something) turns on [*thing* が]
30	つながる		(something) connects [*thing* が／に]

31	なおす	直す	to repair [*thing* を]; to correct [*mistake* を]
32	なくす		to lose [*thing* を]
33	はる		to post; to stick [*thing* を *place* に]
34	ぶつかる		to bump into; to crash into [*thing/person* に]
35	みずをだす	水を出す	to turn on the water
36	もっていく	持っていく	to take (along) (to a different location) [*place* に *thing* を]
37	よごす	汚す	to make (something) dirty [*thing* を]
38	わる	割る	to shatter; to crack; to break [*thing* を]

SURU-VERBS / SURU-VERB PHRASES

39	あさねぼう(を)する	朝ねぼう(を)する	to oversleep (in the morning)
40	あんないする	案内する	to guide [*person* を *place* に]; to show around [*person* に *place* を]
41	けがをする		to get injured
42	ボランティア(を)する		to volunteer
43	リラックスする		to relax
44	れんらくする	連絡する	to contact; to get in touch [*person/place* に]
	れんらくがある	連絡がある	to be contacted; to hear (from) [*person/place* から]

I-ADJECTIVE

45	くさい		foul-smelling; stinky

NOUNS

46	アレルギー		allergy
47	いりぐち	入口／入り口	entrance
48	でぐち	出口	exit
49	おばけ	お化け	ghost; spooky imaginary creature
50	おしり		(one's) backside; buttocks
51	おもいで	思い出	memory
52	かぎ		key; lock
53	かんばん	看板	sign; signboard
54	きょうしつ	教室	classroom
55	くすり	薬	medicine; drug
56	くだもの	果物	fruit
57	くび	首	neck
58	けいさつ	警察	police
59	せいかく	性格	personality; character
60	せき		cough
61	そば		buckwheat (noodles)
62	ち	血	blood
63	でんき	電気	light; electricity
64	にんぎょう	人形	doll
65	のど		throat
66	ひ	火	fire
67	ふつかよい	二日よい	hangover
68	まちがい	間違い	mistake; error
69	ゆか		floor
70	ろうそく		candle

ADVERBIAL NOUN

71	おととい		the day before yesterday

OTHER WORDS AND PHRASES

72	さいあく	最悪	worst **Ex.** さいあくの日 the worst day
73	じどうで	自動で	automatically
74	Noun のこと		about Noun

漢字（かんじ）

Kanji

197	開	カイ	開会式（かいかいしき） opening ceremony　開始する（かいし） to start [formal]　開店する（かいてん） to open (a store)
		あ(ける) あ(く) ひら(く)	開ける（あ） to open (something)　かぎを開ける（あ） to unlock 開く（あ） (something) opens　穴が開く（あな あ） a hole opens up 開く（ひら） to open (a book, eyes, etc.); to turn to (a page)
	to open		開開開開開開開開開開開開
198	閉	ヘイ	閉会式（へいかいしき） closing ceremony　閉店する（へいてん） to close (a store); (a store) closes
		し(める) し(まる) と(じる)	閉める（し） to close (something)　閉まる（し） (something) closes 閉じる（と） to close (a book, eyes, etc.)
	to close		閉閉閉閉閉閉閉閉閉閉閉
199	消	ショウ	消化する（しょうか） to digest　消費する（しょうひ） to consume　消防車（しょうぼうしゃ） fire engine
		け(す) き(える)	消す（け） to turn off (the lights, etc.); to erase; to delete (messages, etc.)　消しゴム（け） eraser 消える（き） (something) turns off/goes out
	to turn off; to disappear		消消消消消消消消消消
200	汚	オ	汚染（おせん） pollution
		きたな(い) よご(す) よご(れる)	汚い（きたな） dirty; messy 汚す（よご） to make (something) dirty　汚れる（よご） (something) becomes dirty
	dirty		汚汚汚汚汚汚
201	乗	ジョウ	乗車券（じょうしゃけん） ticket (for a train, a bus, etc.)　乗馬（じょうば） horseback riding
		の(る)	乗る（の） to get on; to ride　乗り遅れる（の おく） to miss (a train, a bus, etc.) 乗りかえる（の） to transfer (trains, buses, etc.)　乗り物（の もの） ride; vehicle
	to ride		乗乗乗乗乗乗乗乗乗
202	遅	チ	遅刻する（ちこく） to be late
		おく(れる) おそ(い)	遅れる（おく） to be late　乗り遅れる（の おく） to miss (a train, a bus, etc.) 遅い（おそ） slow; late　遅くなる（おそ） to become late/slow　夜遅く（よるおそ） late at night
	late		遅遅遅遅遅遅遅遅遅遅遅遅
203	困	コン	困難(な)（こんなん） difficult; troublesome
		こま(る)	困る（こま） to be in trouble; to have a hard time
	trouble		困困困困困困困

Lesson 14

204 運	運 運		
	ウン	運転する うんてん to drive	運動する うんどう to (get) exercise; to work out
		運転手 うんてんしゅ driver	運がいい うん lucky / 運が悪い うん わる unlucky
	はこ(ぶ)	運ぶ はこ to carry; to transport	
to transport; luck			

205 転	転 転		
	テン	運転する うんてん to drive	自転車 じてんしゃ bicycle; bike
		回転寿司 かいてんずし conveyor belt sushi	転校する てんこう to transfer to another school
	ころ(ぶ) ころ(がる)	転ぶ ころ to fall over; to trip	転がる ころ to roll
to rotate; to roll			

206 痛	痛 痛		
	ツウ	苦痛 くつう suffering; pain	頭痛 ずつう headache / 腹痛 ふくつう stomachache
	いた(い)	痛い いた painful; sore; to hurt; to ache	
pain			

207 医	医 医		
	イ	医者 いしゃ doctor [medical]	医学 いがく medical science / 医学部 いがくぶ medical school
		歯医者 はいしゃ dentist	
doctor; medicine			

208 者	者 者		
	シャ	医者 いしゃ doctor [medical] / 科学者 かがくしゃ scientist	学者 がくしゃ scholar / 記者 きしゃ reporter
		技術者 ぎじゅつしゃ engineer; technician / 研究者 けんきゅうしゃ researcher	作者 さくしゃ author; writer; creator
		読者 どくしゃ reader	歯医者 はいしゃ dentist
	もの	若者 わかもの young people	
person			

209 薬	薬 薬		
	ヤク ヤッ	薬学 やくがく pharmacology	薬局 やっきょく pharmacy
	くすり ぐすり	薬 くすり medicine; drug	風邪薬 かぜぐすり cold medicine
medicine			

210 服	服 服		
	フク	服 ふく clothes / 服装 ふくそう outfit; attire	制服 せいふく uniform
		洋服 ようふく Western-style clothes	和服 わふく Japanese-style clothes
clothing			

211	店 (店 店)	テン	店員（てんいん） sales clerk; shop staff　店長（てんちょう） store manager
			チェーン店（てん） chain store　売店（ばいてん） kiosk; stand　本店（ほんてん） main store; head office
		みせ	(お)店（みせ） shop; store; restaurant　店（みせ）をやる／する to run a shop
store		店店店店店店店店	
212	部 (部 部)	ブ	～部（ぶ） ... club (Ex. 野球部（やきゅうぶ） baseball club)　一部（いちぶ） part; portion
			学部（がくぶ） department [undergraduate university division]　全部（ぜんぶ） all　全部で（ぜんぶ） in total
			部員（ぶいん） club member　部長（ぶちょう） department head; club president　部分（ぶぶん） part; section
		へ	部屋（へや） room
part; section		部部部部部部部部部部部	
213	屋 (屋 屋)	オク	屋上（おくじょう） rooftop　屋内（おくない） indoors
		や	～屋（や） ... shop; ... store (Exs. 本屋（ほんや） bookstore, 花屋（はなや） flower shop)
			部屋（へや） room　屋根（やね） roof
roof; shop		屋屋屋屋屋屋屋屋屋	
214	教 (教 教)	キョウ	教会（きょうかい） church　教室（きょうしつ） classroom　教育（きょういく） education
			教科書（きょうかしょ） textbook　教授（きょうじゅ） professor　宗教（しゅうきょう） religion
		おし(える)	教える（おし） to teach; to tell
to teach		教教教教教教教教教教教	
215	室 (室 室)	シツ	教室（きょうしつ） classroom　温室（おんしつ） greenhouse　会議室（かいぎしつ） conference room
			研究室（けんきゅうしつ） (instructor's) office　地下室（ちかしつ） basement room
			待合室（まちあいしつ） waiting room　和室（わしつ） Japanese-style room
room		室室室室室室室室室	

新しい読み方

The following are new readings for kanji that you have already learned. Read each word aloud.

1) 入口（いりぐち）／入（い）り口（ぐち）　2) 出口（でぐち）　3) お化（ば）け　4) 最悪（さいあく）　5) 火（ひ）

習（なら）った漢字（かんじ）で書ける新しい単語（たんご）

The following are other new vocabulary in this lesson that contain kanji you have already leaned. Read each word aloud. (* indicates a word with a special reading.)

1) 思（おも）い出（で）　2) 自動（じどう）で　3) せきが出（で）る　4) 電気（でんき）　5) 二日（ふつか）よい*
6) 水（みず）を出（だ）す　7) 持（も）っていく

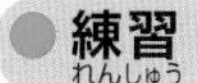

練習(れんしゅう)

1 Read the following words 1-13 aloud.

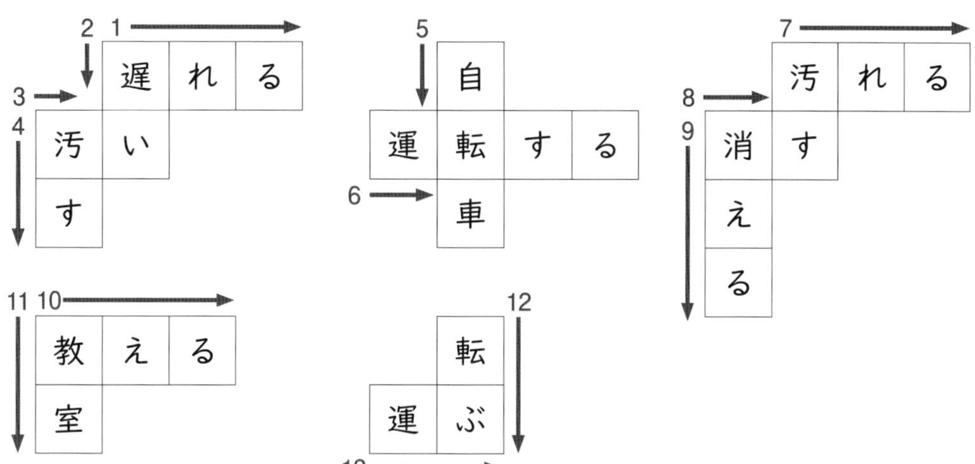

2 Complete sentences 1)-7) by selecting the most appropriate kanji word from a.-h. in the box below. First, conjugate the verb appropriately, then write the letter and reading of each kanji word in (　　).

a. 開ける　b. 閉まる　c. 消す　d. 運ぶ　e. 汚れる　f. 乗る　g. 遅れる　h. 困る

Ex. 毎日電車に（　f. のっ　）て、仕事に行きます。

1）いつも電気を（　　　　　）てから出かけます。

2）テーブルからピザが落(お)ちて、ゆかが（　　　　　）ました。

3）道が分からなくて（　　　　　）ている人がいたら、助(たす)けなくてはいけないと思う。

4）窓(まど)を（　　　　　）たら、鳥の声(こえ)が聞こえました。

5）友達が引(ひ)っこしをするから、荷物を（　　　　　）のを手伝(てつだ)いました。

6）レストランに晩(ばん)ご飯(はん)を食べに行ったけど、休みで（　　　　　）ていました。

7）今日は朝(あさ)ねぼうしたから、授業(じゅぎょう)に（　　　　　）ました。

3 Smith-san uploaded the following post on social media. Read his post aloud, then write the readings for the underlined words.

最悪の一日

今日は大変な一日だった。昨日の夜(よる)、遅く寝(ね)たから、朝(あさ)ねぼうしてしまった。走って駅(えき)に行く時に、自転車にぶつかって転んだ。とても痛かった。そして、電車に乗り遅れて、日本語の授業(じゅぎょう)に遅刻(ちこく)してしまった。授業(じゅぎょう)中、先生が文法(ぶんぽう)を教えている時に寝(ね)てしまった。授業(じゅぎょう)の後で、教室でコーヒーを飲んでいる時、コーヒーのカップを落(お)としてしまった。服が汚れてしまったから、すぐに家に帰った。部屋に帰ったら、ネコのタマが元気がなくて、週末に店で買った新しいえさ (feed) を全然(ぜんぜん)食べていなかった。だから、友達の車を運転して病院(びょういん)に連(つ)れていった。医者にもらった薬を飲んだから、明日は元気になるかなあ。今日は本当に最悪だった。

漢字(かんじ)の話 The Story of Kanji

■ Kanji readings with sequential voicing

By combining two words, such as 旅行(りょこう) and 会社(かいしゃ), you can make a new compound word, such as 旅行会社(りょこうがいしゃ) (travel agency). When a word is combined with another word, the initial sound of the second word frequently changes from a voiceless sound (the か-, さ-, た-, and は-lines) to its voiced counterpart (the が-, ざ-, だ-, and ば-lines), as shown in Exs.1-4 below. This phenomenon is called "sequential voicing." There are some exceptions, but this is a basic rule that you can memorize.

	Word 1		Word 2		New compound word
Ex.1	りょこう	+	かいしゃ	→	りょこうがいしゃ
Ex.2	てまき (hand-roll)	+	すし	→	てまきずし
Ex.3	ほん	+	たな (shelf)	→	ほんだな
Ex.4	ごみ	+	はこ (box)	→	ごみばこ

練習(れんしゅう)

Write the readings of the words below using the sound change rule explained above.

Ex. 手 ＋ 紙(かみ) → 手紙
[て] [てがみ]

1) 山 ＋ 田 → 山田(さん)
[ ] [ ] [ ]

2) 花 ＋ 火 → 花火
[ ] [ ] [ ]

3) アマゾン ＋ 川 → アマゾン川
[ ] [ ]

文法(ぶんぽう)

1 Transitive verbs and intransitive verbs

In general, there are two kinds of verbs, i.e., transitive verbs (Vt) and intransitive verbs (Vi).

[1-a]

Actor		Direct object		Transitive verb (Vt)
トムさん	は	ドア	を	閉(し)めました。
Tom closed the door.				

Transitive verbs (e.g., 閉(し)める, 食(た)べる, 起(お)こす) depict a situation in which someone/something (= Actor) acts to change the state of someone/something else (= Direct object). In [1-a], for example, 閉(し)める is a transitive verb, Tom is the actor, who acted upon the door, and the door is the direct object.

[1-b]

Undergoer of change		Intransitive verb (Vi)
ドア	が	閉(し)まりました。
The door closed.		

Intransitive verbs (e.g., 閉(し)まる, 歩(ある)く, 起(お)きる), on the other hand, depict a situation in which someone/something undergoes a change without acting on anything else; as such, an intransitive verb does not take a direct object. In [1-b], for example, 閉(し)まる is an intransitive verb, and what changes state is the door, which just closed and did not act on anything. Thus, there is no direct object in this sentence.

In English, in most cases, the same verb can be used both transitively and intransitively (e.g., "open," "close," "drop"). In Japanese, by contrast, transitive and intransitive meanings of a concept must almost always be expressed with separate verbs. As a result, there are a great number of transitive/intransitive verb pairs in Japanese.

The table below shows common transitive and intransitive pairs:

Transitive verb	Intransitive verb	Transitive verb	Intransitive verb
(～を) 開(あ)ける open something	(～が) 開(あ)く something opens	(～を) 閉(し)める close something	(～が) 閉(し)まる something closes
(～を) つける turn on something	(～が) つく something turns on	(～を) 消(け)す turn off something	(～が) 消(き)える something turns off
(～を) 入(い)れる put something (in something)	(～が) 入(はい)る someone/something enters (somewhere)	(～を) 出(だ)す take out something	(～が) 出(で)る someone/something comes out
(～を) こわす break something	(～が) こわれる something breaks	(～を) 汚(よご)す make something dirty	(～が) 汚(よご)れる something becomes dirty
(～を) 落(お)とす drop something	(～が) 落(お)ちる something drops	(～を) 止(と)める stop something	(～が) 止(と)まる something stops
(かぎを) かける lock something	(かぎが) かかる something gets locked	(お湯(ゆ)を) わかす boil (water)	(お湯(ゆ)が) わく (water) boils
(～を) 割(わ)る shatter something	(～が) 割(わ)れる something shatters	(～を) つなげる connect something	(～が) つながる something connects

Exs. (1) A: 電気をつけましょう (Vt)。 *Let's turn on the light.*

B: そのボタンを押したら、電気がつきますよ (Vi)。

When you press that button, the light will turn on.

(2) <車の中で>

右のドアが開かないから (Vi)、左のドアを開けて降りてください (Vt)。

The right-side door doesn't open, so please open the left-side door to get off (lit. please open the left-side door and get off).

(3) 母　：どうしておもちゃをこわしたの (Vt)？ *Why did you break your toy?*

子ども：こわしたんじゃないよ (Vt)。こわれたんだよ (Vi)。 *I didn't break it! It broke!*

2 Intransitive verb+ている [State resulting from change]

[2]

Subject		Vi-*te*	
窓	が	開いて	います。
The window is open.			

Using the *te*-form of an intransitive verb (Vi) and いる, you can describe the state of something/someone (X) as the result of a change that has happened to X. The intransitive verb here represents what has happened to X. For example, [2] means that the window opened at some point in the past, and that state of having opened remains the same at the moment of speech, as illustrated below. (See L6 #4-2.)

① At some point in the past something happened to X (= 窓).

② At the moment of speech, the state of X (= 窓) resulting from ① remains the same.

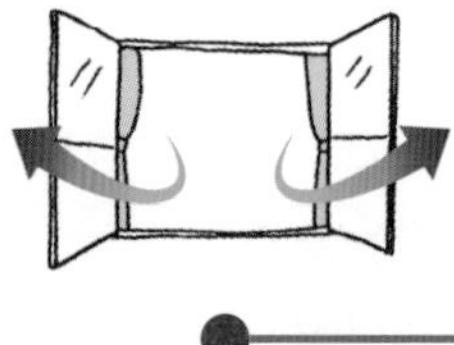

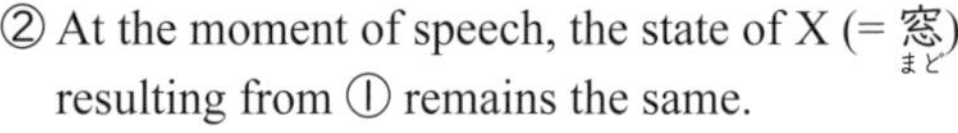

窓が開いた。 *The window opened.*

窓が開いている。 *The window is open.*

Exs. (1) 家の前に車が止まっています。誰が止めたんですか。

A car is parked in front of the house. Who parked it?

(2) 今、スマホがこわれているから、何もできません。

Because my smartphone is broken, I cannot do anything right now.

(3) 人がたくさん入っているレストランはたいてい安くておいしいです。

The restaurants with lots of people in them (lit. where many people have entered and stay there) are usually cheap and delicious.

☞ GID (vol.1): E. Auxiliaries 2. (V-*te*) いる

3 Transitive verb + てある [State resulting from purposeful action] 

[3]

Subject		Vt-*te*	
窓(まど)	が	開(あ)けて	あります。
The window has been opened (for a certain purpose).			

Using the *te*-form of a transitive verb (Vt) and ある, you can describe the state of something as the result of an action taken by someone for some purpose. For example, [3] describes the state of the window, which was opened by someone at some point in the past for some purpose (e.g., in order to let fresh air in).

Note that [2] (Viている sentence) and [3] (Vtてある sentence) are similar but not identical in meaning. The difference between the two is that [2] simply describes the state of the window, whereas [3] not only describes the state of the window but also implies that there is someone's intention behind that state.

① At one point in the past, someone did something to X (= 窓(まど)) for some purpose.

② At the moment of speech, the state of X (= 窓(まど)) resulting from the action in ① remains the same.

誰(だれ)かが窓(まど)を開(あ)けた。*Someone opened the window.*

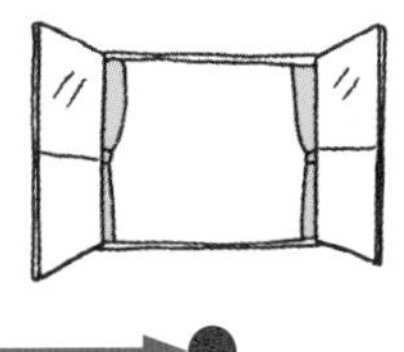

窓(まど)が開(あ)けてある。*The window has been opened.*

In this sentence structure, the actor is not mentioned explicitly. Instead, the direct object of the transitive verb is presented as the subject or the topic.

Note that V-*te*ある is not used just with transitive verbs that have intransitive counterparts. In fact, this construction is often used with transitive verbs that have no corresponding intransitive verbs, as in (2) and (3).

Exs. (1) A: あ、オーブンがついているよ。*Oh, the oven is on.*

B: つけてあるんだ。今(いま)からケーキを焼(や)くから。

It's been turned on. [It's because] I'm baking a cake now.

(2) 先生(せんせい)：この宿題(しゅくだい)は誰(だれ)のですか。名前(なまえ)が書(か)いてありませんよ。

Whose homework is this? There's no name [written] on it.

(3) <パーティーの前(まえ)に>

A: あれ？ ピザは？ *Huh? Where's the pizza?*

B: もう注文(ちゅうもん)してあるから、もうすぐ来(く)るよ。*It's been ordered, so it'll come soon.*

In some situations, もう occurs with V-*te*ある, as in (3)-B.

☞ GID (vol.2): C. Auxiliaries 2. V-*te*おく vs. V-*te*ある

4 ～てしまう "V (to one's regret); finish V-ing" できるII

[4-a]

	V-te	
日本語のクラスに	遅れて	しまいました。
I was late for Japanese class (to my regret).		

You can express your regret or disappointment that something has been done using the past form of V-*te*しまう, as in [4-a]. Although it is not as common as the past form, the non-past form can also be used, as in (3).

Exs. (1) 今日のミーティングの時間を忘れてしまいました。
I forgot the time of the meeting today (to my regret).

(2) 今日のテストでたくさん間違えてしまったから、次はもっと勉強しておきます。
Because I made a lot of mistakes on today's test, I will study harder next time.

(3) 私はいつも日本語の「ビル」と「ビール」を間違えて、「ビルを飲む」と言ってしまいます。
I always mix up ビル (building) and ビール (beer) in Japanese and say "ビルを飲む" (to my regret).

⚠ Note that the past form of V-*te*しまう conveys a feeling of regret or disappointment that a certain action has been done. Therefore, when you regret that something has not been done, this form cannot be used. The following sentence, for example, is ungrammatical:

× 宿題をしなくてしまいました／しないでしまいました。

→ 宿題をすればよかったです。*I wish I had done my homework.*

(More about ～ばよかった in L16 #4-2.)

In casual speech, the contracted forms ～ちゃう／じゃう are often used.

Regular form	Contracted form
（言っ）てしまう／（言っ）てしまった	（言っ）ちゃう／（言っ）ちゃった
（読ん）でしまう／（読ん）でしまった	（読ん）じゃう／（読ん）じゃった

Exs. (4) あ、もうすぐ8時になっちゃう。早く帰ろう。
Oh, it's almost 8 o'clock, unfortunately. Let's go home now.

(5) A: あれ？ 私の牛乳がない。*That's weird. I can't find my milk.*
B: ごめん、今朝飲んじゃった。*Sorry, I drank it this morning.*

[4-b]

	V-te	
論文を全部	書いて	しまいました。
I finished writing all (the sections) of my (academic) paper.		

V-*te*しまう can also be used to express the idea that an action has been completely finished, as in [4-b].

Ex. (6) もう宿題をしてしまったから、どこかに遊びに行きませんか。
I already finished my homework, so would you like to go out somewhere?

The original meaning of V-*te*しまう is that an action is irrevocable, i.e., that you cannot get back to the state of affairs that existed before the action was complete. The two uses of V-*te*しまう introduced above have both been derived from this original meaning.

5 ～かもしれない [Uncertainty; possibility] "may; might; it is possible that ~"

[5]

S-plain	
リサさんはパーティーに来(こ)ない	かもしれません。
Lisa may not come to the party.	

You can express uncertainty or possibility using ～かもしれない. Sentences before かもしれない are always in the plain form except when the predicate is a *na*-adjective or a noun, in which case だ does not appear. Thus, the following sentence is ungrammatical:

× 上田(うえだ)さんは{魚(さかな)がきらい／大学院生(だいがくいんせい)}だかもしれません。

→ 上田(うえだ)さんは{魚(さかな)がきらい／大学院生(だいがくいんせい)}ø かもしれません。

Ueda-san might {not like fish / be a graduate student}.

Exs. (1) 今日(きょう)はすごく寒(さむ)いから、雪(ゆき)が降(ふ)るかもしれません。*It's very cold today, so it might snow.*

(2) 少(すこ)し熱(ねつ)があります。かぜをひいたかもしれません。

I have a little fever. I might have caught a cold.

(3) A: このプロジェクトは前(まえ)のより大変(たいへん)かもしれないね。

This project might be tougher than the previous one.

B: うん。でも、やってみたら楽(たの)しいかもしれないよ。がんばろう。

Yeah. But it might be fun once we take it on. Let's try our best.

☞ **GID** (vol.2): E. Special topics 7. Adj(*na*)/Nだ: Why does だ drop in some situations?

6 ～すぎる "too Adj; V too much/many (N)"

[6-a]

	Adj(*i*)-stem	
この車(くるま)は	高(たか)	すぎます。
This car is too expensive.		

[6-b]

	Adj(*na*)	
ワンさんは	まじめ	すぎます。
Wang-san is too serious.		

[6-c]

	V-*masu*	
コーラを	飲(の)み	すぎました。
I drank too much cola.		

You can express the idea that someone/something is excessive in degree, amount, etc. by attaching the auxiliary verb すぎる to the end of an *i*-adjective stem or a *na*-adjective dictionary form, as in [6-a] and [6-b]. You can also express the idea that someone does something excessively by using V-*masu*すぎる, as in [6-c].

Exs. (1) この食堂の料理はまずすぎます。*The food at this cafeteria is too gross.*

(2) このゲームは簡単すぎます。*This game is too easy.*

すぎる is a *ru*-verb, so its plain non-past negative form is すぎない, its plain past affirmative form is すぎた, and its *te*-form is すぎて.

Exs. (3) <美容院で> 後ろの髪を少し切ってください。あ、でも切りすぎないでください。

Please trim the hair in back a little. Oh, but don't cut it too much.

(4) 昨日のテストは難しすぎたから、全然分かりませんでした。

Yesterday's test was too difficult, so I didn't understand it at all.

(5) 圭太さんが作ったたこ焼きがとてもおいしかったから、食べすぎてしまいました。

The takoyaki *Keita made was very tasty, so I ate too much of it (which is regrettable).*

(6) 週末カレーを作りすぎたから、今週は毎日カレーを食べています。

I made too much curry over the weekend, so I have beeen eating it every day this week.

[6-d]

		V-*nai*		
山田さんは	最近のニュースを	知ら	なさ	すぎます。
Yamada-san knows too little about recent news.				

すぎる can be used with the negative forms of verbs and adjectives. In this case, the negative ending ない changes to なさ before すぎる, as in [6-d].

Ex. (7) あの先生の授業はおもしろくなさすぎます。*That teacher's class is too uninteresting.*

7 S_1し、S_2し [Multiple reasons] "S_1 and S_2, so"

[7]

Topic	S_1 (reason 1)		S_2 (reason 2)		S_3 (main clause)
今のアパートは	家賃が安い	し、	大学にも近い	し、	とてもいいです。
My current apartment offers cheap rent and is close to the university, too, so it's very good.					

You can present multiple reasons using ～し. S_1 and S_2 are commonly in the plain form. The particle も often occurs in S_2.

Exs. (1) このレストランは安いし、メニューもたくさんあるし、人気があります。

This restaurant is cheap and has a lot on its menu, too, so it is popular.

(2) 夏休みは山でキャンプをしたし、海にも行ったし、楽しかったです。

I went camping in the mountains and also went to the beach, so my summer break was fun.

(3) このアプリは便利だし、ただだし、おすすめですよ。

This app is convenient and free of charge, so I recommend it.

In some situations, S_3 is not said or is left partially unsaid, as in (4)-B below.

Ex. (4) A: 今日、一緒に晩ご飯を食べに行かない？
Would you like to go out to dinner with me tonight?

B: ごめん。今日はアルバイトがあるし、お金もないし、ちょっと…
Sorry. I've got to go to my part-time job today and have no money, so... (I can't.)

In conversation, "S_1し、S_2し" sometimes occurs after S_3, as in (5).

Ex. (5) 今のアパートはとてもいいです。家賃が安いし、大学にも近いし。(cf. [7])
My current apartment is very good. It offers low rent and is close to the university, too.

When "S_1し、S_2し" presents multiple reasons, the last し can be replaced by から, as in (6).

Ex. (6) このレストランは安いし、メニューもたくさんあるから、人気があります。(cf. (1))
This restaurant is cheap and has a lot on its menu, too, so it is popular.

See the GID for uses of し other than presenting multiple reasons.

☞ GID (vol.2): D. Sentence patterns 3. S_1し、S_2し

8 ～てほしい "want (someone) to V"

[8-a]

	Actor			V-*te*	
私は	トムさん	に	明日のパーティーに	来て	ほしいです。
I want Tom to come to the party tomorrow.					

You can express the idea that you want someone to do something using V-*te*ほしい. In this sentence construction, the actor whom the speaker wants to do something is marked by に.

[8-b]

	Actor			V-*nai*		
私は	リサさん	に	あまり	心配し	ないで	ほしいです。
I don't want Lisa to worry too much. (lit. I want Lisa not to worry too much.)						

When you want to say that you don't want someone to do something, you use V-*nai*ないでほしい, as in [8-b].

Exs. (1) 私はルームメートに自分の皿を洗ってほしいです。それから、リビングで寝ないでほしいです。
I want my roommate to wash his dishes. And I don't want him to sleep in the living room.

(2) 子どもの時、私は母にディズニーランドに連れていってほしかったです。
When I was a child, I wanted my mother to take me to Disneyland.

(3) 私は海をきれいにするボランティアをしています。みんなにごみの問題を知ってほしいです。それから、プラスチックを使いすぎないでほしいです。
I do ocean cleanup volunteer work. I want everyone to know about the litter issue and don't want them to use too much plastic.

V-*te*ほしいんですが can be used to make a request indirectly, as in (4) below:

Ex. (4) A: あの、すみません。ちょっと手伝(てつだ)っ<u>てほしいんですが</u>…

Um, excuse me. Could you give me a bit of help? (lit. I'd like you to help me a little, but...)

B: ええ、いいですよ。*Yes, sure.*

⚠ ～てほしい should not be confused with ～たい. ～たい is used when the speaker himself/herself wants to do something, whereas ～てほしい is used when the speaker wants someone else to do something. (See L7 #5 ～たい.) Compare the following sentences:

Exs. (5) a. 私(わたし)は研(けん)さんと一緒(いっしょ)にゲームがし<u>たい</u>です。*I want to play games with Ken.*

b. 私(わたし)は研(けん)さんに一緒(いっしょ)にゲームをし<u>てほしい</u>です。*I want Ken to play games with me.*

9 ～たらどうですか [Suggestion] "How about V-ing?; Why don't you V?"

[9]

	V-plain.past		
田中(たなか)さんに	聞(き)いた	ら	どうですか。
How about asking Tanaka-san? (lit. How is it if you ask Tanaka-san?)			

You can make a suggestion using たら (L12 #4) with どうですか.

Exs. (1) A: おなかが痛(いた)いんです。*My stomach hurts.*

B: だいじょうぶですか。ちょっとそこで休(やす)ん<u>だらどうですか</u>。

Are you okay? Why don't you rest over there for a bit?

(2) A: 今晩(こんばん)、田中(たなか)さんとデートするんだ。*I'm going out on a date with Tanaka-san tonight.*

B: じゃ「ラ・ポルタ」というレストランに行(い)っ<u>たらどう</u>？　とてもおいしいよ。

Why don't you go to the restaurant called La Porta, then? It's really good (lit. tasty).

(3) A: 漢字(かんじ)が覚(おぼ)えられないんです。{どうしたらいいですか／どうしたらいいと思(おも)いますか}。*I cannot memorize kanji. {What should I do? / What do you think I should do?}*

B: じゃ、このアプリを使(つか)ってみ<u>たらどうですか</u>。

Well, why don't you try using this app?

～たらどうですか is not used with negative sentences. Thus, the following sentence is not grammatical:

× パーティーに行(い)かなかっ<u>たらどう</u>ですか。**Intended meaning:** *How about not going to the party?*

→ パーティーに行(い)くのをやめたらどうですか。*Why don't you forget about going to the party?*

話しましょう

Activities

▶ **Words written in purple** are new words introduced in this lesson.

できる I　Describe the state of things and places in detail.

できるI-A　Transitive and intransitive verbs

1 Describe the following pictures using transitive or intransitive verbs.  L14-6

Ex.1 ドアを開(あ)けます。　**Ex.2** ドアが開(あ)きます。

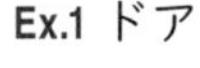 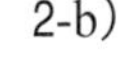

Ex.1 ドア　Ex.2　1-a) ドア　1-b)　2-a) 電気　2-b)

 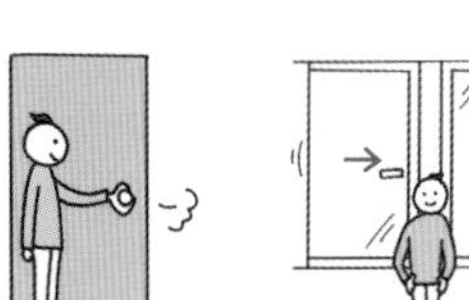   

3-a) 服(ふく)　3-b)　4-a) かぎ　4-b)　5-a) アイスクリーム　5-b)

  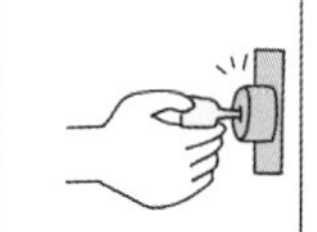   

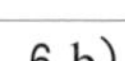 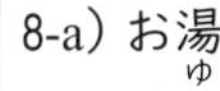 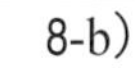

6-a) スマホ　6-b)　7-a) お皿(さら)　7-b)　8-a) お湯(ゆ)　8-b)

2 Oh, no! You are right in the middle of a huge typhoon.

Step 1 Tweet about what has happened outside. L14-7

Ex. antenna / fall → あ！　アンテナが落(お)ちました！

1) umbrella / break　2) window / shatter

3) train / stop　4) light / off

5) your own

Step 2 After the typhoon, your landlord has come over to check on things in your room. Take turns with your partner and go over the problems together as in the example. L14-8

Ex. water / run

Landlord: 水を出してみてください。

You　　: はい。あ！　水が出ません。(← Respond that it does not work.)

1) window / open　2) window / lock　3) TV / turn on　4) Wi-Fi / connect　5) light / turn on

3 Suppose you live in a smart house, but your partner does not. Take turns describing what happens or what you do on certain occasions in your respective houses.

Possible topics 電気　窓(まど)　ドア　カーテン　ブラインド　かぎ　テレビ　お湯(ゆ)　水

Ex. A: 私の家はスマートハウスだから、自動で電気がつきます。

B: いいですね。私は自分で電気を {つけます／つけなくてはいけません}。

できるI-B State resulting from change Viている

1 Practice describing the state of things around you.

Step 1 Describe the state of the following things. L14-9

Ex. 窓(まど)が開(あ)いています。

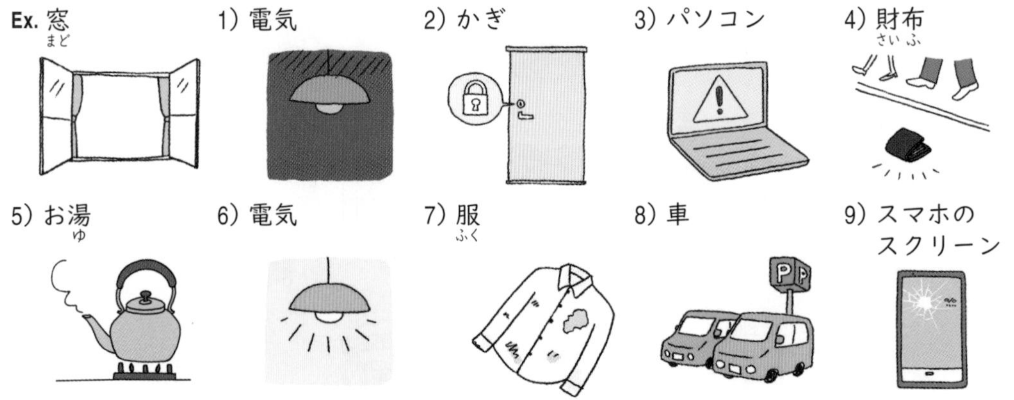

Step 2 Describe the state of things in your room or classroom.

Possible topics 窓(まど)　カーテン／ブラインド　ドア　プロジェクター　電気　ゆか　ごみ

2 Suppose your parents are coming over to your apartment in 30 minutes but you are not ready. Ask your roommate for help. L14-10

Ex. A: すみません、時計が止まっているから、直(なお)してくれませんか。

B: はい、分かりました。直(なお)します。

3 Suppose you live in an apartment named とびらアパート. Your neighbor's room, 201, was broken into.

Step 1 Report what happened to the police.

Role A You are a police officer. Ask the caller (your partner) questions and fill in Picture A with drawings/notes based on the responses you receive.

Role B You have just encountered the situation depicted in Picture B. (See p.155.) Call the police and report what you see.

Picture A

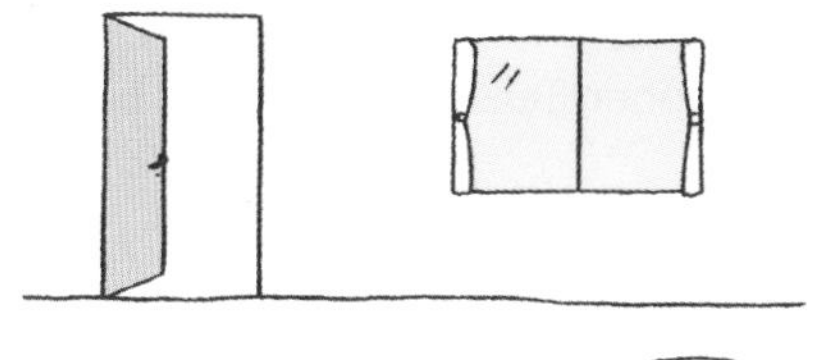

Ex. A: はい、警察(けいさつ)です。

B: 大変です！　あの、「とびらアパート」の201の部屋(へや)で人がたおれて (to fall over) います。

A: そうですか。部屋(へや)についてもう少(すこ)し教(おし)えてください。

B: はい。えっと、ドアが開(あ)いています。それから… <Continue>

Role B ➡p.155

Step 2 Now, both of you are police officers on the scene. Make some logical inferences based on what you see in Picture B on p.155.

Ex. A: ドアが開(あ)いているから、犯人(はんにん) (criminal) はドアから外に出たみたいです。

B: そうですね。{でも／それから}、窓(まど)が… <Continue>

できるI-C State resulting from purposeful action Vtてある

1 Suppose you are visiting Japan. Describe the state of the things you encounter on the street using the words in the box with ～てある。 L14-11

Useful vocabulary	書く	はる	かざる	置(お)く	出す

Ex. かべにメニューが {書いて／はって} あります。

Ex. かべ／メニュー

1) 看板(かんばん)／店(みせ)の行き方

2) 駅(えき)／大きいポスター

写真：Rodrigo Reyes Marin/アフロ

3) 新しい店(みせ)の前／きれいな花

4) 店(みせ)／「招(ま)き猫(ねこ)」というネコ

5) レストランの前／ランチの見本(みほん) (sample)

6) ラーメン屋(や)のテーブル／箸(はし)やしょうゆ

7) 温泉(おんせん)のかべ／富士山(ふじさん)の絵

2 You have prepared dinner for your roommate, who is not home yet.

Step 1 Describe the state of things based on the cues provided, as shown in the examples.

Ex.1 ○サラダを作った → サラダが作ってあります。

Ex.2 ×サラダにドレッシングをかけた → サラダにドレッシングはかけてありません。

1) ○カレーを作った　2) ○テーブルに皿(さら)を出した　3) ○コーラを冷蔵庫(れいぞうこ)に入れた

4) ○ケーキを買った　5) ○果物(くだもの)を冷(ひ)やした　6) ×サラダにチーズをのせた

7) ×ケーキを切った　8) ×果物(くだもの)を洗(あら)った

Step 2 Your roommate comes back after you have finished dinner. Tell them what has been done.

Ex.1 A: サラダが作ってあるから、食べてください。

B: はい、ありがとうございます。

Ex.2 A: サラダにドレッシングはかけてないから、食べる前にかけてください。

B: はい、分かりました。

3 Suppose you have noticed something unusual in the Japan House. Talk to Tao (= your partner) about it, and she will explain the reason for it.

Ex. あなた：あれ？　テーブルの上に牛乳(ぎゅうにゅう)が出ていますよ。

タオ　：あ、出してあるんです。後でパンケーキを作るから…

Ex. milk / out on the table　1) windows / open　2) TV / off

3) oven（オーブン）/ on　4) cake / in the refrigerator　5) water / boiled　6) your own

Ask and answer questions about troubles someone is having.

できるII-A Regret ～てしまう

1 Let's practice talking about regrettable or disappointing situations. Describe the unfortunate occurrences that happened to you today based on the cues provided. L14-13

Ex. 朝(あさ)ねぼうしてしまいました。

Ex. 朝(あさ)ねぼうする　1) バスに乗(の)り遅(おく)れる　2) 教室(きょうしつ)を間違(まちが)える　3) 宿題(しゅくだい)をやるのを忘(わす)れる

4) データがなくなる　5) けがをする　6) スマホがこわれる　7) your own

2 Talk about your own regret or disappointment with your partner.

Ex. A: はあ～ (sigh)。

B: 元気がないですね。

A: 昨日、スマホがこわれてしまいました。

B: え、それは大変ですね。データはだいじょうぶでしたか。(← Follow-up question)

<Continue>

3 Have you ever made a mistake mixing up two different words?

Step 1 Recall some words you always mix up with each other.

Ex. 日本語の「野菜(やさい)」と「やさしい」は似(に)ています。

Step 2 Share your experience involving those words with your partner.

Ex. A: 日本語の言葉(ことば)を間違(まちが)えたことがありますか。

B: はい、あります。「野菜(やさい)」と「やさしい」を間違(まちが)えて、「私の母は野菜(やさい)です」と言ってしまいました。

A: え、お母さんは野菜(やさい)？　おもしろいですね。私は…　<Continue>

4 Practice showing your regret or disappointment casually using ～ちゃった.

Step 1 Practice conjugating verbs into ～てしまった then into ～ちゃった. L14-14

Ex. 食(た)べる → 食(た)べてしまった → 食(た)べちゃった

1) 寝(ね)る	2) 忘(わす)れる	3) 行(い)く	4) 飲(の)む	5) する
6) 来(く)る	7) 乗(の)り遅(おく)れる	8) 間違(まちが)える	9) 汚(よご)れる	10) 消(き)える
11) 転(ころ)ぶ	12) こわす	13) ぶつかる	14) けがをする	15) 朝(あさ)ねぼうする

Step 2 Now, describe the happenings described in できるII-A-1 in casual speech. L14-15

Ex. 朝(あさ)ねぼうしちゃった。

5 Oops! Something unfortunate has just happened to you. Describe your regret or disappointment to your partner.

Ex. A: あっ！

B: どうしたの？

A: 今日の宿題(しゅくだい)、忘(わす)れちゃった。

B: え、本当？

できるⅡ-B Uncertainty and possibility ～かもしれない

1 Let's practice ～かもしれません conjugations as in the example. L14-16

Ex. 行く

	affirmative	negative
non-past	行くかもしれません	行かないかもしれません
past	行ったかもしれません	行かなかったかもしれません

1) できる　2) ある　3) なる　4) する　5) 来る　6) 住んでいる　7) 安い
8) おもしろい　9) 静か　10) 便利　11) 学生　12) 休み　13) 間違える　14) なくす
15) けがをする　16) こわれている　17) くさい　18) アレルギー

2 Suppose you live in the Japan House. It seems like you are the only one at home today, and you don't know where the other members are. Speculate on their whereabouts and/or circumstances. L14-17

Ex.1 リーマン／図書館にいます → リーマンさんは図書館にいるかもしれません。
Ex.2 リーマン／部屋にいません → リーマンさんは部屋にいないかもしれません。

1) マーク／今、友達と勉強しています
2) マーク／今日は家に帰りません
3) 圭太／剣道の練習に行きました
4) 圭太／帰る時、バスに乗り遅れました
5) リーマン／私に連絡できませんでした
6) にゃんた／今、とてもさびしいです
7) タオ／ボランティアの仕事が大変です
8) タオ／今、ボランティア中です

3 Suppose you are preparing to go camping with your partner. Considering all possibilities, discuss how you should prepare.

Ex. 朝と夜は寒いです
A: 朝と夜は寒いかもしれませんね。
B: ええ、セーターを持っていきましょう。
or かばんにセーターを入れておきましょう。

1) 近くにコンビニがありません　2) 虫が多いです　3) 毎日雨です
4) 夜はひまです　5) たくさん歩かなくてはいけません　6) your own

4 Suppose you are talking with your partner about a classmate who looks happy, sad, etc. Guess what happened to them.

Ex. A: ○○さん、スミスさんは今日うれしそうですね。
B: そうですね。テストがよくできたかもしれませんね。
A: そうかもしれませんね。それから、スミスさんは…

<Continue>

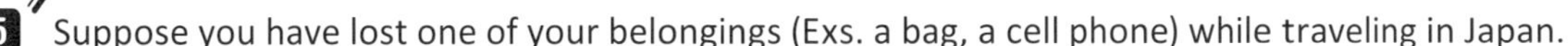

ROLE PLAY

5 Suppose you have lost one of your belongings (Exs. a bag, a cell phone) while traveling in Japan.

Role A You are working at the lost and found at a train station. Ask the questions on the checklist below to the owner of the lost belonging.

Role B You are now talking with a station attendant. Answer the attendant's questions.

Lesson 14

Questions:

- What does the belonging look like?
- What is in the belonging?
- Where did the owner lose it? etc.

Ex. A: どうしましたか。

B: あの、かばんをなくしてしまったんですが…

A: そうですか。えっと、どんなかばんですか。

B: 大きくて青(あお)いかばんです。英語で South Face と書いてあります。

A: そうですか。かばんの中に何が入っていますか。

B: えっと、財布(さいふ)や薬(くすり)が入っています。

A: どこでなくしましたか。

B: 分かりません。東京駅(えき)のトイレかもしれません。

A: <Looking at a monitor> あ、今、東京駅(えき)にありますよ。

B: そうですか、よかったです。ありがとうございます。

できるII-C ～すぎる

1 First, practice using the expression ～すぎる with adjectives. Describe the various conditions at the dorm you live in that you find excessive. L14-18

Ex. 部屋(へや)／せまい → 部屋(へや)がせますぎます。

1) トイレ／くさい　2) リビング／汚(きたな)い　3) ルール／多(おお)い　4) ご飯(はん)／まずい

5) となりの部屋(へや)の人／うるさい　6) ルームメート／まじめ　7) 寮(りょう)の生活(せいかつ)／大変

8) your own

2 Now, practice using the expression ～すぎる with verbs. Say what you and the Japan House members did too much of yesterday. L14-19

Ex. 圭太(けいた)／剣道(けんどう)の練習(れんしゅう)をする

→ 圭太(けいた)さんは昨日、剣道(けんどう)の練習(れんしゅう)をしすぎました。

1) タオ／カラオケで歌(うた)う　2) リーマン／数学(すうがく)について話す

3) アイ／ネットの動画を見る　4) マーク／将来(しょうらい)について考(かんが)える

5) にゃんた／your own　6) 私／your own

3 Talk to your partner about your frustration with something you find excessive.

Possible topics	アルバイト	町	大学	○○の授業(じゅぎょう)	ルームメート	寮(りょう)

Ex. A: 私のアルバイトは最悪(さいあく)です。

B: え、どうしてですか。

A: 毎日忙(いそが)しすぎるんです。一日に８時間も働かなくてはいけません。

B: え、大変ですね。どんなアルバイトをしているんですか。(← Follow-up question)

<Continue>

できるⅡ-D Describing physical conditions

1 Let's practice using expressions for common health problems.

Step 1 Explain your physical condition based on the cues provided. L14-20

Ex. 熱(ねつ)があります。

Ex. 

1) 

2) 

3) 

4) 

5) feel unwell 

6) caught a cold 

7) got injured 

Step 2 You don't feel well today. Using the cues in Step 1, describe your symptoms to your teacher and ask for permission to miss class, go home, etc.

Ex. あなた：あの、先生、実(じつ)はおとといから熱(ねつ)があって、せきが出るんです。
今日は単語(たんご)テストの後で帰ってもいいですか。

先生　：それは大変ですね。いいですよ。お大事に。

2 You are not feeling well today because you did too much of something yesterday.

Step 1 Explain each of your symptoms listed below along with a cause you come up with.

Ex. のどが痛(いた)い → 昨日カラオケで歌(うた)いすぎたから、のどが痛(いた)いです。

1) 二日よい　2) つかれている　3) おなかが痛(いた)い　4) ○○が痛(いた)い　5) your own

Step 2 Using the cues in Step 1, talk about your situation casually with your friend.

Ex. A: あれ？　元気がないね。どうしたの？

B: 実(じつ)は、昨日カラオケで歌(うた)いすぎたから、のどが痛(いた)いんだ。

A: だいじょうぶ？　何時間ぐらい歌(うた)ったの？

<Continue>

3 Suppose you are doing a homestay in Japan and you don't feel well today. Express your physical condition to your host mother.

Lead-in sentence
Physical symptom
Possible cause

Ex. A: お母さん、ちょっといいですか。
B: うん、どうしたの？
A: ちょっとおなかが痛(いた)いんですけど…
B: え、だいじょうぶ？
A: 昨日の夜(よる)、冷(つめ)たい物を食べすぎてしまったかもしれません。今日は学校を休もうと思います。
B: 分かった。じゃ、後で部屋(へや)に薬(くすり)を持っていくね。

できる III Ask for and give suggestions about familiar topics.

できるIII-A Multiple reasons S_1し、S_2し

1 Let's review plain forms and practice using them with ～し。 L14-21

Ex. 行(い)く

1) がんばる　2) ある　3) 高(たか)い　4) 便利(べんり)　5) きらい　6) 雨(あめ)
7) 日曜日(にちようび)　8) 間違(まちが)える　9) 食(た)べすぎる　10) くさい　11) 性格(せいかく)がいい　12) アレルギー

2 Using the cues provided, add multiple reasons to each statement in the speech bubbles. L14-22

Ex. 新しいです／大学に近(ちか)いです
新しいし、大学に近(ちか)いし、「アルン」というカフェはいいですよ。

1) 安いです／きれいな店(みせ)です　2) おいしいコーヒーが飲めます／いつも静(しず)かです

3) 果物(くだもの)がおいしかったです／海がきれいでした
4) ハワイに行くのは夢(ゆめ)でした／いい思い出ができました
5) リラックスできました／仕事をしなくてもよかったです

先週は大変でした。

6) 休みがありませんでした／友達に会えませんでした

7) 忙しすぎました／かぜをひいてしまいました

8) 毎日夜遅くまで働きました／朝早く起きなくてはいけませんでした　9) your own

Group Work

3 Exchange recommendations for places, classes, etc. with your classmates. Make sure to give multiple reasons for each recommendation.

Possible topics	スーパー	カフェ	授業	旅行先 (travel destination)	バンド／歌手

Ex. A: あのう、おすすめのスーパーがありますか。

B:「ケロガー」というスーパーがいいですよ。値段が安いし、あまり混んでいないし、おすすめです。

C: 私のおすすめは「メイヤー」です。先週、めずらしい果物を売っていたし、肉も安かったし。

A: そうですか。じゃ、ケロガーとメイヤーに行ってみようと思います。

4 Invite your partner to do an activity together. Your partner will decline your invitation for multiple reasons. Try to convince your partner to join you with reasons of your own.

Invite	**Ex.** A: 今日、晩ご飯食べに行かない？
Decline with reasons	B: え、今日？　うーん、ごめん。今日は漢字の宿題をしなくてはいけないし、お金もないし、ちょっと…
Convince with reasons	A: そっか。でも、宿題は明日してもいいし、安いレストランもあるし、行かない？
Accept/Decline	B: そうだね。じゃ、行くよ。or うーん、ちょっと…

できるⅢ-B　～てほしい

1 Let's practice using the expression ～てほしい in the affirmative and negative forms. L14-23

Ex. 行く → 行ってほしい → 行かないでほしい

1) 言う　2) 話す　3) がんばる　4) 教える　5) 心配する　6) 安くする
7) 連れてくる　8) かぎをかける　9) あきらめる　10) 消す　11) 連絡する

2 Talk about what you want people to do and not to do.

Step 1 You live in the Japan House. Say what you want the members to do or not to do. L14-24

Ex. 私はタオさんにマレーシアの料理を作ってほしいです。

でも、私がきらいな野菜(やさい)を使わないでほしいです。

Ex. タオ　：○マレーシアの料理を作る　×私がきらいな野菜(やさい)を使う

1) 圭太(けいた)　：○剣道(けんどう)をがんばる　×けがをする

2) にゃんた：○もっと動く　×やせすぎる

3) リーマン：○数学(すうがく)を教(おし)える　×難(むずか)しい説明(せつめい)をする

4) マーク　：○留学(りゅうがく)のアドバイスをする　×私のことを心配する

Step 2 Talk about a family member or friend of yours. What do you want them to do or not to do?

Ex. A: 私は父に毎日もっと歩(ある)いてほしいです。

B: そうですか。どうしてですか。

A: 父は甘(あま)い物が好きだし、全然運動(ぜんぜんうんどう)しないからです。それから父に…　<Continue>

Group Work

3 Is there anything you would like to suggest to a company, university, etc?

Possible topics	レストラン	私の大学の{寮(りょう)／食堂(しょくどう)}	ゲーム	町	映画	アニメ

Step 1 Choose a topic and brainstorm its issue(s) with your groupmates.

・トピックは？　・誰(だれ)に何を{してほしい／しないでほしい}？

Step 2 Make a presentation based on your discussion in Step 1. See which group can gain the most agreement from the rest of the class.

Ex. 「モンスター」というゲームは最近(さいきん)つまらなすぎるし、値段(ねだん)も高すぎるし、よくないと思います。だから、私達はゲームを作る人にもっとクエストをおもしろくしてほしいです。それから、値段(ねだん)を高くしないでほしいです。

4 Practice asking your partner for help.

Useful vocabulary	貸(か)す	作る	連(つ)れていく	紹介(しょうかい)する	一緒(いっしょ)に○○する

Lead-in sentence	**Ex.** A: ごめん、ちょっとお願(ねが)いがあるんだけど… B: 何？
Request + reasons	A: ちょっと自転車(じてんしゃ)を貸(か)してほしいんだけど… 牛乳(ぎゅうにゅう)がないし、お菓子(かし)も買いたいし、コンビニに行きたいんだ。 B: うん、いいよ。

できるⅢ-C Suggestion ～たらどうですか

1 Let's practice using the expression ～たらどうですか. First, change the verbs below into their plain past forms, then form the ～たらどうですか construction with them. L14-25

Ex. 聞く → 聞いた → 聞いたらどうですか

1) 寝る　2) 休む　3) 入る　4) やってみる　5) 買っておく
6) 相談する　7) 来る　8) あきらめる　9) 持っていく　10) ボランティアをする

2 Give some suggestions to the people below. Don't forget to make an empathetic comment before providing your suggestion. L14-26

Ex. A: 気分が悪いんです。

B: え、だいじょうぶですか。（← Comment）

このいすに座って休んだらどうですか。

気分が悪いんです。

お金が
ないんです。

みんなを幸せに
したいんです。

Ex. sit on this chair and take a rest	4) start a part-time job	8) try volunteering
1) be absent from today's class	5) bring a boxed lunch to school	9) teach kids Japanese
2) drink a lot of water	6) sell your ○○	10) become a ○○
3) your own	7) your own	11) your own

3 Your parter is worried about something. Give them a suggestion, and provide reasons for your suggestion.

Possible topics			
	最近寝られない	友達ができない	毎日つまらない
	成績が悪い	前に付き合っていた人が忘れられない	

Concerns
Suggestion with reasons

Ex. A: あのう、最近寝られないんです。どうしたらいいと思いますか。

B: そうですね… じゃ、ヨガをしてみたらどうですか。

A: え、ヨガ？

B: ええ、リラックスできるし、ストレスもなくなるし、いいと思います。

A: じゃ、そうしてみます。ありがとうございます。

4 Your partner is making a plan for tonight. Give them a suggestion on what to do or where to go, and provide reasons for your suggestion.

Opening
Ask for a suggestion
Suggestion with reasons

Ex. A: ちょっと教えてほしいんだけど…

B: うん、何？

A: 今晩ネットで晩ご飯を注文したいんだけど、おすすめ、ある？

B: じゃ、「ムンバイ」でチキンカレーを注文したらどう？ 鳥肉がたくさん入っているし、おいしいし、私もよく注文するよ。

A: へえ、じゃ、注文してみる。

Review

Now you can describe things around you in detail. What familiar place or item would you want to introduce to people around the world? First, write a detailed script for a presentation on it. Then, if you can, make a video of your presentation.

Introduction
Description including current conditions, reasons, your wishes, etc. ・Place/item 1 ・Place/item 2
Statement/question to the audience

Ex. こんにちは。今日はみなさんに私の大学の寮を紹介します。

まず、ここは寮の入口です。ウェストホールと書いてあります。イベントのポスターがはってあります。

危ない人が来るかもしれないから、寮の入口にはいつもかぎがかかっています。

次に、ここは寮の食堂です。私はメニューの中でピザが一番好きです。おいしいし、色々なトッピングもあるから、いつも食べすぎてしまいます。

私の寮の生活は楽しいです。みなさんの寮も紹介してほしいです。

できるI-B **3** Step 1

Role B

Picture B

Ex. A: はい、警察です。

B: 大変です！ あの、「とびらアパート」の201の部屋で人がたおれて (to fall over) います。

A: そうですか。部屋についてもう少し教えてください。

B: はい。えっと、ドアが開いています。

それから… <Continue>

読みましょう

Reading

Getting information from a website: Event information

1 文化祭 (cultural festivals) and 学園祭 (school festivals) are unique events that are held in spring or fall on high school and college campuses in Japan. Many people, including the students' families and friends as well as general public, visit to enjoy these festivals.

1） Below is the main menu on a 学園祭 website. Talk with your classmates about what kind of events and activities are offered at this festival. Try to guess the meaning of any unknown words on the menu buttons.

2） The following are some images on the website. Can you tell which of the above categories ①-⑩ each image belongs in?

a
あなたの将来をうらないます。
b
KARAOKE
ボカロと一緒にカラオケ、レッツゴー！
c
SNS映えする食べ物がたくさんあるよ！
d
どのコスプレがかっこいい？
e
3
手作りジェットコースターに乗ってみない？
f
リアル脱出ゲーム：早くここを出よう！

3） Discuss the following questions with your classmates based on 1) and 2) above.

(1) ⑤の「ゆるキャラ」は『とびらⅠ』(L7, p254) にもありましたが、何ですか。

(2) ⑨の「ショー＆パフォーマンス」では、どんなことをすると思いますか。

(3) ⓒの「SNS映えする」はどんな意味だと思いますか。

(4) ⓕの「リアル脱出ゲーム」では、どんなことをすると思いますか。

(5) ⓐ～ⓕの中で、どれを経験してみたいですか。どうしてですか。

4） あなたの学校でも文化祭や学園祭がありますか。その行事ではどんなことをしますか。

2 Ai and her classmates, Emma from Italy and Dewi from Indonesia, are visiting a haunted house at a college festival. Let's read about their experience!

お化けやしき：haunted house　顔出しパネル：face cutout (for people to stick their faces through)

デヴィ：あ、この教室はお化けやしきだよ。こわいかなぁ…
エンマ：私、こわいのはきらいなんだけど…
アイ　：だいじょうぶ、おもしろそうだよ！　入ってみようよ。

<お化けやしきの中に入る>

エンマ：あ、部屋の入口に変な字が書いてある。
デヴィ：それは「のろい」という漢字。英語で "curse" という意味だよ。
アイ　：デヴィさん、すごい！　私のジャパンハウスの友達のリーマン君みたい。

<お化けやしきの中を歩く>

デヴィ：あ、机の上にろうそくがある。火がついてるよ。
　　　　んっ、消えた！　あー、暗くて部屋の中がよく見えない。
エンマ：きゃっ！　痛い…
アイ　：ど、どうしたの、エンマさん？
エンマ：机にぶつかって、転んじゃった…
アイ　：だいじょうぶ？　あ、服が汚れちゃったね。
エンマ：うん。あっ、机の下に人形が落ちてる。
デヴィ：えっ、本当？　うわっ、人形の目から血が出てるよ。こわすぎる！
アイ　：あ、いすの後ろにテレビがあるよ。きゃっ、テ、Ex.1 テレビがついた！
エンマ：えっ、Ex.2 誰がつけたの？　ひえー、テレビの前に誰かいる！
デヴィ：え、本当？　お化けかもしれない…
エンマ：えっ、お化け!?　逃げようよ。出口はどこかなぁ。早くドアを開けなくちゃ。
デヴィ：あー、だめ。ドアが閉まってるし、かぎもかかってるし、開かないよ。
アイ　：あ、いすの上にかぎがあるよ。デヴィさん、そのかぎで開けてみたらどう？
デヴィ：あ、開いた！　早く外に出よう。

<外に出る>

アイ　：ふうー、こわかった。でも、おもしろかったね。
エンマ：あ、私、転んだ時にたこ焼きのチケットを落としたかもしれない。
デヴィ：えっ、チケットをなくしちゃったの？　困ったね。
エンマ：うん、ポケットに入れてあったんだけど…
アイ　：だいじょうぶ。私、2枚持ってるから、1枚あげるよ。
エンマ：え、本当？　どうもありがとう！
デヴィ：あ、お化けの顔出しパネルがあるよ。3人で写真をとろうよ。
アイ　：いいね！　デヴィさん、その写真をSNSにアップしてほしいんだけど…
デヴィ：うん、もちろん。おもしろいの、とろう！

Visualizing

1) Based on the conversation among Ai and her classmates, complete the picture of the haunted house below with the items a.-f. in the box. You may draw each item, or simply write the letter for each into the appropriate place in the picture.

a. ろうそく　b. 人形（にんぎょう）　c. テレビ　d. お化け　e. かぎ　f. たこ焼（や）きのチケット

Understanding Japanese sentence structure: Transitive and intransitive verbs

2) To understand transitive and intransitive verb sentences, do the following for each of the underlined verbs, as shown in the examples.

Ex.1 l.17 [テレビ](が) I ついた　　**Ex.2** l.18 誰（だれ）が T つけたの　[テレビ](を)

Step 1 Put T (transitive verb) or I (intransitive verb) in front of the verb.

Step 2 Draw a box around the subject of each intransitive verb and the object of each transitive verb and circle the accompanying particle. If the subject of a intransitive verb or the object of a transitive verb is omitted, insert it and its accompanying particle into the sentence.

Comprehension check

3) Mark ◯ if the statement is true and × if it is false.

(　　) デヴィもエンマもアイも、お化けやしきに入りたかった。

(　　) エンマはチケットを落（お）としてしまったから、たこ焼（や）きが食べられないようだ。

(　　) デヴィは顔出（かおだ）しパネルでとった写真（しゃしん）をSNSにアップするようだ。

4) l.7 アイはどうして「デヴィはジャパンハウスのリーマン君（くん）みたい」と言ったと思いますか。

5) There are some interesting and funny interjections which are shaded in the conversation (Exs. きゃっ, うわっ, etc.). Guess what emotion is expressed by each interjection and think about its intonation. You can use your own language for your discussion.

書く練習（れんしゅう）

おもしろくてこわいお化けやしきを自分で考（かんが）えて、それについて説明（せつめい）を書きましょう。

Listening

聞きましょう

リスニング・ストラテジー：Listening strategy

Getting the gist

You can get the gist of a conversation even if you do not understand everything in it. Use the strategies that you have learned so far—picking up keywords, predicting, guessing the meaning of unknown words—to facilitate your comprehension of the conversation as a whole.

L14-27

1 **Pre-listening activity:** Listen to the following conversation and answer the questions to grasp its main idea.

食中毒（しょくちゅうどく）: food poisoning

1） Where does this conversation take place?
2） Why did the male speaker come to this place?
3） What problem does the female speaker think that the male speaker has?

L14-28

2 **Listening:** Listen to conversations 1)-3) between friends. After each conversation, you will hear three statements a.-c. about the conversation. Try to grasp the main point of each conversation and choose the most appropriate statement based on what you have heard.

1) <In a classroom>

a.　b.　c.

2) 箱（はこ）: box

a.　b.　c.

3)

a.　b.　c.

Exit Check ☑

Now it's time to go back to the DEKIRU List for this chapter (p.123) and do the exit check to see what new things you can do now that you've completed the lesson.

言語ノート Language Note

Quantifiers

Words that indicate the number or amount of something are called quantifiers. Most quantifiers in Japanese consist of a number and a counter (e.g., 二つ, 3本, 5枚), but there are also a small number of single-word quantifiers (e.g., たくさん, 少し, ちょっと, 全部).

Japanese quantifiers are used in different ways from those found in English. First, when they are used to quantify a subject or a direct object, they usually occur after the subject marker or the direct object marker, as in (1) and (2).

(1) a. このクラスには学生が30人います。*There are thirty students in this class.*
 b. この作文には間違いがたくさんあります。*This composition contains many errors.*

(2) a. 昼ご飯にハンバーガーを二つ食べました。*I ate two hamburgers for lunch.*
 b. パーティーで日本語を少し話しました。*I spoke some Japanese at the party.*

Note that quantifiers consisting of a number and a counter do not occur immediately before nouns, while single-word quantifiers can occur in that position, as in (3).

(3) a. ?? このクラスには30人学生がいます。Cf. (1a)
 b. パーティーで少し日本語を話しました。Cf. (2b)

Second, when quantifiers modify nouns to form noun phrases, の is necessary between the quantifier and the noun, as in (4).

(4) a. 3びきのネコ（×3びきネコ）*three cats*
 b. 2台の車（×2台車）*two cars*
 c. たくさんの間違い（×たくさん間違い）*many errors*

Third, when quantifiers modify verbs, they occur before them with no particle, as in (5).

(5) a. 毎日4キロ走っています。*I run four kilometers every day.*
 b. 山田さんはたくさん食べます。*Yamada-san eats a lot.*

Lesson 15 ちょっと分かりにくいと思うんですけど…

I think it might be a little difficult to understand...

DEKIRU List

できるCheck ☑

できる I **Offer help to someone in your daily life.**
日常生活で、誰かに手伝いを申し出ることができる。
Entry ☐ Exit ☐

できる II **Express your gratitude when someone does something for you.**
何かしてもらった時に、お礼を言うことができる。
Entry ☐ Exit ☐

できる III **Express your thoughts and give suggestions when asked.**
相談されたことについて、自分の考えやアドバイスを言うことができる。
Entry ☐ Exit ☐

STRATEGIES

Conversation Tips .... • Indicating that something is acceptable/satisfactory "Nounでいい"

Reading .... • Getting information from thank-you messages
• Understanding Japanese sentence structure: Nominalizers (の and こと)
• Grasping the relationship between clauses
• Summarizing

Listening .... • Shadowing (1)

GRAMMAR

1. ～ていく "V and then go; V on one's way" できる I
2. ～てくる "go and V (and come back)" できる I
3. ～ましょうか [Offering to do something] できる I
4. ～て{あげる／くれる／もらう} [Doing/receiving a favor] できる II
5. ～て{くれてありがとう／くださってありがとうございます} "Thank you for V-ing for me/us" できる II
6. {～た／～ない}方がいい [Strong suggestion] できる III
7. Vないで "without V-ing; instead of V-ing" できる III
8. ～やすい／にくい "easy/hard to V" できる III

Conversation

会話

1 できるI Ai is visiting Naoshima with her new classmate, Kim-san.

L15-1

直島(なおしま) (See L12, 会話④)　最高(さいこう): awesome

アイ　：直島(なおしま)は本当にいい所ですね。

キム　：そうですね。最高(さいこう)です。

アイ　：あ、キムさん、見てください。あれは私が大好きな草間彌生(くさまやよい)の作品(さくひん)です。

キム　：わあ、とてもユニークできれいですね！

アイさん、よかったら、あそこで写真(しゃしん)をとりましょうか。

天気がいいし、海もきれいだし、いい写真(しゃしん)がとれると思いますよ。

アイ　：はい、お願(ねが)いします。あのう、キムさん、実(じつ)は私、ちょっといいカメラを持ってきたんです。これでとってくれませんか。

キム　：ええ、いいですよ。

<Kim-san takes pictures of Ai.>

キム　：アイさん、写真(しゃしん)はこれでいいですか。

アイ　：わあ、すごくいいですね。キムさん、どうもありがとう。

キム　：いえいえ。あのう、ちょっとつかれたから、カフェで休んでいきましょうか。

アイ　：そうしましょう。のどがかわきましたね。

2 できるII Ai and Kim-san are talking at a café.

L15-2

キム　：何を注文しましょうか。

アイ　：私はアイスコーヒーとチーズケーキにします。キムさんは？

キム　：うーん、私はかき氷(ごおり)と…　飲み物は水でいいです。

かき氷(ごおり)

<They enjoy their treats.>

アイ　：ここは島(しま)中が美術館(びじゅつかん)みたいですね。

キム　：はい。私は初めて草間彌生(くさまやよい)の作品(さくひん)を見たんですが、大好きになりました。

アイさん、今日はさそってくれて、本当にありがとう。

アイ　：こちらこそ、一緒(いっしょ)に来てくれてありがとう。

あ、キムさん、後でおみやげを買いに行きませんか。

今朝(けさ)、ホストファミリーのお父さんに駅(えき)まで送(おく)ってもらったから、何か買っていってあげたいんです。

キム　：じゃ、後でカフェの人に聞いてみましょうか。
　　　　いいおみやげを教えてくれるかもしれませんよ。

アイ　：そうですね。そうしましょう。

3 できるⅢ Ai and Kim-san are taking the train back to Kyoto.

L15-3

キム　：もう５時ですね。

アイ　：あ、そうですね。夕方(ゆうがた)は道が混(こ)んでいるから、駅(えき)からバスに乗らないで
　　　　電車で帰った方がいいかなあ。

キム　：そうですね、そうしましょう。
　　　　京都(きょうと)は電車もあるし、地下鉄(ちかてつ)もあるし、便利(べんり)ですね。

アイ　：はい、道もとても分かりやすいし、本当にいい町ですね。

キム　：ええ。でも、京都(きょうと)の方言(ほうげん)はちょっと分かりにくいと思うんですけど…

アイ　：私もそう思います。だから、ホームステイの家族(かぞく)は私に方言(ほうげん)を使わないで、
　　　　分かりやすい言葉(ことば)で話してくれるんですよ。

キム　：へえ、そうですか。

アイ　：でも、方言(ほうげん)はおもしろそうだから、ちょっと習(なら)ってみたいんです。

キム　：私も！　アイさん、一緒(いっしょ)に習(なら)いませんか。

Lesson 15

CONVERSATION TIPS

Indicating that something is acceptable/satisfactory "Nounでいい": You can use "Nounでいい" to convey "Noun is OK" or "I would be fine with Noun." When asked 飲み物は？, responding 水がいいです indicates a strong preference for water, whereas saying 水でいいです simply means that you would be fine with water.

1) 学生：先生、この宿題(しゅくだい)は今日出さなくてはいけませんか。
　　先生：いいえ、明日でいいですよ。

2) A：明日のデートの服、これでいい？
　　B：うん、いいと思うよ。

Vocabulary with Pictures

単語(たんご)

▶ **The words written in gray** are supplemental vocabulary.

生活(せいかつ) Daily life

親切・好意(こうい) Making a good impression

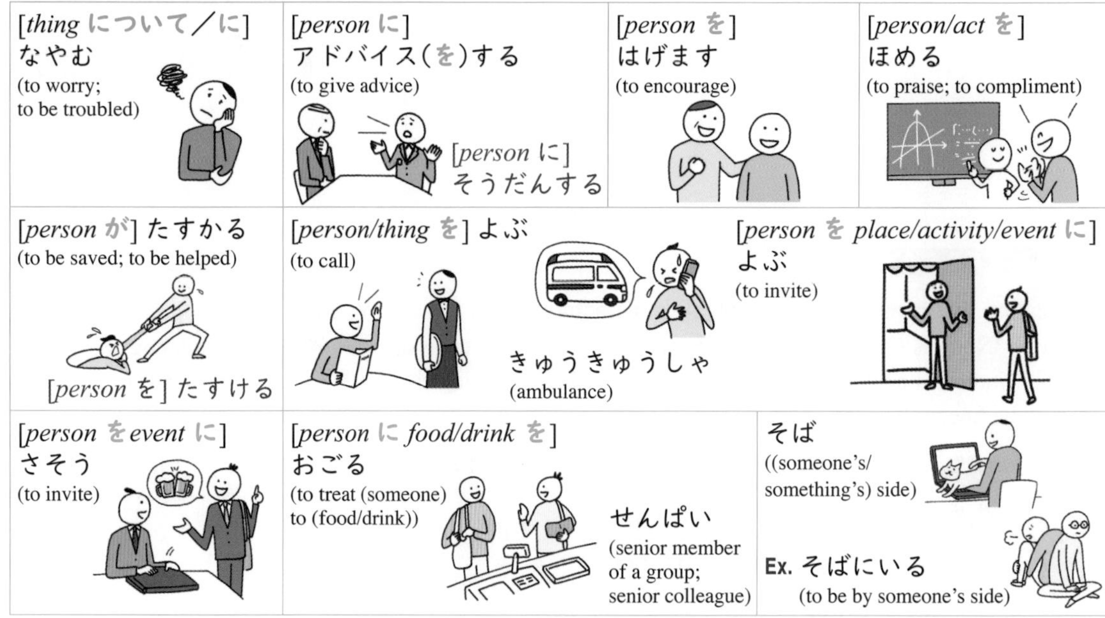

[thing について／に] なやむ
(to worry; to be troubled)
[person に] アドバイス(を)する
(to give advice)
[person に] そうだんする
[person を] はげます
(to encourage)
[person/act を] ほめる
(to praise; to compliment)
[person が] たすかる
(to be saved; to be helped)
[person を] たすける
[person/thing を] よぶ
(to call)
きゅうきゅうしゃ
(ambulance)
[person を place/activity/event に] よぶ
(to invite)
[person を event に] さそう
(to invite)
[person に food/drink を] おごる
(to treat (someone) to (food/drink))
せんぱい
(senior member of a group; senior colleague)
そば
((someone's/something's) side)
Ex. そばにいる
(to be by someone's side)

働く Work

[*old clothes* を *new clothes* に] きがえる (to change clothes)	ひげをそる (to shave (one's) face/beard)	かみをとかす (to comb (one's) hair) かがみ (mirror)	プレゼン(を)する (to give a presentation) プレゼン (presentation)	べんきょうになる (to be informative; to teach one something)
[*thing/person* を] みつける (to find) [*thing/person* が] みつかる	[*company/ organization* に] つとめる (to work (for))	[*mail/person* に] へんじをする (to answer; to respond) へんじ (reply)	むり(を)する (to push oneself too hard)	はつおんする (to pronounce (words))
かいぎ (meeting; conference) かいぎにでる	いけん (opinion) いけんをいう	じょうほう (information) [*thing/person* を] しんじる (to believe (in))		らくご (traditional Japanese comic storytelling) らくごか (*rakugo* storyteller)

社会・自分 Society and self

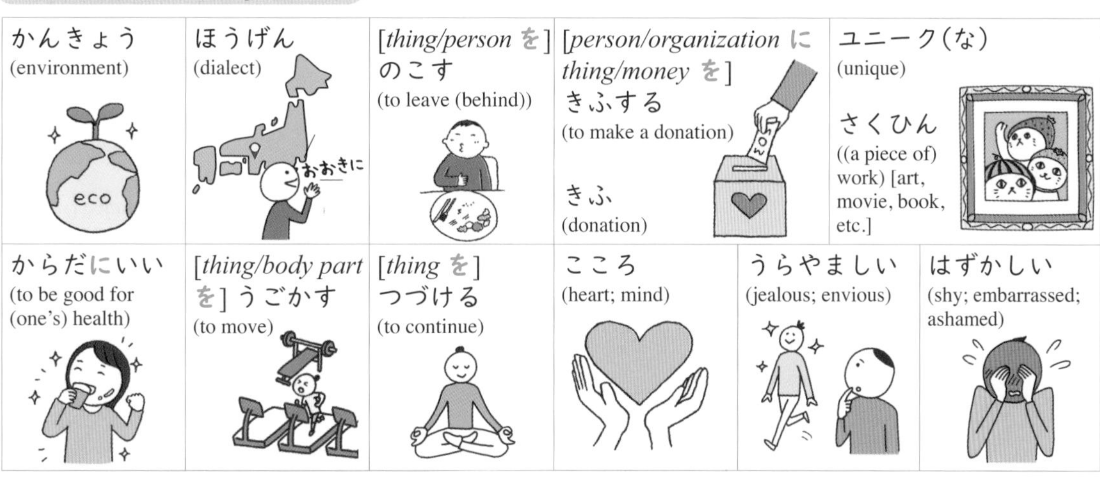

かんきょう (environment)	ほうげん (dialect)	[*thing/person* を] のこす (to leave (behind))	[*person/organization* に *thing/money* を] きふする (to make a donation) きふ (donation)		ユニーク(な) (unique) さくひん ((a piece of) work) [art, movie, book, etc.]
からだにいい (to be good for (one's) health)	[*thing/body part* を] うごかす (to move)	[*thing* を] つづける (to continue)	こころ (heart; mind)	うらやましい (jealous; envious)	はずかしい (shy; embarrassed; ashamed)

そのほかの表現(ひょうげん) Other expressions

- これからも (in the future as well)
- できるだけ (as much as possible)
- いつでも (any time; whenever; always)
- どこでも (anywhere; wherever; everywhere)
- なんでも (anything; whatever; everything)
- Noun のために (for Noun)

どうしたら (how can (one) do something)

どうしたらいいですか (What should I do?)

Vocabulary List

単語(たんご)リスト

L15-5

▶**Highlighted kanji words** contain kanji you have learned previously.

RU-VERBS

1	きがえる	着替える	to change clothes [*old clothes* を *new clothes* に]
2	しんじる	信じる	to believe (in) [*thing/person* を]
3	たりる	足りる	to be sufficient [*thing/person* が]
	たりない	足りない	to be not sufficient [*thing/person* が]
4	つづける	続ける	to continue [*thing* を]
5	つとめる	勤める	to work (for) [*company/organization* に]
6	ほめる		to praise; to compliment [*person/act* を]
7	みつける	見つける	to find [*thing/person* を]

U-VERBS / *U*-VERB PHRASES

8	いる	要る	to need [*thing* が]
9	うごかす	動かす	to move [*thing/body part* を]
10	えさをやる		to feed [*animal* に]
11	おごる		to treat (someone) to (food/drink) [*person* に *food/drink* を] [mainly used among friends]
12	かくす		to hide [*thing/person* を *place* に]
13	かみをとかす	髪をとかす	to comb (one's) hair
14	さそう	誘う	to invite [*person* を *event* に]
15	たすかる	助かる	to be saved; to be helped [*person* が]
16	たたむ		to fold [*clothes* を]
17	なやむ	悩む	to worry; to be troubled [*thing* について／に]
18	のこす	残す	to leave (behind) [*thing/person* を]
19	はげます		to encourage [*person* を]
20	ひげをそる		to shave (one's) face/beard
21	べんきょうになる	勉強になる	to be informative; to teach one something
22	よぶ	呼ぶ	to call [*person/thing* を]; to invite [*person* を *place/activity/event* に]

SURU-VERBS / *SURU*-VERB PHRASES

23	アドバイス(を)する		to give advice [*person* に]
24	かじをする	家事をする	to do housework/household chores
25	きふする	寄付する	to make a donation [*person/organization* に *thing/money* を]
26	せわをする	世話をする	to take care (of) [*person/animal* の]
27	ていでんする	停電する	to lose power; to have a power outage
28	はつおんする	発音する	to pronounce (words)
29	プレゼン(を)する		to give a presentation
30	へんじをする	返事をする	to answer; to respond [*mail/person* に]
31	むり(を)する	無理(を)する	to push oneself too hard

I-ADJECTIVES / *I*-ADJECTIVE PHRASE

32	うらやましい		jealous; envious
33	からだにいい	体にいい	to be good for (one's) health
34	はずかしい		shy; embarrassed; ashamed

NA-ADJECTIVE

35	ユニーク		unique

NOUNS

36	いけん	意見	opinion
37	えさ		feed; animal food
38	エレベーター		elevator
39	かいぎ	会議	meeting; conference
40	かがみ	鏡	mirror
41	かぐ	家具	furniture
42	かんきょう	環境	environment
43	きゅうきゅうしゃ	救急車	ambulance
44	こおり	氷	ice
45	こころ	心	heart; mind
46	さくひん	作品	(a piece of) work [art, movie, book, etc.]
47	じょうほう	情報	information
48	せんたくき		washing machine
49	せんたくもの	せんたく物	laundry [clothes/linens that have been/will be laundered]
50	せんぱい	先輩	senior member of a group; senior colleague
51	そば		(someone's/something's) side
52	どうぐ	道具	tool
53	ほうげん	方言	dialect
54	みずぎ	水着	swimsuit
55	ゆうびん	郵便	mail
56	らくご	落語	traditional Japanese comic storytelling
57	らくごか	落語家	*rakugo* storyteller

ADVERBIAL NOUN

58	ゆうがた	夕方	early evening

OTHER WORDS AND PHRASES

59	いつでも		any time; whenever; always
60	どこでも		anywhere; wherever; everywhere
61	なんでも	何でも	anything; whatever; everything
62	これからも		in the future as well
63	できるだけ		as much as possible
64	どうしたら		how can (one) do something Ex. どうしたらいいですか What should I do?
65	Noun のために		for Noun

漢字 (かんじ)

Kanji

▶＊Special reading

216	続	to continue	ゾク	接続詞 (せつぞくし) conjunction [grammar]
			つづ(ける) つづ(く)	続ける (つづ) to continue (something) 続く (つづ) (something) continues　続き (つづ) continuation
217	助	to help	ジョ	救助する (きゅうじょ) to rescue　助詞 (じょし) particle [grammar]
			たす(ける) たす(かる)	助ける (たす) to save; to help 助かる (たす) to be saved; to be helped
218	調	tune; to investigate	チョウ	体調 (たいちょう) physical condition　調査する (ちょうさ) to investigate 調子がいい (ちょうし) to be in a good condition　調和する (ちょうわ) to harmonize; to be in harmony
			しら(べる)	調べる (しら) to look up/into
219	忘	to forget	ボウ	忘年会 (ぼうねんかい) year-end party
			わす(れる)	忘れる (わす) to forget; to leave behind　忘れ物 (わすもの) lost item
220	図	map; drawing	ト ズ	図書館 (としょかん) library　意図する (いと) to intend 図 (ず) figure [explanatory diagram]　地図 (ちず) map
221	館	building	カン	映画館 (えいがかん) movie theater　大使館 (たいしかん) embassy　図書館 (としょかん) library 水族館 (すいぞくかん) aquarium　体育館 (たいいくかん) gymnasium　博物館 (はくぶつかん) museum 美術館 (びじゅつかん) art museum　領事館 (りょうじかん) consulate　旅館 (りょかん) traditional Japanese inn
222	質	substance; quality	シツ シチ	質問する (しつもん) to ask a question　質 (しつ) quality　物質 (ぶっしつ) material 質屋 (しちや) pawnshop

223	問 問 問	モン	質問する(しつもん) to ask a question　問題(もんだい) problem; question　疑問(ぎもん) question; doubt
		と(い) と(う)	問い(と) question (on tests, quizzes, etc.)
			問う(と) to question
	question		
224	宿 宿 宿	シュク	宿題(しゅくだい) homework　宿泊する(しゅくはく) to lodge; to stay
		やど やど(る)	宿(やど) inn　雨宿りする(あまやど) to take shelter from rain
	lodging		
225	題 題 題	ダイ	宿題(しゅくだい) homework　問題(もんだい) problem; question　課題(かだい) task; assignment
			題名(だいめい) title　話題(わだい) topic of conversation
	subject; theme; topic		
226	試 試 試	シ	試験(しけん) test; exam　中間／期末試験(ちゅうかん／きまつしけん) midterm/final exam
			入学試験(にゅうがくしけん) entrance exam (for school)　試合(しあい) game; match [competition]
		ため(す)	試食する(ししょく) to taste　試す(ため) to try
	test; to try		
227	験 験 験	ケン	試験(しけん) test; exam　経験する(けいけん) to experience
			実験する(じっけん) to perform an experiment　受験する(じゅけん) to take an (entrance) examination
			体験する(たいけん) to experience firsthand; to try
	verification; test		
228	受 受 受	ジュ	受験する(じゅけん) to take an (entrance) examination　受賞する(じゅしょう) to be awarded a prize
		う(ける) う(かる)	受ける(う) to take (tests, etc.); to undergo (a medical procedure)　受け入れる(う い) to accept
			受付(うけつけ) receptionist　受身形(うけみけい) passive form　受かる(う) to pass (an exam)
	to accept; to undergo		
229	練 練 練	レン	練習する(れんしゅう) to practice
			訓練(くんれん) training; drill　避難訓練(ひなんくんれん) evacuation drill
	to practice		
230	習 習 習	シュウ	練習する(れんしゅう) to practice　学習する(がくしゅう) to learn [formal]　習慣(しゅうかん) custom; habit
			復習する(ふくしゅう) to review　予習する(よしゅう) to do preparatory study/research
		なら(う)	習う(なら) to learn
	to learn		

231 飯 (飯 / 飯)	ハン	ご飯(はん) meal; cooked rice 朝(あさ)ご飯(はん) breakfast 昼(ひる)ご飯(はん) lunch 晩(ばん)ご飯(はん) dinner; supper 夕飯(ゆうはん) dinner
	めし	焼(や)き飯(めし) fried rice
meal; cooked rice	飯	

232 族 (族 / 族)	ゾク	家族(かぞく) my family; family [general term] 親族(しんぞく) relatives 水族館(すいぞくかん) aquarium 民族(みんぞく) ethnic group
tribe; family	族	

233 夕 (夕 / 夕)	ゆう	夕方(ゆうがた) early evening 夕暮(ゆうぐ)れ dusk 夕食(ゆうしょく) dinner 夕飯(ゆうはん) dinner 夕日(ゆうひ) setting sun 夕(ゆう)べ evening; yesterday evening 七夕(たなばた)* the Star Festival (July 7)
evening	夕	

Kanji as elements

This kanji is used in many other kanji as an element, so you will encounter it frequently as you continue to study Japanese.

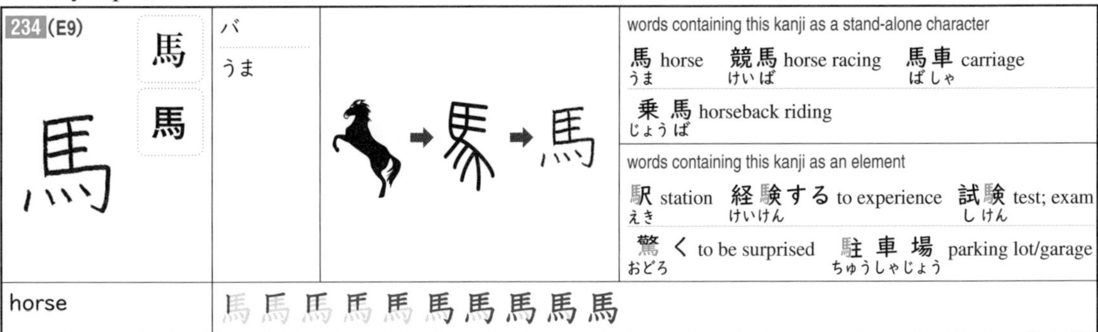

234 (E9) 馬 (馬 / 馬)	バ うま	words containing this kanji as a stand-alone character: 馬(うま) horse 競馬(けいば) horse racing 馬車(ばしゃ) carriage 乗馬(じょうば) horseback riding words containing this kanji as an element: 駅(えき) station 経験(けいけん)する to experience 試験(しけん) test; exam 驚(おどろ)く to be surprised 駐車場(ちゅうしゃじょう) parking lot/garage
horse	馬	

新しい読み方

The following are new readings for kanji that you have already learned. Read each word aloud.

1) 意見(いけん)　2) 動(うご)かす　3) 心(こころ)　4) 大使館(たいしかん)　5) 足(た)りる　6) 方言(ほうげん)
7) 水着(みずぎ)　8) 夕方(ゆうがた)

習(なら)った漢字(かんじ)で書ける新しい単語(たんご)

The following are other new vocabulary in this lesson that contain kanji you have already leaned. Read each word aloud.

1) 家事(かじ)をする　2) 体(からだ)にいい　3) 着(き)がえる　4) 世話(せわ)をする　5) せんたく物(もの)
6) 何(なん)でも　7) 勉強(べんきょう)になる　8) 返事(へんじ)をする　9) 見(み)つける

1 Your classmates are talking about their New Year's resolutions. Complete their statements 1) and 2) by selecting the most appropriate kanji from a.-d. in the box below. First, conjugate the verb appropriately, then write the letter and reading of each kanji word in (　　).

a. 忘	b. 助	c. 続	d. 調

Ex. よくテストの時、漢字(かんじ)を（a. わすれ）てしまうから、今年は毎日三時間勉強しようと思います。

1）図書館の仕事がしたいから、そのために大学院(だいがくいん)で勉強したいです。ネットで（　　　　　）て、先生の意見も聞いてから大学院(だいがくいん)を決(き)めようと思います。それから、日本語の勉強も（　　　　　）たいです。

2）今年は毎日がんばってイヌの世話をしようと思っています。イヌと外で体を動かして、一緒(いっしょ)に遊(あそ)びたいです。それから、困っている人を見たら、すぐに（　　　　　）と思います。

2 Rahim-san wrote an email to her Japanese teacher. Read her email aloud, then write the readings for the underlined words.

> 本田先生、
>
> こんにちは。日本語のクラスのラヒムです。実(じつ)は、今日習った文法(ぶんぽう)がよく分からないんですが、明日のオフィスアワーに質問しに行ってもいいですか。宿題にも答(こた)えが分からない問題があるんです。宿題の質問の後で、一緒(いっしょ)に話す練習をしてほしいんですが、先生は時間がありますか。
>
> それから、来週の水曜日にビザの面接(めんせつ)があって、大使館に行かなくてはいけません。水曜日は試験がありますが、木曜日に受けてもいいですか。
>
> どうぞよろしくお願(ねが)いします。
>
> ラヒム

3 You are looking at online reviews for a new restaurant in your neighborhood. Read the review aloud, then write the readings for the underlined words.

みんなのレビュー　　レストラン「おいしいとびら」

ようこ

1) 土曜日の<u>夕方</u>、<u>ご飯</u>を食べに行きましたが、<u>家族</u>で来ている人が多(おお)かったようです。料理は<u>何でも</u>おいしかったです。

★★★★★

ケイ

2) 昨日予約(よやく)のメールを出したら、すぐに<u>返事</u>があって、予約(よやく)をすることができました。今日行きましたが、場所は<u>映画館</u>の前で、便利(べんり)でした。

★★★★☆

ミッチ

3) 五人で予約(よやく)をしておきましたが、店に着いたらテーブルにいすが一つ<u>足りませんでした</u>。

★☆☆☆☆

漢字(かんじ)の話 The Story of Kanji

■ Creating your own kanji sentences

You have already learned one method of memorizing kanji in Lesson 10: creating kanji stories. In this lesson, you will practice another useful memorization strategy, which is creating kanji sentences. It is helpful to memorize a kanji within a meaningful context, associating the kanji with its meaning. In order to do this, you can create a sentence that contains a kanji together with its meaning(s) and reading(s) that you want to memorize. For example, you can make the following sentences if you want to memorize the kanji 転 and 習.

Ex.1 自転車は自分で運転する車です。
Ex.2 新しく習った漢字(かんじ)はたくさん書いたり読んだりして、練習します。

As you can see in Exs.1 and 2, you first choose a word that includes the kanji you want to memorize (i.e., 自転車, 練習する). Then, you create a sentence that explains the meaning of that word. Now, it's your turn—what kind of sentences can you come up with for 転 and 習? Try making your own kanji sentences to better memorize new kanji!

練習(れんしゅう)

Write the readings for the words 1)-3) in (　　), then choose the most appropriate sentence from a.-d. that explains the meaning of each word.

Ex. 映画館（えいがかん）——— a. 映画を見る建物(たてもの)です。
1) 家事　（　　　　　）・　　・b. 水の中で泳(およ)ぐ時に着る服です。
2) 水着　（　　　　　）・　　・c. 手紙(てがみ)やメールにメッセージを書いて返すことです。
3) 返事　（　　　　　）・　　・d. 家でそうじやせんたくや料理をすることです。

文法

1 ～ていく "V and then go; V on one's way"

[1]

	V-*te*	
明日のパーティーにすしを	作って	いきます。
I will make sushi and take it to tomorrow's party.		

Using V-*te*いく, you can express the idea that someone does something and then goes somewhere (i.e., someone does something before going somewhere).

Ex. (1) 12時から授業がある日は、いつもうちで昼ご飯を食べていきます。
I always eat lunch at home (and go to class) on days when I have a class that starts at noon.

This expression can also be used to express the idea of "(do something) on the way," as in (2) and (3)-B below.

Exs. (2) 学校に行く時、たいていコンビニに寄っていきます。
I usually stop by the convenience store on my way to school.

(3) A: 今晩、ゲームをしに来ない？ *Wanna come play games tonight?*
B: いいね。じゃ、スーパーで何かお菓子を買っていくね。
Sounds good. I'll buy some snacks at the supermarket and bring them, then.

The following graphics illustrate the situations in which [1] and (2) are used.

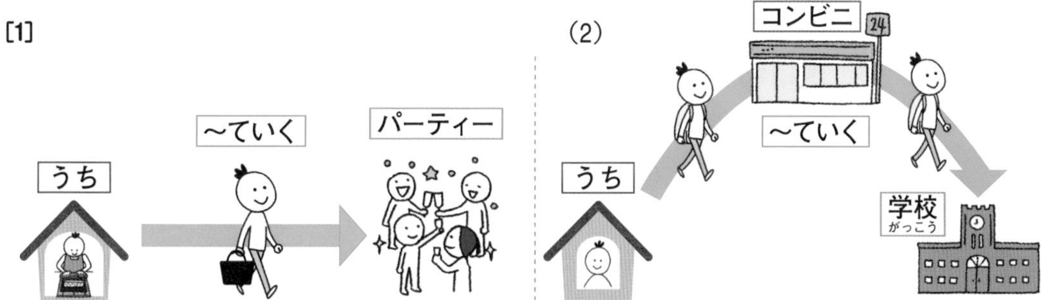

V-*te*いく is often used with 持つ "have (in one's hand); hold" and 連れる "take (someone); be attended by," as in (4) and (5). In this case, too, the subject takes the action of V-*te* at home or somewhere else and then goes to the destination.

Exs. (4) 私はいつも学校にお弁当を持っていきます。*I always take my boxed lunch to school.*

(5) 明日のバーベキューに友達を連れていくかもしれません。
I may take my friend with me to the BBQ tomorrow.

V-*te*いく is also used with momentary verbs such as 乗る and 着る, as in (6) and (7). In this case, the state after taking the action is maintained while the subject moves to the destination. Here, タクシーに乗って and 着物を着て indicate how the subject goes to the destination.

Exs. (6) 時間があまりないから、タクシーに乗っていきましょう。
We don't have much time, so let's take a taxi (lit. let's take a taxi and go).

(7) パーティーに着物を着ていこうと思います。*I'm thinking of going to the party in a kimono.*

2 ～てくる "go and V (and come back)" 

[2]

	V-*te*	
研さんに自転車を	借りて	きます。
I'll go and borrow a bike from Ken. (lit. I'll borrow a bike from Ken and come back.)		

Using V-*te*くる, you can express the idea that someone performs an action somewhere and then comes to the present location of the speaker (i.e., someone does something somewhere before coming to where the speaker is). If the person performing the action is the speaker, it means that he/she goes somewhere to do something and then returns to his/her original location. The literal meaning of V-*te*くる is "V and come," but in this case, the meaning is more like "V and come back." In English, this concept tends not to be expressed explicitly, with most speakers opting to simply say "go and V" and have the listener infer from context that they will return.

Exs. (1) コンビニで牛乳を買ってきます。
I'm going to go buy milk at the convenience store [and then come back].

(2) A: どこに行くの？ *Where're you going?*
B: ちょっとジムのプールで泳いでくるよ。
I'm going to go take a swim at the gym pool [and then come back].

(3) 公園に散歩に行ってきます。*I'm going to go to the park to take a walk [and then come back].*

If the person performing the action is someone other than the speaker, then V-*te*くる is used when that person does something somewhere and then comes to where the speaker is, as in (4) and (5).

Exs. (4) リサさんはケーキを作るのが上手だから、明日ケーキを作ってきてくれませんか。
Lisa, you're good at making cakes, so could you make a cake and bring it tomorrow?

(5) 田中さん、ピザが注文してあるから、今晩私の家に来る時に取ってきてくれませんか。*Tanaka-san, I ordered pizza, so could you pick it up on your way here (lit. when you come to my place) tonight?*

The following graphics illustrate the situations in which [2], (4), and (5) above are used.

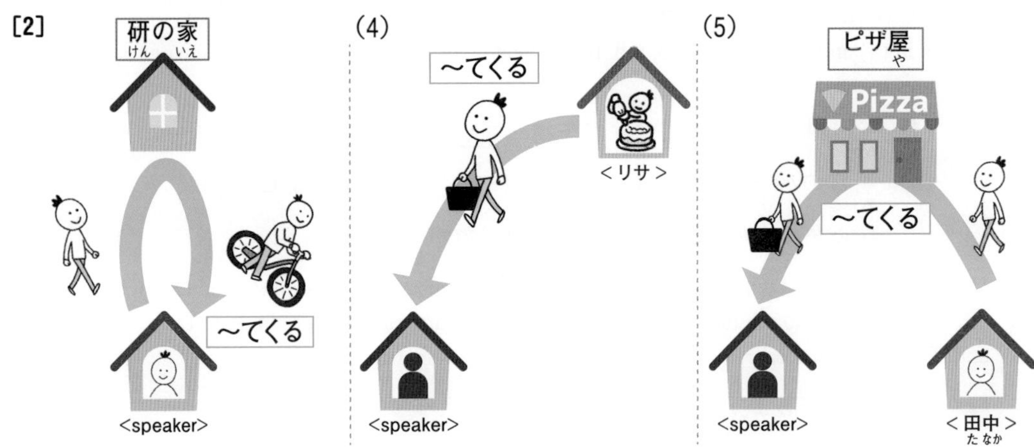

持(も)つ, 連(つ)れる, and momentary verbs (e.g., 乗(の)る) are also used in this sentence structure, as in (6)-(8). (See #1.)

Exs. (6) 今日(きょう)のパーティーにデザートを持(も)ってきます。*I'll bring a dessert to the party today.*

(7) バーベキューに友達(ともだち)を連(つ)れてきてもいいですか。

Would it be okay to bring my friend to the BBQ?

(8) 友達(ともだち)は自転車(じてんしゃ)に乗(の)ってきました。*My friend came by bicycle.*

☞ **GID** (vol.2): E. Special topics 6. Viewpoint 6-1. 行(い)く and 来(く)る; 6-2. ～ていく and ～てくる

Lesson 15

3 ～ましょうか [Offering to do something] "Shall I ~?; Would you like me to ~?; How about I ~?"

[3]

	V-*masu*	
引(ひ)っこしを	手伝(てつだ)い	ましょうか。
Shall I help with your move?		

You can offer to do something politely using ～ましょうか. (This use of ～ましょうか is different from the use of ～ましょうか that means "Shall we ~?" (See L3 #7.))

Exs. (1) A: その荷物(にもつ)は重(おも)そうですね。一緒(いっしょ)に運(はこ)びましょうか。

Those bags look heavy. Shall I carry them with you?

B: あ、お願(ねが)いします。*Oh, yes, please.*

(2) A: 暗(くら)いですね。電気(でんき)をつけましょうか。*It's dark, isn't it? Shall I turn on the light?*

B: あ、だいじょうぶです。ありがとうございます。*Oh, no, that's fine. Thank you, though.*

(3) A: かぜをひいたんですか。薬(くすり)を買(か)ってきましょうか。

Have you caught a cold? Shall I buy some medicine [for you and come back]?

B: ありがとうございます。お願(ねが)いします。*Thank you. I'd appreciate it.*

Note that in this sentence structure, 私(わたし)は is not used. Thus, the following sentence is ungrammatical:

× 私(わたし)は引(ひ)っこしを手伝(てつだ)いましょうか。→ 引(ひ)っこしを手伝(てつだ)いましょうか。(= [3])

In casual speech, V-volか is used instead of V-*masu*ましょうか, as in (4) below. (See L13 #1.)

Ex. (4) 引(ひ)っこしを手伝(てつだ)おうか。*Want me to help with your move?* (cf. [3])

Note that the question marker か cannot be dropped after V-vol, even though か is usually dropped in questions in casual speech.

4 ～て{あげる／くれる／もらう} [Doing/receiving a favor]

In this lesson, we are going to study あげる, くれる, and もらう as auxiliary verbs. These auxiliary verbs are used with the *te*-forms of verbs and express the ideas of "someone does something for someone," "someone does something for me," "have someone do something," etc. Before reading #4-1 through #4-3 below, review the following diagrams of あげる, くれる, and もらう taken from Lesson 7. You can refer to these diagrams when you use these verbs as auxiliary verbs as well.

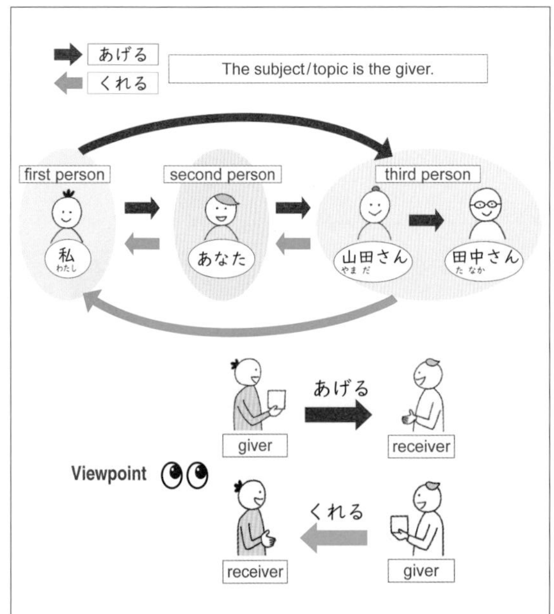

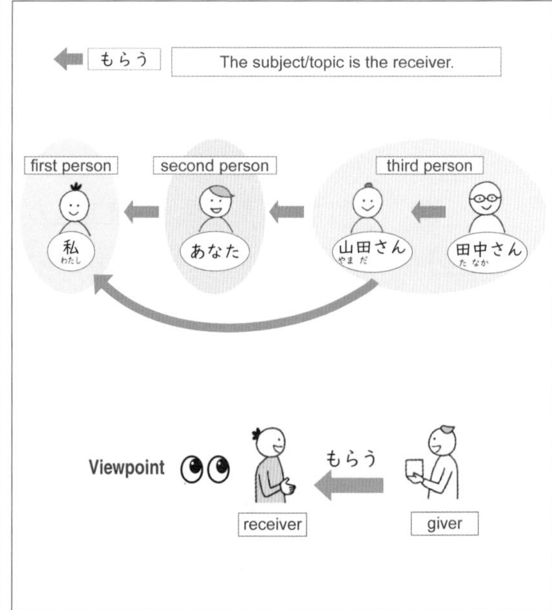

4-1 V-*te*あげる "V (for someone)"

[4-a]

Giver of benefit	Receiver of benefit (not the speaker)			V-*te*	
私は	田中さん	に	まんがを	貸して	あげました。
I lent a comic book to Tanaka-san. (lit. I did Tanaka-san the favor of lending him a comic book.)					

Using V-*te*あげる, you can express the idea of doing someone a favor, as in [4-a]. In this sentence pattern, the speaker cannot be in the position of the benefit receiver.

Exs. (1) 私はリーマンさんにたこ焼きの作り方を教えてあげました。
I taught Riemann how to make takoyaki.

(2) A: 子どもの時、母の日にお母さんに何かしてあげましたか。
Did you do anything for your mother on Mother's Day when you were a child?

B: はい、毎年兄と一緒に朝ご飯を作ってあげました。
Yes, I made breakfast (for her) with my older brother every year.

You can see the meaning of V-*te*あげる clearly by comparing [4-a] with the sentence below:

私は田中さんにまんがを貸しました。*I lent a comic book to Tanaka-san.*

While [4-a] expresses the idea that the speaker did Tanaka-san a favor by lending him a comic book, the sentence above simply describes the fact that the speaker lent Tanaka-san a comic book and doesn't convey the idea that the speaker did that as a favor to Tanaka-san.

In the sentence pattern [4-a], the benefit giver can also be someone other than the speaker. In this case, the sentence describes the situation from the benefit giver's point of view.

Ex. (3) アイさんは圭太さんにサンドイッチを作ってあげました。*Ai made a sandwich for Keita.*

In [4-a], (1), and (2), the benefit receiver is marked by に, but this is not always the case. For example, in (4) and (5) below, the benefit receivers (i.e., the highlighted people) are marked by を and の, respectively.

Exs. (4) 私(わたし)は山田(やまだ)さんを病院(びょういん)に連(つ)れていきました。

→ 私(わたし)は山田(やまだ)さんを病院(びょういん)に連(つ)れていってあげました。*I took Yamada-san to the hospital.*

(5) トムさんは研(けん)さんの部屋(へや)をそうじしました。

→ トムさんは研(けん)さんの部屋(へや)をそうじしてあげました。*Tom cleaned Ken's room for him.*

Here, the benefit receivers in the V-*te*あげる sentences are marked by the same particles as the ones in the sentences that do not involve V-*te*あげる.

Note that in (4) and (5), nothing is transferred to the receiver as the result of the action, while when に is used to mark the benefit receiver, something *is* transferred to the receiver as the result of the action (i.e., a comic book in [4-a], knowledge of *takoyaki* making in (1), breakfast in (2), and a sandwich in (3)).

Because V-*te*あげる explicitly conveys the idea of doing someone a favor, it may sound imposing or even rude if you use it when you offer help to the listener. Particularly when you are offering to do a person of higher status a favor, this expression is not appropriate, as in the following sentence:

× 先生(せんせい)、そのかばんを持(も)ってあげましょうか。

→ 先生(せんせい)、そのかばんを持(も)ちましょうか。*Professor, shall I carry your bag?*

4-2 V-*te*くれる "V for me; kindly V"

[4-b]

Giver of benefit (not the speaker)	Receiver of benefit (the speaker)			V-*te*	
山田(やまだ)さんは	（私(わたし)	に）	まんがを	貸(か)して	くれました。
Yamada-san kindly lent me a comic book.					

You can express your feeling of thankfulness for someone's action using V-*te*くれる, as in [4-b]. In this sentence pattern, the receiver of the benefit is typically the speaker. When the receiver of the benefit is clear from the context, it is usually omitted.

Ex. (1) リーマンさんは（私(わたし)に）漢字(かんじ)を教(おし)えてくれました。*Riemann taught me kanji.*

In the V-*te*くれる structure, too, when something is transferred to the benefit receiver as the result of the action, the receiver is marked by に, as in [4-b] and (1). On the other hand, when nothing is transferred to the benefit receiver as the result of the action, the receiver is marked by the same particle as the one in the corresponding sentence that does not involve V-*te*くれる, as in (2) and (3).

Exs. (2) みかさんは私(わたし)をはげましました。

→ みかさんは私(わたし)をはげましてくれました。*Mika encouraged me.*

(3) トムさんは私(わたし)の部屋(へや)をそうじしました。

→ トムさんは私(わたし)の部屋(へや)をそうじしてくれました。*Tom cleaned my room for me.*

4-3 V-*te*もらう "have someone V; get someone to V"

[4-c]

Receiver of benefit	Giver of benefit (not the speaker)			V-*te*	
私(わたし)は	山田(やまだ)さん	に	まんがを	貸(か)して	もらいました。
I got Yamada-san to lend me a comic book.					

Sentences with V-*te*くれる can be rephrased using V-*te*もらう. For example, [4-b] in the previous section can be rephrased as [4-c] above. Note that in V-*te*もらう sentences, the benefit giver is always marked by に.

One of the differences between [4-b] (= V-*te*くれる sentence) and [4-c] (= V-*te*もらう sentence) is that [4-c] would be used when the speaker asked Yamada-san to lend her a comic book, while [4-b] would usually be used when Yamada-san voluntarily lent the speaker a comic book.

Another difference between [4-b] and [4-c] is that while you use V-*te*くれる only when the benefit receiver is the speaker, a member of the speaker's family (including a pet), and such, there is no such restriction with V-*te*もらう. If you use V-*te*もらう with a third person as the benefit receiver, you are describing the situation from that person's point of view. For example, (1) below is a description from Tom's point of view, and (2) is a description from Lisa's point of view.

Exs. (1) トムさんは研(けん)さんに部屋(へや)をそうじしてもらいました。*Tom got Ken to clean his room for him.*

(2) リサさんはみかさんに病院(びょういん)に連(つ)れていってもらいました。
Lisa had Mika take her to the hospital.

Note that in V-*te*もらう sentences, the benefit giver cannot be the speaker. If the benefit giver is the speaker, V-*te*あげる has to be used, as shown below:

× トムさんは私(わたし)に部屋(へや)をそうじしてもらいました。

→ 私(わたし)はトムさんの部屋(へや)をそうじしてあげました。*I cleaned Tom's room for him.*

☞ **GID** (vol.2): E. Special topics 6. Viewpoint 6-3. あげる, くれる and もらう

5 ～て{くれてありがとう／くださってありがとうございます} "Thank you for V-ing for me/us"

[5]

	V-*te*		
引(ひ)っこしを	手伝(てつだ)って	くれて くださって	ありがとう。 ありがとうございます。
Thank you for helping with my move.			

You can express your gratitude to the listener for what he/she did for you using ～てくれてありがとう (casual) or ～てくださってありがとうございます (very polite). くださって in the latter phrase is the *te*-form of くださる, which is the honorific form of くれる. (For more about honorific forms, see L19 #4 Honorific expressions.)

Exs. (1) スミスさん、昼(ひる)ご飯(はん)を買(か)ってきてくれてありがとう。
Thanks for buying lunch for me/us, Smith-san.

(2) 先輩(せんぱい)、留学(りゅうがく)についてアドバイスしてくださってありがとうございました。
Sempai, thank you for giving me advice about studying abroad.

(3) 黒田先生(くろだせんせい)、漢字(かんじ)の間違(まちが)いを直(なお)してくださってありがとうございました。
Thank you for fixing my kanji mistakes for me, Prof. Kuroda.

When you want to express thanks for something the listener gave you, you simply say "Nounをありがとう(ございます)," as follows:

× ケーキをくれてくれてありがとう。 → ケーキをありがとう。*Thank you for the cake.*

In the sentence pattern in [5], the actor (i.e., the person being thanked) is not mentioned as the topic or the subject. The following sentence with × is ungrammatical. The actor can be included as the addressee, as in the correct sentence below:

× 先生(せんせい){は/が}推薦状(すいせんじょう)を書(か)いてくださってありがとうございます。

→ (先生(せんせい)、)推薦状(すいせんじょう)を書(か)いてくださってありがとうございます。

(Professor,) Thank you for writing a letter of recommendation for me.

⚠ Note that when expressing your gratitude to the listener using the sentence pattern in [5], not including くれて or くださって would be rude and off-putting to the listener because this portion is what indiactes that you are aware that he/she did you a favor. In other words, if you drop くれて or くださって, it sounds like you are not aware of the favor you received from the listener even if you actually are.

× みかさん、宿題(しゅくだい)を手伝(てつだ)って ø ありがとう。

→ みかさん、宿題(しゅくだい)を手伝(てつだ)ってくれてありがとう。*Thank you for helping with my homework, Mika.*

× 先生(せんせい)、推薦状(すいせんじょう)を書(か)いて ø ありがとうございました。

→ 先生(せんせい)、推薦状(すいせんじょう)を書(か)いてくださってありがとうございました。

Thank you for writing a letter of recommendation for me, Professor.

6 {～た/～ない}方(ほう)がいい [Strong suggestion] "should (not)"

[6-a]

	V-plain.past (affirmative)	
それはブラウン先生(せんせい)に	相談(そうだん)した	方(ほう)がいいです。
You should consult Prof. Brown about that.		

[6-b]

	V-plain.non-past (negative)	
それはワンさんに	言(い)わない	方(ほう)がいいです。
You should not tell that to Wang-san.		

You can suggest that someone do something or not do something using V-plain and 方(ほう)がいい. Note that when you suggest someone do something using 方(ほう)がいい, you use the plain past affirmative form of the verb, but when you suggest someone not do something with this expression, you use the plain non-past negative form of the verb.

Exs. (1) 今日(きょう)は雨(あめ)が降(ふ)りそうだから、かさを持(も)っていった方(ほう)がいいですよ。

As it looks like it's going to rain today, you should take an umbrella with you.

(2) 試験(しけん)の前(まえ)は勉強(べんきょう)しすぎない方(ほう)がいいですよ。そして、よく寝(ね)た方(ほう)がいいですよ。

It's best not to study too much before an exam. Also, you should get a good night's sleep (lit. sleep well).

(3) あのホテルは人気(にんき)があるから、早(はや)く予約(よやく)しておいた方(ほう)がいいよ。

That hotel is popular, so you should make a reservation early.

Note that when you talk to a person whose status is higher than yours, using ～方がいい is not appropriate, as in the following sentence:

× 先生、この文法を説明する時、絵を使った方がいいです。
Professor, you should use a drawing when you explain this grammar.

☞ **GID** (vol.2): D. Sentence patterns 4. ～たらどうですか vs. {～た／～ない}方がいい

7 Vないで "without V-ing; instead of V-ing"

[7-a]

	V-plain.neg		
時々朝ご飯を	食べない	で	学校に行きます。
I sometimes go to school without eating breakfast.			

[7-b]

	V-plain.neg		
たいてい本屋に	行かない	で	ネットで本を買います。
I usually buy books on the internet instead of going to the bookstore.			

You can express the idea of "without V-ing" or "instead of V-ing" using Vないで.

Exs. (1) 兄は時々ひげをそらないで会社に行きます。
My older brother sometimes goes to work without shaving.

(2) 勉強しないで試験を受けたから、全然できませんでした。
Because I took the exam without studying, I didn't do well at all.

(3) 弟はたいてい野菜を食べないで肉だけ食べている。もっと野菜を食べた方がいいと思う。
My little brother usually eats just meat without any vegetables. I think he should eat more vegetables.

(4) 今日は天気がいいから、バスに乗らないで自転車に乗って学校に行こうと思う。
The weather's nice today, so I think I'll take my bike to school instead of the bus.

☞ **GID** (vol.2): B. Connecting sentences 5. ～ないで vs. ～なくて

8 ～やすい／にくい "easy/hard to V"

[8-a]

Topic		V-*masu*	
このペンは	とても	書き	やすいです。
This pen is very easy to write with.			

[8-b]

Topic		V-*masu*	
本田さんは	ちょっと	話し	にくいです。
Honda-san is a little hard to talk to.			

You can express the idea that something/someone is "easy/hard to V" using V-*masu*やすい／にくい. Here, やすい and にくい are used as auxiliaries to add the meaning above. やすい and にくい behave as *i*-adjectives, and thus, the basic sentence pattern with this expression is "XはAdj(*i*)." Compare the two sentences below:

この漢字は難しいです。*This kanji is difficult.*

この漢字は書きにくいです。*This kanji is difficult to write.*

Note that the direct object marker を is not used after 漢字. The following sentence is ungrammatical:

× この漢字を書きにくいです。

Likewise, other particles such as で, に, etc. do not occur, as seen in the sentences below:

× このペンでとても書きやすいです。 → [8-a]

× 本田さんにちょっと話しにくいです。 → [8-b]

Exs. (1) このかばんは持ちやすいですね。*This bag is easy to carry, isn't it?*

(2) この町は住みやすいと思いますか。

Do you think this town is a good place to live (lit. easy to live in)?

(3) 昨日勉強した「あたたかかった」という言葉は言いにくかったです。

The word "atatakakatta" I studied yesterday was hard to say.

(4) このサイトは買い物しやすいです。*This website is easy to shop at.*

Just like *i*-adjectives, V-*masu*やすい／にくい can also modify nouns.

Exs. (5) 使いやすい漢字のアプリを探しています。*I'm looking for an easy-to-use kanji app.*

(6) 歩きにくいくつは買わない方がいいですよ。

It's better not to buy shoes that are hard to walk in.

⚠ When you are talking about academic subjects or skill-related topics (e.g., sports, cooking) and want to say "X is difficult/easy (to study, play, etc.)," you simply say "Xは{難しい／やさしい}です" rather than using ～にくい or ～やすい. For example, if you want to say, "Japanese is difficult (to study)" because of there being too many kanji to learn, complex grammar, etc., the following sentence on the left does not convey such a meaning.

?? 日本語は勉強しにくいです。 → 日本語(の勉強)は難しいです。

☞ GID (vol.2): C. Auxiliaries 3. V-*masu*にくい vs. 難しい

話しましょう

▶ **Words written in purple** are new words introduced in this lesson.

Offer help to someone in your daily life.

できるI-A ～ていく

1 Ai received a phone call from the host of the BBQ party she's going to tonight. Recreate the conversation based on the cues provided. L15-6

Ex. H（Host）：もしもし、アイさん、飲み物がちょっと足りないんですが…

A（Ai）　：じゃ、お茶とジュースを買っていきます。

Ex. 飲み物がちょっと足りないんですが…	**Ex.** お茶とジュースを買う
H1）何かデザートがほしいんですが…	A1）ケーキを焼く
H2）何もゲームがないんですが…	A2）みんなでできるゲームを考える
H3）誰か友達を連れてきませんか	A3）美術のクラスの友達をさそう
H4）エンマさんと一緒に来てほしいんです	A4）エンマさんの家に寄る
H5）アイさんに絵を描いてほしいんです	A5）絵を描く道具を準備する
H6）夜、ちょっと寒くなるかもしれません	A6）ジャケットを着る

2 Let's practice describing what people do when they go to certain places.

Step 1 Say what Mari does based on the pictures below. L15-7

Ex.1 まりさんは海に行く時、水着を持っていきます。

Ex.1

1）

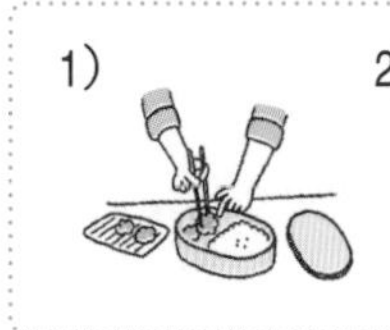

2）

3）サンダル

4）友達の車

Ex.2 まりさんは学校に行く時、天気予報を見ていきます。

Ex.2

5）　6）　7）

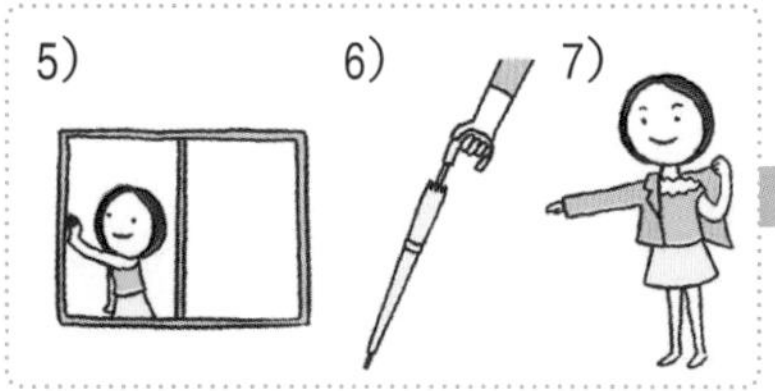

8）　9）

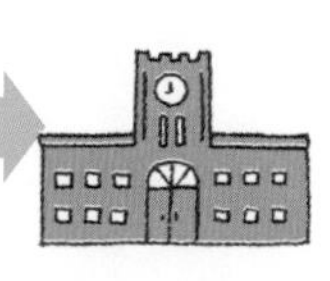

Step 2 Now, talk with your partner about what you do when you're on your way to the beach, mountains, school, etc.

できるI-B　～てくる

1 Have conversations with your partner in the following two situations based on the cues provided.

Step 1 Your friend has come to give you a ride to the airport, but there are some things you've forgotten to take care of before you leave for the trip. L15-8

Ex. 友達　：おはようございます。行けますか。

あなた：あ、すみません。郵便(ゆうびん)をチェックしてきます。

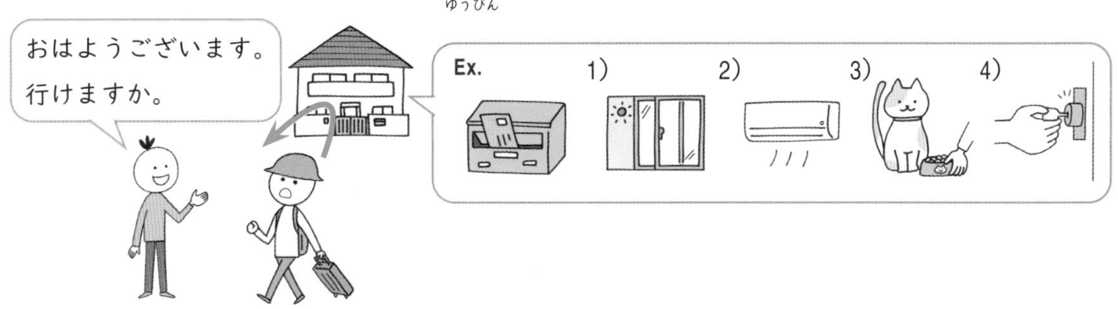

Step 2 After the trip, you are talking with your classmates about your trip. L15-9

Ex. 友達　：日本に行ってきたそうですね。

あなた：はい、東京に行ってきました。

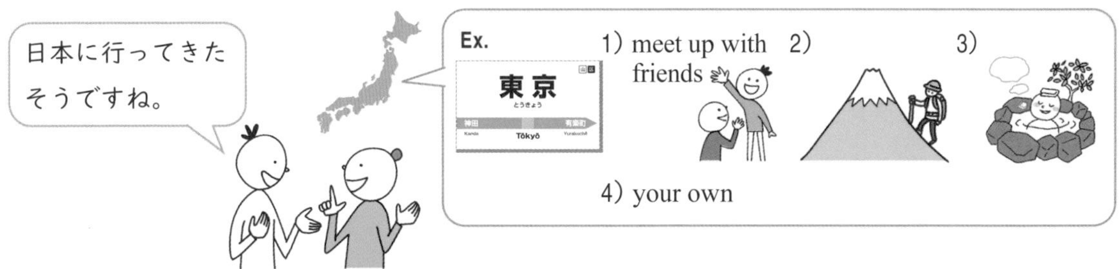

2 You are hosting a dinner at your house tonight. Ask your guests for the following favors.

Ex. あなた：すみませんが、今晩(こんばん)来る時、大きいなべを持ってきてくれませんか。

ゲスト：大きいなべですね。分かりました。持っていきます。

あなた

Ex. bring a big pot　　1) buy ice
2) make a salad　　3) bring your *senpai*
4) bring tools for making *takoyaki*　　5) your own

ゲスト

3 Suppose you are living with a roommate and are going out for a short while. Answer your roommate's questions.

Ex. A: あ、出かけるの？

B: うん、ちょっと散歩(さんぽ)してくる。

A: 分かった。何時ごろ帰ってくる？ (← Follow-up question)

B: すぐ帰ってくるよ。

できるI-C Offering to do something ～ましょうか

1 You are a very kind person. Offer help to the people around you based on the cues provided.

L15-10

Ex. 写真(しゃしん)をとる　A: 写真(しゃしん)をとりましょうか。

B: ありがとうございます。お願(ねが)いします。

or いいえ、だいじょうぶです。ありがとうございます。

1) 荷物を持つ　2) 荷物を運ぶ　3) 電気をつける　4) 窓(まど)を開ける　5) 水を持ってくる

6) エアコンを消す　7) 仕事を手伝(てつだ)う　8) (私が)払(はら)う　9) 案内(あんない)する　10) 救急車(きゅうきゅうしゃ)を呼(よ)ぶ

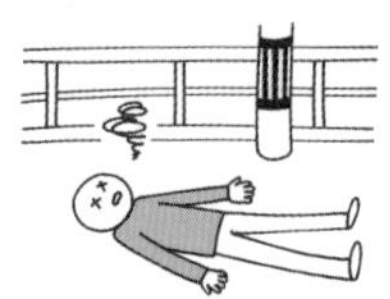

2 You are studying abroad in Japan and living with a host family. Look at the picture below and offer each member of your host family the help they need.

L15-11

Ex. あなた　：お母さん、いすを直(なお)しましょうか。

お母さん：ありがとう。じゃ、お願(ねが)いします。

3 You are visiting a sick classmate and offering to help them in various ways.

Ex. 何か／作る

A: だいじょうぶですか。何か作りましょうか。

B: すみません。じゃ、おかゆ (rice porridge) を作ってくれませんか。(← Request)

A: おかゆですね。分かりました。作ってきます。(← Appropriate response)

1) 何か／家事をする　2) 何か／持ってくる　3) 何か／買ってくる

4) 病院(びょういん)／連(つ)れていく　5) 家族(かぞく)／連絡(れんらく)する　6) your own

Lesson 15

4 Reproduce the dialogues in the previous exercise using casual speech. If you don't remember the volitional forms of verbs, review them first.

Ex. A: だいじょうぶ？　何か作ろうか？

B: ごめん。じゃ、おかゆを作ってくれない？(← Request)

A: おかゆだね。分かった。作ってくる。(← Appropriate response)

できるII Express your gratitude when someone does something for you.

できるII-A Doing/receiving a favor ～てあげる／くれる／もらう

1 Do you often help others? Describe what you (私) and Ai did for each of the people below. Pay attention to the particles you use. (See Grammar on p.176 as needed.) L15-12

Ex.1 私はおじいさんに道を教えてあげました。

Ex.2 アイさんは友達の話を聞いてあげました。

Ex.1 おじいさん／道／教える　Ex.2 友達の話／聞く

私

1) おばあさんの荷物／持つ

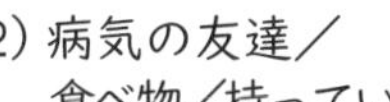

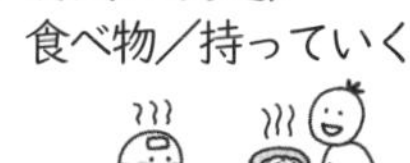

2) 病気の友達／食べ物／持っていく

3) ルームメイト／お金／貸(か)す

4) 友達のイヌの世話／する

5) 友達の弟の宿題(しゅくだい)／見る

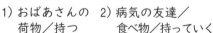

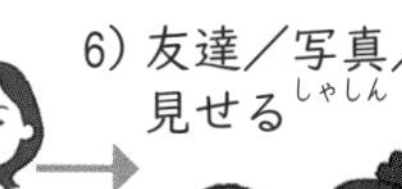

アイ

6) 友達／写真(しゃしん)／見せる

7) クラスメート／コーヒー／おごる

8) 友達／空港(くうこう)／連(つ)れていく

9) 友達の弟／一緒(いっしょ)に遊(あそ)ぶ

2 You are surrounded by warm-hearted people who care about you.

Step 1 Describe what each of these people does for you (私) when you are feeling down. Pay attention to the particles you use. (See Grammar on p.177 as needed.) L15-13

Ex. (私が) 元気がない時、祖母(そぼ)は (私に) おいしい物を送(おく)ってくれます。

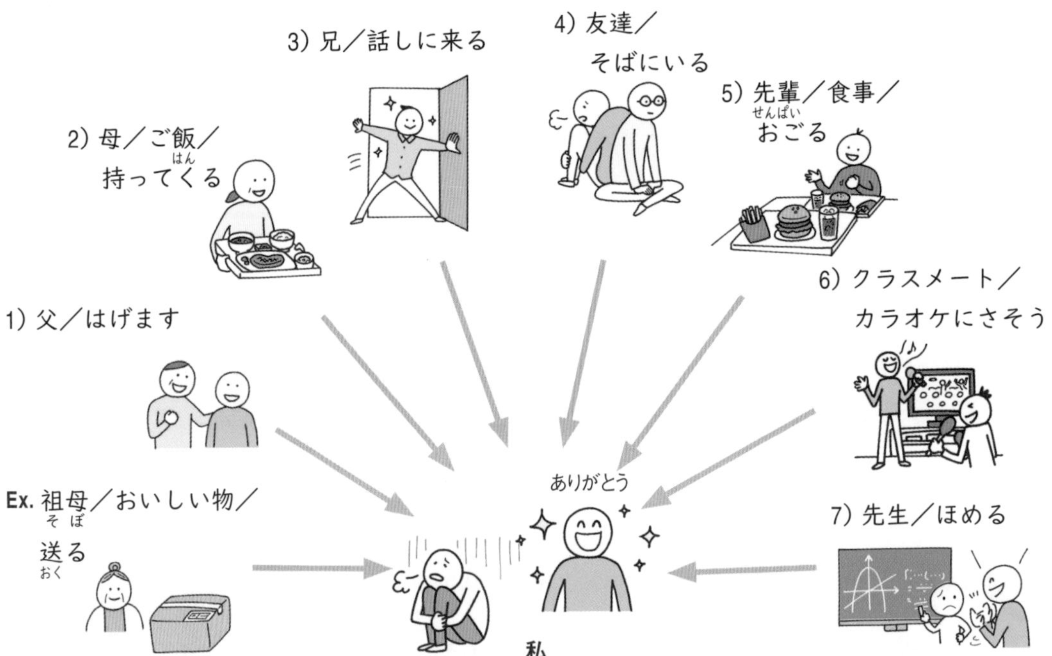

Step 2 Using Step 1 as a reference, talk about your support system when you are feeling down and describe who does what for you.

Ex. A: 私が元気がない時、母は私においしい物を作ってくれます。だから、感謝(かんしゃ)しています。

B: そうですか。やさしいお母さんですね。私はルームメートに感謝(かんしゃ)しています。私が落(お)ち込(こ)んでいる時、ルームメートは私と一緒(いっしょ)に映画を見てくれるんです。

A: いいルームメートですね。

3 Suppose you asked the people in the previous exercise for the favors. Rephrase what each of these people did for you using ～てもらう. L15-14

Ex. 祖母(そぼ)は (私に) おいしい物を送(おく)ってくれました。

→ 私は祖母(そぼ)においしい物を送(おく)ってもらいました。

4 Talk with your partner about the people who helped you during a difficult time.

Possible topics	悩(なや)んでいる時	落(お)ち込(こ)んでいる時	困った時	病気の時

Ex. A: ○○さんは大変な時、誰(だれ)に助(たす)けてもらいますか。

B: そうですね、たいてい友達に助(たす)けてもらいます。例えば、私が将来(しょうらい)について悩(なや)んでいる時、友達は話を聞いて、一緒(いっしょ)に考(かんが)えてくれました。

A: へえ、すごくいい友達ですね。

B: △△さんは大変な時、誰(だれ)に助(たす)けてもらいますか。

A: 私は病気の時… <Continue>

5 The Japanese proverb 一日一善(いちにちいちぜん) encourages you to do one good deed for each day. It doesn't have to be anything big; it's the eagerness to do good deeds that is important. Talk with your partner about the good deeds you have done or will do today.

Ex. A: ○○さんは、今日、何かいいことをしましたか。

B: いいえ、何もしていません。でも、私は漢字(かんじ)を覚(おぼ)えるのが得意(とくい)だから、クラスメートにいい漢字(かんじ)の覚(おぼ)え方を教えてあげようと思います。△△さんは？

A: 私はもういいことをしました。今朝(けさ)、私のイヌを散歩(さんぽ)に連(つ)れていって、たくさん遊(あそ)んであげました。

6 You are happy because someone did something nice for you. Talk about what happened with your friend. 👕

Ex. A: ○○、うれしそうだけど、何かいいこと、あった？

B: 実(じつ)は友達にすごくいい人を紹介(しょうかい)してもらったんだ。

A: へえ、どんな人？（← Follow-up question）

<Continue>

できるⅡ-B ～て{くれてありがとう／くださってありがとうございます}

1 Let's practice conjugating the following verbs first with ～てくれてありがとう and then with ～てくださってありがとうございます。 L15-15

Ex. 書(か)く → 書(か)いてくれてありがとう → 書(か)いてくださってありがとうございます

1) 見(み)せる 2) 教(おし)える 3) 助(たす)ける 4) 手伝(てつだ)う 5) 話(はな)す 6) 聞(き)く
7) 作(つく)る 8) 言(い)う 9) 直(なお)す 10) する 11) 迎(むか)えに来(く)る 12) ほめる
13) おごる 14) さそう 15) アドバイスをする

2 Suppose you understand what Nyanta is saying. On his behalf, thank Ai for what she did for him based on the cues provided. 👕 L15-16

Ex. アイちゃん、<u>拾ってくれてありがとう。</u>

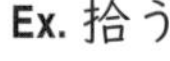
Ex. 拾う　　1) 毎日世話をする　　2) やさしくする　　3) いつもそばにいる　　4) おいしいえさ　　5) your own

3 Your friend did the following things for you, so you want to show your gratitude. Make up your own dialogues based on the pictures below and act them out. 👕 L15-17

Ex. あなた：助(たす)けてくれてありがとう。本当に助(たす)かった。(← Comment)
友達　：どういたしまして。

1)

2)

3)

4)

5) your own

4 Express your gratitude to your teacher for the things they have done for you.

Step 1 Think up short dialogues in which you thank your teacher for the following favors. L15-18

Ex. giving me advice about studying abroad

あなた：先生、<u>留学(りゅうがく)についてアドバイスし</u>てくださってありがとうございました。
先生　：いえいえ、どういたしまして。

1) writing me a letter of recommendation　　2) correcting my homework
3) teaching me about Japanese culture　　4) doing job interview practice together
5) helping me prepare for my presentation　　6) email　　7) your own

Step 2 Now, think of something your teacher has actually done for you and express your gratitude.

Ex. あなた：先生、今学期(こんがっき)、日本語と日本文化を教えてくださってありがとうございました。とても勉強になりました。
先生　：そう言ってくれてありがとう。うれしいです。

5 Write thank-you notes to your classmates and teacher to show your gratitude and hand them out.

Exs.

今学期(こんがっき)、ゴルドさんと一緒(いっしょ)に勉強できて、とても楽しかったです。分からない時、漢字(かんじ)の読み方を教えてくれてありがとう。
ミミ

黒田(くろだ)先生、私がとても落(お)ち込(こ)んでいる時、はげましてくださってありがとうございました。うれしかったです。

ミミ・マスク

できる III Express your thoughts and give suggestions when asked.

できるIII-A Strong suggestion {～た／～ない} 方がいい

1 First, practice conjugating verbs with the expression ～方がいい. L15-19

Ex. 寝(ね)る → 寝(ね)た方がいいです → 寝(ね)ない方がいいです

1) 見(み)る　2) やめる　3) 考(かんが)える　4) あきらめる　5) 行(い)く　6) 言(い)う
7) 使(つか)う　8) 休(やす)む　9) する　10) 来(く)る　11) 信(しん)じる　12) 続(つづ)ける
13) かくす　14) さそう　15) 悩(なや)む

2 When your roommate has problems, what advice can you give them?

Step 1 Your roommate is addicted to games. Tell them what they should do.

Ex. 少(すこ)し勉強する → 少(すこ)し勉強した方がいいですよ。

1) 学校に行く　2) ゲームをやめる　3) パソコンを消す
4) みんなと話す　5) ちょっと体を動(うご)かす　6) your own

Step 2 Your roommate doesn't look well. Tell them what they should not do.

Ex. × 落(お)ち込(こ)む →（あまり）落(お)ち込(こ)まない方がいいですよ。

1) × 一人で悩(なや)む　2) × 一日中家にいる　3) × 何でも信(しん)じる
4) × 心配する　5) × 考(かんが)えすぎる　6) × your own

3 Your friend seems to have a problem. Give them some good suggestions.

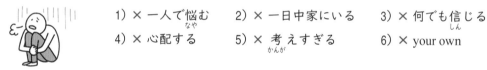

Useful vocabulary	無理(むり)する	落(お)ち込(こ)む	考(かんが)えすぎる	心配しすぎる	謝(あやま)る

Ex. A: ○○、元気がないね。どうしたの？
B: 実(じつ)はかぜ{ひいたんだ／ひいちゃったんだ}。
A: え、かぜ？　家に帰って、休んだ方がいいよ。
無理(むり)しない方がいいよ。
B: ありがとう。そうする。

Ex. かぜをひく

B's problem

1) 頭(あたま)が痛い
2) 好きな人と別(わか)れた
3) 親とけんかした
4) ペットが病気
5) your own

4 Talk about what children should or should not do before elementary school.

Step 1 First, practice forming sentences using ～方がいい to say that children should and should not do the following.

Ex. 家事を手伝う(てつだ) → 子どもは家事を手伝(てつだ)った方がいいと思います。
→ 子どもは家事を手伝(てつだ)わない方がいいと思います。

1) スマホを持つ　2) 外で遊(あそ)ぶ　3) ゲームをする　4) 外国語を勉強する　5) your own

Step 2 Exchange opinions with your partner about whether children should or should not do the things listed in Step 1.

Ex. A: 私は子どもは家事を手伝(てつだ)った方がいいと思います。小さい時から手伝(てつだ)ったら、家事が上手になるからです。〇〇さんはどう思いますか。

B: 私も手伝(てつだ)った方がいいと思います。料理やそうじが好きになるからです。
or 私は手伝(てつだ)わない方がいいと思います。勉強する時間がなくなってしまうからです。

Group Work

5 Choose a topic from the options below and discuss it with your groupmates.

Possible topics

- 朝(あさ)ご飯(はん)を食べる vs できるだけ長く寝(ね)る
- 休みが１か月あったら、留学(りゅうがく)する vs 旅行(りょこう)する
- つまらないけれど、やさしいクラスを取(と)る vs 難(むずか)しいけれど、おもしろいクラスを取(と)る

Ex. A: みなさんは朝(あさ)ご飯(はん)を食べた方がいいと思いますか。
それとも (or)、できるだけ長く寝(ね)た方がいいと思いますか。

B: 私は長く寝(ね)た方がいいと思います。寝(ね)なかったら、授業(じゅぎょう)中に寝(ね)てしまうからです。

C: 私は朝(あさ)ご飯(はん)を食べた方がいいと思います。何も食べなかったら、体によくないからです。〇〇さんはどう思いますか。

A: 私は…　<Continue>

できるⅢ-B　Vないで

1 Let's practice forming the expression ～ないで.　L15-22

Ex. 食(た)べる → 食(た)べないで

1) 見(み)る　2) 考(かんが)える　3) 捨(す)てる　4) 言(い)う　5) 話(はな)す　6) 行(い)く
7) 使(つか)う　8) やる　9) 持(も)つ　10) する　11) 着(き)がえる　12) 続(つづ)ける
13) かくす　14) 残(のこ)す　15) 無理(むり)する

2 Describe what parts of his daily routine Tanaka-san skips when he oversleeps. If only picture cues are given, think of the appropriate words to use on your own. L15-23

Ex.1 × シャワーを浴(あ)びる

→ 田中さんは朝(あさ)ねぼうした時、シャワーを浴(あ)びないで、学校に行きます。

1) × 顔(かお)を洗(あら)う　2) × 着がえる　3) × 髪(かみ)をとかす　4) × ひげをそる
5) × 化粧(けしょう)する　6) × 鏡(かがみ)を見る　7) × ペットにえさをやる

Ex.2

→ 田中さんは朝(あさ)ねぼうした時、シャワーを浴(あ)びないで、顔(かお)だけ洗(あら)って出かけます。

8)　9)　10)
11)　12)　13)

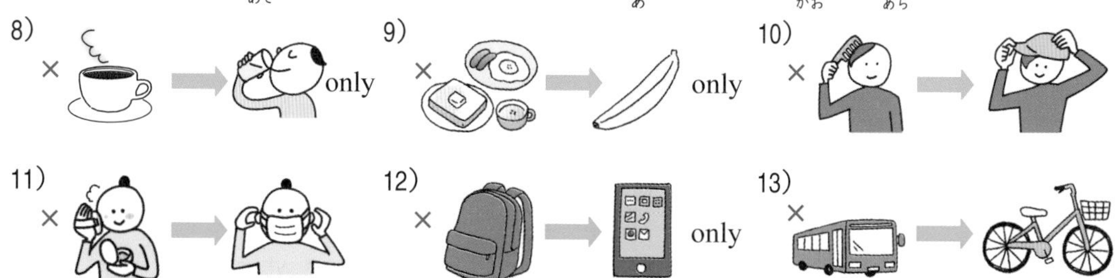

3 Talk with your partner about what parts of your daily routine you skip in the situations below.

Ex. お金がない時

A: ○○さんはお金がない時、どうしますか。

B: そうですね、私は肉や魚を食べないで、毎日キャベツを食べます。

△△さんは？

A: 私は家にいないで、友達の家に行きます。そして、友達にご飯(はん)を作ってもらいます。

B: そうですか。頭(あたま)がいいですね。(← Comment)

1) お金がない時　2) 試験(しけん)がある時　3) すごくつかれた時　4) 停電(ていでん)した時　5) your own

Group Work

4 How eco-friendly are you? Discuss what environmentally-friendly alternatives you can try.

Step 1 Look at the pictures below and brainstorm ideas for eco-friendly practices.

Ex. いらない家具(かぐ)を捨(す)てないで、寄付(きふ)します。

Ex. いらない家具(かぐ)　1) 食べ物　2) 車　3) エレベーター　4) こわれた物　5) your own

Step 2 Now, talk about the eco-friendly practices that you are doing now and those you would like to start implementing in your daily routine.

ペットボトル

Ex. A: みなさんは、環境(かんきょう)のために何かしていますか。
B: 私はペットボトルを捨(す)てないで、リサイクルしています。
C: そうですか。私はできるだけ新しい物を買わないで、古い物を使っています。
A: そうですか。いいですね。私は… <Continue>

できるⅢ-C ～やすい／にくい

1 Let's practice forming the expressions ～やすいです and ～にくいです. L15-24

Ex. 書(か)く → 書(か)きやすいです → 書(か)きにくいです

1) 食(た)べる　2) 見(み)る　3) 覚(おぼ)える　4) 分(わ)かる　5) 住(す)む　6) 使(つか)う
7) 行(い)く　8) 歩(ある)く　9) 話(はな)す　10) 入(はい)る　11) する　12) 見(み)つける

2 Ai has sent you a message about her experiences in Japan. Report what she said.

Ex.1 アイさんによると、ホストファミリーの人達は話しやすいそうです。
Ex.2 日本人の名前は覚(おぼ)えにくいそうです。

Ex.1 ○ ホストファミリーの人達に話す
Ex.2 × 日本人の名前を覚(おぼ)える
1) ○ 日本に住む　2) ○ 京都(きょうと)の道を覚(おぼ)える
3) ○ 京都(きょうと)で生活(せいかつ)する　4) × 京都(きょうと)の方言(ほうげん)が分かる
5) × レストランに一人で入る　6) × カニを食べる

3 What do you think about the following things? Exchange impressions with your partner.

Ex.

A: このタッチペンは使いやすそうですね。
B: そうですね。{きれいに描(か)けそうですね／高いかもしれませんね}。(← Comment)

1)

2) 鬱
3)

4)

5) キーボード

6) your own

4 How is your study of Japanese (pronunciation, grammar, characters, etc.) going? Exchange experiences with your partner related to your study of Japanese so far.

Useful vocabulary 発音（はつおん）する　間違（まちが）える　覚（おぼ）える　言う　読む　分かる

Ex. A: ○○さんは日本語で発音（はつおん）しにくい音がありますか。

B: はい、あります。私は「ら」がちょっと発音（はつおん）しにくいです。△△さんは？

A: 私は長い音が間違（まちが）えやすいです。例えば、間違（まちが）えて、よく「こうこう」を「ここ」と言ってしまいます。　<Continue>

Group Work

5 Compare and contrast two things and exchange opinions about them with your groupmates.

Possible topics 都会（とかい） vs いなか／住みやすい　アプリ：○○ vs △△／使いやすい

Ex. A: 都会（とかい）といなかとどちらの方が住みやすいと思いますか。

B: いなかは自然（しぜん）が多（おお）いし、家賃（やちん）が安いから、私はいなかの方が住みやすいと思います。

C: 私はちょっと違（ちが）う意見（いけん）です。車を使わないで生活（せいかつ）できるから、私は都会（とかい）の方が住みやすいと思います。○○さんはどう思いますか。

<Continue>

Review

Now you can give strong suggestions and express your opinions about familiar things. If you could make suggestions to your past self, what would you like to say?

Step 1 Brainstorm what you would like to say to your past self.

- 今、残念（ざんねん）だと思うことは？
- どうして？
- その時の自分に言いたいこと（アドバイス）は？
- 自分に感謝（かんしゃ）したいことは？

Step 2 Present your message to the class. Your classmates will ask some questions after your presentation.

Regret/disappointment Reason + strong suggestion	**Ex.** 私は高校生になってから、ピアノをやめてしまいました。でも、ピアノがひけたら、かっこいいし、楽しいから、今ちょっと残念（ざんねん）だと思います。だから、15才（さい）の時の私に「ピアノをやめないで続（つづ）けた方がいいよ」と言いたいです。
Gratitude	それから、16才（さい）の私に「日本のアニメを好きになってくれてありがとう」と言いたいです。　<Continue>
============	
Q & A	Q: ○○さんはどうしてピアノをやめてしまったんですか。

Reading

読みましょう

Getting information from thank-you messages

1 下の「ありがとう」のメッセージを読んでみましょう。1)～5)のメッセージは誰(だれ)が誰(だれ)に書いたメッセージだと思いますか。(　　　)に書いてください。

Ex.

今日は私達の日本語のクラスで落語(らくご)の話をしてくださってありがとうございました。とても勉強になりました。初めて本当の落語(らくご)を聞いて、感動(かんどう)しました！

(日本語のクラスの学生)が
(　　落語家(らくごか)　　)に書いた

1)

ケリー、お誕生日(たんじょうび)おめでとう！
いつもはげましてくれて、
ありがとう。
本当に感謝(かんしゃ)しています。
プレゼントを気(き)に入(い)ってくれたら、
うれしいです。　はる

気(き)に入(い)る：to like

(　　　　　　　　)が
(　　　　　　　　)に書いた

2)

いつもおいしい給食(きゅうしょく)を作ってくださって、ありがとうございます。小学校の給食(きゅうしょく)はとてもおいしいです。だから、野菜(やさい)が好きじゃなかったけれど、今は何でも食べられます。これからもおいしい給食(きゅうしょく)を作ってください。

給食(きゅうしょく)：school lunch

(　　　　　　　　)が
(　　　　　　　　)に書いた

3)

一年間茶道(さどう)を教えてくださって、
ありがとうございました。
茶道(さどう)部で先生に教えてもらった
ことを忘れないで、
これからもがんばります。

茶道(さどう)：tea ceremony

(　　　　　　　　)が
(　　　　　　　　)に書いた

4) 公衆(こうしゅう) (public) トイレで見るメッセージ

いつもきれいに
使ってくださって
ありがとうございます。

トイレを(　　　　　　　　)が
トイレを(　　　　　　　　)に書いた

5)

三木(みき)です。
クリスさん、今日は会議(かいぎ)でするプレゼンの英語を直(なお)してくれてありがとう！
今度、ご飯をおごるね。和食(わしょく)かイタリアンだったら、どっちがいい？

(　　　　　　　　)が
(　　　　　　　　)に書いた

2 下の悩み相談 (requests for advice) を読んで、質問に答えてください。

Case **A** はっち 19才

今、大学生で、寮で生活しています。最近、インターネットを見る[Ex.] の をやめられません。昨日も勉強しないで、[Ex.] 6時間ぐらい続けてネットを見てしまいました。少し時間があったら、すぐにおすすめの動画を見たり、何かを調べたり、好きなSNSをチェックしたりしてしまいます。

学生は勉強しなくてはいけないから、勉強してからネットを見た方がいい[a.] こと は分かっています。でも、やめられないんです。長い時間ネットを見てしまうから、宿題や試験の勉強や、やらなくてはいけないことをする時間がなくなります。目が痛くなるし、成績も悪くなるし、自分で考えないでネットに書いてあることを何でも信じてしまうし、問題がたくさんあります。

ネットを見る時間を決めたり、スマホを部屋に持っていかないでかくしたりしてみましたが、だめでした。僕は心が弱いです。どうしたらネットがやめられますか。

Case **B** ドレミ 24才

ITの会社に勤めています。私は小さい時から友達を作る[b.] の が苦手で、友達がいません。友達がたくさんいたら、誰かと話したい時、会って話したり、一緒にご飯を食べたりできます。でも、私にはそういう (such) 友達がいないから、みんなが楽しそうにしている[c.] の を見て、うらやましくなります。そして、友達がたくさんいない[d.] こと をはずかしいと思います。

私が誰にも連絡しないから、誰も私に連絡してくれません。姉は私に「自分からさそってみたらどう？」「友達を紹介してあげようか？」と言いますが、自分からさそってみて、いい返事がもらえなかったら落ち込むし、よく知らない人とは話しにくいし、何もできません。

一人でいる[e.] の はきらいじゃありませんが、いつでも、何でもしゃべれる友達がほしいです。

Understanding Japanese sentence structure: Nominalizers (の and こと)

1） Do you remember the nominalizers の and こと that you learned in L8 and L11, respectively? Nominalizers convert a verb or an entire sentence into a noun equivalent. Underline the nominalized verb phrases for a.-e., as in the example below.

Ex. 最近、インターネットを見る[Ex.] の をやめられません。

Grasping the relationship between clauses

2） The underlined parts in the above requests show connective expressions that indicate the relationship between clauses. Insert the most appropriate letter from the box below after each underlined expression to identify its function.

Ex. 6時間ぐらい続けて **S** ネットを見てしまいました。

S = Sequential relationship	**O** = Opposing ideas
R = Causal relationship [reason/cause]	**C** = Conditional relationship

Lesson 15

Summarizing

3） List the main points of each 悩み相談 in your own words, as shown in the examples.

■ Case A：はっちさんの相談

Main problem	
Specific problems	・宿題や試験の勉強や、やらなくてはいけないことをする時間がない。 ・ ・ ・
Unsuccessful solutions	・ ・

■ Case B：ドレミさんの相談

Main problem	
Specific problems	・[　　　　　　　　　　　　　　　　　　]、うらやましくなる。 ・[　　　　　　　　　　　　　　　　　　]、はずかしいと思う。
Unsuccessful solutions (advice from her sister)	・ ・

Comprehension check

4） Mark ○ if the statement is true and × if it is false.

（　　　）はっちさんはネットでよくゲームをしたり動画を見たりしているみたいだ。

（　　　）はっちさんはネットの情報を信じやすい人のようだ。

（　　　）ドレミさんは友達が多い人がうらやましいと思っているようだ。

（　　　）ドレミさんは一人でいるのはさびしいから好きじゃない。

（　　　）ドレミさんは話しやすい友達をほしがっている。

5） What advice would you give? Choose one person and give your advice using the template provided below.

私は {はっちさん／ドレミさん} に「＿＿＿＿＿＿＿＿＿＿＿＿＿＿＿＿」と言います。

＿＿＿＿＿＿＿＿＿＿＿＿＿＿＿＿＿＿＿＿＿＿＿＿からです。

Referring to Cases A and B, write your own 悩み相談.

聞きましょう

リスニング・ストラテジー : Listening strategy

Shadowing (1)
Shadowing is a language learning technique in which you listen to some audio input in the target language and echo it back, repeating what you hear as exactly as possible and with as little lag as you can manage. In this lesson, we practice this shadowing technique step by step to improve your listening comprehension.

Lesson 15

1 Pre-listening activity: L15-26

Step 1 Listen to the audio without looking at the script. Try to figure out what each sentence is about. You can listen to the audio as many times as you want.

Step 2 Read the script on the *TOBIRA* website to check if you understood the audio correctly. Pay close attention to the part(s) that you could not comprehend and look up the words and expressions that you didn't know.

Step 3 Read each sentence aloud along with the audio while looking at the script (="overlapping"). Repeat this step until you can keep pace with the audio.

Step 4 Practice shadowing without looking at the script. Listen to the audio and echo it back. Repeat this step until you can echo what you hear with confidence.

2 Listening: Now let's try shadowing using a different audio input. L15-27

1) Practice Steps 1-4 above as many times as you like.

2) Record yourself shadowing and evaluate your recording for proficiency in the following categories. (Mark ○ for "good," △ for "so-so," and × for "not good.")

a. Pacing / Fluency		b. Accuracy (grammar, pronunciation)	

How did it go? If you feel confident, challenge yourself using longer or more difficult sentences on the Conversation pages, etc. If you don't feel confident, practice shadowing using phrases you can find in the Activities pages.

Exit Check

Now it's time to go back to the DEKIRU List for this chapter (p.161) and do the exit check to see what new things you can do now that you've completed the lesson.

文化ノート Culture Note　【ウチ・ソト】の考え方

ウチ？ ソト？

とびら先生、先輩が「【ウチ・ソト】は日本の文化や言葉を勉強する時、とても大切だよ」と教えてくれたんですが、【ウチ・ソト】はどんな意味ですか。

にゃんた君、それはとてもいい質問ですね。【ウチ・ソト】について日本語で説明するのはちょっと難しいから、英語で説明します。

You've learned the words うち "home" (or "inside") and そと "outside" as ways to refer to physical locations, but these words also have another, metaphorical usage. When written in katakana as ウチ and ソト, they refer to the inner and outer areas of a person's social space and to the people in those areas. This conception of social space reflects a way of thinking that is important to understanding Japanese society and culture.

So, how does this metaphorical conception of ウチ・ソト work? In Japanese society, there is a tendency to divide others into these two groups: ウチ, or the "in-group" of people to which one belongs, and ソト, the "out-group" of people to which one does not. Japanese people will adjust their speech, attitude, and behavior based on whether the person they are interacting with is ウチ or ソト. For example, people will speak casually to their family, who are ウチ, but will speak politely to customers or clients at work, who are ソト. The boundaries between these two groups change depending on context and relationship dynamics: someone you just met would be ソト, and you would want to speak politely to them, but as you become closer, you might come to consider them ウチ and start to speak more casually.

So, how do Japanese people decide if a person is ウチ or ソト? Look at the diagram below. The farther away you go from the 私 in the center, the more likely a person in that social space is to be considered ソト. The diagram isn't absolute, because whether you think of someone as ウチ or ソト will change based not just on your relationship with the person, but also on the context of the interaction and other social dynamics. Generally speaking, however, anyone up to the "friend" and "same group" (people from the same college, company, etc.) levels would be considered ウチ, while anyone beyond that point would be ソト. Note that the forms of address introduced in the *TOBIRA I* Culture Note "Addressing and referring to people in Japanese" (p.256) become easier to understand if you reference this diagram.

Q: Based on what you have learned, select the appropriate way of referring to your mother: 母 or お母さん.

1) <パーティで>　私：私は３人家族です。【母・お母さん】は高校の先生です。弟が一人います。
　初めて会った人：へえ、そうですか。【母・お母さん】は何を教えていますか。
　私：【母・お母さん】は、日本語を教えています。

2) <家で>　私：あれ？　【母・お母さん】は？　弟：【母・お母さん】は買い物に行ったよ。
　母：ただいま！　私：あ、【母・お母さん】、お帰りなさい！

As you continue to learn more about Japanese culture and language, social distinctions like these will become more natural to you. However, if you find yourself not understanding differences in speech levels or what the proper way to talk in a specific situation is, try thinking from the perspective of ウチ・ソト.

Lesson 16

一日しか会えなくて残念です…

ざんねん

It's too bad we can only meet up for one day...

Instructional Video Lesson 16

DEKIRU List

できるCheck ✓

できる I **Express your feelings about good and bad experiences.**
よかったことや大変だったことについて、気持ちを表現することができる。
Entry ☐ Exit ☐

できる II **Talk about things that did not go well and things you regret.**
うまくいかなかったことや後悔していることについて、話すことができる。
Entry ☐ Exit ☐

できる III **Explain facts about famous things and places and provide information about them.**
有名な物や場所について、事実や情報を話すことができる。
Entry ☐ Exit ☐

STRATEGIES

Conversation Tips .... ・～って as a colloquial quotative particle

Reading .... ・Getting information from infographics
・Understanding demonstratives: こ-words
・Identifying omitted words
・Scanning

Listening .... ・Shadowing (2)

GRAMMAR

1. ～て [Reason] できるI
2. Passive forms of verbs and passive sentences できるI,III
3. ～しか～ない "nothing/nobody but ~; only~" できるII
4. *Ba*-conditional forms of verbs and ～ばよかった "I should (not) have V-ed" できるII
5. Vつもり "be planning to V; be going to V; intend to V" できるII
6. 間／間に "while" できるII

会 話

1 できるI Jean has come to Kyoto to see Ai.

L16-1

ジャン　：アイちゃん、久しぶりだね。京都はどう？
アイ　　：とても楽しいです。来る前は色々なことを心配していたけど、
　　　　　今は日本に来て本当によかったって思っています。
ジャン　：アイちゃん、日本語が上手になったね。
アイ　　：そうですか？　お店のお客さんにも時々ほめられるんですけど、まだまだです。
　　　　　特に京都の方言で話されたら、全然分からなくて…
ジャン　：へえ、そうなんだ。
アイ　　：ええ、昨日も「どっからきはったん？」って聞かれて
　　　　　困りました。
ジャン　：え？　「どっからきはったん」？
アイ　　：ええ、「どこから来たんですか」っていう意味です。
ジャン　：へえ、全然違うんだね。

Ai is at Kyoto Station to see Jean off to Tokyo.

L16-2

アイ　　：ジャンさん、今日は会いに来てくださって、どうもありがとうございました。
　　　　　とても楽しかったです。
ジャン　：僕も楽しかったよ。京都を案内してくれてありがとう。
アイ　　：今日、一日しか会えなくて残念です…
ジャン　：そうだね。でも、一緒に色々な所に行けてよかったよ。
　　　　　伏見稲荷大社、それから、清水寺…
アイ　　：実は私が住んでいる町も案内するつもりだったんですけど…
ジャン　：ああ、宇治？　実は僕も新幹線に乗っている間、
　　　　　ずっと宇治について調べていたんだ。
アイ　　：え、そうなんですか。じゃ、宇治にも行けばよかった…
ジャン　：だいじょうぶ。次は宇治に連れていってくれる？
　　　　　京都にはまた来るつもりだから…
アイ　　：はい、私がホームステイしている間に、ぜひもう一度来てください！

伏見稲荷大社

提供：伏見稲荷大社

清水寺

On another day, Ai is talking with her classmate Kim-san. L16-3

キム　：アイさん、一緒(いっしょ)に美術館(びじゅつかん)でボランティアをしませんか。

アイ　：え、ボランティアですか。

キム　：はい、子ども達に美術(びじゅつ)について教えるボランティアです。

アイ　：へえ、おもしろそうですね。ぜひやってみたいです！

<Ai is giving a talk at the museum about a famous artist.>

みなさん、この絵を見たことがありますか。
とてもおもしろい絵ですね。
これはピカソという画家によって描(か)かれました。
ピカソの絵は世界中の美術館(びじゅつかん)にあって、
たくさんの人に知られています。
ピカソは天才(てんさい)だったと言われています。
それから、とてもユニークな人で、
ピカソについて色々な本が書かれたり、
映画が作られたりしています。
今日は一緒(いっしょ)にピカソの絵を見てみましょう。

CONVERSATION TIPS

～って as a colloquial quotative particle: When speaking, you can use ～って instead of the quotative particle と. Note that this is not used in formal speech or writing.

1）父：あれ？　アイちゃんは？

姉：東京から来た友達に京都(きょうと)を案内(あんない)するって言ってたよ。

2）ジャン：宇治(うじ)は何が有名？

アイ　：平等院(びょうどういん)っていうお寺が有名ですよ。お金の十円玉(じゅうえんだま)のお寺です。

ジャン：あ、そのお寺、前から一度見てみたいって思ってたんだ。

十円玉(じゅうえんだま)

Vocabulary with Pictures

単語（たんご）

生活（せいかつ） Daily life

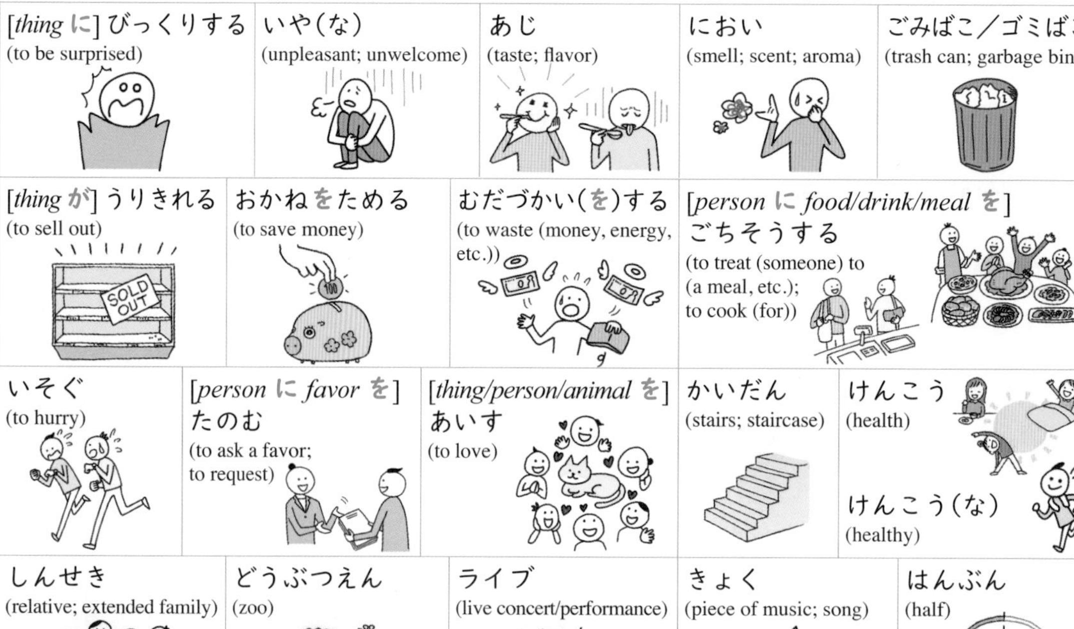

- [*thing* に] びっくりする (to be surprised)
- いや(な) (unpleasant; unwelcome)
- あじ (taste; flavor)
- におい (smell; scent; aroma)
- ごみばこ／ゴミばこ (trash can; garbage bin)
- [*thing* が] うりきれる (to sell out)
- おかねをためる (to save money)
- むだづかい(を)する (to waste (money, energy, etc.))
- [*person* に *food/drink/meal* を] ごちそうする (to treat (someone) to (a meal, etc.); to cook (for))
- いそぐ (to hurry)
- [*person* に *favor* を] たのむ (to ask a favor; to request)
- [*thing/person/animal* を] あいす (to love)
- かいだん (stairs; staircase)
- けんこう (health)
- けんこう(な) (healthy)
- しんせき (relative; extended family)
- どうぶつえん (zoo)
- ライブ (live concert/performance)
- きょく (piece of music; song)
- はんぶん (half)

いやな経験（けいけん） Bad experience

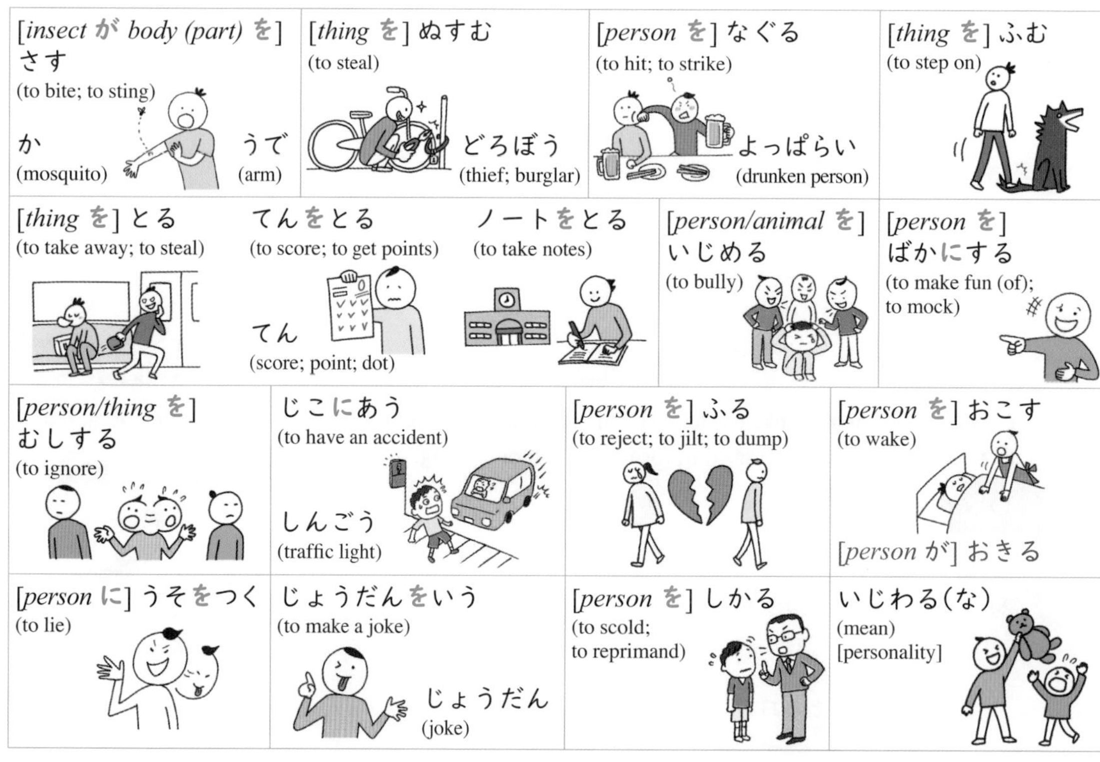

- [*insect* が *body (part)* を] さす (to bite; to sting)
  - か (mosquito)
  - うで (arm)
- [*thing* を] ぬすむ (to steal)
  - どろぼう (thief; burglar)
- [*person* を] なぐる (to hit; to strike)
  - よっぱらい (drunken person)
- [*thing* を] ふむ (to step on)
- [*thing* を] とる (to take away; to steal)
- てんをとる (to score; to get points)
  - てん (score; point; dot)
- ノートをとる (to take notes)
- [*person/animal* を] いじめる (to bully)
- [*person* を] ばかにする (to make fun (of); to mock)
- [*person/thing* を] むしする (to ignore)
- じこにあう (to have an accident)
  - しんごう (traffic light)
- [*person* を] ふる (to reject; to jilt; to dump)
- [*person* を] おこす (to wake)
  - [*person* が] おきる
- [*person* に] うそをつく (to lie)
- じょうだんをいう (to make a joke)
  - じょうだん (joke)
- [*person* を] しかる (to scold; to reprimand)
- いじわる(な) (mean) [personality]

数える（かぞ） Counting

～だい (Counter for cars/machines/mechanical devices)

1	2	3	4	5	6	7	8	9	10	?
いちだい	にだい	さんだい	よんだい	ごだい	ろくだい	ななだい	はちだい	きゅうだい	じゅうだい	なんだい

～てん (Counter for points/score)

0	1	2	3	4	5	6	7	8	9	10	?
れいてん	いってん	にてん	さんてん	よんてん	ごてん	ろくてん	ななてん	はってん	きゅうてん	じ(ゅ)ってん	なんてん

～キロ	～メートル
(... kilometer(s); ... kilogram(s)) 1km≒0.62 mi; 1,093 yd; 1kg≒2.2 lb	(... meter(s)) 1m≒39 in; 3.28 ft; 1.09 yd

Lesson 16

説明する（せつめい） Explaining

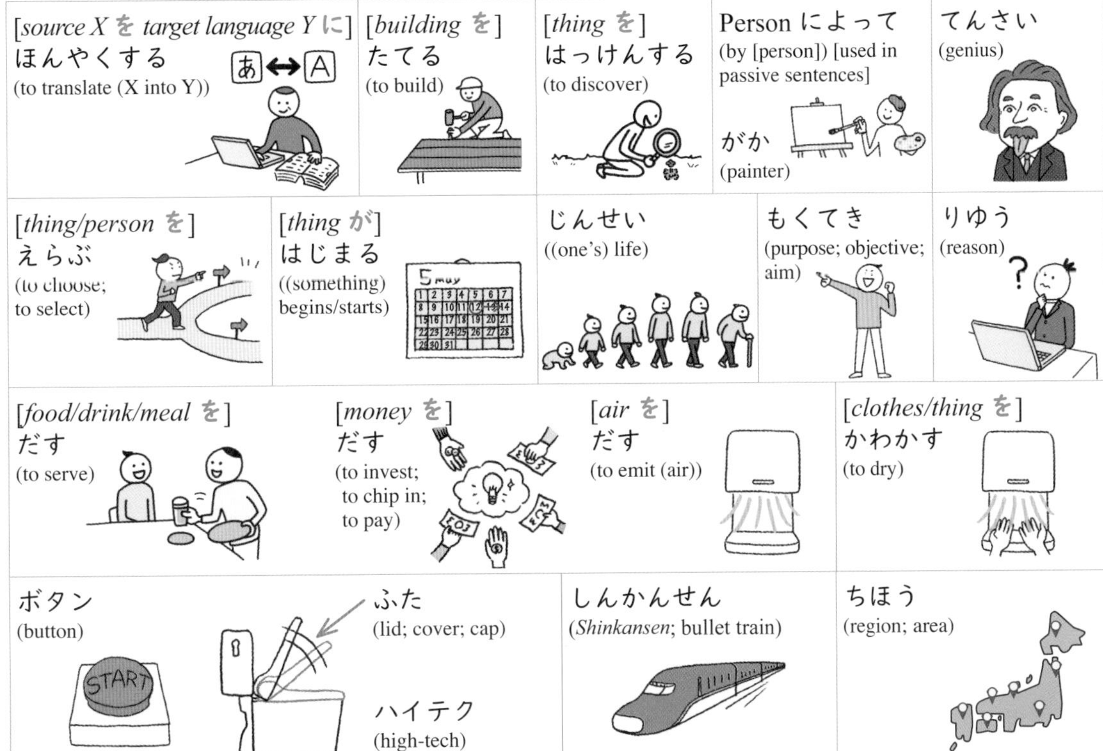

[source X を target language Y に] ほんやくする (to translate (X into Y))
あ↔A
[building を] たてる (to build)
[thing を] はっけんする (to discover)
Person によって (by [person]) [used in passive sentences]
がか (painter)
てんさい (genius)
[thing/person を] えらぶ (to choose; to select)
[thing が] はじまる ((something) begins/starts)
5 may
じんせい ((one's) life)
もくてき (purpose; objective; aim)
りゆう (reason)
[food/drink/meal を] だす (to serve)
[money を] だす (to invest; to chip in; to pay)
[air を] だす (to emit (air))
[clothes/thing を] かわかす (to dry)
ボタン (button)
START
ふた (lid; cover; cap)
ハイテク (high-tech)
しんかんせん (Shinkansen; bullet train)
ちほう (region; area)

そのほかの表現（ひょうげん） Other expressions

げんきをだして(ください) ((Please) cheer up.)

にほんごがじょうずになりましたね (Your Japanese has become better, hasn't it?)

いいえ、**まだまだです** (No, there is still a long way to go.)

おととし (the year before last)	いままで ((up) until now; before now)	ずっと (the whole time; all throughout)	また ((once) again)	とくに (in particular)
まえ (before [earlier in time])	まえの Noun (previous Noun) **Ex.** まえのやすみ (previous break)	Duration まえ ([duration] ago) **Ex.** ２ねんまえ (two years ago)	Duration ご ([duration] later; from now) **Exs.** １しゅうかんご (one week later)　３ねんご (three years later)	

単語リスト

L16-5

▶ **Highlighted kanji words** contain kanji you have learned previously.
▶ ＊ See vocabulary index at the end of the book for other meanings.

RU-VERBS / RU-VERB PHRASE

1	いじめる		to bully [*person/animal* を]
2	うりきれる	売り切れる	to sell out [*thing* が]
3	おかねをためる	お金を貯める	to save money
4	たてる	建てる	to build [*building* を]

U-VERBS / U-VERB PHRASES

5	あいす	愛す	to love [*thing/person/animal* を] **Ex.1** みんなが(ネコを)あいしている everyone loves (the cat) **Ex.2** みんながあいするネコ a cat everyone loves [あいする is used to modify nouns.]
6	いそぐ	急ぐ	to hurry
7	うそをつく		to lie [*person* に]
8	えらぶ	選ぶ	to choose; to select [*thing/person* を]
9	おこす	起こす	to wake [*person* を]
10	かわかす		to dry [*clothes/thing* を]
11	さす		to bite; to sting [*insect* が *body (part)* を]
	かがさす		a mosquito bites
12	しかる		to scold; to reprimand [*person* を]
13	じこにあう	事故にあう	to have an accident
14	じょうだんをいう	冗談を言う	to make a joke
15	だす＊	出す	to serve [*food/drink/meal* を]; to invest; to chip in; to pay [*money* を]; to emit (air) [*air* を]
16	たのむ		to ask a favor; to request [*person* に *favor* を] [たのむ tends not to be used toward one's superior.]
17	とる＊	取る	to take away; to steal [*thing* を]
	てんをとる	点を取る	to score; to get points
	ノートをとる	ノートを取る	to take notes
18	なぐる		to hit; to strike [*person* を]
19	ぬすむ		to steal [*thing* を]
20	はじまる	始まる	(something) begins/starts [*thing* が]
21	ふむ		to step on [*thing* を]
22	ふる		to reject; to jilt; to dump [*person* を]

SURU-VERBS / SURU-VERB PHRASE

23	ごちそうする		to treat (someone) to (a meal, etc.); to cook (for) [*person* に *food/drink/meal* を]
24	ばかにする		to make fun (of); to mock [*person* を]
25	はっけんする	発見する	to discover [*thing* を]
26	びっくりする		to be surprised [*thing* に]
27	ほんやくする		to translate (X into Y) [*source X* を *target language Y* に]
28	むしする	無視する	to ignore [*person/thing* を]
29	むだづかい(を)する		to waste (money, energy, etc.)

NA-ADJECTIVES

30	いじわる		mean [personality]

31	いや		unpleasant; unwelcome Ex. いやなけいけん unpleasant experience
32	けんこう	健康	healthy

NOUNS

33	あじ	味	taste; flavor
34	うで		arm
35	か		mosquito
36	かいだん	階段	stairs; staircase
37	がか	画家	painter
38	きょく	曲	piece of music; song
39	けんこう	健康	health
40	ごみばこ／ ゴミばこ	ごみ箱／ ゴミ箱	trash can; garbage bin
41	しんかんせん	新幹線	*Shinkansen*; bullet train
42	しんごう	信号	traffic light
43	じんせい	人生	(one's) life
44	しんせき	親せき	relative; extended family
45	ちほう	地方	region; area
46	てん	点	score; point; dot
47	てんさい	天才	genius
48	どうぶつえん	動物園	zoo
49	どろぼう		thief; burglar
50	におい		smell; scent; aroma
51	ハイテク		high-tech
52	はんぶん	半分	half
53	ふた		lid; cover; cap
54	ボタン		button
55	まえ*	前	before [earlier in time]
	Duration まえ	～前	[duration] ago Ex. ２年前 two years ago
	まえの Noun	前の～	previous Noun Ex. 前の休み previous break
56	Duration ご	～後	[duration] later; from now Ex.1 １週間後 one week later Ex.2 ３年後 three years later
57	もくてき	目的	purpose; objective; aim
58	よっぱらい		drunken person
59	ライブ		live concert/ performance
60	りゆう	理由	reason

ADVERBIAL NOUNS

61	いままで	今まで	(up) until now; before now
62	おととし		the year before last

ADVERBS

63	ずっと		the whole time; all throughout
64	とくに	特に	in particular
65	また		(once) again

COUNTERS

66	～だい	～台	[counter for cars/ machines/mechanical devices]
67	～てん	～点	[counter for points/ score]
68	～キロ		... kilometer(s); ... kilogram(s) 1km ≒ 0.62 mi; 1,093 yd 1kg ≒ 2.2 lb
69	～メートル		... meter(s) [length; distance] 1m ≒ 39 in; 3.28 ft; 1.09 yd

OTHER WORDS AND PHRASES

70	げんきをだして （ください）	元気を 出して （ください）	(Please) cheer up.
71	まだまだです		There is still a long way to go.
72	Person によって		by [person] [used in passive sentences]

Lesson 16

漢字 (かんじ)

▶ ＊Special reading

235	取 (to take)	シュ	取材する (しゅざい) to interview; to gather information on [reporting]
		と(る)	取る (と) to take (class, notes, etc.); to steal　聞き取る (き と) to catch (what has been said)
			点を取る (てん と) to score　ノートを取る (と) to take notes　年を取る (とし と) to grow old
236	泣 (to cry)	な(く)	泣く (な) to cry　泣き声 (な ごえ) sound of crying; sob　泣き虫 (な むし) crybaby
237	笑 (to laugh)	わら(う) え	笑う (わら) to laugh; to smile
			笑顔 (えがお) smiling face
238	起 (to get up)	キ	起床する (きしょう) to get up (in the morning)　起立する (きりつ) to stand up
		お(こす) お(きる) お(こる)	起こす (お) to wake (someone)
			起きる (お) to get up; to wake up　起こる (お) to happen; to take place
239	始 (to start)	シ	開始する (かいし) to start [formal]
		はじ(める) はじ(まる)	始める (はじ) to begin/start (something)　書き始める (か はじ) to start writing　始め (はじ) beginning; start
			始まる (はじ) (something) begins/starts
240	終 (to end)	シュウ	最終 (さいしゅう) last; final　終電 (しゅうでん) last train　終了する (しゅうりょう) to bring/come to an end
		お(わる) お(わり)	終わる (お) to (come to an) end　書き終わる (か お) to finish writing
			終わり (お) end
241	決 (to decide)	ケツ ケッ	解決する (かいけつ) to solve; to resolve; to settle　決定する (けってい) to make a decision
		き(める) き(まる)	決める (き) to decide
			決まる (き) to be decided　決まり (き) rules; customs

242	歌 (歌 歌)	カ	歌手（かしゅ） singer　歌詞（かし） lyrics　国歌（こっか） national anthem
		うた うた(う)	歌（うた） song
			歌う（うたう） to sing
	to sing; song		
243	洗 (洗 洗)	セン	洗剤（せんざい） detergent; cleaner　洗濯機（せんたくき） washing machine
			洗濯する（せんたくする） to do the laundry; to wash (in the laundry)
		あら(う)	洗う（あらう） to wash　お手洗い（おてあらい） bathroom; restroom; toilet
	to wash		
244	台 (台 台)	ダイ タイ	～台（だい） [counter for cars/machines/mechanical devices] (Ex. 一台（いちだい） one car/machine)
			台所（だいどころ） kitchen
			台風（たいふう） typhoon
	table; stand		
245	旅 (旅 旅)	リョ	旅館（りょかん） traditional Japanese inn　旅行する（りょこうする） to travel (to/in/around)
			海外旅行（かいがいりょこう） overseas trip　観光旅行（かんこうりょこう） sightseeing trip　旅行会社（りょこうがいしゃ） travel agency
		たび	旅（たび） trip; travel　一人旅*（ひとりたび） solo travel
	journey		
246	駅 (駅 駅)	エキ	駅（えき） train station　東京駅（とうきょうえき） Tokyo Station
			駅員（えきいん） station attendant　駅弁（えきべん） boxed lunch sold at stations
	station		
247	朝 (朝 朝)	チョウ	早朝（そうちょう） early morning　朝食（ちょうしょく） breakfast
		あさ	朝（あさ） morning　朝ご飯（あさごはん） breakfast　朝ねぼう(を)する（あさねぼう(を)する） to oversleep (in the morning)
			朝早く（あさはやく） early in the morning　毎朝（まいあさ） every morning　今朝*（けさ） this morning
	morning		
248	昼 (昼 昼)	チュウ	昼食（ちゅうしょく） lunch
		ひる	昼（ひる） daytime; midday　昼ご飯（ひるごはん） lunch　昼寝(を)する（ひるね(を)する） to take a nap
			昼間（ひるま） daytime　昼休み（ひるやすみ） lunch break
	daytime		
249	晩 (晩 晩)	バン	晩（ばん） night; evening　晩ご飯（ばんごはん） dinner; supper
			今晩（こんばん） tonight; this evening　毎晩（まいばん） every night/evening
	nightfall		

250 夜	ヤ よる よ	今夜（こんや） tonight; this evening　深夜（しんや） the middle of the night　徹夜する（てつや） to stay up all night 夜（よる） night; evening　夜遅く（よるおそ） late at night 真夜中（まよなか） midnight; the middle of the night　夜中（よなか） late at night
night	夜夜夜夜夜夜夜夜	

251 漢	カン	漢字（かんじ） kanji; Chinese character　漢字辞典（かんじじてん） kanji dictionary
China; The Han Dynasty	漢漢漢漢漢漢漢漢漢漢漢漢漢	

252 字	ジ	漢字（かんじ） kanji; Chinese character　字（じ） character; letter　数字（すうじ） number [numeral]; digit 文字（もじ） character; letter [symbol used to write words]　名字（みょうじ） family name ローマ字（じ） Roman character; romanized Japanese
character; letter	字字字字字字	

Kanji as elements

This kanji is used in many other kanji as an element, so you will encounter it frequently as you continue to study Japanese.

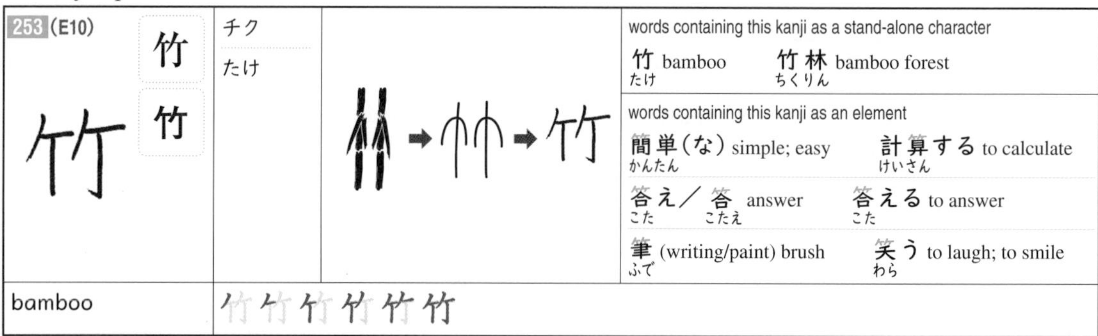

253 (E10) 竹	チク たけ	words containing this kanji as a stand-alone character 竹（たけ） bamboo　竹林（ちくりん） bamboo forest words containing this kanji as an element 簡単（かんたん）(な) simple; easy　計算する（けいさん） to calculate 答え（こた）／答（こたえ） answer　答える（こた） to answer 筆（ふで） (writing/paint) brush　笑う（わら） to laugh; to smile
bamboo	竹竹竹竹竹竹	

新しい読み方

The following are new readings for kanji that you have already learned. Read each word aloud.

1) 味（あじ）　2) 歌手（かしゅ）　3) 半分（はんぶん）　4) 文字（もじ）　5) 旅行（りょこう）する

習った漢字（かんじ）で書ける新しい単語（たんご）

The following are other new vocabulary in this lesson that contain kanji you have already leaned. Read each word aloud.

1) 今（いま）まで　2) 売（う）り切（き）れる　3) お金（かね）（を貯（た）める）　4) 画家（がか）
5) 元気（げんき）を出（だ）して（ください）　6) Duration 後（ご）　7) （冗談（じょうだん）を）言（い）う　8) 人生（じんせい）
9) 親（しん）せき　10) （食事（しょくじ）／飲（の）み物（もの）／お金（かね）／風（かぜ）を）出（だ）す　11) 前（まえ）　12) 理由（りゆう）

練習

1 取る and 出す have multiple meanings. First, read the following sentences aloud, then choose the most appropriate meaning for each use of 取る and 出す from a.-f. in the box. Write your answers in (　　).

a. to serve　b. to be enrolled in　c. to steal　d. to invest　e. to write down　f. to turn in

1) 私は今、映画のクラスを取っているんですが、先生が速(はや)く話すから、ノートを取るのが大変です。
(　　)　(　　)

2) 昨日の晩、漢字の宿題をしたけれど、今日出すのを忘れてしまいました。
(　　)

3) 私の家の近(ちか)くに安くておいしい昼ご飯を出すレストランがあります。
(　　)

2 Find and circle six kanji words that contain kanji you have learned so far, then write the words and their readings in the spaces provided. The words may appear either vertically or horizontally.

Ex.

旅	館	図
行	今	朝
歌	晩	漢
手	文	字

Ex. 旅行 (りょこう)

1) ________ (　　　　)　2) ________ (　　　　)

3) ________ (　　　　)　4) ________ (　　　　)

5) ________ (　　　　)　6) ________ (　　　　)

3 Atsuo-san is known as an "intense guy (熱(あつ)い男)." He is talking about his high school days. Read the speech bubbles aloud, then write the readings for the underlined words.

1) 親せきに画家のおじ (uncle) がいます。仕事をがんばるし、よく泣いたり 笑ったりする熱(あつ)い人で、旅行が趣味(しゅみ)です。僕(ぼく)はおじが大好きで、高校の時、よくおじに会いに行きました！

2) 高校一年生の時、朝早く 起きて勉強をすることに決めました！　毎朝４時半に起きて宿題をしたり、試験の勉強をしたりしました！　起きられない時は、兄に起こしてもらいました。

3) 毎晩、夜遅くまで車を洗うアルバイトをしました！　バイトは、午後４時に始まって、10時に終わりました！　一日に 50 台も洗った時は、つかれすぎて晩ご飯が食べられませんでした。

■ Fun facts about kanji

Q1. How many kanji do I need to learn?

Q2. How many kanji do people in Japan know on average?

Q3. Were all words written in kanji originally created in China?

A1. As of 2017, the total number of kanji taught in Japanese elementary and middle schools is 2,136 (1,026 and 1,110 respectively). It is said that if you master about 2,000 kanji, you will be able to read newspapers, magazines, most books, and other general documents you encounter in daily life in Japan. These kanji are called 常用漢字(じょうようかんじ) (kanji for daily use).

A2. There is another set of 863 kanji called 人名用漢字(じんめいようかんじ) (kanji for use in personal names). The total number of 常用漢字(じょうようかんじ) plus 人名用漢字(じんめいようかんじ) is 2,999. It is said that Japanese adults can usually read about 3,000 kanji.

A3. No, there are also many kanji compound words that were created in Japan. As you learned in Lesson 3, people in Japan started writing with kanji introduced from China in the 6th century. In addition to these, many new kanji compound words were also invented in Japan in the 19th century. These are called 和製漢語(わせいかんご) (Japanese-made kanji compound words), and most of them were invented to describe abstract concepts that were newly introduced from Western countries, including words related to science, the humanities, etc. Many of these words then spread to China, Korea, and other East Asian countries.

練習

Read aloud the following words 1)-10) that you have already learned. Do you remember their meanings? Which words do you think are 和製漢語(わせいかんご)?

1) 自由　2) 映画　3) 文学　4) 音楽　5) 運動

6) 社会　7) 学校　8) 時間　9) 自転車　10) 時計

文法(ぶんぽう)

1 〜て [Reason] "~ and/so"

[1-a]

S₁ (reason)		S2
	Te-form	
このクラスは宿題(しゅくだい)が	多(おお)くて	大変(たいへん)です。
There is a lot of homework for this class, so it's tough.		

You can express reasons using *te*-forms. For example, in [1-a], the *te*-form sentence このクラスは宿題(しゅくだい)が多(おお)くて represents the reason for the statement 大変(たいへん)です.

In this sentence pattern, there is no explicit reason expression such as から, but it is understood from the context that the *te*-form sentence is the reason for what is said in S_2.

In many cases, S_2 expresses the speaker's emotion with such expressions as うれしい, いい, 大変(たいへん), 感動(かんどう)する, and 困(こま)る. The negative forms of verbs that express one's capability (e.g., 分(わ)からない, 読(よ)めない, 見(み)えない) also occur often in S_2, in which case they imply the speaker's disappointment, frustration, etc. as in (3).

Exs. (1) 日本語(にほんご)の勉強(べんきょう)は大変(たいへん)ですが、日本(にほん)の文化(ぶんか)が<u>分(わ)かって</u>うれしいです。
Studying Japanese is hard, but I am glad to (be able to) understand Japanese culture.

(2) この町(まち)は<u>静(しず)かで</u>いいですね。*This town is nice and quiet (lit. This town is quiet and nice).*

(3) スライドの字(じ)が<u>小(ちい)さすぎて</u>読(よ)めません。*The characters on the slides are too small to read.*

[1-b]

S₁ (reason)		S2
	V (negative *te*-form)	
漢字(かんじ)が	覚(おぼ)えられなくて	困(こま)っています。
I'm having trouble because I can't {remember/memorize} kanji.		

When the reason sentence is in the negative form, なくて is used rather than ないで, as in [1-b] and (4).

Ex. (4) 友達(ともだち)がい<u>なくて</u>さびしいです。*I have no friends and (so I) feel lonely.*

☞ **GID** (vol.1): G. Connecting verbs, adjectives, and sentences using *te*-forms
(vol.2): B. Connecting sentences 5. 〜ないで vs. 〜なくて

2 Passive forms of verbs and passive sentences

Sentences that involve passive forms are called passive sentences. Passive sentences describe someone's action or an event from the viewpoint of the person who was affected by the action or event.

2-1 Passive forms

You can make passive forms as follows:

(a) *Ru*-verbs: Change the final る of the dictionary form to られる.

Exs. 食(た)べ~~る~~ → 食(た)べ<u>られる</u>; 見(み)~~る~~ → 見(み)<u>られる</u>

(b) *U*-verbs: Change the final /u/ sound of the dictionary form to the /a/ sound and attach れる.

Ex. 読(よ)む (/yomu/) → 読(よ)まれる (/yoma/ + れる)

When the dictionary form ends in う (e.g., 言(い)う, 買(か)う), change the /u/ sound to /wa/ and attach れる.

Ex. 言(い)う (/iu/) → 言(い)われる (/iwa/ + れる)

(More examples of *u*-verb passive forms are shown in the *u*-verb conjugation table on the inside of the back cover.)

(c) Irregular verbs: する → される; 来(く)る → 来(こ)られる

Passive forms are all *ru*-verbs regardless of the category of the original verb. For example, 読(よ)む is an *u*-verb, but its passive form 読(よ)まれる becomes a *ru*-verb and conjugates as follows:

	Polite		Plain		*Te*-form
Non-past	読(よ)まれます	読(よ)まれません	読(よ)まれる	読(よ)まれない	読(よ)まれて
Past	読(よ)まれました	読(よ)まれませんでした	読(よ)まれた	読(よ)まれなかった	

2-2 Passive sentences

Passive sentences are used in several different patterns, as explained below.

2-2-1 [Person 1] は [Person 2] に V-passive "[Person 1] is/was V-ed by [Person 2]"

Passive sentences in this pattern have corresponding active sentences. For example, [2-a] is the active sentence that corresponds to the passive sentence [2-b].

[2-a] **Active sentence**

Topic (actor)		Direct object		Vt
黒田先生(くろだせんせい)	は	アイさん	を	ほめました。
Prof. Kuroda praised Ai.				

[2-b] **Passive sentence**

Topic		Actor		Vt (passive)
アイさん	は	黒田先生(くろだせんせい)	に	ほめられました。
Ai was praised by Prof. Kuroda.				

In the active sentence [2-a], the subject 黒田先生(くろだせんせい) (also the topic of the sentence) is the actor (= the person who does something), the verb ほめる is a transitive verb, and the direct object アイさん (= the person who receives the action ほめる) is marked by を.

In the passive sentence [2-b], on the other hand, アイさん, who receives the action, is the subject (and also topic) of the sentence, the verb is the passive form of ほめる, and 黒田先生(くろだせんせい), who is the actor, is marked by に.

Passive sentences are used when you describe an action from the viewpoint of the person on the receiving end of that action, as in (1) and (2).

Exs. (1) 私(わたし)はよく先生(せんせい)にオフィスに呼(よ)ばれます。

My teacher often calls me to her office. (lit. I am often called to [my teacher's] office by my teacher.)

(2) 子(こ)どもの時(とき)、私(わたし)はゲームをしすぎてよく父(ちち)にしかられました。

When I was a child, I played video games too much and was often scolded by my father.

[2-c] Active sentence

Topic (actor)		Indirect object		Direct object		Vt
黒田先生(くろだせんせい)	は	アイさん	に	質問(しつもん)	を	しました。
Prof. Kuroda asked Ai a question.						

[2-d] Passive sentence

Topic		Actor		Direct object		Vt (passive)
アイさん	は	黒田先生(くろだせんせい)	に	質問(しつもん)	を	されました。
Ai was asked a question by Prof. Kuroda.						

Lesson 16

Active sentences with verbs that require "N (human) に" also have corresponding passive sentences. For example, the active sentence [2-c], which involves the indirect object アイさん marked by に, has the corresponding passive sentence [2-d], in which アイさん is presented as the subject (also the topic) of the sentence, the verb is the passive form of する, and 黒田先生(くろだせんせい), the actor, is marked by に.

Other verbs that require "N (human) に" include たのむ "request," 注意(ちゅうい)する "warn," 相談(そうだん)する "consult," and 言(い)う "tell."

Exs. (3) タオさんはアイさんににゃんたの世話(せわ)をたのまれました。

Tao was asked by Ai to take care of Nyanta.

(4) 宿題(しゅくだい)を3回(かい)も出(だ)さなかったから、先生(せんせい)に（そのことを）注意(ちゅうい)されました。

I didn't submit my homework (as many as) three times, so I was admonished by my teacher (about that).

(5) にゃんたはジャパンハウスの人達(ひとたち)によくかわいいと言(い)われます。

Nyanta is often told that he is cute by the people in the Japan House.

Note that in general, passive sentences are not as commonly used in English as in Japanese; therefore, literally translating Japanese passive sentences into English sometimes yields unnatural results.

☞ GID (vol.2): E. Special topics 6. Viewpoint 6-4. Passive sentences

2-2-2 [Person 1] は [Person 2] に [Direct object] を V-passive

"[Person 2] V [Direct object], which (negatively) affects [Person 1]"

In this type of passive sentence, the topic person X is not the object, direct or indirect, of the corresponding active sentence. Rather, X is the person affected by the action presented in the corresponding active sentence.

Note that this type of passive sentence is often used when the topic person X is negatively affected, although this is not always the case. Whether X is negatively affected or not is determined by the context.

[2-e] Active sentence

Topic (actor)		Direct object				Vt
ルームメート	は	私(わたし)	の	牛乳(ぎゅうにゅう)	を	飲(の)みました。
My roommate drank my milk.						

[2-f] Passive sentence

Topic (affected person)		Actor		Direct object		Vt (passive)
私(わたし)	は	ルームメート	に	牛乳(ぎゅうにゅう)	を	飲(の)まれました。
I had my milk drunk by my roommate [and I'm upset].						

Here, the topic person of the passive sentence [2-f] (i.e., 私(わたし)) is the person affected by her roommate's drinking her milk. Note that in the active sentence [2-e], the person affected appears as the possessor of the direct object (i.e., the milk). Because the main purpose for the use of this type of passive sentence is to indicate who is affected by someone's action, the following sentence, while not ungrammatical, is unnatural:

× 私(わたし)の牛乳(ぎゅうにゅう)はルームメートに飲(の)まれました。*My milk was drunk by my roommate.*

Exs. (1) 昨日(きのう)、私(わたし)は（誰(だれ)かに）自転車(じてんしゃ)をぬすまれました。
I had my bike stolen (by someone) yesterday.

(2) 電車(でんしゃ)で知(し)らない人(ひと)に足(あし)をふまれました。*I had my foot stepped on by a stranger on the train.*

2-2-3 [Person 1] は [Person 2/Thing] に ([Direct object] を) V-passive
"[Person 2] V ([Direct object]), which (negatively) affects [Person 1]"

This type of passive sentence is similar to those in #2-2-2. The difference is that the person affected by the action, who becomes the topic of the passive sentence, does not appear in the corresponding active sentence at all.

[2-g] Active sentence

Subject (actor)		Vi
雨(あめ)	が	降(ふ)りました。
It rained.		

[2-h] Passive sentence

Topic (affected person)		Actor		Vi (passive)
山田(やまだ)さん	は	雨(あめ)	に	降(ふ)られました。
Yamada-san got rained on.				

[2-i] Active sentence

Subject (actor)		Direct object		Vt
となりの人(ひと)	が	タバコ	を	吸(す)いました。
The person next to me smoked.				

[2-j] Passive sentence

Topic (affected person)		Actor		Direct object		Vt (passive)
私(わたし)	は	となりの人(ひと)	に	タバコ	を	吸(す)われました。
The person next to me smoked [and I was bothered by it].						

While they can often be translated roughly as "[Person] had [something] V-ed" or "[Person] got V-ed," there are no fixed English equivalents for passive sentences of this type or those in #2-2-2.

Exs. (1) （私(わたし)は）電車(でんしゃ)でよっぱらいにとなりに座(すわ)られて、いやでした。
A drunk person sat next to me on the train, which was annoying.

(2) 映画館(えいがかん)でとなりの人(ひと)に大(おお)きい声(こえ)で話(はな)されて、うるさかったです。
The people next to me at the movie theater were talking (lit. talked in a loud voice), and it was irritatingly loud.

(3) 昨日(きのう)は夜遅(よるおそ)く弟(おとうと)にギターをひかれて、寝(ね)られませんでした。
I could not sleep yesterday because my younger brother was playing the guitar late at night.

The kinds of passive sentences introduced in #2-2-2 and #2-2-3 are used when someone was affected (in many cases, negatively) by someone else's action or an event. The following diagram illustrates the conditions for the use of these passive sentences:

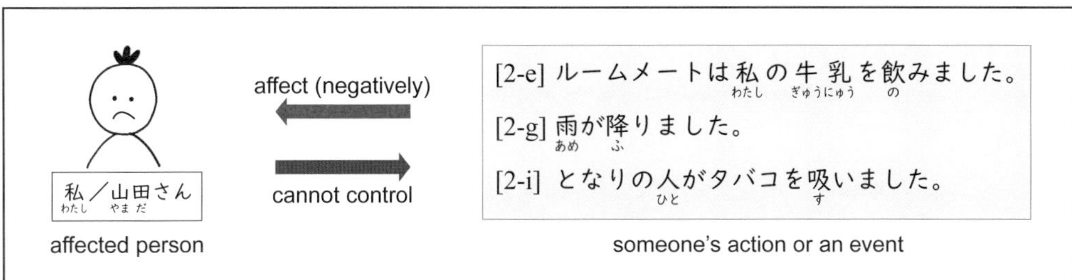

While it is possible to use this passive construction to describe situations in which someone is affected by someone else's action in some way other than negatively, if you want to describe a situation in which someone received some benefit from someone else's action, you should use V-*te*もらう or V-*te*くれる. (See L15 #4.) Compare (4), (5), and (6):

Exs. (4) 私はみかさんに私のレポートを読まれました。*Mika read my report [and I was upset].*

(5) 私はみかさんに私のレポートを読んでもらいました。
I got Mika to read my report (e.g., to receive comments for improvement) [and I appreciated it].

(6) みかさんは私のレポートを読んでくれました。
Mika read my report for me (e.g., to give me comments for improvement) [and I appreciated it].

2-2-4 [Thing] は ([Person] によって) V-passive "[Thing] is/was V-ed (by [Person])"

[2-k]

Topic (thing)		Actor		Vt (passive)
この絵	は	ピカソ	によって	描かれました。
This picture was painted by Picasso.				

Passive sentences are often used when you introduce things like art pieces, famous architecture, books, invented/discovered objects, etc. In this case, the creators/discoverers are marked by によって rather than に, as in [2-k].

[2-l]

Topic (thing)			V-*te* (passive)	
この作家の本	は	世界中で	読まれて	います。
This author's books are read all over the world.				

Passive sentences are also used when it is not necessary to mention the actor(s) or when the actor(s) cannot be specified, as in [2-l]. ～ています is used when the action is ongoing.

Exs. (1) 『ロミオとジュリエット』はシェイクスピアによって書かれました。
"Romeo and Juliet" was written by Shakespeare.

(2) 京都には100年ぐらい前に建てられた家がたくさんあります。
There are many houses in Kyoto that were built about 100 years ago.

(3) 英語は世界中で話されています。*English is spoken all around the world.*

(4) 魚を食べるのは体にいいと言われています。
It is said that eating fish is good for one's health.

3 ～しか～ない "nothing/nobody but ~; only ~"

[3-a]

			V (negative)
弟(おとうと)は	まんが	しか	読(よ)みません。
My younger brother reads nothing but comics.			

[3-b]

		Prt		V (negative)
この本(ほん)は	ネット	で	しか	買(か)えません。
You can buy this book only on the internet.				

You can express the idea of "nothing/nobody but" and "only" using しか with negative predicates.

The particles は, が, and を do not appear with しか, as in [3-a], and (1) and (2). へ and に as the direction/time marker are optional, as in (3). The other particles always appear before しか, as in [3-b] and (4).

Exs. (1) 父(ちち)は英語(えいご)しか分(わ)かりません。*My father only understands English.*

(2) 祖母(そぼ)しかこのおいしいクッキーの作(つく)り方(かた)を知(し)りません。
My grandma is the only one who knows how to make these delicious cookies.

(3) 土曜日(どようび)(に)しかアルバイトができません。
I can only work [at my part-time job] on Saturdays.

(4) 子(こ)どもの時(とき)、シャイだったから、家族(かぞく)としか話(はな)しませんでした。それから、家(いえ)でしか遊(あそ)びませんでした。
When I was a child, I was so shy that I only talked with my family. Also, I only played at home.

[3-c]

Number + Counter			V (negative)
3人(にん)	しか	パーティーに	来(き)ませんでした。
Only three people came to the party.			

You can express the idea of "only" or "no more than" using しか with a number and a counter. In this use, too, the predicate must be in the negative form. しか emphasizes the speaker's impression that the number is small or the amount is little.

Exs. (5) 今(いま)、500円(えん)しか持(も)っていません。*All I have now is 500 yen.*

(6) 昨日(きのう)は2時間(じかん)しか寝(ね)られませんでした。*I could sleep only two hours yesterday.*

☞ GID (vol.2): E. Special topics 2. しか vs. だけ

4 *Ba*-conditional forms of verbs and ～ばよかった

Here, we will learn the *ba*-conditional forms of verbs and an idiomatic expression that involves them. (We will learn more about the use of *ba*-conditional forms in Lesson 18 #6.)

4-1 *Ba*-conditional forms of verbs

The rules for making the *ba*-conditional forms of verbs are as follows:

(a) *Ru*-verbs: Change the final る of the dictionary form to れば.

Exs. 食(た)べ~~る~~ → 食(た)べれば; 見(み)~~る~~ → 見(み)れば

(b) *U*-verbs: Change the final /u/ sound of the dictionary form to the /e/ sound and attach ば.

Exs. 飲(の)む (/nomu/) → 飲(の)めば (/nome/+ば); 話(はな)す (/hanasu/) → 話(はな)せば (/hanase/+ば)

(More examples of *u*-verb *ba*-conditional forms are shown in the *u*-verb conjugation table on the inside of the back cover.)

(c) Irregular verbs: する → すれば; 来(く)る → 来(く)れば

In fact, the above three rules (i.e., (a), (b), and (c)) can be summarized into one single rule as follows:

Verbs: Change the final /u/ sound of the dictionary form to the /e/ sound and attach ば.

Exs. 見(み)る (/miru/) → 見(み)れば (/mire/+ば); 飲(の)む (/nomu/) → 飲(の)めば (/nome/+ば);
する (/suru/) → すれば (/sure/+ば); 来(く)る (/kuru/) → 来(く)れば (/kure/+ば)

(d) Negative ending: Change ～ない to ～なければ.

Exs. 食(た)べる → 食(た)べ~~ない~~ → 食(た)べなければ
飲(の)む → 飲(の)ま~~ない~~ → 飲(の)まなければ
する → し~~ない~~ → しなければ

4-2 ～ばよかった "I should (not) have V-ed; I wish I had (not) V-ed"

[4-a]

	V-cond *	
先生(せんせい)にプロジェクトのトピックを	相談(そうだん)すれば	よかったです。
I should have consulted my teacher about my project topic.		

* V-cond indicates the *ba*-conditional form of a verb.

[4-b]

	V-*nai*		
昨日(きのう)パーティーに	行(い)か	なければ	よかったです。
I wish I hadn't gone to the party yesterday.			

You can express your feelings of regret about your own action (or non-action) in the past using ～ばよかった, i.e., the *ba*-conditional forms of verbs (or the *ba*-conditional form of ～ない) with the past form of いい.

Exs. (1) 朝(あさ)ねぼうしてしまいました。2時(じ)までゲームをしなければよかったです。もっと早(はや)く寝(ね)ればよかったです。

To my regret, I overslept this morning. I shouldn't have played games until two. I should've gone to bed earlier.

(2) テストが30点(てん)！ もっと勉強(べんきょう)すればよかった。昨日(きのう)出(で)かけなければよかった。

[I only got] 30 points on the test! I should have studied more. If only I hadn't gone out yesterday.

(3) 見(み)てよかったと思(おも)う映画(えいが)と、見(み)なければよかったと思(おも)う映画(えいが)は何(なん)ですか。

What are some movies you are glad you watched and some you wish you hadn't?

～ばよかった is a counter-factual expression. That is, the preferred situation described with the *ba*-conditional form is not in fact what happened. If the speaker is glad about the way things turned out, ～てよかった is used, as in (3).

5 Vつもり "be planning to V; be going to V; intend to V"

[5-a]

	V-plain.non-past (affirmative)		
夏休みに日本に	行く	つもり	です。
I'm planning to go to Japan over summer break.			

[5-b]

	V-plain.non-past (negative)		
今年の夏休みは、どこにも	行かない	つもり	です。
I'm planning not to go anywhere this summer break.			

You can express your plan or intention to do something using the plain non-past forms of verbs with つもり. つもり is a type of noun, so you need to follow it with です or its variation (e.g., でした, だ, だった).

Ex. (1) このアパートの家賃は高いから、来月引っこしする<u>つもりです</u>。
The rent for this apartment is expensive, so I intend to move next month.

When you want to express the idea of "not planning to V," you negate the verb before つもり rather than です, as in [5-b] and (2) below. Therefore, 行くつもりじゃないです and 出かけるつもりじゃないです are not used.

Ex. (2) お金がないから、週末は出かけ<u>ないつもりです</u>。
Because I don't have money, I won't be going out over the weekend.

You can use Vつもりでしたが to discuss a plan or intention of yours that was not realized, as in (3) and (4).

Exs. (3) 夏休みに旅行する<u>つもりでした</u>が、忙しくて行けませんでした。
I planned to travel over summer break, but I was busy, so I couldn't go.

(4) 今月はむだづかいし<u>ないつもりだった</u>けど、ゲームを三つも買っちゃった。
I planned not to waste money this month, but I bought three games [which is too many].

Vつもりですか is not an appropriate way to question a person whose status is higher than yours.

× 先輩、明日練習に来るつもりですか。 → 先輩、明日練習に来ますか。
Senpai, are you planning to come to practice tomorrow?

☞ **GID** (vol.2): D. Sentence patterns 7. ～ようと思う vs. つもり

6 間／間に "while"

[6-a]

S1			S2 (main clause)
	V-plain.non-past		
日本に	いる	間、	古い日本の家に住みたいです。
I want to live in an old Japanese house while I'm in Japan.			

[6-b]

S1			S2 (main clause)
	V-plain.non-past		
日本に	いる	間に、	一度、歌舞伎を見たいです。
I want to watch a *kabuki* play once while I'm in Japan.			

You can express the idea of "while" using 間 or 間に. 間 is used when the action represented in S_2 is performed for the entire period represented by S_1, as in [6-a]. If the action represented in S_2 is not performed for the entire period represented by S_1, 間に is used, as in [6-b]. The following diagrams illustrate the difference between 間 and 間に:

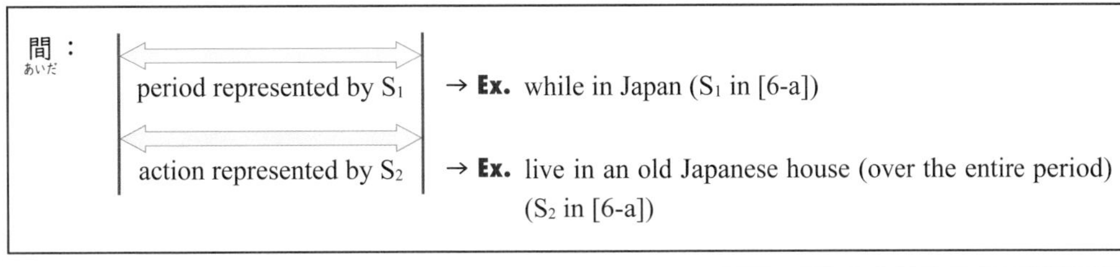

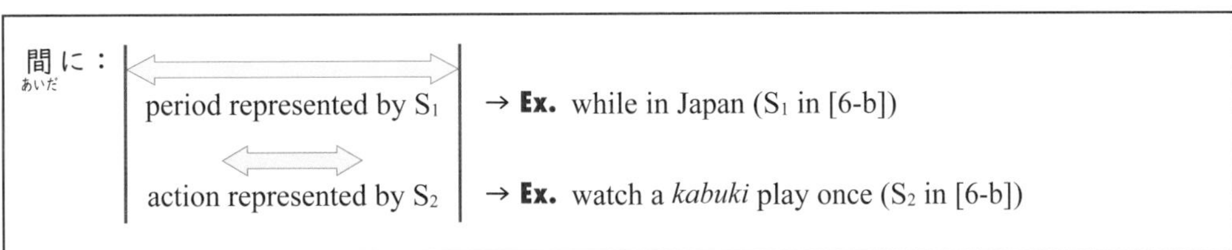

Exs. (1) 電車に乗っている間、ずっと本を読んでいました。

I was reading a book the whole time I was on the train.

(2) トムさんは京都を旅行している間に、清水寺に行きました。

While Tom was traveling in Kyoto, he visited [the temple] Kiyomizu-dera.

As seen in (1) and (2), when the verb in S_1 is an action verb (e.g., 乗る, 作る), V-*te*いる is used before 間(に).

[6-c]

<table>
<tr><td colspan="3">S_1</td><td rowspan="2"></td><td rowspan="2">S_2 (main clause)</td></tr>
<tr><td></td><td>V-te</td><td></td></tr>
<tr><td>母が晩ご飯を</td><td>作って</td><td>いる</td><td>間、</td><td>私はゲームをしていました。</td></tr>
<tr><td colspan="5">While my mother was fixing our dinner, I was playing games.</td></tr>
</table>

In the "S_1 間(に) S_2" structure, when the subjects of S_1 and S_2 are different, the subject in S_1 is marked by が, as in [6-c] and (3) and (4).

Exs. (3) 私が勉強している間、ルームメートは寝ていました。

While I was studying, my roommate was sleeping.

(4) <パーティーの準備で>

友達が買い物をしている間に、私は部屋をそうじしておきました。

While my friend was shopping, I cleaned the room.

間(に) can also be used with nouns. In this case, the form is Nの間(に), as in (5).

Ex. (5) 夏休みの間、ずっとアルバイトをしました。

I worked part-time all throughout the summer break.

☞ **GID** (vol.2): A. Time expressions 3.ながら vs. 間

話しましょう

▶ **Words written in purple** are new words introduced in this lesson.

Express your feelings about good and bad experiences.

できるI-A Reason ～て

1 Suppose you are about to leave Japan after studying there for a semester. What made you feel happy, inconvenienced, or surprised during your stay? L16-6

Ex. 日本に来て、よかったです。

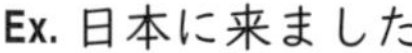

Ex. 日本に来ました
1) 日本語が上手になりました
2) たくさん友達ができました
3) 色々な所に行けました

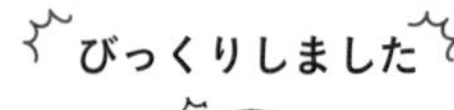

4) 毎日電車が混(こ)んでいました
5) 漢字(かんじ)が読めませんでした
6) 時々クレジットカードが使えませんでした
7) 町にごみ箱(ばこ)がありませんでした

8) ラーメンがすごくおいしかったです
9) 地下鉄(ちかてつ)の駅(えき)の階段(かいだん)が長かったです
10) コンビニがとても便利(べんり)でした
11) トイレがきれいでした
12) your own

2 Describe what you cannot do with a reason. L16-7

Ex. この本は難(むずか)しくて、読めません。

 読む(×)	食べる(×)	live ticket  買う(×)
Ex. 難(むずか)しい 1) 漢字(かんじ)が多(おお)い 2) 字(じ)が小さすぎる 3) 汚れている	4) まずい 5) 味(あじ)がない 6) においが変	7) 高い 8) ファンが多(おお)い 9) ウェブサイトにつながらない 10) もう売り切れてしまった

3 Talk about events in your childhood and your feelings about them.

Step 1 Brainstorm happy events/memories with your partner.

Useful vocabulary	楽しい	幸(しあわ)せ	うれしい	感動(かんどう)する	びっくりする

Ex.1 子どもの時、動物園(どうぶつえん)に行って、楽しかったです。

Ex.2 子どもの時、宿題がなくて、幸(しあわ)せでした。

Group Work

Step 2 Share some of your happy experiences with your groupmates.

Ex. A: みなさんの幸(しあわ)せな経験(けいけん)について教えてください。

B: 私は子どもの時、宿題がなくて、幸(しあわ)せでした。

C: えっと、私は子どもの時、家族と動物園(どうぶつえん)に行ったり、親(しん)せきの家に行ったりして、楽しかったです。 <Continue>

できるI-B Passive forms of verbs and passive sentences

1 Let's practice passive form conjugations. L16-8

Ex. 食(た)べる → 食(た)べられる → 食(た)べられます

1) 見(み)る　2) 捨(す)てる　3) ほめる　4) 間違(まちが)える　5) 死(し)ぬ　6) 言(い)う
7) 連(つ)れていく　8) 取(と)る　9) する　10) 来(く)る　11) いじめる　12) ふむ
13) なぐる　14) たのむ　15) 起(お)こす　16) うそをつく　17) ばかにする

2 Let's tell the story of Cinderella in Japanese. Use the passive form to restate the sentences below from Cinderella's point of view. L16-9

Ex.1 お母さんはシンデレラをしかりました

→ シンデレラはお母さんにしかられました。

1) お母さんはシンデレラをいじめました

2) お母さんはシンデレラを無視(むし)しました

3) お姉さんはシンデレラを朝早(あさ)く起(お)こしました

4) お姉さんはシンデレラをばかにしました

5) お姉さんはシンデレラを全然(ぜんぜん)ほめませんでした

Ex.2 王子様(おうじさま)はシンデレラに名前を聞きました

→ シンデレラは王子様(おうじさま)に名前を聞かれました。

王子様(おうじさま) (prince)

6) 魔法使(まほうつか)いはシンデレラをはげましました

7) 魔法使(まほうつか)いはシンデレラにアドバイスをしました

8) 王子様(おうじさま)はシンデレラに結婚(けっこん)を申(もう)し込(こ)みました (to propose)

9) 王子様(おうじさま)はシンデレラに「一緒(いっしょ)に幸(しあわ)せになってください」と言いました

10) 王子様(おうじさま)はシンデレラをずっと愛(あい)しました

11) 王子様(おうじさま)はシンデレラに感謝(かんしゃ)しました

3 Describe what happened to you today from your own viewpoint. 

Ex. 私は先生に名前を呼(よ)ばれました。

Ex. 先生は私の名前を呼(よ)びました

1) 友達は私のテストを見ました

2) 先生は私の作文をほめました

3) よっぱらいは私の顔(かお)をなぐりました

4) どろぼうは私の財布(さいふ)をぬすみました

5)（誰(だれ)かが）私の足をふみました

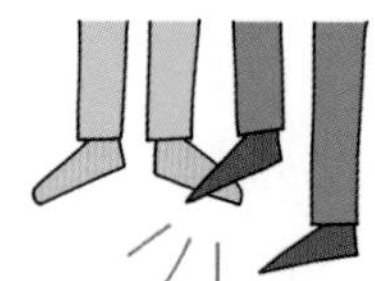

6) かは私のうでをさしました

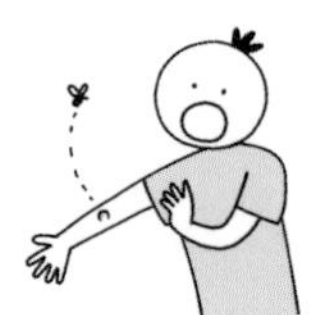

7) 付(つ)き合(あ)っている人は私のスマホをチェックしました

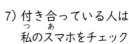

4 Talk about your negative experiences involving your roommate.

Step 1 Describe how you were negatively affected by your roommate's annoying behaviors, using the cues provided. L16-11

Ex. ルームメートは夜(よる)遅く帰ってくる

→（私は）ルームメートに夜(よる)遅く帰ってこられました。困りました。(← Your feeling)

1) ルームメートは朝(あさ)までゲームをする
2) ルームメートはおもしろくない冗談(じょうだん)を言う
3) ルームメートは大きい声(こえ)で電話する
4) ルームメートは（私の）部屋で泣(な)く
5) ルームメートはリビングでたばこを吸(す)う
6) ルームメートは毎晩(まいばん)ギターをひく
7) ルームメートはキッチンを汚す
8) ルームメートは大きい音で音楽を聞く

Step 2 Suppose you were affected by your roommate's behavior. Complain about it to your partner. You may use the cues from Step 1.

Ex. A: 昨日は最悪でした。ルームメートに夜(よる)遅く帰ってこられて、困りました。

B: それは大変でしたね。ルームメートは何時に帰ってきたんですか。

(↖ Follow-up question)

<Continue>

B: 実(じつ)は、私も昨日は最悪でした。

<Continue>

5 People can see the same thing differently depending on their perspective.

Step 1 Describe each of the following situations from ハッピーさん's viewpoint first. Then, describe the same thing from アンハッピーさん's viewpoint. L16-12

Ex. ルームメートは私の部屋をそうじする

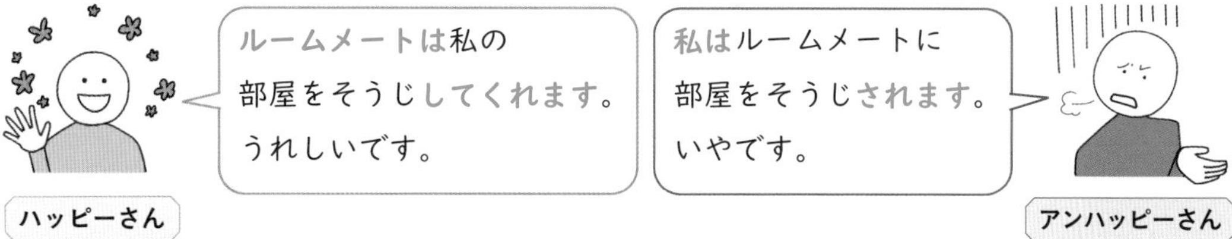

ルームメートは私の
部屋をそうじしてくれます。
うれしいです。
私はルームメートに
部屋をそうじされます。
いやです。
ハッピーさん
アンハッピーさん

1) 友達は毎朝(まいあさ)私を起(お)こす　　2) 母は毎日私に電話する

3) 父は毎月私を動物園(どうぶつえん)に連(つ)れていく　　4) 友達はいつも SNS に私の写真(しゃしん)をアップする

5) 今、付(つ)き合(あ)っている人は毎日私に会いに来る　　6) your own

Step 2 What if the people described in Step 1 did the same things to you? Describe the situations from your own perspective. Are you more like ハッピーさん or アンハッピーさん?

Ex.1 私はルームメートが私の部屋をそうじしてくれたら、うれしいです。
それから… <Continue> だから、私はハッピーさんだと思います。

Ex.2 私はルームメートに部屋をそうじされたら、いやです。それから… <Continue>
だから、私はアンハッピーさんかもしれません。

できる II Talk about things that did not go well and things you regret.

できるII-A ～しか～ない

1 Talk about things you do on your day off to relax and save your energy.

Step 1 Describe the only things you do on your day off based on the cues provided.  L16-13

Ex.1 まんが → 休みにまんがしか読みません。

1) お菓子(かし)　2) ゲーム　3) コーラ　4) スマホ

Ex.2 家族に会う → 休みに家族にしか会いません。

5) ネコとしゃべる　6) トイレとキッチンに行く　7) 家の中で遊(あそ)ぶ　8) SNS で話す

Step 2 Now, talk about what you actually did on your recent day off to relax and save your energy.

Ex. A: 休みはどうでしたか。
B: 何もしませんでした。コンビニにしか行きませんでした。
A: そうですか。私は一日中、動画しか見ませんでした。
<Continue>

2 Let's practice using ～しか～ない with counters.

Step 1 First, let's review some counters. For each item below, say "one X," "two Xs," and "three Xs" using the appropriate counter. L16-14

Ex. 

1)  2)  3)  4)  5) 

6) times 7) hours 8) days 9) weeks

休み

10) months 11) years

準備(じゅんび)の時間

Step 2 Now, say that there is only one of each item in Step 1, as in the example. 

Ex. 皿(さら)が一枚(いちまい)しかありません。

3 Suppose you live a minimalist lifestyle. Describe your life based on the cues provided. 

Ex. Tシャツを持っています (1) → 私はTシャツを一枚(いちまい)しか持っていません。

1) パソコンがあります (1)
2) 毎週アルバイトをします (1 hour)
3) 毎日水を飲みます (1 cup)
4) 昼(ひる)におにぎりを食べます (1)
5) 毎日お金を使います (100 yen)
6) 毎日スマホを使います (30 minutes)

4 Take a look at バリバリさん and ゴロゴロさん's routines.

Step 1 Describe what both バリバリさん and ゴロゴロさん do based on the cues provided. 

Ex. バリバリさんは毎日日本語を5時間も勉強しますが、
ゴロゴロさんは10分しか勉強しません。

	バリバリさん	ゴロゴロさん
Ex. study Japanese	5 hours	10 minutes
1) exercise	2 hours	5 minutes
2) do homework	5 assignments (counter: つ)	1 assignment
3) read academic papers	30 pages (ページ)	1 page
4) check social media	10 times	once
5) walk	10 kilometers	100 meters

Step 2 Talk about both your active and lazy traits with your partner. You may use the cues in Step 1.

Ex. A: 私は毎日日本語を 30 分しか勉強しないから、ゴロゴロさんみたいです。
でも、SNS を 10 回もチェックするから、時々バリバリさんかもしれません。
B: そうですか。私は… <Continue>

5 Talk about your favorite things with your partner.

Step 1 Find out if you know each other's favorite things.

Useful expressions	～回しか	時々しか	少(すこ)ししか	名前しか	週末(に)しか

Ex. A: ○○さんは「トビラッテ」というゲームを知っていますか。
B: ええ、{私も好きです／でも、一回しかしたことがありません／でも、名前しか知りません}。or いいえ、知りません。
<Continue>

Step 2 Make a three-sentence presentation about one of your favorite things to your classmates.

What you like **Reason + limitation** **Conclusion** (invitation, request, suggestion, etc.)

Ex.1 私は「トビラッテ」というゲームが大好きです。
でも、時間がなくて、週末(に)しかできません。
みなさん、今度一緒(いっしょ)にしませんか。

Ex.2 私は「さくら」という日本料理の店が大好きです。
でも、高すぎて、一年に一回しか行けません。
誰(だれ)かさくらで私においしいおすしをごちそうしてくれませんか。

できるII-B Feelings of regret ～ばよかった

1 Let's practice conjugating verbs into their *ba*-conditional forms.

Step 1 First, change the verbs below into their *ba*-conditional forms. L16-18

Ex. 食(た)べる → 食(た)べれば → 食(た)べなければ

1) 起(お)きる	2) 見(み)る	3) ほめる	4) 続(つづ)ける	5) がんばる
6) 買(か)う	7) 読(よ)む	8) する	9) 来(く)る	10) 行(い)ってみる
11) してもらう	12) しておく	13) うそをつく	14) 無視(むし)する	

Step 2 This time, practice forming the expression ～ばよかったです in both the affirmative and the negative using the cues in Step 1. L16-19

Ex. 食(た)べる → 食(た)べればよかったです → 食(た)べなければよかったです

2 Talk about your regrets about what you did or didn't do.

Step 1 Describe your feeling of regret for the past actions and inactions listed below. 

Ex.1 おなかがすいてしまいました。朝(あさ)ご飯を食べればよかったです。

Ex.2 おなかが痛くなってしまいました。アイスクリームを三つも食べなければよかったです。

Ex.1 おなかがすく  ➡ 朝(あさ)ご飯を食べる	Ex.2 おなかが痛くなる  ➡ ×アイスクリームを三つも食べる	1) 私のイヌが5キロも太(ふと)る  ➡ 散歩(さんぽ)に連(つ)れていく
2) 事故(じこ)にあう  ➡ ×信号(しんごう)を無視(むし)する	3) バスに乗り遅れる  ➡ もっと急(いそ)ぐ	4) パソコンがこわれる  ➡ ×安いのを買う
5) 友達にいじめられる  ➡×いじわるなことを言う	6) 好きな人にふられる  ➡ ×うそをつく	7) 先生にしかられる  ➡ your own

Step 2 Suppose you are in the same situations listed in Step 1. Express regret for actions and inactions of your own choosing.

Ex. はあ (sigh)。おなかがすいてしまいました。お菓子(かし)を持ってくればよかったです。

3 Suppose you are regretting something you couldn't do. Talk about it with your partner.

Opening	**Ex.** A: はあ (sigh) …。 B: どうしたんですか。
Reason + unsatisfactory event	A: 実(じつ)は数学(すうがく)の試験が難(むずか)しくて、30点(てん)しか取(と)れなかったんです。 B: ああ、あの試験は難(むずか)しかったですね。
Regret(s)	A: ええ、1週間前から勉強しておけばよかったです。 B: そうですか。大変でしたね。 A: それから、昨日遊(あそ)びに行かなければよかったです。 B: だいじょうぶですよ。元気を出してください。

できるⅡ-C　Plan/intention Vつもり

1 Practice using the expression 〜つもり to talk about your plans/intentions for this semester.

Ex. 自分で料理します → 今学期は<u>自分で料理する</u>つもりです。

1) お金を貯めます　2) 毎日階段を使います　3) 漢字を 300 覚えます
4) 日本のドラマをほんやくしてみます　5) むだづかいしません　6) うそをつきません
7) 甘い物を少ししか食べません　8) エレベーターに乗りません　9) your own

2 Describe your life last year and state a resolution to make this year better, as in the example. (Possible topics for your resolution include your study habits, hobbies, health, etc.) Your partner will ask you follow-up questions.

Ex. A: 去年は SNS でしか友達と話さなかったし、休みにあまり出かけなかったし、つまらなかったです。今年は大学で友達をたくさん作るつもりです。
それから、SNS をしすぎないつもりです。

B: そうですか。〇〇さんはどの SNS をよく使っていますか。

<Continue>

3 What are your plans for your next break?

Step 1 Talk about your plans for a break or weekend with your partner.

マヤ遺跡 (Mayan Ruins)

Ex. A: １週間後は春休みですね。何をしますか。

B: メキシコにマヤ遺跡を見に行くつもりです。

A: え、マヤ遺跡？　おもしろそうですね。ツアーに参加しますか。

B: 安かったら、参加するつもりです。〇〇さんは何をしますか。

A: どこにも出かけないで、毎日、本を読んだり、映画を見たりするつもりです。

<Continue>

Step 2 Now, talk about your plans for a break casually with your friend.

Ex. A: １週間後は春休みだね。何する？

B: メキシコにマヤ遺跡を見に行くつもり(だよ)。

A: え、マヤ遺跡？　おもしろそうだね。ツアーに参加する？

B: 安かったら、参加するつもり(だよ)。〇〇さんは何する？

A: どこにも出かけないで、毎日、本を読んだり、映画を見たりするつもり(だよ)。

<Continue>

4 Now, let's talk about plans that didn't work out.

Step 1 Describe your plan(s) for this past weeked that didn't work out.

Ex.1 週末、親(しん)せきの家に行く**つもりでした**が、行けませんでした。

Ex.2 週末、日本語の宿題をする**つもりでした**が、{少(すこ)ししか／半分(はんぶん)しか／全然(ぜんぜん)}できませんでした。

Step 2 Now, talk about the failed plan(s) you described in Step 1 with your partner. Make sure to include how the plan(s) went wrong and express your regret.

Ask about the weekend	**Ex.** A: 週末はどうでしたか。
Failed plan(s)	B: ちょっと大変でした。日本語の宿題をするつもりでしたが、かぜをひいて、少(すこ)ししかできませんでした。
	A: そうですか。
Regret	B: もっと早く宿題を始(はじ)めればよかったです。

できるII-D 間／間に

1 Describe what you plan to do while visiting Japan, using 間 and 間に as appropriate. L16-22

Ex.1

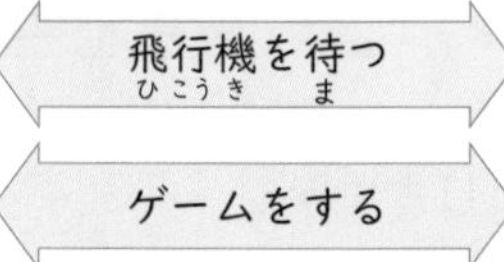

→ 飛行機(ひこうき)を待(ま)っている**間**、ずっとゲームをするつもりです。

1) 飛行機(ひこうき)に乗る／映画を見る
2) 観光(かんこう)する／日本語しか話さない
3) 日本にいる／旅館(りょかん)に泊(と)まる
4) 旅行(りょこう)／夜(よる)は旅館(りょかん)でゆっくりする

Ex.2

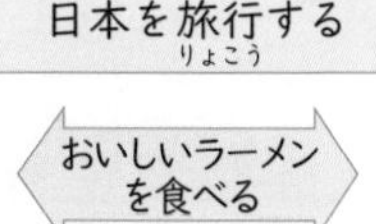

→ 日本を旅行(りょこう)している**間に**、おいしいラーメンを食べるつもりです。

5) 東京を観光(かんこう)する／SNSに写真(しゃしん)をアップする
6) 旅館(りょかん)に泊(と)まる／温泉(おんせん)に入ってみる
7) 日本にいる／新幹線(しんかんせん)に乗る
8) 散歩(さんぽ)／おもしろい写真(しゃしん)をとる

2 Describe two things occurring at the same time.

Step 1 Suppose you are doing a homestay in Japan now. Describe how your daily routine lines up with your host father's, using 間 or 間に as appropriate. L16-23

Ex. 私がシャワーを浴びている間、お父さんは朝ご飯を作ります。

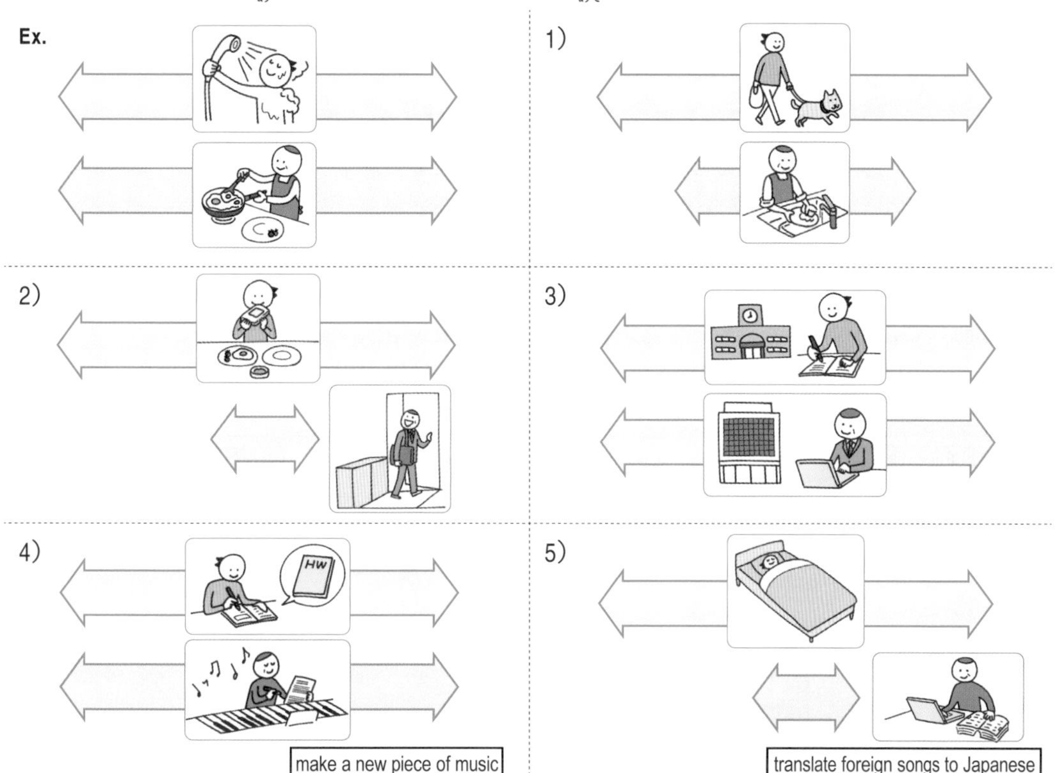

Step 2 Recall and describe how your actions lined up with someone else's (e.g., your roommate, family member, pet) yesterday, using the same format as in Step 1.

Ex. 私がシャワーを浴びている間、私のネコは朝ご飯を待っていました。

Group Work

3 Discuss with your groupmates what you would like to complete, achieve, etc. while you are in a certain place or at a certain stage in life.

Possible topics	大学生	○○に住んでいる	日本に{留学/旅行}している

Ex. A: みなさんは大学生の間に何がしたいですか。

B: 私は大学生の間に留学してみたいです。日本に行って色々な地方の文化を知りたいです。

C: いいですね。私は大学にいる間、ずっとフランスの美術を勉強するつもりです。特にドランという画家について研究しようと思っています。

A: そうですか。私は大学生の{間/間に}… <Continue>

Group Work

4 Are you afraid that you might be addicted to something?

Step 1 Check if you are addicted to your smartphone and social media. Mark ○ if you do each of the following things, and × if you don't. Who has the most ○s?

(　　　)友達とご飯を食べている間に、スマホを時々チェックしてしまう。

(　　　)学校にいる間、スマホがなかったら、心配になる。

(　　　)よく「スマホを見ないで、勉強すればよかった」と思う。

(　　　)毎日 SNS をしすぎて、少(すこ)ししか勉強できない。

(　　　)SNS でしか友達と話さない。

(　　　)明日からもっとスマホを見る時間を短(みじか)くするつもりだ。

Step 2 Choose three sentences from Step 1 to use as a model and make three questions to check if someone is addicted to a different topic of your choice. Then, ask your questions to your groupmates or classmates to see if they are addicted.

Possible topics ゲーム　アニメ　スポーツ／筋(きん)トレ　(SNS の)○○　ペット

できる III Explain facts about famous things and places and provide information about them.

できるIII-A Passive sentences to describe objective facts

1 Let's practice making the passive forms of verbs used when discussing famous creations, inventions, and discoveries. L16-24

Ex.1 書(か)く → 書(か)かれる → 書(か)かれました

1) 見(み)つける　2) 作(つく)る　3) 描(か)く　4) 建(た)てる　5) 発見(はっけん)する

Ex.2 書(か)く → 書(か)かれている → 書(か)かれています

6) 考(かんが)える　7) 楽(たの)しむ　8) 話(はな)す　9) 知(し)る　10) 言(い)う　11) 愛(あい)す

2 How much do you know about arts and culture?

Step 1 State by whom the following things were created or discovered. L16-25

Ex. 『泣(な)く女』(という絵)はピカソによって描(か)かれました。

Ex.『泣(な)く女』／ピカソ　1)『ハリー・ポッター』／J. K. ローリング　2)『モナリザ』／ダ・ビンチ　3)『となりのトトロ』／宮崎駿(みやざきはやお)

4) アップル／スティーブ・ジョブズ　5) 重力(じゅうりょく) (gravity)／ニュートン　6)『ボレロ』／ラヴェル　7) your own

Step 2 Choose some of the works, creations, or discoveries from Step 1 and make a three-sentence presentation for each to describe them in detail.

Useful vocabulary ほんやくする　知る　愛(あい)す　読む　使う　聞く

Ex. ① みなさんは『泣(な)く女』という絵を知っていますか。(← Introduction)
② 『泣(な)く女』はピカソによって描(か)かれました。(← Creator/discoverer)
③ 世界中で知られています。(← Current state)

3 Make questions about what you think is number one in the world in various categories based on the cues provided, as in the example. Then, discuss with your partner and try to guess the answer to each question.

Ex. A: 世界で一番よく話されている言葉(ことば)は何だと思いますか。
B: 英語だと思います。
A: 私もそう思います。or そうですか。私は中国語だと思います。

Ex. 話す／言葉(ことば)　1) 読む／本 or 作家　2) 作る／野菜(やさい)
3) ダウンロードする／アプリ　4) 歌(うた)う／曲(きょく)　5) 楽しむ／ゲーム

4 Make a brief presentation on your favorite artwork, book, etc.

Title
Details: • author/creator • objective facts
Your opinions
Recommendation

Ex. みなさん、『1Q84』という本を知っていますか。
『1Q84』は村上春樹(むらかみはるき)によって書かれました。
色々な言葉(ことば)にほんやくされて、世界中の人に読まれています。
私もおととし読んで、とても感動(かんどう)しました。
読みやすいし、おもしろいメタファーもあるし、おすすめです。
みなさんもぜひ読んでみてください。

Review

Now you can express your feelings about your experiences as well as your regrets. Suppose 死神 (The Angel of Death) has appeared in front of you, and, for some reason, he only speaks in Japanese. Convince 死神 that you should live longer.

Step 1 Brainstorming: Read over the shaded box below and reflect on your life so far.

Step 2 Convince 死神 to let you live longer by listing up some of your regrets in life.

Talk about your good memories with reason(s)

List up your regrets about:

- things you were able to experience only once or a few times
- bad experiences caused by others' actions
- failed plans

Ex.

死神　：今までの人生はどうでしたか。
あなた：とても楽しかったです。
死神　：どうしてですか。
あなた：日本語を勉強して、いい友達ができたからです。この大学に来てよかったです。
死神　：そうですか。じゃ、もう十分 (enough) ですね。
あなた：え、待ってください！　私はまだ死にたくないです。まだ日本に一回しか行ったことがありません。
死神　：そうですか。
あなた：それから、昨日好きな人にふられました。一緒にいる間に、もっと出かければよかったです。だから、もう一度チャンスをください。
死神　：残念ですが…
あなた：あっ、それから、週末に新しいゲームをするつもりでしたが、少ししかできませんでした。だから…
死神　：時間です。行きましょう！
あなた：あーっ！　…あ、夢…

読みましょう

Getting information from infographics

1 日本の「駅弁(えきべん)」について聞いたことがありますか。駅で売られているお弁当(べんとう)を「駅弁(えきべん)」と言います。

いか：squid　かに：crab　さけ：salmon

駅弁(えきべん)マップ

A. 4月10日は「駅弁(えきべん)の日」 1885年〜

青森県(あおもりけん) B.「いかめし」 780円

北海道(ほっかいどう) C.「さけ弁当(べんとう)」 1,030円

鳥取県(とっとりけん) D.「かにずし」 1,080円

東京都(とうきょうと) E.「野菜天ぷら弁当(やさいてんぷらべんとう)」 900円

福岡県(ふくおかけん) F.「鳥親子弁当(おやこべんとう)」 850円

兵庫県(ひょうごけん) G.「すきやきステーキ弁当(べんとう)」 1,200円

愛知県(あいちけん) H.「みそかつサンドイッチ」 670円

I. 4月1日(水)〜8日(水)
ことびらデパート 8F
全国(ぜんこく)有名駅弁(えきべん) うまいもの市(いち)

上の駅弁(えきべん)マップを見て、1)〜6)の質問に日本語で答(こた)えてください。____には答(こた)え、(　　)にはその情報(じょうほう)が分かる写真(しゃしん)のアルファベット A.〜I. を書いてください。

Ex.「駅弁(えきべん)の日」はいつですか。　　<u>4月10日です。</u>（ **A.** ）

1) 駅弁(えきべん)は何年前から売られていますか。　　__________（　　）

2) 北海道(ほっかいどう)で売られている駅弁(えきべん)の名前は何ですか。　　__________（　　）

3) 野菜(やさい)しか食べない人が食べられる駅弁(えきべん)はどれですか。　　__________（　　）

4) パンが使われている駅弁(えきべん)の名前は何ですか。　　__________（　　）

5) 駅弁(えきべん)が買えるのは駅だけですか。　　__________（　　）

6) B.からH.の中で、どの駅弁(えきべん)を食べてみたいですか。それはいくらですか。

__________（　　）

2 日本のすごいものについて書いてあるネットの記事を読んで、質問に答えてください。

留学生の声

日本の①これにびっくり！

大ファン：big fan

日本で勉強している留学生に、日本に住んでおどろいたものについて聞いてみました。その答えの中から、二つ紹介します。

01 駅弁

- 私の国では電車の中で食べ物を食べてはいけないから、日本の新幹線の中でお弁当を食べている 人 を見てびっくりしました。
- 駅で色々な駅弁がたくさん売られていて、おどろきました。ほしいお弁当が決められなくてずっと Ex. 見ていたら、店の人が「(A) これは (B) この駅でしか買えない駅弁ですよ」と教えてくれました。その地方でしか買えない 駅弁 があるのを知ってびっくりしました。
- 日本の駅弁に感動しました。昔から日本にあるし、きれいだし、おいしいし、(a) すばらしい日本の文化だと思います。私は駅弁の大ファンです。
- 僕の旅行の目的はまだ食べたことがない駅弁を食べに行く こと で、僕の旅行は駅弁を選ぶ時から始まります。日本にいる間にできるだけ色々な駅弁を食べるつもりです。
- 駅弁の動画を見て、すごい食べ物があると思いました。旅行に行けないから、食べるのをあきらめていましたが、最近、時々デパートで地方の駅弁が買えることを知りました。留学が終わって国に帰る時「駅弁を食べればよかった」と泣きたくないから、今度絶対にデパートに駅弁を買いに行こうと思います。

02 トイレ

- トイレがとてもきれいでおどろきました。特に、ホテルやデパートのトイレはすごくきれいだし、ただで使えるから、いつも感動します。
- 毎朝、早く起きてトイレをそうじする 友達 にその理由を聞いたら、「日本ではトイレをきれいにしたら、いいことがあると (b) 信じられているんだよ」と教えてくれました。日本には『トイレの神様』という歌もあると聞いて、おもしろいと思いました。
- ハイテクのトイレにびっくりしました。ボタンで色々なことができるし、自動でふたが開いたり閉まったりするし、すごいと思います。でも、読めない漢字があったから、初めは使い方が分からなくて困りました。
- 私は家でお湯でおしりを洗ったり、風を出して (b) かわかしたりしてくれる トイレ を使っているんですが、②このトイレが大好きです。私の国にも③このすごく便利なトイレがほしいです。

おもしろい声がたくさんありますね。みなさんは日本の駅弁やトイレをどう思いますか。他に何か日本ですごいと思ったものがありますか。それから、みなさんが外国に行って、おどろいたり、おもしろいと思ったりしたものがあったら、それについても教えてください。

Understanding demonstratives: こ-words

In Lesson 4, we learned that demonstrative pronouns and adjectives are used to make spatial references to tangible things, as shown in [A]これ and [B]この駅 in the article on the left.

This lesson focuses on another use of demonstratives: to refer to items that appear elsewhere in writing. In this usage, そ-words are most commonly used (See L10 p.367.) while あ-words seldom appear. There are some situations, however, where こ-words are more likely to be used instead:

a. To introduce an upcoming topic (そ-words do not have this function.)

Ex. この話は誰にも言わないでください。実は、私は…

b. To refer to things the writer feels temporally, spatially, or psychologically close to

Ex. 昨日うちの近くのレストランでパスタを食べた。私はこのレストランが大好きで、よく食べに行く。

Lesson 16

練習 Choose the most appropriate function between a. and b. above for the following こ-words found in the article.

①これ (in the title) ②このトイレ (l.28) ③このすごく便利なトイレ (l.28)

Identifying omitted words

1） Identify the omitted words to fill in [ ] and supplement the underlined words (a)-(c).

Ex. 見ていた [駅弁]を見ていた (a) すばらしい [ ]はすばらしい

(b) 信じられている [ ]に信じられている (c) かわかした [ ]をかわかした

Scanning

2） 留学生の声を読んで、日本の駅弁とトイレについて分かったことを書いてください。

おどろいたもの	分かったこと（四つずつ (each)）
駅弁	・新幹線の中でお弁当を食べてもいい
トイレ	

Comprehension check

3） Underline the part of the text modifies each boxed word.

4） あなたは日本の何がすごいと思いますか。理由も言ってください。

書く練習

Write about something exclusive or unique to your country/culture that you think would impress people from other countries/cultures.

聞きましょう

リスニング・ストラテジー : Listening strategy

Shadowing (2)

In this lesson, we will practice expressing emotion through volume, pitch, and rate of speech as well as listening to and shadowing longer sentences.

1 Pre-listening activity:

Step 1 Listen to the audio without looking at the script. Try to figure out what each sentence is about and what emotion the speaker is expressing. You can repeat as many times as you want.

Step 2 Read the script on the *TOBIRA* website to check if you understood the audio correctly. Pay close attention to the part(s) that you could not comprehend and look up the words and expressions that you didn't know.

Step 3 Read each sentence aloud along with the audio while looking at the script (="overlapping"). Repeat this step until you can keep pace with the audio.

Step 4 Practice shadowing. Listen to the audio and try to echo it back with as little lag as possible without looking at the script. You may repeat this step until you feel confident.

2 Listening: Now let's try shadowing in a conversational context.

1) The audio contains a conversation between two people. Follow Steps 1-4 above and practice shadowing both roles, paying attention to their emotions.

2) Record yourself shadowing and evaluate your recording for proficiency in the following categories. (Mark ○ for "good," △ for "so-so," and × for "not good.")

a. Pacing/Fluency		b. Accuracy (grammar, pronunciation)		c. Emotion	

How did it go? If you feel confident, challenge yourself using longer or more difficult sentences on the Conversation pages, etc. If you don't feel confident, practice shadowing using phrases you can find in the Activities pages.

Exit Check

Now it's time to go back to the DEKIRU List for this chapter (p.199) and do the exit check to see what new things you can do now that you've completed the lesson.

Lesson 17

お店を手伝わせていただけませんか。

(手伝: てつだ)

Won't you let me help out around the shop?

Instructional Video Lesson 17

DEKIRU List

できるCheck ☑

できるI **Politely express what you want to do and request permission to do it.**
自分がしたいことを丁寧に申し出たり、許可を求めたりできる。
Entry ☐ Exit ☐

できるII **Ask and answer questions about new experiences and discoveries.**
新しい経験や発見について、尋ねたり答えたりできる。
Entry ☐ Exit ☐

できるIII **Talk about your future goals in detail.**
自分の将来の目標について、詳しく話すことができる。
Entry ☐ Exit ☐

STRATEGIES

Conversation Tips .... • Reacting to what others say in casual speech

Reading .... • Getting information from a website: Travel guide
• Identifying omitted words
• Sorting information
• Understanding metaphors

Listening .... • Shadowing (3)

GRAMMAR

1. ～ので [Reason] できるI
2. Causative forms of verbs and causative sentences できるI
3. ～か(どうか) [Embedded question marker] できるII
4. ～と [Conditional conjunction] できるII
5. ～といい できるIII
   - 5-1 ～といいですね "It would be good if ~, wouldn't it?"
   - 5-2 ～といいんですが… "I hope (that) ~"
6. ～ために [Purpose] できるIII
7. Vまで "until ... V" and Vまでに "by the time ... V" できるIII

Conversation

会　話

1 できるI Ai and her host father are talking at the host family's tea shop.

L17-1

あきら：Ai's host brother

アイ　：お父さん、最近(さいきん)、忙(いそが)しそうですね。

父　：うん、バイトの人が急(きゅう)にやめちゃって、困ってるんだ。
明日から、あきらに手伝(てつだ)わせるよ。

アイ　：そうですか。でも、あきらさんは塾(じゅく)に行くので、
よかったら、私にお店を手伝(てつだ)わせていただけませんか。

父　：え、いいの？

アイ　：はい、お店を手伝(てつだ)うのも勉強になると思います。
色々な人と話せるし、お茶について学(まな)べるし…

父　：そっか。アイちゃんが手伝(てつだ)ってくれたら、助かるよ。

アイ　：はい、ぜひ！　何をしたらいいですか。

父　：そうだね…　じゃ、お客(きゃく)さんが来たら、お茶を出してくれない？

アイ　：はい。分かりました。あ、それから、私にお店のそうじもさせてください。

2 できるII On another day, Ai and her host brother, Akira, are talking in the living room.

L17-2

あきら　：アイちゃん、もうすぐアメリカに帰っちゃうんだね。
アイちゃんがいなくなると、さびしくなるよ。

アイ　：私も…

あきら　：アイちゃん、日本にいる間、どんなことにびっくりしたか教えてくれない？

アイ　：びっくりしたこと？　えっと、日本のハイテクのトイレにおどろいた！
トイレに入るとふたが開くし、ボタンを押(お)すとおしりを洗ってくれるし…

あきら　：え、アメリカにはないの？

アイ　：うーん、あるかどうか分からないけど、見たことないよ。
あ、それから、道にゴミが全然(ぜんぜん)落(お)ちていなくて、びっくりした。
日本は本当にきれいだって思う。

あきら　：へえ、そうなんだ。僕(ぼく)の部屋は汚いけどね。

アイ　：うん、それにもびっくりした！

3 できるIII Ai and her host family are talking on the last night of Ai's stay in Japan. L17-3

あっという間(ま)だ：time flies (lit. it's [the time it takes] while saying あっ)　キュレーター：curator

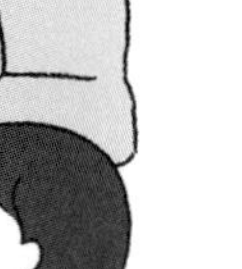

アイ　：みなさん、本当にお世話になりました。

父　：あっという間(ま)だったね。
アイちゃん、店を手伝(てつだ)ってくれてありがとう。

母　：またすぐに会えるといいね。

アイ　：はい、ぜひ。

姉　：私、絶対(ぜったい)にアメリカに行く！　次に会うまで、元気でね。

アイ　：はい、絶対(ぜったい)に来てくださいね。待(ま)ってます！

あきら　：僕(ぼく)もアメリカに行くために、英語の勉強、がんばるよ。

母　：ところで、ジャパンハウスの友達に、何時ごろ着くか知らせた？

アイ　：はい。私が帰るまでに、私の部屋をそうじしておいてくれるそうです。

姉　：そう。やさしいね。

父　：アイちゃん、これからも日本語の勉強、がんばって！

アイ　：はい、日本美術(びじゅつ)のキュレーターになるためにがんばります。
夏(なつ)の間ずっとホームステイをさせてくださって、本当にありがとうございました。とても楽しかったです！

CONVERSATION TIPS

Reacting to what others say in casual speech: You can use そう, そうか, そっか, or そうなんだ when reacting to what someone has said in casual speech. These are the equivalent of そうですか and そうなんですか in polite speech.

A：来月、東京に行くんだ。
B：へぇ、そう。いいね。
A：うん、東京マラソンがあるから。
B：あ、そうなんだ。マラソンに出るの？
A：うん、出るよ。
B：そっか。すごいね。がんばって！

Vocabulary with Pictures

単語(たんご)

▶ **The words written in gray** are supplemental vocabulary.

生活(せいかつ) Daily life

にんげん
(human)

せいかつ(を)する／せいかつをおくる
(to live/lead a life)

ねむる
(to fall asleep; to be asleep)

[*fact/technique/(life) lesson* を]
まなぶ
(to learn)

[*person* に *information* を]
しらせる
(to inform; to notify)

[*person* が *person/thing* に]
ちかづく
(to come close; to approach)

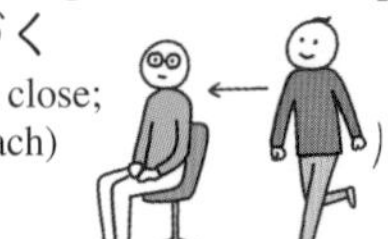

[*time* が]
ちかづく
((time) draws near)

きびしい ⟷ やさしい
(strict; severe; harsh)

[*thing/person* を]
おす
(to push)

ボタン

にほんしょく
(Japanese food)

おおあめ
(heavy rain)

おおゆき
(heavy snow)

きた
(north)

にし
(west)

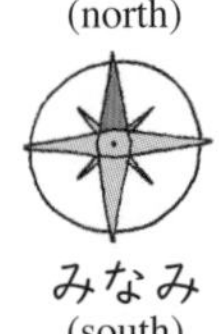

ひがし
(east)

みなみ
(south)

～ぐち
(... entrance/exit)

Exs. きたぐち
(north entrance/exit)

にしぐち
(west entrance/exit)

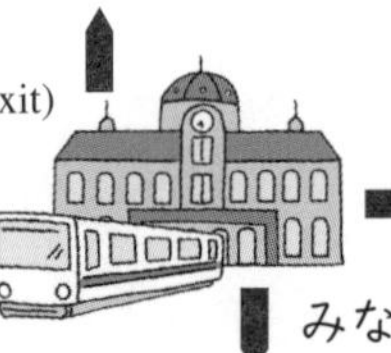

ひがしぐち
(east entrance/exit)

みなみぐち
(south entrance/exit)

働く Work

ぶちょう
(department head/manager; club president)

おきゃくさま
(customer) [formal]

[*person* に]
あいさつ(を)する
(to greet)

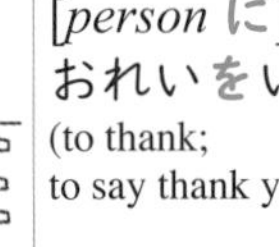

[*person* に]
おれいをいう
(to thank; to say thank you)

おれい
(expression of gratitude)

[*place* に]
しゅっちょう(を)する／しゅっちょうにいく
(to go on a business trip)

[*person* に／の]
おせわになる
(to be in (someone's) care; to be helped (by))

[*person* の] せわをする

[*person* に *message* を／と]
つたえる
(to tell; to pass along; to deliver)

[*person/place* に *thing* が]
とどく
(to arrive; to be delivered)

[*person/place* に *thing* を]
とどける
(to deliver)

しょるい
(document; paperwork)

[*topic* について]
はなしあう
(to discuss; to have a talk)

[*source X* を *target language Y* に]
やくす
(to translate (X into Y))

あ⟷A

[*thing/person* が]
みつかる
(to be found)

[*thing/person* を] みつける

ただしい ⟷ まちがい
(correct; right)

ひょうげん
(expression)

しめきり
(deadline; due date)

人と社会　People and society

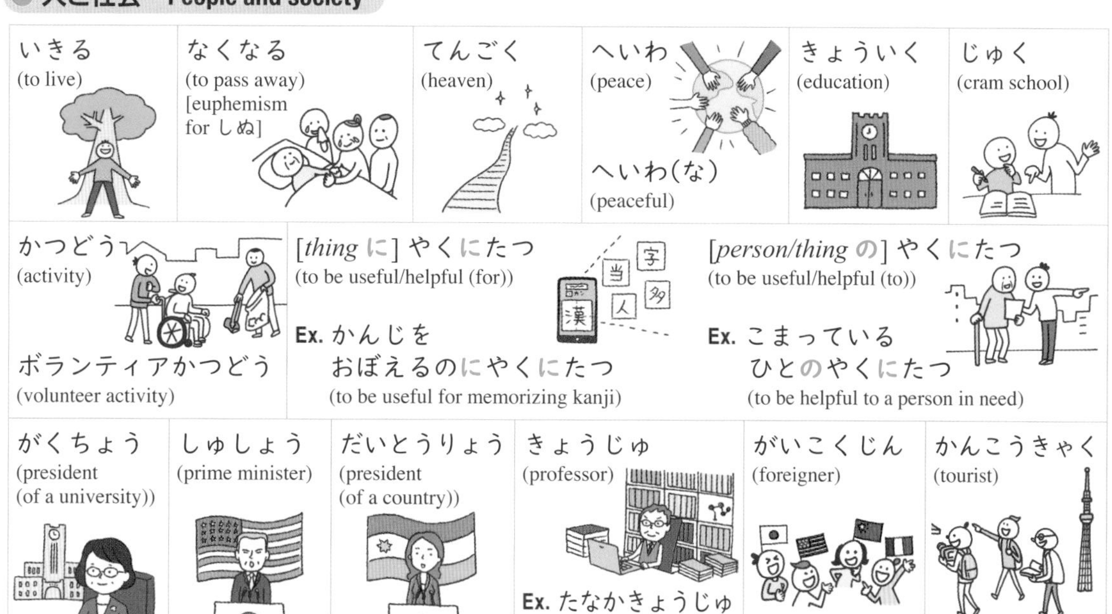

- いきる (to live)
- なくなる (to pass away) [euphemism for しぬ]
- てんごく (heaven)
- へいわ (peace)
- へいわ(な) (peaceful)
- きょういく (education)
- じゅく (cram school)
- かつどう (activity)
- ボランティアかつどう (volunteer activity)
- [*thing* に] やくにたつ (to be useful/helpful (for))
  - **Ex.** かんじを おぼえるのにやくにたつ (to be useful for memorizing kanji)
- [*person/thing* の] やくにたつ (to be useful/helpful (to))
  - **Ex.** こまっている ひとのやくにたつ (to be helpful to a person in need)
- がくちょう (president (of a university))
- しゅしょう (prime minister)
- だいとうりょう (president (of a country))
- きょうじゅ (professor)
  - **Ex.** たなかきょうじゅ (Prof. Tanaka)
- がいこくじん (foreigner)
- かんこうきゃく (tourist)

習慣(しゅうかん)　Customs and practices

- おまいり(を)する／おまいりにいく (to visit/go to a temple/shrine to pray)
- おいのり(を)する (to pray)
- たたく (to clap; to tap; to hit)
- てをたたく (to clap (one's) hands)
- かたをたたく (to tap (one's) shoulder)
- かた (shoulder)
- うわさ(を)する (to gossip; to spread rumors)
- うわさ (gossip; rumor)
- つめ (nail) [finger/toe]
- つめをきる (to clip (one's) nails)
- くしゃみ (sneeze)
- くしゃみをする／くしゃみがでる (to sneeze)
- おもてなし (hospitality)
- [*flower* が] さく (to bloom)
- バラ (rose)
- ゆかた (casual cotton kimono (for summer))
- きせつ (season)
- おんど (temperature (not outside air temperature))

そのほかの表現(ひょうげん)　Other expressions

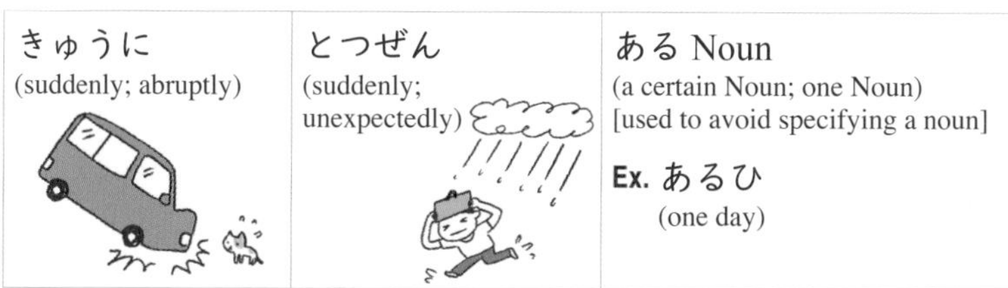

- きゅうに (suddenly; abruptly)
- とつぜん (suddenly; unexpectedly)
- ある Noun (a certain Noun; one Noun) [used to avoid specifying a noun]
  - **Ex.** あるひ (one day)

単語リスト

(たんご)

L17-5

▶ **Highlighted kanji words** contain kanji you have learned previously.

RU-VERBS

1	いきる	生きる	to live
2	しらせる	知らせる	to inform; to notify [*person* に *information* を]
3	つたえる	伝える	to tell; to pass along; to deliver [*person* に *message* を／と]
4	とどける	届ける	to deliver [*person/place* に *thing* を]

U-VERBS / U-VERB PHRASES

5	おす	押す	to push [*thing/person* を]
6	おせわになる	お世話になる	to be in (someone's) care; to be helped (by) [*person* に／の]
7	おれいをいう	お礼を言う	to thank; to say thank you [*person* に]
8	さく		to bloom [*flower* が]
9	ちかづく	近づく	to come close; to approach [*person* が *person/thing* に]; (time) draws near [*time* が]
10	たたく		to clap; to tap; to hit
	てをたたく	手をたたく	to clap (one's) hands
11	とどく	届く	to arrive; to be delivered [*person/place* に *thing* が]
12	なくなる	亡くなる	to pass away [euphemism for しぬ]
13	ねむる	眠る	to fall asleep; to be asleep
14	はなしあう	話し合う	to discuss; to have a talk [*topic* について]
15	まなぶ	学ぶ	to learn [*fact/technique/(life) lesson* を]
16	みつかる	見つかる	to be found [*thing/person* が]
17	やくす	訳す	to translate (X into Y) [*source X* を *target language Y* に] [less formal than ほんやくする]
18	やくにたつ	役に立つ	to be useful/helpful (for/to) [*thing* に] **Ex.** 漢字をおぼえるのにやくに立つ to be useful for memorizing kanji [*person/thing* の] **Ex.** 困っている人のやくに立つ to be helpful to a person in need

SURU-VERBS / SURU-VERB PHRASES

19	あいさつ(を)する		to greet [*person* に]
20	うわさ(を)する		to gossip; to spread rumors
21	おいのり(を)する		to pray
22	おまいり(を)する／にいく	お参り(を)する／に行く	to visit/go to a temple/shrine to pray
23	しゅっちょう(を)する／にいく	出張(を)する／に行く	to go on a business trip [*place* に]
24	せいかつ(を)する／をおくる	生活(を)する／を送る	to live/lead a life

I-ADJECTIVES

25	きびしい	厳しい	strict; severe; harsh
26	ただしい	正しい	correct; right

NA-ADJECTIVE

27	へいわ	平和	peaceful

NOUNS

28	おおあめ	大雨	heavy rain
29	おおゆき	大雪	heavy snow

30	おきゃくさま	お客様	customer [formal]
31	おもてなし		hospitality
32	おれい	お礼	expression of gratitude
33	おんど	温度	temperature (not outside air temperature) Ex. 部屋のおんど room temperature
34	がいこくじん	外国人	foreigner
35	がくちょう	学長	president (of a university)
36	かた	肩	shoulder
37	かつどう	活動	activity
38	かんこうきゃく	観光客	tourist
39	きせつ	季節	season
40	きた	北	north
41	みなみ	南	south
42	ひがし	東	east
43	にし	西	west
44	きょういく	教育	education
45	きょうじゅ	教授	professor Ex. 田中きょうじゅ Prof. Tanaka
46	くしゃみ		sneeze
	くしゃみをする／がでる	くしゃみをする／が出る	to sneeze
47	しめきり	しめ切り	deadline; due date
48	じゅく		cram school
49	しゅしょう	首相	prime minister
50	しょるい	書類	document; paperwork
51	だいとうりょう	大統領	president (of a country)
52	つめ		nail [finger/toe]
	つめをきる	つめを切る	to clip (one's) nails
53	てんごく	天国	heaven
54	にほんしょく	日本食	Japanese food
55	にんげん	人間	human
56	バラ		rose
57	ひょうげん	表現	expression
58	ぶちょう	部長	department head/ manager; club president
59	へいわ	平和	peace
60	ゆかた	浴衣	casual cotton kimono (for summer)

ADVERBS

61	きゅうに	急に	suddenly; abruptly
62	とつぜん	突然	suddenly; unexpectedly

SUFFIX

63	～ぐち	～口	... entrance/exit
	きたぐち	北口	north entrance/exit (of a train station)
	みなみぐち	南口	south entrance/exit (of a train station)
	ひがしぐち	東口	east entrance/exit (of a train station)
	にしぐち	西口	west entrance/exit (of a train station)

OTHER WORDS AND PHRASES

64	ある Noun		a certain Noun; one Noun [used to avoid specifying a noun] Ex. ある日 one day

Lesson 17

漢　字

▶ *Special reading

254	北	ホッ ホク ボク	北海道 (ほっかいどう) Hokkaido [prefecture in Japan]　北極 (ほっきょく) the North Pole 東北地方 (とうほくちほう) the Tohoku region　南北 (なんぼく) north and south　北京* (ペキン) Beijing
		きた	北 (きた) north　北口 (きたぐち) north entrance/exit (of a train station)　北アメリカ (きた) North America
north			北北北北北
255	南	ナン	東南アジア (とうなん) Southeast Asia　南極 (なんきょく) the South Pole 南米 (なんべい) South America　南北 (なんぼく) north and south
		みなみ	南 (みなみ) south　南口 (みなみぐち) south entrance/exit (of a train station)　南アメリカ (みなみ) South America
south			南南南南南南南南南
256	西	サイ ザイ セイ	関西地方 (かんさいちほう) the Kansai region　東西 (とうざい) east and west 西洋 (せいよう) the West; Western countries　南西 (なんせい) southwest　北西 (ほくせい) northwest
		にし	西 (にし) west　西口 (にしぐち) west entrance/exit (of a train station)
west			西西西西西西
257	合	ゴウ	都合がいい (つごう) to be convenient　都合が悪い (つごう わる) to be inconvenient [date, time, etc.]
		あ(う) あ(わせる)	試合 (しあい) game; match [competition]　話し合う (はな あ) to discuss; to have a talk 合う (あ) to fit　付き合う (つ あ) to go out; to date　間に合う (ま あ) to make it in time 合わせる (あ) to put together; to adjust; to combine
to fit			合合合合合合
258	送	ソウ	送信する (そうしん) to send; to transmit (email, data, etc.)　送料 (そうりょう) shipping fee 放送する (ほうそう) to broadcast
		おく(る)	送る (おく) to send; to give a ride; to drop off　生活を送る (せいかつ おく) to live/lead a life
to send; to escort			送送送送送送送送送
259	活	カツ	活動 (かつどう) activity　生活 (せいかつ) daily life; lifestyle　生活(を)する／を送る (せいかつ おく) to live/lead a life 活躍する (かつやく) to play an active part 活用する (かつよう) to make good use; to utilize; to conjugate (a word)
lively			活活活活活活活活活
260	近	キン	最近 (さいきん) recently　近所 (きんじょ) neighborhood; vicinity　近代的(な) (きんだいてき) modern
		ちか(い) ちか(づく)	近い (ちか) near; nearby; close　近く (ちか) near; nearby 近づく (ちか) to come close; to approach; (time) draws near　身近(な) (みぢか) familiar; close to home
near			近近近近近近近

261 歩 歩 歩

ホ / ポ	歩行者（ほこうしゃ） pedestrian　歩道（ほどう） sidewalk
	散歩する（さんぽ） to take a walk
ある(く)	歩く（ある） to walk　歩いて（ある） on foot

to walk

262 急 急 急

キュウ	急に（きゅう） suddenly; abruptly　救急車（きゅうきゅうしゃ） ambulance
	急行（きゅうこう） express (train)　特急（とっきゅう） limited express (train)
いそ(ぐ)	急ぐ（いそ） to hurry　急いで（いそ） hurriedly

to hurry; sudden

263 授 授 授

ジュ	教授（きょうじゅ） professor　授業（じゅぎょう） class　授業中（じゅぎょうちゅう） in class
	授業料（じゅぎょうりょう） tuition

to impart

264 卒 卒 卒

ソツ	卒業する（そつぎょう） to graduate　卒業式（そつぎょうしき） graduation ceremony
	卒業生（そつぎょうせい） graduate; alumnus/alumna　卒業論文（そつぎょうろんぶん） graduation thesis

to graduate

265 業 業 業

ギョウ	授業（じゅぎょう） class　授業中（じゅぎょうちゅう） in class　授業料（じゅぎょうりょう） tuition
	卒業する（そつぎょう） to graduate　営業中（えいぎょうちゅう） open (for business)
	残業する（ざんぎょう） to work overtime　職業（しょくぎょう） occupation

business

266 写 写 写

シャ	写真（しゃしん） photograph　写真家（しゃしんか） photographer　描写する（びょうしゃ） to describe; to portray
うつ(す)	写す（うつ） to copy [visually]

to copy; photograph

267 真 真 真

シン	写真（しゃしん） photograph　写真家（しゃしんか） photographer　真剣(な)（しんけん） serious; earnest
ま	真っ黒（ま くろ） pitch-black　真っ白（ま しろ） snow-white　真ん中（ま なか） middle
	真似する（まね） to imitate; to mimic　真夜中（まよなか） midnight; the middle of the night

true

268 研 研 研

ケン	研究する（けんきゅう） to research　研究室（けんきゅうしつ） (instructor's) office
	研究者（けんきゅうしゃ） researcher

to polish

269 究 究 究	キュウ	研究する(けんきゅう) to research　研究室(けんきゅうしつ) (instructor's) office 研究者(けんきゅうしゃ) researcher
to research; to master	究究究究究究究	
270 顔 顔 顔	かお がお	顔(かお) face　顔色(かおいろ) complexion 笑顔(えがお) smiling face　似顔絵(にがおえ) portrait
face	顔顔顔顔顔顔顔顔顔顔顔顔顔顔顔顔顔顔	
271 幸 幸 幸	コウ	幸福(こうふく) happiness　不幸(ふこう)(な) unhappy
	しあわ(せ)	幸せ(しあわ)(な) happy 幸せ(しあわ) happiness
happiness	幸幸幸幸幸幸幸幸	
272 正 正 正	ショウ セイ	(お)正月(しょうがつ) New Year's (holiday)　正午(しょうご) noon; midday　正直(しょうじき)(な) honest 改正する(かいせい) to revise (rules, law, etc.)
	ただ(しい)	正しい(ただ) correct; right　礼儀正しい(れいぎただ) well-mannered
correct	正正正正正	

新しい読み方

The following are new readings for kanji that you have already learned. Read each word aloud.

1) 生(い)きる　2) 東(ひがし)　3) 人間(にんげん)　4) 学(まな)ぶ

習った漢字で書ける新しい単語(たんご)

The following are other new vocabulary in this lesson that contain kanji you have already leaned. Read each word aloud.

1) 大雨(おおあめ)　2) 大雪(おおゆき)　3) お世話(せわ)になる　4) (お参(まい)りに)行(い)く
5) (お礼(れい)を)言(い)う　6) 外国人(がいこくじん)　7) 学長(がくちょう)　8) しめ切(き)り
9) (出張(しゅっちょう)に)行(い)く　10) 知(し)らせる　11) 天国(てんごく)　12) 日本食(にほんしょく)
13) 部長(ぶちょう)　14) 見(み)つかる　15) (役(やく)に)立(た)つ　16) ～口(ぐち) (Ex. 北口(きたぐち))

練習

1 Geography quiz! Read each of the statements 1)-4) aloud, then mark ○ if it is true and × if it is false.

1)（　　　）アメリカの北にカナダがあります。

2)（　　　）日本の東に韓国（かんこく）や中国があります。

3)（　　　）東京の西に京都（きょうと）があります。

4)（　　　）オーストラリアの南に日本があります。

2 Find and circle eight kanji words that contain kanji you have learned so far, then write the words and their readings in the spaces provided. The words may appear either vertically or horizontally.

教	授	試
卒	業	合
生	料	理
活	動	由

Ex.

Ex. 料理（りょうり）

1) ＿＿＿＿（　　　）　2) ＿＿＿＿（　　　）

3) ＿＿＿＿（　　　）　4) ＿＿＿＿（　　　）

5) ＿＿＿＿（　　　）　6) ＿＿＿＿（　　　）

7) ＿＿＿＿（　　　）　8) ＿＿＿＿（　　　）

3 Kim-san wrote about a bad day she had. Read her story aloud, then write the readings for the underlined words.

1) クラスメートと研究プロジェクトについて話し合うつもりでしたが、クラスメートは来ませんでした。

2) 今日の試験に日本のお正月の習慣（しゅうかん）について書く問題がありましたが、正しい答（こた）えが一つも分かりませんでした。

3) 大学から駅までのバスに乗り遅れました。もっと急げばよかったです。

4) 家に帰る時、知らない人が急に近づいてきて、私の写真をとりました。私はこわくて、走って逃（に）げました。

5) 友達が北海道から来たので、駅に迎（むか）えに行きました。私は駅の北口で待（ま）っていましたが、友達は東口にいたので、会えませんでした。

6)「最近顔が暗くて、幸せじゃなさそうですよ。もっと笑った方がいいですよ」と友達に言われました。

漢字の話 The Story of Kanji

■ Guessing the meanings of unknown kanji compound words

One of the advantages of kanji is that many of them are ideograms; if you know the meanings of individual kanji, it will facilitate your understanding of words and sentences containing them. For example, consider the kanji compound word 手話(しゅわ). You may not know this word, but if you remember that 手 means "hand" and 話 means "to talk," you will probably be able to guess that the meaning of 手話(しゅわ) is "sign language." Try this strategy next time you encounter unknown kanji compound words.

練習

The following kanji compound words 1)-5) are made up of kanji that you have already learned. For each word, think of the meanings of the individual kanji, then guess the meaning of the kanji compound word as a whole.

Word	Kanji 1	+	Kanji 2	= ( )
Ex. 手話(しゅわ)	手 [hand]	+	話 [to talk]	= (sign language)
1) 乗り物(のりもの)	乗り [ ]	+	物 [ ]	= ( )
2) 歩道(ほどう)	歩 [ ]	+	道 [ ]	= ( )
3) 近所(きんじょ)	近 [ ]	+	所 [ ]	= ( )
4) 朝食(ちょうしょく)	朝 [ ]	+	食 [ ]	= ( )
5) 国歌(こっか)	国 [ ]	+	歌 [ ]	= ( )

文法

1 ～ので [Reason] "because; so"

[1]

S₁ (reason)		S₂ (main clause)
旅行に行く	ので、	週末ネコの世話をしてくれませんか。
I'm going on a trip, so could you take care of my cat this weekend?		

You can give a reason using ので. The forms before ので are as follows:

Verbs	plain form	+ ので	食べるので 食べたので	食べないので 食べなかったので
I-adjectives	plain form		高いので 高かったので	高くないので 高くなかったので
Na-adjectives / nouns +だ	*Na*-adjectives / nouns ＋な／じゃない		便利なので 便利だったので	便利じゃないので 便利じゃなかったので
	Na-adjectives / nouns ＋だった／じゃなかった		学生なので 学生だったので	学生じゃないので 学生じゃなかったので

Exs. (1) A: 週末買い物に行きませんか。*Would you like to go shopping over the weekend?*

B: すみません。今、お金がないので、ちょっと…

I'm sorry. I don't have any money now, so...

(2) みかさんは絵を描くのが上手なので、みかさんにポスターを作ってもらいましょう。

Mika's good at drawing, so let's get her to make a poster.

(3) 今日はアルバイトが休みだったので、どこにも行かないでうちにいました。

I had a day off from my part-time job today, so I stayed home without going anywhere.

ので presents a reason more implicitly than から does and thus comes across as more polite, so when you ask someone for a favor with a reason, ので is usually the better choice.

Exs. (4) 日本料理を食べたい {ので／?? から}、いいレストランを教えてくれませんか。

I want to eat Japanese food, so could you tell me (the name of) a good restaurant?

(5) 日本に留学する {ので／?? から}、推薦状を書いてくださいませんか。

I'm going to study abroad in Japan, so would you mind writing a recommendation letter for me?

☞ GID (vol.2): B. Connecting sentences 1. ので vs. から

2 Causative forms of verbs and causative sentences

Sentences that involve causative forms are called causative sentences. A causative sentence describes a situation in which someone makes or lets someone else do something.

2-1 Causative forms

You can make causative forms as follows:

(a) *Ru*-verbs: Change the final る of the dictionary form to させる.

Exs. 食べ~~る~~ → 食べさせる; 答え~~る~~ → 答えさせる

(b) *U*-verbs: Change the final /u/ sound of the dictionary form to the /a/ sound and attach せる.

Ex. 読む (/yomu/) → 読ませる (/yoma/ + せる)

When the dictionary form ends in う (e.g., 言う, 買う), change the /u/ sound to /wa/ and attach せる.

Ex. 言う (/iu/) → 言わせる (/iwa/ + せる)

(More examples of *u*-verb causative forms are shown in the *u*-verb conjugation table on the inside of the back cover.)

(c) Irregular verbs: する → させる; 来る → 来させる

Causative forms are all *ru*-verbs regardless of the category of the original verb. For example, 読ませる conjugates as follows:

	Polite		Plain		*Te*-form
Non-past	読ませます	読ませません	読ませる	読ませない	読ませて
Past	読ませました	読ませませんでした	読ませた	読ませなかった	

2-2 Causative sentences "make ~ V; let ~ V; have ~ V; cause ~ to V"

[2-a]

Topic (causer)	Causee			V (causative)
両親は	妹	を／に	大学に	行かせました。
My parents made/let my younger sister go to college.				

[2-b]

Topic (causer)	Causee		Direct object	V (causative)
黒田先生は	学生	に	発表を	させました。
Prof. Kuroda made/had/let the students give a presentation.				

You can express various meanings using causative sentences. The most common meanings they represent are:

(i) Someone (X) forces someone else (Y) to do something (the "forcing causative"); and

(ii) Someone (X) allows someone else (Y) to do something (the "allowing causative").

In either case, because X is the person who causes Y to do something, we call X the "causer" and Y the "causee."

In causative sentences, the causer usually appears as the topic, and the causee is marked by を or に. In [2-b], in which there is a direct object, the causee is always marked by に because one verb cannot have more than one direct object.

Exs. (1) 子どもの時、母は私{を／に}ピアノのレッスンに行かせました。
When I was a child, my mother made/let me go to piano lessons.

(2) お父さんは光君に将来のことを考えさせました。
Hikaru's father made Hikaru think about his future.

(3) 先生になったら、学生に毎日宿題をさせようと思っています。
I intend on having my students do homework every day when I become a teacher.

(4) 小学生にスマホを持たせた方がいいと思いますか。
Do you think it would be better to let elementary school students have a smartphone?

Whether a causative sentence is interpreted as a forcing causative or an allowing causative depends on the context. For example, [2-a] and [2-b] can be either a forcing causative or an allowing causative, but (5) is most likely a forcing causative and (6) an allowing causative.

Exs. (5) 父は弟にゲームを全部捨てさせました。
My father made my little brother throw away all his games.

(6) 父は弟に好きなゲームをさせました。*My father let my little brother play any games he liked.*

In most cases, when the verb is intransitive, the causee can be marked by either を or に, as in [2-a] and (1). However, に cannot be used if the causee is inanimate, as in (7), or the causee's action is uncontrollable, as in (8).

Exs. (7) 私はとうふ{を／×に}くさらせてしまいました。*I caused the tofu to go bad.*

(8) 弟は父{を／×に}怒らせた。*My little brother made my father angry.*

2-3 *Te*-forms of causative forms + あげる／くれる／もらう [Permission] "let ~ V; (kindly) allow ~ to V"

[2-c]

Topic (causer = benefit giver)	Causee (= benefit receiver)		Direct object	V-*te* (causative)	
トムさんは	みかさん	に	ギターを	ひかせて	あげました。
Tom [kindly] let Mika play his guitar.					

You can express the idea that someone kindly allows someone else to do something using V-*te* (causative) あげる. (See L15 #4-1.)

In [2-c], あげました makes it clear that the sentence is an allowing causative. Without あげました, the sentence is ambiguous as to whether it is an allowing causative or a forcing causative, as in the following sentence:

トムさんはみかさんにギターをひかせました。*Tom made/let Mika play his guitar.*

Exs. (1) 私はスミスさんに私のパソコンを使わせてあげました。
I [kindly] let Smith-san use my PC.

(2) 将来、子どもに好きなことをさせてあげようと思います。
In the future, I think I'll let my children do what they like.

[2-d]

Topic (causer = benefit giver)	Causee (= benefit receiver)		Direct object	V-*te* (causative)	
山田さんは	（私	に）	プリンターを	使わせて	くれました。
Yamada-san [kindly] allowed me to use his printer.					

[2-e]

Topic (causee = benefit receiver)	Causer (= benefit giver)		Direct object	V-*te* (causative)	
私は	山田さん	に	プリンターを	使わせて	もらいました。
I got Yamada-san to let me use his printer.					

You can express your gratitude for someone allowing you to do something using the *te*-form of a causative verb with くれる or もらう, as in [2-d] and [2-e].

In the sentence pattern [2-d], the causee (= the benefit receiver) is often the speaker. When the benefit receiver is clear from the context, it is omitted. (See L15 #4-2 and #4-3 for the difference between V-*te*くれる and V-*te*もらう.)

Exs. (3) a. 両親は私を大学に行かせてくれました。*My parents let me go to university.*

b. 私は両親に大学に行かせてもらいました。*I got my parents to let me go to university.*

(4) a. 小学生の時、母は（私を）友達の家に泊まらせてくれませんでした。

When I was in elementary school, my mother wouldn't let me sleep over at my friends' houses.

b. 小学生の時、私は母に友達の家に泊まらせてもらえませんでした。

When I was in elementary school, I couldn't get my mother to let me sleep over at my friends' houses.

⚠ Note that in (4b), もらえません (the negative potential form of もらう) is used instead of もらいません. This is because in this situation, the speaker wanted to do something but couldn't rather than didn't. In other words, if you said もらいませんでした, it would mean that you chose not to do the action and thus chose not to get permission for it.

2-4 *Te*-forms of causative forms + いただけませんか, くださいませんか, etc. [Request]

"May/Could I V?; Could you let me V?; Please let me V"

[2-f]

	V-*te* (causative)	
この部屋を	使わせて	いただけませんか／くださいませんか。(very polite) もらえませんか／くれませんか。(moderately polite) もらえない？／くれない？ (casual) ください。(direct)
Would you let me use this room? / Could I get you to let me use this room? (～ください: Please let me use this room.)		

You can make a request using the *te*-forms of causative verbs with いただけませんか, くださいませんか, もらえませんか, くれませんか, etc., as in [2-f]. Among these, いただけませんか and くださいませんか are very polite, and もらえませんか and くれませんか are moderately polite, while もらえない？ and くれない？ are casual. ください expresses a direct request.

Note that in [2-f], the person who wants to use the room is the speaker and the person who allows that is the listener. In this sentence structure, 私に is usually left unsaid. 私に is included only when it is the information being emphasized (e.g., a sentence like "Could you let ME use this room?").

⚠ Note also that いただけませんか, もらえませんか, and もらえない are all potential forms. When making a request, you cannot use the non-potential forms (i.e., いただきませんか, もらいませんか, and もらわない) because they indicate your own volition. The equivalent English would be "Will I have the favor of V-ing from you?" Compare the two sentences in (1) below to see how one syllable can change the meaning entirely:

Exs. (1) a. この部屋を使わせていただけませんか。[Asking for permission]
Could you let me use this room?

b. この部屋を使わせていただきませんか。[Making a suggestion]
Shall we use this room? (lit. Shall we have (someone) let us use this room?)

(2) <部長に> あのう、私にその仕事をさせていただけませんか。
Um... could I ask for your permission to do that work?

(3) <ホームステイの家で> あのう、晩ご飯の準備を手伝わせてください。
Um, please let me help you prepare for dinner.

(4) <友達に> おもしろそうなゲームだね。僕にもさせてくれない？
That game looks interesting. Can I play? (lit. Will you let me play [it], too?)

3 ～か(どうか) [Embedded question marker] "if; whether or not"

[3-a]

Embedded question			
S-plain			
明日会議がある	か	どうか	知っていますか。
Do you know whether or not we have a meeting tomorrow?			

[3-b]

Embedded question				
S-plain				
	Q-word			
会議が	いつ	ある	か	教えてください。
Please tell us when the meeting will be held.				

By embedding a question in a sentence, you can do the following:

(i) Asking questions such as "Do you know if ~?" and "Do you remember where ~?"

(ii) Making statements such as "I don't remember if ~" and "I know who ~."

(iii) Making requests such as "Tell me if ~" and "Could you ask someone when ~?"

Note that when the embedded question is a yes-no question, かどうか "whether or not" is used, while when there is a question word, どうか is not necessary. Note also that embedded questions are always in plain form.

The verbs that follow embedded questions include: 知っている, 教える, 分かる, 聞く "ask," 忘れる, and 覚えている.

[3-c]

Embedded question					
	Adj(*na*)				
スミスさんが魚(さかな)が	好(す)き	ø	か	どうか	知(し)りません。
I don't know whether or not Smith-san likes fish.					

[3-d]

Embedded question				
	N			
これは誰(だれ)の	本(ほん)	ø	か	分(わ)かりますか。
Do you know whose book this is?				

だ after *na*-adjectives and nouns is omitted in most cases, as in [3-c] and [3-d].

Exs. (1) 黒田先生(くろだせんせい)に、プロジェクトのトピックを変(か)えてもいいかどうか聞(き)いてみましょう。
Let's ask Prof. Kuroda if it's okay to change our project topic.

(2) 田中(たなか)さんにお金(かね)を借(か)りたかどうか忘(わす)れました。
I forgot if I borrowed money from Tanaka-san or not.

(3) <レストランで> 何(なに)が一番(いちばん)おいしいか教(おし)えてください。
Please tell me what is the best (lit. the most delicious).

(4) 田中(たなか)さんの出身(しゅっしん)はどこか覚(おぼ)えてる？ *Do you remember where Tanaka-san is from?*

In embedded sentences, the subject is often marked by が, as in [3-a] through [3-c], (1) and (3) above, but は may also be used, as in [3-d] and (4).

4 ～と [Conditional conjunction] "if; when"

[4-a]

S1			S2
	V-plain.non-past		
「OK」を	クリックする	と、	ダウンロードが始(はじ)まります。
With a click on "OK," (lit. If you click on "OK,") the download starts.			

[4-b]

S1			S2
	V-plain.non-past		
ここは春(はる)に	なる	と、	桜(さくら)がたくさんさいて、とてもきれいです。
In spring (lit. When it becomes spring), many cherry blossoms bloom here and it's very pretty.			

You can express the idea of "if; when" using the plain non-past forms of sentences with と. This と is a conjunction. The structure "S_1 と、S_2" is commonly used in situations in which S_2 is the case whenever S_1 takes place. When S_1 occurs without fail, the equivalent English is "when" rather than "if," as seen in [4-b].

Exs. (1) この道(みち)をまっすぐ行(い)くと、銀行(ぎんこう)があります。
If you go straight down this street, there will be a bank.

(2) このホテルはオンラインで予約(よやく)すると、10パーセント安(やす)くなります。
If you make a reservation for this hotel online, it's 10% cheaper.

(3) 成績(せいせき)がよくないと、この大学(だいがく)には入(はい)れないと言(い)われました。
I was told that you can't get into this university if your grades aren't good.

(4) このインターンシップの仕事(しごと)は日本語(にほんご)が下手(へた)だとできません。
You can't do this internship if you're poor at Japanese.

The core idea of "S_1 と、S_2" is that whenever S_1 takes place, S_2 accompanies it. Thus, S_2 cannot represent a future action that the actor can take of his/her own will. Requests, volitional sentences and such, therefore, do not occur in S_2. The following sentences are ungrammatical:

× ホテルに着(つ)くと、電話(でんわ)をください。→ ホテルに着(つ)いたら、電話(でんわ)をください。
Intended meaning: *Please give me a call when you've arrived at the hotel.*

× お金(かね)がないと、大学(だいがく)に行(い)きません。→ お金(かね)がなかったら、大学(だいがく)に行(い)きません。
Intended meaning: *I will not go to college if I don't have money.*

However, (5) is grammatical because S_2 represents one's ability, which is not a future action the actor can take of his/her own will.

Ex. (5) お金(かね)がないと、大学(だいがく)に行(い)けません。*I cannot go to college if I don't have money.*

(6) is also grammatical because S_2 represents a habitual action.

Ex. (6) 日本人(にほんじん)は桜(さくら)がさくと、花見(はなみ)に行(い)きます。
Japanese people go cherry blossom viewing when the flowers bloom.

⚠ When S_1 in "S_1と、S_2" represents something that occurs without fail, S_2 cannot be the state of something/someone (often expressed with an adjective), as in the following example:

× この町(まち)は4月(がつ)になると、暖(あたた)かいです。
Intended meaning: *It is warm in this town when April comes around.*

→ この町(まち)は4月(がつ)になると、暖(あたた)かくなります。*It gets warm in this town when April comes around.*

☞ GID (vol.2): B. Connecting sentences 4. たら, と, ば, and なら

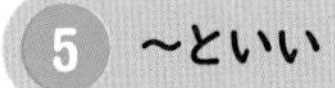

~といい is an idiomatic expression that consists of the conditional conjunction と and the adjective いい. The literal meaning of Xといい is "it's good if X." Using ~といい, you can express your wishes and hopes.

5-1 ~といいですね "It would be good if ~, wouldn't it?; I hope (that) ~"

[5-a]

S-plain.non-past		
日本(にほん)で仕事(しごと)ができる	と	いいですね。
I hope you can work in Japan. (lit. It would be good if you could work in Japan, wouldn't it?)		

Using ~といいですね, you can express your wish that something will happen when you assume that the listener shares your wish. This expression is often used when you want to encourage someone or show sympathy for someone. When the subject is the listener, it is usually omitted, as in [5-a].

Ex. (1) ＜病気の友達に＞

早く元気になるといいですね。*I hope you'll get well soon!*

⚠ Sentences preceding といいですね must represent an uncontrollable action or state. For this reason, potential verbs often occur in the predicate position of the preceding sentence. The following sentence is ungrammatical because 日本で仕事をする is a controllable action.

× 日本で仕事をするといいですね。(cf. [5-a])

Exs. (2) A: 来年日本に留学するんです。*I'm going to study in Japan next year.*

B: そうですか。日本人の友達がたくさんできるといいですね。

Is that so? I hope you can make many Japanese friends.

(3) A: 土曜日に友達とテニスをするんです。*I'm playing tennis with my friend on Saturday.*

B: そうですか。雨が降らないといいですね。*Oh, really? I hope it doesn't rain.*

(4) みか：間違えて研さんのジュース、飲んじゃった。*I accidentally drank Ken's juice…*

リサ：そう。研さんが気がつかないといいね。*You did? Hopefully Ken won't notice…*

5-2 ～といいんですが… "I hope (that) ~"

[5-b]

S-plain.non-past		
奨学金がもらえる	と	いいんですが…
I hope I can get the scholarship.		

Using ～といいんですが, you can express your hope or wish that something will happen or be the case. When the subject is the speaker, it is usually omitted.

The final が indicates that the sentence is not complete. The omitted sentence would be something like どうなるか分かりません "I don't know what'll happen."

Exs. (1) 来年、卒業するんです。いい仕事が見つかるといいんですが…

I graduate next year. I hope I can find a good job.

(2) 来週、ジャパンハウスに新しい人が引っこしてきます。いい人だといいんですが… *A new person will be moving into the Japan House next week, I hope he is nice.*

(3) 来月、ジャンさんのバンドのライブに行くんだ。いい席が取れるといいんだけど… *I'm going to see Jean's band play live next month. I hope I can get a good seat.*

～といいんですが is a colloquial expression. In written language and formal presentations, ～といいと思う is used instead.

Exs. (4) ＜作文＞ 来年、卒業する。いい仕事が見つかるといいと思う。

I graduate next year. I hope I can find a good job.

(5) ＜発表＞ 世界がもっとよくなるといいと思います。

I hope the world will become a better place.

6 ～ために [Purpose] "in order to; for (the purpose of)"

[6-a]

	V-plain.non-past		
車を	買う	ために	両親にお金を借りました。
I borrowed money from my parents in order to buy a car.			

[6-b]

	N			
みかさんは	ヨーロッパ旅行	の	ために	お金を貯めています。
Mika is saving money for a trip to Europe.				

You can express purposes using "V-plain.non-past ために" or "Nのために." When a verb precedes ために, it must represent a controllable action. Potential verbs (e.g., 話せる, できる, 分かる) and the negative forms of verbs (e.g., 遅れない, (かぜを)ひかない) do not occur before ために.

Exs. (1) アイさんは将来キュレーターになるために今、日本で美術を勉強しています。
Ai is studying art in Japan now in order to become a curator in the future.

(2) 世界をもっとよくするために何をしたらいいと思いますか。
What do you think we should do [in order] to make the world a better place?

(3) A: みなさんは何のために働いていますか。*Why (lit. For what) do you work, everyone?*

B: 私はお金のために働いています。*I work for money.*

C: 私は人生を楽しむために働いています。*I work to enjoy life.*

(4) 健康のために毎日1時間歩いています。*I walk an hour every day for my health.*

☞ GID (vol.2): D. Sentence patterns 5. V-*masu* に行く・来る vs. Vために

7 Vまで "until ... V" and Vまでに "by the time ... V"

[7-a]

	V-plain.non-past		Main clause
大学を	卒業する	まで	この寮にいるつもりです。
I plan to be in this dorm until I graduate from university.			

[7-b]

	V-plain.non-past		Main clause
今学期が	終わる	までに	レポートを書かなくてはいけません。
I have to write a paper by the time this semester is over.			

You can express the idea of "until someone does something (or something happens)" using まで, and the idea of "by the time someone does something (or something happens)" using までに. In [7-a], the main clause must represent an action or a state that lasts until the time the まで clause indicates, while in [7-b], the main clause must represent an action (often one with no duration) that is completed before the time the までに clause indicates. The following diagrams illustrate the difference between まで and までに:

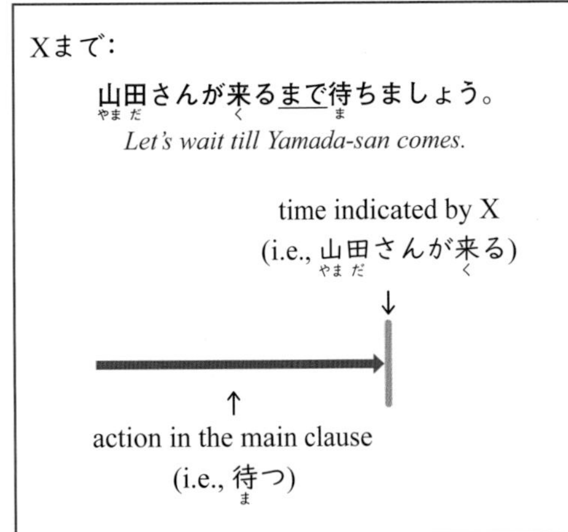

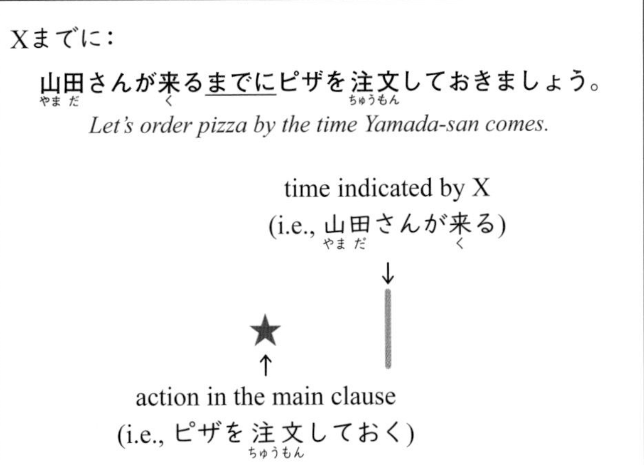

Note that when a verb precedes まで／までに, the verb must be in the non-past form regardless of the tense of the main clause. Therefore, the following sentence is ungrammatical:

× 大学を卒業したまでこの寮にいました。
→ 大学を卒業するまでこの寮にいました。*I was in this dorm until I graduated from the university.*

Exs. (1) 料理ができるまで待っていてください。*Please wait until the meal is ready.*

(2) 彼は死ぬまで一緒にいると言ったけど、他の人と結婚してしまった…
He said he would be with me until he died, but he married someone else…

(3) お客さんが来るまでに部屋をそうじしておかなくてはいけません。
I have to clean the room before our guests come.

(4) 留学が終わるまでに漢字を 2,000 覚えたいです。
I want to memorize 2,000 kanji before my study abroad ends.

As seen in [7-b], (3), and (4), the main clause in the までに structure often represents someone's obligation, desire, or request.

Another note is that までに can also be used with time nouns such as 明日, 来週, and 金曜日, as in (5).

Ex. (5) この宿題は金曜日までに出してください。*Please turn in this homework by Friday.*

話しましょう

▶ **Words written in purple** are new words introduced in this lesson.

できる I　Politely express what you want to do and request permission to do it.

できるI-A　Reason ～ので

1 Let's practice giving various reasons.

Step 1 State reasons to explain why you want to go to Japan. L17-6

Ex. 夏休み(なつ)は長いです → 夏休み(なつ)は長いので、日本に行きたいです。

1) 日本の文化に興味(きょうみ)があります　2) 日本語を習っています　3) 飛行機(ひこうき)のチケットが安いです
4) 日本食が好きです　5) おもしろそうです　6) 専攻(せんこう)は日本語です　7) your own

Step 2 State reasons to explain why you will not go to the party tonight. L17-7

Ex. お酒(さけ)が飲めません → お酒(さけ)が飲めないので、今晩パーティーに行きません。

1) 友達が行きません　2) 時間がありません　3) 気分がよくないです
4) パーティーが好きじゃないです　5) 宿題をしなくてはいけません　6) your own

2 Match the reasons below with their results/consequences and connect the two sentences using ～ので. L17-8

Ex. 急(きゅう)に気分が悪くなったので、病院(びょういん)に行きました。

Ex. 急(きゅう)に気分が悪くなりました。	・お金がありません。
1) むだづかいをしました。	・お礼(れい)を言いました。
2) 大雨でした。	・病院(びょういん)に行きました。
3) 友達にアドバイスをしてもらいました。	・ゲームを買ってもらえませんでした。
4) かぎをなくしてしまいました。	・出かけられませんでした。
5) 母が厳(きび)しかったです。	・家に入れません。

3 Ask your teacher the following favors, providing your own reasons for asking.

Ex. 簡単(かんたん)な本を紹介(しょうかい)する

Opening	あなた：あのう、先生、ちょっとお願(ねが)いがあるんですが… 先生　：はい、何ですか。
Reason + request	あなた：日本語の本を読んでみたいので、簡単(かんたん)な本を紹介(しょうかい)してくださいませんか。 先生　：日本語の本ですか。どんな本が読みたいですか。 <Continue>
Closing	あなた：ありがとうございます。

1) 推薦状(すいせんじょう)を書く　2) 一緒(いっしょ)に会話の練習をする　3) 文法(ぶんぽう)をもう一度説明(せつめい)する　4) your own

4 Your *senpai* invites you to an activity. Give an appropriate reason and decline the invitation.

Ex. A: 今日の夕方、一緒にジムに筋トレに行かない？

B: ○○先輩、すみません。今日は宿題をしなくてはいけないので、ちょっと…

A: そっか。じゃ、明日はどう？

B: 明日はアルバイトをしなくてはいけないし、プロジェクトのしめ切りがあるので、ちょっと…　すみません。

<Continue>

できるI-B Causative forms of verbs and causative sentences

1 Let's practice conjugating verbs into their causative forms. L17-9

Ex. 食べる → 食べさせる → 食べさせます

1) 覚える　2) 受ける　3) (お茶を)いれる　4) 休む　5) 手伝う　6) 運ぶ
7) 迎えに行く　8) 勉強する　9) 来る　10) 届ける　11) 学ぶ　12) 話し合う　13) 出張する

2 Compare demanding and undemanding teachers.

Step 1 Say what these teachers do or do not make their students do.

Ex.1 毎日新しい漢字を覚える

→ スパルタ先生は学生に<u>毎日新しい漢字を覚えさせ</u>ます。

→ ジェントル先生は学生に<u>毎日新しい漢字を覚えさせ</u>ません。

Ex.2 毎週日本のイベントに行く

→ スパルタ先生は学生{を／に}<u>毎週日本のイベントに行かせ</u>ます。

→ ジェントル先生は学生{を／に}<u>毎週日本のイベントに行かせ</u>ません。

1) 教科書を何ページも読む　2) 長い作文を書く　3) 難しい試験を受ける
4) 日本語で質問する　5) 毎週ボランティアに参加する　6) 毎週オフィスアワーに来る

Step 2 If you became a teacher, what would you make your students do? When answering, use the cues in Step 1 as a reference.

Ex. A: ○○さんが先生だったら、学生にどんなことをさせますか。

B: 漢字が苦手な学生が多いので、私は学生に毎日新しい漢字を覚えさせます。

A: 私も同じです。学生に毎日漢字を覚えさせます。漢字は大切だからです。

or 私はちょっと違います。学生に毎日漢字を覚えさせません。単語や文法の復習をしてほしいからです。

3 In the near future, AI may come to play a large role in our lives.

Step 1 Describe the things you'd like to make AI robots do for you. (L17-11)

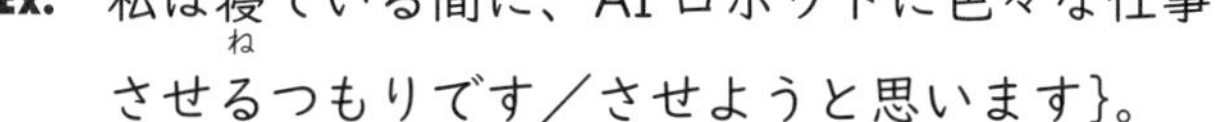

Ex. 私は寝(ね)ている間に、AIロボットに色々な仕事を{させたいです／させるつもりです／させようと思います}。

Ex. while I am sleeping / do various jobs

1) tidy up my room

2) every morning / choose my clothes

3) from home to work (lit. company) / drive the car

4) at work (lit. company) / greet customers

5) at work (lit. company) / make coffee

6) while I am napping / take care of my pet

Group Work

Step 2 Suppose you are making a new AI robot. Brainstorm with your classmates about how you would like to make use of it.

Ex. A: 新しいAIロボットにどんなことをさせたいですか。

B: そうですね。もっと寝(ね)たいので、寝(ね)ている間に、朝ご飯を作らせたいです。

C: いいですね。それから、せんたく物をたたませるのはどうですか。 <Continue>

Step 3 Share your ideas with other classmates.

Ex. 私達は寝(ね)ている間に、新しいAIロボットに朝ご飯を作らせたいです。それから、私達はなまけ者(もの) (lazy person) なので、せんたく物をたたませようと思います。このAIロボットがいたら、人間(にんげん)はもっと自由に時間が使えます。

4 Do you come from a strict household or a more laid-back family?

Step 1 First, let's practice forming the expression "V-*te* (causative) くれる." 

Ex. ☺ 私の親はやさしかったです。(親は) 私にジュースを飲ませてくれました。

☹ 私の親は厳(きび)しかったです。(親は) 私にジュースを飲ませてくれませんでした。

Ex. 飲む　1) 持つ　2) 使う　3) 飼(か)う　4) たくさん食べる　5) 泊(と)まる　6) する

friend's house

Step 2 Now, let's practice forming the expression "V-*te* (causative) もらう" using the cues in Step 1. L17-13

Ex. ☺ 私は親に<u>ジュースを飲ませ</u>てもらいました。

☹ 私は親に<u>ジュースを飲ませ</u>てもらえませんでした。

Step 3 Talk with your partner about whether or not your parent allowed you to do the activities in Step 1 when you were a child using "V-*te* (causative) もらう／くれる."

Ex. A: 私の親はやさしかったです。子どもの時、親は私にジュースを飲ませてくれました。〇〇さんはどうでしたか。

B: 私も飲ませてもらいましたよ。

or 私の親は厳(きび)しかったので、私は飲ませてもらえませんでした。 <Continue>

5 Do you think you would be a strict or permissive parent if you decided to have children? Exchange your opinions with your partner.

Useful phrases	私も〇〇さんと同じです	私は〇〇さんとちょっと違(ちが)います

Ex. A: 〇〇さんは親になったら、子どもに何をさせてあげようと思いますか。

B: 私は子どもにゲームをたくさんさせてあげようと思います。

A: どうしてですか。

B: ゲームをしたら、頭(あたま)がよくなると思うからです。例えば、「クラフト」は頭(あたま)をたくさん使わなくてはいけません。△△さんはどう思いますか。

A: 私は〇〇さんとちょっと違(ちが)います。ゲームをしすぎたら、目が悪くなるので、私は子どもにあまりゲームをさせません。

できるI-C Requests using the *te*-forms of causative verbs

1 Let's practice using causative forms to request permission.

Step 1 First, practice forming the expression "V-*te* (causative) ください." L17-14

Ex. 仕事を手伝(てつだ)う → <u>仕事を手伝(てつだ)わせ</u>てください

1) 書類(しょるい)を届(とど)ける　2) 荷物を運ぶ　3) お客様(きゃくさま)と話(はな)し合(あ)う　4) 書類(しょるい)を英語に訳(やく)す
5) 一緒(いっしょ)に出張(しゅっちょう)に行く　6) 仕事を休む　7) 今日早く帰る　8) データを説明(せつめい)する

Step 2 Now, request permission from your *senpai*/boss using the cues in Step 1.

Exs. 先輩(せんぱい)、<u>仕事を手伝(てつだ)わせ</u>て{くれませんか／もらえませんか}。

部長、<u>仕事を手伝(てつだ)わせ</u>て{くださいませんか／いただけませんか}。

2 You have just started an internship in Japan. Show your boss how motivated you are to be working there. L17-15

Ex. 誰(だれ)か手伝(てつだ)ってほしいんだけど…

Ex. 私に手伝(てつだ)わせてください！

1) 誰(だれ)かこの書類(しょるい)を田中さんに届(とど)けてほしいんだけど…
2) 誰(だれ)かこれを説明(せつめい)してほしいんだけど…
3) 誰(だれ)かこの英語の表現(ひょうげん)を訳(やく)してほしいんだけど…
4) 誰(だれ)か荷物を運んでほしいんだけど…
5) 誰(だれ)かお客様(きゃくさま)を駅の北口(きたぐち)に迎(むか)えに行ってほしいんだけど…
6) your own

3 You are talking with some other interns after work. Make some requests of them.

Ex. A: この雑誌(ざっし)はおもしろいですよ。
B: へえ、じゃ、（私にも）ちょっと読ませて｛くれませんか／もらえませんか｝。
A: もちろん。どうぞ。

1)

2)

3)

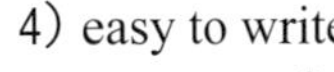

4) easy to write

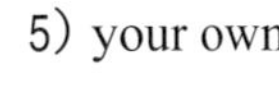

5) your own

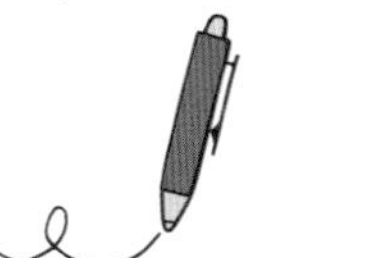

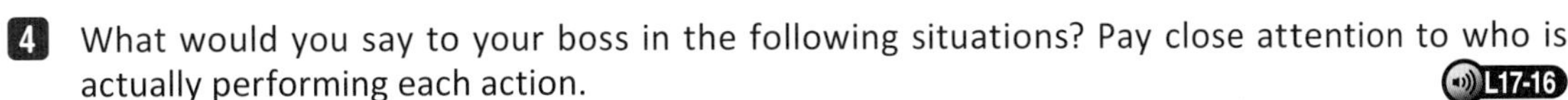

4 What would you say to your boss in the following situations? Pay close attention to who is actually performing each action. L17-16

Ex.1 すみませんが、写真(しゃしん)をとって｛くださいませんか／いただけませんか｝。
Ex.2 すみませんが、写真(しゃしん)をとらせて｛くださいませんか／いただけませんか｝。

Ex.2 take a photo (of this slide)
BOSS
YOU

1) check my document
2) explain today's activity to me again
3) give (lit. say) my opinion about this plan
4) teach me how to use this software（ソフト）
5) take a business Japanese test next Tuesday
6) take a day off next Tuesday

5 During your internship, there are times when you need to request permission for something from your boss. How would you politely make the following requests? Make sure to provide reason(s) for what you want to do.

	Ex.
A: Opening	A: すみません、部長、ちょっとお願いがあるんですが…
	B: はい、何ですか。
A: Reason + request	A: 仕事で使う日本語をもっと勉強したいので、来週日本語のワークショップに参加させて {いただけませんか／くださいませんか}。
B: Follow-up Q or comment	B: それは役に立ちそうですね。ワークショップは何曜日ですか。
	A: 金曜日の午後です。
B: Permission	B: 金曜日の午後ですね。いいですよ。
A: Closing	A: どうもありがとうございます。

Ex. participate in a workshop next week　1) take a day off tomorrow　2) go home early today
3) do a job where I can use more Japanese　4) your own

できるII Ask and answer questions about new experiences and discoveries.

できるII-A Embedded questions ～か(どうか)

1 Look at the pictures below and say if you know the answer to each of the following questions about the place and person depicted. L17-17

Ex.1 ここは日本ですか。 → ここが日本かどうか分かりません。

1) 若い人はよくここに行きますか。
2) ここは今、寒いですか。
3) ここは平和ですか。
4) 季節は秋ですか。
5) your own

Ex.2 この人の名前は何ですか。 → この人の名前が何か分かりません。

6) この人は明日何をしますか。
7) この人はどうして笑っていますか。
8) この人の仕事は何ですか。
9) この人は誰ですか。
10) your own

2 Who has a better memory? Ask your partner if they can answer the following questions.

Ex. 昨日の晩、何を食べましたか。

A: ○○さんは昨日の晩、何を食べたか覚えていますか。

B: はい、何を食べたか覚えています。ラーメンを食べました。

or いいえ、何を食べたか覚えていません。

A: そうですか。私 {は／も} … <Continue>

1) おとといい、よく眠れましたか。
2) 最近、いつつめを切りましたか。
3) 最近、誰にお礼を言いましたか。
4) 先週の土曜日は楽しかったですか。
5) ５年前の○○（country name）の {首相／大統領} は誰でしたか。
6) your own

3 How much do you know about your classmates? Ask if your partner knows the answers to the following questions about a classmate of your choice.

Ex. A: ○○さんの専攻は何か知っていますか。

B: はい、{工学です／工学だと思います}。or いいえ、知りません。

Ex. 専攻は何ですか。
1) 出身はどこですか。
2) 週末によく何をしますか。
3) 今、何年生ですか。
4) どんな音楽が好きですか。
5) アルバイトをしていますか。
6) 日本に行ったことがありますか。
7) 昨日何をしましたか。
8) your own

4 とびらの父 is a famous palm reader. You are visiting him today to ask about many things in your future.

Step 1 First, choose what questions you want to ask とびらの父.

＜質問リスト＞

Ex. 将来、私は有名になりますか。

☐ いい仕事が見つかりますか。

☐ 10年後、どこに住んでいますか。

☐ 将来、私はどんな生活を送っていますか。

☐ your own: ______________________________

ROLE PLAY

Step 2 Now, you are meeting with とびらの父.

Role A You are a client. Ask とびらの父 the questions you've prepared.

Role B You are とびらの父. Answer your client's questions with your psychic powers.

Ex. A: あの、将来、私が有名になるかどうか教えてくれませんか。

B: そうですね… はい、有名になりますよ。

A: そうですか。何になりますか。(← Follow-up question)

B: ○○さんはまず、この大学の教授になって、突然学長になります。

<Continue>

できるⅡ-B Conditional conjunction ～と

1 You are staying at a hotel room with various convenient features. Describe how they work, as in the example. L17-18

Ex. このホテルの部屋はとても便利(べんり)です。手をたたくと電気がつきます。

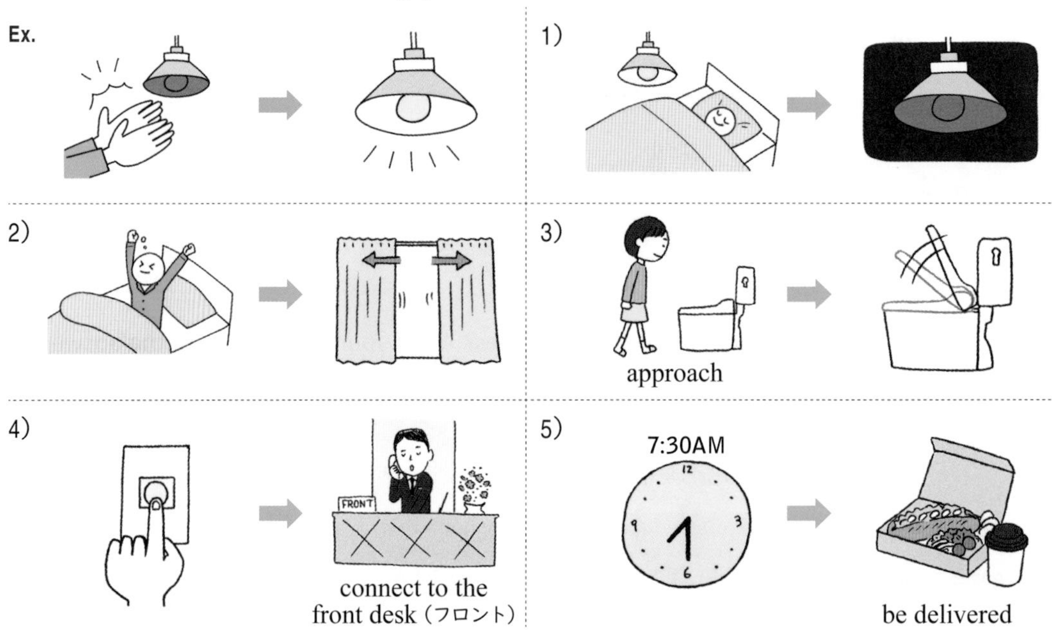

2 What kind of seasonal events do the countries you are familiar with have?

Step 1 Below is a list of seasonal events/traditions in Japan. Describe them in Japanese. L17-19

Ex. 日本では４月になると、学校が始まります。

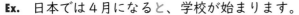

Step 2 Talk with your classmate about seasonal events in the countries you are familiar with.

Ex. A: インドでは春(はる)になると、「ホーリー」というお祭(まつ)りをします。

B: へえ、そうですか。それはどんなお祭(まつ)りですか。 <Continue>

3 There are various superstitions around the world.

Step 1 How much do you know about superstitions? Match each cause with its supposed effect.

Ex. 黒(くろ)いネコを見ると、不幸(ふこう) (unhappy) になります。  L17-20

Ex. 黒(くろ)いネコを見ます。	• いいことがあります。
1) 13日が金曜日です。	• お願(ねが)いがかないます (to come true)。
2) 四(よ)つ葉(ば)のクローバーを見つけます。	• 不幸(ふこう) (unhappy) になります。
3) 誰(だれ)かにうわさをされます。	• 悪いことがあります。
4) 流(なが)れ星(ぼし)においのりをします。	• くしゃみが出ます。
5) 耳が大きいです。	• お金持ちになります。
6) ネコが顔(かお)を洗います。	• 雨が降(ふ)ります。

Step 2 Are there any superstitions that you believe in or find interesting? Brainstorm some superstitions from the countries/cultures you are familiar with.

Ex. くしゃみが３回出る ➡ 次の日はいい天気になる

Step 3 Share one of the superstitions that you brainstormed in Step 2 with your classmates.

Ex. A: オランダ (Netherlands) では、くしゃみが３回出ると、次の日はいい天気になると言われています。

B: へぇ、おもしろい迷信(めいしん) (superstition) ですね。 <Continue>

4 The Butterfly Effect refers to an idea that a single occurrence, no matter how small, can result in large differences later on.

Step 1 Make sentences describing a chain of events based on the cues provided. Pay attention to the verb forms. L17-21

Ex.1 ペンをなくすと、ノートが取れません。

Ex.2 ノートが取れないと、勉強ができません。

Ex.1 Lose your pen ➡ **Ex.2** Can't take notes ➡ 1) Can't study ➡ 2) Can't get good grades ➡ 3) Can't graduate ➡ 4) Can't get a full-time job ➡ 5) Can't buy food ➡ Die

Step 2 Now, create your own chain of events with your partner and share it with the class.

Lesson 17

できる III Talk about your future goals in detail.

できるIII-A Expressing wishes and hopes ～といい

1 Your partner has fallen in love with Tanaka-san and is completely smitten. Encourage your partner using ～といいですね. Your partner will respond with their own wish using ～といいんですが. L17-22

Ex. 田中さんの電話番号(ばんごう)が分かります

A: 田中さんの電話番号(ばんごう)が分かるといいですね。

B: ええ、分かるといいんですが…

1) もうすぐ田中さんに会えます
2) 田中さんに気持ちを伝(つた)えられます
3) 今日、田中さんから連絡(れんらく)が来ます
4) 田中さんに好きな人がいません
5) 田中さんも〇〇さんが好きです
6) your own

2 Suppose your partner is going to study abroad in Japan soon. What do you hope your partner will be able to do/experience there? L17-23

Ex. A: 日本で友達がたくさんできるといいですね。

B: ええ、そうですね。いい友達が見つかるといいんですが…

Ex. find many friends
1) eat tasty Japanese food
2) participate in interesting activities
3) go to famous temples and shrines to pray
4) live a fun life
5) there are no earthquakes
6) not get homesick
7) professors are not very strict
8) your own

3 What are your plans for the following occasions?

Step 1 Talk about your plans with your partner and express your wishes for them.

Possible topics	週末	〇〇休み (Ex. 夏(なつ)休み)	卒業(そつぎょう)の後

Ex. A: 週末、何か予定(よてい)がありますか。

B:「ブラックストーン」というレストランに晩ご飯を食べに行くつもりです。

A: ああ、あの人気があるレストランですね。混(こ)んでいないといいですね。

B: はい、待(ま)たないで、入れるといいんですが…

Step 2 Now, talk about your plans casually with your friend.

Ex. A: 週末、何か予定(よてい)ある？

B:「ブラックストーン」っていうレストランに晩ご飯食べに行くつもり。

A: ああ、あの人気があるレストランだね。混(こ)んでいないといいね。

B: うん、待(ま)たないで、入れるといいんだけど…

できるⅢ-B　Purpose ～ために

1 The *TOBIRA* characters are talking about their future plans. Report their plans by matching each goal with an accompanying action. L17-24

Ex. 将来アイさんは日本の美術を世界に紹介するために、キュレーター (curator) になりたいそうです。

Ex. アイ 日本の美術を世界に紹介します。	•	• 大学院で数学を研究するつもりです。
1) ジャン 有名なミュージシャンになります。	•	• キュレーターになりたいです。
2) リーマン 大学で数学を教えます。	•	• YouTube に動画をアップしています。
3) マーク 世界を平和にします。	•	• ビジネススクールに入ろうと思っています。
4) 圭太 自分の会社を作ります。	•	• 色々な国でボランティア活動がしたいです。

2 Talk about your own actions and the purposes behind them.

Step 1 Ask what your partner does to achieve the following goals.

Ex. 健康　A: 〇〇さんは健康のために、何かしていますか。
B: はい、一週間に三回ぐらいジョギングをしていますよ。
or いいえ、何もしていません。もっと運動した方がいいですね。

1) 健康　2) 将来　3) 環境　4) 楽しい生活を送る　5) いい成績を取る

Step 2 Let's think philosophically. Ask what your partner's purposes are for the following actions.

Ex. 生きています
A: 〇〇さんは何のために、生きていますか。
B: そうですね… 私は社会の役に立つために、生きていると思います。
A: そうですか。例えば、社会のためにどんなことをしていますか。(← Follow-up question)
<Continue>

1) 生きています　2) 大学で勉強しています　3) 働きます　4) your own

3 Have you ever participated in any volunteer activities?

Step 1 Describe one volunteer activity you have taken part in. If you have never participated in any, think what kind of volunteer activities you would like to do.

__________ために、__________で__________ボランティア
(目的は？)　(どこで？)　(何をする？)

Step 2 Share your experience with your partner.

Ex. A: ○○さんは、何かボランティアをしたことがありますか。

Yes	No
B: はい、あります。 A: どんなボランティアをしましたか。 B: 子どものIT教育(きょういく)のために、小学校でプログラミングを教えるボランティアをしました。 A: そうですか。どうでしたか。 <Continue>	B: いいえ、ありません。 A: じゃ、してみたいボランティアがありますか。 B: はい、町をよく知ってもらうために、観光客(かんこうきゃく)に町を案内(あんない)するボランティアがしたいです。 A: そうですか。 <Continue>

4 Talk with your classmate about what kind of things you would make people do to achieve your goals if you were in the following positions.

Possible positions and purposes

大学の学長（大学を知ってもらう）　大学の学長（環境(かんきょう)）

○○のコーチ（チームを強くする）　国の首相(しゅしょう)／大統領(だいとうりょう)（国を平和(へいわ)にする）

Ex. A: もし○○さんが大学の学長だったら、大学を知ってもらうために、誰(だれ)に何をさせたいですか。

B: 私が学長だったら、学生にSNSで大学のプロモーション活動(かつどう)をさせます。

A: それは役(やく)に立ちそうですね。私が学長だったら… <Continue>

できるIII-C Vまで and Vまでに

1 How busy are you tomorrow?

Step 1 Describe Ai's schedule using まで／までに based on the cues provided. L17-25

Ex.1 アイさんは7時まで寝(ね)ます。

Ex.2 アイさんは9時50分までに学校に行きます。

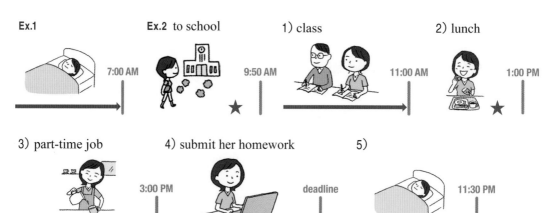

Step 2 Using Step 1 as a model, describe your schedule for tomorrow to your partner.

Ex. 私は明日の朝、クラスがないので、10時まで寝(ね)ます。それから、授業(じゅぎょう)は1時から始まるので、12時50分までに学校に行きます。3時まで授業(じゅぎょう)があります。

2 What are your wishes for your life? Ask the following questions to your partner and expand the conversation by asking follow-up questions.

Ex. A: ○○さんは、死(し)ぬまで続けたいことがありますか。

B: はい、死(し)ぬまでヨガを続けたいと思います。体にいいし、楽しいからです。

A: そうですか。ヨガはいつ始めましたか。 <Continue>

1) 死(し)ぬまで続けたいこと　2) 死(し)ぬまでにしてみたいこと　3) 死(し)ぬまでに行ってみたい所

Group Work

3 By failing to prepare, you are preparing to fail. Time to start thinking about your life plan!

Step 1 List what you would like to achieve in life and when you want to achieve it by. Also, list what preparations you will have to make to achieve your goals. Be ambitious and creative!

Possible goals ○○に行く／留学(りゅうがく)する　○○と会う　○○になる (Exs. 社長, 首相(しゅしょう), 大統領(だいとうりょう))

いつ／何才(なんさい)まで or までに？	目標(もくひょう) (goal) は？	準備(じゅんび)は？
Ex. 四年生になるまでに	日本に留学(りゅうがく)する	いい留学(りゅうがく)プログラムを探(さが)す

Step 2 Choose a few of your life goals and share your life plan in a group. Your classmates will make comments and ask follow-up questions.

Ex. A: 私の人生の計画について話します。まず、四年生になるまでに日本に留学(りゅうがく)しようと思っています。そのために、今からいい留学(りゅうがく)プログラムを探(さが)しておくつもりです。次に30才(さい)になるまでに… <Continue>

B: そうですか。いいプログラムが見つかるといいですね。(← Comment)

C: 日本のどこに留学(りゅうがく)しようと思っていますか。(← Follow-up question)

Review

Now you can talk in detail about your goals for the future. Suppose you are planning to launch a crowdfunding compaign.

Step 1 Brainstorm your crowdfunding plan.

1) クラウドファンディングの目的(もくてき)は何ですか。

2) いつまでに、いくら集めたいですか。

3) お金を集めるために、どんなことをしますか。

Step 2 Suppose your partner is a possible sponsor. Present your crowdfunding plan to your partner.

What your crowdfunding is for

Details about your product/service

Details about funding:
- how much/by when
- actions for achieving your goal

=============

Sponsor's opinion & decision

Ex. A: どんなクラウドファンディングがしたいですか。

B: 日本語が練習できるゲームを作るためにお金を集めたいです。

A: そうですか。どんなゲームを作ろうと思っていますか。

B: 漢字のリズムゲームを作るつもりです。これを使うと、楽しく漢字が勉強できます。

A: おもしろそうですね。いつまでにいくらぐらい集めたいですか。

B: 来年の夏(なつ)までに 1,000 ドルぐらい集めたいです。

A: 1,000 ドル集めるために何をしますか。

B: そのゲームがどうして役(やく)に立つか SNS で説明(せつめい)するつもりです。

A: なるほど。 <Continue>

A: とてもいい計画だと思います。ぜひ私に 100 ドル出させてください。

読みましょう

Getting information from a website: Travel guide

1 日本は「おもてなしの国」と言われています。色々な場所で外国にはないユニークなサービスが経験できるので、外国から来る観光客は感動するようです。

1）下のランキングはある調査 (survey) の「外国人が日本でやりたいこと」です。ランキングを見て、(1)～(4)の質問について話し合ってみましょう。

外国人が日本でやりたいこと

1 ?
2 にぎやかなエリアを歩いて、ショッピングを楽しむ
3 旅館に泊まって温泉に入る
4 季節や自然を楽しむ
5 日本の歴史や文化を知る

(1) ランキングの1番は何だと思いますか。
(2) 4番と5番はどんなことをすると思いますか。
(3) もし日本に行ったら、このランキングの中で何がしてみたいですか。どうしてそれをしてみたいですか。
(4) 他に日本でどんなことがしてみたいですか。

2）温泉旅館では色々なおもてなしが経験できます。下の写真はそのおもてなしの紹介です。

 IYO / PIXTA a. 旅館の前で温かくあいさつしてくれる	 b. 旅館に着くと、初めにお茶やお菓子を出してくれる	 写真：イメージマート c. 好きな浴衣を選んで着ることができる
 d. 外にある大きくてきれいなおふろにゆっくり入れる	 写真：AID / アフロ e. 泊まる部屋でおいしい日本料理が食べられる	 f. 寝る前に、布団を準備してくれる

(1) 温泉旅館に行ったことがある人 → どのおもてなしを経験したことがありますか。
温泉旅館に行ったことがない人 → どのおもてなしを経験してみたいですか。
(2) a.～f. の中で、あなたの出身や今住んでいる国にないおもてなしはどれですか。
(3) あなたの国では、観光客のためにどんなおもてなしがありますか。

Possible topics ホテル　空港　駅　レストラン　店

2 ショートストーリーを読んでみましょう。読んだ後で質問に答えてください。

鈴木(すずき)教授の幸せな生活

鈴木(すずき)教授は大学でAIの研究をしています。毎日とても忙(いそが)しくて家事をする時間がないので、色々な世話をしてくれるAIロボットを[Ex.]作りました。ロボットが何でもしてくれるから、朝起きてから大学に着くまで(a)何もしなくてもいいです。朝7時半になると、ロボットが(b)起こしてくれます。それから、(c)顔を洗って、(d)ご飯を食べさせてくれます。(e)服を着がえさせて、くつ下もくつもはかせてくれます。その後、車で大学に送っていって、(f)仕事が終わると(g)迎(むか)えに来てくれます。自分でそうじやせんたくをしなくてもいいし、(h)手と足のつめも切ってくれるし、大学まで歩かなくてもいいし、教授の生活はバラ色になりました。

教授は魚も野菜(やさい)もきらいなので、ロボットに肉の料理だけ作らせます。大学でも食堂(しょくどう)のランチは食べないで、ロボットが作ったお弁当(べんとう)を食べるから、(i)毎日肉しか食べません。水は全然(ぜんぜん)飲まないで、仕事中にコーヒーを10ぱいも飲みます。(j)大学から帰ってくるまでにロボットがそうじをしておいてくれるから、家の中はいつもきれいです。部屋の温度(おんど)もチェックしてくれるから、暑(あつ)くないし寒(さむ)くないし、鈴木(すずき)教授は毎日とても幸せな生活を送っていました。

ある朝、ロボットは教授を大学に送ってきて研究室のいすに座(すわ)らせた後、いつものように家に帰っていきました。研究室にいた学生が「鈴木(すずき)先生、おはようございます」とあいさつをしました。でも、教授は何も言いません。学生が机(つくえ)の上にコーヒーを置(お)きましたが、教授は全然(ぜんぜん)コーヒーを飲みません。「先生、どうしたんですか」学生がそう言いながら、教授に近づいて(k)肩(かた)に手を置(お)くと、体が氷(こおり)のように冷(つめ)たいです。「大変だ。誰(だれ)か、病院(びょういん)に知らせてください！」すぐにお医者さんが来てくれました。お医者さんによると、教授は前の晩、眠(ねむ)っている間に亡(な)くなったそうです。

夕方になると、ロボットが教授を迎(むか)えに来ました。学生が「先生は亡(な)くなりましたよ」と伝(つた)えたら、ロボットは突然(とつぜん)動かなくなってしまいました。「ロボットも先生と一緒(いっしょ)に天国に行けるといいんだけど…」と学生は思いました。

A commission based on the plot of Shinichi Hoshi's *A Well-Kept Life* (『ゆきとどいた生活』)

In this story, the expressions describing Prof. Suzuki are written in the first person, instead of the third person, to narrate the story from his viewpoint.

☞ GID (vol.2): E. Special topics 6-5. Protagonist's viewpoint in fiction

Identifying omitted words

1） Who did what in the story, and to whom? Insert the appropriate character from P, R, and S into each (　　).

P＝鈴木(すずき)教授　**R**＝ロボット　**S**＝学生

Ex. （ **P** ）は AI ロボットを作りました　　(a)（　　）は何もしなくてもいい

(b) ロボットが（　　）を起こしてくれます　　(c)（　　）が（　　）の顔を洗って

(d)（　　）にご飯を食べさせてくれます　　(e)（　　）が（　　）に服を着がえさせて

(f)（　　）が仕事が終わる　　(g)（　　）が（　　）を迎(むか)えに来てくれます

(h)（　　）が（　　）の手と足のつめも切ってくれる

(i)（　　）は毎日肉しか食べません　　(j)（　　）が大学から帰ってくる

(k)（　　）が（　　）の肩(かた)に手を置(お)く

Sorting information

2） このロボットができることに○、できないことに×を入れてください。

（　　）色々な家事をする　（　　）体のためにいい食べ物かどうか分かる

（　　）お弁当(べんとう)を作る　（　　）何かを運ぶ　（　　）車を運転する

（　　）部屋の温度(おんど)をコントロールする　（　　）悲(かな)しくて泣く

Understanding metaphors

3） 次の表現(ひょうげん)はメタファーです。どんな意味か、あなたが知っている言葉(ことば)にも同じような言い方があるか話し合ってください。自分の国の言葉(ことば)で話してもいいです。

l.9 バラ色になる（なりました）　l.20 氷(こおり)のように冷(つめ)たい　l.25 天国に行ける

Comprehension check

4） 正しい文(ぶん) (sentence) には○、正しくない文(ぶん)には×を入れてください。

（　　） 鈴木(すずき)教授は、自分でできることはロボットにさせないで、全部(ぜんぶ)自分でした。

（　　） 大学の食堂(しょくどう)のランチには魚や野菜(やさい)が入っているようだ。

（　　） 鈴木(すずき)教授はロボットと生活して、とても幸せだったようだ。

（　　） ロボットは、鈴木(すずき)教授が眠(ねむ)っている間に亡(な)くなったことを知っていた。

5） このストーリーを書いた人は何が言いたいと思いますか。

書く練習　Writing Practice

自分が作ってみたいと思う AI ロボットの絵を描(か)いて、そのロボットに誰(だれ)のためにどんなことをさせたいか、どうしてそれをさせたいか説明(せつめい)してください。

Lesson 17

聞きましょう

リスニング・ストラテジー：Listening strategy

Shadowing (3)

This is the last section of this textbook's series of shadowing exercises. In this lesson, practice your shadowing without reading the script. Try to pay attention to the meaning of the passage in addition to focusing on the speaker's emotion, volume, pitch, and rate of speech.

1 **Pre-listening activity:** Start practicing shadowing with three short sentences.  L17-26

Step 1 Listen to the audio and try to figure out what each sentence is about and what emotion the speaker is expressing. You can repeat as many times as you want.

Step 2 Practice shadowing. Listen to the audio and try to echo it back with as little lag as possible. You may repeat this step until you feel confident.

L17-27

2 **Listening:** Now, practice shadowing with a longer text. This time, pay extra attention to the meaning of the passage.

1） Follow Steps 1-2 above and practice shadowing.

2） Comprehension check: Mark ○ if the statement is true and × if it is false. Did you pay attention to the overall passage content to figure out the answers?

a. (　　　)　この人は自分の両親(りょうしん)をいい両親(りょうしん)だと思っているようだ。

b. (　　　)　この人は子どもの時、スポーツをするのがきらいだったようだ。

c. (　　　)　この人は将来(しょうらい)親になったら、自分の子どもにしたいことをさせるつもりだ。

3） Record yourself shadowing and evaluate your recording for proficiency in the following categories. (Mark ○ for "good," △ for "so-so," and × for "not good.")

a. Pacing/Fluency		b. Accuracy (grammar, pronunciation)		c. Emotion	

How did it go? If you feel confident, challenge yourself using longer or more difficult sentences on the Conversation pages, etc. If you don't feel confident, practice shadowing using phrases you can find in the Activities pages.

Exit Check

Now it's time to go back to the DEKIRU List for this chapter (p.237) and do the exit check to see what new things you can do now that you've completed the lesson.

Unit5 チャレンジ

1 Reading for fun

Step 1 One way to improve your reading skills is 多読 (extensive reading). 多読 does not simply mean to read a lot of books; rather, it is a reading method with the following rules:

・簡単な本から読みましょう。
・辞書を使わないで読みましょう。
・分からないところはとばしましょう (to skip)。
・本が {つまらなかったら／難しかったら}、他の本を読みましょう。

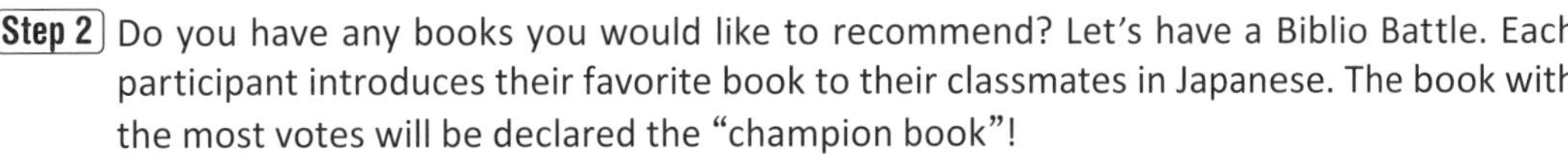

Step 2 Do you have any books you would like to recommend? Let's have a Biblio Battle. Each participant introduces their favorite book to their classmates in Japanese. The book with the most votes will be declared the "champion book"!

Lesson 17

You can find some useful links on the *TOBIRA* website for both 多読 and Biblio Battle.

2 Top 3 spots for ◯◯ lovers

You have learned about various aspects of Japanese culture through *TOBIRA*. What aspect are you interested in the most? Choose one topic (e.g., ramen, museums), search the best three spots for it in Japan, and share them with your classmates.

Ex. 私は「日本の博物館 (museum) トップスリー」を選びました。まず、「カップヌードルミュージアム 横浜」を紹介します。この場所は、インスタントラーメンの秘密 (secrets) について教えてくれるし、自分だけのカップヌードルが作れるし、とても楽しそうだと思います。次に… <Continue>

提供：カップヌードルミュージアム 横浜

3 Japanese slang

Do you know what kind of expressions are used among young people in Japan? Ask your Japanese friends or search online for current popular Japanese slang, then share the words you found interesting with your classmates.

Ex. みなさんは「やばい」という言葉を聞いたことがありますか。「やばい」は本当は「危ない」という意味でしたが、今は「とてもいい」という意味でも使われます。例えば、「このラーメンやばい！」「この映画やばい！」と言います。

文化ノート Culture Note

カタカナ語はおもしろい！

みなさんは今まで色々なカタカナ語を勉強しましたが、カタカナ語は難しいと思いますか。カタカナ語はテクノロジー、ファッション、音楽、スポーツの分野 (field) でたくさん使われているので、上手に使えると、とても便利です。ここでは毎日の生活でよく使われていて、ちょっとおもしろいカタカナ語を見てみましょう。

1) 最近は「チェックする」(L11) のように、「カタカナ語＋する」が多く使われます。下の言葉の意味が分かりますか。

a. シェアする　b. レンタルする　c. カットする　d. スタートする　e. ストップする

2) コンピュータやスマホを使う時、色々なカタカナ語を使います。下の言葉は何をする時に使うと思いますか。他にどんな言葉があると思いますか。

a. ログインする　b. アクセスする　c. アップする　d. クリックする　e. ダウンロードする

3)『とびらⅠ&Ⅱ』で「コンビニ」「プレゼン」「スマホ」のように、長いカタカナ語を短くした言葉を学びました。次の言葉の意味が分かりますか。

a. コピペ　b. コスパ　c. ポテチ　d. アポ　e. コラボ

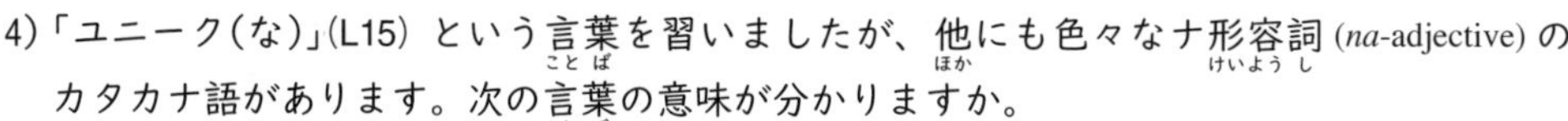

4)「ユニーク(な)」(L15) という言葉を習いましたが、他にも色々なナ形容詞 (*na*-adjective) のカタカナ語があります。次の言葉の意味が分かりますか。

a. グローバル(な)　b. カジュアル(な)　c. シャイ(な)　d. ネガティブ(な)　e. シンプル(な)

5)「サボる」(L11) という動詞 (verb) を習いましたが、「カタカナ語＋る」の言い方はたくさんあって、カジュアルに話す時に使います。下の言葉はどんな意味か分かりますか。

a. メモる　b. ミスる　c. ググる　d. ダブる　e. ハモる

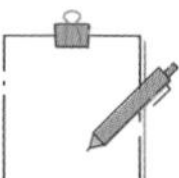

質問　今までにどんなカタカナ語を見たり聞いたりしましたか。それは上の 1)～5) のどのタイプのカタカナ語だと思いますか。

どうですか。カタカナ語はおもしろくて便利だと思いませんか。でも、何でもカタカナ語にするのはやめた方がいいです。例えば、仕事の面接の時に、カタカナ語を使いすぎるのはよくないです。カタカナ語は便利だけれど、気をつけて使いましょう。

Unit 6

世界とつながる

Connecting with the world

06

Pre-activity

Unit6の前に

The theme of this unit is “Connecting with the world.” Just as many Japanese people play an active role in the world outside Japan (Unit 4, p.12), countless people from all over the world have come to Japan and become cultural liaisons between Japan and their countries. They are making an impact on the world in their own unique ways based on their experiences with Japanese culture.

1 日本で活躍している (to play an active role) 外国人を誰か知っていますか。その人の名前、仕事、{やっている／やった} ことについて、クラスメートと話してみましょう。

2 下の写真は日本で活躍して、日本と世界をつなげた人達です。知っている人がいますか。

① 

② 

③ 

提供：公益財団法人 日本棋院

④ 

3 上の写真の人達の紹介文を読んでみましょう。

1） まず、紹介文の中の仕事と出身に線を引いて (to draw a line) ください。
2） 次に、A～Dは①～④のどの人の紹介文か考えてください。
3） それから、興味がある人を一人選んで、紹介文をよく読んでください。
4） 最後に、3）で分かったことと、どうしてその人に興味があるかを話してください。

紹介文

A ダイアン吉日 (Diane Kichijitsu)

落語家、バルーンアーティスト
出身：イギリス・リバプール
・バイリンガルの落語家。英語でも日本語でも落語ができる。
・モットーは「笑いを通じて (through laughter) 世界を一つに」。
・日本の中学の英語の教科書でも紹介された。

B 趙治勲 (Cho Chi Hun)

囲碁のプロ棋士 (professional *Go* player)
出身：韓国・釜山
・プロ棋士になるため、6才の時に日本に来て、11才9か月でプロ棋士になった。
・世界で初めてグランドスラム（7つのタイトル）を取って、1500回も勝った (to win)。

 マーティ・フリードマン (Marty Friedman)

ギタリスト、音楽家、作曲家 (composer)
出身：アメリカ・メリーランド
・音楽のジャンルはハードロックとヘヴィメタル。
・2004年から日本で活動を始めた。色々な日本の歌手とコラボをしたり、日本の音楽をヘヴィメタにアレンジして世界に紹介したりしている。

 オーサ・イェークストロム (Åsa Ekström)

まんが家
出身：スウェーデン・ストックホルム
・子どもの時、『セーラームーン』を見て、日本のアニメやまんがはおもしろいと思った。
・スウェーデンでまんがを描いていたが、日本でまんが家になるために東京に来た。
・2015年に日本語でまんがを描いてデビューした。

Lesson 18

好きなことをしなさい。

Do what you like.

DEKIRU List

できるCheck ☑

できる I **Talk about times when you were forced to do something you did not like.**
させられて嫌だった経験について話すことができる。
Entry ☐ Exit ☐

できる II **Talk about unexpected occurrences and express your feelings about them.**
予期していなかった結果や、それに対する気持ちを伝えることができる。
Entry ☐ Exit ☐

できる III **Encourage people close to you and show empathy towards them.**
身近な人を励ましたり、気遣ったりできる。
Entry ☐ Exit ☐

できる IV **Reading comprehension: Understand essays about personal experiences by connecting them with your own experiences.**
読解：自分の経験と結び付けて、体験談を理解することができる。
Entry ☐ Exit ☐

STRATEGIES

Conversation Tips .... • Inverted sentences in casual speech

Listening .... • Integration (1): Predicting and listening for keywords

GRAMMAR

1. V-*masu* なさい [Mild commands] できる I
2. Causative-passive forms of verbs and causative-passive sentences できる I
3. まだ "still" and もう "no longer" できる II
4. ～のに "in spite of the fact that ~; even though ~" できる II
5. ～はずだ [Expectation/anticipation] できる III
6. ～ば "if" できる III

会話

Ai, now on a flight back to the US, is talking to the elderly Japanese woman (おばあさん) seated next to her. L18-1

おばあさん：アメリカの学生さん？

アイ　　　：はい、そうです。夏(なつ)の間、京都(きょうと)に留学(りゅうがく)していました。

おばあさん：そうですか。今の若い人は好きなことができていいですね。

私も若い時、留学(りゅうがく)したかったけど、親に「やめなさい」って言われて、あきらめさせられたんですよ。

アイ　　　：へえ、そうなんですか。私の両親(りょうしん)はいつも「好きなことをしなさい」って言ってくれます。

おばあさん：そうですか。いいご両親(りょうしん)ですね。ところで、落語(らくご)を知っていますか。

アイ　　　：落語(らくご)ですか…　あ、はい、授業で少し勉強したことがあります。

おばあさん：ああ、そう。実(じつ)は今度、ここで落語(らくご)のイベントをするんですよ。

<The woman hands Ai a flyer.>

アイ　　　：おもしろそうなイベントですね。あ、ここ、私の大学の近くです！

あの、よかったら、私に何か手伝(てつだ)わせていただけませんか。

おばあさん：そうですか。じゃ、今度ボランティアの面接(めんせつ)があるから、申(もう)し込(こ)んでみてください。

アイ　　　：はい、ぜひそうします。

The Japan House members are waiting for Ai to come back. L18-2

タオ　　：もう7時なのに、アイちゃん、まだ帰ってこないね。

圭太(けいた)　　：え、まだ空港(くうこう)にいるの？

タオ　　：うーん、もう空港(くうこう)にはいないと思うけど…　ちょっと心配。

リーマン：今チェックしたら、アイさんの飛行機(ひこうき)は4時ごろ空港(くうこう)に着いたみたいですよ。

圭太(けいた)　　：えっ、4時？

マーク　：だいじょうぶだよ。もう子どもじゃないし…

アイ　：ただいま！

みんな　：あ、アイちゃん、おかえり！

アイ　：みんな、久(ひさ)しぶり！　ごめんね、遅くなって…

にゃんた：ニャー!!!

In the meantime, Ai's host mother and host brother, Akira, are talking at home in Kyoto. L18-3

そう言えば: speaking of which

あきら　：あれ？　お父さんは？

母　：仕事があるって言ってたから、まだ店にいるはずだよ。

あきら、ご飯の時間だから、手伝(てつだ)いなさい。

あきら　：ええ!?　どうしていつも僕(ぼく)だけ手伝(てつだ)わされるの？

お姉ちゃんがいれば、やってくれるのに…

母　：お姉ちゃんはまだ会社で残業(ざんぎょう)してるから、

文句(もんく)を言わないで、早くしなさい。

あきら　：はーい。あ、アイちゃんはもういないのに、

アイちゃんの箸(はし)、出しちゃった。

母　：そう言えば、アイちゃん、もうアメリカに着いたはずだね。

あきら　：うん。アイちゃんがいないと、さびしいね。

CONVERSATION TIPS

Inverted sentences in casual speech: When speaking informally, the order of sentences and phrases is often inverted. In particular, conjunctive phrases that end with て, し, から, のに, and けど frequently appear at the end in casual speech. Note that you should not use this type of inversion when speaking and writing formally.

1）A：あのう、今日の晩ご飯、一緒(いっしょ)に行けないんだ。忙(いそが)しくて…

B：え、行けないの？　レストラン、予約(よやく)したのに…

A：うん、ごめん。ちょっと時間ないんだ。明日、試験があるし…

2）A：僕(ぼく)のスマホ、知らない？　ここに置(お)いたんだけど…

B：え、スマホ？　知らないよ。

Vocabulary with Pictures

単語（たんご）

▶ **The words written in gray** are supplemental vocabulary.

生活　Daily life

[*person* と] なかよくする
(to get along; to act friendly)

[*person* と] なかよくなる
(to become good friends)

[*thing* を] がまんする
(to be patient; to put up with)

[*clothes* に] アイロンをかける
(to iron)

アイロン
(iron) [appliance]

[*thing* に] あながあく
(a hole opens up)

Ex. あながあいているふく
(clothes with holes)

あな
(hole)

[*home, etc.* を] るすにする
(to be away)

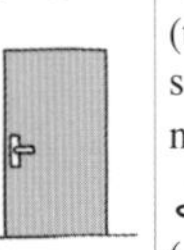

るす
(absence; being away (from home, etc.))

ようじがある
(to have an errand/ something that needs to be done)

ようじ
(errand; something that needs to be done)

つごうがわるい ↔ つごうがいい
(to be inconvenient) [date, time, etc.] / (to be convenient) [date, time, etc.]

ゆきがつもる
(snow accumulates)

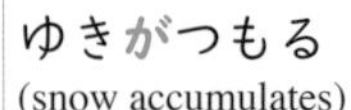

[*road, etc.* を] わたる
(to cross)

しんごう

こうさてん
(intersection)

きけん(な) ↔ あんぜん(な)
(dangerous)

だいじ(な)
(precious; important)

ふべん(な) ↔ べんり(な)
(inconvenient)

からて
(karate) [martial art]

はいしゃ
(dentist)

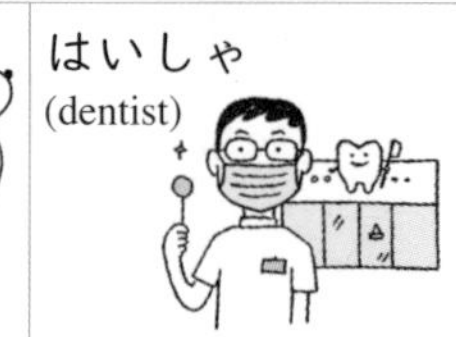

学校・仕事　School and work

[*place* に] かよう
(to commute; to attend)

[*event/activity* に] まにあう
(to make it in time; to be in time)

[*rule/timeline* を] まもる
(to stick to)

じかんをまもる
(to be on time; to be punctual)

しめきりをまもる
(to meet a deadline)

[*thing/person* を] まもる
(to protect)

ちきゅうをまもる
(to protect the Earth)

ちきゅう
(the Earth)

Noun にやさしい
(nice to Noun)

Ex. ちきゅうにやさしい
(environmentally (lit. earth) friendly)

せんぱい

こうはい
(junior member of a group)

ざんぎょうする
(to work overtime)

[*thing* に／を] しっぱいする
(to fail; to be unsuccessful)

[*person/thing* に] もんくをいう
(to complain)

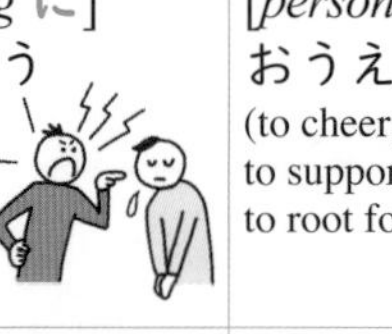

もんく
(complaint)

[*person/team/thing, etc.* を] おうえんする
(to cheer; to support; to root for)

[*thing* の] にんきがでる
(to become popular)

[*place* が] すく
(to get less crowded)

[*place* が] すいている
(to be not crowded)

あんしんする ↔ ふあん(な)
(to feel relieved/ at ease) / (uneasy)

なやみ
(worry; problem)

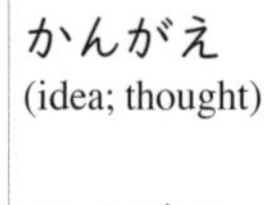

なやみがある
(to have worries)

かんがえ
(idea; thought)

アイデア
(idea; thought)

けいざい
(economy)

はじめ ↔ おわり
(beginning; start) / (end)

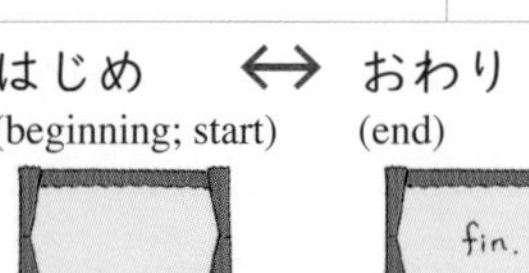

しょうテスト
(quiz) [academic]

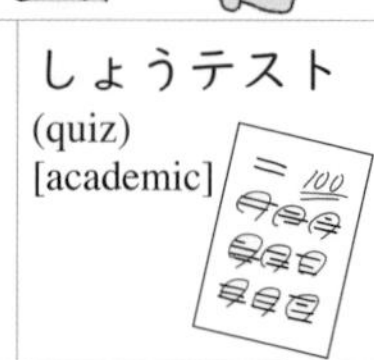

読み物に出てくる言葉 Vocabulary for the Reading section

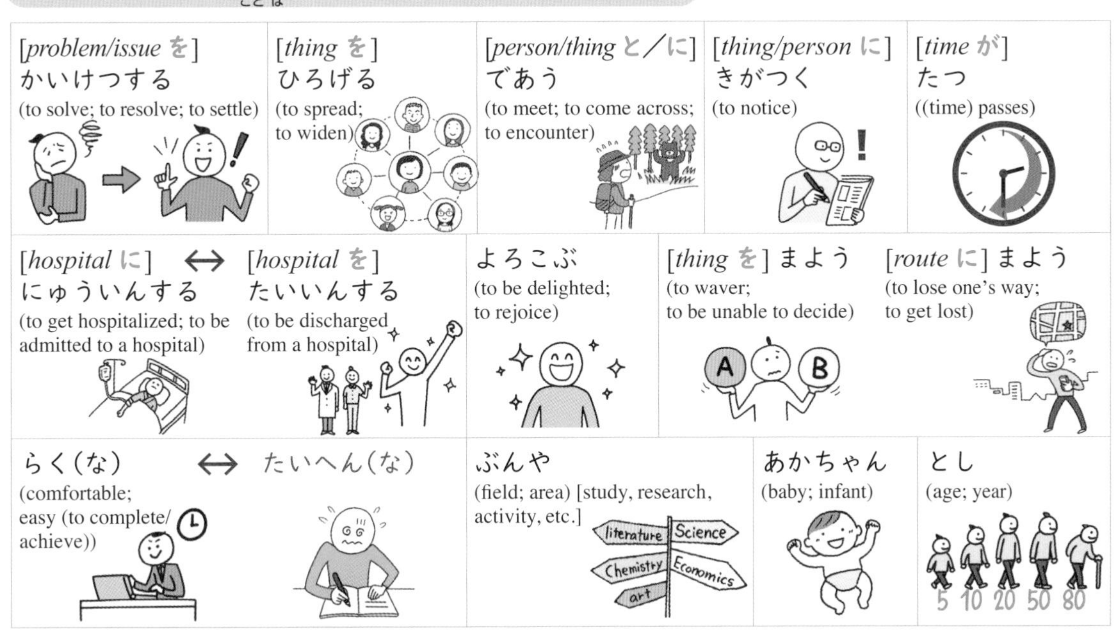

[problem/issue を] かいけつする (to solve; to resolve; to settle)
[thing を] ひろげる (to spread; to widen)
[person/thing と／に] であう (to meet; to come across; to encounter)
[thing/person に] きがつく (to notice)
[time が] たつ ((time) passes)
[hospital に] にゅういんする (to get hospitalized; to be admitted to a hospital) ↔ [hospital を] たいいんする (to be discharged from a hospital)
よろこぶ (to be delighted; to rejoice)
[thing を] まよう (to waver; to be unable to decide)
A
B
[route に] まよう (to lose one's way; to get lost)
らく(な) (comfortable; easy (to complete/achieve)) ↔ たいへん(な)
ぶんや (field; area) [study, research, activity, etc.]
literature
Science
Chemistry
Economics
art
あかちゃん (baby; infant)
とし (age; year)
5 10 20 50 80

指示文でよく使われる表現 Expressions commonly used in instructions

こえにだす (to say aloud)

せんをひく (to draw a line)
せん (line) 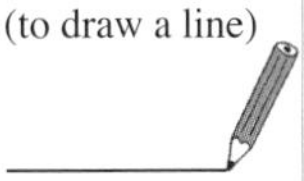

やじるし (arrow)

まる (true; correct) ○
ばつ (X-mark; false; incorrect) ×

さんかく (triangle) △
しかく □

ひょう (chart; table)

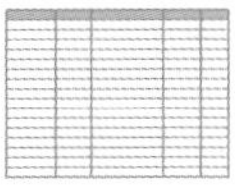

ず (figure)

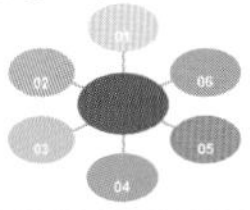

じゅんばん (order; sequence) 1 → 2 → 3 → 4 → 5

ぶぶん (part; section)

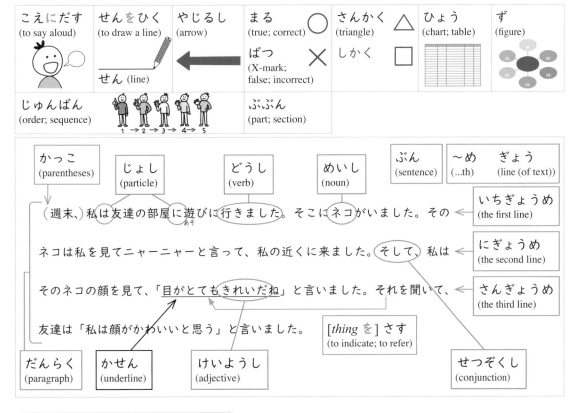

かっこ (parentheses)
じょし (particle)
どうし (verb)
めいし (noun)
ぶん (sentence)
～め (...th)
ぎょう (line (of text))

（週末、）私は友達の部屋に遊びに行きました。そこにネコがいました。その ← いちぎょうめ (the first line)

ネコは私を見てニャーニャーと言って、私の近くに来ました。そして、私は ← にぎょうめ (the second line)

そのネコの顔を見て、「目がとてもきれいだね」と言いました。それを聞いて、 ← さんぎょうめ (the third line)

友達は「私は顔がかわいいと思う」と言いました。

[thing を] さす (to indicate; to refer)

だんらく (paragraph)
かせん (underline)
けいようし (adjective)
せつぞくし (conjunction)

そのほかの表現 Other expressions

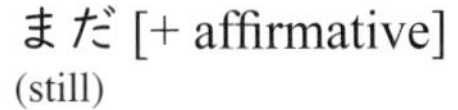

もう [+ negative] (no longer)

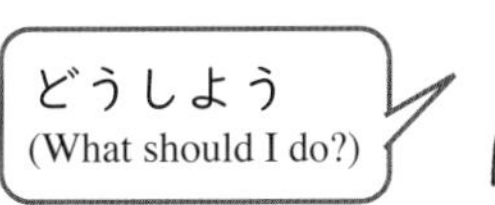

単語(たんご)リスト

L18-5

▶**Highlighted kanji words** contain kanji you have learned previously.
▶✱ See vocabulary index at the end of the book for other meanings.

RU-VERB / RU-VERB PHRASES

1	アイロンをかける		to iron [*clothes* に]
2	にんきがでる	人気が出る	to become popular [*thing* の]
3	ひろげる	広げる	to spread; to widen [*thing* を]

U-VERBS / U-VERB PHRASES

4	あながあく	穴が開く	a hole opens up [*thing* に] Ex. あながあいているふく clothes with holes
5	かよう	通う	to commute; to attend; to frequent [*place* に]
6	きがつく	気がつく	to notice [*thing/person* に]
7	すく		to get less crowded [*place* が]
	すいている		to be not crowded [*place* が]
8	たつ	経つ	(time) passes [*time* が]
9	であう	出会う	to meet; to come across; to encounter [*person/thing* と／に]
10	まにあう	間に合う	to make it in time; to be in time [*event/activity* に]
11	まもる*	守る	to stick to [*rule/timeline* を]; to protect [*thing/person* を]
	じかんをまもる	時間を守る	to be on time; to be punctual
	しめきりをまもる	しめ切りを守る	to meet a deadline
	ちきゅうをまもる	地球を守る	to protect the Earth
12	まよう	迷う	to waver; to be unable to decide [*thing* を]; to lose one's way; to get lost [*route* に]
13	もんくをいう	文句を言う	to complain [*person/thing* に]
14	ゆきがつもる	雪が積もる	snow accumulates
15	ようじがある	用事がある	to have an errand/something that needs to be done
16	よろこぶ	喜ぶ	to be delighted; to rejoice
17	わたる		to cross [*road, etc.* を]

SURU-VERBS / SURU-VERB PHRASES

18	あんしんする	安心する	to feel relieved/at ease
19	おうえんする	応援する	to cheer; to support; to root for [*person/team/thing, etc.* を]
20	かいけつする	解決する	to solve; to resolve; to settle [*problem/issue* を]
21	がまんする		to be patient; to put up with [*thing* を]
22	ざんぎょうする	残業する	to work overtime
23	しっぱいする	失敗する	to fail; to be unsuccessful [*thing* に／を]
24	なかよくする	仲良くする	to get along; to act friendly [*person* と]
25	にゅういんする	入院する	to get hospitalized; to be admitted to a hospital [*hospital* に]
26	たいいんする	退院する	to be discharged from a hospital [*hospital* を]
27	るすにする	留守にする	to be away [*home, etc.* を]

I-ADJECTIVE PHRASE

28	つごうがわるい	都合が悪い	to be inconvenient [date, time, etc.]
	つごうがいい	都合がいい	to be convenient [date, time, etc.]

NA-ADJECTIVES

29	きけん	危険	dangerous

30	だいじ	大事	precious; important
31	ふべん	不便	inconvenient [place, location, etc.]
32	らく	楽	comfortable; easy (to complete/achieve)

NOUNS

33	アイロン		iron [appliance]
34	あかちゃん	赤ちゃん	baby; infant
35	おわり	終わり	end
	はじめ	始め	beginning; start
36	からて	空手	karate [martial art]
37	かんがえ	考え	idea; thought
38	けいざい	経済	economy
39	こうさてん	交差点	intersection
40	こうはい	後輩	junior member of a group
41	しょうテスト	小テスト	quiz [academic]
42	ちきゅう	地球	the Earth
43	とし	年	age; year
44	なやみ	悩み	worry; problem
	なやみがある	悩みがある	to have worries
45	はいしゃ	歯医者	dentist
46	ぶんや	分野	field; area [study, research, activity, etc.]
47	るす	留守	absence; being away (from home, etc.)

ADVERBS

48	まだ [+ affirmative]*		still
49	もう [+ negative]*		no longer

OTHER WORDS AND PHRASES

50	どうしよう		What should I do?
51	Noun にやさしい		nice to Noun; easy on Noun Ex. ちきゅうにやさしい environmentally (lit. earth) friendly

Lesson 18

指示文(しじぶん)でよく使われる表現(ひょうげん) Expressions commonly used in instructions

U-VERB / U-VERB PHRASES

1	こえにだす	声に出す	to say aloud
2	さす	指す	to indicate; to refer [*thing* を]
3	せんをひく	線を引く	to draw a line

NOUNS

4	ぎょう	行	line (of text)
5	だんらく	段落	paragraph
6	ぶん	文	sentence
7	けいようし	形容詞	adjective
8	じょし	助詞	particle
9	せつぞくし	接続詞	conjunction
10	どうし	動詞	verb
11	めいし	名詞	noun
12	さんかく	三角	triangle
13	ばつ		X-mark; false; incorrect
14	まる*	丸	true; correct
15	ず	図	figure [explanatory diagram]
16	ひょう	表	chart; table
17	せん	線	line
18	かせん	下線	underline
19	やじるし	矢印	arrow
20	かっこ		parentheses
21	じゅんばん	順番	order; sequence
22	ぶぶん	部分	part; section

SUFFIX

23	～め	～目	...th Ex.1 １ぎょう目 the first line Ex.2 １だんらく目 the first paragraph Ex.3 一つ目 the first (one)

漢　字

▶ ＊Special reading

273	院	institution	イン	大学院(だいがくいん) graduate school　大学院生(だいがくいんせい) graduate student　病院(びょういん) hospital 入院する(にゅういん) to get hospitalized　退院する(たいいん) to be discharged from a hospital 美容院(びよういん) hair salon
274	通	to pass; to commute	ツウ	交通(こうつう) traffic; transportation　通学する(つうがく) to commute to school 通勤する(つうきん) to commute to work　通訳(つうやく) interpretation; interpreter [oral translation] 普通(ふつう) usually; normally
			かよ(う) とお(る)	通う(かよ) to commute; to attend; to frequent　通る(とお) to pass
275	考	to consider	コウ	参考(さんこう) reference
			かんが(え) かんが(える)	考え(かんが) idea; thought 考える(かんが) to think; to consider　考え方(かんが　かた) a way of thinking
276	答	to answer	トウ	解答する(かいとう) to give an answer　返答する(へんとう) to give a response
			こた(え) こた(える) こたえ	答え(こた)／答(こたえ) answer 答える(こた) to answer
277	残	to leave	ザン	残業する(ざんぎょう) to work overtime　残念(な)(ざんねん) unfortunate; regrettable; disappointing
			のこ(す) のこ(る)	残す(のこ) to leave (something behind) 残る(のこ) to be left; to remain
278	留	to keep; to stay	リュウ ル	留学する(りゅうがく) to study abroad　留学生(りゅうがくせい) international student 留守(るす) absence; being away (from home, etc.)　留守にする(るす) to be away (from home, etc.) 留守番(るすばん) house-sitting　留守番電話(るすばんでんわ) answering machine; voicemail
			と(める)	留める(と) to fasten
279	重	heavy; to pile up	ジュウ チョウ	重要(な)(じゅうよう) important; significant　体重(たいじゅう) body weight 貴重品(きちょうひん) valuables
			おも(い) かさ(ねる)	重い(おも) heavy [weight]　重ねる(かさ) to pile up; to layer

280 便 便 便

convenience

ベン ビン	便利(な)(べんり) convenient; useful　不便(な)(ふべん) inconvenient [place, location, etc.] 便(びん) flight [airplane]　郵便(ゆうびん) mail　郵便局(ゆうびんきょく) post office

281 利 利 利

profit

リ	便利(な)(べんり) convenient; useful　権利(けんり) right; privilege　利益(りえき) profit 利用する(りよう) to utilize; to take advantage
き(く)	左利き(ひだりき) left-handed　右利き(みぎき) right-handed

282 不 不 不

non-; un-; in- [negative prefix]

フ	不便(な)(ふべん) inconvenient [place, location, etc.]　不安(な)(ふあん) uneasy 不可能(な)(ふかのう) impossible　不幸(な)(ふこう) unhappy 不公平(な)(ふこうへい) unfair　不思議(な)(ふしぎ) mysterious

283 弱 弱 弱

weak

ジャク	弱者(じゃくしゃ) the weak; the vulnerable　弱点(じゃくてん) weak point
よわ(い)	弱い(よわ) weak　弱く(よわ) weakly [adverbial form of 弱い(よわ)]

284 用 用 用

to use

ヨウ	用事がある(ようじ) to have an errand　活用する(かつよう) to make good use; to conjugate (a word) 使用する(しよう) to make use　使用中(しようちゅう) in use　生活用品(せいかつようひん) daily necessities 用意する(ようい) to prepare　利用する(りよう) to utilize; to take advantage

285 地 地 地

ground; land; earth; place

チ ジ	地下(ちか) basement; underground　地球(ちきゅう) the Earth　地図(ちず) map 地方(ちほう) region; area　地下鉄(ちかてつ) subway　地理(ちり) geography 地震(じしん) earthquake

286 球 球 球

sphere

キュウ	地球(ちきゅう) the Earth　野球(やきゅう) baseball　気球(ききゅう) hot-air balloon

287 野 野 野

field

ヤ	分野(ぶんや) field; area [study, research, activity, etc.]　野球(やきゅう) baseball　野菜(やさい) vegetable
の	長野(ながの) Nagano [prefecture/city in Japan]　野口さん(のぐち) Noguchi-san [last name] 野原(のはら) field; plain [open grassy area]

Lesson 18

288 空 (空 / 空)	クウ そら から	空港(くうこう) airport　空気(くうき) air; atmosphere 空(そら) sky　青空(あおぞら) blue sky 空手(からて) karate [martial art]　空(から)(の) empty
empty; sky	空空空空空空空空	
289 港 (港 / 港)	コウ みなと	空港(くうこう) airport　香港(ホンコン)* Hong Kong 港(みなと) harbor; port　港町(みなとまち) port city/town
harbor	港港港港港港港港港港港港	
290 両 (両 / 両)	リョウ	ご両親(りょうしん) (someone else's) parents　両親(りょうしん) my parents 両替(りょうがえ)する to exchange (currencies)　両手(りょうて) both hands 両方(りょうほう) both (sides/parties)
both	両両両両両両	
291 他 (他 / 他)	タ ほか	その他(た)／その他(ほか) other; something else; the rest　他人(たにん) other people; unrelated person 他(ほか)に besides　他(ほか)の Noun other/another Noun
other	他他他他他	

新しい読み方

The following are new readings for kanji that you have already learned. Read each word aloud.

1) 安心(あんしん)する　2) 地下(ちか)　3) 地図(ちず)　4) 入院(にゅういん)する　5) 広(ひろ)げる
6) 間(ま)に合(あ)う　7) 楽(らく)(な)　8) 留守(るす)／留守(るす)にする　9) 図(ず)

習った漢字で書ける新しい単語(たんご)

The following are other new vocabulary in this lesson that contain kanji you have already leaned. Read each word aloud.

1) (穴(あな)が)開(あ)く　2) 終(お)わり　3) 気(き)がつく　4) 小(しょう)テスト　5) 大事(だいじ)(な)
6) (都合(つごう)が)悪(わる)い　7) 出会(であ)う　8) 年(とし)　9) 人気(にんき)が出(で)る　10) 始(はじ)め
11) (時間(じかん)／しめ切(き)り／地球(ちきゅう)を)守(まも)る　12) (文句(もんく)を)言(い)う　13) 雪(ゆき)(が積(つ)もる)　14) 行(ぎょう)
15) (声(こえ)に)出(だ)す　16) 文(ぶん)　17) 部分(ぶぶん)　18) ～目(め) (Ex. 一行目(いちぎょうめ))

練習

1 Write the reading for each word 1)-7) in (　　), then match each word with the corresponding definition from a.-h.

Ex. 地球	（ ちきゅう ）	———	a. 今私達が住んでいる惑星(わくせい) (planet)
1) 空港	（　　　　）		b. どこかに出かけて、家に誰(だれ)もいないこと
2) 残業する	（　　　　）		c. しなくてはいけないことがあること
3) 不便な	（　　　　）		d. 飛行機(ひこうき)に乗ったり降(お)りたり (to get off) する所
4) 答える	（　　　　）		e. 毎日学校や仕事に行くこと
5) 通う	（　　　　）		f. 都合(つごう)がよくないことや便利じゃないこと
6) 留守にする	（　　　　）		g. 働く時間の後も会社で仕事をすること
7) 用事がある	（　　　　）		h. 質問に返事をしたり、自分の意見や考えを言ったりすること

2 Three students wrote about their good memories on their social media. Read their stories aloud, then write the readings for the underlined words.

1) 高校三年生の時、両親が日本の長野に留学させてくれました。長野は冬(ふゆ)にたくさん雪が積(つ)もって、きれいでいい所でした。山に登(のぼ)った時、山の中に自動販売機(じどうはんばいき) (vending machine) があってびっくりしましたが、とても便利でした。スマホの地図を見ながら色々な所に出かけて、たくさんの人に出会えました。ずっと忘れられない思い出です。

2) 私は大学で政治(せいじ)や経済(けいざい)について勉強しました。そして、社会の色々な問題をどうしたら解決(かいけつ)できるかよく考えていました。卒業の後も研究を続けたいと思ったから、大学院に入りました。大学院では他の 分野も勉強しています。社会の役(やく)に立つ研究をして、いい論文(ろんぶん)を書いて残したいです。

3) 中学の時、体が弱かったから、スポーツをして、体を強くしようと思いました。空手が好きだったけど、チームでするスポーツがしたかったから、野球部に入りました。毎日重い物を持って走るトレーニングをしました。そして、その後もトレーニングを続けていたら、体が強くなりました。トレーニングは楽じゃなかったけど、チームメートとがんばったことは大事な思い出になりました。

漢字の話 The Story of Kanji

■ Sound elements

A	B

As you learned in Lesson 7, many kanji are formed from two or more elements. In the left-right construction, the left element (A) usually represents the meaning of the kanji, and the right element (B) usually represents its sound (*on-yomi*). For example, the meanings and sound elements of the kanji 時 and 持 are shown below. The two kanji share the sound element 寺 and the *on-yomi* ジ, which is the same as the *on-yomi* of the stand-alone kanji 寺, as in 東大寺(とうだいじ).

	Meaning	Sound		Meaning	Sound
時 *kun-yomi*: とき *on-yomi*: ジ	日	寺(ジ)	持 *kun-yomi*: も(つ) *on-yomi*: ジ	扌	寺(ジ)

More than 70% of Japanese kanji have this characteristic. So, you can often guess the reading of an unknown kanji if you already know the *on-yomi* of its sound element. Whenever you learn a new kanji, try to memorize its sound element's meaning and reading together. This will help you increase the number of kanji you can read and recognize.

練習

1)～3)の漢字の言葉(ことば)には同じ部分(ぶぶん)があって、同じ音(おん)読みがあります。1)～3)の漢字の同じ部分(ぶぶん)に○をして、漢字の音(おん)読みを書いてください。

	音(おん)読み
Ex. (寺) 時 持つ 待つ	ジ
1) 文化　花	
2) 受ける　授業　教授	
3) 九　研究	

文法

1 V-*masu* なさい [Mild commands] "V."

[1]

	V-*masu*	
5時までに家に	帰り	なさい。
Come back home by five o'clock.		

You can tell the listener to do something using V-*masu*なさい. A common situation in which this form is used is when parents tell their children to do something. It is rarely used in conversation between adults.

V-*masu*なさい is also used in written instructions for test questions and exercises, as in (3) below.

Exs. (1) お母さん：ゲームをやめなさい。それから、宿題をしなさい。
Stop playing games and do your homework.

(2) 子どもの時、よく父に「野菜を食べなさい」と言われました。
When I was a child, I was often told, "Eat your vegetables!" by my father.

(3) <試験で> 次の文を読んで質問に答えなさい。
Read the following sentences and answer the questions [about it].

V-*masu*なさい is not used to express negative commands (i.e., "Don't V").

Lesson 18

2 Causative-passive forms of verbs and causative-passive sentences

In the previous two lessons, we learned passive sentences, which are used when someone is affected by another person's action, and causative sentences, which are employed when someone makes another person do something. In this lesson, we will learn causative-passive sentences, which like causative sentences describe situations in which someone makes someone else (X) do something, but unlike causative sentences, the description is from X's point of view. With these sentences, you can express your negative feelings when someone makes you do something you don't want to.

2-1 Causative-passive forms of verbs

You can make causative-passive forms as follows:

Step 1 Make the causative form from a verb. (See L17 #2-1.)

Exs. 食べる → 食べさせる; 読む → 読ませる; する → させる; 来る → 来させる

Step 2 Change the final る of the causative form to られる. (= the rule to make the passive form from a *ru*-verb)

Exs. 食べさせ~~る~~ → 食べさせられる; 読ませ~~る~~ → 読ませられる;
させ~~る~~ → させられる; 来させ~~る~~ → 来させられる

For *u*-verbs, there is also a more casual short form. The short form is made by changing the final /u/ sound of the dictionary form to the /a/ sound and attach される.

Ex. 読む (/yomu/) → 読まされる (/yoma/ + される)

When the dictionary form ends in う (e.g., 言う, 買う), change the /u/ sound to /wa/ and attach される.

Ex. 言う (/iu/) → 言わされる (/iwa/ + される)

Exception: This form is not used for verbs whose dictionary forms end with す (e.g., 話す, 探す, 返す). For these verbs, the longer forms are the only option.

× 話さされる → 話させられる

(More examples of *u*-verb causative-passive forms are shown in the *u*-verb conjugation table on the inside of the back cover.)

2-2 Causative-passive sentences "be made to V"

[2-a] Causative sentence

Topic (causer)	Causee			Vt (causative)
母は	弟	に	ブロッコリーを	食べさせました。
My mother made my little brother eat broccoli.				

[2-b] Causative-passive sentence

Topic (causee)	Causer			Vt (causative-passive)
弟は	母	に	ブロッコリーを	食べさせられました。
My little brother was made to eat broccoli by my mother.				

[2-a] is a causative sentence, and [2-b] is a causative-passive sentence. [2-a] describes the event from the causer's point of view, while [2-b] describes the same event from the viewpoint of the causee (= the person who was made to do something).

Using causative-passive sentences, you can express the idea that someone is forced to do something by someone else and suffers from it. In other words, causative-passive sentences always come with a nuance of duress and adversity. In this sentence structure, the causee, who is negatively affected by the causer's act, commonly occurs as the topic, and the causer is marked by に.

Exs. (1) 私は子どもの時、親に毎週部屋をそうじさせられました。
When I was a child, I was made to clean my room by my parents every week.

(2) 私は昨日、友達に30分も待たされてしまいました。
I was made to wait by my friend yesterday for 30 whole minutes.

(3) 私の歴史のクラスでは毎週本を100ページぐらい読まされたり、レポートを書かされたりします。 *We are made to read about 100 pages of a book and write a report (among other things) in my history class every week.*

3 まだ "still" and もう "no longer"

[3-a]

			V, Adj(*i*), etc. (affirmative)
トムさんは	まだ	ゲームを	しています。
Tom is still playing the game.			

[3-b]

		V, Adj(*i*), etc. (negative)
シャワーを浴(あ)びたので、	もう	ねむくないです。
I took a shower, so I'm no longer sleepy.		

You can express the idea of "still" using まだ with affirmative sentences, and that of "no longer" using もう with negative sentences. In general, まだ is used when the state of X has not changed since some previous point in time, while もう is used when the current state of X has changed. (See L6 #6 for other uses of もう and まだ.)

☞ GID (vol.1): D. Aspect 2.もう and まだ

Exs. (1) 東京(とうきょう)の9月(がつ)はまだ暑(あつ)いです。*It is still hot in Tokyo in September.*

(2) 私(わたし)は二十歳(はたち)だし、一人(ひとり)で住(す)んでいるし、もう子(こ)どもじゃないです。
I'm twenty years old and living on my own—I'm not a child anymore.

(3) A: あのう、まだ寮(りょう)に住(す)んでいますか。*Um, are you still living in the dorm?*

B: いいえ、もう住(す)んでいません。今(いま)はアパートに住(す)んでいます。
No, I'm not living there anymore. I live in an apartment now.

Lesson 18

4 ～のに "in spite of the fact that ~; even though ~" できる II

[4-a]

S₁			S₂
	V-plain		
あまりお金(かね)が	ない	のに	高(たか)い車(くるま)を買(か)いました。
In spite of the fact that I do not have much money, I bought an expensive car.			

[4-b]

S₁				S₂
	Adj(*na*)			
この歌手(かしゅ)は歌(うた)が	上手(じょうず)	な	のに	あまり人気(にんき)がありません。
In spite of the fact that this singer is good at singing, she is not very popular.				

[4-c]

S₁				S₂
	N			
一君(はじめくん)は	まだ5才(さい)	な	のに	漢字(かんじ)がたくさん読(よ)めます。
Hajime can read many kanji in spite of the fact that he is still five years old.				

You can express the idea of "in spite of" using のに. That is, S_1のに is used when something happens (or something is the case) contrary to what would naturally be expected from S_1. Because of this, のに often conveys the speaker's surprise, discontent, disappointment, and such. For example, while the sentence with the conjunction が in (1a) below simply states S_1 and S_2 as contrastive information, (1b) conveys the speaker's surprise, discontent, etc. because のに is used.

Exs. (1) a. あの新(あたら)しいレストランは高(たか)いですが、あまりおいしくないです。
That restaurant is expensive, but it isn't very good.

b. あの新(あたら)しいレストランは高(たか)いのに、あまりおいしくないです。
Even though that restaurant is expensive, it's not very good.

The forms before のに are always plain forms except that だ after *na*-adjectives and nouns changes to な, as seen in [4-b] and [4-c]. This connection rule is the same as that for ～ので and ～んです. (See L17 #1 and L9 #2.)

Exs. (2) 明日(あした)テストがある<u>のに</u>、まだ勉強(べんきょう)していません。
Even though I have a test tomorrow, I haven't studied (for it) yet.

(3) 昨日(きのう)はいい天気(てんき)だった<u>のに</u>、一日中(いちにちじゅう)家(いえ)にいました。
Even though the weather was nice yesterday, I stayed home all day.

(4) 今年(ことし)の夏(なつ)、本当(ほんとう)は二人(ふたり)で花火(はなび)が見(み)たかった<u>のに</u>…
I really wanted the two of us to watch the fireworks together this summer, though…
(lit. In spite of the fact that I wanted the two of us to watch the fireworks together this summer, [we can't].)

As in (4), in some situations, the main clause is left unsaid because it is understood from the context or situation.

Note that S_2 cannot be a sentence that expresses the speaker's volition or desire. The following sentences are ungrammatical:

× お金(かね)がないのに、旅行(りょこう)に{行(い)くつもりです／行(い)きたいです／行(い)こうと思(おも)います}。

Intended meaning: *In spite of the fact that I don't have money, {I'm going to take a trip / I want to take a trip / I think I will take a trip}.*

Neither can S_2 be a command, a request, advice, a suggestion, or an invitation. The following sentences are also ungrammatical:

× お金(かね)がないのに、この本(ほん)を{買(か)いなさい／買(か)ってください／買(か)った方(ほう)がいいです／買(か)ったらどうですか／買(か)いましょう}。

Intended meaning: *In spite of the fact that you don't have money, {buy this book. / please buy this book. / you'd better buy this book. / why don't you buy this book? / let's buy this book.}*

☞ **GID** (vol.2): B. Connecting sentences 2.のに vs. けれど／けど

5 ～はずだ [Expectation/anticipation] "I expect; should; be supposed to; must"

[5-a]

Topic (third person)		V-plain (affirmative)	
研(けん)さんは	今(いま)、大阪(おおさか)に	住(す)んでいる	はずです。
I expect Ken is living in Osaka now.			

[5-b]

Topic (third person)		V-plain (negative)	
田中(たなか)さんは	今晩(こんばん)のパーティーに	来(こ)ない	はずです。
I don't expect Tanaka-san to come to this evening's party.			

You can express your expectation or anticipation using はずだ. This expectation/anticipation cannot be a mere hope or guess; it should be the result of reasoning based on solid information.

The forms before はず are always plain forms except when it is preceded by *na*-adjectives and nouns. Instead, you attach な to *na*-adjectives and の to nouns before はず, as in (1) and (2).

Exs. (1) スミスさんは東京に10年住んでいるから、日本の文化をよく知っているはずです。それから、日本語が上手なはずです。 *Smith-san has lived in Tokyo for 10 years, so he must know Japanese culture well. Also, he must be good at Japanese.*

(2) みかさんの弟さんは去年大学に入ったから、今二年生のはずです。
Mika's younger brother started college last year, so he must be a sophomore now.

(3) 今日、面接を受けた会社から連絡があるはずです。とても緊張しています。
Today, I'm supposed to hear from the company I had an interview with. I'm really nervous.

(4) マーク：あれ？ 圭太は？ *Wait, where's Keita?*
アイ　：今日は水曜日だから、剣道の練習に行ったはずですよ。晩ご飯の時間まで帰らないはずです。 *Today is Wednesday, so he must have gone to* kendo *practice. He's not supposed to be back till dinner time.*

You cannot use はず in the first person for future actions. The following sentence is ungrammatical:

× 私はパーティーに行くはずです。→ 私はパーティーに行こうと思います。
I think I'll go to the party.

6 ～ば "if"

We studied ～ばよかった in Lesson 16 #4-2. In this lesson, we will learn more general ways of using *ba*-conditional forms. First, let us study how to make *ba*-conditional forms out of verbs, *i*-adjectives, and {Adj(*na*)/N}だ.

(a) Verbs: See L16 #4-1 for the *ba*-conditional forms of verbs.

Exs. *Ru*-verbs: 食べる → 食べれば　　*U*-verbs: 話す → 話せば
Irregular verbs: する → すれば; 来る → 来れば

(b) *I*-adjectives: Adj(*i*)-stem + ければ

Exs. 高(い) → 高ければ; おもしろ(い) → おもしろければ

Exception: いい → よければ

The negative ending ～ない conjugates in the same way as *i*-adjectives; thus, the *ba*-conditional form of ～ない is ～なければ.

Exs. 話さない → 話さなければ; 安くない → 安くなければ; 静かじゃない → 静かじゃなければ

(c) {Adj(*na*)/N}だ: {Adj(*na*)/N}なら(ば) (ば is usually omitted.)

Exs. 上手だ → 上手なら; 日曜日だ → 日曜日なら

[6-a]

S₁ (conditional clause)		S₂ (main clause)
	V-cond	
スミスさんの電話番号(でんわばんごう)は田中(たなか)さんに	聞(き)けば	分(わ)かると思(おも)います。
I think you can get Smith-san's phone number from Tanaka-san. (lit. As for Smith-san's phone number, I think you will know [it] if you ask Tanaka-san.)		

[6-b]

S₁ (conditional clause)			S₂ (main clause)
	Adj(*i*)-stem		
家賃(やちん)が	高(たか)	ければ	借(か)りません。
If the rent is expensive, I won't rent it.			

[6-c]

S₁ (conditional clause)			S₂ (main clause)
	Adj(*na*)/N		
場所(ばしょ)が	便利(べんり)／便利(べんり)な所(ところ)	なら	借(か)りたいです。
If it is in a convenient location (lit. If the location is convenient/a convenient place), I want to rent it.			

Using *ba*-conditional forms, you can express a condition under which someone does something, something occurs, or something is the case.

Ba-conditional sentences have some usage restrictions. First, S_2 cannot be in the past tense. For example, the following sentence is ungrammatical:

× 図書館(としょかん)に行(い)けば、山田(やまだ)さんに会(あ)いました。

→ 図書館(としょかん)に行(い)ったら、山田(やまだ)さんに会(あ)いました。*When I went to the library, I ran across Yamada-san.*

Second, when S_1 represents someone's action, S_2 cannot be a command, a request, or a volitional sentence. Therefore, the following sentences are ungrammatical:

× 田中(たなか)さんが来(く)れば、{電話(でんわ)をください／電話(でんわ)します}。

→ 田中(たなか)さんが来(き)たら、{電話(でんわ)をください／電話(でんわ)します}。

{Give me a call / I'll call you} if Tanaka-san comes.

Exs. (1) 美術館(びじゅつかん)に行(い)く時(とき)は、駅(えき)からバスに乗(の)れ<u>ば</u>いいですよ。*When you go to the museum, you can get there by bus from the station. (lit. if you get on the bus from the station, it will be good.)*

(2) 学生(がくせい)：あぁ… 先生(せんせい)、もう漢字(かんじ)は覚(おぼ)えられません。

Oh, man... Professor, I can't memorize any more kanji.

先生(せんせい)：あきらめな<u>ければ</u>覚(おぼ)えられます。がんばってください。

You'll be able to if you don't give up. Hang in there.

(3) A: これ、筋(きん)トレのアプリだって。*This is a workout app, I hear.*

B: へえ、本当(ほんとう)に便利(べんり)<u>なら</u>使(つか)うけど… *Hmm, if it really is useful, I'll give it a try.*

☞ GID (vol.2): B. Connecting sentences 4. ば, たら, と, and なら

話しましょう

▶ **Words written in purple** are new words introduced in this lesson.

できる I Talk about times when you were forced to do something you did not like.

できるI-A Mild commands ～なさい

1 Let's practice the expression ～なさい. Tell a child to do the following. L18-6

Ex. 本を読む → 本を読みなさい。

1) 野菜を食べる　2) 早く寝る　3) ゲームをやめる　4) 車に気をつける
5) 部屋を片づける　6) 歯医者に行く　7) 急ぐ　8) 時間を守る
9) 仲良くする　10) がまんする

2 Suppose you are working as a camp counsellor for Japanese-speaking kids this summer. Prepare a list of useful phrases with your partner to use with the kids who do not behave well.

Ex. 早く起きなさい。

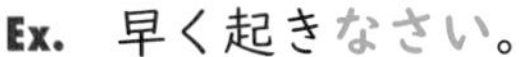

3 You see the following sentences on a test. What are you supposed to do? Match the Japanese instruction sentences with those in English in the box below.

Ex. 番号を入れなさい。 (a.)

1) 質問に答えなさい。 (　　)　2) 2行目を見なさい。 (　　)
3) ○か×を入れなさい。 (　　)　4) (　) に助詞を入れなさい。 (　　)
5) 意見を書きなさい。 (　　)　6) 正しい答えを選びなさい。 (　　)
7) 2段落目を読みなさい。 (　　)　8) 簡単に説明しなさい。 (　　)

a. Insert the appropriate number.	**b.** Read the second paragraph.	**c.** Choose the correct answer.
d. Insert ○ or ×.	**e.** Write your opinions.	**f.** Explain it briefly.
g. Answer the question.	**h.** Look at the second line.	**i.** Insert the appropriate particle in the parentheses.

できるI-B Causative-passive forms of verbs and causative-passive sentences

1 Let's practice conjugating verbs into their causative-passive forms. 

Ex.1 食べる → 食べさせる → 食べさせられる → 食べさせられます
Ex.2 読む → 読ませる → 読まされる → 読まされます

1) 調べる　2) やめる　3) あきらめる　4) 行く　5) 習う　6) 持つ
7) 書く　8) 飲む　9) 話す　10) 勉強する　11) 持ってくる
12) アイロンをかける　13) 時間を守る　14) 通う　15) 残業する

2 Let's talk about your classes. Describe the pictures from both the teacher's and the students' viewpoints. L18-8

Ex. 毎日小テストを受ける

→ スパルタ先生は学生に毎日小テストを受けさせます。

→ 学生はスパルタ先生に毎日小テストを受けさせられます。

1) 作文を書く

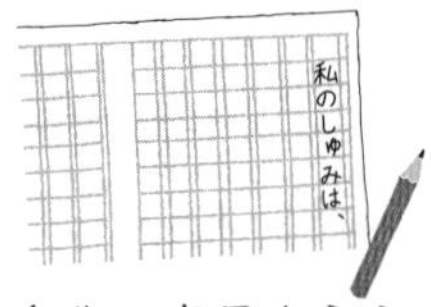

2) 毎週発表(はっぴょう)する

3) 世界について考(かんが)える

4) 経済(けいざい)について調べる

5) 自分の意見を言う

6) 分かるまで読む

7) 何時間も宿題をする

8) your own

3 Let's talk about what you are forced to do.

Step 1 アンハッピーさん is working under the worst manager in the world, while ハッピーさん has the best manager ever. Describe their working conditions. L18-9

Ex. アンハッピーさんは部長にいつも残業(ざんぎょう)させられます。

でも、ハッピーさんは毎日５時に{帰れます／帰ってもいいです}。

アンハッピーさん	ハッピーさん
Ex. いつも残業(ざんぎょう)する	Ex. 毎日５時に帰る
1) 危険(きけん)な仕事をする	1) 好きな仕事をする
2) 毎朝７時に会社に来る	2) 好きな時間に会社に来る
3) 時々週末も働く	3) 時々１週間休む
4) 部長が好きな野球(やきゅう)チームを応援(おうえん)する	4) 自分が好きな野球(やきゅう)チームを応援(おうえん)する
5) 絶対(ぜったい)にしめ切りを守る	5) 自分でしめ切りを決める
6) アイロンをかけたシャツを着る	6) Ｔシャツを着て仕事をする
7) your own	7) your own

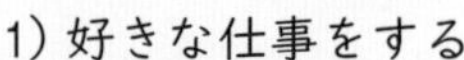

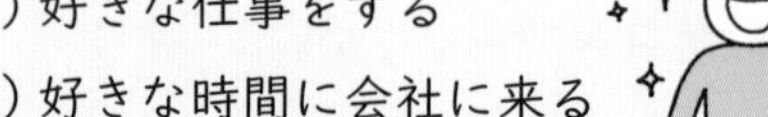

Step 2 Talk with your partner about your hardest class this semester and explain its requirements.

Ex. A: ○○さん、ねむそうですね。最近、忙(いそが)しいですか。

B: ええ、実(じつ)は経済(けいざい)のクラスが大変なんです。毎週教科書(きょうかしょ)を100ページぐらい読まされます。

A: え、100ページも読まされるんですか。それは大変ですね。

B: はい。△△さんは大変なクラスがありますか。

<Continue>

4 Recall what you were forced to do when you were a child and talk about it with your partner.

Ex. A: 私は子どもの時、ブロッコリーが大きらいでした。

　　でも、母に「食べなさい」と言われて、食べさせられました。

B: そうですか。今はブロッコリーが好きになりましたか。(← Follow-up question)

<Continue>

5 Listen to the audio on the *TOBIRA* website and choose the most appropriate option for each question. L18-10

Ex. 子どもはお母さんに

　a. 勉強されます　　b. 勉強させます　　c. 勉強させられます

1) お母さんは子どもにお菓子(かし)を

　a. 食べさせました　　b. 食べさせてあげました　　c. 食べさせられました

2) お母さんは子どもにゲームを

　a. してあげました　　b. させてあげました　　c. させられました

3) 学生は先生に今日試験を

　a. 受けられます　　b. 受けさせます　　c. 受けさせられます

4) 私は田中さんにケーキを

　a. 食べさせました　　b. 食べられました　　c. 食べさせられました

5) 私は田中さんにケーキを

　a. 食べさせました　b. 食べられました　c. 食べさせられました　d. 食べさせてあげました

できるII Talk about unexpected occurrences and express your feelings about them.

できるII-A まだ and もう ("still" and "no longer")

1 Describe the given topics using まだ and もう.

Step 1 Let's practice using まだ+affirmative form ("still") and もう+negative form ("no longer").

Ex. このドラマはおもしろいです

→このドラマはまだおもしろいです → このドラマはもうおもしろくないです

1) 今は忙(いそが)しいです　2) 9月は暑(あつ)いです　3) 私達は仲(なか)がいいです

4) 公園(こうえん)の桜(さくら)はきれいです　5) 16才(さい)は子どもです

桜(さくら)

Step 2 State your opinions about the questions below, using まだ+affirmative form or もう+negative form.

Ex. 9月は夏(なつ)ですか。

A: 私は9月はまだ夏(なつ)だと思います。毎日Tシャツを着ているからです。

B: そうですか。私も9月はまだ夏(なつ)だと思います。

or 私は9月はもう夏(なつ)じゃないと思います。 <Continue>

1) 3月は寒(さむ)いですか。 2) 16才(さい)は子どもですか。 3) カタカナを読むのは難(むずか)しいですか。

4) 宇宙(うちゅう) (space) に旅行をするのは夢(ゆめ)ですか。 5) your own

2 You've run into your Japanese friend from high school for the first time since graduation. Answer your friend's questions based on the cues provided. L18-12

Ex. A: ○○さんは高校の時、(よく) サッカーをしていましたが、

今もまだ (サッカーを) していますか。

B: ○ はい、まだしています。or × いいえ、もうしていません。

Ex. ○ / ×

1) ○

Japanese

2) ×

3) ○

commuted to guitar lessons (ギター教室)

4) ×

Tigers (← team name)

5) ○

lived near the school

6) ×

with Tanaka-san

7) your own

3 What was a big hit when you were a child/high school student? Talk about it with your partner.

Step 1 Brainstorm what was popular in your childhood/high school days.

Possible topics よく○○ていたお菓子(かし)／ゲーム／音楽

Step 2 Pick a topic from Step 1 and talk about it with your partner.

Ex. A: ○○さんが子どもの時、よく食べていたお菓子(かし)は何ですか。

B:「うまいよ」というお菓子(かし)です。

A: へえ、そうですか。どんなお菓子(かし)ですか。(← Follow-up question)

B: チョコレートのお菓子(かし)です。

A: 今もまだよく食べていますか。

B: ええ、まだよく食べていますよ。or いいえ、もう食べていません。

<Continue>

Step 3 Report to the class what you and your partner still do and/or no longer do.

4 You are now doing a monthly house cleaning with your friend. Talk to each other and decide whether or not you should keep the items below.

Ex. A: 祖母(そぼ)が使っていたアイロン、まだ使えると思う？

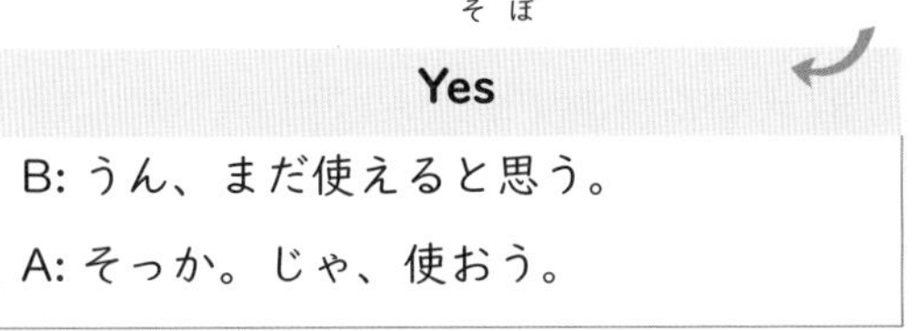

Yes
B: うん、まだ使えると思う。
A: そっか。じゃ、使おう。

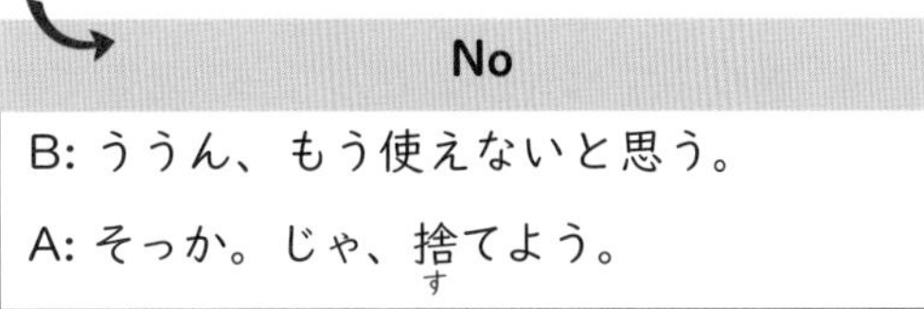

No
B: ううん、もう使えないと思う。
A: そっか。じゃ、捨(す)てよう。

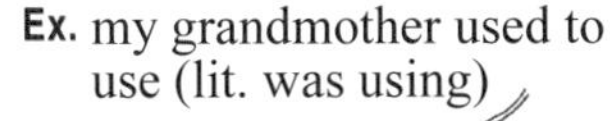

Ex. my grandmother used to use (lit. was using)　1) bought last week　2) bought yesterday　3) bought 5 years ago

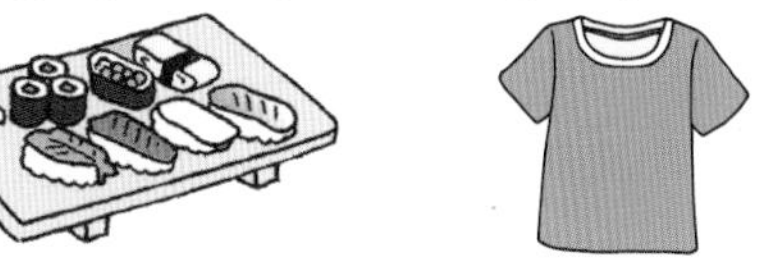

4) with a hole　5) bought 4 years ago　6) made a week ago　7) your own

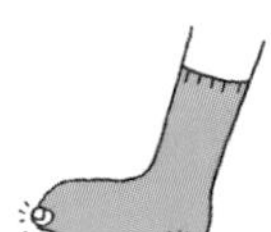

Group Work

5 What will the world be like 50 years from now? For example, will people still do the things we do now? Will they still use the same devices? Exchange your opinions.

Possible topics	車を運転する　〇〇を使う　〇〇で映画を見る　〇〇に乗る　〇〇（place/device）で音楽を聞く／勉強する

Ex. A: 50年後、みんなまだ車を運転していると思いますか。

B: 車は自動運転になるから、50年後、人間はもう運転していないと思います。

C: 私は〇〇さんの｛意見／考(かんが)え｝とちょっと違(ちが)います。車の運転は楽しいから、みんなまだ車を運転していると思います。 <Continue>

できるII-B　～のに "in spite of the fact that ~"

1 Let's review the forms used before ～のに.　L18-13

Ex. 食(た)べる

	affirmative	negative
non-past	食べるのに	食べないのに
past	食べたのに	食べなかったのに

1) 見(み)る　2) 買(か)う　3) ある　4) する　5) 来(く)る　6) 寒(さむ)い　7) いい
8) きらい　9) 休(やす)み　10) 大事(だいじ)　11) 終(お)わり

2 Your classmate Tanaka-san is missing/has missed an important project meeting. Express your surprise/discontent. L18-14

Ex.1 大事な話をします

→ <u>大事な話をする</u>のに、田中さんはミーティングに来ません。

1) みんなが待(ま)っています　2) 田中さんの考(かんが)えも聞きたいです　3) 都合(つごう)が悪くないです
4) 来なくてはいけません　5) 元気です　6) 大事な会議(かいぎ)です

Ex.2 大事な話をしました

→ <u>大事な話をした</u>のに、田中さんはミーティングに来ませんでした。

7)「行く」と言いました　8) 大事な用事(ようじ)がありませんでした
9) 田中さんに来てほしかったです　10) 来なくてはいけませんでした
11) 元気でした　12) プレゼンの準備(じゅんび)の日でした

3 You've found the following images on social media. Talk about each of them with your partner, showing your surprise about it. L18-15

Ex. ハワイです

A: あ、見てください。ハワイなのに、雪が降(ふ)っています。

B: あ、本当ですね。めずらしいですね。(← Comment)

1) 天気がいいです

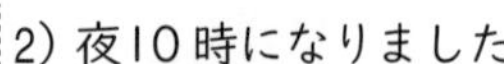

2) 夜10時になりました

3) 仕事中です

4) サルです

5) 信号(しんごう)が赤(あか)です

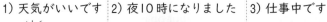

intersection

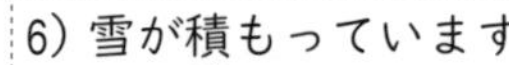

6) 雪が積(つ)もっています

7) もう子どもじゃないです

8) テストが悪かったです

delighted

4 The same things happened to やっぱりさん and びっくりさん. やっぱりさん had expected them to happen, while びっくりさん had not. Add more details using ので or のに as in the underlined part in the example.

Exs.

やっぱりさん (I-thought-so)

<u>朝ご飯を食べなかった</u>ので、

びっくりさん

<u>朝ご飯をたくさん食べた</u>のに、

<u>おなかがすきました</u>。

1) テストが100点(てん)でした
2) 今、幸せです
3) スピーチを失敗(しっぱい)しました
4) この町は不便(ふべん)です
5) ○○は人気があります
6) your own

5 Talk with your partner about your surprise or discontent over how certain things went.

Possible topics	週末	テスト	旅行	デート	○○休み (Ex. 冬(ふゆ)休み)

Ex. A: 週末はどうでしたか。

B: 最悪でした。ゲームがしたかったのに、宿題があって、できませんでした。

A: そうですか。どんなゲームがしたかったんですか。(← Follow-up question)

<Continue>

6 Let's tweet in Japanese! Make as many sentences as possible on the hashtag #どうしよう, expressing your surprise or discontent with もう／まだ. Share your tweets with your classmates.

Ex.1 #どうしよう　もう一年生じゃないのに、まだひらがなを間違(まちが)えてしまう

Ex.2 #どうしよう　まだ月曜日なのに、つかれている

できるⅢ Encourage people close to you and show empathy towards them.

できるⅢ-A Expectation/anticipation ～はずだ

1 Let's review the forms used before ～はず. L18-16

Ex. 食(た)べる

	affirmative	negative
non-past	食べるはずです	食べないはずです
past	食べたはずです	食べなかったはずです

1) できる　2) 分(わ)かる　3) ある　4) する　5) 来(く)る　6) 安(やす)い

7) いい　8) 静(しず)か　9) 学生(がくせい)　10) 手伝(てつだ)ってくれる　11) 仲良(なかよ)くなれる

12) 人気(にんき)が出(で)る　13) 気(き)がつく　14) 失敗(しっぱい)する　15) 残業(ざんぎょう)している

2 Match the sentences below to describe your reasoned assumptions about Ai's host family. L18-17

Ex. <u>お父さんはお茶の店をしている</u>ので、<u>おいしいお茶をよく知っている</u>はずです。

Ex. お父さんはお茶の店をしています。 •	• 不便(ふべん)です。
1) お母さんは京都(きょうと)の方言を話しません。 •	• おいしいお茶をよく知っています。
2) お父さんはタイガースを応援(おうえん)しています。 •	• タイガースのファンです。
3) お姉さんは明日用事(ようじ)があります。 •	• 家を留守(るす)にします。
4) お父さんは日曜日も仕事をしています。 •	• 出身(しゅっしん)は京都(きょうと)じゃないです。
5) お姉さんは昨日残業(ざんぎょう)させられました。 •	• 日曜日の昼は都合(つごう)が悪いです。
6) 弟さんは先週テストでいい点(てん)を取りました。 •	• 家に帰るのが遅かったです。
7) 家の近くにコンビニがありません。 •	• お母さんは安心(あんしん)しました。

3 Suppose you are looking for a new apartment with your partner.

Step 1 Look at the information on the two apartments below. Discuss some of their features and share your expectations based on them.

アーバー

- college students only
- few lights outside
- near convenience stores and restaurants
- within walking distance of campus (= can walk to campus)

ハイム

- located on a mountain
- (doors) lock automatically
- (units have) a big kitchen
- environmentally friendly

Useful vocabulary うるさい　静(しず)か　便利(べんり)　不便(ふべん)　危険(きけん)　安心(あんしん)できる　大学に通(かよ)いやすい　住みやすい　住みにくい

Ex. A: アーバーは、大学生しかいないから、うるさいはずです。

B: そうですか。ハイムは山の中にあるから、静(しず)かなはずです。

<Continue>

Step 2 Decide which apartment to move into.

Ex. A: どちらのアパートにしましょうか。

B: 私は静(しず)かな所がいいから、ハイムがいいと思います。

A: そうですか。私 {は／も} … <Continue>

B: じゃ、{アーバー／ハイム} にしましょう。

4 Suppose it's 10PM on Wednesday and your meeting has just ended.

Step 1 You are starving. Look at the signs below and decide where to go with your partner. Make a suggestion based on your expectations.

Useful expressions すいている　混(こ)んでいる　まだ開いている　もう開いていない　休み

レストラン　ララ	バーガーバーガー	カフェ　アルン
午前 11:30 ～午後 11:30 休み：水曜日	24H Fast food	午前 10:00 ～午後 8:30 休み：ありません

Ex. A: おなかがすいたね。どこかに食べに行かない？

B: そうだね。じゃ、ララに食べに行かない？　もう 10 時だから、店はすいているはずだよ。

A: うーん、でも、今日は水曜日だから… <Continue>

Step 2 What would you do or where would you go if you were starving late at night in your city? Discuss with your partner using the conversation in Step 1 as a model.

できるIII-B Conditional ～ば

1 Let's practice *ba*-conditional form conjugations. L18-18

Ex. 行(い)く → 行(い)けば → 行(い)かなければ

1) できる　2) 急(いそ)ぐ　3) ある　4) する　5) 来(く)る
6) してもらう　7) しておく　8) してみる　9) 食(た)べられる　10) 安(やす)い
11) 便利(べんり)　12) 雨(あめ)　13) 都合(つごう)がいい　14) 危険(きけん)

2 Suppose you are planning to buy a new phone. State your conditions for purchase. 

Ex. 安い → 安ければ買います。でも、安くなければ買いません。

1) 今買える　2) 好きな色がある　3) 使いやすい　4) デザインがいい
5) 地球(ちきゅう)にやさしい　6) 色がきれい　7) 今と同じブランド　8) your own

Lesson 18

3 Your friends are facing some problems.

Step 1 Give advice to your friends. L18-20

Ex.1

朝ねぼうしてしまいました。

自転車に乗れば、{だいじょうぶですよ／間(ま)に合(あ)いますよ}。

Ex.1 ride a bike　1) run　2) hurry　3) don't eat breakfast

Ex.2

漢字が覚(おぼ)えられないんです。

何回も書けば、{だいじょうぶですよ／覚(おぼ)えられますよ}。

Ex.2 write over and over　4) use an application called ○○
5) memorize kanji with Riemann　6) don't think that kanji are difficult

Step 2 Suppose your partner is facing some problems. Using Step 1 as a model, give them some advice.

Group Work

4 Work with your groupmates to come up with some advice for making studying Japanese, your school life, or life in general better, then share it with the class. Whose advice do you think is the best?

Ex.

「人にも地球(ちきゅう)にもやさしくしなさい。
そうすれば、みんな幸せになれるはずです。」

5 You have concerns about something you are being made to do. Talk about it with your partner, who is very positive and easygoing.

A: Lead-in sentence	**Ex.** A: ちょっと悩(なや)みがあるんですけど… B: どうしたんですか。
A: Problem = what you are forced to do	A: 私は作りたくないのに、いつもルームメートに晩ご飯を作らされるんです。
B: Empathy + opinion	B: そうですか。それは大変ですね。 でも、料理したくなければ、しなくてもいいと思いますよ。 A: え、本当にそう思いますか。 B: ええ、がまんしない方がいいと思います。
A: Your decision	A: そうですね。じゃ、いやな時はもう作りません。

Group Work

6 You are a member of a committee in your community (Exs. Japanese course, dining hall, dorm, fan club). Make suggestions to improve your community and share your expectations for the results of your proposed improvements.

Step 1 Decide what to work on and brainstorm ideas to improve it.

Useful expressions 〇〇をもっと{多(おお)く／よく／楽しく／おいしく／きれいに}する

Ex. 大学の食堂(しょくどう)をもっとよくする

A: 大学の食堂(しょくどう)をもっとよくするために、どうすればいいと思いますか。

B: メニューコンテストをしたらどうですか。コンテストで一番になったメニューが食べられれば、もっと食堂(しょくどう)の人気が出るはずです。

C: それはいい考(かんが)えですね。それから、デザートを多(おお)くしたらどうですか。そうすれば、みんな喜(よろこ)ぶはずです。

<Continue>

Step 2 Make a brief presentation about your plans to the class.

Ex. 私達は、大学の食堂(しょくどう)をもっとよくするために、まずメニューコンテストをしようと思います。コンテストをすれば… <Continue>

Review

You can now give a presentation on your experience about overcoming fear, hardship, or difficulty (learning to play a sport/musical instrument, learning a new language, etc.).

Step 1 Decide on a topic and brainstorm each category listed below.

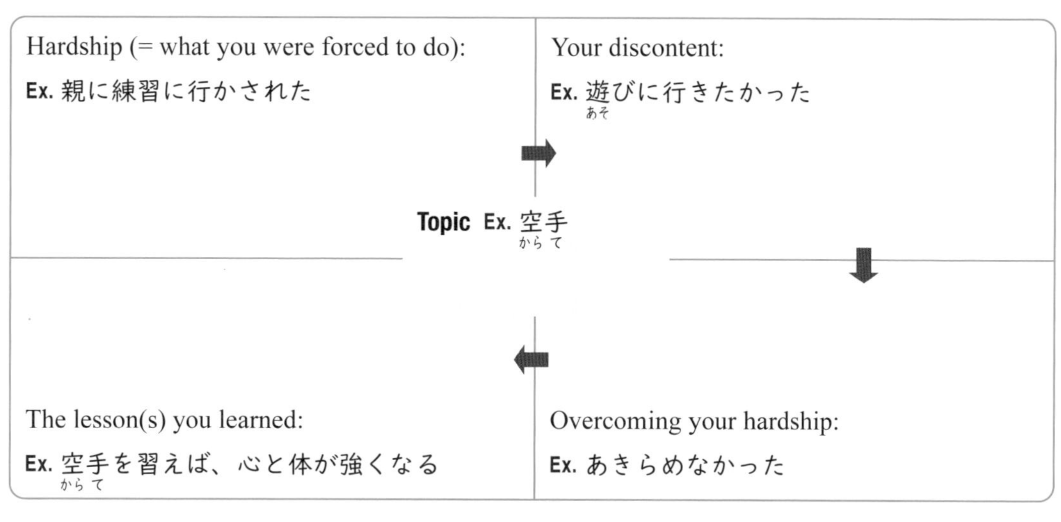

Step 2 Make a brief presentation about your experience. Your classmates will ask you questions after the presentation.

Topic introduction

Your hardship:
- what you were forced to do
- your discontent
- overcoming your hardship

Your message(s)/ lesson(s)

=============

Q&A

Ex. みなさんは空手(からて)をしたことがありますか。私は５才(さい)の時からずっと空手(からて)を習っていますが、初めは大変でした。例えば、遊(あそ)びに行きたかったのに、親に練習に行かされました。毎日練習したのに、上手になりませんでした。でも、私はあきらめないで空手(からて)をずっと続けました。今もまだ練習に通(かよ)っています。
みなさんにもぜひ空手(からて)を始めてほしいです。空手(からて)を習えば、心と体が強くなるはずです。

Q: 私も空手(からて)を習いたいんですが、どこに行けばいいですか。

読みましょう

Understand essays about personal experiences by connecting them with your own experiences.

読み物を読む前に

1 世界には色々なボランティア活動があります。下の写真は日本のボランティア情報サイトで紹介されている世界の色々なボランティア活動の例です。

Step 1 下の写真の(1)～(6)はどんなことをするボランティアだと思いますか。クラスメートと話し合いなさい。

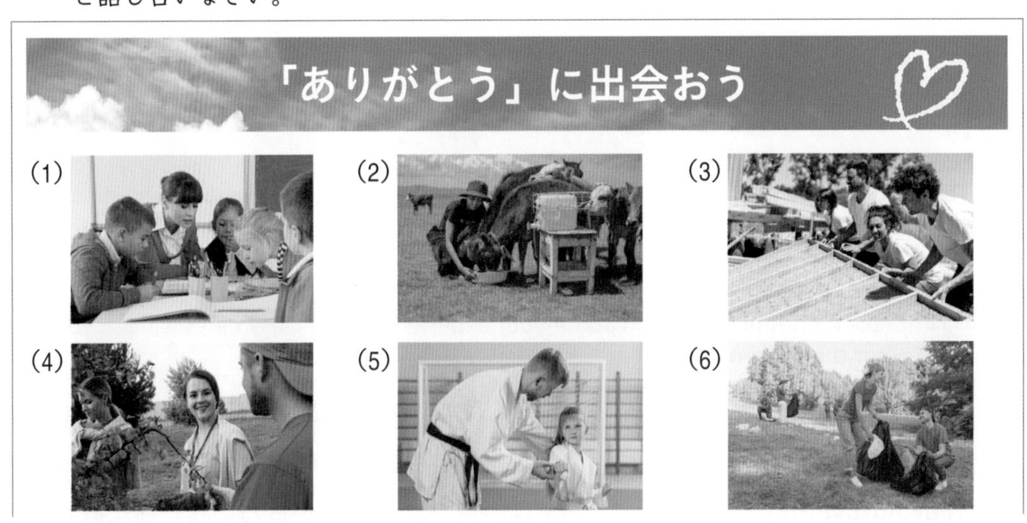

Step 2 下のa.～f.は、上の(1)～(6)のどの写真の説明か選びなさい。

a. 子ども達に勉強を教える（Ex.(1)）　　b. 動物の世話をする（　　）
c. ごみを拾う（　　）　　d. 家を建てる（　　）
e. 子ども達にスポーツを教える（　　）　　f. 木を植える（　　）

2 あなたが今住んでいる国にはどんなボランティアがありますか。クラスメートと話しなさい。

3 あなたはボランティアをしたことがありますか。
したことがある人 → 下のa.～e.のどの分野のボランティアをしましたか。
したことがない人 → 下のa.～e.のどの分野のボランティアをしてみたいですか。

a.

b.

c.

d.

e.

読み物を読もう

ジニーさんは日本に留学中に、日本語スピーチコンテストに参加しました。ジニーさんのスピーチの原稿 (script) を読んで質問に答えましょう。

苦しむ：to suffer　だく：to hold　食べ始める：to start eating

「私の世界を広げてくれた経験」　ジニー・ウィリアムズ（オーストラリア）

子どもの時、みなさんの夢は何でしたか。私はピアニストになるのが夢で、小学校の時から毎日がんばってピアノを練習していました。でも、高校三年生の時に指にひどいけがをして、その夢をあきらめました。大学に入って何を専攻するか決めなくてはいけませんでしたが、ピアノの他にしたいことがなかったし、将来何になりたいか分からなかったから困りました。悩んでいたら、ある先輩が「ボランティアをしてみたら、やりたいことが見つかるかもしれないよ」とアドバイスしてくれました。そして、このアドバイスが私を変えてくれました。

オーストラリアの大学生は色々なボランティア活動をします。例えば、ホームレスの人のために食事を作るボランティアや動物園でコアラの世話をするボランティアです。地球の環境を守るために木を植えたり、海や山や公園でゴミを拾ったりするボランティアもあります。何をしようか迷ったけれど、私は子どもの病院でボランティアをすることに決めました。家から近くて通うのが便利だったし、子どもの病院だったら、子ども達と一緒に遊べばいいから仕事は楽なはずだと思ったからです。でも、実は全然楽じゃありませんでした。

そこは0才から16才の子ども達が入院している病院で、私の仕事は入院中の子ども達の世話をすることでした。病気が軽い子ども達に本を読んであげたり、一緒に散歩したりするのは楽しかったです。でも、重い病気で苦しんでいる1才の赤ちゃんをだいていた時は、私がこの赤ちゃんにしてあげられることは何もないと思って心が痛くなりました。そして、ボランティアをやめたいと思いました。

11月の終わりに、まりえちゃんという日本人の子どもが入院してきました。まりえちゃんは小学生で、年は6才でしたが、日本からオーストラリアに来てまだ3か月しか経っていなかったから、英語がよく分からなくて大変そうでした。私は大学で日本語のクラスを取っていたので、まりえちゃんに「こんにちは」と言ってみました。まりえちゃんはすごくびっくりした顔で「日本語が分かるの？」と聞きました。「うん、分かるよ」と言ったら、まりえちゃんの顔が明るくなりました。この日から1か月間、私はまりえちゃんの世話をしました。私はまだ日本語が下手だったので、私達は日本語と英語で話しました。ある日、まりえちゃんはご飯を食べたくなさそうでした。「元気になるために食べなさい」と[Ex.]言ったけれど、「いやだ。食べたくない」という[(a)]返事しかしませんでした。「分かった。じゃ、私が食べるね。『いただきます！』」と[(b)]言ったら、まりえちゃんが "Hey! That's mine!" と言ってご飯を[(c)]食べ始めました。そして、一緒に大きい声で[(d)]笑いました。その後で、まりえちゃんのご両親に「ま

Lesson 18

りえはジニーに会っている時、とても楽しそうだし、英語を話すのも好きになったようです。この病院でジニーと出会えたことをとても(e)喜んでいるんですよ。どうもありがとう」と言われました。その時は本当にうれしかったです。まりえちゃんが退院してから２年経ちますが、私達は今もまだ仲良くしていて、時々会って話します。

私はボランティアをする前には、やりたいことがありませんでした。将来、どんな仕事をすればいいか分かりませんでした。でも、このボランティアをして二つのことに気がつきました。それは、人に何かしてあげて「ありがとう」と言われたらうれしくなること、そして、外国語ができれば誰かの役に立てることです。

今、私の夢は大学を卒業したら日本に行って、子ども達に英語を教える［こと］です。将来は学校の先生になりたいと思っています。そのために時々大学の近くの小学校に行って、外国から来た子ども達に英語やオーストラリアの文化を教えるボランティアをしています。病院でボランティアをしなければ、この夢を持てなかったと思います。私の世界を広げてくれたボランティアと日本語の勉強に感謝しています。

読み物を読んだ後で、考えてみよう

1 ［　　］の言葉を修飾している (to modify) 部分に線を引きなさい。

2 １行目から14行目までを読んで、次の質問に答えましょう。

1）まず一度読んで、(1)と(2)の質問に答えなさい。

(1) 1段落目 ジニーさんはどんなことに悩んでいましたか。その部分に線を引きなさい。

(2) 2段落目 ジニーさんはその問題を解決するために何をしましたか。その部分に線を引きなさい。

2）もう一度読んで、(1)～(4)の質問に答えなさい。

(1) ジニーさんの子どもの時の夢は何でしたか。

(2) 7行目「アドバイスしてくれました」とありますが、誰がジニーにどんなアドバイスをしてくれましたか。

(3) ジニーさんが決めたボランティアはどんなボランティアでしたか。どうしてそれに決めましたか。

(4) 14行目「でも、実は全然楽じゃありませんでした」は、どうして楽じゃなかったと思いますか。自分の考えを言いなさい。

3 15行目から34行目までを読んで、次の質問に答えましょう。

1）15行目 そこはどこですか。

2）ジニーさんはどんな仕事をしましたか。

3）ジニーさんはどんな時にそのボランティアをやめたいと思いましたか。

4) ジニーさんとまりえちゃんはどうして仲良(なかよ)くなったと思いますか。自分の考えを言いなさい。

5) 次の表現(ひょうげん)はメタファーです。どんな意味だと思いますか。日本語で答えなさい。

16行目(ぎょうめ)と17行目(ぎょうめ) 病気が軽(かる)い／重い病気＝＿＿＿＿＿＿＿＿＿＿＿＿

18行目(ぎょうめ) 心が痛くなりました＝＿＿＿＿＿＿＿＿＿＿＿＿

25行目(ぎょうめ) 顔が明るくなりました＝＿＿＿＿＿＿＿＿＿＿＿＿

6) (a)～(e)は誰(だれ)がしたことですか。(　　)にJ（＝ジニーさん）、M（＝まりえちゃん）を入れなさい。

Ex. 言った　(J)　　(a) 返事しかしませんでした (　　)

(b) 言った　(　　)　　(c) 食(た)べ始(はじ)めました　(　　)

(d) 笑いました (　　)　　(e) 喜(よろこ)んでいる　(　　)

7) 正しい文には○を、正しくない文には×を入れなさい。

(　　) 子どもの病院のボランティアは全部(ぜんぶ)難(むずか)しい仕事だった。

(　　) まりえちゃんは病院にいる間、全然(ぜんぜん)英語を話さなかった。

(　　) まりえちゃんはご飯が食べられない病気だった。

(　　) ジニーさんとまりえちゃんは今も友達で、時々会う。

4 35行目(ぎょうめ)から43行目(ぎょうめ)までを読んで、次の質問に答えましょう。

1) ジニーさんについて(1)～(3)の質問に答えなさい。

(1) ジニーさんが病院のボランティアをして気がついたことは何ですか。二つ書きなさい。

(2) ジニーさんの将来(しょうらい)の夢(ゆめ)やしたいことは何ですか。二つ書きなさい。

(3) ジニーさんが今しているボランティアは何ですか。

2) ジニーさんは何が自分の世界を広げてくれたと思っていますか。二つ書きなさい。

3) ジニーさんのスピーチ原稿(げんこう)を読んで、あなたはどう思いましたか。三つの文で答えなさい。

【　　】には下から接続詞(せつぞくし)を一つ選(えら)んで書きなさい。

でも　　だから　　それから　　例えば

まず、＿＿＿＿＿＿＿＿＿＿＿＿＿＿＿＿＿＿＿＿＿＿。

【　　　】、＿＿＿＿＿＿＿＿＿＿＿＿＿＿＿＿＿＿＿＿。

【　　　】、＿＿＿＿＿＿＿＿＿＿＿＿＿＿＿＿＿＿＿＿。

みんなで話してみよう

1 あなたは大学に入った時に何か悩(なや)みがありましたか。悩(なや)みがあった人はどうやって解決(かいけつ)しましたか。(Cf. ll.2-6)

2 あなたは友達や後輩(こうはい)が専攻(せんこう)や将来(しょうらい)について悩(なや)んでいたら、どんなアドバイスをしてあげますか。どうしてそのアドバイスをしますか。(Cf. ll.4-8)

3 オーストラリアの大学生がするボランティアの中で、あなたはどのボランティアをしてみたいですか。それはどうしてですか。(Cf. ll.9-14)

4 あなたはジニーさんがしたボランティアの仕事をしてみたいですか。どうしてそう思いますか。(Cf. ll.15-34)

5 日本語の勉強はジニーさんの世界を広げました。あなたも日本語を勉強して、何か変わったことがありますか。例えば、どんなことですか。(Cf. ll.35-43)

> **変わったことの例**
> 興味(きょうみ)　すること　性格(せいかく)　好きなもの　したいこと　考え方　人間関係(にんげんかんけい) (personal relationships)

6 このスピーチの原稿(げんこう)を読んで、ジニーさんにどんな質問をしてみたいですか。

7 ボランティア活動のクラブを作ろうと思います。あなたは誰(だれ)のために、どんなボランティアをするクラブを作りたいですか。理由も言いなさい。

書く練習

あなたの「自分の世界を広げてくれた経験(けいけん)」について書きなさい。

> **トピックの例**
> アルバイト　クラブ活動　留学　大変だったこと　SNS　学校の勉強　友達

聞きましょう

リスニング・ストラテジー：Listening strategy

Integration (1): Predicting and listening for keywords

In this lesson, we will practice listening to a short news clip as an integration exercise. There are websites where you can listen to simplified Japanese news created for Japanese language learners. You can find a link to one of them on the *TOBIRA* website.

1 Pre-listening activity: The pictures below show the people appearing together in the news clip you will listen to later. Look at the pictures and talk with your classmate in Japanese about what you think you will hear in the news.

2 Listening:

1) Listen to the news clip about a group of Santa Clauses' visit to Japan and answer the questions a.-e. in the table below in Japanese. While listening to the news clip, take notes (in a language of your choice) on any keywords that might help you answer the questions. Try to guess the meaning of any unfamiliar words from the context.

佐賀県（さがけん）：Saga Prefecture　技（わざ）：skill; technique　隠（かく）れる：to hide

a. いつ？	b. どこで？	c. 誰（だれ）が？
	佐賀県（さがけん）の＿＿＿＿＿＿	
d. 何をした？		
e. それはどうだった？		

2) Discuss your reactions to this news clip with your classmates in Japanese. What do you think about it? Was it interesting or strange? Why do you think so?

Now it's time to go back to the DEKIRU List for this chapter (p.281) and do the exit check to see what new things you can do now that you've completed the lesson.

文化ノート　Culture Note

日本語の歌を歌ってみよう

みなさんはどんな日本語の歌を知っていますか。『世界で一つだけの花』という歌を聞いたことがありますか。この歌は歌詞 (lyrics) がとてもいいし、メロディも難しくないので、人気があって色々な人に歌われています。まず歌を聞いてみてください。

- 歌を聞いてどう思いましたか。
- 下にこの歌の歌詞 (lyrics) があります。歌を聞きながら、一緒に歌ってみましょう。

世界に一つだけの花

作詞・作曲 (songwriting)：槇原敬之　　歌：SMAP

A
No.1にならなくてもいい
もともと特別な Only one

花屋の店先に並んだ
いろんな花を見ていた
ひとそれぞれ好みはあるけど
どれもみんなきれいだね
この中で誰が一番だなんて
争うこともしないで
バケツの中誇らしげに
しゃんと胸を張っている

それなのに僕ら人間は
どうしてこうも比べたがる？
一人一人違うのにその中で
一番になりたがる？

B
そうさ　僕らは
世界に一つだけの花
一人一人違う種を持つ
その花を咲かせることだけに
一生懸命になればいい

もともと：originally; by nature　特別な：special　店先＝店の前　いろんな＝色々
ひと(人)それぞれ：each person　好み：taste; preference　なんて：such a thing as　争う：to compete
バケツ：bucket　誇らしげに：proudly　しゃんと胸を張る：to stand straight and tall
僕ら＝僕達　こうも：like this　そうさ＝そうです　種：seed

1) この歌のタイトルはどんな意味だと思いますか。
2) この歌にはどんなメッセージがあると思いますか。
3) 歌の中のどの言葉やメロディがいいと思いましたか。
4) あなたが知っている日本語の歌をみんなに紹介して、みんなで歌ってみましょう。

Lesson 19

明日はどんな話をなさいますか。

What story will you be telling tomorrow?

Instructional Video Lesson 19

DEKIRU List

できるCheck ☑

できる I **Introduce yourself appropriately in a formal setting.**
フォーマルな場面で自己紹介ができる。
Entry ☐ Exit ☐

できる II **Use *keigo* to ask questions politely to someone of a higher status or someone you are meeting for the first time.**
目上の人や初めて会った人に、敬語を使って質問することができる。
Entry ☐ Exit ☐

できる III **Familiarize yourself with polite offers and other common phrasing involving humble expressions.**
申し出などのよく使われる謙譲表現に慣れる。
Entry ☐ Exit ☐

できる IV **Understand common public announcements and signs that contain *keigo*.**
公共の場所での敬語の案内や注意を理解することができる。
Entry ☐ Exit ☐

できる V **Reading comprehension: Identify the characters, setting, and storyline of a *rakugo* story and enjoy the humor in *rakugo*.**
読解：落語の内容を理解し、落語のおもしろさを楽しむことができる。
Entry ☐ Exit ☐

STRATEGIES

Conversation Tips .... • Repeating for more natural conversation
Listening .... • Integration (2): Predicting based on context and visual clues

GRAMMAR

1. Introduction to *keigo*
2. Courteous expressions できるI
3. ～でしょうか [Extra-polite question] できるII
4. Honorific expressions できるII
5. Humble expressions できるIII
6. おV-*masu*ください・お／ごVNください "Would you please V?" できるIV

会 話

1 できる I,II Ai is interviewing for a volunteer position at a *rakugo* event.

L19-1

面接官(めんせつかん)：interviewer

面接官(めんせつかん)　：簡単(かんたん)な自己紹介(じこしょうかい)をお願(ねが)いします。

アイ　：初めまして。アイ・ブルーノと申(もう)します。ゴーブル大学から参(まい)りました。

今、二年生で、美術(びじゅつ)と日本語を勉強しております。

面接官(めんせつかん)　：ブルーノさんですね。どうしてこのボランティアに申(もう)し込(こ)みましたか。

アイ　：落語(らくご)に興味(きょうみ)を持ったからです。

面接官(めんせつかん)　：そうですか。今までに何かボランティアをしたことがありますか。

アイ　：はい。日本に留学中に美術館(びじゅつかん)でしたことがあります。

面接官(めんせつかん)　：そうですか。分かりました。

<The interview continues.>

面接官(めんせつかん)　：最後に何か聞きたいことがありますか。

アイ　：はい。私は落語(らくご)についてあまりよく知らないんですが、いいでしょうか。

面接官(めんせつかん)　：あ、それは心配しなくてもいいですよ。

アイ　：分かりました。どうぞよろしくお願(ねが)いいたします。失礼(しつれい)します。

2 できる II Ai got the volunteer position at the *rakugo* event and is now talking with a performer who is going to appear in it.

師匠(ししょう)：master of Japanese traditional arts

アイ　：師匠(ししょう)はいつアメリカにお着きになりましたか。

落語家(らくごか)　：えっと、3日前です。

アイ　：アメリカはいかがですか。

落語家(らくごか)　：みなさんが色々な所に連(つ)れていってくださって、楽しいですよ。

アイ　：そうですか。あのう、師匠(ししょう)は何年ぐらい落語(らくご)をなさっていますか。

落語家(らくごか)　：50年です。

アイ　：え、50年ですか！

あのう、落語(らくご)の話はいくつぐらい覚(おぼ)えていらっしゃいますか。

落語家(らくごか)　：うーん、数(かぞ)えたことはありませんが、100ぐらい話せると思います。

アイ　：え、100も！　すごいですね。

明日はどんな話をなさいますか。

落語家(らくごか)　：『まんじゅうこわい』という話をします。

楽しみにしていてください。

3 できる III,IV The *rakugo* performer arrives at the event venue.

L19-3

(それ)では：polite equivalent of じゃ

アイ　：師匠(ししょう)、荷物をお持ちしましょうか。

落語家(らくごか)　：いえいえ、だいじょうぶですよ。

アイ　：あのう、何かお飲み物は…

落語家(らくごか)　：あ、じゃ、冷(つめ)たいお茶をお願(ねが)いします。

アイ　：はい、分かりました。では、こちらでお待(ま)ちください。

<Ai brings out some tea.>

アイ　：師匠(ししょう)、どうぞおめしあがりください。

落語家(らくごか)　：あ、どうもありがとう。

<After a while>

アイ　：それでは、会場(かいじょう)にご案内(あんない)します。こちらへどうぞ。

CONVERSATION TIPS

L19-4

Repeating for more natural conversation: In conversations, repeating/rephrasing a keyword or a key phrase that the other person has used can allow you to either: 1) confirm that your understanding is correct, or 2) show your surprise.

1) アイ：あのう、すみません、ブルーノと申(もう)しますが…

受付(うけつけ)(receptionist)：はい、ブルーノさんですね。あちらに座(すわ)って、お待(ま)ちください。

2) A：夏(なつ)休みに北海道に行ったんだ。

B：え？　北海道？　いいね。何したの？

A：えっと、温泉(おんせん)に入ったり、動物園(どうぶつえん)でペンギンの散歩(さんぽ)を見たり…

B：えっ、ペンギンが散歩(さんぽ)するの？　おもしろそうだね。

Vocabulary with Pictures

単語（たんご）

▶ **The words written in gray** are supplemental vocabulary.

あらたまった表現（ひょうげん） Courteous expressions

Ordinary expressions	Courteous expressions	
いう	もうす	もうします
いく	まいる	まいります
いる	おる	おります
くる	まいる	まいります
する	いたす	いたします
たべる／のむ	いただく	いただきます
～ている	～ておる	～ております

けいご
(*keigo*; honorific language)

Ordinary expressions	Polite expressions
これ／ここ／この人	こちら
それ／そこ／その人	そちら
あれ／あそこ／あの人	あちら
どこ	どちら
どう	いかが
だれ	どなた

人に会う Meeting people

[*person* に] じこしょうかいする
(to introduce oneself)

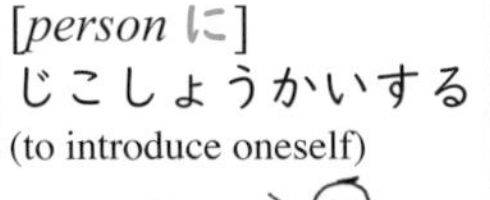

[*thing/person* に] きょうみをもつ
(to take an interest (in))

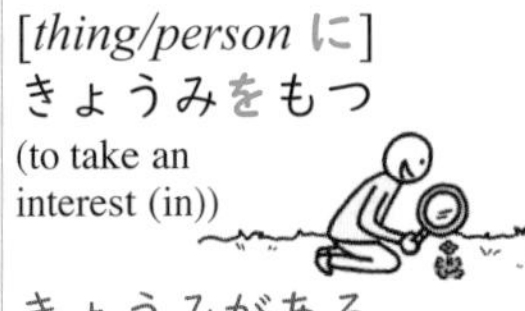

きょうみがある
(to be interested (in))

[*thing* に] チャレンジする
(to take on a challenge; to try)

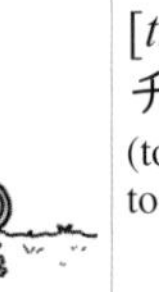

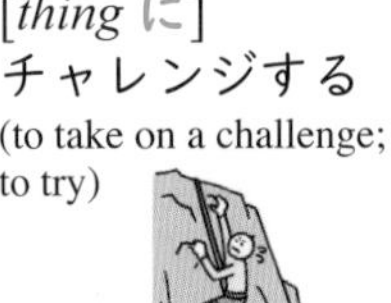

ひつよう(な)
(necessary)

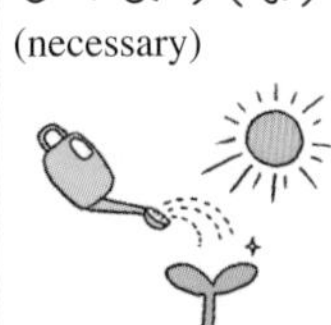

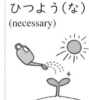

なぜ
(why)

[*home* に] あがる
(to go inside someone's home (in Japan))

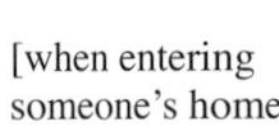

[when entering someone's home]

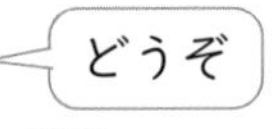

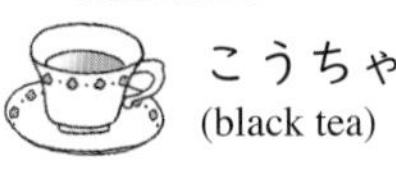

こうちゃ
(black tea)

[to signal you will soon be leaving someone's home, etc.]

おじゃましました

[when leaving someone's home, etc.]

人・場所 People and places

せいじか
(politician)

えいがかんとく
(film director)

おとこのこ (boy)
おんなのこ (girl)

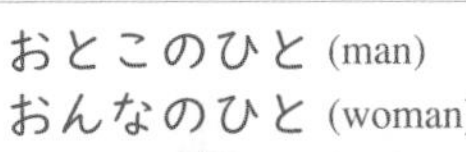

[*thing* を] りようする
(to utilize; to take advantage)

かいじょう
(venue; meeting place)

こうじょう
(factory)

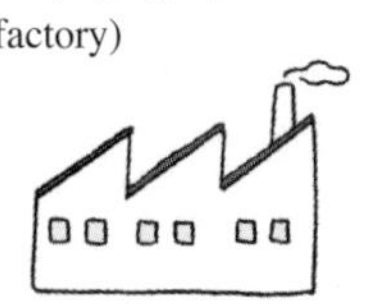

じゅうしょ
(address)

おもに
(mostly; mainly)

尊敬語(そんけいご) Honorific expressions

Ordinary expressions	Honorific expressions		Ordinary expressions	Honorific expressions	
いう	おっしゃる	おっしゃいます	する	なさる	なさいます
いく／くる	いらっしゃる	いらっしゃいます	たべる／のむ	めしあがる	めしあがります
いる	いらっしゃる	いらっしゃいます	ねる	おやすみになる	おやすみになります
～ている	～ていらっしゃる	～ていらっしゃいます	みる	ごらんになる	ごらんになります
くれる	くださる	くださいます			
～てくれる	～てくださる	～てくださいます			

生活 Daily life

[*thing* を] かぞえる
(to count)

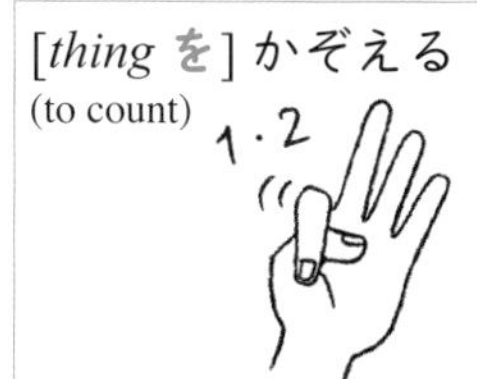

[*place* に] ならぶ
(to stand in line; to line up)

れつ
(line; row)

[*seat* に] かける
(to sit down
(on a chair, sofa, etc.))

でんわをきる
(to hang up the phone)

えんりょする
(to hold back; to refrain)

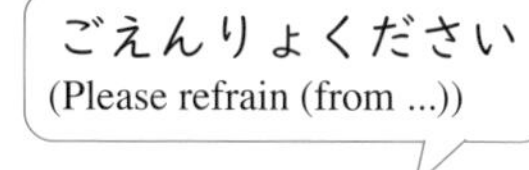

ふくろ
(bag; sack)

いっしょうけんめい(に)
(with one's utmost effort;
with all one's might)

読み物に出てくる言葉(ことば) Vocabulary for the Reading section

[*event* が]
おこる
(to happen; to take place)

[*building/thing* が]
ゆれる
(to shake; to sway)

[*thing* が]
たおれる
(to fall down)

[*tree* が]
たおれる
(to fall over)

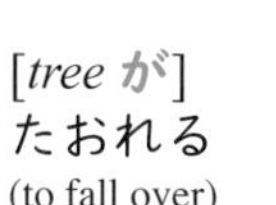

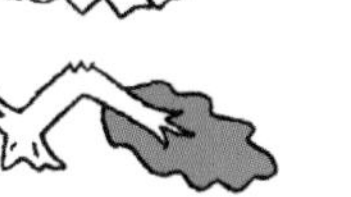

[*person* が]
たおれる
(to pass out)

はく
(to throw up;
to vomit)

[*surgery/medical exam* を]
うける
(to undergo
(a medical
procedure))

[*person* を]
だます
(to deceive;
to trick)

[*memory/thing/person* を]
おもいだす
(to recall;
to be reminded)

クモ
(spider)

ヘビ
(snake)

まんじゅう
(steamed bun with
bean paste filling)

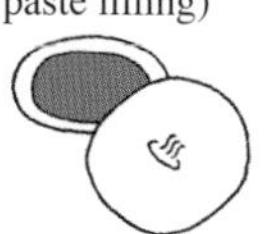

ちゅうしゃ
(injection; shot)

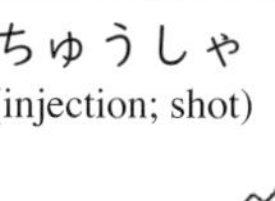

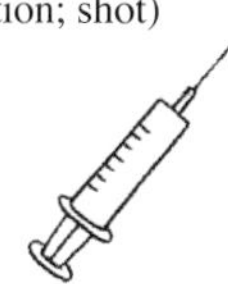

[*thing/person* が]
あつまる
(to be collected;
to gather together)

[*thing/person* を] あつめる

Lesson 19

Vocabulary List

単語(たんご)リスト

L19-5

▶ Purple words are *keigo*.
▶ **Highlighted kanji words** contain kanji you have learned previously.
▶ ＊ See vocabulary index at the end of the book for other meanings.

RU-VERBS

1	うける*	受ける	to undergo (a medical procedure) [*surgery/medical exam* を]
2	かける*		to sit down (on a chair, sofa, etc.) [*seat* に] [not used when you sit down on the floor]
3	かぞえる	数える	to count [*thing* を]
4	たおれる		to fall down [*thing* が]; to fall over [*tree* が]; to pass out [*person* が]
5	ゆれる		to shake; to sway [*building/thing* が]

U-VERBS / *U*-VERB PHRASES

6	あがる	上がる	to go inside someone's home (in Japan) [*home* に]
7	あつまる	集まる	to be collected; to gather together [*thing/person* が]
8	おこる	起こる	to happen; to take place [*event* が]
9	おもいだす	思い出す	to recall; to be reminded [*memory/thing/person* を]
10	きょうみをもつ	興味を持つ	to take an interest (in) [*thing/person* に]
11	だます		to deceive; to trick [*person* を]
12	でんわをきる	電話を切る	to hang up the phone
13	ならぶ	並ぶ	to stand in line; to line up [*place* に]
14	はく		to throw up; to vomit
15	いたす いたします		courteous expression for する [*thing* を]
16	いただく いただきます		courteous expression for 食べる and 飲む [*thing* を]
17	おる おります		courteous expression for いる [*place* に]
18	～ておる ～ております		courteous expression for ～ている
19	まいる まいります	参る	courteous expression for 行く and 来る [*place* に]
20	もうす もうします	申す	courteous expression for 言う [*name* と]
21	いらっしゃる いらっしゃいます		honorific expression for 行く, 来る, and いる [*place* に]
22	～ていらっしゃる ～ていらっしゃいます		honorific expression for ～ている
23	おっしゃる おっしゃいます		honorific expression for 言う [*sentence/name* と]
24	おやすみになる おやすみになります	お休みになる	honorific expression for ねる
25	くださる くださいます		honorific expression for くれる [*thing* を]
26	～てくださる ～てくださいます		honorific expression for ～てくれる
27	ごらんになる ごらんになります	ご覧になる	honorific expression for 見る [*thing* を]
28	なさる なさいます		honorific expression for する [*thing* を]
29	めしあがる めしあがります		honorific expression for 食べる and 飲む [*thing* を]

SURU-VERBS

30	えんりょする	遠慮する	to hold back; to refrain
31	じこしょうかいする	自己紹介する	to introduce oneself [*person* に]
32	チャレンジする		to take on a challenge; to try [*thing* に]
33	りようする	利用する	to utilize; to take advantage [*thing* を]

NA-ADJECTIVE

34	ひつよう	必要	necessary

NOUNS

35	えいがかんとく	映画監督	film director
36	おとこのこ	男の子	boy
37	おんなのこ	女の子	girl
38	かいじょう	会場	venue; meeting place
39	クモ		spider
40	けいご	敬語	*keigo*; honorific language
41	こうじょう	工場	factory
42	こうちゃ	紅茶	black tea
43	じゅうしょ	住所	address
44	せいじか	政治家	politician
45	ちゅうしゃ	注射	injection; shot
46	ふくろ	袋	bag; sack
47	ヘビ		snake
48	まんじゅう		steamed bun with bean paste filling
49	れつ	列	line; row

DEMONSTRATIVES

50	こちら		this; here; this way; this person [polite equivalent of これ／ここ／この人]
51	そちら		that; there; that way; that person [polite equivalent of それ／そこ／その人]
52	あちら		that over there; over there; that way over there; that person over there [polite equivalent of あれ／あそこ／あの人]

ADVERBS

53	いっしょうけんめい(に)		with one's utmost effort; with all one's might
54	おもに	主に	mostly; mainly

QUESTION WORDS

55	いかが		how [polite equivalent of どう]
56	どちら*		where; which way [polite equivalent of どこ]
57	なぜ		why [used with no emotional tone]

OTHER WORDS AND PHRASES

58	おじゃまします		[polite greeting used when entering someone's home, etc.]
	おじゃましました		[polite greeting used when leaving someone's home, etc.]
59	そろそろしつれいします	そろそろ失礼します	[polite greeting used to signal you will soon be leaving someone's home, etc.]

Lesson 19

Polite phrases you often hear at restaurants, stores, etc.

1	いらっしゃい／いらっしゃいませ	Welcome!
2	何名様(なんめいさま)でしょうか	How many (people in your party)?
3	よろしいですか／よろしいでしょうか	Is it/that/this alright? [polite equivalent of いいですか]
4	申(もう)し訳(わけ)ございません	I am very sorry.
5	少々(しょうしょう)お待(ま)ちください	Please wait a moment.
6	ございます	courteous expression for あります **Ex.** お手洗いはこちらにございます。 The restroom is this way.
7	～でございます	courteous expression for です **Ex.** メニューでございます。 Here is our menu.

▶ *Special reading

292	覚 覚 覚	カク	味覚(みかく) taste [sense]
		おぼ(える) さ(ます) さ(める)	覚える(おぼ) to memorize　目を覚ます(め さ) to wake (oneself) up　目覚まし時計*(めざ どけい) alarm clock
			目が覚める(め さ) to wake up
to memorize; to awaken			覚覚覚覚覚覚覚覚覚覚覚覚
293	貸 貸 貸	タイ	賃貸(ちんたい) lease; rental
		か(す)	貸す(か) to lend
to lend			貸貸貸貸貸貸貸貸貸貸貸貸
294	借 借 借	シャク シャッ	借家(しゃくや) rented house　借金(しゃっきん) debt
		か(りる)	借りる(か) to borrow　借り物(か もの) borrowed item
to borrow			借借借借借借借借借借
295	待 待 待	タイ	期待する(きたい) to expect; to hope for　招待する(しょうたい) to invite
		ま(つ)	待つ(ま) to wait　お待たせ！(ま) Sorry I kept you waiting.
			待ち合わせ(ま あ) meeting up; meetup
to wait			待待待待待待待待待
296	落 落 落	ラク	落語(らくご) traditional Japanese comic storytelling　落語家(らくごか) *rakugo* storyteller
			段落(だんらく) paragraph　落選する(らくせん) to fail to be elected; to lose an election
		お(とす) お(ちる)	落とす(お) to drop (something)
			落ちる(お) (something) drops/falls　落ち込む(お こ) to get depressed　落ち葉(お ば) fallen leaves
to fall; to drop			落落落落落落落落落落落落
297	違 違 違	イ	違反する(いはん) to violate (a law, etc.)　違法(な)(いほう) illegal
		ちが(える) ちが(う)	間違える(まちが) to make a mistake
			違う(ちが) to be different　間違い(まちが) mistake; error　違い(ちが) difference
to differ			違違違違違違違違違違違違違
298	死 死 死	シ	死(し) death　死語(しご) obsolete word; outdated phrase
			必死(の)(ひっし) desperate; frantic
		し(ぬ)	死ぬ(し) to die　死神(しにがみ) The Angel of Death
to die			死死死死死死

299	多	many; much	タ	多数決（たすうけつ） majority vote　多分（たぶん） maybe; probably　多様（たよう）(な) diverse
			おお(い)	多い（おおい） (there are/one has) a lot; numerous; plentiful
				多く（おおく）のNoun many/a lot of Noun(s); most Nouns
300	少	few; little	ショウ	少々（しょうしょう） a little [formal]　少女（しょうじょ） young girl　少年（しょうねん） young boy
			すく(ない)	少ない（すくない） (there are/one has) not much; little; few
			すこ(し)	少し（すこし） a few; a little　少し（すこし）のNoun a few/a little Noun(s)　もう少し（すこし） a little more
301	工	craft	コウ	工学（こうがく） engineering [field of study]　工場（こうじょう） factory
			ク	工業（こうぎょう） industry; manufacturing　伝統工芸（でんとうこうげい） traditional craftsmanship
				人工（じんこう）(の) man-made　人工的（じんこうてき）(な) artificial　大工（だいく） carpenter
302	主	main	シュ	主語（しゅご） subject [grammar]　ご主人（しゅじん） someone's husband　主人公（しゅじんこう） main character
				主婦（しゅふ） housewife　民主主義（みんしゅしゅぎ） democracy
			おも / ぬし	主に（おもに） mostly; mainly　主な（おもな） main; leading; major　飼い主（かいぬし） pet owner
303	員	member	イン	会社員（かいしゃいん） company employee; office worker　駅員（えきいん） station attendant
				会員（かいいん） member (of an association)　公務員（こうむいん） civil servant　全員（ぜんいん） all members
				店員（てんいん） store clerk　部員（ぶいん） member (of a club)　議員（ぎいん） legislator; Diet/Congress member
304	去	gone	キョ / コ	去年（きょねん） last year　過去（かこ） past
			さ(る)	去る（さる） to leave [formal]
305	風	wind; air; appearance	フウ / フ	台風（たいふう） typhoon　扇風機（せんぷうき） electric fan　風景（ふうけい） scenery　風刺（ふうし）する to satirize
				洋風（ようふう） western style　和風（わふう） Japanese style　(お)風呂（ふろ）に入る（はいる） to take a bath
			かぜ	風（かぜ） wind　風邪（かぜ）をひく* to catch a cold
306	経	to pass through	ケイ	経験（けいけん）する to experience　経営（けいえい）する to manage (a business, etc.)　経済（けいざい） economy
				経済学（けいざいがく） economics [field of study]　神経科学（しんけいかがく） neuroscience [field of study]
			た(つ)	経つ（たつ） (time) passes

Lesson 19

307 春	シュン	春分の日(しゅんぶんのひ) the spring equinox
	はる	春(はる) spring　春休み(はるやすみ) spring break　春学期(はるがっき) spring semester
spring	春春春春春春春春春	

308 夏	カ ゲ	初夏(しょか) early summer　夏至(げし) the summer solstice
	なつ	夏(なつ) summer　夏休み(なつやすみ) summer break　夏学期(なつがっき) summer semester
summer	夏夏夏夏夏夏夏夏夏夏	

309 秋	シュウ	秋分の日(しゅうぶんのひ) the autumn equinox
	あき	秋(あき) fall; autumn　秋休み(あきやすみ) fall break　秋学期(あきがっき) fall semester
fall	秋秋秋秋秋秋秋秋秋	

310 冬	トウ	冬至(とうじ) the winter solstice
	ふゆ	冬(ふゆ) winter　冬休み(ふゆやすみ) winter break　冬学期(ふゆがっき) winter semester
winter	冬冬冬冬冬	

新しい読み方

The following are new readings for kanji that you have already learned. Read each word aloud.

1) 上(あ)がる　2) 集(あつ)まる　3) 起(お)こる　4) 会場(かいじょう)　5) 工場(こうじょう)　6) 住所(じゅうしょ)　7) 台風(たいふう)

習った漢字で書ける新しい単語(たんご)

The following are other new vocabulary in this lesson that contain kanji you have already leaned. Read each word aloud.

1) 受(う)ける　2) 映画(えいが)(監督(かんとく))　3) 男(おとこ)の子(こ)　4) 女(おんな)の子(こ)　5) 思(おも)い出(だ)す
6) お休(やす)みになる　7) (興味(きょうみ)を)持(も)つ　8) 電話(でんわ)を切(き)る　9) 利用(りよう)する

練習

1 Four students are talking about their concerns. Read their concerns aloud, then write the readings for the underlined words.

1) 友達に大事な本を貸しましたが、なくされてしまいました。

2) 私はデートの日によく朝ねぼうして彼（かれ）を待たせてしまいます。どうしたら早く起きられますか。

3) 死ぬまでにやりたい五つのことは何ですか。私はずっと考えていますが、まだ決められないんです。

4) 私の行きたい大学は、授業料が高いので、お金を借りて大学に行く学生が多いそうです。でも、卒業してからお金を返すのは大変そうだから、心配しています。

2 You are looking at an online shopping site. Read the reviews for items 1)-4) aloud, then write the readings for the underlined words.

1) 単語（たんご）を覚える時、使うといいですよ。	2) 届（とど）きませんでした。住所を間違えたかもしれません。	3) 何回も落としたのに、割（わ）れませんでした。	4) 主に 落語を聞いていますが、音がきれいです。
★★★★☆	★☆☆☆☆	★★★★★	★★★★★

3 You found some interesting hashtags on social media. Read the hashtags aloud, then write the readings for the underlined words.

1) 2) 3) 4)

#秋の夕方の空
#台風の後
#風が強かった
#初めての経験
#去年の夏休み
#少しこわかった
#会社員の生活
#三年経った
#冬のファッション
#家の近くの工場の桜（さくら）
#春の雪みたい

漢字の話 The Story of Kanji

■ Kanji prefixes and suffixes

By now you understand that generally kanji are ideographic; that is, they represent meaning. As you will see in the examples below, there are some kanji that function as prefixes or suffixes in kanji compound words. 不 is an example of a prefix that serves as a negative marker; it carries the meaning of "not." 家 is a suffix used to indicate that the kanji compound word denotes a profession. Knowing prefixes and suffixes such as these will help you enhance your kanji vocabulary.

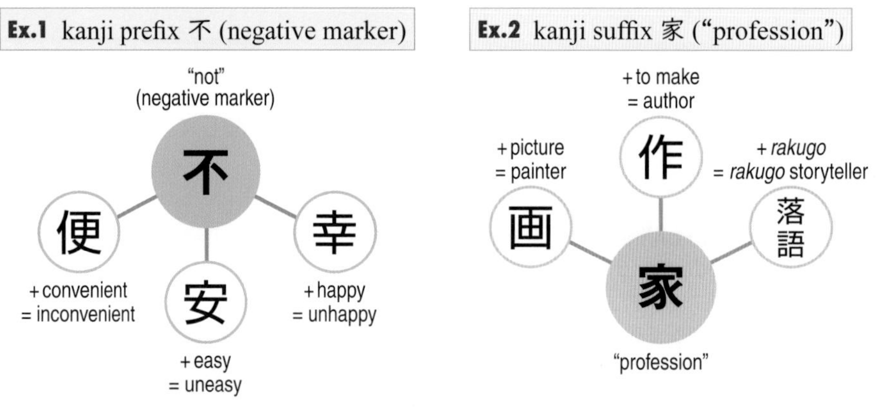

練習

1)～5)の漢字の言葉(ことば)の中には、同じ漢字 (prefix/suffix) が一つあります。その漢字を探(さが)して、意味を考えてください。

	言葉(ことば)	Prefix/Suffix	意味
Ex.	毎日　毎週　毎月(まいつき)　毎年　毎回(まいかい)	毎	every
1)	本屋　花屋　ピザ屋　魚屋　肉屋		
2)	最悪　最近　最新(さいしん)　最古(さいこ)　最高(さいこう)		
3)	会社員　部員(ぶいん)　店員(てんいん)　教員(きょういん)		
4)	社長　学長　校長(こうちょう)　町長(ちょうちょう)　会長(かいちょう)		
5)	旅行用(りょこうよう)　勉強用(べんきょうよう)　仕事用(しごとよう)　そうじ用(よう)		

文法（ぶんぽう）

1 Introduction to *keigo*

In this lesson, we will study *keigo*, or extra-polite expressions. As you know, there are two basic forms in Japanese: polite forms and plain forms. Polite forms are used in polite speech, and plain forms are used in causal speech and also in certain grammatical structures. *Keigo* is yet another set of expressions that are commonly used in both spoken and written Japanese. Here, we first overview the function of *keigo* and its structure. Specific *keigo* expressions will be explained in #2-#6.

Keigo either expresses the speaker's respect for the listener (or someone the speaker talks about) or demonstrates the speaker's courtesy. Thus, it is even politer than polite forms. Just like using polite forms and plain forms properly is essential to establish and maintain good relationships with others, using *keigo* properly is highly important when its use is expected (e.g., when you talk to your teacher, your company president, or your client, or when you talk about those people). The proper use of *keigo* is an indication of how much attention the speaker is paying to the relationships between the speaker and the listener (or the person the speaker is talking about).

There are three major categories in *keigo*: honorific expressions, humble expressions, and courteous expressions. (Here, "expressions" include productive forms and special words.)

(i) **Honorific expressions**: Expressions that are used when the speaker talks about an action/state of someone for whom the speaker wants to show respect, whether the listener or some other third party (e.g., when you talk to a famous professor about his/her research).

(ii) **Humble expressions**: Expressions that are used when the speaker talks about their own action that involves someone for whom the speaker wants to show respect, whether the listener or some other third party (e.g., when you offer help to your company executive).

(iii) **Courteous expressions**: Expressions that are used when the speaker talks very politely about their own action/state that does not involve the listener (e.g., when you introduce yourself to a job interviewer) or the action/state of something else (e.g., when you tell the listener that the taxi has arrived).

Form/expression		Showing:	Talking about:	Subject	Examples
Plain forms			anyone/anything	anyone/ anything	行く; 大きい; 上手だ; 先生だ
Polite forms		politeness to the listener	anyone/anything	anyone/ anything	行きます; 大きいです; 上手です; 先生です
Keigo (Extra-polite expressions)	Honorific expressions	respect to the listener or a third person	an action/state of the listener or a third person (e.g., asking about the listener's travel schedule)	the listener or a third person	いらっしゃいます; お帰りになります; お忙しいです; お上手です; ご病気です
	Humble expressions	respect to the listener or a third person	the speaker's own action (e.g., offering help to the listener)	the speaker	いただきます (receive); お見せします; ご説明します
	Courteous expressions	extra politeness to the listener	· the speaker's own action or state (e.g., self-introduction) · the action/state of something	the speaker, the speaker's possession (e.g., my name, my major), etc.	参ります; 申します; ～でございます

Lesson 19

Note that when referring to a possession of the listener or someone else for whom the speaker wants to show respect, the prefixes お or ご are used. **Exs.** (先生(せんせい)の) お仕事(しごと); お時間(じかん); ご研究(けんきゅう)

In what follows, we will study the forms and meanings of commonly used *keigo* expressions. Some of the expressions introduced here are not for you to produce at this point of your Japanese studies. Rather, they are introduced so that you will be able to understand them when you encounter them in various situations. The goals for *keigo* production in this lesson are: (1) to be able to introduce yourself in a formal setting using courteous expressions; (2) to be able to ask questions using honorific expressions; (3) to familiarize yourself with polite offers and other common phrasing involving humble expressions; and (4) to be able to understand common public announcements and signs that contain *keigo*.

Keigo forms of nouns and adjectives are not introduced here. For them, see 言語(げんご)ノート (Language Note): *Keigo* forms of nouns and adjectives (p.346).

2 Courteous expressions

[2]

		Courteous verb
初(はじ)めまして。	赤井圭太(あかいけいた)と	申(もう)します。
How do you do? I'm Keita Akai. (lit. I call [myself] Keita Akai.)		
日本(にほん)の大阪(おおさか)から		参(まい)りました。
I am (lit. came) from Osaka, Japan.		

You can introduce yourself using courteous expressions. These expressions are used when you talk about yourself to someone formally and very politely (e.g., when you introduce yourself at job interviews, business meetings) and when you give formal presentations. Courteous expressions are also used when you talk about the action or state of something else (e.g., when you tell the listener that something is coming, where something is).

The following is a list of common courteous expressions:

Ordinary expressions	Courteous expressions (*masu*-form)
Verbs	
行(い)く・来(く)る	参(まい)ります
する	いたします
言(い)う	申(もう)します
いる	おります
食(た)べる・飲(の)む	いただきます
ある	ございます*

Auxiliaries	
(～て)いる	(～て)おります
～だ	～でございます*

* (～で)ございます is commonly used by people like hotel clerks and shop attendants. Thus, you need to understand it, but you do not need to use it at this point.

Exs. (1) <自己紹介で>

初めまして。スミスと申します。*Nice to meet you. I'm Smith.*

ゴーブル大学で日本の歴史を専攻しております。

I am majoring in Japanese history at Goble University.

どうぞよろしくお願いいたします。*It's a pleasure to meet you.*

(2) A: コーヒーをどうぞ。*Here is your coffee.*

B: ありがとうございます。いただきます。*Thank you very much. (lit.) [I'll humbly] drink [it].*

Note that the plain forms, *te*-forms, and *masu*-stems (i.e., V-*masu*) of courteous expressions are not commonly used in conversation. For example, the following sentences are unnatural:

?? 私はまだニューヨークに参ったことがありません。

→ 私はまだニューヨークに行ったことがありません。 *I haven't been to New York yet.*

?? 昨日、友達と一緒に料理をいたしてとても楽しかったです。

→ 昨日、友達と一緒に料理をしてとても楽しかったです。

Yesterday, I cooked together with my friend and had a very good time.

?? 来年、日本に留学いたしたいです。

→ 来年、日本に留学したいです。 *I'd like to study abroad in Japan next year.*

3 ～でしょうか [Extra-polite question]

[3-a]

	V-plain	
会議は５時までに	終わる	でしょうか。
Will the meeting be over by five?		

[3-b]

	Adj(*i*)/Adj(*na*)/N *	
先生、明日のテストは	難しい	でしょうか。
Professor, is tomorrow's test difficult?		

* The forms before でしょうか are provided on the next page.

You can ask questions very politely using the extra-polite question ending でしょうか instead of using ますか and ですか. For example, you can say [3-a] to your boss when you are a little hesitant to check if the meeting will be over by five, and thus want to ask this question more politely than usual. Similarly, you can say [3-b] to your teacher when you want to ask this question more politely than usual for some reason.

The forms before でしょうか are as follows:

Verbs	plain form	+ でしょうか	食べるでしょうか 食べたでしょうか	食べないでしょうか 食べなかったでしょうか
I-adjectives	plain form		高いでしょうか 高かったでしょうか	高くないでしょうか 高くなかったでしょうか
Na-adjectives / nouns +だ	*Na*-adjectives / nouns +∅／じゃない		静かでしょうか* 静かだったでしょうか	静かじゃないでしょうか 静かじゃなかったでしょうか
	Na-adjectives / nouns +だった／じゃなかった		休みでしょうか* 休みだったでしょうか	休みじゃないでしょうか 休みじゃなかったでしょうか

*だ is not used before でしょうか. That is, ～だでしょうか is an ungrammatical form.

Exs. (1) 部長、あのう、次のミーティングは何曜日でしょうか。
Uh, sir (lit. department head), what day of the week is the next meeting?

(2) 先生、今日の宿題を明日出してもいいでしょうか。
Professor, may I submit today's homework tomorrow?

(3) <At a tourist information desk>
金閣寺に行きたいんですが、どのバスに乗ればいいでしょうか。
I'd like to go to [the temple] Kinkaku-ji. Which bus should I take?

The politer form of いいですか is いいでしょうか. If you use よろしい instead of いい (i.e., よろしいでしょうか), the question becomes even more polite.

Ex. (4) 部長、明日の会議の書類です。これでよろしいでしょうか。
Ma'am (lit. department head), here is the document for tomorrow's meeting. Would this be all right? (lit. Would it be all right with this?)

4 Honorific expressions

Using honorific expressions, you can very politely talk about the action of someone for whom you want to show respect (i.e., the listener or a third person). For example, students commonly use honorific expressions when they talk about their teacher's actions. Honorific expressions are also commonly used when hotel clerks, shop workers, etc. talk to their customers.

There are several types of honorific expressions. Among them, we will learn special honorific verbs and the おV-*masu*になる form here.

4-1 Special honorific verbs

There is a set of special honorific verbs, some of which are listed below:

Ordinary verb	Special honorific verb (dictionary form)	Special honorific verb (*masu*-form)
いる・行(い)く・来(く)る	いらっしゃる	いらっしゃいます [1]
する	なさる	なさいます [1,2]
食(た)べる・飲(の)む	めしあがる	めしあがります
言(い)う	おっしゃる	おっしゃいます [1]
見(み)る	ご覧(らん)になる	ご覧(らん)になります
寝(ね)る	お休(やす)みになる	お休(やす)みになります
くれる	くださる	くださいます [1]
知(し)っている	ご存知(ぞんじ)だ [3]	ご存知(ぞんじ)です [3]

Ordinary auxiliary verb	Special honorific auxiliary verb (dictionary form)	Special honorific auxiliary verb (*masu*-form)
(～て)いる	(～て)いらっしゃる	(～て)いらっしゃいます [1]

1. The *masu*-form ending is います, not ります.
2. The honorific *masu*-form of VNする is (お／ご)VNなさいます (e.g., (お)電話(でんわ)なさいます, (ご)研究(けんきゅう)なさいます). The polite prefix お occurs with Japanese-origin words and a few kanji compound words, while ご occurs with other kanji compounds. No polite prefix is used with katakana words (e.g., ×おメールなさいます).
3. ご存知(ぞんじ) is a noun. You only need to understand this word; you do not need to learn to use it yet.

[4-a]

	Honorific verb
高田先生(たかだせんせい)は去年(きょねん)この大学(だいがく)に	いらっしゃいました。
Prof. Takada came to this university last year. / Prof. Takada was at this university last year.	

Because いらっしゃいます can mean いる, 行(い)く, or 来(く)る depending on the situation or context, [4-a] is ambiguous if it is used alone.

Exs. (1) ＜部長(ぶちょう)に＞ 明日何時(あしたなんじ)ごろ会社(かいしゃ)にいらっしゃいますか。
Around what time will you be coming to work tomorrow?

(2) ＜レストランで社長(しゃちょう)に＞ 何(なに)をめしあがりますか。*What will you have to eat?*

(3) 黒田先生(くろだせんせい)は明日(あした)のワークショップで日本語(にほんご)のオノマトペについて発表(はっぴょう)なさるそうです。*I heard that Prof. Kuroda is presenting on Japanese onomatopoeia at the workshop tomorrow.*

4-2 お V-*masu* になる

[4-b]

		V-*masu*	
山口先生(やまぐちせんせい)はもう	お	帰(かえ)り	になりましたか。
Has Prof. Yamaguchi already {left / gone home}?			

When a verb does not have a corresponding special honorific verb, おV-*masu*になる is used. However, in most cases, the おV-*masu*になる form is not used when the *masu*-stem is one syllable long (e.g., 似る).

Exs. (1) 黒田先生、この本をもうお読みになりましたか。
Prof. Kuroda, have you read this book already/yet?

(2) 社長はよくクラッシックをお聞きになるそうです。
I heard that the CEO often listens to classical music.

(3) 先生がお書きになった本を読みました。
I read the book you wrote, professor. / I read the book the professor wrote.

(4) 部長はいつもエレベーターをお使いになりません。
The department head doesn't use the elevator all the time.

4-3 なさっています・していらっしゃいます

[4-c]

		Honorific form of している
本田先生は	ロボットの研究を	なさっています／していらっしゃいます。
Prof. Honda is doing research on robots.		

Because しています consists of two parts, して and います, there are two ways to make an honorific form out of it. One uses the honorific form of して (i.e., なさって = the *te*-form of なさいます), and the other uses the honorific form of います (i.e., いらっしゃいます). "Double honorific forms" (e.g., なさっていらっしゃいます) are not commonly used.

Exs. (1) 黒田先生はよく授業を休む学生のことを心配{なさっています／していらっしゃいます}。*Prof. Kuroda worries about students who are often absent from class.*

(2) 社長は先週ヨーロッパに出張{なさっていました／していらっしゃいました}。
The CEO was on a business trip in Europe last week.

(3) 会社員A: 部長は今何を{なさっています／していらっしゃいます}か。
What is the manager doing now?

会社員B: お客様と食事を{なさっています／していらっしゃいます}。
She is dining with her guests/clients.

As mentioned above, "double honorific forms" are usually not used in expressions that involve two verbs. (4) and (5) below provide additional examples:

Exs. (4) 黒田先生はオーストラリアに留学なさったことがあります。
Prof. Kuroda has studied abroad in Australia.

(5) 黒田先生は推薦状を書いてくださいました。
Prof. Kuroda wrote a letter of recommendation for me.

Where an honorific form is used depends on the expression. In (4), for example, the verb before ことがあります is an honorific form (i.e., 留学なさった), and the final element あります is a non-honorific form. In (5), on the other hand, the final element くださいました is an honorific form, and the preceding *te*-form verb 書いて is a non-honorific one.

5 Humble expressions 

Using humble expressions, you can talk about your own actions very politely. These are different from courteous expressions in that they are used for actions that involve someone for whom you want to show respect (usually the listener, but also potentially a third person). You often use humble expressions when you talk to people such as your teachers, clients, and your company's executives. Hotel clerks and shop workers commonly use humble expressions when they talk to their customers as well.

There are two kinds of humble expressions: the おV-*masu*する form and special humble verbs.

5-1 おV-*masu*する

[5]

		V-*masu*	
先生、そのかばんを	お	持ち	します。
Professor, I'll carry that bag.			

[5] provides a sentence pattern with おV-*masu*する.

 The おV-*masu*する form is used only when the speaker's action directly involves someone for whom the speaker wants to show respect, as in [5]. Thus, the following sentences are ungrammatical:

× 私は毎日１キロお泳ぎします。 → 私は毎日１キロ泳ぎます。
I swim one kilometer every day.

× 先生、（私は）お帰りします。 → 先生、（私は）失礼します。*Professor, I'm leaving.*

For *suru*-verbs, お／ごVNします is used (e.g., 電話する → お電話します; 説明する → ご説明します). お occurs with Japanese-origin words and a few common kanji compound words (e.g., お願いする, お電話する), while ご occurs with other kanji compounds (e.g., ご説明する, ご案内する). No polite prefix is used with katakana words (e.g., ×おメールします).

Exs. (1) 黒田先生、お借りしていた本をお返しします。ありがとうございました。
Prof. Kuroda, I'm returning the book that I borrowed from you. Thank you!

(2) 今日は新しいプロジェクトについてご説明します。
Today I'm going to explain our new project.

(3) <To a colleague>
私が社長を駅までお送りするよ。*I am going to take the CEO to the station.*

You can use おV-*masu*しましょうか and お／ごVNしましょうか to offer help to your superiors.

Exs. (4) 部長、コーヒーをおいれしましょうか。*Shall I make coffee, sir (lit. department head)?*

(5) キャンパスをご案内しましょうか。*Shall I show you around the campus?*

5-2 Special humble verbs

Special humble verbs that are commonly used are listed below:

Ordinary verb	Special humble verb (dictionary form)	Special humble verb (*masu*-form)
聞(き)く (to ask)・行(い)く	うかがう	うかがいます
もらう	いただく	いただきます
あげる	さしあげる	さしあげます

Ordinary auxiliary verb	Special humble auxiliary verb (dictionary form)	Special humble auxiliary verb (*masu*-form)
(～て)もらう	(～て)いただく	(～て)いただきます

Exs. (1) 先生(せんせい)、今日(きょう)の午後(ごご)オフィスにうかがってもよろしいでしょうか。

Professor, may I come (lit. go) to your office this afternoon?

(2) 日本(にほん)に留学(りゅうがく)するので、黒田先生(くろだせんせい)に推薦状(すいせんじょう)を書(か)いていただきました。

As I will study abroad in Japan, I had Prof. Kuroda write me a recommendation letter.

6 おV-*masu*ください・お／ごVNください "Would you please V?"

[6-a]

		V-*masu*	
ここで	お	待(ま)ち	ください。
Would you please wait here?			

[6-b]

		VN	
何(なに)かございましたら、メールで	ご	連絡(れんらく)	ください。
If you have any issues (lit. there is something), would you please contact me via email?			

You can make a polite request using おV-*masu*ください, as in [6-a], or お／ごVNください, as in [6-b]. These honorific expressions are used when you make a request for an action to someone to whom you want to be very polite to (e.g., your teachers, customers, your company's executives).

Exs. (1) ＜お寺(てら)で＞ くつをぬいでお入(はい)りください。

Please take your shoes off before entering. (lit. Please take off your shoes and enter.)

(2) <On a box of free maps at a visitor's center>

ご自由(じゆう)にお取(と)りください。*Please feel free to take one. (lit. Please take one freely.)*

(3) ＜美術館(びじゅつかん)で＞ お写真(しゃしん)はご遠慮(えんりょ)ください。*Please refrain from photography.*

話しましょう

▶ **Words written in purple** are new words introduced in this lesson.

できる I　Introduce yourself appropriately in a formal setting.

できるI-A　Courteous expressions

1 Let's practice changing ordinary verbs into courteous expressions used in a formal setting.

Ex. 食べます → いただきます 

1) 行きます　2) 来ます　3) します　4) 言います　5) います
6) 飲みます　7) しています　8) 住んでいます　9) お願いします

2 Let's learn how to exchange Japanese business cards, or *meishi*. Write your name on a small piece of paper before starting the activity.

○○と申します。どうぞよろしくお願いいたします。
△△と申します。こちらこそ、どうぞよろしくお願いいたします。

How to exchange *meishi*

1) Small quick bow
2) Exchange *meishi*
3) Receive with both hands
4) Hold at chest height

3 Riemann is introducing himself to a Japanese guest speaker who came to his class.

Step 1 Suppose you are Riemann. Give a formal self-introduction using courteous expressions for the underlined parts of the sentences.

なぞとき：brainteaser　L19-7

① 始めのあいさつ＋名前	初めまして。リーマン・ゴルドと<u>言います</u>。
② ～年生＋専攻	一年生で、数学を専攻し<u>ています</u>。
③ 出身	出身はインドのニューデリーです。 or インドのニューデリーから<u>来ました</u>。
④ 趣味や好きなこと	趣味はなぞときと漢字を覚えることです。
⑤ 他の情報	高校の時、日本語の文字に興味を持ったので、日本語の勉強を始めました。
⑥ 終わりのあいさつ	どうぞよろしく<u>お願いします</u>。

Group Work

Step 2 Now, introduce yourself using the format from Step 1 as a model.

4 Your Japanese friend has brought you to their parents' house. Practice useful expressions for the occasion.

Step 1 First, choose the most appropriate response to each of the following utterances. L19-8

玄関(げんかん)：entrance (to a house); entryway

Ex. ＜玄関(げんかん)で＞ いらっしゃい。どうぞ上(あ)がってください。 •	• ありがとうございます。いただきます。
1) ＜部屋で＞ お茶をどうぞ。 •	• こんにちは。おじゃまします。
2) ＜部屋で＞ ゆっくりしていってくださいね。 •	• はい。そろそろ失礼(しつれい)します。
3) ＜部屋で＞ もう帰るんですか。 •	• ありがとうございます。
4) ＜玄関(げんかん)で＞ 気をつけて帰ってくださいね。 •	• はい。おじゃましました。

(Ex. is connected by a line to "こんにちは。おじゃまします。")

Step 2 To make a good impression on your friend's parents, respond politely to their questions and comments below. L19-9

Ex. ご両親：いらっしゃい。
どうぞ上(あ)がってください。

Ex. あなた：こんにちは。
おじゃまします。

1) お茶とお菓子(かし)をどうぞ。
2) 大学では何を勉強しているんですか。
3) ずっと○○に住んでいるんですか。
4) ゆっくりしていってくださいね。

－－－－－－－－－－ <After a while> －－－－－－－－－－

5) もう帰るんですか。
6) 気をつけて帰ってくださいね。

できる II Use *keigo* to ask questions politely to someone of a higher status or someone you are meeting for the first time.

できるII-A Extra-polite question ～でしょうか

1 Let's practice how to ask questions politely.

Step 1 Make extra-polite questions using the cues provided. L19-10

Ex. 終(お)わる？

	affirmative	negative
non-past	終わるでしょうか	終わらないでしょうか
past	終わったでしょうか	終わらなかったでしょうか

1) できる？ 2) 見(み)える？ 3) 聞(き)こえる？ 4) ある？ 5) 来(く)る？ 6) 多(おお)い？
7) いい？ 8) 問題(もんだい)？ 9) 必要(ひつよう)？

Step 2 Change the following commonly asked questions into their extra-polite equivalents.

Ex. 今いいですか → 今いいでしょうか (L19-11)

1) 今話してもいいですか　2) どうすればいいですか　3) どこでできますか

4) いつまでにしなくてはいけませんか　5) いつ行かなくてはいけませんか

6) なぜですか　7) 届きましたか　8) いくらでしたか

2 Think about some possible questions that you may ask your teachers before, during, and after class. Person A asks the questions, and person B pretends to be a teacher and answers A's questions appropriately.

Possible questions	～てもいいですか [permission]　～なくてはいけませんか [obligation] ～んですが、{どうすればいいですか／Q-word がいいですか} [advice]

Ex. A: 先生、英語で質問してもいいでしょうか。

B: はい、いいですよ。or いいえ、日本語で話してください。

3 What would you want to know if you were going to live in or travel to Japan? Think of at least two Japan-related questions to post on an internet forum, then share them with your partner.

Ex. A: 私の一つ目の質問は「12月の京都はどのぐらい寒いでしょうか」です。
二つ目は「すもうに興味を持っているんですが、いつ、どこで見られるでしょうか」です。 <Continue>

B: どちらもいい質問ですね。私の一つ目の質問は… <Continue>

できるII-B Honorific expressions

1 Let's practice basic honorific expressions. (L19-12)

A. Special honorific verbs

Ex.1 来る → いらっしゃる → いらっしゃいます

Ex.2 している → していらっしゃる → していらっしゃいます

1) いる　2) 行く　3) する　4) 食べる　5) 飲む　6) 言う　7) 見る　8) くれる

9) 寝る　10) 説明する　11) 出張する　12) 研究している　13) 住んでいる

B. おV-*masu*になる

Ex. 話す → お話しになる → お話しになります

1) 出かける　2) 考える　3) 聞く　4) 読む　5) 書く　6) 会う　7) 使う　8) 作る　9) 帰る

C. V-*te*くださる

Ex. 言う → 言ってくださる → 言ってくださいます

1) ほめる　2) 一緒に考える　3) 話を聞く　4) はげます　5) 一緒に喜ぶ

6) する　7) 来る

2 Using honorific expressions, talk about the action or state of someone for whom you want to show respect. L19-13

Step 1 You are doing an internship at a Japanese company. Talk about the CEO using the appropriate honorific expressions.

Ex.1 社長は７時ごろ会社に**いらっしゃいます**。　ラジオ体操(たいそう)：exercises guided by radio broadcast

Ex.1 ７時ごろ会社に来ます

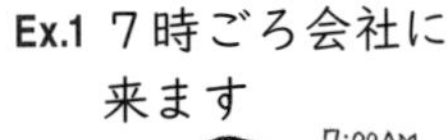

1) 紅茶(こうちゃ)を飲みます

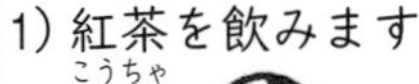

2) 世界のニュースを見ます

3) みんなとラジオ体操(たいそう)をします

4) あまり自分のオフィスにいません

5) 時々海外に出張(しゅっちょう)します

6) みんなにおみやげをくれます

7) 文句(もんく)を言いません

8) よくみんなと昼ご飯を食べます

9) お子さんがいます

10) 会社の近くに住んでいます

11) 12時ごろ寝(ね)ます

Ex.2 社長はフランス語が**お分かりになります**。

Ex.2 フランス語が分かります

12) 英語と中国語を話します

13) 時々仕事で政治家(せいじか)に会います

14) 毎月本を何冊(さつ)も読みます

15) クラシックを聞きます

16) エレベーターに乗りません

17) いつも階段(かいだん)を使います

18) この会社を作りました

19) 本を書きました

20) 今日はもう帰りました

Step 2 Now, talk with your partner about an action/a state of your teacher or your boss at work.

Ex. 経済(けいざい)の先生はたいてい授業の10分前にクラスにいらっしゃいます。
それから…　<Continue>

3 (Information gap) A VIP from another company, President Son, will be visiting your company next week, and you and your colleague will be attending to his needs during the visit. Confirm the schedule for the visit with your partner.

Ex. A: ソン社長は何時に空港にお着きになりますか。

B: 水曜日の午後６時にお着きになります。

Student A

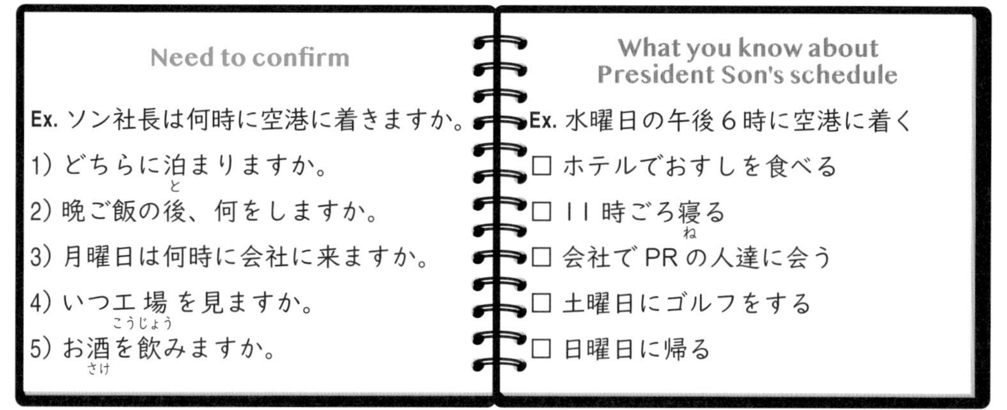

Need to confirm
Ex. ソン社長は何時に空港に着きますか。
1) どちらに泊(と)まりますか。
2) 晩ご飯の後、何をしますか。
3) 月曜日は何時に会社に来ますか。
4) いつ工場(こうじょう)を見ますか。
5) お酒(さけ)を飲みますか。
What you know about President Son's schedule
Ex. 水曜日の午後６時に空港に着く
□ ホテルでおすしを食べる
□ 11時ごろ寝(ね)る
□ 会社でPRの人達に会う
□ 土曜日にゴルフをする
□ 日曜日に帰る

Student B ➡p.345

4 You are going to attend a Japanese language exchange with business people in your city.

Step 1 Practice asking the following questions using honorific expressions for the parts of the sentences with **continuous underlines** and extra-polite questions ending in でしょうか for the parts with **dotted underlines**. L19-14

Ex.1 お名前は何と言いますか。 → お名前は何とおっしゃいますか。

Ex.2 海外の生活はいかがですか。 → 海外の生活はいかがでしょうか。

1) 今、どちらに住んでいますか。
2) どんな（お）仕事をしていますか。
3) 週末はよく出かけますか。
4) 何かスポーツをしますか。
5) どんな音楽をよく聞きますか。
6) 最近、何か映画を見ましたか。
7) 大学では何を専攻(せんこう)しましたか。
8) よく日本に帰りますか。
9) こちらに来て一番おどろいたことは何ですか。
10) 日本食の店はどこがおすすめですか。
11) おすすめの日本食がありますか。
12) your own

Step 2 Now you are at the language exchange. In pairs, ask questions politely to someone of a higher status you met there. You may use the questions in Step 1. When answering the questions, you do not need to use *keigo*.

Ex. A: あの、○○さんは今、どちらに住んでいらっしゃいますか。

B: この近くに住んでいます。△△さんは？ <Continue>

ROLE PLAY

5 You have a chance to interview a famous person for your school newspaper. Conduct a good interview.

Step 1 First, ask your partner which famous person they will be (e.g., athlete, movie star, author, politician, scientist). Then, think of some interesting questions for that person, who no matter their actual abilities can for some reason speak Japanese in this scenario.

インタビューする人：＿＿＿＿＿＿＿＿＿＿

Q1.＿＿＿＿＿＿＿＿＿＿＿＿＿＿＿　Q2.＿＿＿＿＿＿＿＿＿＿＿＿＿＿＿

Q3.＿＿＿＿＿＿＿＿＿＿＿＿＿＿＿　Q4.＿＿＿＿＿＿＿＿＿＿＿＿＿＿＿

Step 2 Conduct the interview following the interview format below.

Role A Interviewer: interviews B using *keigo*

Role B Famous person: answers A's questions

Ex. インタビューする人：金高監督（有名な映画監督）

Greeting	A: 初めまして。ゴーブル大学のブルーノと申します。どうぞよろしくお願いいたします。 B: 映画監督の金高です。よろしくお願いします。
Questions using appropriate *keigo*	A: 金高監督は大学で映画の勉強をなさっていましたか。 B: はい、私は子どもの時から動画や映画を見るのが大好きで、大学では映画研究を専攻していました。 A: そうですか。最近はよくどんな映画をご覧になりますか。 B: そうですね、主にアジアの映画を見ます。 <Continue>
Gratitude	A: 今日は質問に答えてくださって、どうもありがとうございました。 B: こちらこそ、ありがとうございました。楽しかったです。

6 Let's learn some useful phrases for shopping and eating out in Japan. Listen to the questions on the *TOBIRA* website and take an educated guess at the most appropriate response to each from the box below. L19-15

Expressions to use ・はい。　・はい、お願いします。　・〇〇をお願いします。
・いいえ、{いりません／だいじょうぶです}。

A. ＜コンビニで＞

B. ＜レストランで＞

Familiarize yourself with polite offers and other common phrasing involving humble expressions.

できるIII-A Humble expressions

1 To facilitate your comprehension, let's practice some basic humble expressions.

Ex.1 聞(き)く → お聞(き)きする → お聞(き)きします

1) 答(こた)える　2) 調(しら)べる　3) 話(はな)す　4) 待(ま)つ　5) 会(あ)う　6) 送(おく)る　7) 持(も)つ
8) 手伝(てつだ)う　9) 貸(か)す　10) 電話(でんわ)する

Ex.2 紹介(しょうかい)する → ご紹介(しょうかい)する → ご紹介(しょうかい)します

1) 説明(せつめい)する　2) 案内(あんない)する　3) 連絡(れんらく)する

2 Suppose you are doing an internship at a Japanese company.

Step 1 Your *senpai*, Ichikawa-san, seems to need some help. Say you will do the work for her.

Ex. 市川(いちかわ)さん、(私が) 仕事をお手伝(てつだ)いします。

Ex. 仕事を手伝(てつだ)う

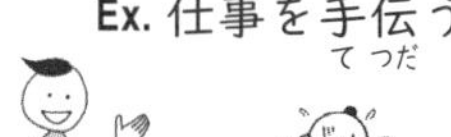

1) 荷物を持つ

2) 必要(ひつよう)なことを調べる

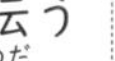

3) 書類(しょるい)を作る

4) お話を聞く

5) 電話を貸(か)す

6) 仕事の後、家まで送る

7) 使い方を教える

8) お客様(きゃく)を案内(あんない)する

9) このデータについて説明(せつめい)する

Step 2 Using the same cues as in Step 1, offer help to your *senpai* politely.

Ex. A: 市川(いちかわ)さん、よかったら、仕事をお手伝(てつだ)いしましょうか。
B: ありがとう。じゃ、お願(ねが)い(します)。　(← Respond appropriately)

3 Suppose you want to post a short video on social media.

Step 1 Practice the following useful phrases for your presentation using humble expressions.

Ex. 話(はな)します → お話(はな)しします

1) 教(おし)えます　2) 見(み)せます　3) 紹介(しょうかい)します　4) 会(あ)いましょう　5) 待(ま)っています

Step 2 Choose a topic that you would like to share with others and talk about it as in the example.

Introduce yourself	**Ex.** みなさん、こんにちは。ジャンです。
Introduce the topic	今日は私が好きな美術館(びじゅつかん)について**お話しします**。
Main message + details	今日みなさんに**ご紹介(しょうかい)したい**美術館(びじゅつかん)は直島(なおしま)にある地中美術館(ちちゅうびじゅつかん)です。自然(しぜん)とアートを一緒(いっしょ)に楽しめる美術館(びじゅつかん)で、こちらがその写真です。行ったら絶対(ぜったい)に感動(かんどう)すると思うので、おすすめです。
Closing	では、次の動画で**お会いしましょう**。みなさんのコメントを**お待(ま)ちしています**。

Chichu Art Museum
Photo: FUJITSUKA Mitsumasa

できるIV Understand common public announcements and signs that contain *keigo*.

できるIV-A Polite requests おV-*masu*ください

1 Make polite requests using the following verbs, as in the examples. L19-20

Ex.1 座(すわ)る → **お座(すわ)りください**　**Ex.2** 連絡(れんらく)する → **ご連絡(れんらく)ください**

1) 入(はい)る　2) 使(つか)う　3) 読(よ)む　4) 待(ま)つ　5) 取(と)る　6) 注意(ちゅうい)する
7) (いすに) かける　8) 上(あ)がる　9) 並(なら)ぶ　10) めしあがる　11) 遠慮(えんりょ)する

2 You will see various signs in Japan.

Step 1 Match each of the following signs with the corresponding English meaning from the box below.

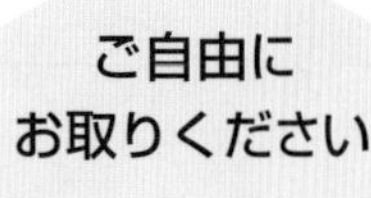

1) (a.)

セルフサービス
ご自由に
お飲みください
2) (　　)

コンセント
ご自由にお使いください

3) (　　)

4) (　　)

5) (　　)

6) (　　)

7) (　　)

お早めに
おめしあがりください
8) (　　)

a. Please feel free to take (one).　b. Please help yourself (to drinks).
c. Please refrain (from using it).　d. Please eat (it) while (it's) fresh.
e. Please enter with your shoes on.　f. Please form two lines.
g. Please feel free to use (it).　h. Please beware of the dog.

Step 2 Talk about where you think you can find these signs.

3 You are at a job interview. What should you do if you hear the following requests? Act it out.

Ex. こちらにお名前とご住所(じゅうしょ)をお書きください。

1) こちらでお待(ま)ちください。　　2) 携帯(けいたい)電話をお切りください。

3) どうぞお入りください。　　4) どうぞおかけください。

5) 面接(めんせつ)はこれで終わりです。気をつけてお帰りください。

Review

Now you can understand basic *keigo* and use simple *keigo* expressions in both speech and writing. Create a video letter to your future host family in Japan.

Read the example below, then write a script for your video letter using the example as a model.

Opening:
- introduce yourself

Body:
- reasons for studying abroad in Japan
- your interests/ questions for your host family

Closing:
- say you're excited to meet them

Ex. ホストファミリーのみなさん、初めまして。

アデリナ・マルケスと申(もう)します。私の出身(しゅっしん)は南アメリカのコロンビアです。19才(さい)です。今、ゴーブル大学の二年生で、生物学(せいぶつがく) (biology) を専攻(せんこう)しております。

私は将来(しょうらい)、日本の大学で研究したいです。早く日本語が上手になりたいので、日本に留学しようと思いました。

私は料理を作るのが大好きなので、みなさんにコロンビアの料理をご紹介(しょうかい)したいです。それから、私は日本の祭(まつ)りに興味(きょうみ)があるんですが、近くで祭(まつ)りを見ることができるでしょうか。みなさんはよくどんなことをなさいますか。

夏(なつ)にみなさんに会えるのを楽しみにしております。

お世話になりますが、どうぞよろしくお願(ねが)いいたします。

できるII-B **3** Student B

Need to confirm

Ex. ソン社長は何時に空港に着きますか。

6) 晩ご飯は何を食べますか。

7) 何時ごろ寝(ね)ますか。

8) 会社で誰(だれ)と会いますか。

9) 週末ゴルフをしますか。

10) いつ帰りますか。

What you know about President Son's schedule

Ex. 水曜日の午後6時に空港に着く

☐ スカイホテルに泊(と)まる

☐ 晩ご飯の後、ホテルで温泉(おんせん)に入る

☐ 月曜日は朝9時に会社に来る

☐ 金曜日の午後、工場(こうじょう)を見る

☐ お酒(さけ)を飲む

言語ノート Language Note *Keigo* forms of nouns and adjectives

You can make your statements and questions politer using the *keigo* (or extra-polite) forms of nouns and adjectives when you talk about the hearer's possessions/states or those of someone for whom you want to show respect. For most nouns and adjectives, the *keigo* forms can be made by attaching the polite prefix ご or お to them, as in (1) and (2). (Note that you don't use these polite forms when you talk about your own possessions/states.)

(1) a. 先生のご家族 *the professor's family* Cf. 私の家族 *my family*
    b. 社長のお話 *the president's talk* Cf. 私の話 *my talk*

(2) a. スミス先生はとてもお忙しいです。*Prof. Smith is very busy.*
        Cf. 私はとても忙しいです。*I am very busy.*
    b. 社長はゴルフがお好きです。*The president likes golf.*
        Cf. 私はゴルフが好きです。*I like golf.*

In general, the polite prefix お is used with Japanese-origin words and a few kanji compound words, and ご is used with most Chinese-origin words. Note that お is usually not used with the following words:

(i) Katakana words: ×おペン, ×おスマホ
(ii) Words that begin with お: ×お大きい, ×お遅い

The following tables provide the *keigo* forms of some nouns and adjectives. As seen here, some words do not occur with either お or ご. Rather, they have special polite forms.

Nouns	*Keigo* forms	Nouns	*Keigo* forms	Nouns	*Keigo* forms
名前	お名前	子ども	お子さん	住所	ご住所
仕事	お仕事	兄	お兄さん	出身	ご出身
電話	お電話	姉	お姉さん	趣味	ご趣味
時間	お時間	弟	弟さん	返事	ご／お返事
話	お話	妹	妹さん	(ほかの)人	(ほかの)方
国	お国	兄弟	ご兄弟	これ／ここ	こちら
家	お宅	両親	ご両親	それ／そこ	そちら
飲み物	お飲み物	家族	ご家族	あれ／あそこ	あちら

Adjectives	*Keigo* forms
忙しい	お忙しい
元気	お元気
好き	お好き
きらい	おきらい
上手	お上手
親切	ご親切

Q-words	*Keigo* forms
だれ	どなた
どこ	どちら
どう	いかが

Expression	*Keigo* form
久しぶりです	お久しぶりです

読みましょう

Identify the characters, setting, and storyline of a *rakugo* story and enjoy the humor in *rakugo*.

読み物を読む前に

1 はじめに「とびら WEB サイト」にある「落語」の動画を見ましょう。
どの動画を見てもいいですが、見た後で下の質問に答えなさい。

1）落語家は話をする時、

a. 何を着ていますか。　　　b. 何に座(すわ)って話をしていますか。

c. 小道具(こどうぐ) (prop) は何を使いますか。それは、例えばどんな物になりますか。

2）落語の動画を見て、他にどんなことに気がつきましたか。

2 落語は江戸時代(えどじだい) (the Edo Period: 1603-1868) に始まった伝統芸能(でんとうげいのう) (traditional performing art) ですが、今の若い人達にも人気があって、色々なところで楽しまれています。

1）下の①～⑤を見て、分かることを話し合いなさい。

1

『マンガでわかる落語』
春風亭昇吉［著］　誠文堂新光社

2

『じょしらく(6)<完>』
ヤス［著］　久米田康治［原作］　講談社

3

大学落語研究部
新春寄席
1月22日（日）
開場 13:30　開演 14：00
<場所> くろしお寺

4

5

ライブ配信や動画など、オンラインで楽しめる落語の情報が満載！
落語情報サイト
こばなし

2）①～⑤を説明(せつめい)している文を下の a.～e. の中から選(えら)びなさい。

a. ある大学の落語研究部の学生達のパフォーマンス。場所はお寺で、1月にある。
b. 飲み物を飲みながら、落語家の話を楽しむことができる。
c. 女の子が落語にチャレンジするまんが。まんがが人気が出たので、アニメも作られた。
d. ネットで見たり聞いたりできる落語の情報(じょうほう)が見つかる。
e. 色々な落語の話をまんがで紹介(しょうかい)してある。落語をライブで楽しむ前に読んでおくと、話が分かりやすい。

Lesson 19

読み物を読もう

読み物１　小話（短くてちょっとおもしろい話）

小話１

学生：神様、どうぞ次のテストで100点を取らせてください。

神様：そのために何でもしますか。

学生：はい、何でもします！

神様：分かりました。じゃ、勉強しなさい。

小話２

患者(patient)：先生、私、手術を受けるの、初めてなんですけど、だいじょうぶでしょうか。

医者　　　：心配しなくてもいいですよ！　私も手術をするのは今日が初めてですから！

小話３

A：本はお好きですか。

B：はい、大好きです。

A：そうですか。シェークスピアの『ロミオとジュリエット』はお読みになりましたか。

B：はい、「ロミオ」は読みましたけど、「ジュリエット」はまだです。

A：(T_T)??

1) 小話を声に出して読んでみてください。どの小話が一番おもしろいと思いましたか。

2) 小話を一つ選んで～～の部分を他の言葉に変えて、パロディを作ってみましょう。

読み物２　『まんじゅうこわい』（落語の有名な話）

読む前に自分がこわいと思うものについて話し合いなさい。それは下にありますか。

Lesson 19

まんじゅうこわい

ある日、みんながマツの家に集まって、何が一番こわいか話していました。
「僕はヘビが一番こわいよ。ヘビを見ると死にそうになる…」
「私は地震がこわい！　家がぐらぐらゆれたら、動けなくなってしまう」
「私は高い所です。高い所では、こわくて立っていられません」
「僕がこわいのは注射です。だから、絶対に医者に行きたくないです」
マツが笑いながら話を聞いているので、みんなはマツに聞きました。
「マツさんは何がこわいんですか？」
Ex.(マ)「おれ？　おれはこわいものは何もないよ」
「え、ほんと？　クモは？　お化けは？」
「クモ？　全然。お化けがいたら、死ぬまでに一度会ってみたいよ」
「え、ほんと？　すごいね、マツさんは」
「あっ、ちょっと待って。思い出した！　一つだけこわいものがある！」
「え、何？　何？」
「いやだ、言いたくない。こわすぎる」
「え、こわすぎる？　そんなにこわいものは何なの？」
「だめだ。こわくて言えない」
「お願い、教えて、教えて！」
みんながいっしょうけんめいに聞くので、マツはこわそうに答えました。
「まんじゅう。おれはまんじゅうがこわい…」
「え、まんじゅう？　あのお菓子のまんじゅうですか」
「うん。考えると、はきそうになる。オエ」
「マツさん、だいじょうぶ？」
「だいじょうぶじゃない。オエ～。まんじゅうのこと考えたら、気持ちが悪くなったから、休ませてもらうよ」
そう言うと、マツはとなりの部屋に行ってしまいました。
「マツさんはヘビもお化けもこわくないのに、まんじゅうはこわいみたいですね」
「ちょっとマツさんをこわがらせようか」
みんなは店に行ってまんじゅうをたくさん買ってきて、眠っているマツのそばに置きました。
　さて、マツが布団から顔を出すと、目の前にまんじゅうがたくさんあります。
「あ、まんじゅうだ！　わあ、こわい、こわい。もぐもぐ、すっごくこわい、パクパク…」
　マツはまんじゅうを食べ始めました。
　みんなはマツがまんじゅうがこわすぎてたおれているかもしれないと思って、となりの部屋を見てみました。すると、マツは「こわい、こわい！」と言いながら、まんじゅうをおいしそうに食べています。それを見て、みんなはマツにだまされたことに気がつきました。
「マツさん、ひどいですよ」
「マツさんが本当にこわいものはいったい何ですか」
「そうだなあ、今は[　]が一番こわい！」

動けなくなる：to freeze up
おれ：I [used typically by men to show masculinity]
そんなに：that much; to that extent
こわがらせる：to scare (someone)
さて：Now [transition word]
～から顔を出す：to show one's face out of ~
すっごく＝すごく
食べ始める：to start eating
すると：thereupon; when [they] did
いったい：(what) in the world
そうだなあ＝そうですね

読み物を読んだ後で、考えてみよう

1 落語やアニメやまんがには、オノマトペ (onomatopoeia) がたくさん使われます。オノマトペはたいていカタカナで書かれますが、ひらがなで書かれる時もあります。日本語のオノマトペには主に二つのタイプがあります。

Type 1: Mimics sounds of people, animals, objects, and natural phenomena

Type 2: Represents both physical and psychological states as well as manners of action

1) 『まんじゅうこわい』のオノマトペを探しましょう。①～④のオノマトペが文の中のどこにあるか見つけて、線を引きなさい。

① ぐらぐら　② オェ／オェ～　③ もぐもぐ　④ パクパク

2) ①～④のオノマトペは Type 1 と Type 2 のどちらだと思いますか。

3) ①～④はどういう時に使われると思いますか。下の A.～D. の中から選びなさい。

A. おいしそうにたくさん食べる　B. 何も言わないでいっしょうけんめい食べる
C. 気持ちが悪い　D. 地震で地面 (ground) や色々なものがゆれる

4) あなたの知っている言葉にもオノマトペがありますか。例えば、どんなことをどんな言葉で言いますか。

オノマトペは色々な使い方があって、ルールも難しいので、『上級へのとびら』(*TOBIRA: Gateway to Advanced Japanese*) でもっと勉強します。

2 1行目から28行目を読んで、下の質問に答えなさい。

マツのこわすぎるものは何だと思いますか。

3 29行目から44行目を読んで、下の質問に答えなさい。

1) 37行目「そう言うと」の「そう」は何を指していますか。線を引きなさい。

2) 42～44行目 みんながマツのそばにまんじゅうを置いた後で、どんなことが起こると思いますか。

4 45行目から60行目を読んで、下の質問に答えなさい。

1) 54～55行目「それを見て」の「それ」は何を指していますか。線を引きなさい。

2) 60行目 ［　　］にはどんな言葉が入ると思いますか。考えてみましょう。

5 マツはみんなとどんなスピーチスタイルで話していますか。そのことから何が分かりますか。

6 話の順番(じゅんばん)に、(　　)に番号(ばんごう)を入れなさい。

A. (　　)

B. (　　)

C. (　　)

D. (　　)

E. (　　)

F. (　　)

7 この話を声(こえ)に出(だ)して読んでみましょう。

Step 1 マツやみんなが話している文の上に、その文を話している人のマークを入れなさい。

(l.14 Ex.ⓜ) ナレーター＝ⓝ　マツ＝ⓜ　他(ほか)の人達＝ⒶⒷⒸⒹ／ⓜ(＝みんな)

Step 2 読む前に、どの人になって読むか決めなさい。一人の人が色々な人の文を読んでもいいですが、その時は違う声(こえ)と話し方で読んでみてください。

みんなで話し合ってみよう

1 60行目(ぎょうめ)の[　　]の答えは「おいしいお茶」です。自分の答えとどちらの方がおもしろいと思いますか。

2 下のa.～f.は、日本の若い人達が落語が好きな理由です。どの意見がおもしろいですか。どの意見について「なるほど」と思いますか。

落語が好きな理由

a. 話がおもしろくて分かりやすい。
b. SNSのしすぎでつかれた心をリラックスさせてくれる。
c. 落語家が一人で色々な人になって話すのがすごい。
d. 落語を聞きながら笑ったり泣いたりして、色々な気持ちが経験できる。
e. 着物を着た若い人が、昔の古い話をしゃべるのがクール！
f. 落語は言葉(ことば)の情報(じょうほう)が多すぎないから、自由に想像(そうぞう)(to imagine)できて楽しい。

自分の話を作ってみよう

あなたの『〇〇こわい』という話を作ってみましょう。こわいものは食べ物や家族、友達、大学、社会、国、何でもいいです。おもしろいパロディを作ってください。

Listening

聞きましょう

リスニング・ストラテジー : Listening strategy

Integration (2): Predicting based on context and visual clues

You will hear many expressions with *keigo* in public while in Japan, and it is important to be able to understand them. In this lesson, we will practice listening to some common *keigo* expressions in day-to-day situations using the strategies you have learned.

L19-21

1 Pre-listening activity: a.～c. は日本でよく聞く敬語(けいご)です。その表現(ひょうげん)を(1)～(5)のどの場面(ばめん) (situation)で聞くか、選(えら)んでください。

1) ＜駅や電車の中で＞ a. ________ b. ________ c. ________

(1)  (2)  (3)  (4)  (5) 

2) ＜旅館に泊(と)まっている時＞ a. ________ b. ________ c. ________

(1)  (2)  (3)  (4)  (5) 

2 Listening:

1) スミスさんは、仕事で日本に行って、会議(かいぎ)に出ました。休みの時間に、日本の会社の人がスミスさんに質問をしました。a.～c. の質問について、正しい答えを１番から３番の中から選(えら)んでください。

a. ________ b. ________ c. ________

2) スミスさんは、会議(かいぎ)の後でレストランに行って、レストランの人と話しました。a.～d. の質問について、正しい答えを１番から３番の中から選(えら)んでください。

a. ________ b. ________ c. ________ d. ________

Exit Check

Now it's time to go back to the DEKIRU List for this chapter (p.317) and do the exit check to see what new things you can do now that you've completed the lesson.

Lesson 20

みんな、これからどうするの?

What's everyone doing next?

DEKIRU List

できるCheck ☑

できる I **Talk about your personal growth, changes in society, and the future to come.**
自分の成長や社会の変化、将来について話すことができる。
Entry ☐ Exit ☐

できる II **Discuss briefly how you can do your part to make the world a better place.**
社会に役に立つにはどんなことをしたらいいか、簡単に話すことができる。
Entry ☐ Exit ☐

できる III **Reading comprehension: Understand and enjoy the expressions and characteristics of Japanese poems.**
読解：日本語の詩の表現や特徴を理解して、楽しむことができる。
Entry ☐ Exit ☐

STRATEGIES

Conversation Tips .... ・Confirming assumptions

Listening .... ・Integration (3): Predicting, getting the gist, and listening for keywords

GRAMMAR

1. ～ても "even" できるI
2. Vようになる "come to V" できるI
3. Vことにする "decide to V" and Vことにしている "make it a practice/rule to V" できるII
4. ～なら [Conditional conjunction] できるII
5. ～でしょう／だろう [Conjecture] できるII

Conversation 会話

1 できる I **Ai, Mark, and Tao are chatting in the living room of the Japan House.** L20-1

師匠(ししょう)：master of Japanese traditional arts

マーク　：最近、みんな忙(いそが)しくて、あまりゆっくり話せなかったね。
アイ　　：そうですね。私も落語のイベントがあったし…
タオ　　：落語の師匠(ししょう)に敬語(けいご)で話すのは大変だったでしょう？
アイ　　：うん、ちょっと。
マーク　：敬語(けいご)は難(むずか)しいからね。
　　　　　ところで、アイちゃん、留学はどうだった？
アイ　　：すごくよかったです！　色々なことが経験できたし、
　　　　　日本語で話しても緊張(きんちょう)しなくなったし…
タオ　　：へえ、どうやって緊張(きんちょう)しないで話せるようになったの？
アイ　　：話が全部(ぜんぶ)分からなくても、気にしなくなったんだ。
　　　　　そうしたら、もっと楽に会話ができるようになったよ。
タオ　　：え、でも、分からないことがあったら、困るでしょう？
アイ　　：分からない時は、分からないって言えば、教えてもらえるよ。
タオ　　：そっか。

2 できる II **Ai, Keita, and Riemann are chatting in the living room.** 

リーマン：アイさん、留学して何か変わりましたか。
アイ　　：うーん、そうだね…　日本についてたくさん学んだけど、
　　　　　自分の国のこともよく分かるようになったかなぁ…
リーマン：え、アメリカのこと？
アイ　　：うん、日本でよくアメリカについて聞かれたから、
　　　　　質問に答えるために、アメリカのこともたくさん勉強したんだ。
圭太(けいた)　：じゃ、日本で自分の国について再発見(さいはっけん)できたんだね。
アイ　　：え？　さいはっけん？
圭太(けいた)　：うん、もう一度発見(はっけん)して、もっとよく知るっていう意味。
アイ　　：あ、はい、それです！

圭太(けいた)：僕(ぼく)もよく日本について質問されるから、毎日、日本のニュースを見ることにしてるよ。

リーマン：アイさん、ニュースを見るなら、“Door to the World”というアプリがいいですよ。

3 できる I,II **The seasons have turned, and now it's spring. The Japan House members are having a cherry blossom viewing party.** 

リーマン予想(よそう)を証明(しょうめい)する：to prove the Riemann Hypothesis (a famous mathematical conjecture)

アイ：今年も桜(さくら)がきれいだね。

タオ：うん、1年は早いね。みんな、これからどうするの？

マーク：僕(ぼく)は卒業したら、大学院で国際関係(こくさいかんけい)の研究をすることにしたよ。ジャパンハウスに住んでから、国と国の関係(かんけい)について勉強したいって思うようになったんだ。

リーマン：僕(ぼく)の将来(しょうらい)の目標(もくひょう)は、数学(すうがく)の「リーマン予想(よそう)」を証明(しょうめい)することです！まだ誰(だれ)も答えを見つけていないんですよ。

タオ：すごい！　でも、リーマン君(くん)ならできるかもしれないね。アイちゃんの目標(もくひょう)は日本美術(びじゅつ)のキュレーターでしょ？

アイ：うん。それから、今はアメリカに来た留学生を助けてあげようと思ってる。日本でたくさんの人に助けてもらったから…　圭太(けいた)さんは？

圭太(けいた)：うーん、将来(しょうらい)のことはまだ分からないけど…できれば、子ども達に剣道(けんどう)を教えたいんだ。何か社会の役(やく)に立つことがしてみたいし、剣道(けんどう)なら日本の文化も教えられるし…

タオ：私も何か目標(もくひょう)を見つけよう！　あ、にゃんたの目標(もくひょう)は？

にゃんた：ニャ、ニャ、ニャー！

CONVERSATION TIPS

Confirming assumptions: In addition to the function of ～でしょ(う) explained in the grammar section of this lesson (#5), you can confirm your assumption by using ～でしょ(う) with rising intonation. ～でしょ(う) is used in this way when the speaker assumes that what they are saying is true.

A：おかえり。遅かったね。つかれたでしょう？

B：うん、明日テニスの試合があるから、ずっと練習してて…

A：そっか、おなか、すいたでしょ？　このお菓子(かし)、食べてもいいよ。

Vocabulary with Pictures

単語（たんご）

▶ **The words written in gray** are supplemental vocabulary.

チャレンジ　Challenge

[*thing* が] うまくいく
(to go well)

[*thing* を] きにする
(to care/worry/be concerned (about))

[*person/thing* に] はんたいする
(to be against; to disagree)

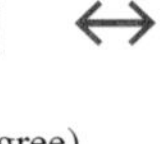

NO

[*person/thing* に] さんせいする

[*thing* に] じしんをもつ
(to have confidence)

じしん
(confidence)

もくひょう
(goal; objective; target)

けっか
(result; outcome)

かんけい
(relationship)

こくさいかんけい
(international relations)

うちゅう
((outer) space; the universe)

うちゅうじん
(alien; extraterrestrial being)

つき
(the Moon)

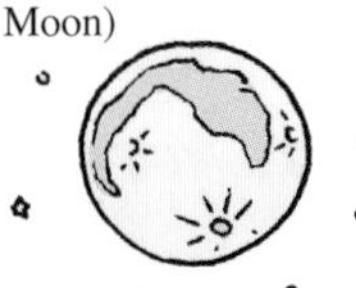

かせい
(Mars)

生活　Daily life

てつやする
(to stay up all night)

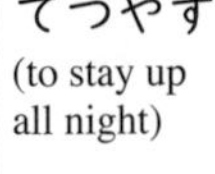

ばんぐみ
program [TV, radio, etc.]

ひとりぐらし(を)する
(to live alone)

せんざい
(detergent; cleaner)

かぎをあける
(to unlock)

[*thing* に] かぎをかける

[*thing/person* が] ぬれる
(to get wet)

[*insect/animal/person, etc.* を] ころす
(to kill)

ふあん(な)
(uneasy)

↔ あんしんする

ばか(な)
(foolish; stupid)

おしゃれ(な)
(stylish; fashionable)

うつくしい
(beautiful)

やさしい
(gentle; tender)

やさしく
(gently; tenderly)

おとな
(adult)

〜まつ
(end of ...)

げつまつ
(end of the month)

Exs. せんしゅうまつ
(last weekend)

こんしゅうまつ
(this weekend)

らいしゅうまつ
(next weekend)

どうする
(What will you do?)

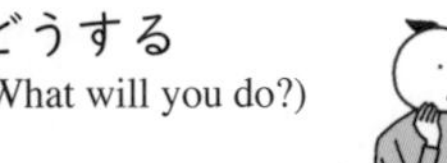

これから**どうしますか**
(What will you do next?)

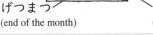

読み物に出てくる言葉(ことば) Vocabulary for the Reading section

し (poem; poetry)

しじん (poet)

さくしゃ (author; writer; creator)

だれでも (anyone; whoever; everyone)

かし (lyrics)

ないよう (content)

しょくぶつ (plant)

は／はっぱ (leaf)

はね (feather; wing)

くうき (air; atmosphere)

[*sentence* と] かんじる (to feel; to sense)

[*thing* が] まわる (to go around; to rotate)

Ex. ちきゅうがまわる (the Earth rotates)

[*thing* を] くりかえす (to repeat; to do over again)

[*thing X* と *thing Y* を] くらべる (to compare (X and Y))

[*thing* が] つづく ((something) continues)

[*thing* を] つづける

Lesson 20

Vocabulary List

単語(たんご)リスト

L20-5

▶**Highlighted kanji words** contain kanji you have learned previously.

RU-VERBS / *RU*-VERB PHRASE

1	かぎをあける	かぎを開ける	to unlock
2	かんじる	感じる	to feel; to sense [*sentence* と]
3	くらべる	比べる	to compare (X and Y) [*thing X* と *thing Y* を]
4	ぬれる		to get wet [*thing/person* が]

U-VERBS / *U*-VERB PHRASES

5	うまくいく		to go well [*thing* が]
6	くりかえす	くり返す	to repeat; to do over again [*thing* を]
7	ころす		to kill [*insect/animal/person, etc.* を]
8	じしんをもつ	自信を持つ	to have confidence [*thing* に]
9	つづく	続く	(something) continues [*thing* が]
10	まわる	回る	to go around; to rotate [*thing* が] **Ex.** ちきゅうがまわる the Earth rotates

SURU-VERBS / *SURU*-VERB PHRASE

11	きにする	気にする	to care/worry/be concerned (about) [*thing* を]
12	てつやする	徹夜する	to stay up all night
13	はんたいする	反対する	to be against; to disagree [*person/thing* に]
14	ひとりぐらし(を)する	一人暮らし(を)する	to live alone

I-ADJECTIVE

15	うつくしい	美しい	beautiful

NA-ADJECTIVES

16	おしゃれ		stylish; fashionable
17	ばか		foolish; stupid
18	ふあん	不安	uneasy

NOUNS

19	うちゅう	宇宙	(outer) space; the universe
	うちゅうじん	宇宙人	alien; extraterrestrial being
20	おとな	大人	adult
21	かし	歌詞	lyrics
22	かんけい	関係	relationship **Ex.** XとYのかんけい relationship between X and Y
23	こくさいかんけい	国際関係	international relations
24	くうき	空気	air; atmosphere
25	けっか	結果	result; outcome
26	さくしゃ	作者	author; writer; creator
27	し	詩	poem; poetry
28	しじん	詩人	poet
29	しょくぶつ	植物	plant
30	せんざい	洗剤	detergent; cleaner
31	つき	月	the Moon
32	ないよう	内容	content
33	は／はっぱ	葉／葉っぱ	leaf
34	はね	羽	feather; wing
35	ばんぐみ	番組	program [TV, radio, etc.]
36	もくひょう	目標	goal; objective; target

ADVERB

37	やさしく		gently; tenderly

SUFFIX

38	～まつ	～末	end of ...
	こんしゅうまつ	今週末	this weekend
	げつまつ	月末	end of the month

OTHER WORDS AND EXPRESSIONS

39	だれでも	誰でも	anyone; whoever; everyone
40	どうする		What will you do? **Ex.** これからどうしますか。 What will you do next?

漢 字

▶ ＊Special reading

No.	Kanji	Meaning	Reading	Words	Stroke order
311	結	to tie	ケッ ケツ	結果（けっか） result; outcome　結婚する（けっこん） to get married　結婚式（けっこんしき） wedding ceremony 結局（けっきょく） after all; in the end　結構（けっこう） fairly; rather　結論（けつろん） conclusion	結
			むす(ぶ)	結ぶ（むす） to tie; to link	
312	婚	marriage	コン	結婚する（けっこん） to get married　結婚式（けっこんしき） wedding ceremony 婚約する（こんやく） to get engaged　婚約者（こんやくしゃ） fiancé/fiancée 離婚する（りこん） to divorce	婚
313	果	fruit; result	カ	結果（けっか） result; outcome　果実（かじつ） fruit　果汁（かじゅう） fruit juice 果樹園（かじゅえん） orchard　効果（こうか） effectiveness; impact 果物＊（くだもの） fruit	果
314	予	in advance	ヨ	予習する（よしゅう） to do preparatory study/research　予定（よてい） schedule; plan 予約する（よやく） to reserve　天気予報（てんきよほう） weather forecast 予算（よさん） budget　予測する（よそく） to predict	予
315	約	to promise; approximate	ヤク	予約する（よやく） to reserve　婚約する（こんやく） to get engaged 約～（やく） approximately ... (Ex. 約百人（やくひゃくにん）)　約束(を)する（やくそく） to make a promise 要約する（ようやく） to summarize	約
316	定	to decide; to determine	テイ	予定（よてい） schedule; plan　定期（ていき） fixed period; regular 定食（ていしょく） set meal　定年（ていねん） retirement age	定
			さだ(める) さだ(まる)	定める（さだ） to decide; to determine　定まる（さだ） to become settled; to be decided/determined	
317	全	all	ゼン	安全(な)（あんぜん） safe; secure　全部（ぜんぶ） all　全部で（ぜんぶ） in total　完全に（かんぜん） completely 全員（ぜんいん） all members　全国（ぜんこく） nationwide　全然（ぜんぜん） (not) ... at all　全体（ぜんたい） whole; entirety	全
			すべ(て) まった(く)	全て（すべ） all　全く（まった） entirely	

Lesson 20

318 伝

伝	デン	伝言 (でんごん) (verbal) message　伝説 (でんせつ) legend; folklore　伝統 (でんとう) tradition
	つた(える) つた(わる)	伝える (つた) to tell; to pass along; to deliver　手伝う* (てつだ) to help 伝わる (つた) to be passed along; to be conveyed; to be introduced
to transmit; to report; legend		

319 感

感	カン	感じる (かん) to feel; to sense　感動する (かんどう) to be moved; to be (emotionally) touched 感謝する (かんしゃ) to thank; to feel grateful　感心する (かんしん) to admire; to be impressed 感想 (かんそう) impression; thought
emotion; feeling		

320 暑

暑	ショ	暑中見舞い (しょちゅうみま) summer greeting (card)
	あつ(い)	暑い (あつ) hot [air temperature]　暑さ (あつ) heat 蒸し暑い (む あつ) muggy; hot and humid
hot		

321 寒

寒	カン	寒中見舞い (かんちゅうみま) winter greeting (card)
	さむ(い)	寒い (さむ) cold [air temperature]　寒さ (さむ) cold; coldness
cold		

322 犬

犬	ケン	愛犬 (あいけん) (one's beloved) pet dog
	いぬ	犬 (いぬ) dog　子犬 (こいぬ) puppy　柴犬 (しばいぬ) *Shiba Inu* [a dog breed native to Japan]
dog		

323 赤

赤	セキ	赤十字 (せきじゅうじ) Red Cross　赤道 (せきどう) equator
	あか あか(い)	赤 (あか) red [noun]　赤い (あか) red [adjective]　赤ちゃん (あか) baby; infant 赤信号 (あかしんごう) red light [traffic signal]
red		

324 青

青	セイ	青年 (せいねん) young person
	あお あお(い)	青 (あお) blue [noun]　青い (あお) blue [adjective] 青信号 (あおしんごう) green light [traffic signal]　青空 (あおぞら) blue sky
blue		

325 白

白	ハク	白紙 (はくし) blank (sheet of) paper　白鳥 (はくちょう) swan
	しろ しろ(い)	白 (しろ) white [noun]　白い (しろ) white [adjective] 白黒 (しろくろ) black and white　面白い (おもしろ) interesting; funny　真っ白 (ましろ) snow-white
white		

326 黒 (黒 / 黒)	コク	黒板(こくばん) blackboard
	くろ / くろ(い)	黒(くろ) black [noun]　黒い(くろい) black [adjective]　黒田(くろだ)さん Kuroda-san [last name]
		白黒(しろくろ) black and white　真っ黒(まっくろ) pitch-black
black		黒
327 銀 (銀 / 銀)	ギン	銀行(ぎんこう) bank　銀(ぎん) silver　銀色(ぎんいろ) silver [color]　銀河(ぎんが) galaxy
silver		銀
328 紙 (紙 / 紙)	シ	表紙(ひょうし) (book) cover　用紙(ようし) (blank) form [document]　和紙(わし) traditional Japanese paper
	かみ / がみ	紙(かみ) paper
		手紙(てがみ) letter [correspondence]　折り紙(おりがみ) *origami* (paper-folding craft)
paper		紙
329 葉 (葉 / 葉)	ヨウ	紅葉(こうよう) autumn color (of leaves); fall foliage
	は / ば	葉(は)／葉(は)っぱ leaf　葉書(はがき) postcard
		言葉(ことば) word; phrase; language　落ち葉(おちば) fallen leaves
leaf		葉

新しい読み方

The following are new readings for kanji that you have already learned. Read each word aloud. (* indicates a word with a special reading.)

1) 大人(おとな)*　2) 言葉(ことば)　3) 月(つき)　4) 続(つづ)く　5) 回(まわ)る

習った漢字で書ける新しい単語(たんご)

The following are other new vocabulary in this lesson that contain kanji you have already leaned. Read each word aloud.

1) かぎを開(あ)ける　2) 気(き)にする　3) 空気(くうき)　4) くり返(かえ)す　5) 作者(さくしゃ)
6) (自信(じしん)を)持(も)つ　7) 一人(ひとり)(暮(ぐ)らしをする)　8) 不安(ふあん)(な)　9) ～末(まつ) (Ex. 今週末(こんしゅうまつ))

練習

1 Find and circle nine kanji compound words that contain kanji you have learned so far, then write the words and their readings in the space provided below. The words may appear either vertically or horizontally.

Ex.

手	結	果	物
紙	婚	銀	行
予	約	感	動
定	安	全	部

Ex. 結婚 （ けっこん ）

1) ______ （　　　） 2) ______ （　　　）

3) ______ （　　　） 4) ______ （　　　）

5) ______ （　　　） 6) ______ （　　　）

7) ______ （　　　） 8) ______ （　　　）

9) ______ （　　　）

2 Tanaka-san wrote the following blog entries about various things he found interesting recently. Read the entries aloud, then write the readings for the underlined words.

1) 私のペットの犬は体が黒いから、名前は「クロ」だ。犬は頭(あたま)がいい動物で、人間の言葉が分かるが、クロもすごく頭(あたま)がよくて、英語も日本語も分かる。それから、クロは人の気持ちを感じることもできるみたいだ。先週末、クロを姉の家に連(つ)れていった時、赤ちゃんが泣く前に分かったみたいだった。

2) 動画を見ていたら、世界の国旗(こっき) (national flag) には赤と青と白を使ったものが29もあると言っていた。

3) 今日、おもしろい詩(し)を読んだ。この詩(し)の作者は同じ言葉をくり返して自分の気持ちを伝えたいようだ。

4) 私の両親は部屋の温度(おんど)についてよくけんかしている。父が暑いと感じる時、母は寒いと感じるそうだ。弟は大人になってからほこり (dust) のアレルギーになったから、空気がきれいかどうかいつも気にしている。来週末、空気清浄機(せいじょうき) (air purifier) を買いに行く予定だそうだ。

漢字の話 The Story of Kanji

■ 日本の漢字文化

There are many different ways in which Japanese people enjoy and show appreciation for their kanji culture.

今年の漢字® (Kanji of the Year)

Each year, The Japanese Kanji Aptitude Testing Foundation announces the Kanji of the Year. Chosen by popular vote, the kanji best symbolizes the sentiment as well as notable events of that particular year. The following are some kanji that were previously chosen as the Kanji of the Year. See the *TOBIRA* website to learn more about 今年の漢字.

Year	Kanji	Reading	Meaning	Notable event(s) of the year
2005	愛	あい	love	People were constantly reminded of the power of "love" by many celebrity marriages, relief efforts for natural disasters, and also a number of cruel incidents caused by lack of love.
2011	絆	きずな	human bonds	After the Great East Japan Earthquake and tsunami, people throughout Japan gained renewed appreciation for their "bonds" with loved ones.
2016	金	きん	gold; money	This year brought to mind different aspects of the kanji 金, including the record-high 12 "gold" medals in the Olympics and many "money" scandals in politics.

Check out this/last year's 今年の漢字 using the QR code above and write it in the table.

芸術(げいじゅつ)としての漢字 (Kanji as art)

Have you ever tried your hand at Japanese calligraphy? In class, you may have been instructed by your teacher to write kanji neatly. In fact, writing kanji can also be an art form. See the *TOBIRA* website for the following topics using the QR code above.

1. **Sisyu** (紫舟(ししゅう)): Sisyu is a famous Japanese professional calligrapher. The characters she writes are considered to be works of art. (See p.12 Unit 4の前に.)
2. **The Japan Kanji Museum & Library** (漢字ミュージアム): In this museum located in Kyoto, you can enjoy various exhibitions related to kanji.
3. **National High School Calligraphy Performance Championship** (書道パフォーマンス甲子園(こうしえん)): In this national competition, teams of high school students write kanji on large pieces of paper with oversized brushes while moving in rhythm with music. They are judged based on the beauty of both their calligraphic art and choreography.

提供：書道パフォーマンス甲子園実行委員会

Lesson 20

Grammar

文法(ぶんぽう)

1 ～ても "even"

1-1 Sても "even if; even though"

[1-a]

S₁ (ても clause)			S2
	V-*te*		
辞書(じしょ)で	探(さが)して	も	このスラングは見(み)つかりませんよ。
You cannot find this slang even if you look it up in the dictionary.			

You can express the idea of "even if; even though" using {V-*te*/Adj(*i*)-*te*/Adj(*na*)で/Nで} + も. "S_1 ても S_2" is used in the following situation:
(i) it is expected that if the action in S_1 is performed (or the state in S_1 is the case), something will happen, but
(ii) something contrary to the expectation in (i) takes place.
In [1-a], for example, the listener expects that the slang can be found if he/she looks it up in the dictionary, but the speaker is saying that it cannot be found, contrary to the listener's expectation. Similarly, in (1), the speaker expected that taking medicine would take care of his/her headache, but it didn't happen.

Note that "S_1 たら S_2" ("if S_1, S_2") expresses an idea contrastive to that of "S_1 ても S_2." (See (3) below.)

Exs. (1) 薬(くすり)を飲(の)んでもまだ頭(あたま)が痛(いた)いです。*Even though I took some medicine, I still have a headache.*

(2) この文法(ぶんぽう)は難(むずか)しくて、勉強(べんきょう)しても分(わ)かりませんでした。
This grammar is difficult; even though I studied it, I didn't understand it.

(3) アイさんはそばを食(た)べたらアレルギーが出(で)ますが、タオさんはそばを食(た)べてもだいじょうぶです。 *Ai gets an allergic reaction if she has buckwheat, but Tao has no problem with it (lit. even if Tao eats it, she is all right).*

[1-b]

S₁ (ても clause)			S2
	V (negative *te*-form)		
ここの漢字(かんじ)は辞書(じしょ)で	調(しら)べなくて	も	意味(いみ)が分(わ)かります。
I can figure out the meanings of the kanji characters here {even if I don't look them up / without looking them up} in a dictionary.			

When S_1 is a negative sentence, なくても occurs in the end of S_1.

Exs. (4) リーマンさんはアプリを使(つか)わなくても、漢字(かんじ)が覚(おぼ)えられます。
Riemann can memorize kanji without using an app (lit. even if he doesn't use an app).

(5) このお菓子(かし)はお店(みせ)に行(い)かなくても、ネットで買(か)えます。
You can buy this snack on the internet without going to the store (lit. even if you don't go to the store).

The permission expression ～てもいい ("may") and the non-obligation expression ～なくてもいい ("do not have to") are set phrases that involve ～ても and ～なくても. Their literal meanings are "good/okay even if～" and "good/okay even if～not," respectively. (See L8 #10 and L13 #7.)

The predicate of S_1 can also be an *i*-adjective, a *na*-adjective, or a noun.

[1-c]

S₁ (ても clause)			S₂
	Adj(*i*)-*te*		
他(ほか)の車(くるま)より	高(たか)くて	も	この車(くるま)を買(か)うつもりです。
I'm going to buy this car even if it's more expensive than other cars.			

[1-d]

S₁ (ても clause)			S₂
	Adj(*na*)		
歌(うた)が	下手(へた)	でも	カラオケは楽(たの)しいです。
Karaoke is fun {even though I'm / even if you're} not good at singing.			

[1-e]

S₁ (ても clause)			S₂
	N		
明日(あした)	雨(あめ)	でも	ハイキングに行(い)きましょう。
Even if it rains tomorrow (lit. Even if (the weather) is rain tomorrow), let's go hiking.			

Exs. (6) 難(むずか)しくても日本語(にほんご)の勉強(べんきょう)を続(つづ)けるつもりです。
Even if it's difficult, I intend to keep studying Japanese.

(7) このアパートは古(ふる)いから、静(しず)かで安全(あんぜん)でも借(か)りたくないです。
Because this apartment building is old, I don't want to rent it even if it is quiet and safe.

(8) 私(わたし)は会議(かいぎ)が夜(よる)でもだいじょうぶです。*Even if the meeting is (held) at night, it is okay with me.*

☞ **GID** (vol.2): B. Connecting sentences 3. のに vs. ても

1-2 Nでも "even N"

[1-f]

	N		
この言葉(ことば)の意味(いみ)は	先生(せんせい)	でも	分(わ)かりませんでした。
Even my teacher couldn't figure out the meaning of this word.			

You can express the idea of "even X" using X でも. This expression is used when one thing is expected of X (an action or lack of action, an ability or inability, etc.) but in fact the opposite is true.

Exs. (1) ニュースキャスターでも時々(ときどき)敬語(けいご)を間違(まちが)えます。
Even newscasters sometimes make mistakes with keigo.

(2) この本(ほん)はやさしい言葉(ことば)で書(か)かれているから、子(こ)どもでも読(よ)めます。
This book is written in simple language, so even children can read it.

This use of Nでも must be distinguished from the use in [1-e] in #1-1. That is, the Nでも in [1-e] is part of the ても clause (the English equivalent is "even if/though ~ is N"), while the Nでも in [1-f] is part of the main clause (the English equivalent is "even N").

2 Vようになる "come to V"

In Lesson 10 #2, we studied なる with the adverbial forms of adjectives in order to express a change of a state (e.g., 野菜が高くなった, 私は漢字が好きになった). Here, we will learn how to use なる with verbs.

[2]

	V-plain.non-past	
日本語でメールが	書ける	ようになりました。
I've come to be able to write emails in Japanese.		

When you use なる with verbs, you add ように to their plain non-past forms. Using Vようになる, you can express:

(i) a gradual change in one's ability to do something ([2], (1), and (2)),

(ii) a gradual change in one's daily habits ((3)), and

(iii) a gradual change in the accessibility of facilities, services, etc. ((4)).

Note that when sentences are about a change in one's ability and in the availability of something, the potential forms of verbs are used before ようになる.

Exs. (1) 前は起きられなかったけれど、最近、朝早く起きられるようになった。
I didn't use to be able to, but recently I've come to be able to get up early in the morning.

(2) 毎日練習したら、難しいヨガのポーズができるようになりますよ。
If you practice every day, you'll start to be able to do difficult yoga poses.

(3) 一人暮らしを始めてから自分で料理するようになった。
Since I began living by myself, I started to do my own cooking (lit. to cook on my own).

(4) 6月になると、公園のプールが使えるようになります。
When June comes around, we can start using the swimming pool in the park.

You can express a change in one's ability from "being able to do X" to "not being able to do X" or in one's habit from "doing X" to "not doing X," using either Vないようになる or Vなくなる. Although the difference between the two is subtle, Vなくなる is more commonly used.

Exs. (5) 高校生の時はフライドチキンとピザとポテトを一度に食べられたが、今は食べられなくなった／ないようになった。*When I was in high school, I could eat fried chicken, pizza, and French fries all at once, but now I can't anymore (lit. I have come to not be able to eat).*

(6) スマホがこわれて友達に連絡できなくなって／ないようになってしまった。
Because my smartphone broke, I cannot (lit. have come to be unable to) contact my friends.

3 Vことにする "decide to V" and Vことにしている "make it a practice/rule to V"

[3-a]

	V-plain.non-past		
来年は一人でアパートに	住む	こと	にします。
I think I'll (lit. I choose to) live in an apartment by myself next year.			

[3-b]

	V-plain.non-past		
来学期も日本語を	取る	こと	にしました。
I've decided to take Japanese next term, too.			

[3-c]

	V-plain.non-past		
毎日４キロ	走る	こと	にしています。
I make it a practice to run four kilometers every day.			

You can express what you have decided to do (or not to do) using Vことにする. The verbs before こと are always in the plain non-past from.

There are three sentence patterns that involve Vことにする:

(i) **Vことにする**: This pattern is used when you decided to do (or not to do) something just before the moment of speech. (See [3-a].)

Exs. (1) A: 明日のイベントに行きますか。*Will you go to the event tomorrow?*

B: うーん、そうですね。明日は時間があるから、行く<u>ことにします</u>。

Umm... Well, I've got time tomorrow, so I'll (lit. I choose to) go.

(2) 今日、また朝ねぼうしちゃった。明日からもっと早く起きる<u>ことにしよう</u>。

I overslept again this morning. I'll (lit. I choose to) get up earlier from tomorrow on.

(ii) **Vことにした**: This pattern is used when you decided to do (or not to do) something some time ago and the decision hasn't changed. (See [3-b].)

Exs. (3) ずっと悩んでいましたが、日本の映画を研究するために大学院に行く<u>ことにしました</u>。

I was torn about it for a long time, but I've decided to go to graduate school to study Japanese movies.

(4) 夏休みは東京に留学するつもりだったけど、奨学金がもらえなかったので、行かない<u>ことにした</u>。*I was planning to study in Tokyo during summer break, but I decided not to go because I couldn't get a scholarship.*

(iii) **Vことにしている**: This pattern is used when you decided to do (or not to do) something some time ago and that action has become your routine practice. (See [3-c].)

Exs. (5) 大学に入ってからずっと日曜日の朝は公園を散歩する<u>ことにしています</u>。

I've made a habit of taking a walk in the park every Sunday morning since I started college.

(6) 健康のためにインスタントラーメンを食べない<u>ことにしています</u>。

For my health, I make it a rule not to eat instant ramen.

4 ～なら [Conditional conjunction] "if it is the case that ~; if it is true that ~; would"

[4-a]

S_1 (なら clause)			S_2
	V-plain/Adj(*i*)-plain		
トムさんが	来る	なら、	私は帰ります。
<At a party> If (it's true that) Tom is coming, I'll go home.			

[4-b]

S_1 (なら clause)			S_2
	Adj(*na*)/N		
場所が	不便	なら、	そのアパートは借りません。
If the location is inconvenient, I won't rent that apartment.			

You can express the idea "if something is the case (or true)" using Sなら. Sなら is commonly used when you hear S as a fact, or hear something that implies that S is the case. For example, [4-a] may be a response to アリスさんはトムさんもパーティーに呼んだそうです (I heard that Alice invited Tom to the party, too.) when the speaker doesn't want to see Tom for some reason.

Note that in [4-a], the action in S_1 (= Tom's coming) has not been completed before the action in S_2 (= the speaker's going home). The other conditional expressions (i.e., たら, と, and ば) cannot be used for such situations. In other words, in S_1 たら S_2, S_1 と S_2, and S_1 ば S_2, the action in S_1 is always completed before the action in S_2. (See L12 #4, L17 #4, and L18 #6.) For example, in the following sentence, Tom's coming takes place before the speaker's going home.

トムさんが来たら、私は帰ります。*When/If Tom comes, I will go home.*

The connection patterns for なら are as follows:

Verbs	plain form	＋なら	食べるなら 食べたなら	食べないなら 食べなかったなら
I-adjectives	plain form		高いなら 高かったなら	高くないなら 高くなかったなら
Na-adjectives / nouns ＋だ	*Na*-adjectives / nouns ＋ø／じゃない		便利なら* 学生なら*	便利じゃないなら 学生じゃないなら
	Na-adjectives / nouns ＋だった／じゃなかった		便利だったなら 学生だったなら	便利じゃなかったなら 学生じゃなかったなら

*だ is not used before なら. That is, ～だなら is an ungrammatical form.

Exs. (1) 日本語を勉強するなら、『とびら』という教科書がいいですよ。
If you're going to study Japanese, TOBIRA *is a good textbook (lit. the textbook called* TOBIRA *is good).*

(2) お酒を飲むなら、車で来ないでください。そして、お酒を飲んだら、車を運転して帰らないでください。
If you (plan to) drink, don't come by car. And if you do drink, don't drive home.

(3) 最近(さいきん)つかれているみたいだけど、アルバイトが大変(たいへん)なら、やめたらどう？
You look tired lately. If your part-time job's too hard, why don't you quit?

(4) A: 週末(しゅうまつ)、ご飯(はん)を食(た)べに行(い)かない？ *Do you wanna go out to eat over the weekend?*
B: うん、土曜日(どようび)ならいいよ。*Yeah, Saturday would work (lit. if it's Saturday, it's good).*
C: うん、韓国料理(かんこくりょうり)なら行(い)きたい。
Year, if we're getting Korean food (lit. If it's Korean food), I want to go.

Because the core meaning of なら is "if it is the case/true," it cannot be used when S_1 is always the case or true. For example, the following sentence is ungrammatical:

× ここは春(はる)になるなら、桜(さくら)がきれいです。
→ ここは春(はる)に {なったら／なると}、桜(さくら)がきれいです。
This place is beautiful in the spring (lit. when it becomes spring).

[4-c]

A:	落語(らくご)に興味(きょうみ)があります。		
	I'm interested in *rakugo*.		
B:	S_1 (なら clause)		S_2
	落語(らくご)に興味(きょうみ)がある	なら、	今度一緒(こんどいっしょ)に聞(き)きに行(い)きませんか。
	If you're interested in *rakugo*, would you like to go see a show (lit. listen [to it]) together sometime?		

Using なら, you can topicalize what the listener has just said and make a recommendation or suggestion about it, as seen in Speaker B's line in [4-c].

Exs. (5) A: 今度(こんど)の休(やす)みに北海道(ほっかいどう)に行(い)くんです。*I'm going to Hokkaido over our next break.*
B: 北海道(ほっかいどう)に行(い)くなら、ぜひおいしいラーメンを食(た)べてみてください。
If you're going to Hokkaido, definitely try the delicious ramen (there).

(6) A: あー、痛(いた)い… *Ooh, [my head] hurts...*
B: 頭(あたま)が痛(いた)いなら、今日(きょう)は帰(かえ)ったらどう？
If you've got a headache, why don't you go home for the day?

☞ GID (vol.2): B. Connecting sentences 4. たら, と, ば, and なら

5 ～でしょう／だろう [Conjecture] "probably"

FYI

[5-a]

	V-plain / Adj(*i*)-plain	
山田さんもパーティーに	来る	でしょう。
Yamada-san will probably come to the party, too.		

[5-b]

	Adj(*na*) / N	
明日のテストは	簡単	でしょう。
Tomorrow's test will probably be easy.		

You can say something you're not certain about using でしょう or だろう. だろう is the plain form of でしょう and is used in casual speech and in written language. Note that でしょう／だろう cannot be used for the speaker's own uncertain action in the future. Therefore, the following sentence is ungrammatical:

× 私も明日のパーティーに行くでしょう。

Intended meaning: *I'll probably go to tomorrow's party, too.*

→ 私もたぶん明日のパーティーに行くと思います。

The connection pattern for でしょう／だろう is as follows:

Verbs	plain form	+ でしょう／だろう	食べるでしょう 食べたでしょう	食べないでしょう 食べなかったでしょう
I-adjectives	plain form		高いでしょう 高かったでしょう	高くないでしょう 高くなかったでしょう
Na-adjectives / nouns +だ	*Na*-adjectives / nouns +ø／じゃない		便利でしょう* 学生でしょう*	便利じゃないでしょう 学生じゃないでしょう
	Na-adjectives / nouns +だった／じゃなかった		便利だったでしょう 学生だったでしょう	便利じゃなかったでしょう 学生じゃなかったでしょう

*だ is not used before でしょう／だろう. That is, ～だ{でしょう／だろう} is an ungrammatical form.

Exs. (1) 7時の天気予報です。明日東京は雨でしょう。大阪は晴れでしょう。
This is the 7 o'clock weather forecast. Tokyo will be rainy tomorrow. Osaka will be sunny.

(2) A: 圭太さんがいませんね。*Keita isn't here, is he?*

B: 今たぶん剣道の練習をしているでしょう。*He is probably practicing* kendo *now.*

(3) AIロボットと生活するようになったら、私達の世界は大きく変わるだろうと思います。*When AI robots become part of our daily lives (lit. When we begin to live with AI robots), I think our world will probably change greatly.*

Note that assertive endings with no でしょう (e.g., 明日東京は雨です, 大阪は晴れです) are not used in Japanese weather forecasts, as in (1), while "probably" is not used in English weather forecasts.

話しましょう

▶ **Words written in purple** are new words introduced in this lesson.

Talk about your personal growth, changes in society, and the future to come.

できるI-A ～ても

1 Let's practice forming the expression ～ても. L20-6

Ex. 見る → 見ても → 見なくても

1) 食べる　2) いる　3) できる　4) ある　5) なる　6) 言う　7) 聞く
8) 分かる　9) する　10) 来る　11) 高い　12) いい　13) 大変　14) 大人

2 Describe the following topics, combining two sentences into one using ～ても.

ランナーさん

Ex.1 ランナーさんは雨が降っても、走ります。

Ex.1 雨が降ります　1) つかれています
2) 寒いです　3) 大変です
4) 旅行中です　5) 時間がありません
6) 走りたくないです
} + 走ります

このスマホ

Ex.2 このスマホはマイナス 30 度でも、こわれません。

Ex.2 マイナス 30 度です　7) とても暑い所です
8) 落とします　9) ふみます
10) ぬれます　11) 注意して使いません
} + こわれません

Lesson 20

3 Are you a positive thinker or a negative thinker?

Step 1 Describe how positive and negative people tend to think using the cues provided. L20-8

Ex. ネガティブさんはいやなことを言われたら、怒ります。
ポジティブさんはいやなことを言われても、怒りません。

Ex. いやなことを言われる／怒る　1) 失敗する／あきらめる　2) 反対される／不安になる
3) トラブルがある／文句を言う　4) 難しい／できないと思う　5) 結果がよくない／気にする
6) うまくいかない／落ち込む　7) 仕事がいや／すぐやめる　8) your own

Step 2 Now, pair up and ask each other five questions from Step 1 to find out how positive or negative your partner is. Count your partner's "positive" answers.

Ex. A: ○○さんはいやなことを言われたら、怒りますか。
B: はい、怒ります。or いいえ、私はいやなことを言われても、怒りません。
△△さんはいやなことを言われたら、怒りますか。
A: 私 {は／も} … <Continue>

Step 3 Tell your partner the result based on the chart below.

Ex. ○○さんの答えによると、結果はポジティブ度100%でした。

あなたのポジティブ度 (degree of positivity)

ポジティブな答え	5つ	4つ	3つ	2つ	1つ
ポジティブ度	100%	80%	60%	40%	20%

Group Work

4 Visualize the person you want to be.

Step 1 First, brainstorm the traits of positive people you know (e.g., personality, attitude, resilience). List up several traits.

Ex. ・うまくいかなくても、すぐあきらめない　・友達が落ち込んでいたら、はげます

Step 2 Pick two traits you came up with in Step 1, then present them to your groupmates.

Ex. 私は「うまくいかなくても、すぐあきらめない人」、そして「人に言われなくても、自分で考えてやる人」になりたいです。がんばります。

できるI-B　Vようになる

1 What happens when you live on your own?

Step 1 First, describe how living alone has changed Mei's life. L20-9

Ex.1 一人暮らしを始めてから、メイさんは料理ができるようになりました。

Ex.2 メイさんは高い物を{買わなく／買わないように}なりました。

Ex.1 料理をする　ability	Ex.2 ×高い物を買う　daily habit
1) せんたくやそうじをする	7) よく徹夜する
2) 朝早く起きる	8) 親に感謝する
3) ゴミの出し方が分かる	9) ひとりごとを言う (to talk to herself)
4) ゴキブリ (cockroach) を殺す	10) ×部屋をかたづける
5) 自分で考えて決める	11) ×むだづかいする
6) 自分に自信を持つ	12) ×一人でこわい映画やテレビ番組を見る

Step 2 Now, talk about how living away from your family has changed your life. If you live with your family, use your imagination.

Ex. A: ○○さんは今、一人暮らしをしていますか。寮に住んでいますか。

B: 私は寮に住んでいます。

A: そうですか。寮で生活を始めてから、何が変わりましたか。

B: そうですね、家族と会えなくなったので、よく家族と電話で話すようになりました。それから、料理ができるようになりました。△△さんは？

2 Did you know that mobile phones were only used to make calls in the past? The first smartphone was invented in 1992. Talk about how smartphones have changed the world.

Step 1 Describe how people's daily habits have changed with smartphones. L20-10

Ex.1 play games

→ スマホができて、スマホでゲームをするようになりました。

Ex.2 not use game consoles

→ スマホができて、あまりゲーム機(き)を使わなくなりました。

1) send messages　2) listen to music　3) take photos　4) enjoy social media　5) not get lost　6) not write by hand　7) your own

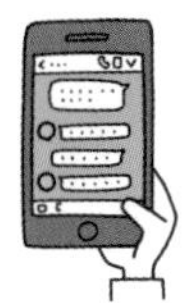

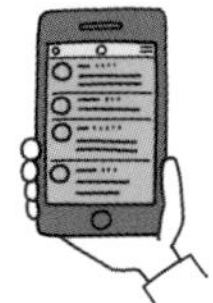

Step 2 Now, describe how availability of facilities, services, etc. has changed with smartphones.

Ex. can unlock the door L20-11

→ テクノロジーが進(すす)んで (to advance)、スマホでかぎを開けられるようになりました。

1) can pay money　2) can send money　3) can take a class　4) can make videos　5) can look up anything immediately　6) your own

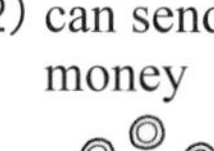
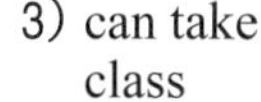
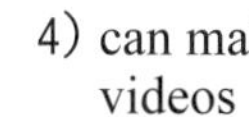

3 Pick a technology or service from the box below and exchange opinions about how it has changed people's lifestyles.

Possible topics	動画サイト	ストリーミング	ビデオ会議(かいぎ)アプリ	SNSアプリ
	デリバリーサービス			

Ex. A: まずYouTubeについて話しましょう。YouTubeができて、どう変わったと思いますか。

B: 簡単(かんたん)に動画がアップできるようになったから、誰(だれ)でも有名になれるようになったと思います。

A: そうですね。それから、YouTubeで料理の作り方が分かるから、料理の本を買わなくなりましたね。

<Continue>

Lesson 20

4 Talk with your partner about the changes that have happened to you since you started something new (a new school, club, hobby, etc.).

Possible topics		
大学に入って	○○（club）に入って	○○（hobby, sports, SNS, etc.）を始めて

Ex. A: ○○さんは大学に入って何が変わりましたか。

B: そうですね、まず授業が難（むずか）しくなったから、テストがなくても勉強するようになりました。

A: あー、分かります。

B: それから、新しい友達を作るために、色々な人と話すようになりました。

A: なるほど。新しい友達がたくさんできましたか。（← Follow-up question）

<Continue>

5 How has your Japanese improved over time? Look back on your progress to move further forward.

Step 1 Briefly write down what you can/can't do using Japanese now.

	話す・聞く	読む・書く	日本の文化
🙂	Ex. 自分のことが話せる	短（みじか）い話が読める	落語について少し分かる
🙁	Ex. アニメや映画の日本語が少ししか分からない	漢字がたくさん書けない	知らないことがたくさんある

Step 2 Talk about what you can/can't do using Japanese now with your partner.

Ex. A: ○○さんは日本語でどんなことができるようになったと思いますか。

B: 私は日本語の二年生になってから、自分のことがたくさん話せるようになりました。でも、日本語でアニメや映画を見ている時、まだ少ししか分かりません。△△さんはどうですか。

A: そうですね、私は…　<Continue>

Group Work

Step 3 What do you want to do using Japanese? Write down your goals in the space provided below, then present them to the class.

①日本語でできるようになりたいこと：＿＿＿＿＿＿＿＿

②その理由や例：＿＿＿＿＿＿＿＿

③そのために、しようと思っていること：＿＿＿＿＿＿＿＿

Ex. ①私は字幕 (subtitles) を見なくても、日本語でアニメや映画が楽しめるようになりたいです。②それができたら、もっとおもしろいと思うし、若い人の話し方も学べるからです。③だから、同じアニメをくり返して見てみようと思っています。

Group Work

6 What will our world look like in the year 2100?

Step 1 Consider the changes in technology, climate, and society that may have occurred by 2100. Use your imagination and describe them in detail.

Ex. 宇宙エレベーターに乗って、簡単に月に旅行に行けるようになると思います。それから、薬を飲んで、食事をしなくなるかもしれません。

Step 2 Make three predictions about the year 2100 based on what you discussed, then present them to the class.

Ex. 私達は 2100 年までに宇宙エレベーターに乗って、簡単に月に旅行に行けるようになると思います。それから、月や火星 (Mars) に住めるようになるかもしれません。でも、宇宙人から地球を守らなくてはいけなくなるかもしれません。

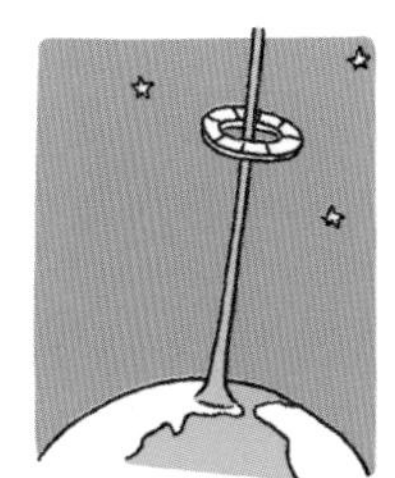

できるII Discuss briefly how you can do your part to make the world a better place.

できるII-A Vことにする

1 You have just decided to do the following things to make your life better. Describe your decisions. L20-12

Ex. 私は健康な生活を送るために、たくさん野菜を食べることにします。

Purpose	Decision
Ex. live a healthy life	→ eat a lot of vegetables
1) make more friends	→ join a tennis club at university
2) go to outer space	→ save money
3) learn about cultures in other countries	→ read more news on international relations
4) live happily	→ not to care about small mistakes
5) live in a new apartment	→ not to waste money
6) have more confidence	→ not to compare yourself with other people
7) your own	

2 Ask your partner if they have any New Year's resolutions that they have made for a better life.

Ex. A: ○○さんは今年の抱負(ほうふ) (resolutions) がありますか。

B: はい、私はいい成績(せいせき)を取るために、試験の前の日だけ徹夜(てつや)しないで、毎日復習(ふくしゅう)することにしました。

A: そうですか。私はもっとポジティブになるために、失敗(しっぱい)をしても気にしないことにしました。 <Continue>

3 Share your summer plans with your partner.

Ex. A: ○○さんは今年の夏休みに何をするかもう決めましたか。

Yes

B: はい、インターンシップをすることにしました。

A: そうですか。どんなインターンシップですか。 <Continue>

No

B: いいえ、まだ決めていません。自分の部屋をおしゃれにしたいと思っているんですが…

A: そうですか。じゃ、YouTube でおしゃれな部屋の作り方の動画を調べてみたらどうですか。色々な国の家具(かぐ)やインテリアの動画がたくさんあって、役(やく)に立つと思いますよ。

<Continue>

B: じゃ、私は夏休みの間に研究して、部屋をおしゃれにすることにします。

4 What are you studying for your major?

Step 1 Brainstorm some aspects of your major or the field you are interested in by filling in the blanks below.

① 専攻(せんこう)／興味(きょうみ)がある分野：________________

② 理由：________________________________

③ 勉強・研究していること／したいこと：________________

Step 2 Explain your major to your partner. Your partner will ask follow-up questions.

Ex. A: ○○さんの専攻(せんこう)は何ですか。

B: 神経科学(しんけいかがく)です。英語で "neuroscience" です。

A: そうですか。どうしてそれを専攻(せんこう)することにしたんですか。

B: 将来(しょうらい)、新しい VR のゲームを作りたいからです。

A: いいですね。今どんなことを勉強していますか。(← Follow-up question)

<Continue>

できるII-B Vことにしている

1 Match each purpose below with a habitual action and make a sentence. L20-13

Ex. 環境(かんきょう)を守るために、できるだけ洗剤(せんざい)を使わないことにしています。

Purpose	Habitual action
Ex. 環境(かんきょう)を守る	• 毎日筋(きん)トレをします
1) 健康(けんこう)で強い体を作る	• できるだけ洗剤(せんざい)を使いません
2) 心の健康(けんこう)	• 服やお金を寄付(きふ)します
3) 日本語の表現(ひょうげん)を学ぶ	• アニメや日本のドラマを見ます
4) 自分の将来(しょうらい)	• いやなことをあまり考えません
5) 困っている人を助ける	• お金を貯(た)めます

2 Do you have any specific habits or rules for yourself?

Step 1 Using the purpose cues 1)-5) in 1, talk with your partner about whether you have formed any habits or made any rules for yourself.

Ex. A: ○○さんは環境(かんきょう)を守るために、何をしていますか。

B: 環境(かんきょう)を守るために、できるだけプラスチックを使った物を買わないことにしています。

A: 例えば、どんな物ですか。(← Follow-up questions)

<Continue>

Step 2 Report to the class what kind of rules/habits your partner has.

できるII-C Conditional ～なら

1 Let's practice giving tips and recommendations.

Step 1 Your partner is looking for a place to go this weekend. Recommend Tobira Park based on the following preferences or plans your partner has told you about. L20-14

Ex. 自然(しぜん)が好きなら、「とびら公園(こうえん)」がおすすめですよ。

Ex. likes nature　1) will take a walk　2) will take a dog
3) looking for a quiet place　4) wants to see beautiful scenery
5) likes lakes　6) (it's) a date　7) your own

Step 2 Think of some travel recommendations for a country/city you are familiar with in response to a post on social media.

Ex. 4月にノルウェーに行くなら、船(ふね)でクルーズをするのがおすすめです。
景色(けしき)が美(うつく)しいし、フィヨルド(fjord)も見られるし、いいですよ。

2 Say you are inviting ピッキーさん, who is known for being very picky, to dinner this weekend. How would she respond to your invitation? L20-15

Ex. あなた　：ピッキーさん、週末に一緒(いっしょ)に晩ご飯を食べに行きませんか。

ピッキー：うーん、<u>日曜日の晩</u>なら、いいですよ。

Ex. 日曜日の晩です　1) アイさんが来ます　2) おいしいパスタが食べられます
3) ○○さんがおごってくれます　4) 店が広いです　5) 店がおしゃれです
6) 行ったことがない店です　7) 家から遠(とお)くないです　8) your own

3 You are talking with your friend about the coming weekend. Give a recommendation based on what your friend tells you.

Ex. A: 今週末、何する？

B: 今週末？　来週試験があるから、カフェで勉強することにした。

A: あ、カフェ（で勉強する）なら、「マイティー」っていうカフェがいいよ。
混(こ)んでいないし、静(しず)かだし、勉強しやすいよ。コーヒーもおいしいし…

B: へえ、そのカフェはどこにあるの？　<Continue>

Ex. カフェで勉強する　1) 友達とレストランで食事する　2) アルバイトを探(さが)す
3) アニメか映画を見る　4) 何か楽しいことをする　5) your own

4 Try making an advice pamphlet for those who are learning first-year Japanese from your point of view as a *senpai*.

Group Work

Step 1 Brainstorm about your Japanese learning experiences with your groupmates.

Possible topics	活用(かつよう) (conjugation)	文法(ぶんぽう)	助詞(じょし)	発音(はつおん)	漢字	読む	書く	聞く	話す

1) 日本語は特(とく)に何が難(むずか)しいと思いますか。　**Ex.** 活用(かつよう)
2) どうすれば 1)が上手になると思いますか。**Ex.** 役(やく)に立つアプリを使う。例えば…

Step 2 Share your group's ideas with the class.

Difficulty **Solution** **Details**	**Ex.** 私達は日本語は活用(かつよう)が特(とく)に難(むずか)しいと思います。だから、後輩(こうはい)に役(やく)に立つアプリを教えてあげることにしました。私達のおすすめは「かっちゃん」というアプリです。「かっちゃん」なら、教科書(きょうかしょ)の単語(たんご)の活用(かつよう)を発音(はつおん)を聞きながら簡単(かんたん)に練習することができます。　<Continue>

Step 3 Talk about how you can share your advice with your *koohai* (social media, a meetup, etc.), then share it with them.

Review

Now you can discuss your personal growth as well as your contributions to society. Let's think about how you can make a contribution to your community.

Step 1 The following are some common themes for sustainable development. Brainstorm with your partner by answering the following questions.

健康

教育

ジェンダー

環境

平和

1) どのコミュニティ（例えば大学や町）のどんな問題？

Ex. コミュニティ：大学の寮　　問題：寮のイベントでたくさんゴミが出る

2) 1)の問題は、どのテーマに関係がある？

Ex. 環境

3) 1)の問題を解決したいなら、何をした方がいい？

Ex. イベントには「マイカップ」と「マイプレート」を持っていく

Step 2 Present your ideas for contributing to your community to the class. Your audience will ask follow-up questions.

Problem to work on
Your idea(s) for improvement
Change(s) you expect to see
Conclusion
=============
Q&A

Ex. 私達が選んだテーマは環境です。大学の寮では、イベントでゴミがたくさん出ます。だから、その問題について考えてみました。

ゴミを少なくしたいなら、寮のイベントに、みんな自分の「マイカップ」と「マイプレート」を持っていった方がいいと思います。

そうしたら、寮のゴミも少なくなるし、みんなもっと環境について考えるようになるし、とてもいいと思います。

だから、みなさん、これからマイカップとマイプレートを使うことにしましょう！

Q: マイカップやマイプレートを洗う時、水も洗剤もたくさん使います。それについてどう思いますか。

言語ノート Language Note　たら, と, ば, and なら

In this volume, we have learned four conditional expressions: たら, と, ば, and なら. Let us review some important points of these expressions here.

1. たら (L12 #4)

"S_1たらS_2" is used when the action, event, or state in S_1 triggers that in S_2. たら can be used in most situations in which "if" is used in English. (1) provides examples:

(1) a. 今晩パーティーをします。時間があったら来てください。
I'm throwing a party this evening. Please come if you have time.
b. 雨が降ったら試合はないでしょう。*If it rains, there'll be no game, I guess.*
c. 日本で仕事ができたらとてもうれしいです。*I'd be very happy if I could work in Japan.*

"S_1たらS_2" can also be used when there is no question as to whether or not S_1 will occur, in which case, the idea of S_1たら is expressed using a temporal expression in English, as in (2).

(2) a. 6時になったら帰りたいです。*I want to go home at six (lit. when it has become six).*
b. 授業が終わったら私のオフィスに来てください。*Please come to my office after class.*

When S_1 and S_2 in "S_1たらS_2" both represent an action, S_1 must be completed before S_2. Thus, (3) is not grammatical.

(3) ×空港に行ったら電車で行った方がいいですよ。
Intended meaning: *If you're going to the airport, you'd better go by train.* (See 4. なら below.)

2. と (L17 #4)

The fundamental meaning of "S_1とS_2" is that S_2 always accompanies S_1. (4) provides examples:

(4) a. 私は難しい本を読むと頭が痛くなります。*My head aches whenever I read a difficult book.*
b. コンビニに行くとコピー機が使えます。
If you go to a convenience store, you can use a copier.

Because its core meaning is "S_2 is always the case when S_1 takes place," "S_1とS_2" cannot be used when S_2 represents a one-time action or event in the future, as in (5).

(5) a. ×今晩パーティーをします。時間があると来てください。Cf. (1a)
b. ×雨が降ると試合はないでしょう。Cf. (1b)

3. ば (L18 #6)

"S_1ばS_2" also means "If S_1, S_2." Thus, some sentences that involve たら can be paraphrased using ば, as in (6).

(6) a. 今晩パーティーをします。時間があれば来てください。Cf. (1a)
b. 雨が降れば試合はないでしょう。Cf. (1b)
c. 日本で仕事ができればとてもうれしいです。Cf. (1c)

When both ば and たら can be used, the difference between the ば version and the たら version is subtle. The たら version may sound a little more casual than the ば version to some speakers.

However, because ば is a conditional expression in a more strict sense, it cannot be used in some situations in which たら can be used. For example, "S_1ばS_2" is ungrammatical when S_2 represents a past event, as in (7).

(7) カフェに{×行けば／行ったら}ユミさんがいました。
When I went to the café, I found Yumi there (lit. Yumi was there).

4. なら (L20 #4)

The core meaning of "S_1ならS_2" is "if S_1 is {the case/true}, S_2." なら is different from たら, と and ば in that the action in S_1なら does not have to be completed before the action in S_2, as in (8). Here, たら, と, and ば cannot be used.

(8) a. 空港に行くなら電車で行った方がいいですよ。Cf. (3)
b. 引っこしするなら私の車を貸してあげますよ。*If you're moving, I'll lend you my car.*

Another difference is that "S_1ならS_2" cannot be used when S_1 takes place without fail, as in (9). たら, と, and ば, on the other hand, can all be used here.

(9) ×ここは夜になるならすずしくなります。**Intended meaning:** *It gets cool here at night.*

(10) shows the differences in meaning among the four different conditional expressions.

(10) a. 学校が忙しくなったらアルバイトをやめます。
I'll quit my part-time job {if/when} I get busy with my school work.
b. ×学校が忙しくなるとアルバイトをやめます。
c. 学校が忙しくなればアルバイトをやめます。
I'll quit my part-time job if I get busy with my school work.
d. 学校が忙しくなるならアルバイトをやめます。
I'll quit my part-time job if it's true that I'll get busy with my school work.

(10a) can mean two different things as shown in the English translations. That is, たら can be used both when the speaker knows that S_1 will take place and when the speaker is not certain that S_1 will take place. In either case, the event in S_1 occurs before the action in S_2.
(10b) is ungrammatical because S_2 represents a one-time action in the future.
(10c) basically means the same thing as (10a) if the speaker is not certain that S_1 will takes place. That is, S_1ば only means "if S_1."
(10d) is different from (10a) and (10c) in that the action in S_2 is taken before the event in S_1. That is, the speaker will quit her part-time job when she determines that she is going to get busy with her school work rather than when her school work actually gets busy.

See **GID** (vol.2): B. Connecting sentences 4.たら, と, ば, and なら for more comprehensive information on these conditional expressions.

読みましょう

できる III Understand and enjoy the expressions and characteristics of Japanese poems.

読み物を読む前に

1 次の質問に答えなさい。答えは日本語じゃなくてもいいです。

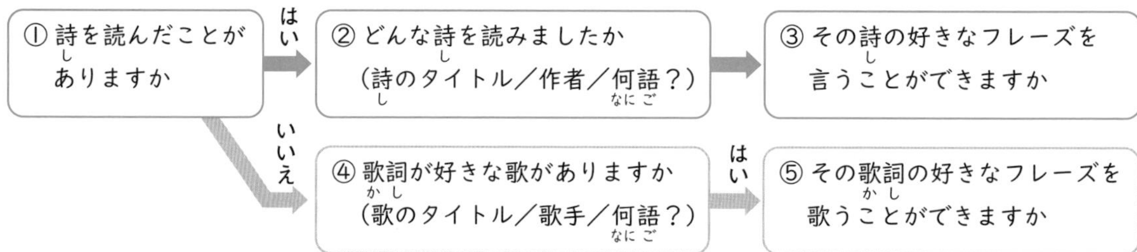

① 詩を読んだことがありますか
はい
② どんな詩を読みましたか（詩のタイトル／作者／何語？）
③ その詩の好きなフレーズを言うことができますか
いいえ
④ 歌詞が好きな歌がありますか（歌のタイトル／歌手／何語？）
はい
⑤ その歌詞の好きなフレーズを歌うことができますか

2 音とリズムを楽しむ

下の二つの詩は、谷川俊太郎という詩人の『ことばあそびうた』という本の中の詩です。

いるかいるか　いないかいるか
いないいないいるか　いつならいるか
よるならいるか　またきてみるか

いるかいないか　いないかいるか
いるいるいるか　いっぱいいるか
ねているいるか　ゆめみているか

かっぱかっぱらった
かっぱらっぱかっぱらった
とってちってた
かっぱなっぱかった
かっぱなっぱいっぱかった
かってきってくった

『ことばあそびうた』より　谷川俊太郎［詩］　福音館書店［刊］

1) 詩を声に出して何回も読んでみてください。ラップのように読んでもいいです。
　読み方：まず左から右に読んで、それから次の行を読む。
2) 詩の中でどの言葉がくり返されていますか。その言葉に ◯ をしましょう。
3) 「いるか」は "dolphin" で、「かっぱ」は水の中に住む妖怪 (See *TOBIRA I*, p.216) です。詩の意味が全部分からなくてもいいですが、この二つの詩を読んで、どう思いましたか。
4) みんなの前で声に出して読んでみましょう。

3 メタファーを考える

みなさんは「緑」と聞いて何をイメージしますか。日本語でイメージするのは、野菜や木や自然です。だから、日本では緑という言葉はよく植物や自然のメタファーとして (as) 使われます。

色々な言葉のイメージ（メタファー）について話し合ってみましょう。日本語で言えなかったら、分かる言葉で話してもいいです。

1）あなたの（国の）言葉では「緑」にはどんな意味がありますか。何をイメージしますか。

2）あなたの（国の）言葉では「赤」「青」「黒」にはどんな意味がありますか。何をイメージしますか。

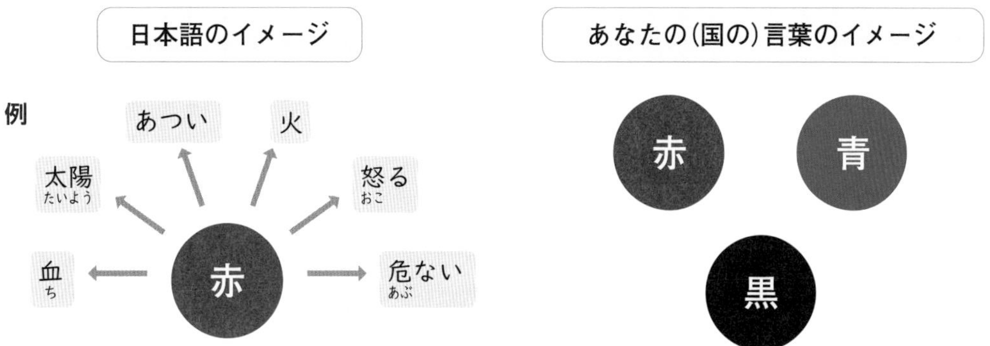

3）あなたの（国の）言葉では「鳥」「山」「雪」について、どんなことをイメージしますか。

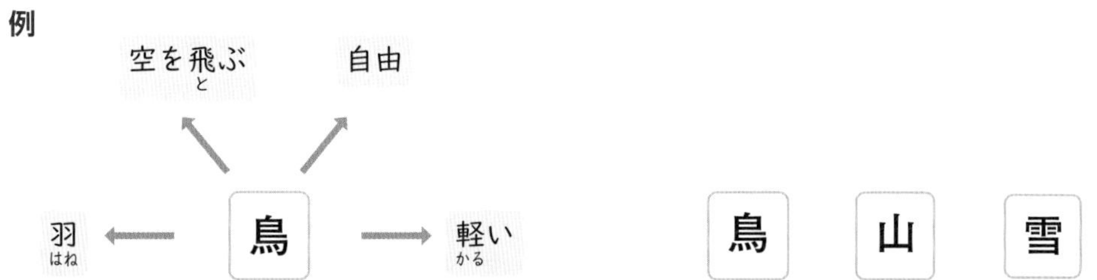

読み物：詩を読んでみよう

1 金子みすゞという詩人の『こだまでしょうか』という詩を読んでみましょう。詩を読む時に一つの言葉の色々な意味を考えると、作者の伝えたいことが分かるようになります。

> みすゞ＝みすず　あすぼう＝あそぼう　〜っていう＝〜と言う　あすばない＝あそばない
> そうして＝そして　さみしくなって＝さびしくなって

こだまでしょうか

金子みすゞ

「あすぼう」っていうと
「あすぼう」っていう。
「馬鹿」っていうと
「馬鹿」っていう。
「もうあすばない」っていうと
「あすばない」っていう。
そうして、あとで
さみしくなって、
「ごめんね」っていうと
「ごめんね」っていう。
こだまでしょうか、
いいえ、誰でも。

『金子みすゞ童謡全集』（JULA 出版局）より

1）『こだまでしょうか』の詩について話し合ってください。

①「こだま」は何だと思いますか。誰と誰が話していると思いますか。

②「さみしくなって」という文がありますが、さびしくなるのは誰でしょうか。

③ 最後の行の「いいえ、誰でも」の後には、どんな言葉が続くと思いますか。

2） この詩を読んでどう感じましたか。感じた気持ち全部に ◯ をしてください。

おもしろい　かわいい　さびしそう　うれしそう　悲しそう
静か　空気がきれい　その他 (other)：＿＿＿＿＿＿

3） 2)で選んだ気持ちで『こだまでしょうか』を声に出して読んでみてください。一人で読んでも、ペアやグループで読んでもいいです。自分の好きな読み方を見つけましょう。

2 谷川俊太郎の『生きる』という詩を読んでみましょう。

1）「生きる」という言葉にどんなイメージを持っていますか。どんな言葉を連想 (to associate) しますか。

Step 1 詩を読む前に「生きる」という言葉のマインドマップを作りましょう。自分で作っても、グループで作ってもいいですが、できるだけ日本語を使って書いてください。

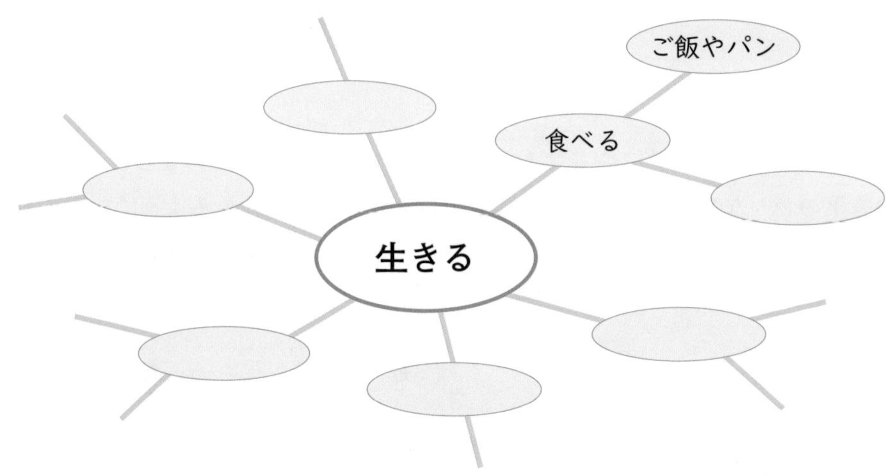

Step 2 みんなでマインドマップを比べてみましょう。他の人と同じ言葉やよく似ている言葉がありますか。全然違う言葉は何ですか。

Step 3 なぜその言葉を連想 (to associate) したか話し合ってみましょう。

生きる

谷川俊太郎

生きているということ
いま生きているということ
それはのどがかわくということ
木漏れ日がまぶしいということ
ふっとあるメロディを思い出すということ
くしゃみすること
あなたと手をつなぐこと

生きているということ
いま生きているということ
それはミニスカート
それはプラネタリウム
それはヨハン・シュトラウス
それはピカソ
それはアルプス
すべての美しいものに出会うということ
そして
かくされた悪を注意深くこばむこと

生きているということ
いま生きているということ
泣けるということ
笑えるということ
怒れるということ
自由ということ

生きているということ
いま生きているということ
いま遠くで犬が吠えるということ
いま地球がまわっているということ
いまどこかで産声があがるということ
いまどこかで兵士が傷つくということ
いまぶらんこがゆれているということ
いまいまがすぎてゆくこと

生きているということ
いま生きているということ
鳥ははばたくということ
海はとどろくということ
かたつむりははうということ
人は愛するということ
あなたの手のぬくみ
いのちということ

『生きる』より　谷川俊太郎［詩］　福音館書店［刊］

まぶしい：dazzling
ふっと：suddenly
手をつなぐ：to hold hands
すべての：all
かくされた悪：hidden evil
注意深く：carefully
こばむ：to refuse

吠える：to bark
産声があがる：(a baby) gives its first cry
兵士：soldier
傷つく：to be wounded
ぶらんこ：swing [playground equipment]
すぎてゆく(＝すぎていく)：to pass by

はばたく：to flap (wings)
とどろく：(a wave) roars
かたつむりははう：a snail crawls
ぬくみ(＝ぬくもり)：gentle warmth
いのち：life

木漏れ日

2) 詩を声に出さないで読んでみてください。

3) 詩の内容や詩が伝えたいことについて考えてみましょう。

① この詩の中に、1) のマインドマップに書いたのと同じ言葉がありますか。

②「生きる」の英語の意味には "to live; to be alive; to exist; to survive; to subsist" がありますが、この詩にはどの意味が合う (to fit) と思いますか。

③ 意味が分からないフレーズがあったら、どんな意味か話し合ってみましょう。

④ この詩のどの言葉やフレーズが好きですか。

4) 詩の段落は連 (stanza) と言いますが、『生きる』には連が五つあります。

1番目の連：1～7行目　　2番目の連：8～17行目　　3番目の連：18～23行目

4番目の連：24～31行目　　5番目の連：32～39行目

① それぞれの連 (each stanza) のトピックは下のどれか考えてみましょう。一つじゃなくてもいいです。

今、生き物がしていること	気持ちや感情 (emotions)	美しいと思うもの
体で感じたりしたりすること	今、地球で起こっていること	その他：________

② それぞれの連 (each stanza) は、どんな読み方がいいと思いますか。

強く読む	やさしく読む	うれしそうに読む	悲しそうに読む
静かにゆっくり読む		速く元気に読む	その他：__________

5) あなたなら、10行目から14行目のカタカナのところにどんなカタカナの言葉を入れますか。入れた後で、どんな言葉にしたかみんなで話し合ってみましょう。

Group Work

6) 4) の②で考えた読み方でこの詩を声に出して読んでみてください。

2番目の連 (stanza) のカタカナの言葉は、5) で入れた自分の言葉に変えてもいいです。

グループで読むなら、はじめに誰がどの連 (stanza) を読むか決めてください。

練習した後で、みんなの前で読んでみましょう。

詩を書いてみよう

この『生きる』という詩のそれぞれの連 (each stanza) のトピックやフォーマットを使って、自分の「生きる」という詩を作ってみましょう。

フォーマットの例

生きているということ
いま生きているということ
それは________________________________ということ
________________________________ということ
____

聞きましょう

リスニング・ストラテジー：Listening strategy

Integration (3): Predicting, getting the gist, and listening for keywords
In this lesson, you will listen to a speech as a part of our integration exercises. First, try to understand the main points and some details, then practice asking questions.

1 **Pre-listening activity:** 日本語スピーチコンテストにスピーチを聞きに来ました。次はグエンさんのスピーチです。グエンさんのスピーチのタイトルは「初めて落語にチャレンジ」です。グエンさんはどんなスピーチをすると思いますか。スピーチのタイトルから内容（ないよう）を考えてみましょう。

2 **Listening:** L20-16

1） グエンさんのスピーチを聞きましょう。グエンさんがこのスピーチで一番言いたいことは何ですか。スピーチの後で a.～c. の文を聞いて一つ選（えら）んでください。

小話（こばなし）：brief comic story　けいこ：lesson; rehearsal　拍手（はくしゅ）：applause

グエンさんがスピーチで一番言いたいこと　　a.　　b.　　c.

2） グエンさんのスピーチをもう一度聞いて、下の a.～c. の質問に日本語で答えてください。

a. グエンさんはどうして落語のイベントに出ましたか。
b. グエンさんはどうして小話（こばなし）をやめたいと思いましたか。
c. グエンさんが小話（こばなし）をやめたいと思った時、クラスメートと先生はどうしましたか。

3） あなたが1でした予測（よそく）(prediction) は正しかったですか。クラスメートと話し合ってください。

4） スピーチの後で、グエンさんにスピーチの内容（ないよう）について質問します。グエンさんにしたい質問を二つ考えましょう。

質問１：＿＿＿＿＿＿＿＿＿＿＿＿＿＿＿＿＿＿＿＿

質問２：＿＿＿＿＿＿＿＿＿＿＿＿＿＿＿＿＿＿＿＿

Exit Check
Now it's time to go back to the DEKIRU List for this chapter (p.353) and do the exit check to see what new things you can do now that you've completed the lesson.

Challenge Unit6 チャレンジ

1 Best Japanese music playlist

Do you have any favorite Japanese songs?

Step 1 Share your favorite song(s) with your classmates and make a playlist together.

Step 2 Try translating the lyrics (in part or in whole) into other languages you know and explain the song to your classmates. You may sing the song if you like.

Ex. みなさんは『手紙～拝啓 十五の君へ～』という歌を聞いたことがありますか。
これは日本の卒業式 (graduation ceremony) でよく歌われる歌です。
歌詞はちょっと難しいですが、感動するし、歌いやすいので、
みなさんにおすすめしたいです。特に好きな歌詞は… <Continue>

2 Kanji of the semester

As explained in 漢字の話 on p.363, in Japan, the kanji of the year is announced each year to symbolize notable events of that year. Think of one kanji that describes this semester or year for you and explain it to your classmates.

Ex. 私の今学期の漢字は「会」です。今年は日本語のクラスで色々な人に会って、日本語で会話をして、いい友達になりました。それから、日本の会社でインターンシップをして、楽しかったです。
これからは小さくても、何か社会の役に立つことをしたいと思っています。だから、私は「会」を選びました。

3 Connecting with the world

Through *TOBIRA*, you have learned not only the Japanese language but also many aspects of Japanese culture. Now, it is your turn to share your own culture with Japanese speakers outside of the classroom.

Step 1 Brainstorm a topic by answering the following questions.

1) トピックは何？	**Ex.** ベトナム映画
2) 何を伝えたい？	**Ex.** あまり知られていないけれど、ベトナム映画はおもしろい
3) どうやって伝えたい？	**Ex.** 日本語で動画を作って、SNS にアップする

おすすめの
ベトナム映画 10

Step 2 Create a presentation about your topic, share it with your classmates, and comment on their presentations.

単語さくいん Vocabulary Index

[u] = u-verb, [ru] = ru-verb, [irr.] = irregular verb
* = additional meaning (See the right-most column for the lesson in which it appears.)
See p.287 for expressions commonly used in instructions.

あ	あいさつ(を)する		to greet [*person* に]	L17
	あいす [*u*]	愛す	to love [*thing/person/animal* を]	L16
	アイロン		iron [appliance]	L18
	アイロンをかける [*ru*]		to iron [*clothes* に]	L18
	あかちゃん	赤ちゃん	baby; infant	L18
	あがる [*u*]	上がる	to go inside someone's home (in Japan) [*home* に]	L19
	あきらめる [*ru*]		to give up [*thing* を]	L14
	あく [*u*]	開く	(something) opens [*thing* が]	L14
	あける [*ru*]	開ける	to open [*thing* を]	L14
	あさねぼう(を)する	朝ねぼう(を)～	to oversleep (in the morning)	L14
	あじ	味	taste; flavor	L16
	あたためる [*ru*]	温める	to warm; to heat up [*thing* を]	L11
	あちら		that over there; over there; that way over there; that person over there [polite equivalent of あれ/あそこ/あの人]	L19
	あつまる [*u*]	集まる	to be collected; to gather together [*thing/person* が]	L19
	あつめる [*ru*]	集める	to collect; to gather [*thing/person* を]	L12
	アドバイス(を)する		to give advice [*person* に]	L15
	あながあく [*u*]	穴が開く	a hole opens up [*thing* に]	L18
	あやまる [*u*]	謝る	to apologize [*person* に]	L13
	ある Noun		a certain Noun; one Noun	L17
	アレルギー		allergy	L14
	あんしんする	安心する	to feel relieved/at ease	L18
	あんないする	案内する	to guide [*person* を *place* に]; to show around [*person* に *place* を]	L14
い	いかが		how [polite equivalent of どう]	L19
	いきる [*ru*]	生きる	to live	L17
	いけん	意見	opinion	L15
	いじめる [*ru*]		to bully [*person/animal* を]	L16
	いじわる(な)		mean [personality]	L16
	いそぐ [*u*]	急ぐ	to hurry	L16
	いたす [*u*]		courteous expression for する	L19
	いただく [*u*]		courteous expression for 食べる and 飲む	L19
	いためる [*ru*]		to stir-fly [*thing* を]	L11
	いっしょうけんめい(に)		with one's utmost effort; with all one's might	L19
	いつでも		any time; whenever; always	L15
	いなくなる [*u*]		to disappear [*person/animal* が]	L12
	いままで	今まで	(up) until now; before now	L16
	いや(な)		unpleasant; unwelcome	L16
	いらっしゃる [*u*]		honorific expression for 行く, 来る, and いる	L19
	いりぐち	入口／入り口	entrance	L14
	いる [*u*]	要る	to need [*thing* が]	L15
	いれる [*ru*]	入れる	to put (Y) in (X); to insert (Y in X) [*thing X* に *thing Y* を]	L11
う	うえる [*ru*]	植える	to plant [*plant* を]	L13
	うける [*ru*]	受ける	to take [*exam/quiz* を]; to undergo (a medical procedure) [*surgery/medical exam* を]*	L8 L19
	うごかす [*u*]	動かす	to move [*thing/body part* を]	L15
	うごく [*u*]	動く	(something/someone) moves; (something) functions [*thing/person* が]	L12
	うそをつく [*u*]		to lie [*person* に]	L16
	うちゅう	宇宙	(outer) space; the universe	L20
	うちゅうじん	宇宙人	alien; extraterrestrial being	L20
	うつくしい	美しい	beautiful	L20
	うで		arm	L16
	うまくいく [*u*]		to go well [*thing* が]	L20
	うまれる [*ru*]	生まれる	to be born [*person/animal* が]	L12
	うらやましい		jealous; envious	L15
	うりきれる [*ru*]	売り切れる	to sell out [*thing* が]	L16
	うわさ(を)する		to gossip; to spread rumors	L17
え	えいがかんとく	映画監督	film director	L19
	えさ		feed; animal food	L15
	えさをやる [*u*]		to feed [*animal* に]	L15
	えらぶ [*u*]	選ぶ	to choose; to select [*thing/person* を]	L16
	エレベーター		elevator	L15
	えんりょする	遠慮する	to hold back; to refrain	L19
お	おいのり(を)する		to pray	L17
	おうえんする	応援する	to cheer; to support; to root for [*person/team/thing, etc.* を]	L18
	おおあめ	大雨	heavy rain	L17
	おおゆき	大雪	heavy snow	L17

おかねをおろす [*u*]	お金を～	to withdraw money	L12
おかねをためる [*ru*]	お金を貯める	to save money	L16
おきゃくさま	お客様	customer [formal]	L17
おきゃくさん	お客さん	guest; customer	L13
おく [*u*]	置く	to put; to place [*thing* を *place* に]	L14
おこす [*u*]	起こす	to wake [*person* を]	L16
おこる [*u*]	怒る	to get angry	L11
おこる [*u*]	起こる	to happen; to take place [*event* が]	L19
おごる [*u*]		to treat (someone) to (food/drink) [*person* に *food/drink* を]	L15
おじゃましました		[polite greeting used when leaving someone's home, etc.]	L19
おじゃまします		[polite greeting used when entering someone's home, etc.]	L19
おしゃれ(な)		stylish; fashionable	L20
おしり		(one's) backside; buttocks	L14
おす [*u*]	押す	to push [*thing/person* を]	L17
おせわになる [*u*]	お世話に～	to be in (someone's) care; to be helped (by) [*person* に/の]	L17
おちこむ [*u*]	落ち込む	to get depressed; to feel down	L12
おちる [*ru*]	落ちる	(something) drops/falls [*things* が]	L14
おっしゃる [*u*]		honorific expression for 言う	L19
おとこのこ	男の子	boy	L19
おとす [*u*]	落とす	to drop [*thing* を]	L14
おととい		the day before yesterday	L14
おととし		the year before last	L16
おとな	大人	adult	L20
おどり		(traditional Asian) dance	L13
おどろく [*u*]		to be surprised	L11
おにぎり		rice ball [Japanese food]	L12
おばけ	お化け	ghost; spooky imaginary creature	L14
おまいり(を)する／にいく [*u*]	お参りに行く	to visit/go to a temple/shrine to pray	L17
おもいだす [*u*]	思い出す	to recall; to be reminded [*memory/thing/person* を]	L19
おもいで	思い出	memory	L14
おもてなし		hospitality	L17
おもに	主に	mostly; mainly	L19
おや	親	parent	L12
おやすみになる [*u*]	お休みに～	honorific expression for ねる	L19
おゆ	お湯	hot water	L11
おゆがわく [*u*]	お湯が～	water boils	L14
おゆをわかす [*u*]	お湯を～	to boil water	L14
おる [*u*]		courteous expression for いる	L19
おれい	お礼	expression of gratitude	L17
おれいをいう [*u*]	お礼を言う	to thank; to say thank you [*person* に]	L17
おわり	終わり	end	L18
おわる [*u*]	終わる	to (come to an) end [*thing* が]	L11
おんど	温度	temperature	L17
おんなのこ	女の子	girl	L19
か			
か		mosquito	L16
かいがい	海外	overseas	L13
かいぎ	会議	meeting; conference	L15
かいけつする	解決する	to solve; to resolve; to settle [*problem/issue* を]	L18
がいこくじん	外国人	foreigner	L17
かいじょう	会場	venue; meeting place	L19
かいだん	階段	stairs; staircase	L16
かいわ	会話	conversation	L11
かえす [*u*]	返す	to return; to give back [*person/place* に *thing* を]	L12
かえる [*ru*]	変える	to change (X into Y) [*thing X* を *thing Y* に]	L12
がか	画家	painter	L16
かがくしゃ	科学者	scientist	L12
かがさす [*u*]		a mosquito bites	L16
かがみ	鏡	mirror	L15
かぎ		key; lock	L14
かぎがかかる [*u*]		(something) locks (itself) [*thing* に]	L14
かぎをあける [*ru*]	～を開ける	to unlock	L20
かぎをかける [*ru*]		to lock [*thing* に]	L14
かぐ	家具	furniture	L15
かくす [*u*]		to hide [*thing/person* を *place* に]	L15
がくちょう	学長	president (of a university)	L17
かける [*ru*]		to pour/drizzle/sprinkle (Y onto X) [*thing X* に *thing Y* を]; to sit down (on a chair, sofa, etc.) [*seat* に]*	L11 L19
かさ		umbrella	L13
かさをさす [*u*]		to hold up an umbrella	L13
かざる [*u*]		to display (as decoration) [*thing* を *place* に]; to decorate [*thing/room* を]	L14

かし	歌詞	lyrics	L20
かじをする	家事を〜	to do housework/household chores	L15
かぞえる [*ru*]	数える	to count [*thing* を]	L19
かた	肩	shoulder	L17
がっき	楽器	musical instrument	L12
かつどう	活動	activity	L17
がまんする		to be patient; to put up with [*thing* を]	L18
かみさま	神様	deity; god	L13
かみをそめる [*ru*]	髪を染める	to color (one's) hair	L13
かみをとかす [*u*]	髪を〜	to comb (one's) hair	L15
ガムをかむ [*u*]		to chew gum	L13
かよう [*u*]	通う	to commute; to attend; to frequent [*place* に]	L18
からだにいい	体にいい	to be good for (one's) health	L15
からて	空手	karate [martial art]	L18
かわかす [*u*]		to dry [*clothes/thing* を]	L16
かんがえ	考え	idea; thought	L18
かんきょう	環境	environment	L15
かんけい	関係	relationship	L20
かんこうきゃく	観光客	tourist	L17
かんしゃする	感謝する	to thank; to feel grateful [*person/thing* に]	L13
かんじる [*ru*]	感じる	to feel; to sense [*sent.* と]	L20
かんたん(な)	簡単(な)	simple; easy [not used for people]	L11
かんどうする	感動する	to be moved; to be (emotionally) touched [*thing* に]	L11
カンニング(を)する		to cheat (on a test, etc.)	L13
かんばん	看板	sign; signboard	L14
き			
きえる [*ru*]	消える	(something) turns off/goes out [*thing* が]	L14
きがえる [*ru*]	着替える	to change clothes [*old clothes* を *new clothes* に]	L15
きがつく [*u*]	気が〜	to notice [*thing/person* に]	L18
きけん(な)	危険(な)	dangerous	L18
きじ	記事	(media) article	L13
きせつ	季節	season	L17
きた	北	north	L17
きたぐち	北口	north entrance/exit (of a train station)	L17
きにする	気に〜	to care/worry/be concerned (about) [*thing* を]	L20
きびしい	厳しい	strict; severe; harsh	L17
きふする	寄付する	to make a donation [*person/organization* に *thing/money* を]	L15
きまる [*u*]	決まる	to be decided [*thing* が]	L12
きもち	気持ち	feeling; mood	L13
きもちがいい	気持ちがいい	nice-feeling; comfortable; pleasant	L13
きもちがわるい	気持ちが悪い	to feel sick/creepy/gross/unpleasant	L13
きゅうきゅうしゃ	救急車	ambulance	L15
きゅうに	急に	suddenly; abruptly	L17
ぎゅうにく	牛肉	beef	L11
ぎゅうにゅう	牛乳	milk	L13
きょういく	教育	education	L17
ぎょうじ	行事	(seasonal/annual) event	L13
きょうしつ	教室	classroom	L14
きょうじゅ	教授	professor	L17
きょうみをもつ [*u*]	興味を持つ	to take an interest (in) [*thing/person* に]	L19
きょく	曲	piece of music; song	L16
きる [*u*]	切る	to cut [*thing* を]	L11
〜キロ		... km; ... kg	L16
きをつける [*ru*]	気を〜	to be careful; to watch out; to take care [*thing* に]	L13
きんちょうする	緊張する	to get nervous; to feel tense	L12
きんトレ(を)する	筋トレ(を)〜	to do strength training; to lift weights	L12
く			
くうき	空気	air; atmosphere	L20
くさい		foul-smelling; stinky	L14
くしゃみ		sneeze	L17
くしゃみをする／がでる [*ru*]	〜が出る	to sneeze	L17
くすり	薬	medicine; drug	L14
くださる [*u*]		honorific expression for くれる	L19
くだもの	果物	fruit	L14
〜ぐち	〜口	... entrance/exit	L17
くつした	くつ下	sock	L11
くび	首	neck	L14
クモ		spider	L19
くらべる [*ru*]	比べる	to compare (X and Y) [*thing X* と *thing Y* を]	L20
くりかえす [*u*]	くり返す	to repeat; to do over again [*thing* を]	L20
くるまをとめる [*ru*]	車を止める	to park/stop a car	L13
け			
けいかく	計画	plan	L12
けいかくをたてる [*ru*]	計画を立てる	to make a plan	L12
けいけんする	経験する	to experience [*thing* を]	L12

けいご	敬語	*keigo*; honorific language	L19
けいざい	経済	economy	L18
けいさつ	警察	police	L14
けいさんする	計算する	to calculate [*thing* を]	L12
けがをする		to get injured	L14
けしき	景色	scenery; view	L11
けしゴム	消しゴム	eraser	L11
けしょうする	化粧する	to put on makeup	L13
けす [*u*]	消す	to turn off (the lights, etc.); to erase; to delete (messages, etc.) [*thing* を]	L14
けっか	結果	result; outcome	L20
げつまつ	月末	end of the month	L20
げんきをだして(ください)	元気を出して〜	(Please) cheer up.	L16
けんこう	健康	health	L16
けんこう(な)	健康(な)	healthy	L16

こ

〜こ	〜個	[counter for small objects]	L13
Duration ご	〜後	[duration] later; from now	L16
こうこうせい	高校生	high school student	L13
こうさてん	交差点	intersection	L18
こうじょう	工場	factory	L19
こうちゃ	紅茶	black tea	L19
こうはい	後輩	junior member of a group	L18
コーヒー/おちゃをいれる [*ru*]	お茶を〜	to make coffee/tea	L13
こおり	氷	ice	L15
こくさいかんけい	国際関係	international relations	L20
こころ	心	heart; mind	L15
ごちそうする		to treat (someone) to (a meal, etc.); to cook (for) [*person* に *food/drink/meal* を]	L16
こちら		this; here; this way; this person [polite equivalent of これ/ここ/この人]	L19
こと		(intangible) thing	L12
ことば	言葉	word; phrase; language	L11
コピーする		to make a copy [*thing* を]	L12
こまる [*u*]	困る	to be in trouble; to have a hard time	L12
{ごみ/ゴミ}ばこ	〜箱	trash can; garbage bin	L16
こむ [*u*]	混む	to get crowded [*place* が]	L11
ごらんになる [*u*]	ご覧になる	honorific expression for 見る	L19
これからも		in the future as well	L15
ころす [*u*]	殺す	to kill [*insect/animal/person, etc.* を]	L20
ころぶ [*u*]	転ぶ	to fall over; to trip	L14
こわす [*u*]		to break; to damage [*thing* を]	L14
こわれる [*ru*]		(something) breaks [*thing* が]	L14
こんしゅうまつ	今週末	this weekend	L20

さ

さいあく	最悪	worst	L14
さいご	最後	final; last	L11
さいごに	最後に	finally	L11
さいごの Noun	最後の〜	final Noun; last Noun	L11
さいしょ	最初	the first	L13
ざいりょう	材料	ingredient; material	L11
さく [*u*]		to bloom [*flower* が]	L17
さくしゃ	作者	author; writer; creator	L20
さくひん	作品	(a piece of) work	L15
さす [*u*]		to bite; to sting [*insect* が *body (part)* を]	L16
さそう [*u*]	誘う	to invite [*person* を *event* に]	L15
〜さつ	〜冊	[counter for bound/printed materials]	L13
ざっし	雑誌	magazine	L11
さとう	砂糖	sugar	L11
サボる [*u*]		to skip (work, class, etc.) [*work/class* を]	L13
さわぐ [*u*]		to make noise	L13
さんかする	参加する	to participate [*event* に]	L13
ざんぎょうする	残業する	to work overtime	L18

し

し	詩	poem; poetry	L20
シートベルトをする		to fasten a seat belt; to buckle up	L13
しお	塩	salt	L11
しかく	四角	square; box (on a form) [noun]	L11
しかくい	四角い	square; box-shaped	L11
しかる [*u*]		to scold; to reprimand [*person* を]	L16
じかんをまもる [*u*]	時間を守る	to be on time; to be punctual	L18
じこ	事故	accident [traffic, etc.]	L12
じこしょうかいする	自己紹介する	to introduce oneself [*person* に]	L19
じこにあう [*u*]	事故に〜	to have an accident	L16
しじん	詩人	poet	L20
じしんをもつ [*u*]	自信を持つ	to have confidence [*thing* に]	L20
しぜん	自然	nature	L11
しっぱいする	失敗する	to fail; to be unsuccessful [*thing* に/を]	L18
じどうで	自動で	automatically	L14
じぶん	自分	oneself	L11
じぶんで	自分で	by oneself; on one's own	L11

しま	島	island	L12
しまる [*u*]	閉まる	(something) closes [*thing* が]	L14
しめきり	しめ切り	deadline; due date	L17
しめきりをまもる [*u*]	しめ切りを守る	to meet a deadline	L18
しめる [*ru*]	閉める	to close [*thing* を]	L14
しゃかい	社会	society	L13
しゃべる [*u*]		to chat; to talk; to speak [*person* と] [informal]	L13
じゆう	自由	freedom	L12
じゆう(な)	自由(な)	free	L12
じゆうに	自由に	freely	L12
～じゅう	～中	(all) throughout [*place* + 中] [*duration* + 中]	L13
じゅうしょ	住所	address	L19
しゅうしょくする	就職する	to get a (full-time) job [*workplace* に]	L12
じゅく		cram school	L17
しゅくだいがでる [*ru*]	宿題が出る	homework is assigned	L13
しゅじゅつする	手術する	to undergo surgery; to perform surgery [*body part* を]	L12
しゅしょう	首相	prime minister	L17
しゅっちょう(を)する／にいく [*u*]	出張に行く	to go on a business trip [*place* に]	L17
しょうがくせい	小学生	elementary school student	L13
しょうがっこう	小学校	elememtary school	L13
じょうだんをいう [*u*]	冗談を言う	to make a joke	L16
しょうテスト	小テスト	quiz [academic]	L18
じょうほう	情報	information	L15
しょうゆ		soy sauce	L11
しょくじ(を)する	食事(を)～	to have a meal; to dine	L12
しょくぶつ	植物	plant	L20
しょるい	書類	document; paperwork	L17
しらせる [*ru*]	知らせる	to inform; to notify [*person* に *information* を]	L17
(お)しろ	(お)城	castle	L12
しんかんせん	新幹線	*Shinkansen*; bullet train	L16
しんごう	信号	traffice light	L16
しんじる [*ru*]	信じる	to believe (in) [*thing/person* を]	L15
じんせい	人生	(one's) life	L16
しんせき	親せき	relative; extended family	L16
しんぱいする	心配する	to worry [*thing* を/について]	L12

す

すうじ	数字	number [numeral]; digit	L11
すく [*u*]		to get less crowded [*place* が]	L18
ずっと		the whole time; all throughout	L16
すばらしい		wonderful; fantastic	L12

せ

せいかく	性格	personality; character	L14
せいかつ(を)する／をおくる [*u*]	生活を送る	to live/lead a life	L17
せいじか	政治家	politician	L19
せき		cough	L14
せきがでる [*ru*]	～が出る	to cough	L14
ぜったい(に)	絶対(に)	definitely	L13
せつめいする	説明する	to explain [*person* に *thing* を]	L11
せわをする	世話を～	to take care (of) [*person/animal* の]	L15
せんざい	洗剤	detergent; cleaner	L20
せんたくき		washing machine	L15
せんたくもの	せんたく物	laundry [clothes/linens that have been/will be laundered]	L15
せんぱい	先輩	senior member of a group; senior colleague	L15

そ

そちら		that; there; that way; that person [polite equivalent of それ/そこ/その人]	L19
そつぎょうする	卒業する	to graduate [*school* を]	L12
そば		buckwheat (noodles)	L14
そば		(someone's/something's) side	L15
そろそろしつれいします	～失礼します	[polite greeting used to signal you will soon be leaving someone's home, etc.]	L19

た

～だい	～台	[counter for cars/machines/ mechanical devices]	L16
たいいんする	退院する	to be discharged from a hospital [*hospital* を]	L18
だいじ(な)	大事(な)	precious; important	L18
たいしかん	大使館	embassy	L12
だいとうりょう	大統領	president (of a country)	L17
タオル		towel	L13
たおれる [*ru*]		to fall down [*thing* が]; to fall over [*tree* が]; to pass out [*person* が]	L19
たからくじ	宝くじ	lottery (ticket)	L12
たからくじ{に／が}あたる [*u*]	宝くじ～当たる	to win a lottery	L12
だす [*u*]	出す	to submit; to turn in [*thing* を]; to take out [*thing* を]; to serve [*food/drink/meal* を]*; to invest; to chip in; to pay [*money* を]*; to emit (air) [*air* を]*	L6 L16

たすかる [*u*]	助かる	to be saved; to be helped [*person* が]	L15
ただ		free of charge	L12
ただしい	正しい	correct; right	L17
たたみ	畳	*tatami* [traditional Japanese straw mat]	L13
たたむ [*u*]		to fold [*clothes* を]	L15
～たち	～達	[plural marker for people, animal, etc.]	L12
たつ [*u*]	経つ	(time) passes [*time* が]	L18
たてる [*ru*]	建てる	to build [*building* を]	L16
たとえば	例えば	for example	L11
たのしみ	楽しみ	pleasure; enjoyment	L12
たのしみにしています	楽しみに～	to look forward to [*event/activity* を]	L12
たのしむ [*u*]	楽しむ	to enjoy [*thing* を]	L12
たのむ [*u*]		to ask a favor; to request [*person* に *favor* を]	L16
たまご	卵／玉子	egg	L11
だます [*u*]		to deceive; to trick [*person* を]	L19
たりない	足りない	to be not sufficient [*thing/person* が]	L15
たりる [*ru*]	足りる	to be sufficient [*thing/person* が]	L15
だれでも	誰でも	anyone; whoever; everyone	L20
たんい	単位	(academic) credit	L12
ち			
ち	血	blood	L14
チェックする		to check (out/on) [*thing* を]	L11
ちがう [*u*]	違う	(X is) different (from Y) [*thing X* は *thing Y* と]; (X and Y are) different [*thing X* と *thing Y* は]	L12
ちかづく [*u*]	近づく	to come close; to approach [*person* が *person/thing* に]; (time) draws near [*time* が]	L17
ちきゅう	地球	the Earth	L18
ちこくする	遅刻する	to be late [*activity/event* に]	L13
ちず	地図	map	L12
ちほう	地方	region; area	L16
チャレンジする		to take on a challenge; to try [*thing* に]	L19
～ちゅう	～中	(with)in; during; in the middle of [*activity* + 中]	L13
ちゅういする	注意する	to pay attention [*thing/person* に]; to warn [*person* に/を]	L13
ちゅうがく／ちゅうがっこう	中学／中学校	junior high school; middle school	L13
ちゅうがくせい	中学生	junior high school student	L13
ちゅうしゃ	注射	injection; shot	L19
ちゅうもんする	注文する	to order [*thing* を]	L11
つ			
つき	月	the Moon	L20
つきあう [*u*]	付き合う	to go out; to date [*person* と]	L12
つぎ	次	next	L11
つぎに	次に	next [sequencer]	L11
つぎの Noun	次の～	next Noun	L11
つく [*u*]	着く	to arrive [*place* に]	L11
つく [*u*]		(something) turns on [*thing* が]	L14
つける [*ru*]		to spread (Y on X); to dip (X in Y) [*thing X* に *thing Y* を]	L11
つける [*ru*]		to turn on (the lights, etc.) [*thing* を]	L14
つごうがいい	都合がいい	to be convenient [date, time, etc.]	L18
つごうがわるい	都合が悪い	to be inconvenient [date, time, etc.]	L18
つたえる [*ru*]	伝える	to tell; to pass along; to deliver [*person* に *message* を/と]	L17
つづく [*u*]	続く	(something) continues [*thing* が]	L20
つづける [*ru*]	続ける	to continue [*thing* を]	L15
つとめる [*ru*]	勤める	to work (for) [*company/organization* に]	L15
つながる [*u*]		(something) connects [*thing* が/に]	L14
つなげる [*ru*]		to connect [*thing* を/に]	L14
つめ		nail [finger/toe]	L17
つめをきる [*u*]	～を切る	to clip (one's) nails	L17
つりをする		to fish	L13
て			
データ		data	L12
であう [*u*]	出会う	to meet; to come across; to encounter [*person/thing* と/に]	L18
ていでんする	停電する	to lose power; to have a power outage	L15
～ていらっしゃる [*u*]		honorific expression for ～ている	L19
～ておる [*u*]		courteous expression for ～ている	L19
できあがりです		It is done; It is ready (to eat).	L11
できる [*ru*]		to come into existence; to gain [*person/thing* が]; to do well; to be good at [*thing* が]	L14
できるだけ		as much as possible	L15
～てくださる [*u*]		honorific expression for ～てくれる	L19
でぐち	出口	exit	L14

てつやする	徹夜する	to stay up all night	L20
でる [ru]	出る	to go/come out [*thing* が]; to exit; to leave [*place* を]; to attend; to appear [*meeting/event/media* に]	L13
てをたたく [u]	手を～	to clap (one's) hands	L17
てん	点	score; point; dot	L16
～てん	～点	[counter for points/score]	L16
でんき	電気	light; electricity	L14
てんごく	天国	heaven	L17
てんさい	天才	genius	L16
でんしレンジ	電子～	microwave (oven)	L11
でんわにでる [ru]	電話に出る	to answer the phone	L13
でんわをかける [ru]	電話を～	to make a phone call [*person* に]	L13
でんわをきる [u]	電話を切る	to hang up the phone	L19
てんをとる [u]	点を取る	to score; to get points	L16
と			
～ど	～度	... time(s)	L13
どうが	動画	video; animated image	L12
どうぐ	道具	tool	L15
どうしたら		how can (one) do something	L15
どうしよう		What should I do?	L18
どうする		What will you do?	L20
どうぶつえん	動物園	zoo	L16
とくに	特に	in particular	L16
どこでも		anywhere; wherever; everywhere	L15
ところで		by the way	L13
とし	年	age; year	L18
どちら		which (of two); where; which way [polite equivalent of どこ]*	L10 L19
とつぜん	突然	suddenly; unexpectedly	L17
とどく [u]	届く	to arrive; to be delivered [*person/place* に *thing* が]	L17
とどける [ru]	届ける	to deliver [*person/place* に *thing* を]	L17
とぶ [u]	飛ぶ	to fly [*sky, etc.* を]; to jump	L12
とまる [u]	止まる	(something) stops [*thing* が]	L13
とめる [ru]	止める	to stop [*thing* を]	L13
とりにく	鳥肉／鶏肉	chicken (meat)	L11
とる [u]	取る	to take [*thing* を]; to take away; to steal [*thing* を]*	L8 L16
どろぼう		thief; burglar	L16
な			
ないよう	内容	content	L20
なおす [u]	直す	to repair [*thing* を]; to correct [*mistake* を]	L14
なかよくする	仲良くする	to get along; to act friendly [*person* と]	L18
なかよくなる [u]	仲良くなる	to become good friends [*person* と]	L12
なくす [u]		to lose [*thing* を]	L14
なくなる [u]		to disappear [*thing* が]	L12
なくなる [u]	亡くなる	to pass away [euphemism for しぬ]	L17
なぐる [u]		to hit; to strike [*person* を]	L16
なさる [u]		honorific expression for する	L19
なぜ		why	L19
なべ		(cooking) pot	L11
なやみ	悩み	worry; problem	L18
なやみがある [u]	悩みが～	to have worries	L18
なやむ [u]	悩む	to worry; to be troubled [*thing* について/に]	L15
ならぶ [u]	並ぶ	to stand in line; to line up [*place* に]	L19
なるほど		That makes sense; I get it.	L13
なんでも	何でも	anything; whatever; everything	L15
に			
におい		smell; scent; aroma	L16
にげる [ru]		to escape; to run away	L14
にし	西	west	L17
にしぐち	西口	west entrance/exit (of a train station)	L17
にほんしょく	日本食	Japanese food	L17
にもつ	荷物	package; baggage	L12
Noun にやさしい		nice to Noun; easy on Noun	L18
Person によって		by [person]	L16
Noun によると		according to Noun	L13
にゅういんする	入院する	to get hospitalized; to be admitted to a hospital [*hospital* に]	L18
にる [ru]	似る	to resemble; to be similar/alike [*thing/person* に/と] [*thing/person X* と *thing/person Y* は/が]	L14
にわ	庭	garden; yard	L11
にんきがでる [ru]	人気が出る	to become popular [*thing* の]	L18
にんぎょう	人形	doll	L14
にんげん	人間	human	L17
ぬ			
ぬぐ [u]		to take off; to remove [*clothes/shoes* を]	L11
ぬすむ [u]		to steal [*thing* を]	L16
ぬれる [ru]		to get wet [*thing/person* が]	L20
ね			
ねだん	値段	price [monetary]	L12
ねむる [u]	眠る	to fall asleep; to be asleep	L17

の	ノートをとる [*u*]	～を取る	to take notes	L16
	のこす [*u*]	残す	to leave (behind) [*thing/person* を]	L15
	Noun のこと		about Noun	L14
	のせる [*ru*]		to put (Y) on (X); to top (X) with (Y) [*thing X* に *thing Y* を]	L11
	Noun のために		for Noun	L15
	のど		throat	L14
	のりおくれる [*ru*]	乗り遅れる	to miss (a train, bus, etc.) [*transportation* に]	L14
は	は／はっぱ	葉(っぱ)	leaf	L20
	～はい	～杯	[counter for food/drink in cups, glasses, bowls, etc.]	L13
	はいしゃ	歯医者	dentist	L18
	ハイテク		high-tech	L16
	ばか(な)		foolish; stupid	L20
	ばかにする		to make fun (of); to mock [*person* を]	L16
	はく [*u*]		to throw up; to vomit	L19
	はげます [*u*]		to encourage [*person* を]	L15
	はこぶ [*u*]	運ぶ	to carry; to transport [*place* に *thing/person* を]	L11
	はさむ [*u*]		to put/insert/sandwich (Y) between (X) [*thing X* に *thing Y* を]	L11
	はじまる [*u*]	始まる	(something) begins/starts [*thing* が]	L16
	はじめ	始め	beginning; start	L18
	はじめ	初め	beginning; first	L12
	はじめて	初めて	for the first time	L11
	ばしょ	場所	place; area; location	L11
	はしる [*u*]	走る	to run	L12
	はずかしい		shy; embarrassed; ashamed	L15
	はつおんする	発音する	to pronounce (words)	L15
	はっけんする	発見する	to discover [*thing* を]	L16
	はっぴょうする	発表する	to present; to announce [*thing* を/について]	L12
	はなしあう [*u*]	話し合う	to discuss; to have a talk [*topic* について]	L17
	はね	羽	feather; wing	L20
	バラ		rose	L17
	はらう [*u*]	払う	to pay [*money* を]	L12
	はる [*u*]		to post; to stick [*thing* を *place* に]	L14
	ばんぐみ	番組	program [TV, radio, etc.]	L20
	はんたいする	反対する	to be against; to disagee [*person/thing* に]	L20
	はんぶん	半分	half	L16
ひ	ひ	火	fire	L14
	ひがし	東	east	L17
	ひがしぐち	東口	east entrance/exit (of a train station)	L17
	ひげをそる [*u*]		to shave (one's) face/beard	L15
	ビジネス		business	L13
	ひだりて	左手	left hand	L12
	びっくりする		to be surprised [*thing* に]	L16
	ひつよう(な)	必要(な)	necessary	L19
	ひどい		terrible [thing/person]; serious [injury]	L12
	ひとびと	人々	the general public; people [unspecified]	L13
	ひとりぐらし(を)する	一人暮らし(を)～	to live alone	L20
	ひやす [*u*]	冷やす	to chill; to cool down [*thing* を]	L11
	びよういん	美容院	hair salon	L13
	ひょうげん	表現	expression	L17
	ひるね(を)する	昼寝(を)～	to take a nap	L12
	ひろう [*u*]	拾う	to pick up (off the ground) [*thing* を]	L13
	ひろげる [*ru*]	広げる	to spread; to widen [*thing* を]	L18
	びんぼう(な)	貧乏(な)	poor [lacking money/food/ possessions to live]	L12
ふ	ふあん(な)	不安(な)	uneasy	L20
	ふくしゅうする	復習する	to review [*thing* を]	L12
	ふくろ	袋	bag; sack	L19
	ふた		lid; cover; cap	L16
	ぶたにく	豚肉	pork	L11
	ぶちょう	部長	department head/manager; club president	L17
	ふつかよい	二日よい	hangover	L14
	ぶつかる [*u*]		to bump into; to crash into [*thing/person* に]	L14
	ふとい	太い	thick [line]; big [body shape]	L11
	ふとん	布団	*futon* [Japanese-style bedding]	L13
	ふべん(な)	不便(な)	inconvenient [place, location, etc.]	L18
	ふむ [*u*]		to step on [*thing* を]	L16
	フライパン		frying pan	L11
	ふる [*u*]		to reject; to jilt; to dump [*person* を]	L16
	プレゼン(を)する		to give a presentation	L15
	ぶんや	分野	field; area [study, research, activity, etc.]	L18
へ	へいわ	平和	peace	L17
	へいわ(な)	平和(な)	peaceful	L17

ヘビ		snake	L19
べんきょうになる [u]	勉強に～	to be informative; to teach one something	L15
へんじをする	返事を～	to answer; to respond [mail/person に]	L15
(お)べんとう	(お)弁当	boxed lunch	L12
ほ ほうげん	方言	dialect	L15
ほかに	他に	besides	L12
ほかの Noun	他の～	other/another Noun	L12
ほそい	細い	thin [line]; small [body shape]	L11
ボタン		button	L16
ほめる [ru]		to praise; to compliment [person/act を]	L15
ボランティア(を)する		to volunteer	L14
～ほん	～本	[counter for long, cylindrical objects]	L13
ほんやくする		to translate (X into Y) [source X を target language Y に]	L16
ま まいる [u]	参る	courteous expression for 行く and 来る	L19
まえ	前	front; in front of [thing/person の]; before [earlier in time]*	L5 L16
Duration まえ	～前	[duration] ago	L16
まえの Noun	前の～	previous Noun	L16
まがる [u]	曲がる	to turn [road/corner を direction に]	L13
まず		first; to begin with	L11
まぜる [ru]	混ぜる	to mix [thing を]	L11
また		(once) again	L16
まだ		not yet [+negative]; still [+affirmative]*	L6 L18
まだまだです		There is still a long way to go.	L16
まちがい	間違い	mistake; error	L14
まちがえる [ru]	間違える	to make a mistake [thing を]	L14
～まつ	～末	end of ...	L20
(お)まつり	(お)祭り	festival	L13
まなぶ [u]	学ぶ	to learn [fact/technique/(life) lesson を]	L17
まにあう [u]	間に合う	to make it in time; to be in time [event/activity に]	L18
まもる [u]	守る	to follow; to keep [rule/promise を]; to stick to [rule/timeline を]*; to protect [thing/person を]*	L13 L18
まよう [u]	迷う	to waver; to be unable to decide [thing を]; to lose one's way; to get lost [route に]	L18
まる	丸	circle; oval [noun]	L11
まるい	丸い	circular; round	L11
まわる [u]	回る	to go around; to rotate [thing が]	L20
まんじゅう		steamed bun with bean paste filling	L19
み みがく [u]		to polish [thing を]; to brush (one's teeth) [teeth を]	L12
みぎて	右手	right hand	L12
みずぎ	水着	swimsuit	L15
みずをだす [u]	水を出す	to turn on the water	L14
みせをやる [u] / する	店を～	to run a shop	L11
みつかる [u]	見つかる	to be found [thing/person が]	L17
みつける [ru]	見つける	to find [thing/person を]	L15
みなみ	南	south	L17
みなみぐち	南口	south entrance/exit (of a train station)	L17
む むしする	無視する	to ignore [person/thing を]	L16
むだづかい(を)する		to waste (money, energy, etc.)	L16
むり(を)する	無理(を)～	to push oneself too hard	L15
め ～メートル		... m [length; distance]	L16
めしあがる [u]		honorific expression for 食べる and 飲む	L19
めずらしい		rare; unusual; unique	L12
めんせつ	面接	(job) interview	L12
も もう		already [+affirmative]; no longer [+negative]*	L6 L18
もうしこむ [u]	申し込む	to apply (to/for) [thing に]	L13
もうす [u]	申す	courteous expression for 言う [name と]	L19
もうすぐ		soon	L12
もくてき	目的	purpose; objective; aim	L16
もくひょう	目標	goal; objective, target	L20
もじ	文字	character; letter [symbol used to write words]	L11
もし(～たら)		if [emphasizes the conditional meaning]	L12
もちろん		of course; certainly	L12
もっていく [u]	持っていく	to take (along) (to a different location) [place に thing を]	L14
もってくる [irr.]	持ってくる	to bring (along) (to the speaker's location) [place に thing を]	L13
もんくをいう [u]	文句を言う	to complain [person/thing に]	L18
もんだい	問題	problem; question; issue	L11
や やく [u]	焼く	to bake; to broil; to grill; to toast; to sear [thing を]	L11

	やくす [*u*]	訳す	to translate (X into Y) [*source X* を *target language Y* に]	L17
	やくそく(を)する	約束(を)〜	to make a promise; to make an appointment [*person* と]	L12
	やくにたつ [*u*]	役に立つ	to be useful/helpful (for/to) [*thing* に] [*person/thing* の]	L17
	やさしく		gently; tenderly	L20
	やめる [*ru*]		to stop (doing); to quit [*thing* を]	L13
	やる [*u*]		to do [*thing* を] [more casual than する]	L11
ゆ	ゆうがた	夕方	early evening	L15
	ゆうびん	郵便	mail	L15
	ゆか		floor	L14
	ゆかた	浴衣	casual cotton kimono (for summer)	L17
	ゆきがつもる [*u*]	雪が積もる	snow accumulates	L18
	ゆっくりする		to relax; to stay for long	L11
	ゆでる [*ru*]		to boil (in water to cook) [*thing* を]	L11
	ユニーク(な)		unique	L15
	ゆび	指	finger	L12
	ゆれる [*ru*]		to shake; to sway [*building/thing* が]	L19
よ	ようじがある [*u*]	用事が〜	to have an errand/something that needs to be done	L18
	よごす [*u*]	汚す	to make (something) dirty [*thing* を]	L14
	よごれる [*ru*]	汚れる	(something) becomes dirty [*thing* が]	L14
	よしゅうする	予習する	to do preparatory study/research [*thing* を]	L12
	よっぱらい		drunken person	L16
	よぶ [*u*]	呼ぶ	to call [*person/thing* を]; to invite [*person* を *place/activity/event* に]	L15
	よやくする	予約する	to reserve [*thing/place* を]	L11
	よる [*u*]	寄る	to stop by [*place* に]	L11
	よろこぶ [*u*]	喜ぶ	to be delighted; to rejoice	L18
ら	ライブ		live concert/performance	L16
	らく(な)	楽(な)	comfortable; easy (to complete/achieve)	L18
	らくご	落語	traditional Japanese comic storytelling	L15
	らくごか	落語家	*rakugo* storyteller	L15
り	りゆう	理由	reason	L16
	りようする	利用する	to utilize; to take advantage [*thing* を]	L19
	リラックスする		to relax	L14
	りれきしょ	履歴書	résumé	L12
	りんご		apple	L11
る	るす	留守	absence; being away (from home, etc.)	L18
	るすにする	留守に〜	to be away [*home, etc.* を]	L18
れ	れい	例	example	L11
	れいぞうこ	冷蔵庫	refrigerator	L11
	れつ	列	line; row	L19
	れんらくがある [*u*]	連絡が〜	to be contacted; to hear (from) [*person/place* から]	L14
	れんらくする	連絡する	to contact; to get in touch [*person/place* に]	L14
ろ	ろうそく		candle	L14
	ろんぶん	論文	thesis; dissertation; academic paper	L12
わ	わしょく	和食	Japanese cuisine	L11
	わたる [*u*]		to cross [*road, etc.* を]	L18
	わる [*u*]	割る	to shatter; to crack; to break [*thing* を]	L14
	われる [*ru*]	割れる	(something) shatters/cracks/breaks [*thing* が]	L14

著者紹介

※以下アルファベット順

岡(おか) まゆみ • Mayumi Oka［編著］

現職　ミシガン大学日本研究センター研究員
ミドルベリー日本語学校日本語大学院プログラム講師

教歴　ミシガン大学アジア言語文化学科日本語学課長
プリンストン大学専任講師, コロンビア大学専任講師, 上智大学講師

著書　『中・上級者のための速読の日本語 第2版』(2013);『マルチメディア日本語基本文法ワークブック』共著(2018)(以上、ジャパンタイムズ出版);『上級へのとびら』(2009);『きたえよう漢字力』(2010);『中級日本語を教える教師の手引き』(2011);『これで身につく文法力』(2012);『日英共通メタファー辞典 』(2017);『初級日本語 とびらⅠ』(2021);『とびらⅠワークブック 1』(2022);『とびらⅠワークブック 2』(2023) (以上共著、くろしお出版); その他

その他　全米日本語教師学会理事(2007-2010)
ミシガン大学 Matthews Underclass Teaching Award(2019)

近藤(こんどう) 純子(じゅんこ) • Junko Kondo［編著］

現職　南山大学外国人留学生別科専任語学講師

教歴　ミシガン大学アジア言語文化学科専任講師, マドンナ大学講師

著書　『上級へのとびら』(2009);『きたえよう漢字力』(2010);『中級日本語を教える教師の手引き』(2011);『これで身につく文法力』(2012);『初級日本語 とびらⅠ』(2021);『とびらⅠワークブック 1』(2022);『とびらⅠワークブック 2』(2023) (以上共著、くろしお出版)

筒井(つつい) 通雄(みちお) • Michio Tsutsui［文法解説］

現職　ワシントン大学人間中心設計工学科名誉教授

教歴　コロンビア大学日本語教育夏期修士プログラム講師, ワシントン大学教授, マサチューセッツ工科大学助教授, カリフォルニア大学デービス校客員助教授

著書　『日本語基本文法辞典』(1986);『日本語文法辞典〈中級編〉』(1995);『日本語文法辞典〈上級編〉』(2008);『マルチメディア日本語基本文法ワークブック』(2018)(以上共著、ジャパンタイムズ出版);『上級へのとびら』(2009);『きたえよう漢字力』(2010);『中級日本語を教える教師の手引き』(2011);『これで身につく文法力』(2012);『初級日本語 とびらⅠ』(2021);『とびらⅠワークブック 1』(2022);『とびらⅠワークブック 2』(2023)(以上共著、くろしお出版); その他

その他　全米日本語教師学会理事 (1990-1993, 2009-2012)

森(もり) 祐太(ゆうた) • Yuta Mori

現職　ライデン大学地域研究科講師及び、国際学科日本語プログラムコーディネーター

教歴　ミシガン大学専任講師, ハーバード大学専任講師, ミドルベリー大学夏期日本語学校講師

著書　『初級日本語 とびらⅠ』(2021)(共著、くろしお出版)

奥野(おくの) 智子(ともこ) • Tomoko Okuno

現職　ミシガン大学レジデンシャルカレッジ日本語プログラムコーディネーター

教歴　ミシガン州立大学専任講師, 北海道国際交流センター日本語日本文化講座夏期セミナー講師, 金沢工業大学夏期日本語教育プログラム講師

著書　『初級日本語 とびらⅠ』(2021)(共著、くろしお出版)

榊原(さかきばら) 芳美(よしみ) • Yoshimi Sakakibara

現職　ミシガン大学アジア言語文化学科専任講師

教歴　ミシガン州立大学専任講師, 北海道国際交流センター日本語日本文化講座夏期セミナー講師

著書　『マルチメディア日本語基本文法ワークブック』(2018)(共著、ジャパンタイムズ出版);『初級日本語 とびらⅠ』(2021);『とびらⅠワークブック 1』(2022);『とびらⅠワークブック 2』(2023)(共著、くろしお出版)

曽我部(そがべ) 絢香(あやか) • Ayaka Sogabe

現職　ミシガン大学アジア言語文化学科専任講師

教歴　バンダービルト大学専任講師, ミドルベリー大学夏期日本語学校講師

著書　『初級日本語 とびらⅠ』(2021)(共著、くろしお出版)

安田(やすだ) 昌江(まさえ) • Masae Yasuda

現職　ミシガン大学アジア言語文化学科専任講師

教歴　オークランド大学特別講師

著書　『初級日本語 とびらⅠ』(2021)(共著、くろしお出版)

制作協力

■ 反転授業用動画作成、英語校閲・校正・監修

クリストファー・シャード（Christopher Schad）

現職 ミシガン大学アジア言語文化学科専任講師

教歴 プリンストン大学専任講師, スワスモア大学講師,
ミドルベリー大学夏期日本語学校講師

■ 校正・英語校正

平川(ひらかわ)ワイター永子(えいこ)（Eiko Hirakawa Weyter）

現職 フリーランス日本語教師

教歴 ミシガン大学専任講師, パデュー大学専任講師

■ 英語翻訳協力者

ジェニファー・クリスト（Jennifer Crist）
アンドリュー・グレイグ（Andrew Greig）

■ イラスト

坂木浩子
村山宇希

■ 装丁・本文デザイン

鈴木章宏

■ 音声録音

狩生健志

■ 音声出演協力

カワムラ, 富樫萌々香, 藤野タロウ,
まつむらりょう, 幸

■ 編集

市川麻里子
金髙浩子

■ 写真・画像提供

アフロ
伊賀流忍者道場
一般財団法人印刷朝陽会
岡山後楽園
カップヌードルミュージアム 横浜
株式会社朝日学生新聞社
株式会社朝日新聞出版
株式会社あすなろ書房
株式会社 KADOKAWA
株式会社講談社
株式会社誠文堂新光社
株式会社ハコスタ
旧嵯峨御所 大本山 大覚寺
京都大学 iPS 細胞研究所
京都市メディア支援センター
公益財団法人日本棋院
公益財団法人福武財団
公益社団法人和歌山県観光連盟
高知商工会議所・よさこい祭振興会
紫舟アトリエ
写真 AC
ジョイパックレジャー株式会社
書道パフォーマンス甲子園実行委員会
ダイアン吉日
秩父市役所
築地玉寿司
坂茂建築設計
ぴあ株式会社
伏見稲荷大社
妙心寺 退蔵院
夢アカデミー／夢蔵 MUSASHI
両足院
iStock
KonMari Media Japan
Marty Friedman (Howmic Inc.)
photolibrary
PIXTA
SCRAP 出版

■ 転載協力

音羽山 清水寺
株式会社福音館書店
日本スケート連盟
村上春樹事務所
JASRAC
JULA 出版局

初級日本語 とびらII

TOBIRA II : Beginning Japanese

2022年 7月 4日 第1刷発行
2023年 8月20日 第2刷発行

著 者 岡まゆみ・近藤純子・筒井通雄・森祐太・奥野智子・榊原芳美・曽我部絢香・安田昌江

発行人 岡野秀夫

発行所 くろしお出版
〒102-0084 東京都千代田区二番町4-3
Tel: 03-6261-2867 Fax: 03-6261-2879
URL: https://www.9640.jp Email: kurosio@9640.jp

印 刷 シナノ印刷

ISBN978-4-87424-900-0 C0081

Conjugation Tables

A-1. *U*-verbs

Plain neg.	Non-past		言(い)わ 持(も)た 帰(かえ)ら	飲(の)ま 遊(あそ)ば 死(し)な	話(はな)さ	聞(き)か	泳(およ)が	ない
	Past							なかった
Passive								れる
Causative								せる
Causative-passive								せられる[1]
***Masu*-form**	Non-past	Aff.	言(い)い 持(も)ち 帰(かえ)り	飲(の)み 遊(あそ)び 死(し)に	話(はな)し	聞(き)き	泳(およ)ぎ	ます
		Neg.						ません
	Past	Aff.						ました
		Neg.						ませんでした
Dictionary form (=Plain non-past affirmative form)			言(い)う 持(も)つ 帰(かえ)る	飲(の)む 遊(あそ)ぶ 死(し)ぬ	話(はな)す	聞(き)く	泳(およ)ぐ	
Potential			言(い)え 持(も)て 帰(かえ)れ	飲(の)め 遊(あそ)べ 死(し)ね	話(はな)せ	聞(き)け	泳(およ)げ	る
***Ba*-conditional**			言(い)え 持(も)て 帰(かえ)れ	飲(の)め 遊(あそ)べ 死(し)ね	話(はな)せ	聞(き)け	泳(およ)げ	ば
Volitional			言(い)お 持(も)と 帰(かえ)ろ	飲(の)も 遊(あそ)ぼ 死(し)の	話(はな)そ	聞(き)こ	泳(およ)ご	う
***Te*-form**			言(い)っ 持(も)っ　て 帰(かえ)っ	飲(の)ん 遊(あそ)ん　で 死(し)ん	話(はな)して	聞(き)いて	泳(およ)いで	
Plain past affirmative			言(い)っ 持(も)っ　た 帰(かえ)っ	飲(の)ん 遊(あそ)ん　だ 死(し)ん	話(はな)した	聞(き)いた	泳(およ)いだ	

1. ～される is also used (e.g., 言(い)わされる; 飲(の)まされる). However, (話(はな))さされる is not used. (See L18 #2-1.)

A-2. *Ru*-verbs and irregular verbs

			Ru-verbs	Irregular verbs		
Plain neg.	Non-past		見(み) 食べ(た)	来(こ)	し	ない
	Past					なかった
Passive					*	られる
Causative					ø	させる
Causative-passive					ø	させられる
Masu-form	Non-past	Aff.		来(き)	し	ます
		Neg.				ません
	Past	Aff.				ました
		Neg.				ませんでした

	Ru-verbs	Irregular verbs		
Dictionary form (=Plain non-past affirmative form)		来(く)	す	る
Potential	見(み) 食べ(た)	来(こ)	**	られる
Ba-conditional		来(く)	す	れば
Volitional		来(こ)	し	よう
Te-form		来(き)	し	て
Plain past affirmative		来(き)	し	た

* The passive form of する is される. ** The potential form of する is できる.

B. *I*-adjectives

	Non-past		Past		*Te*-form	Noun modification form	Verb modification form	*Ba*-conditional form
	Affirmative	Negative	Affirmative	Negative				
Plain	大(おお)きい	大(おお)きくない	大(おお)きかった	大(おお)きくなかった	大(おお)きくて	大(おお)きい	大(おお)きく	大(おお)きければ
	いい[1]	よくない	よかった	よくなかった	よくて	いい	よく	よければ
Polite	大(おお)きいです	大(おお)きくないです	大(おお)きかったです	大(おお)きくなかったです	1. いい and いいです are irregular forms.			
	いいです[1]	よくないです	よかったです	よくなかったです				

C. *Na*-adjectives / Nouns + だ

	Non-past				Past				*Te*-form		Noun modification form		Verb modification form		*Ba*-conditional form
	Affirmative		Negative		Affirmative		Negative								
Plain	静(しず)か	だ	静(しず)か	じゃない	静(しず)か	だった	静(しず)か	じゃなかった	静(しず)か	で	静(しず)か	な[1]	静(しず)か	に[1]	なら
	学生(がくせい)		学生(がくせい)		学生(がくせい)		学生(がくせい)		学生(がくせい)		学生(がくせい)	の[1]	学生(がくせい)	X[2]	
Polite	静(しず)か	です	静(しず)か	じゃないです	静(しず)か	でした	静(しず)か	じゃなかったです	1. To be accurate, な, の, and に are particles, and not conjugated forms of だ. 2. Various particles occur in the position of X according to the verb that follows. **Exs.** 学生(がくせい)になる; 本(ほん)を読(よ)む; 海(うみ)で泳(およ)ぐ						
	学生(がくせい)		学生(がくせい)		学生(がくせい)		学生(がくせい)